MEDIA

NOW

Understanding Media, Culture, and Technology

EIGHTH EDITION

JOSEPH STRAUBHAAR
University of Texas, Austin

ROBERT LaROSE
Michigan State University

LUCINDA DAVENPORT
Michigan State University

WADSWORTH
CENGAGE Learning·

Australia • Brazil • Japan • Korea • Mexico • Singapore • Spain • United Kingdom • United States

WADSWORTH
CENGAGE Learning®

Media Now: Understanding Media, Culture, and Technology, Eighth Edition
Joseph Straubhaar, Robert LaRose, and Lucinda Davenport

Publisher: Michael Rosenberg

Development Editor: Megan Garvey

Assistant Editor: Erin Bosco

Editorial Assistant: Rebecca Donahue

Media Editor: Jessica Badiner

Executive Brand Manager: Ben Rivera

Marketing Coordinator: Brittany Blais

Senior Market Development Manager: Kara Kindstrom

Senior Content Project Manager: Michael Lepera

Senior Art Director: Marissa Falco

Print Buyer: Doug Bertke

Senior Rights Acquisition Specialist: Mandy Groszko

Production Service/Compositor/Text Designer: PreMediaGlobal

Cover Designer: Lisa Kuhn, Curio Press

Cover Image: © Veer/gubh83

For product information and technology assistance, contact us at
Cengage Learning Customer & Sales Support, 1-800-354-9706

For permission to use material from this text or product, submit all requests online at **www.cengage.com/permissions.**
Further permissions questions can be emailed to
permissionrequest@cengage.com.

Library of Congress Control Number: 2012947885

ISBN-13: 978-1-133-31136-2

ISBN-10: 1-133-31136-9

Wadsworth
20 Channel Center Street
Boston, MA 02210
USA

Cengage Learning is a leading provider of customized learning solutions with office locations around the globe, including Singapore, the United Kingdom, Australia, Mexico, Brazil and Japan. Locate your local office at **international.cengage.com/region**

Cengage Learning products are represented in Canada by Nelson Education, Ltd.

For your course and learning solutions, visit **www.cengage.com.**

Purchase any of our products at your local college store or at our preferred online store **www.cengagebrain.com.**
Instructors: Please visit login.cengage.com and log in to access instructor-specific resources.

Printed in the United States of America
1 2 3 4 5 6 7 16 15 14 13 12

Brief Contents

Contents

PART TWO   The Media

CHAPTER 3
Books and Magazines   57

CHAPTER 6

Radio   157

CHAPTER 9

CHAPTER 10
Public Relations
285

CHAPTER 11
Advertising
313

CHAPTER 12

The Third Screen: Smart Phones and Tablets   349

CHAPTER 13
Video Games

CHAPTER 16

Media Ethics   475

CHAPTER 17

Global Communications Media   503

Preface

The convergence of old media with new media forms is a continuum and a moving target. There are few corners of media industries or indeed any aspect of modern life that has not been touched by digital media. Such a renewed interest in innovative new media has not been seen since the "Internet bubble" at the turn of the century. Social media are the latest manifestation of media convergence, encroaching on the original mode of human speech communication that was previously conducted face-to-face, and more recently, by telephone.

Our theme is that the convergence of traditional media industries and newer technologies has created a new communications environment that impacts society and culture. Social media are the latest example of transformative media along with smartphones and tablet computers. Our goal throughout this book is to prepare students to cope with that environment as both critical consumers of media and aspiring media professionals.

We reach for that goal by providing an approach to mass media that integrates traditional media (magazines, books, newspapers, music, radio, film, and television) and newer media (the Internet, tablets, e-readers, smartphones, and video games), and emphasizes the intersection of technology, media, and culture.

We have already witnessed astounding changes in the structure of the radio and telecommunications industries and the rapid evolution of the newspaper, film, and television industries. These are changes that affect our society as well as those across the globe and our students need to learn about them in their introductory courses to prepare them to be productive citizens.

NEW TO THIS EDITION

The eighth edition of *Media Now* provides the most current coverage possible of the media industry and reflects the field's latest research as well as the challenges that confront the media industries in transition. Social media represent an overarching trend toward audience-originated content that forces media executives, advertisers and public relations executives as well as dictators around the world to rethink their strategies. We believe that these changes afford "teachable moments" in which students can reflect on the future of the media and their own life plans while recognizing the cyclical nature of the economy and the impact that external events can have on providers of entertainment, information, and communication.

Chapter by chapter, here are examples of the updates you will find in this edition:

- **The Changing Media** asks if social media are a fundamentally new type of communication and examines their impact on media industries.

- **Media and Society** considers the new business models that are emerging in the digital media environment and calls attention to the impact of social media on conventional notions of gatekeeping and popular culture.

- **Books and Magazines** explains the latest trends in electronic publishing and the impact of printing on-demand, self-publishing, e-books and social media.

- **Newspapers** analyzes the exciting opportunities in this evolving industry and the influence of mobile devices and social media on news.

- **Recorded Music** tracks how the music industry is learning to live with declining sales by exploring new outlets for music on the Internet.

- **Radio** examines the Internet "cloud music" trend, evolving Internet radio and their impact on conventional broadcasting.

- **Film and Home Video** analyzes how the industry prospers through premium ticket sales in 3D and IMAX venues, while changing global distribution to fight piracy.

- **Television** explores the growing impact of YouTube, Netflix and Hulu and the prospect of Internet-connected TV sets on the audiences and business prospects of conventional TV providers.

- **The Internet** looks back at the historical origins of social media and looks ahead to the implications of new Internet protocols for their users.

- **Public Relations** describes how social media present new opportunities, tools and challenges for public relations professionals.

- **Advertising** introduces new advertising strategies built around social media and smartphones.

- **The Third Screen** traces the history of smartphones and monitors the latest trends in smartphone technologies and apps.

- **Video Games** considers cutting edge gaming technologies, the rise of social media games, and the latest research on game addictions.

- **Media Uses and Impacts** updates research on the positive and negative impacts of social media and video games and describes new research methods based on the analysis of large data sets obtained from the Internet.

- **Media Policy and Law** examines regulations and legal precedents that apply to social media and updates information about consumer privacy protections.

- **Media Ethics** defines ethics and presents current ethical issues in the various media industries and some new challenges brought about by social media.

- **Global Communications Media** investigates the impact of social media on democratic revolutions in Tunisia, Egypt, and Libya, and accelerating global film and music flows.

UPDATED PROVEN FEATURES

This book comes with a rich set of features to aid in learning, all of which have been updated as necessary:

- **Media Literacy:** Included within each media chapter, these sections focuses on key issues regarding the impact of media on culture and society, encouraging students to think critically and analyze issues related to their consumption of media. In this edition, these sections have been expanded to include "news you can use" tips on how our readers can take practical actions that will empower them as media consumers.

- **Glossary:** Key terms are defined in the margins of each chapter, and a complete glossary is included in the back of the book.

- **Timelines:** Major events in each media industry are highlighted near the beginning of each chapter in Media Then/Media Now lists.

- **Box program:** Four types of boxes appear in the text. Each is designed to target specific issues and further pique students' interest and many are new to this edition:

  - **MEDIA AND CULTURE** boxes highlight cultural issues in the media.

  - **TECHNOLOGY DEMYSTIFIED** boxes explain technological information in a clear and accessible way.

  - **YOUR MEDIA CAREER** guides readers to the "hot spots" in media industries updated with the latest projections from the Bureau of Labor Statistics.

  - **WORLDVIEW** expands thinking from beyond the front door to a more global perspective.

- **Stop & Review:** Appearing periodically throughout each chapter, and available in electronic format on the *Media Now* companion website, these questions help students incrementally assess their understanding of key material.

- **Summary & Review:** Each chapter concludes with the authors' highly praised, engaging summary and review sections, which are presented as questions with brief narrative answers.

TEACHING AND LEARNING RESOURCES

Mass Communication CourseMate for Media Now: This multi-media resource offers a variety of rich learning materials designed to enhance the student experience. These materials include quizzing and chapter-specific tools such as chapter outlines, interactive glossaries and timelines, Stop & Review tutorial questions, and Critical Thinking About the Media exercises. You will also find an Interactive eBook. Use the "Engagement Tracker" to see progress for the class as a whole or for individual students. Identify students at risk early in the course. Uncover which concepts are most difficult for your class. Monitor time on task. Keep your students engaged. Go to cengagebrain.com to access these resources.

- **Note to faculty:** If you want your students to have access to these online textbook resources, please be sure to order them for your course. The content in these resources can be bundled at no additional charge to your students with every new copy of the text. If you do not order them, your students will not have access to these online resources. *Contact your local Cengage Learning sales representative for more details.*

CLASS PREPARATION, ASSESSMENT, AND COURSE MANAGEMENT RESOURCES

Instructor's Resource Manual: *Media Now's* Instructor's Resource Manual provides you with extensive assistance in teaching with the book. It includes sample syllabi, assignments, chapter outlines, individual and group activities, test questions, links to video resources and websites, and more.

- **PowerLecture with JoinIn® CD-ROM:** This all-in-one lecture tool lets you bring together text-specific lecture outlines and art from Cengage Learning texts, along with video and animations from the Internet or your own materials—culminating in a powerful, personalized media-enhanced presentation. In addition, the CD-ROM contains ExamView® computerized testing, and an electronic version of the book's Instructor's Resource Manual. It also includes book-specific JoinIn™ content for response systems tailored to *Media Now,* allowing you to transform your classroom and assess your students' progress with instant in-class quizzes and polls. Our exclusive agreement to offer TurningPoint software lets you pose book-specific questions and display students' answers seamlessly within the Microsoft PowerPoint slides of your own lecture, in conjunction with the "clicker" hardware of your choice. Enhance how your students interact with you, your lecture, and each other.

ACKNOWLEDGMENTS

We wish to thank our spouses, Sandy Straubhaar, Betty Degesie-LaRose, and Frederic Greene for their patience and valuable ideas. We also want to thank a number of our students and graduate assistants, Stuart Davis, Laura Dixon, Julie Goldsmith, Nicholas Robinson, Tim Penning, and Serena Carpenter for their reviews and comments on the chapters. Also, thanks to Rolf and Chris Straubhaar, Julia Mitschke, and to Rachael and Jason Davenport Greene for insights into their culture and concerns. Special thanks to Dr. Alex Games, Dr. Wei Peng, and Tammy Lin, all of the Department of Telecommunications, Information Studies, and Media at Michigan State University, for reviewing drafts of the video games chapter.

We would also like to acknowledge the tremendous efforts of everyone at Cengage Learning who worked with us to create an outstanding book. In particular, we want to mention development editor Megan Garvey for her professionalism, organizational skills, attention to deadlines, sound advice, and good judgment, and for her diplomacy, energy, and work ethic. Great appreciation also goes to photo researcher Jeremy Glover for the patience he was repeatedly called upon to display as we searched for *just* the right image; to assistant editor Erin Bosco for coordinating the ancillaries, to editorial assistant Rebecca Donaue for her quick responses; and to our publisher, Michael Rosenberg, for overseeing the whole process.

We also gratefully acknowledge the assistance of the guest writer of our advertising chapter, Teresa Mastin of DePaul University. Dr. Mastin earned her master's degree from California State–Fullerton and her doctorate in mass media from Michigan State University. She has more than 10 years experience teaching advertising and public relations, formerly at Michigan State University. We thank for writing the Instructor's Resource Manual and Examview quizzes, and for working on the JoinIn resources.

Finally, we wish to thank the following reviewers for their thoughtful suggestions and guidance in the development of the Eighth Edition:

Mark D. Ricci, State University of New York College at Brockport

John S. Nelson, Dakota State University

Matthew Jackson, Penn State University

Jon Arakaki, SUNY College at Oneonta

We also thank the following individuals for their reviews of the previous editions: Robert Abeman, Cleveland State University; Jon Arakaki, State University of New York, College at Oneonta; Thomas Berner, Pennsylvania State University; Elena Bertozzi, Indiana University; Larry Bohlender, Glendale Community College; Sandra Braman, University of Wisconsin, Milwaukee; Dr. Jim Brancato, Cedar Crest College; Michael Brown, University of Wyoming; Erik Bucy, Indiana University; Karyn S. Campbell, North Greenville University; Larry Campbell, University of Alaska, Anchorage; Richard Caplan, University of Akron; Meta Carstarphen-Delgado, University of Oklahoma; Jerry G. Chandler, Jackson State University; Tsan-Kuo Chang, University of Minnesota, Twin Cities; John Chapin, Rutgers University; Joseph Chuk, Kutztown University of Pennsylvania; Dan Close, Wichita State University; Gene Costain, University of Central Florida; Dave D'Alessio, Univeristy of Connecticut, Stamford; Robert Darden, Baylor University; Krishna DasGupta, Worcester State College; Staci Dinerstein, County College of Morris; David Donnelly, University of Houston; Mike Dorsher, University of Wisconsin, Eau Claire; Michael Doyle, Arkansas State University; Dr. Jim Eggensperger, Iona College; Lyombe Eko, University of Maine; Emily Erickson, Louisiana State University; Nick-ieann Fleener, University of Utah, Linda Fuller, Worcester State College; Ivy Glennon, University of Illinois at Urbana-Champaign; Donald Godfrey, Arizona State University; Mark Goodman, Mississippi State University; Tom Grimes, Kansas State University; Larry Haapanen, Lewis and Clark State College; Ken Hadwiger, Eastern Illinois University; Linwood A. Hagin, North Greenville University; Junhao Hong, State University of New York, Buffalo; Kevin Howley, Northeastern University; Jack Hodgson, Oklahoma State University; Rick Houlberg, San Francisco State University; James Hoyt, University of Wisconsin, Green Bay; Susan Hunt-Bradford, St. Louis Community College; Harvey Jassem, University of Hartford; Howard Keim, Tabor College; Randall King, Point Loma Nazarene University; Seong H. Lee, Appalachian State University; Bradley Lemonds, Santa Monica College; Charles Lewis, Minnesota State University, Mankato; William Lingle, Linfield College; Linda

Lumsden, Western Kentucky University; Robert Main, California State University, Chico; Reed Markham, Salt Lake Community College; Judith Marlane, California State University, Northridge; Stephen McDowell, Florida State University; Timothy P. Meyer, University of Wisconsin, Green Bay; Jonathan Millen, Rider College; Suman Mishra, Temple University; Joel Moody, University of Toronto, Mississauga; Jennifer Nelson, Ohio University; Kyle Nicholas, Old Dominion University; Daniel Panici, University of Southern Maine; Karen Pappin, Huntington University, Laurentian; Norma Pecora, Ohio University; Ben Peruso, Lehigh Carbon Community College; Cristina Pieraccini, State University of New York, Oswego; Tina Pieraccini, State University of New York, Oswego; Michael Porter, University of Missouri; Peter Pringle, University of Tennessee, Chattanooga; Hoyt Purvis, University of Arkansas; Arthur Raney, Indiana University; Divyesh K. Raythatha, Delaware State University; Mike Reed, Saddleback College; Humphrey Regis, University of South Florida; Ronald Rice, Rutgers University; Karen E. Riggs, Ohio University; Shelly Rodgers, University of Minnesota, Twin Cities; Marshall Rossow, Mankato State University; Gay Russell, Grossmont College; Joseph Russomanno, Arizona State University; Marc Ryan, Marist College; Christian Sandvig, University of Illinois at Urbana, Champaign; Tom Shaker, Northeastern University; Laura Sherwood, University of Nerasak, Kearney; Roger Soenksen, James Madison University; Jeffrey C. South, Virginia Commonwealth University; Don Stacks, University of Miami; Michelle J. Stanton, California State University, Northridge; Patrick J. Sutherland, Bethany College; Jill D. Swenson, Ithaca College; Michael Ray Taylor, Henderson State University; Don Tomlinson, Texas A&M University; Max Utsler, University of Kansas; Hazel Warlaumont, California State University, Fullerton; Alden L. Weight, Arizona State University, Polytechnic Campus; Susan Weill, Texas State University, San Marcos; Debora Wenger, Virginia Commonwealth University; Clifford Wexler, Columbia-Greene Community College; Glynn R. Wilson, Loyola University, New Orleans; Alan Winegarden, Concordia University; J. Emett Winn, Auburn University; and Phyllis Zagano, Boston University,

About the Authors

DR. JOSEPH D. STRAUBHAAR is the Amon G. Carter Centennial Professor of Communications and Media Studies Director in the Radio-TV-Film Department of the University of Texas at Austin. He was the Director of the Center for Brazilian Studies within the Lozano Long Institute for Latin American Studies. He is also Associate Director for International Programs of the Telecommunication and Information Policy Institute at the University of Texas. He has published books, articles, and essays on international communications, global media, digital inclusion, international telecommunications, Brazilian television, Latin American media, comparative analyses of new television technologies, media flow and culture, and other topics appearing in a number of journals, edited books, and elsewhere. His primary teaching, research, and writing interests are in global media, international communication and cultural theory, the digital divide in the U.S. and other countries, and comparative analysis of new technologies. He does research in Latin America, Asia, and Africa, and has taken student groups to Latin America and Asia. He has presented seminars abroad on media research, television programming strategies, and telecommunications privatization. He is on the editorial board for the *Communications Theory, Studies in Latin American Popular Culture,* and *Revista Intercom.*

Visit Joe Straubhaar on the Web at
http://rtf.utexas.edu/faculty/jstraubhaar.html

DR. ROBERT LaROSE is a Full Professor in the Department of Telecommunication, Information Studies, and Media at Michigan State University and serves as director of the Media and Information Studies Ph.D. program. He won Outstanding Article Award for the year in the field of communication from the International Communication Association, and also the McQuail Award for the Best Article Advancing Communication Theory from Amsterdam School of Communication Research for his 2010 paper, *The Problem of Media Habits.* He conducts research on the uses and effects of the Internet. He has published and presented numerous articles, essays, and book chapters on computer-mediated communication, social cognitive explanations of the Internet and its effects on behavior, understanding Internet usage, privacy, and more. In addition to his teaching and research, he is an avid watercolor painter and traveler.

Visit Robert LaRose on the Web at
http://www.msu.edu/~larose

DR. LUCINDA D. DAVENPORT is the Director of the School of Journalism at Michigan State University. She was recently the Associate Dean for Graduate Education in the College of Communication Arts and Sciences, among other administrative positions. She received the Excellence in Teaching university award from MSU and has earned national awards for her research, which focuses mainly on news media and innovative technology, media history and journalistic ethics. She has professional experience in newspaper, television, public relations, advertising, and online news. Her credentials include a Ph.D. in Mass Communication from Ohio University, an M.A. in Journalism from the University of Iowa, and a B.A. double major in Journalism and Radio/TV/Film from Baylor University. Her master's thesis and doctoral dissertation were firsts in the country on computerized information services and online news.

Visit Lucinda D. Davenport on the Web at **http://jrn.msu.edu.**

MEDIA
NOW

DIGITAL MEDIA reach us anytime, anywhere on a growing array of screens exemplifying the media convergence we will examine in the first chapter.

THE CHANGING MEDIA

THE MEDIA IN OUR LIVES

If you were the typical American media consumer, you would spend over nine and a quarter hours a day with the media! Multiply that by the number of days in a year, and you would spend almost five months of each year with media (see Table 1.1). Since this is the information age we can break that down into the bits and bytes of computer data. It adds up to 34 billion bytes a day per person, or about a third of the capacity of a 100-GB computer hard drive (Bohn & Short, 2009).

We consume information, but we also make it when we update Facebook profiles, upload videos to YouTube, or control avatars in multiplayer online games like "Call of Duty." Most of us will enter careers in which we gather, organize, produce, or distribute information. This includes professional information specialists employed in the media as journalists, movie actors, musicians, television producers, writers, advertising account executives, researchers, Web page designers, announcers, and public relations specialists. Even in traditional manufacturing industries such as the auto industry, information-handling professionals in managerial, technical, clerical, sales, and service occupations make up a third of the workforce (Aoyama & Castells, 2002). So, we now work and play in an **information society**.

[In an **information society**, the exchange of information is the predominant economic activity.]

1455	Gutenberg Bible is published
1910	United States transitions to an industrial society
1960	United States transitions to information society

1991	World Wide Web is launched
1996	Telecommunications Act of 1996 reforms U.S. media policy
2009	United States adopts digital TV

MEDIA IN A CHANGING WORLD

> **Mass communication** is one-to-many, with limited audience feedback.
>
> **Digital** means computer-readable information formatted in 1s and 0s.

Media technology changes with every generation: for example, Mr. McQuitty, who is 45 years old, is a television producer. When he was in a college **mass communication** survey course, our fictional Mr. McQuitty studied books, newspapers, magazines, radio, television, and film. Today, these conventional media have evolved through the advent of **digital** technology. Mr. McQuitty's daughter, Rachael, wants to start her own online channel. She takes some of her college courses on campus and some online and downloads her textbooks from the Internet. Her world revolves around iPods, Androids, the Kindle Fire, Facebook, YouTube, texting, and tweets.

Conventional media forms are combining with new ones in ways that change our media consumption patterns, our lives, and the societies in which we live. Anyone who has ever used a cell phone to download an e-mail, vote for an *American Idol* contestant, view a video clip, or listen to a song has experienced the merging of conventional mass media into new media forms through advances in digital technology and telecommunications networks. New media technologies impact our culture by offering new lifestyles, creating new jobs and eliminating others, shifting media empires, demanding new regulations, and presenting unique new social issues (see Figure 1.1).

The changes are not purely technology driven, however. Our individual creativity and our cultures push back against the technologies and the corporations that deploy them to redefine their uses. The Internet is a prime example. Originally developed to support communication between weapons research labs in the wake of a nuclear holocaust, the Internet has evolved into a tool for entertainment, commerce, and education. Big media corporations now compete for its content with citizen journalists, Facebook users, garage bands, and amateur video producers. Some of those amateurs, such as Rebecca Black, who recorded the music video "Friday" in 2011, can become international phenomenon. Individual users who take precautions to preserve their online privacy also take a stand against control by corporate interests on the Internet.

TABLE 1.1 Annual Media Consumption

MEDIUM	HOURS PER PERSON
Television*	1,693
Radio and satellite* Radio*	744
Internet*	181
Recorded music*	172
Newspapers	169
Magazines	128
Books	112
Video games*	107
Home video	61
Mobile content*	21
Theatrical movies*	12
Total	3,400

*Age 12+, all others 18+.

Source: Veronis Suhler Stevenson, Communications Industry Forecast 22nd ed., 2009.

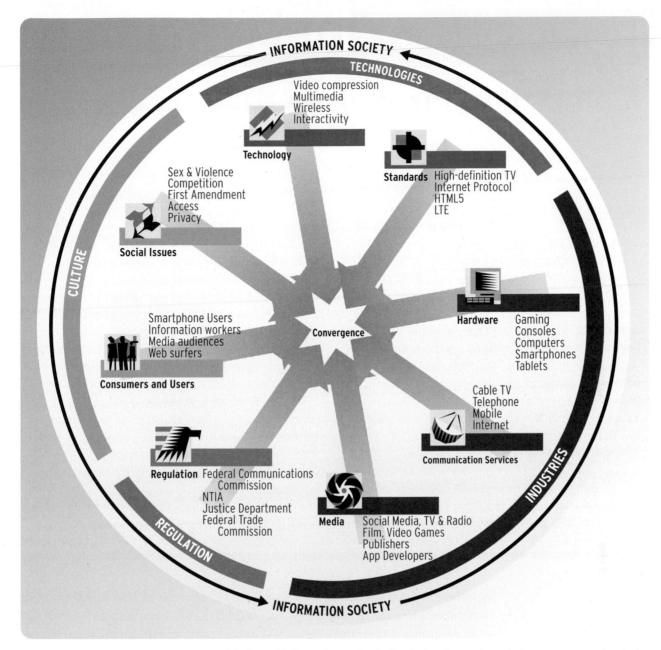

FIGURE 1.1 MEDIA CONVERGENCE Media and information technologies, industries, and regulations are converging to impact our culture in the information society.

MERGING TECHNOLOGIES

There are not many forms of purely **analog** communication still in common use today. We still experience purely analog communication when we are in a room with another person listening to what they say and taking in facial expressions. Handwritten notes are another example, but only for those who don't text or tweet. In a short span of years technology has moved us away from analog communication and into the digital age in which nearly all other forms of communication are created, stored, and transmitted in digital form.

The digital domain now encompasses nearly all radio, television, film, newspapers, magazines, and books with an ever-narrowing list of exceptions. Local talk radio is about the only purely analog medium that remains—local music radio

> **Analog** communication uses continuously varying signals corresponding to the light or sounds originated by the source.

A DIGITAL MEDIA PRIMER

All digital transmissions are composed of only two digits: 1 and 0. These are actually a series of on (for 1s)–off (for 0s) events. These can be encoded in a variety of ways including turning electrical currents or light beams on and off in Internet connections, changing the polarity of tiny magnets on the surface of a computer hard drive, or varying the patterns of pits on the surface of a CD.

Consider a simple landline telephone call. The digital conversion occurs on a computer card that connects your line to the telephone company's switch. First, brief excerpts, or samples, of the electrical waveform corresponding to your voice are taken from the telephone line at a rate of 8,000 samples per second. The size, or voltage level, of each sample is measured and "rounded off" to the closest of 256 different possible readings. Then a corresponding eight-digit binary number is transmitted by turning an electrical current on for a moment to indicate a 1 and turning it off for a 0.

The process is reversed at the receiving end. At 8,000 samples per second and eight digits per sample, the on–off signals are numerous—64,000 each second! Thus, when two lovers are talking on the phone and there is complete (if meaningful) silence on the line, the voltage reading is 0. The corresponding binary number is 00000000. If the lovers begin to quarrel loudly, the voltage reading might jump to the maximum: 11111111. To the couple, it seems that they are talking to each other, but in reality they are listening to computer emulations of their voices. Digital recordings use the same methods, but they employ more numerous samples and allow more volume levels to improve sound quality.

To make computer graphics, a computer stores digital information about the brightness and color of every single point on the computer screen. On many computer screens, there are 1024 points of light (or picture elements, pixels for short) going across and 768 down. Up to 24 bits of information may be required for each point so that millions of colors can each be assigned their own unique digital code.

Similarly, when we type text into a computer, each key corresponds to a unique sequence of eight computer bits (such as 1000001 for A). These sequences are stored inside the computer or transmitted through the Internet, in the form of tiny surges of electricity, flashes of light, or pulses of magnetism. The human senses are purely analog systems, so for humans to receive the message, we must convert back from digital to analog.

stations still transmit analog signals but they play music that is stored on digital recordings. To catch up with the times, the "old media" have responded with digital innovations of their own. Sirius XM digital radio channels host old radio program reruns and specialized music and artists. The music industry increasingly relies on digital distribution through iTunes and other digital music services after facing ruin from free-but-illegal Internet downloads. Many conventional media outlets provide "apps" of themselves for consumption on mobile devices such as smartphones, e-readers and other tablet computers. The latest trend is to "go social" by adding social networking extensions to print and video media so that audience members can engage in interactions that focus on media content.

Digital communication technology converts sound, pictures, and text into computer-readable formats by changing the information into strings of *binary digits* (*bits*) made up of electronically encoded 1s and 0s (see Technology Demystified: A Digital Media Primer, above). People using a telephone today still hear a "W" phonetic sound just as people did a hundred years ago, but only after the phone converts the analog sound to digital pulses and then changes it back to sound for reception by humans (see Figure 1.2). Computers recognize a "W" in the encoded bits of 1010111 when you press the W key on the

DIGITAL MEDIA Avatar raised digital film production to a new level and re-introduced 3-D technology to a wide audience. It serves as an example of the transformation of all media to digital forms.

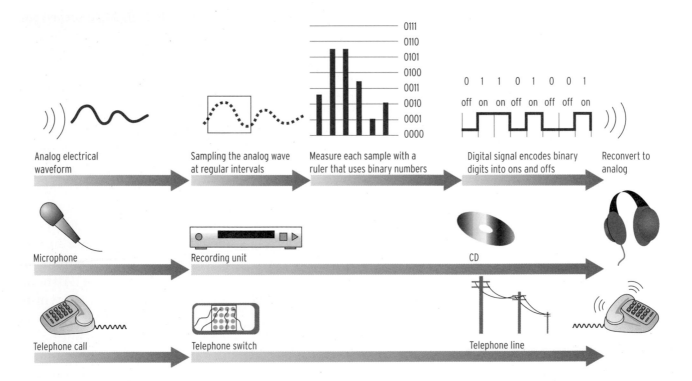

FIGURE 1.2 CONVERTING ANALOG TO DIGITAL The analog-to-digital conversion process occurs in a variety of media. Here we illustrate the examples of a music CD recording and a telephone call.

> A **channel** is an electronic or mechanical system that links the source to the receiver.

keyboard. A particularly useful quality of digital information is that many different sources can be combined in a single transmission medium so that formerly distinct **channels** of communication, such as telephone and television, can be integrated in a common digital medium, such as the Internet or a DVD.

CHANGING INDUSTRIES

> **Convergence** is the integration of mass media, computers, and telecommunications.

The **convergence** of media technologies is propelling changes in media industries as newer media firms like Google, Apple, and Facebook compete with old media companies for dominance (see Figure 1.1, page 5). Apple became the most powerful player in the recorded music industry with iTunes, rocked the telephone industry with the iPhone, and is shaking up print media and video with the iPad. Google has emerged as the largest advertising medium of all as advertisers direct more and more of their dollars to ads tied to online searches. In 2011 Google made a bid to acquire Motorola, a leading cell phone manufacturer, in hopes of besting Apple in the race to move the Internet to mobile devices. Meanwhile, Facebook is prospering as an advertising and content distribution platform for its hundreds of millions of social network users worldwide. Apple and Google, along with Amazon and Netflix, hope to lead a transition to Internet video that could replace conventional broadcast and cable television.

Conventional media firms are struggling to stay in the picture. In 2011 cable television giant Comcast closed a deal to buy NBC Universal after revenues from the NBC television network declined. Also the largest Internet service provider in the United States, Comcast was attracted by NBC's ownership interest in the online video distributor Hulu as well as by NBC's profitable cable channels. Comcast promptly introduced its own video service xfinity and began offering video over the Internet to help maintain the loyalty of its conventional cable television customers. However, many such deals have turned sour. News Corporation, owner of Fox Television, bought MySpace only to see it lose ground to Facebook, finally selling the social networking site in 2011 for less than 10 percent of the price it had paid.

The economic recession of 2007–2009 and the world-wide economic problems that followed weakened the old media just as digital media were beginning to hit their stride. Advertising revenues declined, and many media firms were saddled with debt-ridden deals they made during more prosperous times. Print media were hit the hardest. Although news organizations continued to operate in the black, they decreased their printed output and ramped up their online publishing. The number of two-newspaper cities dwindled, and other daily papers cut back on the number of

Ramin Talaie/Bloomberg via Getty Images

YOUR NEXT TV may be an Internet-capable TV like the Sony model shown here. Internet TV is an example of technological convergence between the Internet and conventional television.

days they made home deliveries or became exclusively online publications. Printed weekly news magazines also suffered as millions turned to the Internet for news and analysis, sometimes from the same news organization online. In 2011 *U.S. News & World Report* became an exclusively online publication, and *Newsweek* merged with an online news organization, The Daily Beast.

Changing industries also mean challenging careers for those entering media professions (see Your Media Career: Room at the Bottom, Room at the Top).

YOUR MEDIA CAREER

ROOM AT THE BOTTOM, ROOM AT THE TOP

The rewards of top-echelon media careers are well publicized: multimillion-dollar salaries, hobnobbing with the rich and famous, globe-hopping lifestyles. From among the tens of thousands who enter the media industry each year from courses like the one you are taking now, only a few make it to the level of Diane Sawyer, Steven Spielberg, Bob Woodward, or Howard Stern. Still, fulfilling professional success can be attained in less visible media occupations, either behind the scenes of global productions or in local markets, where the rewards may come from creative self-expression or from the satisfying feeling of "making a difference."

The challenges of media careers are many. It is often said that media industries "eat their young." Some young college graduates never move beyond internships, often unpaid ones, or entry-level "go-for" positions. Making the jump to steady professional employment sometimes depends on things we do not learn in college, such as having family connections or being born with basic creative talent. Those who progress beyond the entry level may leave after "burning out" on the workload or finding that competitive pressure from yet newer waves of eager college graduates keeps both entry- and mid-level salaries relatively low.

Yet, the media want you. Some media industries, notably music, television, advertising, and film, feed on the creative energies of young professionals who give them insights into young consumers. This means positions are continually opening up at all levels, and talented and well-connected graduates can rise rapidly through the ranks. However, it is also possible to be "washed up" at age 30.

Convergence makes media-related careers highly volatile. Whenever you read about a media merger or a new form of digital media production or distribution, it means that dozens, if not hundreds, of existing media jobs may disappear. In the short term, the challenge will be starting a media career. The Great Recession of 2007–2009 made entry into mass-media fields more difficult than usual (Vlad et al., 2009).

Most people entering the workforce today will have four or five different careers regardless of the field they enter and this is also true of media careers. When we say "different careers," we don't mean working your way up through a progression of related jobs inside an industry, say, from the mailroom at NBC Television to vice president for Network Programming at CBS. For many of our readers it will mean starting out in a media industry but retraining to enter health care, education, or computer careers where employment is expected to grow the fastest over the next decade. To assess your options, you can visit the Occupational Outlook Handbook (http://www.bls.gov/OCO/), an authoritative source of information about the training and education needed, earnings, expected job prospects, what workers do on the job, and working conditions for a wide variety of media occupations. Or, keep reading. In each chapter you will find features about media careers in related fields.

While in college prepare yourself for the challenging career road ahead by diversifying your skills. Multimedia computer skills not only are in demand in media industries but also will help you leap into other careers if necessary. The abilities to write a coherent paragraph and to produce professional photos, videos, audio, and Web pages are in demand across the information economy. Multimedia creators also have entrepreneurial opportunities outside of the walls of the conventional media institutions—from bloggers to Web page designers to YouTube "producers." To take advantage of these opportunities, or to prepare for the day when you might meet the limits of your creative talent, learn as much as you can about all facets of the media, including its economic, legal, marketing, and management aspects. Mix in challenging science and liberal arts courses to further diversify your options. Perfecting your production skills might help you land your first media job but too narrow of a focus might relegate you to low-paying, unsteady freelance production work that does not require a college education. Don't waste yours!

CHANGING LIFESTYLES

When new media enter our lives, media consumption patterns evolve. Each month, for example, more than 180 million U.S. Internet users now watch video online, averaging about 20 hours of viewing monthly (comScore, 2011). Three-fourths of Internet users visited the Internet and a fourth used their cell phones for political purposes during the 2010 elections (Smith, 2011). Top video games like "Call of Duty" make as much money as top movies like *The Twilight Saga*.

A lifestyle change among the college-age population makes media executives take notice: young adults are no longer easily reached by conventional mass media. They spend so much time juggling their iPods, cell phones, and video games (often simultaneously) and maintaining their Facebook identities, that there is little time or interest left for traditional newspapers or television. That's why the old media run websites to sustain interest in *Survivor*, create "buzz" for new movies, or add live discussion forums to printed stories. It's also why media and advertisers look for new ways to recapture the young adult audience, such as making TV shows available online and inserting ads into video games. However, television, broadly defined, is still central to many young people. And much of the new content created on Facebook and Twitter has to do with favorite movies, TV shows, and songs, as old and new media interact in complex ways.

New media introduce us to alternative ways to live, as millions of people now shop, seek health information, get their news, access government information, and keep up with their friends online (Zickuhr, 2010). Others forge new identities (Turkle, 1995), develop new cultures (Lévy, 2001), and find information to make personal decisions online. However, the new media may also displace close human relationships with superficial ones online (Turkle, 2011), lower the quality of public discourse by substituting Internet rumors for professional journalism, or drag popular culture to new lows.

> The **Telecommunications Act of 1996** is federal legislation that deregulated the communications media.

SHIFTING REGULATIONS

With the **Telecommunications Act of 1996**, Congress stripped away regulations that protected publishing, broadcasting, cable and satellite television, telephone, and other media companies from competing with one another. Lawmakers had hoped to spark competition, improve service, and lower prices in all communications media. Unfortunately, the flurry of corporate mergers, buyouts, and bankruptcies has outpaced consumer benefits.

Recent changes in copyright laws shifted the balance of power between media companies and their audiences. The Copyright Term Extension

ahmed Abd El-Latef / Demotix/Demotix/Demotix/Corbis

MEDIA EFFECT The Egyptian government was concerned about the effects the Internet was having on society after it was used to organize a rebellion, so they shut it down. Here Egyptian reporters protest the shutdown. These events mark the start of a new battle between governments and their citizens over control of the Internet.

Act of 1998 broadened the **copyright** protection enjoyed by writers, performers, songwriters, and the giant media corporations that own the rights to such valued properties as Bugs Bunny. The Digital Millennium Copyright Act weakened the fair use rights of students and professors to reproduce copyrighted printed works for noncommercial, educational use. It also cracked down on "sharing" music and videos online and made it a crime to tamper with copy protections on music and videos.

> **Copyright** is the legal right to control intellectual property.

Vital consumer interests are also at stake in the battle over **net neutrality**. This is the principle that Internet providers should remain neutral in handling information on the Internet to avoid favoring content provided by their affiliates and business partners and charging their competitors—and ultimately the public—excessive fees. To win approval for its purchase of NBC Universal, Comcast had to promise federal regulators that it would give fair access to its Internet network to competing online video distributors and also offer video content produced by NBC Universal on an equitable basis to online rivals.

> **Net neutrality** means users are not discriminated against based on the amount or nature of the data they transfer on the Internet.

RISING SOCIAL ISSUES

Social issues are intrinsic to the media. Television is often singled out for the sheer amount of time that impressionable youngsters spend watching it. Children ages 2 to 5 years old average 32 hours a week in front of the television screen (McDonough, 2009). Television has been criticized for its impacts on sexual promiscuity, racial and ethnic stereotypes, sexism, economic exploitation, mindless consumption, childhood obesity, smoking, drinking, and political apathy. The impact of television on violence is an enduring concern of parents and policy makers alike. By the time the average child finishes elementary school, he or she has seen 8,000 murders and 100,000 acts of violence and by the age of 18, has seen 40,000 murders and 200,000 other acts of violence (TV-Free, n.d.).

New media are fast replacing television as the number one concern about media effects. Some researchers believe that video games have a much greater effect on violent behavior than old media and are nearly as powerful inducements to violence as participation in street gangs (Anderson et al., 2006). New media have also made it possible for children to turn into producers of problematic content, including videos of middle school beat downs posted on YouTube and exchanges of self-posed child pornography exchanged as cell phone text messages.

Another issue of concern is whether the spread of the Internet creates a **digital divide** that spawns a new underclass of citizens who do not enjoy equal access to the latest technology and the growing array of public services available online? (See Media and Culture, A New Balance of Power?)

> The **digital divide** is the gap in Internet usage between rich and poor, Anglos and minorities.

On a global scale, a wave of pro-democracy rebellions that swept through the Middle East and saw parallels in the Occupy Wall Street movement in the U.S. in 2011seemed to feed on Facebook, Twitter, text messages, and cell phone videos. However, the Internet can also be manipulated by dictators and terrorists. The Egyptian authorities turned off the Internet in an unsuccessful effort to end

STOP&REVIEW

1. List four examples of the convergence phenomenon.
2. What is meant by the term *information society*?
3. What are three conventional types of mass media?
4. What is the difference between analog and digital?
5. Name areas in which communication regulations are shifting.

MEDIA&CULTURE

A NEW BALANCE OF POWER?

Just how powerful are the media? Do they affect the very underpinnings of the social order, by determining who holds power in society and how they keep it?

The new media can put us all at the mercy of "digital robber barons." The late Steve Jobs was widely praised and much admired upon his death, but he was a prime example of someone who sets out to dominate new media, to create interesting new things, but also to enrich himself at our expense. The dominance of this type of person reduces the diversity of content and raises the cost of information. For example, Apple maintains control over the applications ("apps" for short) that are allowed on its iPhone. Innovative apps developed by entrepreneurs that might save consumers money on music, but that would diminish the profits from Apple's iTunes are not allowed. Meanwhile, old media interests like Disney and Time Warner sue peer-to-peer file sharing services on the Internet like LimeWire to protect their property rights. We might well ask, Is the information society just a new way for the rich to get richer?

Or, do the new media consign the poor to continuing poverty? The digital divide describes the gap in Internet access between whites and minorities, rich and poor (NTIA, 2002). As the Internet grows into an important source of employment, education, and political participation, that digital divide could translate into widening class division and social upheaval. Equal opportunity in the information economy already lags for both minorities and women, who are underrepresented in both the most visible (that is, on-camera) and most powerful (that is, senior executive) positions in the media. And although the gap in Internet access for women has largely closed (except for those who are poor or who are recent immigrants) women are poorly represented in computer-related professions and the proportion of women enrolled in undergraduate computer science majors is now in the low teens, about a third of the peak level in the 1980s (Computing Research Association, 2011). The issue is global. The nations of the world are divided between those with access to advanced communication technology and those without it.

Or, could the new media be a catalyst for a shift away from traditional ruling classes? Social media were integral to pro-democracy revolutions in the Middle East and the Occupy Wall Street movement in the U.S. Blogs raise issues that are ignored by the mainstream press. The diverse and lively communities of the Internet may contribute to the fragmentation of culture and power—for many, identity is defined as much by the Internet communities in which we participate as by the countries we live in or the color of our skin.

---

pro-democracy demonstrations there. In Iran, the government used the Internet to track down and punish participants who posted revolutionary messages online (Morozov, 2011).

CHANGING MEDIA THROUGHOUT HISTORY

Although changes in the media and the accompanying changes in society sometimes appear to be radically new and different, the media and society have always adapted to one another. In this section we examine how the role of the media has evolved as society developed—and vice versa—from the dawn of human civilization (see Figure 1.3, page 13) through agricultural, industrial, and information societies (Bell, 1973; Dizard, 1997; Sloan, 2005).

PREAGRICULTURAL SOCIETY

Before agricultural societies developed, most people lived in small groups as hunters of animals and gatherers of plants. These cultures depended on the spoken words and songs to transmit ideas among themselves and between generations.

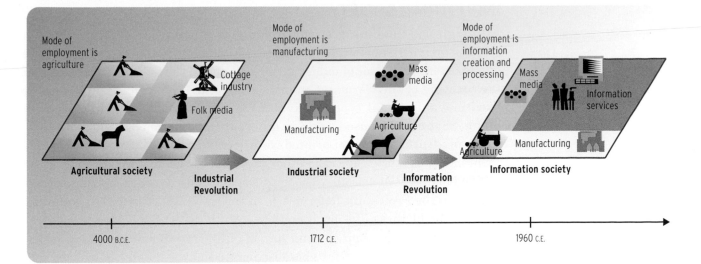

FIGURE 1.3 STAGES OF ECONOMIC DEVELOPMENT The three basic stages of economic development, from agricultural to industrial to informational.

Shamans and storytellers spread the news. The oral tradition is an extremely rich one, bringing to us Homer's *Iliad* and *Odyssey* and the epic stories, folktales, ritual chants, and songs of many other cultures. These works that originated in oral forms live on today in the fairy tales and campfire stories that we tell our children.

AGRICULTURAL SOCIETY

Once agricultural society developed, most work was found on farms or in resource extraction, such as mining, fishing, and logging. Agricultural societies were more settled and more complex than pre-agricultural societies. It was the ancient Sumerian culture, located in what is now modern-day Iraq, that is commonly credited with developing writing in 3100 BCE. The Greco-Roman method of writing developed into our present-day alphabet.

In early civilizations literacy was common only among priests and the upper classes. In some cultures literacy was intentionally limited, because the ruling class wanted to keep the masses ignorant of new ideas. Reproduction of printed works was painstaking. Christian monks copied books by hand. The Chinese developed printing with a press that used carved wooden blocks, paper, and ink. With much of the populace still illiterate, couriers skilled at memorizing long oral messages were valuable communications specialists.

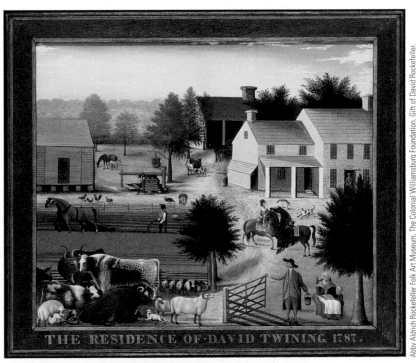

DOWN ON THE FARM Agricultural societies are characterized by resource extraction. Written communication evolved as a specialized function. Literacy expanded in industrial society to provide skilled workers who were able to follow complex written procedures.

INDUSTRIAL SOCIETY

Although the beginning of the Industrial Revolution is often dated to correspond with Thomas Newcomen's invention of the steam engine in 1712, an important precursor of industrialism is found in the field of communication: the printing of the German Gutenberg Bible in 1455. Johannes Gutenberg used movable metal type—individual letters instead of a complete page plate—that could be used again in different combinations. Eventually, thousands of identical copies of printed works could be printed relatively cheaply. Printed copies of the Bible and other religious works, including copies in the native languages of various Western European cultures, were instrumental in spreading the Protestant Reformation of the sixteenth century, which in turn spurred the further diffusion of literacy.

The mass production and the spread of literacy to new classes of society helped create a demand for sporadic printed news sheets that eventually evolved into newspapers. In 1690 Benjamin Harris published the first newspaper in America, *Publick Occurrences, Both Foreign and Domestick,* although the British colonial authorities promptly shut it down after one issue because it was printed without their permission. Fourteen years later, John Campbell printed the first continuously published American newspaper, the *Boston News-Letter.*

North Wind Picture Archives / Alamy

START THE PRESSES! The advent of the printing press in the late fifteenth century was a precursor of mass literacy and the Industrial Revolution. The bibles printed by Johannes Gutenberg and others launched a revolution in religious beliefs and culture in the Western world.

In a sense, the Industrial Revolution extended Gutenberg's methods to the manufacture of not just newsprint, but virtually all types of goods. Industrial production (and higher wages) was centered in large cities, triggering a mass migration from rural areas to cities and from agricultural jobs to manufacturing. Growing urban populations with money to spend on manufactured goods provided ready audiences as newspapers expanded to become the first advertising-supported medium of mass communication.

By 1910 the United States had become an industrial society: manufacturing had outstripped agricultural employment for the first time. Industrialization also encouraged the spread of literacy to cope with more complex job requirements and the demands of urban life. Soon, industrial methods of mass production were applied to speed up the printing process of newspapers and magazines and to invent newer communication technologies for the urban populations. Film, radio, and television, as well as newspapers and magazines, are the characteristic media of industrial societies.

INFORMATION SOCIETY

Today, we live in an information society—our economy depends primarily on the production and consumption of information. When the United States was still an agricultural society, only about 10 percent of the population was employed as **information workers**. The point at which information work starts to dominate the workforce marks the transition to an information society. This transition happened in the United States in 1960, but relatively few other nations have made the transition so far. The proportion of information workers has reached about three-fifths of the U.S. workforce (Wolff, 2006). Since the media reflect the societies that spawn them, it comes as no surprise that the dominant tool in an information society is one that helps to create, store, and process information: the computer.

The evolution of media in the information society can be marked by points at which various media first adopted digital technology and the point at which they became complete, end-to-end digital production and distribution channels. Some of these changes predate the invention of the personal computer in 1975 and the advent of the World Wide Web in 1991.

Telephone. The first consumer communications medium to be digitized was the telephone, beginning in 1962 with digital equipment buried deep within AT&T's network. Today, telephone conversations are converted to digital form in your cell phone handset and travel as computer data throughout the telephone network (see Figure 1.2, page 7). Digital subscriber lines (DSL) make landline phones a practical medium for high-speed Internet access. Apple's iPhone and other smartphones capable of Internet access point us in the direction of using our cell phones for all of our music and video entertainment.

> **Information workers** create, process, transform, or store information.

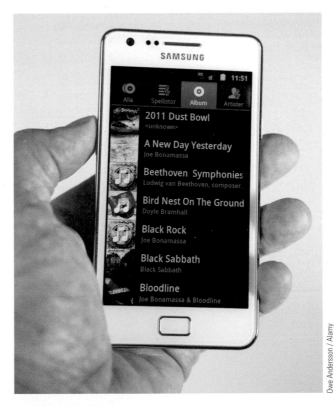

WIRELESS WEB Cell phones that provide wireless Internet access and video (smartphones) represent the new phase of media convergence. They compete for attention with both old media forms such as television and newspapers as well as new media forms such as personal computers and iPods.

NOW AT YOUR LOCAL THEATER Digital Light Projection (DLP) systems using CD-like digital storage media instead of film represent the digital revolution at your local movie theater.

[**Interactive** communication uses feedback to modify a message as it is presented.]

Print Media. Digitization first hit the production rooms of print media in the late 1960s. Now it is only in the final printing process that the words and images are converted from computer code to analog print image. Thousands of newspapers and magazines are also available electronically on the Internet, and e-books and tablets like Apple's iPad and Amazon's Kindle are catching on fast as e-readers.

Film. In Hollywood, the computer movement started with the special effects for *Star Wars* in 1974. Now most film editing is done on computer and digital 35-mm cameras are in widespread use. Computer-generated hit films, beginning with *Toy Story* in 1995, are becoming commonplace. Movie theater sound systems are digital, and the latest Digital Light Projection (DLP) systems use digital technology to project the images as well. *Avatar* pushed digital movies into the third dimension. In the home, Blu-ray high-definition digital video discs and online services like streaming Netflix are making home video all digital from studio to consumer.

Video Games. Video games were digital from the start. First developed on computers in 1962, they moved to arcades and home consoles in 1971–1972, and later onto personal computers and handhelds. The latest video game consoles display such high-quality graphics that they might be considered **interactive** movies.

Recordings. The first digital compact disc (CD) recordings reached consumers in 1982 and outpaced vinyl record album sales a decade later. The file sharing craze sparked by Napster in 1999 introduced millions of music lovers to downloading digital music free from the Internet, eventually paving the way for Apple's iTunes to dominate online digital music distribution.

Cable and Satellite Television. In 1998 cable companies began to convert content to digital form as a way to increase the number of channel offerings on their systems. Cable went digital in part to meet competition from direct broadcast satellites (DBS) that began beaming hundreds of channels of digital programming directly to home dishes in 1995. Now many cable subscribers enjoy high-speed Internet access and telephone service as well.

Broadcasting. High-definition television (HDTV), which uses digital formats to transmit wider and clearer pictures, replaced conventional television completely in 2009. The next generation of radio, digital audio broadcasting (known as high-definition radio), reached the air in 2004 to compete with digital satellite radio services and with streaming audio on the Internet. Meanwhile, digital video recorders like TiVo threaten broadcasters with their ability to skip commercials and to personalize viewing. Internet television distributors like Hulu and online streaming music services like Pandora challenge the basic concept of broadcasting to mass audiences.

Thus, the media are becoming an integral part of our information society. Indeed, employees of newspapers, radio and television stations, and film and recording studios now are grouped together with telecommunications workers and computer programmers as part of the information sector of the economy. Thus, to understand the media now a broad view encompassing telecommunications, consumer computer products, and mass media is required.

STOP&REVIEW

1. What were the media forms in preagricultural society?

2. What media evolved in industrial societies?

3. What changes led to the development of the information society?

4. Which media have become purely digital from end to end?

CHANGING CONCEPTIONS OF THE MEDIA

Reading highly encapsulated accounts of the evolution of the media, such as the above, you might get the mistaken impression that society has always followed a logical, linear progression driven by changes in communication technology. However, many aspects of society—such as economics and politics—must come together for technologies like movable type or computers to develop. This reality raises the fundamental question that we noted earlier and will consider at length in Chapter 2: Do the media determine culture and society, or do culture and society determine the media? Here we will review a conventional model of human communication and then examine how new media challenge that model.

THE SMCR MODEL

The classic SMCR model was first developed by Shannon and Weaver (1949) and later refined by David Berlo (1960) and Wilbur Schramm (1954). They created what is known as the **Source-Message-Channel-Receiver (SMCR)** model.

> The **Source-Message-Channel-Receiver (SMCR)** model of mass communication describes the exchange of information as the message passes from the source to the channel to the receiver, with feedback to the source.

The *source* is the originator of the communication.

The *message* is the content of the communication, the information that is to be exchanged.

An *encoder* translates the message into a form that can be communicated—often a form that is not directly interpretable by human senses.

A *channel* is the medium or transmission system used to convey the message from one place to another.

A *decoder* reverses the encoding process.

The *receiver* is the destination of the communication.

A *feedback mechanism* between the source and the receiver regulates the flow of communication.

Noise is any distortion or errors that may be introduced during the information exchange.

This model can be applied to all forms of human communication, but here we will just illustrate it with a mass communication example, that of television viewing (see Figure 1.4). According to the model, when you are at home watching a television program, the television network (a corporate source)

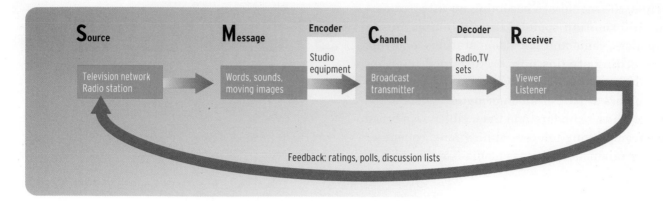

FIGURE 1.4 SMCR MODEL The SMCR model is one way of describing the communication process as applied to broadcast media. In this example we apply the model to television and radio broadcasting.

originates the message, which is encoded by the microphones and television cameras in the television studio. The channel is not literally the number on the television dial to which you are tuned, but rather the entire chain of transmitters, satellite links, and cable television equipment required to convey the message to your home. Although we sometimes call a TV set a "receiver," it is really the decoder, and the viewer is the receiver. Feedback from viewers is via television rating services. Electronic interference with the broadcast and the distractions of the neighbor's barking dogs are possible noise components in this situation.

In this classic view, mass communication is a one-to-many communication, and the mass media are the various channels through which mass communication is delivered; that is, through newspapers, radio, TV, or film, the message is communicated from a single source to many receivers at about the same time, with limited opportunities for the audience to communicate back to the source.

In Wilbur Schramm's time, from the late 1940s to the early 1980s, mass media were produced by large media corporations. There an elite corps of media commentators and professional producers acted as **gatekeepers**, deciding what the audience should receive. These editors and producers, recognizing their own power, were aware of themselves as shapers of public opinion and popular tastes (Schramm, 1982).

Mass-media messages were addressed to the widest possible audience. The underlying motive was to homogenize tastes and opinions to further the goals of a mass-market industrial economy. Feedback was largely limited to reports from audience research bureaus, which took days or weeks to compile in those days. Beyond the basic demographic distinctions of gender and age found in research reports, the audience was an undifferentiated mass, anonymous to the source and a passive receptacle for the message. Social critics like Adorno and Horkheimer (1972) called this approach the industrialization of culture.

Other critics, like Carey (1989), criticized the SMCR model for being too linear, seeing media only as a one-way flow from creators to audiences. He and others began to see communication as a more circular, interactive, or even

> **Gatekeepers** decide what will appear in the media.

ritual process—one in which audiences not only choose from but also interact with media content, changing its meaning.

Facebook, Twitter, and YouTube are **social media** that challenge the SMCR model, and they embody and even extend the critiques of Carey and others. Social media users continually interact with one another and provide instant feedback not only to their own communication partners but also to the creators of conventional mass media productions that are frequent topics of online commentary. Now we create our own media content, share it with hundreds or thousands of our online "friends" and contest the power of authoritative mass media sources in ways and on a scale that neither Schramm nor Carey could anticipate. YouTube videos conform in some ways to the conventional mass communication model in that they are one-to-many but feedback in the form of audience comments is nearly instantaneous and the sources are typically amateur video producers rather than media professionals. So, do social media constitute a fundamentally new type of communication?

MARIO ANZUONI/Reuters /Landov

WOW FACTOR Filmmakers hope 3-D movies will encourage the masses to lay down their game consoles and return to movie theaters. However, 3-D movies are still examples of conventional mass communication in that they address a mass audience with limited feedback.

[**Social media** are media whose content is created and distributed through social interaction.]

TYPES OF COMMUNICATION

Communication is simply the exchange of meaning. This definition covers a lot of ground. It obviously includes talking to your friends, reading a newspaper, watching television, and surfing the Internet. Less obvious examples of communication might include the graphic design on a T-shirt, a fit of laughter, or the wink of an eye. And, the meaning exchanged does not have to be profound: a sonnet by Shakespeare and a verse scratched on a bathroom wall both qualify as communication. In terms of the SMCR model, the exchange is between the source of the message and the receiver.

[**Communication** is an exchange of meaning.]

Mass communication is a major focus of this book but is only one of the possible modes of communication. Another hallmark of the classical approach is to classify communication according to the number of people communicating and to examine processes that are unique to each mode. The basic categories include intrapersonal, interpersonal, small group, and large group, as well as mass communication, shown in Figure 1.5. In this figure, the number of people involved grows from top to bottom, with the width of the pyramids with mass communication forms at the bottom. Now we can also distinguish between analog (on the left) and digital forms of communication (on the right) in each category. As we move from top to bottom we move among types of communication, from intrapersonal to interpersonal,

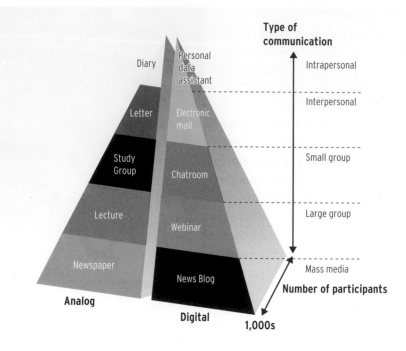

FIGURE 1.5 TYPES OF COMMUNICATION Types of communication may be distinguished according to the number of participants and the nature of the communication process.

from small group to large group, from one to mass communication, and back again. An example of each type is found in the corresponding layer of the pyramid, one for analog and one for digital:

Intrapersonal communication is an exchange of information we have with ourselves, such as when we think over our next move in a video game or sing to ourselves in the shower. Typing a to-do list into a computer or a smartphone is electronically mediated intrapersonal communication.

Interpersonal communication includes exchanges in which two or more people take part, but the term is usually reserved for situations in which just two people are communicating. Sometimes we call that one-to-one communication. Having a face-to-face conversation over lunch and writing a postcard to a friend are everyday examples. When interpersonal communication is electronically **mediated**, as in a telephone conversation, the term *point-to-point communication* is sometimes used.

Group communication is a situation in which three or more people communicate with one another. Not all communication that takes place in a group setting is included, however. When pairs of students talk to each other in a classroom before the start of a lecture, for example, they are engaged in interpersonal communication (see above).

Small-group communication usually involves fewer than a dozen people, extending interpersonal communication into situations where group dynamics become important. For example, when students get together to "scope out" an exam, their interaction is likely to follow one of several well-known patterns of small-group interaction as they define a study plan. For example, one person in the group may dominate. Or, they may take turns speaking and let everyone have their say; we could call that many-to-many communication. Online, small group communication happens in chat rooms and in multi-user video phone calls.

Large-group communication involves anywhere from a dozen to several thousand participants, and the communication situation restricts active involvement to only a few of the parties. However, large-group communication still involves immediate feedback from the receivers of the message, which is not the case with mass communication. Examples of large-group communication are lectures, concerts, and live theatrical performances. When we update our Facebook profiles or post messages to our Twitter "followers" we are engaging in large group communication—provided we have a dozen or more online friends or followers.

Many communication situations do not fit neatly into these categories. Are talk-radio shows, in which audience members provide instant communication back to the source—and even, in a sense, become sources themselves—still true mass-media forms? What about TV shows like *American Idol* that invite viewers to direct the content by voting with their cell phones? We could perhaps call that many-to-one communication. In the social media sphere, wall postings and photo tags are further examples. Other aspects of social media, such as discussion groups in Facebook might be termed many-to-many communication since audience members are also participants who are themselves also the sources of the content.

Also, the number of participants is not always a reliable indicator of the type of communication involved. A college lecture delivered on the last day before spring break to only six students or a Facebook posting made by someone with only a few online friends would still be a large-group communication (because of the style of presentation), even though the audience is a small group in terms of the number of people involved. Thus, both the nature of the communication setting and the size of the gathering must be considered.

Other classifications of communication reflect the setting for the communication or the nature of the communication process. Organizational communication takes place in formally structured organizations, spans the entire spectrum of communication types as classified by size, and is affected by a person's position and function within the organization. For example, in certain highly structured organizations, most communication travels in one direction—from the bosses to the workers—with little flowing either back up the chain of command or laterally, to workers in other departments. Other organizations use social media to promote horizontal communication between employees and "bottom up" feedback from employees to management. Communication can also be distinguished between one-way communication, in which the flow of information goes from the source exclusively to the receiver, and two-way, in which both participants take an active role. Finally, intercultural communication takes place across international or cultural boundaries.

So, are social media a fundamentally new type of communication? That is debatable. Social networking sites like Facebook are unique in that their various functions provide examples of virtually every type of communication we have mentioned here. Social media also bring relatively rare types of communication, such as many-to-one and many-to-many, within the reach of millions and make it routine for their users to originate their own large group communications. Empowering the audience or user to produce media content as well as consume it also occurs in social media venues on a very large scale, but is not entirely unprecedented. Letters to the editor and radio call-in programs are time-honored old media examples of audience-produced content as well.

WHAT ARE THE MEDIA NOW?

At one time, *media* simply meant the mass media of radio, television, newspapers, and film. We now talk about *new media*— a term usually associated with interactive media technology, such as the Internet and video games. Although we sometimes use new media in ways that are not so new and different, such as reading news stories online, old media are acquiring new interactive dimensions, such as voting with our cell phones for our favorite *American Idol* on TV. The defining aspects of the new media are that they are digital, interactive, social, **asynchronous**, multimedia, and **narrowcasted**. These particular characteristics are important in distinguishing a new, audience-focused conception of the media from the older SMCR model, which emphasized the one-way transmission of messages.

Digital. Digital media have become so widespread and their improvements so obvious that we may now sometimes take them for granted. Earlier, we listed some of the important milestones in the transition from analog to digital media. What differences do digital media make? Digitization improves the quality of transmission because digital signals are less susceptible to interference and distortion. Digital messages also can be compressed by allowing multiple channels to be carried where only one was possible before. Many users can also share the same transmission channel simultaneously by taking turns. The Internet uses this approach, which is called *packet switching*: if we cut up the stream of digits for your e-mail into chunks (called "packets"), and cut up the YouTube video file your neighbor is receiving, then both of you can share the same channel. Furthermore, digitization is the key to multimedia— combining text, image, and sound in two-way communication channels—representing an important departure from the old media where each modality was confined to separate channels and was one-way only.

Interactive. We hear about interactive television and interactive websites but just what is "interactivity"? Sometimes the word is used as a synonym for two-way communication, but few interactive media are truly two-way in the same sense as interpersonal communication. In a conversation, two people not only take turns responding to each other but also modify their interaction on the basis of preceding exchanges (Rafaeli, 1988). Social media like Facebook

DIGITAL INTERPERSONAL Cell phones are an example of digital interpersonal communication when used alone, and an example of digital small-group communication if you text messages to your closest friends. Uploading pictures to Facebook from your smartphone is large-group communication while viewing movies on a mobile is mass communication.

Asynchronous media are not consumed simultaneously by all members of the audience.

Narrowcasting targets media to specific segments of the audience.

and Twitter are interactive in that sense, but it is the actions of the people as much as the **affordances** of the technology, such as the Like button found in Facebook, that make it so.

The ultimate form of interactivity would pass the so-called Turing test for artificial intelligence, named after the British computer pioneer Alan Turing (1950). To pass the test, a computer would be able to fool you into thinking that you were interacting with a human. Watson, the computer that trounced human champions on *Jeopardy!* in 2011, would pass that test but only while playing *Jeopardy!*. Watson might not, however, have the answer if you asked directions to the washroom in the *Jeopardy!* studio. Watson may also have had the edge in faster response times when pressing the button in addition to whatever intelligence it possessed.

We will narrow the definition of interactive media to mean those where feedback from the receiver is used by the source—whether human or computer—to continually modify the message as it is being delivered to the receiver. By this definition, selecting alternative plots in an online novel is interactive, but TV remote controls and book indexes are not (no real-time feedback to the source). In video games where the game gets harder as you score more points, there are, in effect, real-time interactions with the game developer. The software reacts just as a human player would.

Interactivity is an important departure from mass communication in the conventional SMCR model, where feedback was weak and delayed by days or weeks. When feedback is instantaneous the audience gains new power, not only to select content but to contest the messages supplied by the media, and even contribute to media content. For example, when *American Idol* viewers vote for a contestant who has been humiliated by one of the judges, they are contesting the mass-mediated message. Although, to fit our definition of interactivity, the results would be presented in real time and the judges would be reversed on the spot, perhaps with the contestants performing taunting "victory dances." As much as any other change in the media, this strengthening of the feedback link alters the nature of the mass communication process, making the audience active participants, rather than passive receivers of media content.

Social Media. Another dimension of audience power in the new media world is the ability of audiences to contribute content of their own, not merely selecting it as in our example of *American Idol*, but actually creating it themselves. Since this involves sharing words and images with other users in the course of social interactions, social media have emerged as an umbrella term for this phenomenon.

Behind the scenes, new technologies have made it possible to strip away the middle layers of media organizations and to shrink the minimum size of media enterprises back to that of small cottage industries and even to individual media entrepreneurs. Giant media corporations are still with us, but the number of people required to turn out a media product within them is shrinking. Affordable TV cameras, audio recorders, digital editing technology, and cell phone cameras put people from all walks of life in the producer's chair.

Perhaps the best-known examples of social media are social networking sites like Facebook and video sharing sites like YouTube. **Blogs** that are

Photos 12 / Alamy

ASYNCHRONOUS HIT Modern Family is the most watched TV show on DVRs. Its audience grows 40 percent among those 18-49 when delayed viewing is counted over a week's time.

filled with personal and professional commentary, content that now often serves as sources for the traditional media, are another example. Twitter is sometimes called a microblog, where the commentary is reduced to 140-character snippets. Wikipedia, reader comments posted on newspaper websites, and consumer-generated product reviews on the Web are other examples of the social media phenomenon.

The ability of social media to define culture may be eroding the power of the conventional media. Ever-growing amounts of the news and entertainment are generated by those who do not work for established "big media" organizations. This trend liberates the creative energies of millions of people and makes it possible for viewpoints that are not acceptable in mainstream media to find an audience. Still, the conventional media provide a valuable public service by separating fact from fiction and weeding out truly awful and harmful content. Perhaps informative and entertaining social media will rise to the top through the recommender systems built into social media—but what if they do not?

Asynchronous Communication. Simultaneity, the notion that everyone in the audience receives the message at about the same time (or *synchronously*), was once another defining characteristic of the mass media. That view made sense before consumer recording technology became commonplace in the 1960s and 1970s. Before then, you had to catch a program the first time it aired or wait for the reruns. However, the notion never applied very well to film, not without stretching "the same time" to cover a period of several weeks.

Situations that lack simultaneity are examples of asynchronous communication. Consumers' ability to "time shift" programs using digital video recorders (DVRs) and Internet video renders the notion of simultaneity obsolete, as they can choose when to watch a program regardless of the time and day it originally airs. The television networks are now time-shifting themselves by uploading their own programs on the Internet within hours of the time of their original broadcast. Both postal mail and e-mail are two common examples of asynchronous interpersonal communication.

Narrowcasting. Another sign of the growing power of the audience in the new media is the practice of targeting content to smaller audiences, sometimes called narrowcasting (as opposed to broadcasting). Advanced audience research methods help the media cater to smaller audiences by enhancing the richness and speed of audience feedback. The result is that narrowcasting—dedicating communication channels to specific audience subgroups, or market segments—is now practical. Demographic characteristics, such as sex and age, once the sole means of defining audiences, are being replaced by a focus on lifestyles and user needs, and even individual preferences including purchasing and online surfing behavior. Rather than homogenize audiences, the new communications media cater to specialized groups and define new niches and even customize content for individuals by sifting through vast databases of information that consumers leave behind as they navigate the Internet. Narrowcasting is also sometimes referred to as deliberate segmentation of audiences into small target groups or fragmentation of large audiences into smaller ones.

Multimedia. Converging technologies break down conventional distinctions between channels of communication so that we can select between modes of presentation. Consider online newspapers that show us the text of the latest story about scandal in high places, but also include links to additional resources such as animated graphics that "follow the money trail" and live video of the congressional hearings on the matter, as well as to instant polls and a discussion group where we can express our outrage. This multitude of news components means we can choose to experience the same story in five different ways, including as a conversation with other audience members. More media are gaining interactive features such as these, which offer consumers new options for selecting information, personalizing content, and participating in a larger conversation. The change means that, increasingly, the mass media of radio, television, newspapers, and film as we once knew them are no longer quite the same.

So what are the media now? Older media forms such as newspapers, television, and film, and conventional media institutions like the *New York Times*, CBS Television, and MGM Studios are still with us and will continue to be for a long time. But throughout the media environment, numerous changes in the media, both big and small, are being driven by the continuing evolution of technology, regulation, media ownership, our economy, our culture, our world, and ourselves. As this evolution continues, the old media of generations past are gradually taking on new media forms such as those we've discussed here.

TIME SHIFTER Personal digital video recorders (like TiVo, shown here) allow viewers to record the TV programs they want and then watch at their own leisure instead of at the show's scheduled airtime. However, they are not interactive in our sense of modifying the content in real time with feedback to the source.

STOP&REVIEW

1. What does the acronym SMCR stand for?
2. Use the SMCR model to describe what happens when you watch TV.
3. Is an automated teller machine interactive? Explain.
4. Name three examples of social media.
5. How do the "new media" differ from the "old media"?

SUMMARY&REVIEW

WHAT IS THE INFORMATION SOCIETY?

The information society is one in which the production, processing, distribution, and consumption of information are the primary economic and social activities. In an information society, an ever-increasing amount of time is spent with digital communications media. Most people are employed as information workers: people who produce, process, or distribute information as their primary work activity. The information society is a further step in the evolution of society from its former bases in agriculture and manufacturing.

HOW ARE MASS MEDIA AND INFORMATION TECHNOLOGIES CONVERGING?

Increasingly, communication is created and distributed in computer-readable digital form. This change means that the same basic technologies can be used to transmit all forms of communication—text, audio, or video—in an integrated communication system such as the Internet. Thus, separate channels of communication are no longer needed for each medium. The mass media, telecommunications, Internet, and computer software industries are all part of the same information sector of the economy—they are, in other words, converging. Laws and public policies governing the media, career opportunities in communications industries, social and personal issues arising from media consumption, and even theories of the media and their role in society are all changing.

WHAT ARE THE COMPONENTS OF THE COMMUNICATION PROCESS?

All communication processes can be described in terms of a simple model in which a corporate or individual source encodes a message and transmits it through a physical channel to the person for whom the message is intended—the receiver. We call this the SMCR model. In most communication situations, feedback is also provided between the receiver and the source. Contemporary views of the process stress that it takes place in the context of a culture shared by the source and the receiver and that both source and receiver contribute to the creation of meaning.

WHAT IS MASS COMMUNICATION?

The conventional view is that mass communication involves large professional organizations, audiences of hundreds or thousands or millions of people, and no immediate feedback between source and receiver. Newspapers, magazines, radio, television, and film are all examples of mass media.

WHAT OTHER TYPES OF COMMUNICATION EXIST?

When the communication channel is an electronic or mechanical device—such as a radio station or a movie projector—we call it mediated communication. Mediated communication may be point-to-point, one-to-many, or multipoint-to-multipoint. Communication can be characterized according to the number of people involved. Intrapersonal communication involves one person, interpersonal communication usually includes only two people, and small-group communication usually encompasses more than two but fewer than a dozen participants. Large-group communication involves dozens or hundreds of people, but feedback is still immediate. Communication can also be characterized according to the setting in which it takes place. For example, organizational communication happens inside a formally structured organization. Social media combine multiple types of communication and empower audiences to contribute content on an unprecedented scale.

WHERE DID THE MASS MEDIA COME FROM?

Although mass media had forerunners in agricultural and pre-agricultural societies, they are generally regarded as creations of the Industrial Age. Mass-production methods coupled with the rise of large urban audiences for media during the Industrial Age led to the rise of print and later mass media.

WHAT IS INTERACTIVITY?

A variety of meanings have been attached to the term *interactive*, ranging from the simple ability to select content from a large number of options to devices that could pass the Turing test by faithfully mimicking human interaction. The term should be reserved for communication situations in which the user modifies the content by providing feedback to the source in real time.

WHAT ARE THE NEW MEDIA?

The long-term trend is to integrate the many specialized channels of communication into all-purpose digital networks that will provide access at the convenience of the audience. Familiar mass-media forms such as newspapers, radio, and television are evolving into, or learning to coexist with, new forms that are all-digital, such as the World Wide Web. Recent interactive capabilities give users a new measure of control over the media channels they consume, where and when they consume the media, and even the content of those channels. Mass media sources are becoming more numerous and also less authoritative and professional. Messages are customized for smaller specialized audience segments, sometimes even using personal forms of address, and are narrowcast to these segments rather than broadcast to a homogeneous audience.

THINKING CRITICALLY
ABOUT THE MEDIA

1. How would you tell the story of the development of the information society to your parents?

2. Describe what convergence has meant in your life and how it affects you.

3. What will your future life in the information society be like?

4. Explain text messaging using the SMCR model.

5. If you send a text message to your entire "friends circle," is that mass communication? Explain.

6. Are social media a fundamentally new type of communication or not? Justify.

KEY TERMS

affordances (p. 23)

analog (p. 5)

asynchronous (p. 22)

blog (p. 23)

channel (p. 8)

communication (p. 19)

convergence (p. 8)

copyright (p. 11)

digital (p. 4)

digital divide (p. 11)

gatekeeper (p. 18)

information society (p. 3)

information worker (p. 15)

interactive (p. 16)

mass communication (p. 4)

mediated (p. 20)

narrowcasting (p. 22)

net neutrality (p. 11)

social media (p. 19)

Source-Message-Channel-Receiver (SMCR) (p. 17)

Telecommunications Act of 1996 (p. 10)

EAGER MEDIA CONSUMERS like these buyers of the final *Twilight Saga* novel help us understand why the media exist. We will examine many other explanations for the media here in this chapter.

2

MEDIA AND SOCIETY

UNDERSTANDING THE MEDIA

This chapter is organized around one of the most fundamental debates about media and society: do media change society or reflect society? For example, is the adoption of the Internet determined by the cost of Internet service or does Internet technology change the economics of media consumption? Or do both take place?

We begin this chapter with the arguments that society drives the changes in media content and technology. Then we'll end the chapter by presenting opposing positions about how media content and media technologies impact society and culture. In between, we will consider viewpoints that occupy the middle ground, emphasizing the mutual relationship between media and culture.

We'll examine the issue through **theories** of media and society. Theories reflect our assumptions about patterns of behavior of individuals and media institutions. Media theories can help us predict future actions in similar circumstances, take a more critical look at what media do, and interpret the broader meaning of the media and their content. In this chapter we will focus on theories about how media institutions function in society. In Chapter 14 we will examine theories of media impacts on individuals. Theories are the work of scholars who are typically employed as university professors, so we would also like to introduce you to that profession (see Your Media Career: Media Scholar, page 32).

> **Theories** are general principles that explain and predict behavior.

29

MEDIA ECONOMICS

If you were to ask people who work in the media why their companies operate the way they do, probably the most frequent answer would be "to make money." Notwithstanding some important nonprofit exceptions such as Public Broadcasting, America is a capitalist society and its media institutions reflect that fact. Accordingly, the first set of theories we will examine explains the media in economic terms.

[**Economics** studies the forces that allocate resources to satisfy competing needs.]

Economics studies the forces that allocate resources to satisfy competing needs (Picard, 2002). Classical economists believe that media institutions, as well as the cultures and societies in which they exist and the media consumption behavior of individuals, reflect economic forces. For these economists, our purchase of Microsoft's Xbox 360 results from a cold and calculated economic comparison of its price and features to Nintendo's Wii and the costs of other competing entertainment alternatives, rather than from our passion to play games.

MASS PRODUCTION, MASS DISTRIBUTION

Throughout the history of the mass media, mass production and mass distribution have been the keys to economic success. Recalling our discussion of the historical development of the media in Chapter 1, we can say that the transition from the folk media that characterized agricultural society to the mass media associated with industrial society came about as standardized media products were distributed to ever-expanding mass markets (see Figure 2.1). In this respect, the media follow an industrial economic model in which profits are reaped by producing many copies of a product at the lowest possible cost to the producer. As media companies get larger, expand their scope, and find larger audiences, they can spread the first-copy costs over more consumers. They reap immense profits if their production costs go down while audiences expand.

Thus, all media companies constantly strive to produce media products more efficiently to reduce their costs, but large firms enjoy some natural—sometimes unfair—advantages in doing so. For example, CBS Television can better afford investments in labor-saving technologies like robotic cameras for the big market television stations it owns than can family-owned, small-town television stations. This is because the large stations produce more programs and sell ads in the programs at higher rates so that they can more quickly

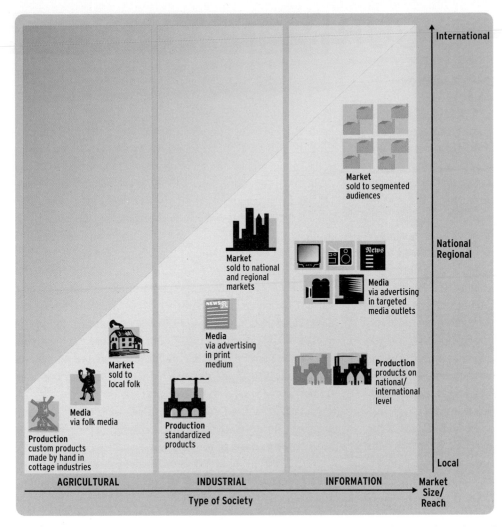

International

National
Regional

Local

Market
sold to segmented
audiences

Market
sold to national
and regional
markets

Media
via advertising
in targeted
media outlets

Media
via advertising
in print
medium

Production
products on
national/
international
level

Market
sold to
local folk

Media
via folk media

Production
standardized
products

Production
custom products
made by hand in
cottage industries

AGRICULTURAL   INDUSTRIAL   INFORMATION   Market
                                                              Size/
Type of Society   Reach

FIGURE 2.1 DEVELOPMENT OF MASS MEDIA Mass media developed during the industrial age by building on economies of scale to reap increasing profits from larger mass markets. They replaced folk media and in turn are being transformed into highly targeted and personalized forms.

recover the cost of the equipment from what they save on labor. They spend more money to make even more money.

Sometimes media organizations combine their companies and slash staff. In the newspaper industry, many formerly independent local papers have been reorganized under common management so that a single advertising sales staff serves two papers instead of one. We call these efficiency measures **economies of scale**. Production efficiencies are hard to come by in the electronic media because each movie, television program, or home page is an original product. Yet the incremental, or marginal, cost of each additional copy is very low after that first copy is made.

Economies of scale also give big media companies an advantage when dealing with the firms that supply their operations with products and services. When a CBS-owned television station places an order for editing equipment, its corporate parent may further fatten the order by buying equipment for several other CBS-owned stations at the same time. To achieve their own economies of scale, equipment suppliers will negotiate a volume discount for CBS, whereas the "mom-and-pop" station pays the full price because they make fewer purchases. However, when the costs of production technologies

> **Economies of scale** result when unit costs go down as production quantities increase.

MEDIA SCHOLAR

On the surface, the job of media scholar looks like a cushy one: between press interviews about her latest research and travel junkets, the scholar may spend only six or seven hours a week to teach her classes, attend the occasional faculty meeting, and manage her teaching assistants. Once she gets tenure, she has the guarantee of lifetime employment and gets a sabbatical year off every few years. Meanwhile she is free to enjoy those long summer, winter, and spring vacations!

In reality, she may never have a real vacation (or a free weekend) from the time she embarks on her career as a scholar until the day she gets tenure. Most of those breaks and all of those sabbaticals are devoted to scholarly work: developing new curricula, writing scholarly journal articles and books, and striving to develop new knowledge for the benefit of her students and society. For every hour she spends in class several more are devoted to preparation, grading, and advising students. Additional hours go into serving on university committees, reviewing scholarship produced by others, and doing outreach in the community. The pursuit and administration of external grants from government agencies like the National Science Foundation, the National Endowment for the Humanities, and the National Institutes of Health may be part of her job as well. It's really four jobs in one (teaching, research, service, grant seeking) that add up to far more than 40 hours a week, with the time allocations varying according to where the institution stands in the academic "pecking order" (e.g., 2-year or 4-year, Ph.D.-granting university or not).

What sustains her is a passion for creating knowledge and a desire to make the world a better place through the students she mentors. Those are the prime qualifications for a career as a media scholar. Four to seven years of formal education beyond a bachelor's degree are also required, during which time the aspiring scholar will serve as a low-paid apprentice while obtaining her "terminal degree." One route is to obtain a Master of Arts (MA) degree followed by a Doctor of Philosophy (Ph.D.) in communication, mass media, or journalism or in a related field such as sociology or psychology. Following that route, she will write articles for scholarly journals such as the *Journal of Communication, Journalism Quarterly, Journal of Advertising Research,* or *Journal of Computer Mediated Communication.* Alternatively, she could obtain a Master of Fine Arts (MFA) degree and become a creative scholar by having her films, videos, photos, or graphics presented at peer-juried creative competitions. Either way, "publish or perish" is her credo, since if she hasn't produced enough scholarship to obtain tenure, usually after 7 years of teaching and 7 years of graduate studies, she may have to find another line of work.

According to the Occupational Outlook (BLS, 2012), employment for postsecondary (i.e., post–high school) teachers is expected to grow at about the same rate as other occupations over the next several years. Increasing enrollments and the retirement of "baby boomer" professors assure continued growth. There are about 30,000 postsecondary teachers in the field of communication. Their median annual salaries are about equal to those for all postsecondary teachers, about $61,000 per year in 2010. However, salaries depend on academic rank, location, and the status of the institution. Full professors at prestigious institutions located on the East or West Coasts earn salaries well into the six figures—and that's for nine or ten months of work—and they can supplement their incomes with consulting fees, publication royalties, and extra money for summer teaching and research.

---

drop rapidly, this barrier to entry declines and smaller producers can take advantage of lower production equipment costs to jump in to parts of the market. For example, small record labels and video producers now compete with "Big Media" companies on the Internet.

THE BENEFITS OF COMPETITION

[The **law of supply and demand** describes the relationship among the supply of products, prices, and consumer demand.]

In the presence of competition, cost savings resulting from economies of scale may be passed along to consumers. When this happens, the **law of supply and demand** dictates that more people will consume the product, leading to further economies of scale, further improvements in production and products, and so on in a spiral effect.

It is perhaps easiest to grasp the benefits of competition using mass-produced consumer products such as color television sets. Improvements in electronics and manufacturing techniques yielded economies of scale that cut the price of a color TV set from $6,000 in 1953 to less than $200 today (in today's dollars). As the price decreased, more people bought color sets, and the most efficient manufacturers earned profits to invest in larger plants and newer, faster production techniques that further lowered the costs relative to their competition and created more and improved products. Lower prices and improved products meant still more sales, and so on. What was a luxury item for an elite few in 1953 has become a fixture in 99 percent of households, as lower prices increased consumer demand for the product. Today, most homes have two or three television sets (TV-Free, n.d.). Other media, such as newspapers and magazines, with substantial **marginal costs** associated with producing each additional copy, follow a similar formula.

> **Marginal costs** are the incremental costs of each additional copy or unit of a product.

Competition still benefits the consumer even when marginal costs are low, such as television programming distribution. For example, cable television operators have to be mindful of the prices and offerings of satellite TV companies and new media options. If they set cable prices too high, the law of supply and demand dictates that their customers will consider signing up with the satellite TV company or watching TV shows on the Internet.

MEDIA MONOPOLIES

What happens when there is little or no competition? The producer of a media product can pocket the cost savings realized from economies of scale in the form of higher profits—especially if there is no competition to undercut the price or introduce attractive new products. In fact, why bother to become more efficient? Sometimes producers can make more money by simply raising prices, provided they are not so steep that consumers forgo making the purchase. For example, when there are two newspapers in town, they compete for subscribers by undercutting each other's prices and adding features to win new readers. But if one drives the other out of business, or if they merge, the newsstand price may rise higher than ever.

Thus, the economics of media industries can lead to ownership patterns that are not in the best interest of consumers. These patterns include **monopoly**, in which one company dominates an industry and can set its prices, and **oligopoly**, in which a few companies dominate (see Figure 2.2). For example, having only one newspaper in town creates a newspaper **monopoly**. New York City has three daily newspapers—that is an **oligopoly**. And when there are two independent outlets, it is called a **duopoly**.

> **Monopoly** is when one single company dominates a market.
>
> **Oligopoly** is when a few firms dominate a market.
>
> A **duopoly** exists when two companies dominate a market.

Big is not invariably bad. The greatest economies of scale should result when there is only a single provider, because the initial costs are spread among the greatest possible number of consumers (Noam, 1983). Unfortunately, big companies can behave badly when they dominate a market. They might not want to invest in product research and development or new equipment to better serve the public. They may abuse their market power with underhanded tactics, such as holding back innovations like digital radio broadcasting because they profit from the status quo. Or, they'll take profits from a business in which they enjoy monopoly dominance, such as personal

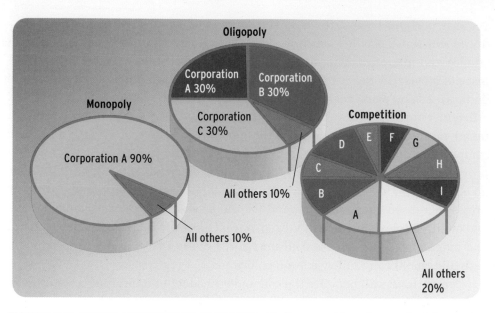

FIGURE 2.2 MEDIA OWNERSHIP PATTERNS Media ownership patterns reflect the number of competing media and how they divide the market. In a monopoly one firm dominates while in an oligopoly a small number of firms split the market among themselves.

computer operating system software, and use those profits to take over other competitive businesses, such as the market for Internet browser software. (Microsoft was found guilty of this.) Another abuse is to slash prices below costs to ruin smaller competitors. For instance, Amazon.com initially offered electronic books at low prices that undercut local bookstores. After the giant has bankrupted its smaller competitor, it can raise prices again to boost profits.

Similarly, monopolies and oligopolies can afford high entry costs that pose **barriers to entry** to new competitors. If a mom-and-pop radio station wanted to retaliate against the big media groups by buying dozens of stations of its own, chances are it could not raise the money necessary. Large media companies can find the financing, even if they are already deeply in debt, because they have a track record with bankers and valuable assets that banks could seize. Newer, smaller entrants have few assets and inspire less confidence in investors. So, the big get bigger and the small are forced out of business, resulting in greater concentration of ownership.

When companies dominate a market, they can raise their prices—and their profits—with impunity. Some communications media are regarded as such necessities that many consumers grudgingly pay far more than the companies' actual costs. Cable television rates have consistently risen well above inflation, for example. And sometimes oligopolies forge "gentlemen's agreements" to fix prices among themselves, with nearly the same effects on the consumer as a monopoly. Major book publishers got together to force Amazon to raise the prices for electronic books to match the retail prices of printed books in support of their traditional business model, for example, even though the e-books cost far less to produce and distribute.

Monopolies in communications media are especially troubling because they can also reduce the diversity of content. What could happen if the same company owned the local newspaper, the leading local TV and radio stations, and the local cable TV franchise and commanded all of its outlets to back the

Barriers to entry are obstacles companies must overcome to enter a market.

same candidate for mayor? It would be very difficult for the other candidates to present their position to the public. Such issues raise questions of regulation. The media industries continually push the Federal Communications Commission to relax prohibitions on such cross-ownership while some consumer advocates would like to see them strengthened (see Chapter 15).

THE PROFIT MOTIVE

Let's change our unit of analysis and examine more closely how economic forces that operate at the industry level affect individual media organizations. For privately owned media companies, everything is ultimately subordinate to the flow of **profits**, including the content of the media and the audiences they seek. The owners of the media must turn a profit after paying all their operating costs and their taxes. They also have to pay back their entry costs, the money they borrowed from banks or their investors to put their production and distribution apparatus in place, with interest. These capital costs for a local newspaper include the printing presses; the building and all of the equipment and furniture in it; and a fleet of trucks to distribute the papers. There are also continuing costs such as the paper and ink the news is printed with and the personnel for reporting, designing, advertising, selling, and distributing the newspaper. Moreover, the rate of profit must match or exceed that which investors could realize if they invested in other types of businesses or just left their money in the bank (Picard, 2002; Vogel, 2007). This economic pressure is so great that media sometimes compromise their public service obligations. For example, (Pew Research Center, 2011) newsroom staffs shrank 30 percent between 2000 and 2010. The result is that fewer reporters cannot adequately cover the community in either quantity or quality of stories.

All media firms have to recoup their costs somehow, but why is there such a wide disparity in their cost to the consumer? Some media, such as broadcast radio and television, are seemingly free, whereas newspapers charge for subscriptions by the month, and movies charge hefty admissions for a single viewing. The answer lies in the different methods the media use to recoup their first-copy costs.

First consider moviemaking, where costs are largely recovered from direct payments from the consumer in the form of movie theater admissions. The first-copy costs include the salaries for the actors and the production staff, rental of the studios and cameras, travel to the locations where the film is shot, the special effects, and all of the management overhead associated with getting the film made and shown to the public. Thus, first-copy costs include everything that goes into making the master print of the film.

The actual production costs for *Avatar* remain a closely guarded secret, but the best estimate is that they ran $280 million. That does not include the development of the innovative 3D technology that director James Cameron created for the movie which he hopes to spread over sequels and license to other

BUSINESSMAN OR MONOPOLIST? The dominance of social networking by Facebook's Mark Zuckerberg raises antitrust issues about monopolistic practices. Has Facebook become so powerful that it limits innovation and discourages competition?

> **Profits** are what is left after operating costs, taxes, and paybacks to investors.

film makers. The incremental cost for showing the movie in each additional theater is minimal, about $1,500 to duplicate and deliver it to each outlet. But *Avatar* opened simultaneously on more than 3,400 screens, adding another $5.1 million. It also opened on about 180 IMAX screens for which the prints cost $50,000 each, tacking on $9 million more. It cost another $150 million in advertising and marketing promotions to fill the theaters. Success was not ensured until all of the first-copy, marketing, and distribution costs were recovered, some $444 million in all by these estimates. In the case of *Avatar*, box office receipts were $761 million in its initial theatrical run in domestic theaters. That made it the top grossing film of all time. However, those box office proceeds have to be split with the theater owners. So, after its domestic run, *Avatar* was actually a flop from the studio's point of view—it lost about $64 million! But it pulled in more than $2 billion from international showings and was the most popular home video in 2010—that added another $183 million. The basic cable and broadcast television rights went for $25 million and the rights for pay per view and pay cable television will add to the profits. Royalties from toys, video games, and other merchandising tie-ins added $150 million more. So, the film should net well over $3 billion for its media conglomerate parent, News Corporation, but it will be years before they know the final "take."

In advertising-supported electronic media such as television, radio, and commercial websites, the cost of each additional copy is virtually zero. That is, whether one person or 20 million people view *Dancing with the Stars*, the cost to the network is the same. But the value to the advertiser increases with the increased number of households. The cost of broadcasting a program to 1,000 homes is the same as broadcasting it to 2,000 homes, but the fee to the advertiser may double. And so, the broadcaster can recoup the first-copy costs exclusively from advertising sales and offer the program "free" to the viewer.

In publishing, the first-copy costs include the salaries of all the writers and editors who prepare the stories and the designers and preproduction workers who get them ready for the printing press and online publication. In addition, newspapers and magazines incur substantial per-unit marginal costs when they print and distribute each copy to their readers—the amount of paper and the ink consumed and the payments to delivery people rise with each copy. To offset these marginal costs, most newspapers and magazines have three revenue streams: advertising sales, subscriptions (now including online subscriptions in many cases), and newsstand purchases. Advertising is usually the most important of the three, typically contributing three-fourths of newspaper revenues. So when advertising declines, as in the 2007–2009 recession, newspapers are in trouble.

When revenues from advertisers and consumers exceed production costs, profits result. The media reinvest some of their profits to make improved products that even more consumers will want. For example,

FIRST COPY COSTS The salaries paid to the stars of the *Twilight Saga* films are examples of the costs of making the first copy of a film that must be spread over millions of moviegoers.

Pictorial Press Ltd/Alamy

television networks invest their profits in new programs that they hope will be hits; newspaper publishers invest in faster printing presses.

But profits are not always paramount. The Public Broadcasting Service (PBS) is the prime example of a not-for-profit media organization in the United States. Government funds and voluntary charitable contributions cover its operating costs so it can be independent of advertisers. No profits are expected. Still, these not-for-profit media are also money-minded; they must continually raise money from grants and corporate donors—and "from viewers like you"— to cover their capital costs and operating budgets.

HOW MEDIA MAKE MONEY

The formula for staying profitable is seemingly simple. The payments received from media consumers (see Figure 2.3) must exceed the total spent on content, distribution, daily operations, taxes, and investment. There are a number of different business models for making money in the media:

- *Direct sales* occur when consumers pay lump sums to purchase products that they own, such as iPods.
- *Rentals* also involve direct payment for a product, except that the consumer only borrows the product, such as DVD rentals. A retail outlet buys the product from a manufacturer and recoups the purchase price by renting it multiple times.

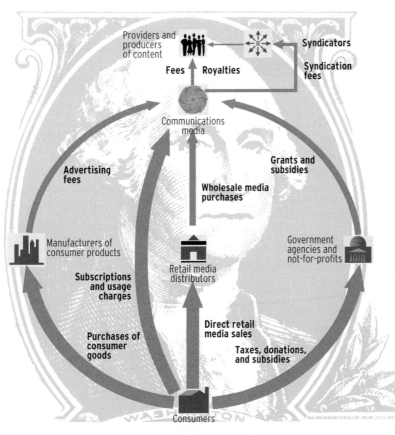

FIGURE 2.3 MEDIA REVENUE SOURCES There are four main ways of paying for media: advertising, direct sales, subscriptions, and public subsidies. Media organizations in turn pay the producers of the content, either directly or through syndication agreements and royalty fees.

- *Subscriptions* are payments for a continuing service rather than a single product. Newspapers, magazines, and cable and satellite companies make money this way.
- *Usage fees* include admission fees to movies or theaters and pay-per-view movies on TV.
- *Advertising* is the main economic base for most newspapers and magazines and all commercial television and radio stations. Advertisers buy commercial time or page space from the media, and the rates are set in relation to the number of people who are likely to be exposed to the ad. The more people who see or hear the ad, the more that media companies can charge advertisers.
- *Syndication* is the rental of content to media outlets, rather than to the consumer. Newspaper cartoons and reruns of old television series are syndicated to the media outlets that distribute them locally.
- *License fees* compensate the creators of media content for the use of their original ideas. For example, songwriters receive a **copyright royalty fee** collected from Internet radio stations that play their songs.
- *Subsidies* are provided for communications media that society considers desirable, but that commercial interests do not find profitable. PBS is subsidized by federal, state, and local taxes.
- *Voluntary donations* are made by corporations, private foundations and individuals to media that provide a public service, like National Public Radio. Also, some creators let you download their software and games, and then pay if you like them.

[A **copyright royalty fee** is a payment for use of a creative work.]

FROM MASS MARKETS TO MARKET SEGMENTS

From our discussion so far, it might seem natural to you that communications media should strive for products that have the broadest possible appeal. Indeed, until recently this was the case. Now, however, technological changes and receptivity by audiences and advertisers encourage media to engage in *narrowcasting*, to target smaller, more specific audience segments with more specialized content. Improvements in the information available about media audiences and markets for consumer products and in the efficiency of media production and distribution brought about by information technologies have converged to make this approach profitable. Revisiting Figure 2.1 (see page 31), this development marks the transition from the mass media of industrial society to the targeted media of the information society.

In television, the 1970s were a time when CBS, NBC, and ABC ruled the screen. Together, they accounted for over 90 percent of the prime-time audience, and top shows like *All in the Family* reached up to half the people watching television. Their sponsors sold

Cheryl Forman

SELLING THE AUDIENCE Advertising is the major revenue source for mass media. The media sell advertising space on the basis of the size of the audience.

mass-market products like Lay's potato chips that appealed to a broad spectrum of viewers. For the sponsors, this was a good deal—a relatively inexpensive way to present a mass-market item to a mass audience.

Now, with competition from specialized cable and satellite channels and Internet video, top-rated network television shows reach about a fifth of the audience they once did, or around 10 percent of possible viewers, and advertisers offer a dizzying array of variations on their products. Several factors contribute to such finely grained audience segmentation. First, information technologies, such as desktop publishing and computerized video editing, have lowered media production costs. That makes

SYNDICATION First-run syndicated programs such as *Wheel of Fortune* are sold directly to individual TV stations which profit from local advertising during the programs.

it possible to profit from smaller audiences. Second, advertisers value small audiences if they contain high proportions of their target market. A computer software ad that appears in *Personal Computing* magazine might reach more potential computer software buyers than one that appears in *People* magazine. Thus, *PC* is more worthwhile to the software advertiser, even though the cost of reaching each individual *People* reader (many of whom are not in the market for software) is lower. Third, sophisticated research techniques and databases of consumer information make it practical to aggregate a large audience of potential customers across multiple, narrowcast media more efficiently than by making a single mass-media buy (see Chapter 11). Finally, conventional media forms like the broadcast TV networks that have lost audiences to narrowcasters have had to respond with more narrowly targeted programs of their own.

NEW MEDIA ECONOMICS

Popular sites on the World Wide Web and social media have pushed segmentation to a new extreme: personalization. The logic behind personalized content, customized for individuals, is similar to that of narrowcasting except the market segments shrink to specific individuals. Personalization works to the advertisers' benefit, giving them the ability to target ads very precisely to specific people who are actually in the market for their products. For example, if someone enters *digital cameras* as a search term into Google, then he or she is greeted with several sponsored links featuring special deals on cameras, but a conventional television station has no way of "knowing" if a viewer is interested in digital cameras. The conventional media can't customize to an audience of one because the first-copy costs could never be recovered through economies of scale. Yahoo! can greet its users by name and personalize their color schemes, news topics, featured sports teams, and advertisements. A TV station attempting the same thing would have to do a separate "take" of the

David McNew/Getty Images

WHICH MODEL? Arcade video games are a new media version of an older media way of making money, the usage fee. Console games rely on the direct sales model.

evening news for each audience member; change the sets, the anchors, and the stories for each one; and operate a separate transmitter and studio for each viewer!

The Internet challenges basic assumptions of media economics, since reproduction and distribution costs are greatly reduced (Kahin & Varian, 2000). That means it may no longer make sense to charge for exclusive access to content as the older media do, but rather to charge only for the timeliness or convenience of information (Gilder, 2000; Odlyzko, 2001). Websites that sell media products like books and CDs can also afford to offer a wider selection of specialized offerings that brick-and-mortar bookstores and record stores cannot afford to stock on their shelves.

Many websites make money in the proven traditional media way—through advertising—but with some interesting twists. For example, Google advertisers bid for prime space at the top and right-hand margins of their search pages, whereas conventional media charge fixed rates for ads. Google charges "by the click" so that advertisers pay only when someone clicks on their ad. Those ad rates can run from a few pennies to as much as $100 per click. By comparison, broadcast TV advertisers reach Super Bowl viewers for only 3 cents each. The difference is that the Google ads reach consumers as they actively seek the product through a keyword search (Google calls them "adwords"), and the click-through assures the advertiser that the consumer is interested in their particular brand. By comparison, the Super Bowl viewer may not notice the ad, may not be in the market for the product, may be the loyal customer of some other company's products, may forget the ad because he or she is not going to shop until the next day, or may not even be in the room when the ad runs.

Websites run by traditional media companies such as the *New York Times* have an edge over those run by Internet companies such as Salon.com. The older media companies have deeper pockets to subsidize unprofitable websites, and they can recycle content that is supported by conventional media cash flows. The incremental advertising dollars from Web ads help cover the cost of running the website. That's why nytimes.com is free, although the paper version costs $2.50. However, now that the Internet is becoming the dominant news medium less and less content is free. Now only about one day's worth of the *Times* each month (10 articles) is free. After that you have to pay a monthly subscription to offset the

STOP&REVIEW

1. What are *economies of scale*?
2. Why is the first copy of a mass-media production the most expensive?
3. What are the basic types of media ownership patterns?
4. How do the mass media make profits? Why are profits necessary?
5. What are some of the ways that websites make money?

decline in print subscriptions. Social media websites, eBay and YouTube included, have a further economic advantage over older media: their content is provided free to the website proprietor. Think about it, when you update your Facebook profile you are providing free content to those who profit from the advertising sales. Where is your cut of the profits from Facebook's initial stock offering? If you contribute popular original content YouTube will give you a 50 percent cut of the ad revenue, with top partners like The Annoying Orange earning hundreds of thousands of dollars a year (O'Neill, 2010).

NEW MODEL The social media site Groupon makes money a new way, by offering discounts to groups of interested buyers and then splitting the price the consumer pays with the advertiser.

CRITICAL STUDIES

Critical scholars have alternative theories for the relationship of media industries, content, and society. They examine the connection between media and society from political-economic, feminist, ethnic, and media criticism perspectives. These perspectives focus on the need for **media literacy** and a critical understanding of media structure and its power, as well as the meaning of its content. That means that we should not just accept the media at face value, as though it were a natural phenomenon like the weather. We should try instead to understand the causes underlying media change and to be skeptical about the motives of the media industry. In contrast to the SMCR model introduced in Chapter 1, the **critical studies** approach emphasizes the feedback link and an active process in which the human receiver "decodes" the messages that the human source encodes.

> **Media literacy** means learning to think critically about the role of media in society.

> **Critical studies** examines the overall impact of media.

POLITICAL ECONOMY

Political economy draws inspiration from the work of nineteenth-century political economist Karl Marx. Marx wrote that society is based on the relations between those who own the means of production (for example, consumer electronics factories and printing presses) and those who work for them. In this view, it is the owners' interests that are reflected by media and culture, because the dominant groups in a society—usually those who own the major corporations—want to create an underlying consensus, or **hegemony**, of ideology favoring their continued domination (Gramsci, 1994). These views of society were reflected in the Occupy Wall Street movement that contested the power of the richest 1 percent over the other 99 percent. Hegemony consists of creating a consensus around certain self-serving ideas, like "the poor will always be with us," through a variety of means, including the media. Although consumer needs and the law of supply and demand still affect the media, they operate in an economic system devoted to preserving the interests of the ruling classes.

> **Political economy** analyzes patterns of class domination and economic power.

> **Hegemony** is the use of media to create a consensus around certain ideas, so that they come to be accepted as common sense.

This analysis suggests that media reflect the interests of media owners, advertisers, and, through the advertisers' corporations, the general nature of what the people in power want said (Altschull, 1995). The same groups of people who

AP Photo/Jim Cooper

WHAT'S YOUR POINT? Do cable talk show shows like *Bill O'Reilly* offer fresh perspectives or do they merely reinforce a hegemony of ideas? When Bill rails against the Occupy Wall Street movement does he act in the interests of "the 1 percent?"

sit on the boards of directors of major media companies also sit on the boards of other major corporations and the banks that support them. Now the same economic class that dominates the older media is asserting control over the new media as well (McChesney, 2007) and the ruling class includes new media entrepreneurs like Mark Zuckerberg of Facebook as well as old media barons like Rupert Murdoch of News Corp. Even public service media like PBS are supported, in part, by businesses through direct donations and through large charitable foundations, such as the Ford Foundation, that are controlled by the same class of people who own the large corporations. Thus, in the recent economic crisis we saw many news reports that criticized major investment firms for causing the crisis. But there was little in the mainstream media criticizing the capitalist banking system until the Occupy Wall Street movement forced the media to pay attention. Even then, much of the media coverage focused on the protest as a civil disturbance involving confrontations with the police rather than the underlying issue of economic inequality.

Communication media support the political and economic status quo in other ways. Citizens who can afford the price of a computer and have the skills to get information from the Internet can participate more fully in politics by accessing coverage of political issues and contributing to blogs. Unequal access remains important in the Information Age. African-Americans and Hispanics are less likely than Anglos to have phone service (Mueller & Schement, 1995) or high speed Internet access (NTIA, 2011), making access to technology a new dimension of social stratification between the "haves/have nots" and the "information rich/information poor" segments of society. However, the tensions arising from such inequalities do not usually undermine the underlying social order, according to Gramsci (1971), who argued that the media (and educational institutions) convince the poor to accept the hegemony of ideas that keeps the ruling class on top. For example, supporters of the underlying social order might offer the excuse that the poor don't want Internet access, rather than being unable to afford it or being excluded from opportunities to learn how to use it effectively.

[**Culture** is a group's pattern of thought and activity.]

Political economy has cultural implications as well. As commercial media reach into more societies, people in different parts of the world become aware of Coca-Cola and Nike shoes. That may undermine ties to their traditional **culture** and spur the growth of consumer culture (Featherstone, 1990). The danger is that commercial messages may impact our innermost desires and perceptions of ourselves, making us feel dependent upon consumer products for our happiness. While we become more indebted, pursuing materialistic dreams, manufacturers become fat with profits.

The *cultural industries* approach (Hesmondhalgh, 2008) offers a more hopeful outlook. While recognizing the tendencies of media conglomerates to control cultural products through copyright restrictions and marketing campaigns, this school of thought also considers the implications of the pre-eminence of creative labor in the information economy. Public policies that subsidize artists and seek to cluster them in creative communities can improve the cultural well-being of society.

The *commodification* of what was once public information, such as census data, into a commodity that can be bought and sold by private companies, such as market research databases, furthers the dominance of the owners of information industries (Schiller, 1996). The modification of copyright and patent laws to favor their owners is another example (Schement & Curtis, 1997). Now, the personal information that we provide to websites (Campbell & Carlson, 2002) or social networks (Koponen, 2009) has also become a commodity. Political economists believe that such actions further reinforce hegemony of power that acts against the interests of common citizens.

FEMINISM ON THE LINE Women reinvented the telephone, converting it to an instrument of social interaction. In doing so, they contested the dominance of a patriarchal society.

FEMINIST STUDIES

Feminist critics of the media have concerns that parallel those of political economists to some degree, but focus on the oppression of women by men rather than the oppression of the working class by the ruling class. Thus, communication media serve the purposes of the patriarchy that runs society. The oppression also has economic dimensions. Women typically earn only about two-thirds of what men make in comparable jobs, so the perpetuation of sexism in the images we see in the media benefits the owners of media organizations and their associates who run corporate America.

Over the years, feminist media scholars have focused on the fact that too few women appear in the media and are limited to a few stereotypical roles (i.e., housewife, mother, nurse, secretary, helper). We will examine those patterns of content and their impact in greater depth in Chapter 14 when we examine media impacts. Here we are concerned more with the reasons why such portrayals exist. These include the underrepresentation of women as media producers and in the corporate decision structure, as well as social norms that prescribe only certain roles for women. For instance, women are bombarded by advertising messages that stress their role as consumers of mass-produced goods and push unrealistic ideals of feminine beauty that in turn drive sales of products targeted to women. These critiques link feminism with political economy in looking at underlying reasons for the structure and content of the media.

Feminists also take issue with the way media are targeted by gender. They argue that media for women, such as romance novels or soap operas, have been denigrated as less serious than male-oriented spy novels. They see the pleasure women take in such media as a form of resistance to male dictates about what is enjoyable (Radway, 1984). Meanwhile, video games (Cassell &

Jenkins, 1998) seem designed to alienate and exclude women and, in so doing, exclude them from the inner world of computer knowledge reserved for men. Other studies examine women's particular subjectivity or sense of interpretation of what media mean (Livingstone, 1998).

Women influence the development of technology. The telephone was intended as an instrument of communication for the (male-dominated) business world, and telephone companies discouraged "trivial" social use of the telephone (mostly by women) to keep the lines clear for important (that is, male-originated) business calls. However, women staged a quiet rebellion against these restrictions, forcing the redesign of the telephone system, by expanding its capacity to handle the social and other uses women made (Fischer, 1992).

We see the "communications specialist" emerge again in new media as women become the dominant bloggers on the Internet (Lin, 2007; Synovate, 2007). But they still communicate from within their homes, limiting personal social contact and continuing the perception that they are not "businessmen."

ETHNIC MEDIA STUDIES

Many of the same issues apply to minority racial and ethnic groups, including African-Americans, Latinos, and Asians. Many scholars (and political groups like La Raza) have criticized media for disproportionately showing African-Americans, Latinos, and Arabs in such stereotypical roles as maids, criminals, or even terrorists. We will examine the extent of ethnic stereotyping and its consequences in Chapter 14 when we examine media impacts.

Scholars such as Herman Gray (1995) critique a deeper level of structural problems with race and media. They argue that racial depictions are a form of ideology, designed to keep whiteness associated with dominance and power, whereas black and brown minorities are pointed toward inferior social roles. The media have been described as a system of racialization that defines race and ethnicity; for example, by portraying African American women as nameless sex objects in music videos (Littlefield, 2008). Those images perpetuate a "new racism" in a society that believes that the problem of racism has been solved even as the sexualized images allow viewers to blame the victims of teen pregnancy and unwed mothers that are enduring consequences of the "old racism." Racial disparities are also reflected in the economics of the media. Advertisers undervalue minority audiences, for example, even after correcting for income levels (Napoli, 2002); that benefits advertisers of products targeted to minorities by reducing their advertising costs. Minorities have a difficult time obtaining financing, which is a barrier to minority ownership in broadcasting (Braunstein, 2000); that reduces competition for white-owned media outlets serving minority communities.

MEDIA CRITICISM

Another critical studies approach looks at the media as a kind of literature and applies traditions of literary criticism (Lotz, 2001). Here, long-standing cultural conventions dictate the content of the media rather than capitalist economics or power relationships in society. This approach focuses on **genres**, categories of creative works that have a distinctive style and format, such as horror or science fiction. Over time, genres become storytelling formulas that evolve out of the interaction between producers and audiences (Allen, 1992).

Genres are distinctive styles of creative works. The term is also used to represent different types or formats of media content.

They transfer from one medium to another. For example, romance and adventure genres were transported from print novels to film, radio, and television. We can also find adventure games (although romance games are hard to find) but game critics caution against applying either conventional film genres (e.g. adventure) or typologies from the game industry (e.g., first person shooters) to video games since game mechanics as well as aesthetic styles play a role (Arsenault, 2009). For example, many first person shooter games require actions other than shooting to destroy or escape from opponents and two-dimensional and three-dimensional shooters might be regarded as separate genres.

Media criticism scholars also probe for verbal and visual symbolism in media (Berger, 1992; Seiter, 1992). In this *semiotic analysis*, words, sounds, and images are interpreted individually as signs or symbols of something other than the literal action. The sign has two components: a concept, or the thing signified, and a sound-image, or signifier. For example, in a *Star Trek* episode a musical theme (signifier) functions as a sign to announce that the starship Enterprise is about to come to the rescue (concept).

MEDIA&CULTURE

POSTMODERNISM

Modern society began with the Enlightenment in the eighteenth century. Modernity is a way of viewing the world in which reason is the source of progress and science has universal explanations for all natural phenomena. Modernity is characterized by technological innovation, dynamism, and seeing change as positive. It is also reflected in social institutions, such as representative forms of government, large companies, and banks. The dawn of the modern era also coincided with the Industrial Revolution, so we can think of it in terms of industrialization, the growth of science and technology, urbanization, and the evolution of mass media and culture.

Many scholars argue that in art, culture, and society we are now in a *postmodern* era. What is taking place is a break with modernity, both in modes of thinking and in economic and political institutions. We have moved from an era of economic determinism, in which economic phenomena determine all others, to a time of cultural determinism (Baudrillard, 1983). Now messages carried by communications technologies take on new meanings, different from or even opposed to what was originally intended. We have moved from an era of universal laws and truths based on rational science to one in which local, particularistic, subjective understandings are more important and more valid. The postmodern view is that there is no universal truth, that what you think depends on your own experience, which depends on what groups you belong to, what media you pay attention to, what your family taught you. And what you think is as valid as what anyone else thinks, even if he or she belongs to a privileged elite and carries a title like "president" or "college professor."

A corollary of this view is that developments in the information society encourage cultural fragmentation. According to French philosopher Jean-Francois Lyotard (1984), the new media permit many new forms of expression, creating new forms of knowledge and new social formations. As more groups express their own ideas through proliferating multimedia channels—and even define their identities in terms of those channels—society becomes more focused on these groups. In consequence, society becomes less concerned with widespread ideas of nation-states and other vestiges of the modern era, creating a postmodern world.

But what comes after postmodernism, and are we already there? The Internet is being used by those who hope to promote new universal ideas, such as radical Islam, whereas nation-states like China try to assert control over online discourse. In the media realm, giant media corporations are beginning to assert themselves on the Internet in ways that may further homogenize popular culture.

STOP&REVIEW

1. What is a political economist?
2. How can the evening TV news create a hegemony of ideas?
3. What is the essence of the feminist critique of the media?
4. How do genres develop?

Where do symbols come from, and what makes some more powerful than others? To answer these questions one can use a related approach—looking for archetypes and symbols taken from psychological theories. Analysis of media content is often seen as analogous to Freud's interpretation of dreams, since both media creators and audiences are relying on images created through psychological processes like condensation (fusing symbols together) and displacement (replacement of one symbol by another) (Freud, 1949). Other scholars draw upon the work of Carl Jung (1970), who interpreted recurring cultural themes as the expression of underlying archetypes, unconscious symbols of concepts like motherhood that all cultures share.

We see that the audience has a role to play in the selection of content. Media creators have to follow certain conventions and produce media that fit the expectations of their audiences. Otherwise, they risk alienating those audiences. So, the audience wields a great deal of power in the media content creative process. Scholars also point out that audiences frequently interpret media in a way very different from what its writers or producers had in mind. So the question of the power of media to impose meanings versus the power of the audience to interpret them remains a lively debate, depending on which studies and scholars you choose to believe.

DIFFUSION OF INNOVATIONS

Individuals and society also have the power to influence the success of media technology. The diffusion of innovations theory has its roots in sociology and helps us understand why people adopt new communication behaviors (Rogers, 1995). **Diffusion** is a process by which an innovation—a new way of doing things—is communicated through media and interpersonal channels over time among the members of a community.

[**Diffusion** is the spread of innovations.]

For example, researcher Everett Rogers (1986) observed that VCRs diffused very quickly in the United States, going from 1 percent of American households in 1980 to 20 percent in 1985 (peaking at 90% in 2006, Nielsen Media Research, 2010). Prices are important in diffusion. VCR prices declined rapidly, from $2,200 in 1975 to under $100 in 2004. Now DVD players and digital video recorders are rapidly replacing VCRs. As a general rule, all new technologies follow a similar price pattern: the first few units sold cost 10 or more times as much as the last units sold, a direct consequence of the economies of scale discussed earlier in this chapter.

WHY DO INNOVATIONS SUCCEED?

How quickly an innovation diffuses depends on several other factors besides its cost: what do people think are the relative advantages of the new idea compared to existing ways of doing things? How compatible is it with existing ways of doing things? How complex is the new technology to operate? How easy is it to try out the new way before committing a lot of time or money to it? Can people observe others using the innovation successfully? Information that we acquire from the media and from observing others forms our expectations of how it will perform for us, persuading us to adopt it or not. For example, a study of the adoption of broadband Internet by rural residents found that the ability to experience the personal benefits of the broadband predicted the adoption of broadband connections in the home (LaRose et al., 2007).

Factors other than the attributes of the innovation affect diffusion of innovations. One factor is the amount of previous experience people have had with similar technologies. For example, among the first people to use broadband Internet are those who had already used dial-up Internet. Some people are naturally more innovative than others and may be more inclined than others to try out new gadgets. Social norms play a role. Cell phones went from being associated with blue-collar delivery truck drivers to being chic for executives to being a fashion accessory for teens. Indeed, cell phones have become a necessity for most students on campus.

BETTER LUCK THIS TIME The new iPad is Apple's second try at a tablet computer. The Newton was a failure due to a faulty handwriting recognition program.

HOW DO INNOVATIONS SPREAD?

Diffusion of new communication technology goes through a predictable sequence of stages. First, we gain knowledge about the new idea from the media and from people we know. For example, we may read about new e-books in an electronics magazine or see our classmate use one. Then we weigh the merits. Does it cost too much? How much do we need the lecture notes that are available only in the e-book version? Finally, we decide to try it and make our purchase. Afterward, we continue to reassess our experience with the innovation and confirm, reject, or modify our use of it. We may find that our own handwritten lecture notes are more useful than the e-book's and regret our purchase. In other words, we decide which innovations to pursue according to the expected outcomes of our adoption decision, and we then continually monitor the fulfillment of those expectations.

People do not adopt new ideas at the same rates (see Figure 2.4). Those who first use an innovation are called *innovators*. People who follow up on

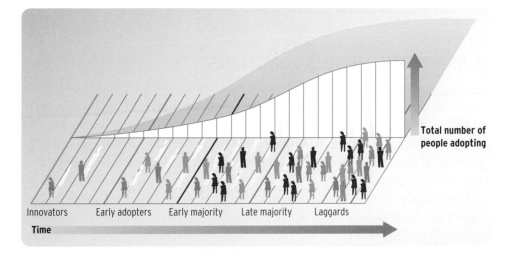

Innovators | Early adopters | Early majority | Late majority | Laggards

Total number of people adopting

Time

FIGURE 2.4 DIFFUSION Some people adopt new ideas earlier than others. The majority of people do so only after innovators and early adopters have forged the way. Growth accelerates when the early majority latch onto new innovations.

NEWSFLASH: IT'S RAINING! The news media perform the surveillance function by alerting us to important things going on around us, such as the approach of a hurricane. Later coverage of events may serve an interpretation function by helping us understand the need for better emergency response procedures.

innovative ideas through specialized media such as trade journals or interpersonal contacts are early adopters. Those who join the trend as it begins to go mainstream make up the early majority. Those who wait to see what most people are going to do constitute the late majority. Those who wait until the very end are called *laggards*.

Interactive communication technologies diffuse in a characteristic way. First, a certain minimum number, or *critical mass*, of adopters is necessary for it to be useful enough for most people to go along with the trend (Lin, 2003). E-mail is a good example. What good was e-mail to the first two Internet users in 1969? They couldn't send messages to their family or friends. E-mail spread very slowly at first. Now over three-fourths of the U.S. population has e-mail, so it is very useful.

Since information technologies are relatively flexible tools, they tend to be used in new, unanticipated ways by their adopters. Rogers (1986) called this *reinvention*. For instance, early adopters of home computers were attracted by educational software for children. Once the children had the computers, they used them to play computer games instead. Then the personal computer was reinvented again, as a tool to send e-mail and obtain information on the Internet. Now the computer is housed in a smart phone and used for instant messages and online access. Thus, in its emphasis on the attributes of innovations, the diffusion-of-innovations approach initially may seem technologically deterministic, but it stresses the ability of people and their cultures to act as influences in the spread of innovations.

WHAT ARE THE MEDIA'S FUNCTIONS?

Now we turn to sociological theories that emphasize the mutual dependence of media and society. These theories represent a middle ground between cultural determinism and **technological determinism**. Functionalism states that society cannot function without the media and that the media exist to serve the needs of our societies and cultures (Wright, 1974). The media help us to achieve these social needs:

[**Technological determinism** explains that the media cause changes in society and culture.]

Surveillance. Certain media specialize in providing information to help people with their surveillance of the environment, alerting them to important events—newspapers and CNN, for example. We also use Facebook, e-mail, Twitter, or text messaging to keep up with what is going on in our personal lives. The World Wide Web is a powerful surveillance tool, because its users can seek out information on topics of interest rather than passively waiting for the older media to bring topics to them.

Interpretation. Information is not of much use until it is processed, interpreted, and correlated with what we already know. Individuals, groups, and the media all contribute to this process. The newspaper editorial page helps us interpret the headlines, *The Daily Show* interprets headlines with humor, and Internet blogs comment upon and interpret current events and social trends.

Values Transmission/Socialization. As soon as human beings had language, they used it to pass on ideas to their children. Today the media have assumed the roles of storytellers, teachers, and even parents. For example, textbooks like this one pass along concepts about the media to a new generation of students. But this function is not limited to media with an obvious educational or informational purpose, such as *Sesame Street*. Generations of movie buffs have learned about the values of loyalty and friendship from watching *The Sting*.

Entertainment. With the exception of magazine-style information programs such as *60 Minutes*, the top 10 programs on network television have always been entertainment oriented. Newspapers complement their news and commentary with entertaining diversions on sports and lifestyle. Americans spend enormous amounts of time and money attending or renting feature films, listening to music, watching television comedies, playing video games, and surfing the Internet just for fun.

New media are bringing about new functions. The Internet has attracted attention for its role in building and maintaining social bonds through the likes of Facebook. Social media like YouTube, Flickr, and blogs also function as outlets for creative self-expression that conventional media afforded only to an elite few.

MEDIA AND PUBLIC OPINION

In this section, we examine social theories that tie together the relationship between the events of the day and the decisions of media professionals about what becomes media content.

GATEKEEPING

Of all the events that happen in a community, who decides which ones will be covered and recorded for posterity and which ones will silently fade into oblivion? The *gatekeeping* theory (Shoemaker, 1991; White, 1949) emphasizes the crucial role of the so-called *gatekeepers*, the media managers and editors who can either open or close "the gate" on a story or shape how it is presented.

Gatekeepers are influential. They can squelch new ideas and suppress the news of events that others might find important. For instance, if an editor decides not to send a camera crew to a local Occupy Wall Street gathering, she excludes the views of the activists from the public debate. However, media outlets compete with each other for audiences, so the gatekeeping actions of any one news editor are unlikely to have much impact. Gatekeepers get fired if they leave out too many stories that their viewers want to see and that the competition is willing to show them. So, the consensus among editors to keep certain stories in the news while excluding others may bias the public

SETTING THE ADENDA Presidents command so much attention from the press that they can define the important issues of the day, attempting to set the agenda of public debate. The President's political rivals contest his agenda and try to set their own.

REUTERS/Joshua Lott

agenda and reinforce a hegemony over ideas.

Some think that the hinges are falling off the gate with the profusion of online news sources, amateur "citizen journalists," bloggers, and tweeters who challenge conventional news editors when determining what is newsworthy and what is not. However, gatekeeping theorists argue that these new sources, even if not conventional media managers, are new manifestations of the gatekeeping phenomenon (Shoemaker, 2009).

AGENDA SETTING

Who sets the public agenda—or topics of interest—in an election year: the media gatekeepers or the candidates? Some figures, like the president, can routinely command media attention (Gandy, 1982). Other public figures and interest groups try to set the agenda by harping on an issue in their public statements or TV ads, but they succeed only if their words are picked up in the news.

Other times, the media set the agenda for the candidates. For instance, media coverage of big bonuses paid to failing financial firms in the midst of the financial crisis of 2009 quickly turned this into a political issue. Thus, agenda setting bestows political power on the media. However, the media are not all-powerful. The media's constant harping on the Clinton-Lewinsky sex scandal had no effect on the president's approval ratings, perhaps because adultery was not a highly relevant issue for the public (Yioutas & Segvic, 2003). Also, the new media environment, with its many competing (and sometimes unprofessional) voices, may be undermining the power of the older media to set the public agenda (Williams & Delli Carpini, 2004).

Agenda-setting theory also describes how media coverage affects public opinion. Merely by publishing some stories and not others, the media set the agenda—or topic of conversation—for what people probably will and won't be discussing that day. We will consider that aspect when we examine media effects in Chapter 14.

FRAMING

Whereas the media's agenda setting tells us *what* topics to think about, the framing of issues tells us *how* to think about those topics. Framing theory examines how writers frame or present a story (Altheide, 1974; Gitlin, 1983). Reporters decide what to include within the view, or frame, of a story and what to leave out, much as a painter chooses what to put on the canvas of a painting. They decide which tone, words, and facts to include, but also the conceptual framework, context, and interpretation of the facts.

Where do frames come from? French media critic Pierre Bourdieu (1998) contends that even in countries where there is supposed to be freedom of expression, there is invisible self-censorship. If they wish to remain employed, journalists realize what is permissible and pre-edit their own work to be consistent with those perceived norms. For example, news producers at ABC "just know" they should avoid stories about animated movies that are not produced by their corporate parent, Disney.

TECHNOLOGICAL DETERMINISM

Now we arrive at the end of the continuum that is opposite cultural determinism. Some social critics maintain that communications media change everything in society. In this view, technology drives social change, so it is sometimes called *technological determinism*. Variations on this theme stress the social effects of media messages, covered in Chapter 14, and the technological culture that gives rise to them.

THE MEDIUM IS THE MESSAGE

The most famous technological determinist, Marshall McLuhan, argued that print (*The Gutenberg Galaxy*, 1962) and electronic media (*Understanding Media*, 1964) were truly revolutionary, an idea captured in his famous aphorism "The medium is the message." He proposed that new communication technologies determine culture and that it is the form of the media rather than their content that matters. For example, in McLuhan's view, the invention of the printing press led to the rise of the scientific method and later to our technological society by forcing thinkers to put their words in linear order and their arguments in a logical progression—just like the words on a printed page. This led to thinking about the natural world in the same linear fashion, instilling the notion that it, too, had a beginning and an end, causes and effects.

McLuhan did not live to witness the Internet, but he coined a phrase that perhaps describes it well. The "global village" draws the entire world together into an electronically mediated small town. "By electricity we everywhere resume person-to-person relations as if on the smallest village scale" (McLuhan, 1964, p. 255). When he wrote that in the 1960s, he was thinking of broadcast television and the telephone, long before the Internet—or CNN—was a reality.

McLuhan further theorized that in society's zeal to conquer technology, we might progress in technology, but we would regress as a culture. Whereas technology could extend human capabilities in one way, it would cut off others. For example, the telephone would

THE MEDIUM IS THE MESSAGE Marshall McLuhan, the late communication scholar, argued that the way we think is determined by the nature of the media we consume. For example, does reading this text in a linear progression from left to right and top to bottom subtlety lead us to believe that the world is an ordered place governed by cause and effect?

extend the voice, but amputate printed correspondence. These amputations could have long-term cultural consequences with new media, too. Digital archives extend memories about prior generations, but cut off the need to save original documents. Sometimes a reversal of the original intent occurs: digital archives save memories, yet in 5 to 10 years the hardware and software used to retrieve the computerized files will be obsolete and the memories gone forever (Davenport, Randle, & Bossen, 2007).

TECHNOLOGY AS DOMINANT SOCIAL FORCE

Other media theorists emphasize that social systems and worldviews promote technology and dominate culture. Neil Postman (1992) argued that computers foster *technopoly*, in which technology is deified and extends its control to all aspects of life. Technopoly compounds the excesses of technocracy, in which the scientific method is applied by experts to technology for the improvement of life, but also to the destruction of culture.

Similarly, French sociologist Jacques Ellul (1990) argued that the pursuit of technological improvement led to the social dominance of an elite tier of scientists, engineers, and managers for whom technology became an end in itself, devoid of moral foundation. But for Ellul, the technologists' efforts were ultimately ineffective. Technologists promise a great deal to ensure their status in a society conditioned to welcome technological progress. But they deliver very little: not even a truly satisfying evening's entertainment on TV, an effective magazine ad, or a true relationship on the Internet.

In *The Rise of the Network Society* (2000) Manuel Castells described the impact of information technologies on society as nothing less than a revolution comparable to the Industrial Revolution of three centuries before (see Chapter 1). In his view, not only have technological innovations changed society, but the process of innovation itself has been accelerated by the application of those technologies, creating a self-perpetuating revolution.

MEDIA DRIVE CULTURE

Still other viewpoints emphasize media content over technology. In the early nineteenth century, Oxford professor and poet Matthew Arnold held that people moving from the countryside into the cities would become refined by coming in contact with "high culture" media such as the ballet and the opera. Implicit was the idea that media should exist to educate, not entertain, a point echoed by some present-day critics, such as Postman (1992).

Sociologist and philosopher Theodor Adorno (Horkheimer & Adorno, 1972) argued, however, that mass-produced cultural goods of low quality replaced high culture and traditional folk culture. If people were easily entertained by pop music, would they ever attend a classical opera? As mass audiences consumed **popular culture**, would everyone begin to think and act alike? For example, they might believe that the perfect 1950s family portrayed in *Leave It to Beaver* was a realistic model for their own family (Real, 1989). Another observation is that mass media overwhelm the "true" culture of the people in the interest of perpetuating class hegemony (Carey, 1972). Postman argued that literacy and reasoning skills decline as a result

[**Popular culture** is made up of elements mass-produced in society for the mass population.]

of overexposure to popular culture. In his words, we are "amusing ourselves to death" (Postman, 1986). Or, in the words of another critic, we are living in a "filter bubble" (Pariser, 2011) in that the personalized algorithms that Google, Amazon, Facebook, and others use to feed us online information trap us in a world where we are never subject to new ideas or people that diverge from those we "liked" to or searched for in the past.

As we learn more about the relationship between media and society, scholars continue to debate which perspective is most valid. Throughout *Media Now* we try to present both sides of the debate so that you, the reader, can decide for yourself what the best explanation is.

STOP&REVIEW

1. Give examples of people who are gatekeepers.
2. What are the main social functions of the mass media?
3. Using the "diffusion of innovations" paradigm, explain how Facebook spread through society.
4. How does technological determinism differ from cultural determinism?

SUMMARY&REVIEW

HOW DO ECONOMICS INFLUENCE THE MEDIA?

First-copy costs in mass media entail virtually all the investment in the production of a work. Economies of scale occur when producers make so many copies of something that they learn how to make each of those copies more cheaply. By the law of supply and demand, cheaper copies can reach far more people, creating a broader audience. Producers want to spread production costs and also their entry costs—the initial costs of establishing a media enterprise—across a broad audience in order to increase profits and satisfy their investors.

HOW IS MEDIA OWNERSHIP STRUCTURED?

Media can be structured as monopolies, where one company dominates the industry; as oligopolies, where a few companies dominate; or in competition, where a number of companies vie for dominance. The patterns of ownership have a great deal to do with the diversity and nature of the media's content, their availability and accessibility to people, and their role in society. Generally speaking, the more the ownership is concentrated in the hands of a few, the less diverse and more expensive the media are.

WHAT ARE THE SOURCES OF MEDIA REVENUE?

Most revenues come directly from the end user of media products. Direct sales of media products occur when consumers pay out a lump sum and take a media product such as a CD home with them. A rental also involves payment for a product, except that the consumer pays only to borrow it, as in a videotape rental. Subscriptions permit newspapers and magazines to be sold on a continuing basis over time for a standard fee. Usage fees are charged for temporary access to media products, such as movie theater admissions, that consumers can't literally take home. The media collect advertising revenues by selling access to their audiences to advertisers, who in turn pay for advertising by charging consumers.

WHAT IS THE ROLE OF PUBLIC SUBSIDIES?

Public subsidies, from either voluntary contributions or taxes, are provided for socially desirable content that commercial interests do not find profitable to provide. The educational and cultural programs on the PBS are prime examples.

WHAT IS SEGMENTATION?

Technological changes, industry changes, and receptivity by audiences and advertisers are all encouraging media to segment their audiences; that is, to focus on smaller, more specific audiences with more specialized programs or contents. The targeting of media content to appeal to the tastes of a particular narrow audience segment is called *narrowcasting*.

WHAT ARE THE NEW MEDIA ECONOMICS?

The Internet takes segmentation to its logical conclusion by personalizing content and ads for individual users. Websites profit from having their users supply the content free of charge and by having users absorb the distribution costs. Others profit by re-purposing content created for conventional media for distribution on the Internet. Unlike conventional media, Internet companies like Google can charge advertisers on the basis of those who respond to their ads (by the click) rather than according to the number who were exposed to the page carrying the ad.

HOW DO POLITICAL ECONOMISTS EXPLAIN MEDIA?

Social structure is determined by the efforts of dominant classes to maintain their wealth and power. The dominant class in society uses its ownership of the media to influence their content. This class creates a consensus, or hegemony, of ideas that reinforces its position of dominance. In this view, maintaining class dominance is furthered by the profitability of media enterprises. This tends to keep media content within the bounds of this hegemonic set of ideas.

WHAT DO FEMINIST AND ETHNIC STUDIES CONTRIBUTE?

The sex-role and ethnic stereotypes that appear in the media may be there for a reason: to perpetuate the dominance of white males in society.

WHAT IS SEMIOTICS?

Semiotics is branch of critical studies. It is a systematic way of looking at media content to examine the symbols and signs contained in it. The signs in media communicate something of symbolic value to the audience; they include visual images, music, camera angles, words, and so on. The producer creates or encodes a meaning into the sign, but the audience may decode or interpret a different meaning.

WHAT ARE GENRES?

In media content, formulas, or genres, evolve over time. These formulas are things like soap operas, mystery novels, and action cartoons. They represent an agreement between producer and audience on what kinds of stories ought to be told and how, or on how a music video ought to look, or on how a talk show host ought to act.

WHAT ARE AGENDA SETTERS AND GATEKEEPERS?

Agenda setters from government, businesses, and political interest groups try to influence what the media cover and what "spin" media give to that coverage. Within the media themselves, a variety of media professionals make decisions about what goes into and what stays out of news and entertainment media. They are the gatekeepers.

WHAT SOCIAL FUNCTIONS DO MEDIA SERVE?

Among the functions sociologists have identified for communications media are surveillance (keeping track of our world or environment), interpretation (making sense of what we learn), value transmission (passing values on from one generation to the next), and entertainment.

HOW DO NEW MEDIA SPREAD?

New technologies spread like a disease, from person to person, slowly at first but gradually picking up speed. People consider an innovation's relative advantages, its compatibility with existing practices, its complexity, and any opportunities they have to observe the innovation in action before they try it out themselves. Some people are innovators, some are early adopters, followed by the majority of adopters, late adopters, and laggards. Interactive technologies seem to require a critical mass of users before large numbers will adopt it.

WHAT IS TECHNOLOGICAL DETERMINISM?

Technological determinists argue that changes in society and culture are driven by advances in media technology and by the content of the media to a large extent. They oppose the view of cultural determinists, who maintain that culture determines the nature of the media and their content.

THINKING CRITICALLY
ABOUT THE MEDIA

1. Is Mark Zuckerberg of Facebook a monopolist or not? Explain your position.

2. How has the hegemony of ideas affected you personally?

3. List all the media you used today and define the functions associated with each one.

4. What is your favorite medium, and how does it make money from you?

5. Twitter was slow to catch on among college students. How can you explain that in diffusion of innovation terms?

KEY TERMS

barriers to entry (p. 34)

copyright royalty fee (p. 38)

critical studies (p. 41)

culture (p. 42)

diffusion (p. 46)

duopoly (p. 33)

economics (p. 30)

economies of scale (p. 31)

genre (p. 44)

hegemony (p. 41)

law of supply and demand (p. 32)

marginal costs (p. 33)

media literacy (p. 41)

monopoly (p. 33)

oligopoly (p. 33)

political economy (p. 41)

popular culture (p. 52)

profits (p. 35)

technological determinism (p. 48)

theories (p. 29)

FROM MANUSCRIPTS hand-copied by medieval monks to e-books distributed through the Internet, publishing the written word is an ever-changing media form.

3

BOOKS AND MAGAZINES

HISTORY: THE PRINTING TO DIGITAL EVOLUTION

Founding father and colonial-era publisher Benjamin Franklin would have appreciated the historical path to the Kindle Fire and its reason for being! As he developed apps for Amazon books and used social media to interact with his magazine audiences, he would have understood that where we are today is the result of a continual cycle of technological innovations and social acceptances, competition between forms and uses of media, consumer demand, growing literacy, and changes in society wrought by media (see Media Then/Media Now, p. 58).

EARLY PRINT MEDIA

Technology influences what formats are possible in media, but it does not define their contents. For example, **novels** flourished with printing because mechanical reproduction allowed quantities of books to be produced less expensively. However, the concepts and forms that characterize the novel originated much earlier: Greek oral poets produced epic works such as the *Odyssey* (Homer, 800 BCE). And the Japanese *Tale of Genji*, recognizable as a novel by

> **Novels** are extended fictional works, usually of book length.

current standards, was written by Lady Murasaki Shikibu in the eleventh century. Thus, the antecedents of novels about daily life, romances, mysteries, and horror existed well before the advent of printing.

The earliest experiments with an alphabet are thought to be from the Middle East in 1900–1800 BCE, and it continued to be developed by the Phoenicians, Greeks, and Romans. However, the oldest script still in existence today is from the Chinese, a country that also developed brushes, ink, and paper in 105 CE. Brushes used a type of ink made from soot or black soil, and Tsai-Lun, the superintendent of a weapons manufacturing factory, created a form of paper by mashing together different plants, rags, and water and drying them on screens of bamboo (Sloan, 2005). The Chinese built upon their knowledge by developing printing blocks—they carved symbols in pieces of wood and inked them—and pressing them on paper, which they used to produce books. These inventions were passed along to the Japanese and Koreans and then to the Arabs. By 1051, the Chinese put together a metal, clay, and wooden press. The Koreans further refined the printing process by developing movable metal type in 1234. Printing did not evolve further (it was difficult to deal with 40,000 Asian characters) until 1455, when Johannes Gutenberg of Germany (re)discovered movable type and printed the first (German) Bible. Innovations continued from there.

Until Gutenberg's press, books were a limited medium throughout the world because they had to be hand-copied. For thousands of years, handwritten and printed materials were available only to the few best-educated people, such as the Mandarin bureaucratic elite of China. In many cultures, rulers did not want their subjects gaining new ideas and questioning government policies. Thus few people in the early civilizations of Greece, Egypt, China, the Middle East, and Rome were literate or had access to libraries.

As the more sophisticated cultures were destroyed by barbarians, reading and writing was carried on by monks, who passed along all sorts of information about farming and irrigation to peasants. Many monks also devoted their lives to copying text and creating beautiful illustrations by hand. Some surviving examples, among them the Irish *Book of Kells* (800 CE), are considered major works of art today. Books tended to build on earlier oral traditions, for instance, early Greek epics such as the *Iliad* (800 BCE), medieval European literature such as Icelandic sagas, and the folk stories and fairy tales collected by the brothers Grimm.

The growth of **literacy** in Europe and the writing of books in the everyday language spoken by most people in a particular region, such as Italian or Swedish, was key for the development of print media. Prior to 1100, written communication was nearly always in Latin, the language of the Roman Catholic Church. Thus, to be literate, people had to learn a second language. By the 1200s, written versions of daily languages were more frequent and, as a result, literacy became more commonplace in the 1300s and 1400s among the political elite, the commercial and trading class, and such professionals as the sea captain Christopher Columbus. Outside this group, though, most people remained illiterate.

Throughout the Middle Ages in Europe, few books other than the Bible and religious or philosophical commentaries were available for people to read. This began to change by the 1300s and 1400s. Universities were established to train more people as clergy and clerks. Also, the most important books printed and circulated in Europe came from the Hebrew Middle East (the Bible, the Torah) or the Arab Middle East (focusing on science, math, astronomy, and navigation). Many also came from ancient Greece: classic works of science, literature, and philosophy, such as Plato's *Republic,* that influenced European ideas of government. Whereas books had survived only in hand-copied form for centuries, the printing of these classic works gave a greater number of people access to ideas about life and work. For instance, in the late 1400s, Columbus learned from an Arab book on geography that he might be able to reach India and Southeast Asia by sailing west across the Atlantic Ocean. It is highly likely that if Columbus had been born 100 years earlier, he would not have had access to such books. Clearly, the European explosion of print technology and printed contents built a much larger world context.

Scala/Art Resource, NY

HANDMADE Among the earliest books were illustrated manuscripts that were carefully created by hand, like this page from Statute of a Council from the fourteenth century.

[**Literacy** is the ability to read and understand a variety of information.]

THE GUTENBERG REVOLUTION

The Gutenberg Bible was published in 1455, the result of Johannes Gutenberg's development of movable type and mechanical printing five years earlier. This German press was a technology breakthrough that made new forms of mass production possible—people could print many more books, handbills, and newsletters at a much lower cost. For example, within 15 years of Gutenberg, a French-printed Bible cost one-fifth of what a hand-copied manuscript had cost. As the new technology gained momentum, printing and reading became a cyclical process that reinforced itself. As more people had sufficient money and interest to buy books, book production increased and benefited from economies of scale, which made individual books cheaper (see Chapter 2). This permitted even more people to buy books (see Media&Culture: Goodbye, Gutenberg, page 60).

MEDIA&CULTURE

GOODBYE, GUTENBERG

Did reading change the way our brains work? As we saw in Chapter 2, Canadian media scholar Marshall McLuhan (1962) argued in *Typographic Man* that printing fostered linear modes of thinking about ordered sequences of events that in turn led to thinking about cause and effect, then science, then the modern industrial world.

At a social level, readers were more likely to identify with people and issues beyond their immediate communities. In another book, *The Imagined Communities*, Benedict Anderson (1991) argued that reading was largely responsible for the development of nationalism: the intense individual identification that countries have with their nations that enables them to command such loyalty that people are willing, even excited, to go to war. Anderson traced such individual passion for the nation to the experience of reading the same novels and newspapers across the breadth of the national territory, so that people began to imagine themselves as part of a larger community defined by all the people reading the same things. As our media today become more fragmented, critics wonder if audiences will, too.

In his later, 1964 book, *Understanding Media*, McLuhan observed that electronic media had further changed most people to a new sort of orientation, not based on the typographical logic, but focused instead on decoding and understanding television. Some studies of learning among young people in the United States and Germany seem to show new patterns in which many children who are not good at reading are sophisticated at learning from computer games and television

Bettmann/Corbis

GUTENBERG'S PRESS The invention of the printing press allowed reading as a leisure activity to flourish, helping people identify with communities beyond their immediate location.

screens with complex arrays of numbers and images (Bachmair, 2006). However, *Typographic Man* still has many advantages in our society. People who are good at deep involvement and comprehension in reading still tend to do better in school, particularly college, which is still the main avenue to the best-paying jobs in our society.

The Bible, prayer books, and hymnals were among the earliest publications. Beyond the Bible and religious pamphlets, new products were often more entertainment oriented and aimed at broader groups of people with less education. *Broadside ballads* were single sheets of words for popular songs, whereas chapbooks were cheaply bound books or pamphlets of poetry, ballads, or prose that were aimed at a broader audience. Libraries provided one means of popularizing books and making them more accessible to the public. Sir Thomas Bodley started the first modern lending library of printed books in 1602 in Oxford, England. Years later, as printing and binding costs continued to decline and thus made books more affordable, publishers began to distribute books directly to the public by selling them through bookstalls in railway stations. Then, book publishing accelerated rapidly: two million titles were issued worldwide in the 1700s and eight million in the 1800s.

THE FIRST AMERICAN PRINT MEDIA

In America, also, print media began with copies of religious books; after all, the colonists came to America to pursue religious freedom. The *Bay Psalm Book* was the first book published in America, printed in 1640 by Elizabeth Glover, who set up the first printing press in the new Massachusetts college called Harvard. As most families encouraged their children to read the Bible, the literacy rate in the colonies was high. As more people could read, other publications followed religious ones. Soon thereafter came newspapers, magazines, and **almanacs**, published in Boston, New York, and Philadelphia (see Chapter 4).

One of the more influential publishing figures in the American colonies was Benjamin Franklin, a major innovator in printing, science, politics, and practical inventions. As a printer, Franklin constantly experimented to see what kinds of publications would attract an audience. (If he had social media, he might have asked them directly!) In 1732, he published one of America's first successful nonreligious books, *Poor Richard's Almanack*, which contained moral advice, farming tips, amusements, and maxims for American colonists. Almanacs, along with educational primers, religious books, and law books, were among the most popular books in the colonies. The oldest regularly published periodical in North America is *The Old Farmer's Almanac*, started by Robert B. Thomas in 1792 with a new issue appearing each September. Franklin and other book printers also produced political pamphlets. Thomas Paine's *Common Sense*, which urged readers to support independence from Great Britain, sold 100,000 copies in 10 weeks.

Franklin also started the first **subscription library** in America, beginning a tradition that greatly helped popularize book reading. Still, the high cost of books and the difficulty of gaining access to them aided the rise of less expensive newspapers and magazines.

Early Magazines. Magazines began to develop in Great Britain in the 1700s. They carried fiction and nonfiction in varying degrees, depending on the readership. The first was the British *Gentleman's Magazine* of 1731, whose editors deliberately left news to the newspapers and focused on elegant and amusing writing about literature, politics, history, biography, and criticism (Riley, 1993). This formula still characterizes much of magazine content: humor; fiction; and essays about politics, literature, music, theater, and famous people.

AP Photo/Jim Cole

CONVENIENT AND USEFUL *The Old Farmer's Almanac* has provided weather forecasts, gardening tips and other useful information since 1792. Farmers wanted it handy throughout the year, so they ran nails and string through the top left corner to hang it on the wall in the kitchen, barn or outhouse. Today, publishers use machinery to punch holes in the press run of 400 million books for the same reason.

[**Almanacs** are book-length collections of useful facts, calendars, and advice.]

[**Subscription libraries** lent books to the public for a fee.]

The first American magazines debuted in 1741 in Philadelphia, the nation's first center for magazines. William Bradford's *American Magazine* lasted for three months, whereas its competitor, Ben Franklin's *General Magazine and Historical Chronicle*, was printed three days later and lived for six months. Publishers tried to popularize several other short-lived magazines prior to the American Revolution, but all were limited by too few readers with leisure time to read, high costs of publishing, and expensive distribution by horse-drawn coaches.

During the American Revolution, magazines became more political. For example, Thomas Paine edited *Pennsylvania Magazine*, which urged revolution. Despite the emphasis on politics, many magazines in the 1700s were called **miscellanies** and appealed to a small, far-flung, and diverse audience. After the American Revolution, magazines took a while to succeed economically. Magazines were given no cost break in postal rates until 1879 (Riley, 1993), so few magazines were widely read or long-lived until the 1800s (Tebbel, 1969).

The fledgling American publishing industry was given a significant economic boost by the first U.S. Congress with the passage of the Copyright Act of 1790. This legislation gave authors and their publishers exclusive rights to their publications for a period of 14 years (renewable for an additional 14 years). During that time, anyone who wished to reproduce the work would have to make a payment, called a *royalty fee*, to the copyright holder for the use of the work.

As the 1700s drew to a close, American magazines were aimed at the better-educated and wealthy elite and a small but growing middle class. Publishers took up political causes, siding with Federalists (promoting a strong central government, a federal system) or their opposition (wanting a state-oriented, decentralized government). The political organ of the Federalist movement, *Port Folio*, was the first magazine to achieve substantial national circulation and contained essays such as Alexander Hamilton's "Federalist Papers," promoting the passage of the Constitution. A formidable anti-Federalist magazine, the *National Magazine of Richmond* was one of the few magazines published outside the dominant publishing centers of Philadelphia, Boston, and New York.

In the early 1800s, there was a new trend toward "literary miscellanies," such as the *Saturday Evening Post*, whose editors moved from reproducing European literature to popularizing American writers. They covered weekly events, history, politics, art, reviews, travelogues, short stories, and serialized fiction. "Special miscellanies" focused on specific topics and audiences. Sarah Josepha Hale's *Ladies' Magazine* of Boston was the first successful American magazine targeted toward women and was soon followed by *Godey's Lady's Book*. By the 1840s, magazines shifted their attention toward broader and more sustainable mass audiences.

During the Civil War era, magazines began to have a much greater impact on public life. Several magazines grew to fame for their coverage and illustrations dramatizing scenes of the war. Magazines such as *Harper's Weekly* created an important new form of publication, the illustrated newsweekly. During the war talented correspondents quickly sketched battle scenes that were sent back home to the magazine for artists to fill in with detail. Then **woodcuts**

Miscellanies were magazines with a wide variety of content.

Woodcuts were used to make illustrations by carving a picture in a block of wood, inking it, and pressing it onto paper.

were quartered so that different parts of the scene could be carved by different artists simultaneously and put back together, so the illustration could be published with its news story as soon as possible.

America Reads. In the mid-1800s, improving social conditions fostered a mass audience for books and magazines. An expanding public education system taught more people to read. As wages increased, young people moved to the cities to work in the burgeoning industrial economy, and an urban middle class grew. Prices fell with economies of scale, improved printing technology, and more demand for print media. Access to books increased as the number of public libraries tripled in the first half of the nineteenth century.

Perhaps most important, however, was the popularization of book content. Many American novelists earned loyal fans by addressing the uniquely American national experience and interests. James Fenimore Cooper wrote compelling stories about the struggles of both white settlers and indigenous people on the frontier. In novels such as *The Last of the Mohicans* (1826), Cooper dramatized the attraction of the West. Immigrants sometimes cited his work as part of what they knew about America, a contributing factor of what drew them to the West.

Novels had political effects. A prime example is Harriet Beecher Stowe's *Uncle Tom's Cabin* (1852), which sold 300,000 copies in its first year and did much to inspire popular opposition to slavery (Davis, 1985).

In the second half of the nineteenth century, a new cheap format popularized reading even more. **Dime novels** (called "Penny Dreadfuls" in Great Britain) were often lurid, gallows humor that involved a broader audience, including working-class people. For instance, Horatio Alger wrote 100 books that collectively sold about 250 million copies. His popular hero was usually a poor boy who managed to rise out of poverty through hard work, honesty, thrift, planning, and other virtues. The phrase "Horatio Alger hero" eventually became a popular term for anyone who gained social mobility and success through hard work and honest living.

As the U.S. Postal system improved, methods of transportation became reliable, and as more people appreciated literature as an important form of knowledge and entertainment, magazines grew into a major mass medium in the 1800s.

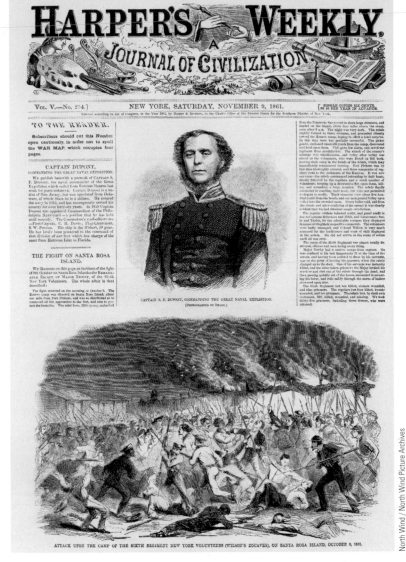

THE CIVIL WAR ILLUSTRATED The vivid illustrations of Civil War action in *Harper's Weekly*, like these images in woodcuts of the attack on Santa Rosa Island and of Mathew Brady's photograph of Capt. S.F. DuPont, attracted large readership in the 1860s. To examine larger and more woodcuts in this issue, see: http://www.sonofthesouth.net/leefoundation/civil-war/battle-santa-rosa-island.htm

[**Dime novels** were inexpensive paperback novels of the nineteenth century.]

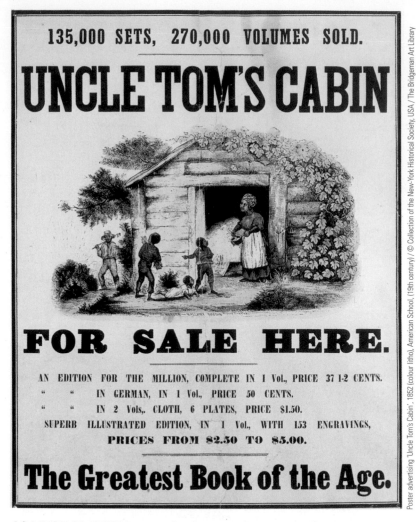

AGAINST SLAVERY Harriet Beecher Stowe's *Uncle Tom's Cabin* was a best seller in its day and also helped set the agenda for opposition to slavery.

Magazines benefited particularly from a major change in their delivery system. The Postal Act of 1879 gave magazines special rates. Within 40 years, the number of magazines grew almost sevenfold—to 1,800 in 1900 (Riley, 1993). This de facto subsidy to magazine distribution continues today: publishers pay lower third-class rates for mailing, whereas their magazines are sent by first-class mail.

Many students today would not recognize a magazine of the 1800s. Most were octavo size (a little larger than 6×9 inches), with matte (nonglossy) pages. Covers had ornate, illustrated woodcut borders and the table of contents, listing titles and authors, was centered in the middle. By the late 1800s, the flowing borders and the table of contents gave way to elaborate artistic drawings surrounding the magazine's name. Color and more sophisticated drawings surrounding teasers about content were new innovations in the early 1900s. And as reliance on advertisers grew, so did the number of pages devoted to ads. Many magazines charged about $250 for full-page ads, which were grouped together in the front and back of the periodical, separately numbered, and often bound together as a pamphlet that could be lifted out of the book. *Harper's New Monthly Magazine* (April 1894) cost 35 cents, whereas the average factory worker's wage was 5 to 20 cents an hour. A sample of the content shows illustrations, including one by Frederic Remington; a story by journalist Richard Harding Davis; vignettes; poems; history; political events and issues; and a "monthly record of current events."

By the twentieth century, most Americans were literate and could afford small luxuries, such as magazines, which were cheaper than ever before. They had more leisure time to read, as both the agricultural and industrial economies developed, and their interest in civic affairs, the arts, professional matters, and politics boomed. New **genres** appeared—investigative magazines, digests, newsmagazines, and pictorial magazines. An increasing sense of openness and freedom in the press expanded the number of topics acceptable to magazine readers. By the early twentieth century, popular "pulp" fiction magazines, named for the cheap, pulpy paper they used, began to push the bounds of social acceptability with sensationalism—police stories, romance, crime mysteries, scandals, science fiction, and fantasy.

[**Genres** are distinctive styles of creative works. The term is also used to represent different types or formats of media content.]

Muckraking. In the late 1800s and early 1900s, magazines began to overtake newspapers in investigative reporting and crusades for reform. Much of this investigative reporting, known as **muckraking**, appeared in *McClure's* and *Collier's*, nationally circulated and inexpensive magazines that reached millions of readers and had a great impact on public opinion. The term refers to reporters being willing to stir up and sift through the unpleasant aspects of public life that most people ignore and to identify and publicize misdeeds by public figures. Magazine journalism looked for crusading reporters who could report and write controversial, striking stories that would draw in a mass audience.

In 1918, during the Progressive Era (which ran from 1890 to the end of World War II), reform politicians, unions, rural associations, and magazine and newspaper reporters protested the power of big business and the conservative politics of the parties in power. Reformers pushed for more social, economic, and political justice, like the regulation of food and drug purity, child labor laws, a shorter workday, a minimum wage, job safety rules, reduced political corruption, and government regulation of big-business excess. Editor Ida Tarbell, from *McClure's*

MUCKRAKER In the early twentieth century, Ida Tarbell gained prominence as one of the leading magazine writers by exposing the abuses of the Standard Oil Company.

[**Muckraking** is investigative journalism that "rakes up the muck"—dirt and filth—to expose corruption and scandal.]

Magazine, wrote a meticulous muckraking exposé that was devoured by the public on the unprincipled rise of Standard Oil Company under John D. Rockefeller's unethical business tactics. The 19-part series is still considered a hallmark in investigative journalism, and it is listed as fifth out of the top 100 influential works in American journalism, according to New York University (http://www.infoplease.com/ipea/A0777379.html).

Muckraking often led to landmark reform legislation in the first decade of the twentieth century. The Pure Food and Drug Act resulted from an article in *Collier's* called "The Great American Fraud" by Samuel Hopkins Adams. The Mann Act, which prohibited transportation of women across state lines for immoral purposes, resulted from an article in *McClure's,* titled "Daughters of the Poor," by Burton J. Hendrick. And Upton Sinclair's *The Jungle,* a book about Chicago slaughterhouses, led to the Meat Inspection Act.

The term *muckraking* has now lost its crusading political meaning and today refers more to the investigation of sexual scandals and other "dirt" on public figures. However, contemporary journalists continue to target corruption and abuse of power with a crusading spirit that often results in positive change. Some current magazines—*The Nation* and *Mother Jones*—still

STOP&REVIEW

1. What key elements of print media developed first outside Europe?

2. What was the impact of printing in Europe?

3. Why and how did magazines develop?

4. What was the role of the print media in the Civil War?

5. What was *muckraking*?

specialize in muckraking journalism. Many Web magazines and blogs have also continued this tradition, such as TomPaine.com with commentary and opinion.

MODERN MAGAZINES

After the 1920s, magazines competed with radio and film for people's leisure time. Some magazines did not adapt well to the competition and disappeared. Some quality magazines like *Harper's Monthly* and *Atlantic Monthly* kept a loyal audience but barely survived. New magazines tried mass appeal—to become everything to everyone (Payne, 1993). The successful magazines sold more copies, were less expensive to produce, and cost less to readers.

Magazines became a major mass medium. The once-popular *Saturday Evening Post* focused on the accomplishments of American business, inspirational success stories, action stories, romance, and some factual reports. However, its formula for appealing to a middle-class audience never adjusted to subsequent competition from television. As advertising shifted to television, the *Post* lost money and went out of business in 1969.

The *Ladies' Home Journal* did much better with a narrower, but loyal, targeted audience and still holds tightly to its place in circulation among the top 15 magazines. It has had to be imaginative and creative to continue to be successful with added competition from the numerous other women's magazine, and competition from other media, such as streaming movies, DVDs, CDs, TV, radio, and online and mobile devices.

————YOUR MEDIA CAREER

WANTED! WRITERS AND EDITORS!

Books and magazines have one of two purposes—to inform or to entertain—or both. Their content is mostly in the form of words, often with visuals.

In this section, we will concentrate on writers, authors, and editors in the book and magazine industries, although these businesses also include visual communicators, sales personnel, and promotion experts, among other professionals.

A wonderful aspect of being a journalist, writer, author, or editor is that—depending on your employer and the organization—you can write at home all day in your Captain America pajamas, or work at the office in your new "Dress for Success" suit, or gather information in the field in your Abercrombie-distressed jeans. The Internet and communications software have made other options, such as freelancing, feasible as self-supporting professions.

Most writers and editors major in journalism, communication, or English. Journalism majors learn how to write fact-based, nonfiction stories. They learn how to gather information through making observations, interviewing sources, researching documents in print or online, and thinking critically. They also learn how to organize and present their information, as they consider the story angle, the audience, and the medium.

Some writers are generalists and can write well about many subjects because of their good research and writing skills. Others are specialists who have perhaps minored or gained expertise in an additional area, such as environment, international affairs, medicine, technology, science, business, sports, or fashion.

The best way to break into the business is to work in student media while in college or job shadow a professional. A good way to get ahead is to do several internships while in school. Internships can help beginners understand the field, and find out what else they need to know to be successful.

Writers and authors put together the story, usually in narrative form for a magazine or book. Writers and editors must master grammar, punctuation, spelling, and word usage.

Editors plan the theme of a magazine and choose appropriate writers. They also review the completed stories. With books, they review proposals and make decisions to hire particular authors. Copy editors and proof readers go over the completed works with a fine-toothed comb to make sure that every letter is in place and that every word conveys the desired meaning.

If you do well as a writer or editor for a publishing company (books, magazines, news), then you've begun to establish a good track record. Their editors will continue to contact you for additional projects.

It's a competitive market, so you need to be good. The Bureau of Labor Statistics (bls.gov) expects the profession of writers and authors to grow 15 percent and editors to increase at the pace of the national average of 8 percent. Many are self-employed. Although the phone and the Internet allow writers and editors to work from anywhere, major media and entertainment markets are located in Boston, Chicago, Los Angeles, New York, and Washington, D. C. The average salary for a writer or author is $66,000, with the highest 10 percent earning about $110,000.

If you are a successful book author, then you can expect book royalties between 8 and 15 percent, depending on how good you are and how well you negotiate. (The more successful you are, the more you might be able to negotiate.) In the current book industry, the costs are divided among the author (10 percent), publisher (30 percent), printer (10 percent), distributor (10 percent), and retailer (40 percent). However, if you are the author of an e-book your cut and the publisher's cut is about the same, but the online company now gets the rest (60 percent). Always, always check the fine print in your contract!

A magazine genre that is struggling to find a new niche is the **newsmagazine.** In 1923, Henry Luce and Briton Hadden started *Time* magazine, and that success led Time Inc. to introduce *Life*, an illustrated photojournalism magazine in 1936. *Life* met the public's desire for a photographic report of the world with pictures of the week's events and fairly short news analyses, creating a visual style of journalism. Competition from an upstart mass medium with moving pictures—television— led to the closing of *Life* four decades later. Other newsmagazines, such as *Time, Economist, The Atlantic,* and *The New Yorker*, which balance photo images with extensive text and in-depth reporting, continued to do well even after television became popular, but are now experiencing the free news sources of the Internet as a challenge.

One of the newsmagazines that experienced troubles with the economy and online competition is *Newsweek*. With its revenues slipping, *Newsweek*'s owner (The Washington Post Company) changed its philosophy from being a general-circulation magazine to providing a niche for a smaller, high-income circulation. That didn't work as circulation dropped lower than 2 million. *Newsweek* finally found a buyer for $1 and assumption of its large debt. The new owner

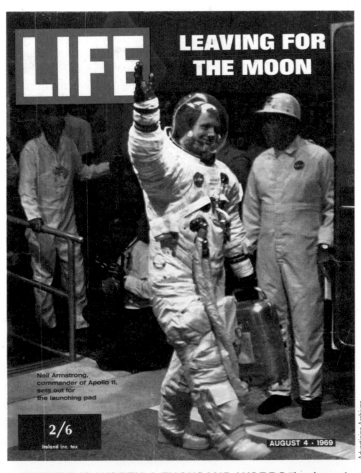

A PICTURE IS WORTH A THOUSAND WORDS The dynamic photojournalism of *Life* magazine pioneered a visual approach to the news that was later copied by television.

Table 3.1 Number Of Magazines—Total and Consumer, 2001–2010

YEAR	TOTAL*	CONSUMER
2010	20,707	7,163
2009**	20,638	7,110
2008**	20,590	7,383
2007	19,532	6,809
2006	19,419	6,734
2005	18,267	6,325
2004	18,821	7,811
2003	17,254	6,234
2002**	17,321	5,340
2001**	17,694	6,336

*Includes, but not limited to, consumer magazines in North America regardless of publishing frequency. Consumer magazines are sold to the general public and are separate from journals and trade publications.

**Represents economic downturn

Note: Fluctuations reflect that the number of magazines changes based on economic conditions.

Source: *National Directory of Magazines*, 2011 (chart found at: http://www.magazine.org/advertising/magazine-media-factbook/84.html)

> **Newsmagazine** is a weekly periodical with coverage (text and visual) on current news events.

rapidly partnered with a successful online news site to form the *Newsweek*/Daily Beast website that claims to attract about 10 million visitors a month and the *Newsweek* magazine now reaches 14 million readers (not all paying subscribers) in the United States and many more with its international editions.

Cutting itself out of the herd and taking a different tact, is the newsmagazine *The Week,* which began in 2003 and continues to grow. It capitalizes on readers' busy schedules and their media information overload. Contrary to the other newsmagazines, it does not do in-depth reporting but summarizes the reporting of recent news events.

Whereas newsmagazines attract general audiences, most magazines target specific audiences and have prospered overall through the years, including this past year, as the industry recovers from the bad economy. In 1950 there were 250 magazines in publication (Alsop, 1997, p. 929). Magazines today number more than 20,700—the highest number recorded by the National Directory of Magazines (see Table 3.1, this page).

Recent decades have seen a proliferation of more specialized magazines for even narrower audiences. This trend has only accelerated. Today there's a magazine to cover almost every hobby, occupation, and interest, from canoeing to dairy farming. And niches within specializations continue to grow. For example, within the past 10 years, the number of ethnic magazines grew by about 560 titles, from almost 420 at the turn of the century to about 980 in 2010.

BOOK PUBLISHING GIANTS

Many publishing houses, such as Harper & Row, have been around since the early 1800s. Some of the most active American hardback publishers, such as McGraw-Hill and Prentice Hall, set up shop in the early twentieth century. As printing costs declined, more Americans could afford hardback books, and the publishing industry grew.

For both books and pulp magazines that specialized in short stories, the first half of the twentieth century was a boom era for detective stories, science fiction, and westerns (Folkerts & Teeter, 1994). Behind this publishing boom was the low "book rate" for mailing books, which made both mail-order sales and marketing via book clubs much cheaper. Mail-order book clubs, such as the Book-of-the-Month Club and the Literary Guild, initially worried publishers but ultimately benefited them by popularizing book reading and buying.

World War II helped popularize reading by ushering in the paperback era. Most of the publishing houses established during this time, such as Pocket Books, Bantam Books, and Penguin Books, profited from paperbacks.

Young people away at war read more, and as they returned home and entered college (assisted by educational benefits for veterans), they read textbooks and mass-marketed paperbacks. As educational institutions and the public demanded more textbooks, publishers of serious literature and nonfiction introduced larger-format trade paperbacks to complement "pocket-size" paperbacks.

The connotation of a **book publisher** is changing. To your grandfather, the term would conjure up a huge publishing building—such as Random House—on a city block in New York, the main publishing center of the United States. For your mother, "publishing" might include the online companies that she can use to publish memoirs of your recent family vacation. No offense to your mother, but the large publishing company might not make enough sales with your mother's book to cover their expenses, no matter how cute you look in her photos. However, the online companies would be happy to take her book, charging different fees for the design, number of books, and optional marketing support. Another alternative for your mother is to take her book to a printing company, instead.

The definition of "book" is changing. Although an **e-book** is electronic, it is still a book. While **audio books** are not read, they are still stories or information that people consume—just in a different form (audio). The number of books overall—no matter the platform—continues to rise, led by the digital categories composed of e-books and downloadable audio books.

Other trends are causing today's book publishing industry to stretch and grow in new directions. Publishers have experimented with distributing books directly to the public themselves, while some bookstore chains have tried publishing their own books. Non-traditional publishing companies took a giant step forward, acting as reprint companies that produce on-demand public domain titles—printed books whose copyright or intellectual property rights have expired.

In the United States and internationally, book publishers and bookstores are redefining themselves. High tech companies including Amazon, Google, and Apple challenge conventional print institutions ranging from publishers to bookstores to public libraries (see Technology Trends, next section). For example, Amazon.com is trying to usurp the role of book publishers and literary agents by publishing and distributing works directly to readers (and is succeeding, in some cases). Google has scanned libraries full of older volumes that it would like to offer free on the Internet even as libraries reduce their book collections to make more room for public access computers. Apple is attempting to extract a generous share of the revenues from magazine publishers who would like to put online versions on iPads.

However, digital technology could also help the conventional print industry. Online surveillance of social media and analysis of massive consumer databases reveals reading patterns—what titles are popular, what format is preferable, how books are being ordered, and how they are being delivered, for example. In China, e-books are read more on **mobile devices** and the Internet than on **e-readers**. Thus, if publishers can win control over new technology they can take advantage of new opportunities to thrive, such as making cell phone "apps" (see Chapter 12) that can be downloaded to mobile devices for a fee.

Book publishers offer an array of services, from editing to promoting to selling a book.

E-books are book content that appears in digital text format. It can be read on mobile devices, computer tablets, and e-readers.

Audio books are books narrated onto CDs. Some can be downloaded.

Mobile devices are hand-held computers or cell phones with display screens. They access and send information using cell phone or WiFi connections to the Internet.

E-readers are devices that are used to read digital content found in books, magazines, and newspapers.

TECHNOLOGY TRENDS: FROM CHAPBOOK TO E-BOOK

In the 500 years since Gutenberg, most improvements in publishing technology have revolved around finding faster ways to press ink on paper, although progress was slow for about 400 years.

AFTER GUTENBERG

The invention of the first rotary press in 1846 was a significant advancement in printing. Unlike previous presses that printed on single sheets of paper one sheet at a time, rotary presses used rotating cylinders of type to print on both sides of large, continuous rolls of paper. Typesetting remained a slow, manual process until linotype machines were introduced, which cast entire lines of type from molten lead instantly.

Printed illustrations had been a staple of magazines since the Civil War (1861–1865), but only a few publications could afford them because they required the painstaking hand carving or engraving of wood (see woodcuts, pp. 62–63) or metal master plates. Lithography speeded the printing of illustrated pages by replacing engraving with a type of chemical etching. Photoengraving transformed illustrated publications by chemically etching images onto the surface of metal plates through a photographic process, a vast improvement over handmade lithographs. After World War II, offset printing was introduced so an entire page of print, complete with illustrations, could be photographed and the photographic image transferred to a smooth metal plate with chemically etched images that could be inked and printed.

PUBLISHING IN THE INFORMATION AGE

At first, computers were put to work assisting typesetters, automatically hyphenating and spacing the type on each line. In the 1970s, computers replaced typesetting machines by transferring text directly to photographic film that in turn was transferred to metal printing plates. The computerization of the layout and paste-up process further simplified printing, as did the digitizing of photographs so that they could be edited and placed on a page electronically. Now companies produce magazines with **computer-to-plate** technology.

Desktop publishing is the process of editing, laying out, and inserting photos using a desktop computer.

Computer-to-plate technology transfers page images composed inside a computer directly to printing plates.

As more power and speed were packed into desktop computers, software enabled users to layout pages on a personal computer and scanning became cheaper. By the late 1990s, **desktop publishing**, inexpensive photocopying, high-speed printing, and the publication of magazines in virtual form lowered the barriers to entry into the magazine business. Now, almost anyone with a personal computer can produce his or her own books, magazines, flyers, and posters.

And, perhaps surprisingly, the advent of electronic cash registers and bar codes has transformed the publishing industry. For book publishers, barcode scanners changed how inventory is tabulated and best-seller lists are compiled, by automating records instead of polling clerks, as in the old days. Another form of bar code, the QR (for Quick Response) code, those squares with jumbles of tiny square dots cropping up in popular magazines, activate interactive ads and editorial features when scanned with a smartphone.

E-PUBLISHING

Four evolutions to the computer age have had an impact on the traditional book publishing industry: e-commerce on the Internet, Kindle's impact toward society's acceptance of e-books, printing books on demand, and Google's digitization of printed books.

Amazon and other companies would not exist without **e-commerce**. Without leaving home, shoppers can "browse" and buy books. The Hunger Games series in hardcopy can be delivered in overnight mail or instantly downloaded to your e-reader. Virtual bookstores "remember" that you purchased *Catching Fire* and the next time you visit, automatically recommend *Mockingjay* or the latest in the series for a pre-purchase and

[**E-commerce** is the ability to buy and sell online.]

TECHNOLOGY DEMYSTIFIED

CUDDLING UP WITH A NICE ELECTRONIC BOOK?

There is something very comfortable to many people about a printed book. Even small paperbacks have their advantages: cheap, portable, no batteries required, durable. Attractively bound books with large type intrigue the romantic and the collector. Both entice us to relax at the beach or curl up by a cozy fire or in bed.

Can a lightweight, high-tech plastic device with a limited battery life ever offer serious competition to print books, the oldest medium around? Electronic books (e-readers) have their appeal. No night-light is required, if the screen has a backlight. You can mark passages electronically, search for key words, or get constant updates for timely material, like tax laws. You can carry a pile of titles around with you much more easily. You can download titles from the Internet anywhere that has cell phone reception. And, with the cost of both e-readers and electronic books dropping fast, they are becoming a viable alternative to printed books, magazines, and newspapers. However, they are not as economical as libraries.

In 2000, publishers became interested in e-books, although few were sold. Until 2007, e-books were read mostly on computers, not separate readers. Now, many students get e-books through their library sites or "e-reserve reading." College students with limited budgets are turning to online or digital books that sell for half the price of the hardback version. The Kindle popularized e-books and competes with Apple's iPad and the Barnes & Noble Nook. Even newer e-readers include Skiff Reader, Plastic Logic Que, enTourage edge, Samsung readers, Sony readers, and a host of others. Smartphones like the Apple iPhone and Google's Android offer an alternative platform.

Oleksiy Maksymenko Photography/Alamy

SUPER BOOK? Technology has allowed companies like Amazon, Barnes and Noble, and Apple to create the e-reader, a device that holds hundreds of books and weighs only a few ounces.

The advent of electronic books may well be one of the ultimate tests of just how well computers can interface with people. Can the advantages of electronic scanning, searching, and built-in lighting compete with a book's simple interface, low cost, portability, and traditional charm?

delivery—even before it is published. It's almost like having a personal librarian and shopper.

Although printed books still sell more than any other book form, the popularity of e-books continues to increase multifold—especially post Christmas when everyone is trying out their new e-readers and buying e-books with bookstore gift cards. During this time, more e-books than printed books sell the 10 most popular book titles. Amazon's e-book annual sales for e-books now surpass printed books.

Custom publishing, or **print-on-demand**, takes advantage of computer-based publishing. Publishers of college texts print just the chapters of a textbook that an instructor requests. Independent online publishers print enough of your mother's vacation memory book for the immediate family or everyone on her Christmas list. And small publishers, who may not have the resources for their own bookstores, take orders for printing requested books, using the vast inventories and searchable databases of the Internet to give new life to **backlisted** books.

Large companies, such as Google, want to take advantage of the Internet to make **orphaned books** available for a price and then keep the royalties! Google is battling a seven-year (so far) lawsuit from opponents who would have profit going toward finding the authors. Google has already scanned about 15 million books, and critics worry that Google's resources could give it a monopoly on all information and access. On the one hand, Google could obtain digital versions of all books in all libraries and special collections in universities and museums, many of which house classical literature and valuable historical works, and make these classics more available. On the other hand, what happens once Google becomes a monopoly of information and can choose whether or not to sell its databases to university and community libraries?

Some authors are simply bypassing conventional publishers altogether and are self-publishing their Great American Novels for just $300 by going through an online company such as www.iuniverse.com. Other authors don't care to see a printed product, but sell their digital versions online. CourseSmart lets students download or read and highlight textbooks online for about half the cost of a printed textbook. Still other authors don't care about royalties or printing their books. OpenCourseWare at MIT shares textbooks and other material online. Connexions goes a step further and allows instructors and students to mix and edit material as long as the originators are credited.

Companies involved with e-books are trying to develop ways to avoid people's swapping of copyrighted works online—the problem that the music industry initially encountered with Napster.com (see Chapter 5). For a fee, you can store large files and share them with your friends on RapidShare, which also has a large amount of pirated material.

A challenge to those who provide digital information is that people don't like reading a lot of text from a computer screen (Davenport, 1987). Computer text is harder—and about 60 percent slower—to read than ink on paper (Frost, 1996). As a result, many people find themselves scanning information online that they would read more thoroughly from print. E-reader displays are easier to read than computer screens, and people find they are enjoying the

---

Print-on-demand technology prints books only when they are ordered by customers.

Backlist books are older books that are not actively promoted but are still in print.

Orphaned books are older books, perhaps still under copyright—whose authors are unknown.

act of reading—and read more. Kindle won the war with the iPad on crisp, easy-to-read text, but other e-readers are catching up. If all else fails, you can have your Kindle read aloud to you.

As with most former print-only publications, the magazine industry also migrated to the Web. Consumer magazines with websites grew 30 percent from 2006 to 2011, although they declined in recent years. Adding multimedia, such as videos, additional photos, slide shows, audio, and animation attract readers to articles they might not have read otherwise (MPA, www.magazinefactbook.org, 2011/12). As magazine websites decrease, e-readers and computer tablets are increasing the popularity of magazines. More than half of the people between your age and your assistant professor's age read magazines electronically. Today, more than half of all tablet and e-reader owners read a magazine on their devices, and that's good news for magazine publishers because tablet and e-reader sales are expected to grow in two years by more than 400 percent worldwide (MPA, 2011).

STOP&REVIEW

1. When did magazines peak as a medium for mass audiences?
2. What form have magazines taken as modern mass media?
3. What is a recent trend in magazine delivery?
4. What is a recent trend in print production?

INDUSTRY: GOING GLOBAL

The Web reaches out to everyone. Publishers can target readers on another continent and consumers enjoy reading international publications. Major industry trends also include corporate consolidation, improvements in magazine circulation and advertising, book and magazine specialization, audience segmentation, and convergence with other digital media.

MAGAZINE ECONOMICS

Magazines are a targeting medium with *segmented* or *mass* audiences. But to be profitable, they strive for the largest possible audience they can reach within their potential target—or market—group, and they still follow such economic rules as economies of scale.

Magazines want to report a large **audience** to advertisers. Magazines with large audiences can charge more for advertising because more people will see the advertisement. Audience is made up of the **circulation** number (subscription and single-copy sales) *multiplied by* the number of people who have seen a copy of the magazine. This second number is called the **pass-along rate**—how many people who read the same copy sitting in the doctor's office or on a bus, for example. Advertisers compare audiences when deciding to advertise in different magazines, online or print publications, radio or TV. The audience formula for magazines is the following:

Circulation (average number of copies) x Readers per copy = Audience

Some advertisers, such as deodorant companies, want the largest exposure possible (shot-gun approach). Others that sell exercise machines, for example, would prefer to advertise to a narrow (health care) audience that will pay attention to their product and not waste money advertising to other segments of the public.

Audience is the number of readers of a magazine.

Circulation is the number of copies distributed to the public, for a price or free.

Pass-along rate is the number of people who see a single copy of the magazine.

Andrew Woodley / Alamy

READ TO GAME Magazine publishing thrives on very specialized audiences, like gamers who want to keep up with the latest trends.

Table 3.2 Editorial And Advertising Pages, 2001-2010

YEAR	% EDITORIAL	% ADVERTISING
2010	54.1	45.9
2009	56.0	44.0
2008	53.8	46.2
2007	52.9	47.1
2006	53.0	47.0
2005	52.8	47.2
2004	51.9	48.1
2003	52.1	47.9
2002	53.4	46.6
2001	54.9	45.1

Note: Sunday magazines excluded

Source: Hall's *Magazine Reports,* 2011(chart found at: http://www.magazine.org/advertising/magazine-media-factbook/99.html)

Magazine revenue comes from advertising, subscriptions, and single-copy sales. Overall, about 60 percent comes from advertising, 30 percent from subscriptions, and the rest from single-copy sales. The mix of revenue from these sources varies greatly among different kinds of magazines. Most **consumer magazines** depend on subscriptions and advertising. Subscriptions account for almost 90 percent of total magazine circulation. Single-copy, or newsstand, sales accounted for the rest (MPA, 2011, p. 14). However, single-copy sales are important: they bring in more revenue per magazine, because subscription prices are typically at least 50 percent less than the price of buying single issues. Further, potential readers explore a new magazine by buying a single issue; all those insert cards with subscription offers are included in magazines to encourage you to subscribe. Some magazines are distributed only by subscription. Professional or **trade magazines**, or highly specialized magazines, such as *Columbia Journalism Review,* are often published by professional associations and may feature a small amount of highly targeted advertising. A few magazines, like Consumer Reports strive for objectivity and therefore contain no advertising.

Advertising is a crucial source of revenue for most magazines, and the competition for ads is very intense. For most consumer magazines, ads are a far more important source of revenue than subscriptions but the magazine must reach the right audience for the advertiser. For example, in the computer and telecommunications industries, many magazines like *Network World* are sent free to professionals who make decisions about purchasing equipment or services that the magazine might advertise. A magazine's decision to cater to such subscribers convinces advertisers, with high-tech equipment to sell, to place their ads in that magazine.

In some magazines, ad pages almost equal the number of editorial pages (see Table 3.2, this page). If ad pages frustrate you, just remember that without advertisers, your magazine might cost more. Some readers find advertising pages informative. Just ask your roommate.

MAGAZINE CIRCULATION AND ADVERTISING TRENDS

The age of the mass-marketed magazine is still with us. Some consider *AARP The Magazine* a mass circulation magazine because its stories touch on all topics, from money matters to weight loss to affordable cities to celebrity news. *Reader's Digest, National Geographic,* and *People* are among the leading magazines distributed through the conventional magazine channels of yearly subscriptions and newsstand sales (see Table 3.3, this page). In alignment with the economy, some are experiencing declines in subscription rates. When people struggle to survive, paying for a magazine subscription is usually considered a luxury. Over the past decade, the circulation of women's magazines has dropped about 1 percent (55.2 to 54.6 million), men's magazines about 6 percent (26.1 to 24.6 million), and general-interest magazines about 18 percent (32.1 to 26.4 million) (Sass, 2009).

As usual when the economy takes a downturn, so do many industries, including magazines. In recent years, more magazines were closed than launched. Lack of advertising revenue—not a lack of readers—is generally the reason magazines close. Businesses advertise less in hard times. Magazines must vie with other media, such as newspaper, television, radio, and online media for advertising dollars. Then, advertising revenue is split among magazines, which threatens the viability of both new and established magazines. New magazine titles appear digitally and in print every year to share the total "pie" of advertising revenue. Fortunately, when the economy turns upward the size of the total pie grows again, making room for new publications.

MAGAZINE DISTRIBUTION AND MARKETING

Consumers get their magazines by subscriptions or at retail outlets, such as supermarkets, drugstores, and bookstores. Readers often subscribe to a magazine by returning the magazines inserts (cards, bind-ins, tip-ins, magna strips!) and a quarter of subscribers buy their subscription online. And, let's not forget the ever-popular school and club fund-raisers that sell magazine subscriptions.

Single-copy or newsstand sales do not make a lot of money for publishers, but they increase the paid circulation rate that they

> **Consumer magazines** are magazines that contain general-interest topics.
>
> **Trade magazines** are magazines that are targeted toward a particular profession.

Table 3.3 Top 25 Consumer Magazines By Paid Circulation

PUBLICATION	TOTAL PAID & VERIFIED 6 MONTHS ENDING 6/30/11
AARP The Magazine	22,395,670
AARP Bulletin	22,236,761
Better Homes And Gardens	7,648,900
Game Informer Magazine	5,954,884
Reader's Digest	5,653,440
National Geographic	4,445,603
Good Housekeeping	4,336,711
Woman's Day	3,863,710
Family Circle	3,816,958
People	3,556,753
Time-The Weekly Newsmagazine	3,376,226
Ladies' Home Journal	3,267,239
Taste Of Home	3,235,718
Sports Illustrated	3,207,861
Cosmopolitan	3,032,211
Prevention	2,903,417
Southern Living	2,830,179
Maxim	2,530,440
AAA Living	2,477,127
O, The Oprah Magazine	2,461,464
American Legion Magazine	2,323,308
Glamour	2,304,146
Parenting	2,227,351
Redbook	2,211,659
Familyfun	2,128,351

Source: Audit Bureau of Circulations (chart found at: http://accessabc.wordpress.com/2011/08/09/the-top-25-consumer-magazines-from-june-2011-fas-fax/)

Table 3.4 Top 25 Consumer Magazines By Single Copy Sale

PUBLICATION	SINGLE-COPY SALES (6 MONTHS ENDING 6/30/11)
Cosmopolitan	1,599,305
Woman's World	1,193,927
People	1,153,774
First	1,094,056
Us Weekly	646,685
In Touch Weekly	646,646
In Style	570,272
O, The Oprah Magazine	546,164
Family Circle	525,358
People Stylewatch	504,504
National Enquirer	502,904
Glamour	453,707
Weight Watchers	449,805
All You	444,815
Star Magazine	442,131
Men's Health	431,792
Real Simple	380,721
Vogue	360,400
Vanity Fair	349,566
Food Network Magazine	339,854
Good Housekeeping	339,528
Woman's Day	339,350
Life & Style Weekly	334,700
Women's Health	315,075
Seventeen	295,530

Source: Audit Bureau of Circulations, chart found at: http://accessabc.wordpress.com/2011/08/09/the-top-25-consumer-magazines-from-june-2011-fas-fax/

can sell to advertisers. Visibility on the newsstand rack also confirms the popularity of the magazine to current subscribers and advertisers and it may entice new subscribers who bought a single copy on an impulse (see Table 3.4, this page).

A crucial link between publishers and retailers is magazine wholesalers and distributors. Distributors have a great influence on getting a magazine to a particular store or newsstand and placing it in a visible location to reach the public. A few publishers find it more efficient to do their own research and promote themselves directly to stores, bypassing distributors. Some retailers, such as Walmart, also bypass distributors to pick the magazines they think will attract their customers. Other stores simply take what the wholesaler delivers, because the wholesalers have the capability to do their own market research or the staff to do selective ordering.

MAGAZINE INDUSTRY: INDIVIDUAL OWNERS TO CONGLOMERATES

New magazines, both conventional and Internet-based, spring up constantly. Most of them die rather quickly or are acquired by larger groups, which can provide them with marketing, publicity, advertising contracts, and better circulation prospects. However, the magazine industry is also one of the media areas where a new entrant or competitor can best break in by appealing to a new segment of the market that is not yet served by other magazines. For instance, *Rolling Stone* magazine went quickly from a small counter-culture or "hippie" magazine in 1969 to a widely read rock music and counter lifestyle magazine in the 1970s to the most popular mainstream music magazine today.

Although many Web and digital magazines are started, new print magazines continued to appear, as well. The most popular topics of new print launches were special interest/lifestyle, crafts and games, and gourmet cooking magazines (see Table 3.5, p. 77).

Although anyone can start a magazine, companies with big bucks have the ready resources to make a new magazine successful quickly. Many of these companies are **conglomerates**. For example, Time Warner owns 20 magazines whose revenues total $3.7 billion. Their combined circulation puts Time Warner at the top. Yet, only 14 percent of the company's revenue is from its magazines (see Table 3.6, p.78). The other 86 percent comes from its filmed entertainment, cable networks, and other publishing holdings that might also appear online (see Chapter 8). Conglomerates are geared to be profitable, and they can create

[**Conglomerates** are big businesses or corporations that own seemingly unrelated holdings. They are made up of diverse parts from across several media industries and are involved in multiple areas of business activity.]

THE ECONOMICS OF BOOK PUBLISHING

Some books are read by millions of people. Book publishing has been transformed by the search for best sellers, just as Hollywood has been transformed by the search for the box office smash. Every publisher gambles on successful authors and stories to find the book that attracts millions of readers. For example, Rick Riordan finished his manuscript of *The Lightning Thief* in 1994 and Bantam Books accepted it three years later. Bantam sold it in an auction to the Miramax Books in 2005, when it was finally published. (The Walt Disney Company owned Miramax Books and then changed its name to Hyperion-Disney.) It sold 1.2 million copies in the next four years and has been translated internationally. Other media adaptations of the book increase sales. The same year it was released in print, *The Lightning Thief* was adapted into an audio book by a division of Random House. Two years later, 20th Century Fox bought the film rights and you went to see it on the big silver screen in 2010 and saw it again on DVD. Since then, Rick Riordan has been busy with guaranteed successful sequels, with a ready-made audience.

There are hundreds of small publishers—academic presses, political groups, and religious organizations—that concede the best sellers to Random House, but still hope to reach many people with their message in book form. They are more motivated by the urge to publish a certain kind of book that they feel is important to the world.

As with magazines, music, and movies, most books reach consumers primarily through intermediaries—book clubs, stores, and bookstores that are brick and mortar or virtual. Specialized books, published by academic or technical presses, are sold to libraries rather than to individuals, although falling library budgets threaten to change that. But even these presses dream of selling a larger number of books to individual buyers, both to increase their revenue and to ensure their books are more widely read.

Now, some authors are cutting publishers out of the picture by building up "buzz" in social media and selling their works directly to the public, paralleling developments in the music business (see Chapter 5). For example, Amanda Hocking, author of popular vampire romances, self-published her early works, publicized them through social media including Twitter and book blogs, and distributed them through Amazon before signing a multi-million dollar deal with a conventional publisher.

synergies (such as cross-promotion or multiple usage of content) with their other holdings.

Table 3.5 New U.S. Magazine Launches By Interest Category

NEW MAGAZINES BY INTEREST CATEGORY, 2010	
Special Interest/Lifestyle	15
Crafts/Games/Hobbies/Models	12
Epicurean	12
Metropolitan/Regional/State	12
Men's	11
Sports	11
Fashion/Beauty/Grooming	8
Ethnic	6
Gay/Lesbian	6
Home	6
Motorcycles	6
Women's	6
Comic Technique/Comics	5
Fishing & Hunting	4
Health	4
Music	4
Politics	4
Automotive	3
Business	3
Camping/Outdoor Recreation	3
Children's	3
Entertainment	3
Literary/Reviews/Writing	3
Religion	3
TV/Radio/Communications	3
Art/Antiques	2
Bridal	2
Dressmaking/Needlework	2
Gaming	2
Media Personalities	2
Science & Technology	2
Teen	2
Travel	2
Aviation	1
Computers	1
Dogs/Pets	1
Fitness	1
Military/Naval	1
Nature/Ecology	1
Photography	1
Popular Culture	1
Total New U.S. Magazine Launches	**180**

Source: http://www.magazine.org/RESEARCH/finance_and_operations/finance_operations_trends_and_magazine_handbook/NewLaunchesbyCategory2010.aspx

Table 3.6 Top Magazine Companies

COMPANY	NUMBER OF MAGA- ZINES	COMBINED CIRCULATION FOR ALL MAGAZINES	TOP MAGAZINE	TOP MAGAZINE'S CIRCULATION	MAGAZINE REVENUE 2009	PERCENTAGE OF REVENUE FROM MAGAZINES
Advance Publications	29	17,528,900	Glamour	2,307,710	unav.	39%
Hachette Filipacchi Media	7	7,876,590	Woman's Day	3,895,810	$286.00 Million	82%
Hearst Corporation	21	22,550,700	Good House- keeping	4,418,400	$1.84 Million	unav.
Meredith Corporation*	29	24,555,600	Better Homes and Gardens	7,677,500	$809.00 Million	74%
Reader's Digest Association	12	16,693,700	Reader's Digest	5,533,040	$724.00 Million	100%
RodaleEmmaus	8	7,868,230	Prevention	2,900,360	$357.00 Million	100%
Time Warner	20	32,477,800	Time	3,314,950	$3.70 Billion	14%
U.S. News & World Report*	1	1,024,960	U.S. News & World Report	1,024,960	unav.	100%
Washington Post	3	3,330,000	Newsweek	2,650,000	$184.00 Million	4%
Wenner Media	3	4,177,800	US Weekly	1,974,970	$588.00 Million	100%

*For these companies, full year financial figures had not been released as of March 11, 2010

Source: http://stateofthemedia.org/media-ownership/magazines/

BOOK PUBLISHING HOUSES

Publishing houses are the organizations that acquire manuscripts and supervise the overall production of "books" in printed, e-book, and audio versions. Their work includes acquiring and investing in new ideas, developing, producing, curating, editing, marketing, protecting copyright, and delivering books in every form and platform.

Book publishing falls into five general categories: 1) trade—fiction, non-fiction, and religious content for all ages, 2) K-12 school, 3) higher education—such as this textbook, 4) professional (journals and digital resources for professionals), and 5) scholarly. The publishing houses might be commercial, independents, universities, religious groups, trade associations, and even vanity presses that will publish anything as long as the author provides the money. Cengage, the publisher of this textbook, is a company devoted to learning, whereas other publishing houses, such as Random House, may have several divisions (AAP, 2011).

Publishers' net sales revenue is $27.9 billion, and continues to increase, according to the Association of American Publishers (2011). Even though the computerized publishing technologies discussed earlier in this chapter make the publication of smaller, more specialized projects possible, major mass-market books continue to be expensive to produce because marketing and other costs have increased. As a result, many publishers feel that they have to concentrate on selling more copies of fewer books.

Publishing houses make room for new formats—or the presentation and distribution—of book content, depending on what consumers want. You probably have bought a variety of book formats for different purposes. As you look around your room, you might see physical books that you can hold (hardcover, **softcover**, mass market paperback, and packaged audiobooks), display devices for non-physical books that have no packaging around the content (e-books, downloaded audiobooks, paid mobile apps, and Internet products) or a combination of printed and digital components that are more common in higher education because of the expense and varied nature of learning.

> **Softcover** books are usually printed and distributed in a manner similar to that of hard cover books. They are larger, exhibit more intricate artwork on the cover and are more expensive than mass market paperbacks.

BOOKSTORES

Publishers stock the shelves of bookstores, which range from national chains to small, independent bookstores and from physical stores to e-stores. Barnes & Noble is the largest bookstore chain in the United States, followed by Books-A-Million or BAM!

Barnes and Noble reinvented itself from a bricks and mortar store to the largest e-bookstore with an inventory of about 1 million printed books and about 1 million e-book titles that can be read on its Nook. The first color

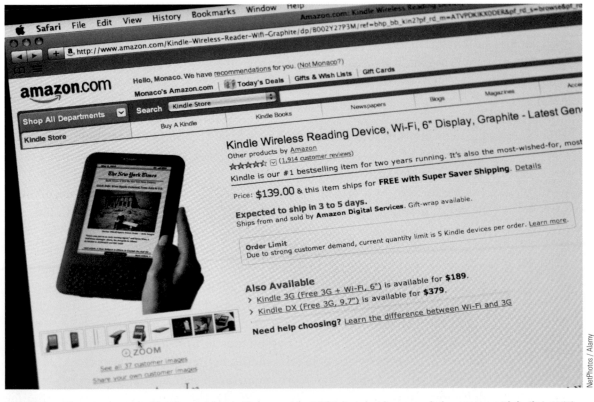

NetPhotos / Alamy

E-INK E-reader users can read books, watch movies, access the Web, download apps and play games with built-in WiFi. Amazon Kindle (with or without the keyboard) has competition from other e-readers such as the Barnes and Noble Nook, Apple iPad, and Sony Reader Touch. Other e-readers include the new Google Nexus 7, BeBook Neo and Kobo e-Reader.

e-reader, Nook, has about 30 percent of the e-reader market, shared mostly with Amazon's Kindle and Apple's iPad. In addition to books, Barnes and Noble sells games, toys, magazines, music, and videos that you can buy online or think about purchasing while having coffee in their bookstores' cafes.

Amazon has never had a storefront, saving lots of capital on real estate storefronts and personnel. When its products are not in its warehouses, it takes orders over the Internet and arranges to have books shipped to customers from publishers or used-book sellers. Amazon has become the nation's largest online retailer with books and e-books as only one line of merchandise. It continues to triple its sales and its e-reader, the Kindle Fire, has been its best-selling product.

AP Photo/Amy Sancetta

READ AS YOU DRIVE The audio book market has exceeded $1.1 billion, and continues to increase sales. The audio book market is made up of CD's (72 percent), downloads (21 percent), preloaded devices (3 percent), and cassettes (3 percent), according to the Audio Publishers Association (http://www.audiopub.org/resources-industry-data.asp).

BOOK PURCHASERS

People love to read. They are buying more books than ever before. About 316,500 new book titles were published in 2010, an increase of 10 percent from two years earlier. In addition, print-on-demand books skyrocketed to more than 3 million, mostly from reprint houses that specialize in public domain works and from publishing houses that cater to people who want to self-publish. New digital technology has made possible the production of a few books at a time on-request, whereas that was not profitable with older printing technology.

More than half of Americans who are older than a tween buy printed books. Who buys the most books? You'll find the answer when you observe men and women's reading habits next time you're in the airport. (The average age is early 40s and women buy about two-thirds of all books, especially detective and thrillers.) As you look around, you'll see that most common nonfiction genres are biographies (Bowker, 2010). And, at the moment, less than 1 percent of all book buyers toss their books. The reasons behind these choices might have an effect on the success of e-books.

And, who buys e-books? The audience is the same as for printed books: women in their early 40s who are reading fiction on a Kindle or Nook. Marketing of e-books becomes even more important because e-book readers are more deliberate in their purchases (Owen, 2011). E-book searchers are looking for a particular book they've already heard about whereas printed book browsers often buy books on a whim while looking through the bookstore shelves—and discovering so many more.

WHAT'S TO READ? MAGAZINE AND BOOK GENRES

In the following sections, we will examine some of the principal genres and forms in books and magazines.

MAGAZINES FOR EVERY TASTE

North American publishing houses churned out 20,700 different magazines in 2010, a number that increases every year, according to the National Directory of Magazines (www.magazine.org/asme/editorial_trends, 2010). Companies define and count "magazines" differently. Whereas some are subscriber based ("consumer magazines"), others are free with a group membership fee. For example, the top magazine is *AARP* and it appears in the mailboxes of people who are paid members of the American Association of Retired Persons. What might also help to keep *AARP* on top is that there are not as many senior citizen magazines (146) com-

peting for similar audiences as there are for health/medicine magazines (1100), which might contribute to *Men's Health* being listed at number 39 and *Women's Health* at number 48 (see the top magazine categories in Table 3.7, on page 82). Thus, a magazine niche, such as health, entertainment, computers, sports, or fashion might experience shake-outs when audience circulation and economic support by advertisers are divided among too many magazines.

Generally, magazines have several advantages as *segmented* media. Although they are somewhat constrained by limited newsstand space, magazines can continue expanding into more specialized topics and treatments until they no longer find audiences large enough to be worthwhile. Also, their formats and economic base are more flexible. A small-circulation magazine can still be profitable if those it reaches are interested enough in its contents to support it or if that audience is important to specific advertisers. Many magazines don't need to compete. There are lots of college alumni magazines, each with a different audience. Your college wants to reach only its alumni, in the hopes they will

RAPID GROWTH Ethnic magazines are the fastest growing interest category with about 980 different titles.

Table 3.7 Growth of Top 10 Magazine Categories

| | TAP 10 MAGAZINE CATEGORIES 2000-2010 | | | |
RANK	CATEGORY	2000	2010	GROWTH IN NUMBER OF TITLES
1	Ethnic	419	978	559
2	Travel	669	829	160
3	Regional Interest	794	939	145
4	Medicine	959	1100	141
5	Real Estate	190	324	134
6	College Alumni	442	569	127
7	Bridal	40	150	110
8	Nursing	130	187	57
9	Golf	98	140	42
10	Senior Citizens	105	146	41

Note: Data as of January 2011. Totals Include cross references and therefore may cc include Canadian and Trade Publications in addition to U.S. Consumer Magazines.

Source: National Directory of Magazines. 2011: Oxbridge Communications and therefore may contain inherent duplication. http://www.magazine.org/ASME/EDITORIAL_TRENDS/GrowthCats2010.aspx]

continue to feel connected to the university, and perhaps offer donations and scholarships to benefit students like you.

Magazines (and books) can perform an important set of communications functions for elite audiences. Political activists are served by a variety of magazines ranging from the liberal, such as *The Nation,* to the conservative, such as the *National Review.* Intellectual magazines, such as the *New York Review of Books,* try to set the stage and agenda for academic and political debates on various issues, often by reviewing books that they hope will help shape those debates. Some government policy–oriented magazines, such as *Foreign Affairs,* pride themselves on having an influential readership and having their articles sometimes affect policy debates.

Similarly, magazines and trade journals can meet the needs of business audiences by providing information about professional development, specific business areas, and current economic trends. Some business magazines, such as *Business Week* and *Fortune,* are fairly general, whereas others cover specific professions, such as *Advertising Age, Columbia Journalism Review,* and *Broadcasting and Cable*. Some trade publications, such as *Variety,* blur the distinction between newspapers and magazines by publishing both daily and weekly editions.

Reader studies show that photos in both articles and advertisements hold much attraction for magazine readers. Visual magazines serve much more specific, targeted audiences. Bridal magazines, fashion magazines, sports magazines, and even rock-music magazines depend a great deal on visual appeal. Do you think *National Geographic* or *Bridal* magazine would sell as well without high-quality photos? While reading print magazines, most magazine readers prefer looking at professional photos and images to looking at the same visual content on the Internet. *Rolling Stone* magazine made photographer Annie Leibovitz famous, and Richard Avedon gained fame from his photos in fashion magazines.

It is still too early to tell, but the popularity of magazine apps might be shifting the landscape for some of these magazines.

BOOK PUBLISHING

The top book genre by far is fiction, which includes romance, detective, horror, and anything else that is a story from the imagination and not real life. Fiction is followed by poetry and drama. Then, cooking, arts, biography, literature, philosophy/psychology, education, religion and business—to round out the top 10. It's sometimes hard to put a book in only one category because it can cross into more. Many of the top works of the 19th and 20th centuries are fiction, history, and biography (see Table 3.8, below).

Books are diverse and hard to characterize in general terms. Some books are sacred, some are sensational, some are eagerly read for pleasure, some are assigned reading in college courses. According to the Association of American Publishers, the major categories of book types are as follows:

> **Trade books.** Hardcover or paperback, including fiction (like Christopher Paolini's *Inheritance*) and most nonfiction, such as cookbooks, biographies, how-to books, and art books.

Table 3.8 Top Books of The 19ᵀʰ and 20ᵀʰ Centuries In Western Literature

TOP TEN WORKS OF THE 20TH CENTURY

1. *Lolita* by Vladimir Nabokov
2. *The Great Gatsby* by F. Scott Fitzgerald
3. *In Search of Lost Time* by Marcel Proust
4. *Ulysses* by James Joyce
5. *Dubliners* by James Joyce
6. *One Hundred Years of Solitude* by Gabriel Garcia Marquez
7. *The Sound and the Fury* by William Faulkner
8. *To the Lighthouse* by Virginia Woolf
9. The complete stories of Flannery O'Connor
10. *Pale Fire* by Vladimir Nabokov

TOP TEN WORKS OF THE 19TH CENTURY

1. *Anna Karenina* by Leo Tolstoy
2. *Madame Bovary* by Gustave Flaubert
3. *War and Peace* by Leo Tolstoy
4. *The Adventures of Huckleberry Finn* by Mark Twain
5. The stories of Anton Chekhov
6. *Middlemarch* by George Eliot
7. *Moby-Dick* by Herman Melville
8. *Great Expectations* by Charles Dickens
9. *Crime and Punishment* by Fyodor Dostoevsky
10. *Emma* by Jane Austen

Source: http://www.theatlantic.com/entertainment/archive/2012/01/the-greatest-books-of-all-time-as-voted-by-125-famous-authors/252209/

Professional books. Reference or occupational education books aimed at professionals, such as doctors, lawyers, scientists, researchers, managers, and engineers (such as *Associated Press Stylebook* and *Briefing on Media Law*).

Elementary, high school, and college textbooks. Such as *Media Now: Understanding Media, Culture, and Technology*.

Mass-market paperbacks. Softbound books, generally smaller in format and less expensive than trade paperbacks (e.g., Kathryn Stockett's *The Help*).

Religious books. The Bible, other sacred texts, hymnals, prayer books, and commentaries.

MAY THE ODDS BE EVER IN YOUR FAVOR

THE
HUNGER GAMES
2012

THEHUNGERGAMESMOVIE.COM · LIONSGATE

Lionsgate/Courtesy Everett Collection

BEST SELLING BOOKS CAN TURN INTO BLOCKBUSTER MOVIES
The Hunger Games three-book series, written by Suzanne Collins, was widely successful on its own. The success of the blockbuster movie that followed was in part because of the already-loyal book fans.

Book club editions. Clubs that publish, sell, and distribute their own editions of mass-market books, professional books, and other specialized books. The Quality Paperback Book Club, for instance, issues trade paperback versions of current hardcover best sellers.

Mail-order publications. Books largely created by publishers to be sold by mail. These are usually classic novels or a specialized series on subjects like U.S. history, wars, cars, and aviation (e.g., the Time-Life Old West series).

Subscription reference books. Books sold as a package or series, including encyclopedias, atlases, dictionaries, glossaries, and thesauri (such as *Merriam-Webster's Dictionary & Thesaurus*). (Similar to print encyclopedias, most of these no longer are published in print in the United States.)

Audiovisual and multimedia. Website materials, DVDs, and CDs marketed primarily to schools, companies, and training groups but also to individuals, by both regular publishing houses and new multimedia publishing companies.

University and scholarly presses. Scholarly or artistic books of primary appeal to scholars and libraries (for instance, *The Quest for Cortisone* by Thom Rooke).

Although digital books and magazines are finding success, it is likely that some genres will remain more popular in print. For example, some people prefer to carry around a book or magazine, instead of an electronic device, for leisure reading and like to put books on their study bookshelves or pass magazines along to friends and family. Other books, however, such as travel guides, might be predisposed to digitization because they can be searched easily while you are on a trip, but won't take up storage space once you return home (similar to maps and GPS systems). They have a one-time use; after all, the prices and restaurants may no longer be viable the next time you visit.

MEDIA LITERACY

As we have seen in this chapter, the role that publishing and literacy play in society is continually evolving. Here we consider some of the issues that confront the publishing industry today.

NEW LITERACIES, OLD LITERACIES

Learning how to create, access, analyze, and evaluate news and information from different media is defined as *media literacy*. The Center for Media Literacy also notes that media literacy "builds an understanding of the role of media in society as well as essential skills of inquiry and self-expression necessary for citizens of a democracy" (www.medialit.org). Instead of simply letting media bombard you with a cacophony of messages, you can learn to use different media effectively to obtain the information you need to make productive decisions. You can be an active seeker of information and an active participant, contributing to the market place of ideas and a democratic form of governance. To become this critical thinker, you have to understand how the different media work—who makes decisions and why and how are they made?

However, conventional literacy in the sense of being able to read and understand the printed word is also a concern. A comprehensive national survey found that 15 percent of adults in the United States had less than basic literacy skills, meaning that although they could sign their names to a document they were not necessarily able to understand what they had signed (National Center for Educational Statistics, 2005). Education makes a difference: five years ago only 1 percent of students enrolled in four year colleges were in that "below basic" category (Baer et al., 2006). However, an additional 6 percent of four-year college students were unable to understand documents as "complex" as a television program guide and 56 percent were unable to synthesize information, such as comparing viewpoints between newspaper editorials.

And, that study was completed before texting and twittering began eroding the literacy skills of youth. OMG!

BOOKS AS IDEAS, BOOKS AS COMMODITIES

Before the Internet, relatively few people had access to media to voice their opinions, except in letters-to-the-editor columns in local newspapers. Yet it has been assumed that competition would bring out diverse points of view and approximate a fairly free discussion among knowledgeable people. Now most of the readership of books is concentrated on the output of a few publishers. To make the best profit, those publishers tend to promote a handful of potential best sellers, rather than a broad catalog of fiction and nonfiction. People wonder whether the trend toward maximizing sales of a few books in the U.S. book publishing industry means a reduction in the ability of a diversity of authors to find publishers for their ideas. Given that books are very important in national intellectual and political life, some writers and publishers fear that it will be hard for manuscripts other than probable blockbuster best sellers to find a publisher if the number of publishing houses were to decline.

This concern is partially met by a steady rise of new, small publishing houses that target different audiences, by the number of people who are self-publishing their own manuscripts through the Internet, and by print-on-demand requests for older books whose ideas and discussion are still relevant today. Although it may seem as if book publishers continue to consolidate and monopolize the decisions for what makes a "good" book, many new publishing houses continue to spring up, signaling growth and diversity in the print industry. These new publishers tend to be small and to reach far fewer people than the largest book publishers; yet, collectively they are a significant force.

The concern about publisher monopolies is met also by the less expensive and wider distribution of books through e-bookstores and through e-books and e-readers, all of which help to promote the spread of different ideas and voices. Now that much of the U.S. population has access to the Internet, new electronic publishers, digital magazines, online bookstores and a growing market certainly increase the potential for competition and a greater diversity of viewpoints.

Unfortunately, members of low-income households may have limited access to the Internet; either because of the cost of computers or mobile devices or because of Internet connection charges. So, although diverse points of view are available, not everyone can access them easily. This is why libraries are important to our democratic society. Anyone is welcomed to read printed material at a library, borrow books or journals, or access information online through a library computer thus becoming exposed to different points of view.

REDEFINING THE ROLE OF MAGAZINES

As magazine publishers compete with an ever-expanding array of media that provide many options for readers, publishing executives must reflect on what they do best—in comparison to other media. Magazines offer high-quality imagery for artwork, photos, and advertisements, which remains key for many industries and readers. And they can offer greater depth than radio, TV, or even newspapers, so people still depend on magazines such as *The Economist* for comprehensive coverage of news and *Rolling Stone* for music news.

Yet, to remain competitive, they must change to accommodate the needs of audiences and the times. Celebrity magazines, for example, have felt the pinch of the economy and competition from the Internet. The *OK!* staff was overhauled, *Star* neared bankruptcy, and *People* and *Us Weekly* are no longer at their peak. Meanwhile, celebrity blogs such as Perez Hilton, TMZ, and Gawker are some of the most popular blogs on the Internet, and they've got photos, gossip, and attitude. They also continue to gain advertising and hits. Celebrity magazines are holding their own, incorporating blogs and video into their online presence. Whereas celebrity blogs are mostly gossip, magazines have in-depth, objective stories, and the resources for better journalism.

The challenge for magazines now is to be an interactive app for a mobile device, tablet or e-reader, such as the iPad, Kindle or Nook. A digital magazine has to offer more than simply replicating the printed magazine, especially when the app costs the same as the printed version. As a digital magazine or mobile app, publications have to worry about their size. Interactivity and multimedia are a trade-off. If consumers want to write interactive letters-to-the editor, vote on products, listen to audio, or watch videos or interactive graphics, such as the blossoming of a pink flower on Martha Stewart's premier *Living* magazine for a tablet, then the magazines will become more bulky to download instead of being instantaneous.

INTELLECTUAL PROPERTY AND COPYRIGHT

Copyright issues have become key points of contention for print media. In recent years, both book publishers and academic journals have cracked down on students who use material that has been copyrighted by publishers. Similarly, publishers are becoming increasingly concerned about the number of "borrowed" images, photos, sections of text, and headlines from printed and online newspapers, magazines, and books. Because publishers and authors are determined to collect royalties from such reproduction and use, new **intellectual property** rules have changed as electronic distribution increases. If you copy a photo of your favorite star onto your website from a magazine, by law, whoever holds the copyright—the photographer, her photo agency, or the magazine itself—would like you to pay for the use of the photo. After all, they had to pay the celebrity and the photographers for the photo shoot and foot the bill for travel, rental of the set, and lighting and camera equipment.

Individual authors and photographers have rights to their intellectual property during their lifetimes, and their heirs have rights for 70 years after the creator's death, so any publication less than 125 years old has to be checked for its copyright status. The duration of copyright protection has increased steadily over the years; the life-plus-70-years standard was set by the Copyright Term Extension Act of 1998, which increased the 50-year limit established by the 1976 Copyright Act (see chapter 15). Supporters of

> **Intellectual property** is a creative work of art, writing, film, or software that belongs to a legally protected owner.

such legislation like to defend these increases with tales of starving writers and their impoverished descendants, but in reality the beneficiaries are more likely to be transnational publishing conglomerates. And note that copyright laws serve a dual purpose. In addition to protecting the rights of authors so as to encourage the publication of new creative works, copyright is also supposed to place reasonable time limits on those rights so that outdated works may be incorporated into new creative efforts. Therefore, the extended copyright protection frustrates new creative endeavors such as including poetry and song lyrics on Internet sites.

And what about starving students who have to pay high fees for course packets and textbooks—who feels sorry for you? One of the basic precepts of copyright law is fair use, the notion that some copyright infringements serve a higher social purpose, such as education, and should be permitted. These "infringements" include making single copies for personal use, citing short passages in scholarly works, and making multiple copies for classroom use. So, if you make your own copy of a course packet, that's fair use and no copyright royalty is owed. Now, what if you are short on time and ask a copy shop to make the copies for you? That is a copyright violation, at least according to a landmark decision that the publishing industry won against Kinko's print shops in 1991—a decision that sharply increased course packet prices. Although Kinko's has gone out of this business, other copy shops now have to pay a copyright fee on materials in course packets. Thus, the continual bolstering of copyright protection and the associated hardball legal tactics of transnational publishing giants have had an effect on the exercise of fair use rights—even if the work is scanned and sent to you electronically.

PUBLIC LIBRARIES, FREEDOM OF SPEECH, AND THE FIRST AMENDMENT

Libraries are great places. Most people aren't concerned about the clothes you wear or your patter in a library. Instead, they'd prefer that you didn't talk. People go to libraries for news, information, and help, especially in times of economic hardship. They look for information in books, computers connected to the Internet, magazines, and journals to help them with decisions about their lives. In addition to borrowing material, most patrons purchase particular authors and other sources of information, as a result of being introduced to them at a library. And, if you are a power patron, then you probably visit a library about once a week and are an active voter. As society changes, so do libraries in an effort to keep relevant in people's lives. Borrowers may find a printed book to their liking, but they also are checking out audio "talking" books and e-books and using their computers to do social media. If you were in your school's library last week, then you probably contributed to one of the 31 million weekly searches on databases and your question to the librarian may have been one of 470,000 questions they answer weekly (ALA, 2010).

Libraries also fight censorship issues in an effort to champion free speech. Thus, First Amendment issues are crucial to the publishing industry. Freedom

Table 3.9 Top Ten Most Frequently Challenged Books List of 2010

1. *And Tango Makes Three*, by Peter Parnell and Justin Richardson
2. *The Absolutely True Diary of a Part-Time Indian*, by Sherman Alexie
3. *Brave New World*, by Aldous Huxley
4. *Crank*, by Ellen Hopkins
5. *The Hunger Games*, by Suzanne Collins
6. *Lush*, by Natasha Friend
7. *What My Mother Doesn't Know*, by Sonya Sones
8. *Nickel and Dimed*, by Barbara Ehrenreich
9. *Revolutionary Voices*, edited by Amy Sonnie
10. *Twilight*, by Stephenie Meyer

Attributed to the Office for Intellectual Freedom, as part of ALA's *State of America's Libraries* report during *National Library Week*.

http://www.oif.ala.org/oif/?p=2008

of speech and of expression in print media is well established in the United States, but over the years, community and religious groups have objected to the contents of various books, magazines, and digital publications. The top reasons for objections are sexually explicit material, offensive language, material unsuitable to an age group, violence, homosexuality, religious viewpoint, and being anti-family (ala.org, 2008). Since the turn of the twentieth century, most books in the United States have been exempt from overt **censorship**, although novels like *Lady Chatterley's Lover* (1928), by D. H. Lawrence, went through periods of being censored. By today's standards, many readers would consider Lawrence's sexually explicit passages fairly tame, but the book challenged the conventional limits of its time.

> **Censorship** is the formal restriction of media or speech content by government, political, or religious authorities.

Even today, books get pulled from library shelves for various reasons. For example, the top most frequently challenged book in recent years is titled *And Tango Makes Three,* by Peter Parnell and Justin Richardson, a child's book about two male penguins who hatch a chick in the New York Zoo. *The Catcher in the Rye* (1951), by J. D. Salinger, has been challenged for rough language, *The Adventures of Huckleberry Finn* (1885), by Mark Twain, for racial stereotypes and epithets, and *Harry Potter* and *Twilight* books for witchcraft and sorcery.

The focal point for discussions about censorship of books is usually the local library or school system, because campaigns to ban books usually focus on what is available through libraries or assigned in schools. Librarians have evolved a number of strategies for reconciling freedom of access with the desire to protect children or other vulnerable audiences from adult content. Some books are not shelved but have to be requested; access to others is restricted by age.

The Internet poses similar challenges for libraries, because local libraries now offer Internet access as one of their services to the public. Their challenge is to figure out how to keep the screen clean for all ages. This is difficult when their search engines can be used to seek out a wide variety of controversial material that may contain sex, violence, or hate speech. (See Chapter 15 for discussions of laws to require libraries to use filtering programs to screen out controversial material.)

SUMMARY&REVIEW

WHAT KEY ELEMENTS OF THE PRINT MEDIA WERE DEVELOPED FIRST OUTSIDE EUROPE?

A number of essential ideas were brought to Europe—for example, using rags to make paper was imported from China. Other printing techniques, such as movable metal type, developed in parallel form outside Europe but were probably not a direct influence on the development of European print media.

WHAT WAS THE IMPACT OF PRINTING IN EUROPE?

The advent of printing by Gutenberg greatly accelerated the growth of literacy by making books cheaper and more widely available. Education became more widespread because texts were easier to get. Printing affected religion by making the Bible widely available, politics by boosting news circulation, and economics by increasing knowledge and skills.

WHY AND HOW DID MAGAZINES DEVELOP?

In 1741, the first U.S. magazines appeared—William Bradford's *American Magazine* and Benjamin Franklin's *General Magazine*. During the American Revolution, many magazines took a more political tone. Few magazines were popular or long-lived during this time. They covered weekly events, politics, and art and contained reviews, travelogues, short stories, and fiction; they were aimed at an educated elite. By the 1820s, magazines of more general interest, such as the *Saturday Evening Post,* began to appear. The number of magazines increased during the Civil War, and they began to reach wider audiences. The Postal Act of 1879 made distribution cheaper.

WHAT WAS THE ROLE OF PRINT MEDIA IN THE CIVIL WAR? HOW DID THE WAR AFFECT THE MEDIA?

Books and magazines affected the issues debated that surrounded the Civil War. *Uncle Tom's Cabin,* for example, is a book widely credited with helping influence northern U.S. opinion against slavery. Several magazines, such as *Harper's Weekly,* grew to fame during the Civil War as a result of their print coverage and their illustrations, which dramatized scenes of the war. Illustrations became prominent tools of magazine journalism. Circulations grew.

WHAT WAS "MUCKRAKING"?

Muckraking characterized the period around 1900, when crusading magazines exposed scandals and corruption in government and among industry cartels.

WHEN DID MAGAZINES PEAK AS A MEDIUM FOR MASS AUDIENCES?

After 1900, many new kinds of magazines sprang up. News photo magazines, such as *Life*, and general-interest magazines, such as the *Saturday Evening Post* and *Collier's*, continued to serve a broad audience up through the 1950s, when both their photojournalism roles and entertainment functions were undercut by television.

WHAT FORM HAVE MAGAZINES TAKEN AS MODERN MASS MEDIA?

They have become increasingly targeted to more segmented audiences. Instead of addressing a broad mass audience, magazines now tend to focus on very specific demographic and interest groups and on audiences particularly interested in politics, hobbies, and other subjects.

WHAT IS A RECENT TREND IN MAGAZINE DELIVERY?

The mail was crucial for enabling magazines to reach a broad audience in an affordable manner. After the 1990s, electronic delivery by the World Wide Web became an alternative for magazine delivery.

WHAT IS HAPPENING WITH BOOK PRINTING?

Desktop publishing is the creation of publication-quality documents using the increased power and speed of desktop computers, laser printers, and scanners that digitize photos or illustrations into computer-readable form. Desktop publishing has done much to decentralize print media. The average person can now produce local or specialized media. This advance in technology has led to the proliferation of books-on-demand, something not possible with older technology.

WHAT ARE THE MAIN TRENDS IN BOOK PUBLISHING?

Increasing numbers of books are being published and purchased by consumers, students, and businesses.

Large publishing houses are consolidating even as smaller ones proliferate.

WHAT TYPES OF MAGAZINES ARE SUCCEEDING?

General-interest magazines have declined as specialized, targeted magazines have grown in numbers and diversity.

WHAT ARE THE MAIN COPYRIGHT ISSUES FOR PRINT MEDIA?

A major issue in print media is the photocopying of copyrighted material. The Copyright Term Extension Act of 1998 extends the period of protection to the life of the author plus 70 years. Many newsletters and new electronic publications borrow images, sections of text, and headlines from newspapers, magazines, and books. Publishers and authors want to collect royalties in return for such use. As electronic distribution increases, new intellectual property rules have been developed.

THINKING CRITICALLY
ABOUT THE MEDIA

1. Which culture should receive the most credit for the invention of printing? Please explain.

2. How has the content of magazines changed over time, and why?

3. How is recent technology changing the way print media is produced, distributed, and read? Is this a good thing?

4. How do conglomerates affect print publishing? Are there positives and negatives associated with conglomerates?

5. Debate the following proposition: Books are an obsolete medium.

KEY TERMS

almanac (p. 61)

audience (p. 73)

audio book (p. 69)

backlist (p. 72)

book publisher (p. 69)

censorship (p. 89)

circulation (p. 73)

computer-to-plate (p. 70)

conglomerate (p. 76)

consumer magazine (p. 75)

desktop publishing (p. 70)

dime novel (p. 63)

e-book (p. 69)

e-commerce (p. 71)

e-readers (p. 69)

genre (p. 64)

intellectual property (p. 87)

literacy (p. 59)

miscellany (p. 62)

mobile devices (p. 69)

muckraking (p. 65)

newsmagazine (p. 68)

novels (p. 57)

orphaned books (p. 72)

pass-along rate (p. 73)

print-on-demand (p. 72)

softcover (p. 79)

subscription library (p. 61)

trade magazine (p. 75)

woodcut (p. 62)

PEOPLE WANT NEWS! Methods of gathering and presenting news have changed from telegraphs and broadsheets to computer-assisted reporting and handheld digital display screens. But no matter how the news is delivered, critical thinking, news judgment, good writing, creativity, and ethical decisions are still paramount.

4

PRINT TO DIGITAL NEWSPAPERS

HISTORY: JOURNALISM IN THE MAKING

The history of newspapers is also the history of our ideas about what journalism should be. Newspapers have always wrestled with commercial interests and political powers, but their history reflects the evolution of a free press from European and American Revolution models. Many publishers and editors worked hard to battle government censorship and commercialism. The struggles are the same today as they were centuries ago, but the circumstances have changed. The story of journalism is crucial to understanding the role and function of journalism today—combating a European stranglehold during colonial times; moving from a party press to an independent press; transforming from a ravaged Civil War existence to an industrialized nation; moving forward from the sensational in yellow journalism to a reformist "muckraking" mind-set in the Progressive Era; and on to modern media. In the history of newspapers, we can see the evolution of social responsibility—the development of better journalistic practices and ethics.

1690	First American newspaper, *Publick Occurrences Both Forreign and Domestick*, published	**1972**	Watergate scandal inspires new era of investigative reporting
1733	John Peter Zenger trial establishes truth as a defense for press against libel charges	**1982**	*USA Today* national daily launched
		1986	Knight Ridder's and Times-Mirror's experiments with videotex close down
1783	First daily newspaper published in America, *Pennsylvania Evening Post, and Daily Advertiser*	**1994**	The development of the World Wide Web signals a change in the newspaper industry
1789	First Amendment to Constitution enshrines freedom of press	**2009**	*Detroit Free Press* and *Detroit News* begin hybrid model of three-day home delivery supplemented by online delivery
1833	The *New York Sun,* first Penny Press daily, begins publication	**2012**	More than half of Americans get news and information from a hand-held device.
1878	New Journalism movement originated by Joseph Pulitzer		

NEWSPAPERS EMERGE

First there were town criers announcing news to an intrigued audience in city courtyards, then there were newsletters. Starting in 59 BCE, Julius Caesar's *Acta Diurna* (Journal of Daily Events) was posted daily for 200 years in public places and announced news concerning the Roman senate, merchant business, weather, disasters, individuals, and later, even gossip. During the 1500s, financial institutions in Europe, particularly Germany's House of Fugger, gathered and published financial and trade news for all interested businesspeople. Meanwhile, Italians were charged a gazetta (about a penny) to hear the daily newsletter on merchant news read aloud. In 1618, patterning their newsletters after German and Belgian newsletters, the Dutch published their **corantos** (currents of news) to include local news and gossip. And England's first newsletter, published weekly in 1641, was the *Diurnal Occurrences in Parliament*, listing government business. In 1702, Mrs. Elizabeth Mallet published the *Daily Courant*—England's first *daily* newspaper—that continued for 33 years. She listed **datelines** and clearly separated objective news from opinion and advertising (Sloan, 2005).

Freedom of the press was nonexistent in the early days of newspapers in Europe. The ruling class granted licenses to printers and had their authorities censor every article before it was printed. Over time, open societies recognized the importance of freedom of speech and criticized censorship. By the early 1600s, British citizens were leaving the country in droves, many of them coming to America in hopes of freedom to practice their religion—and with it the freedom to talk and write about their beliefs. In anger over the Church's refusal to allow publication of his essay on divorce, John Milton wrote his famous *Areopagitica* in 1644 and entreated Parliament to cease licensing and censorship. He advocated that a free press would allow a diversity of voices and that in the **marketplace of ideas,** truth would emerge and rise above.

Corantos were news sheets that appeared around 1600.

Datelines appear at the beginning of a story and note the location where a story happens.

Marketplace of ideas is the concept that the truth and the best ideas will win out in competition.

THE COLONIAL AND REVOLUTIONARY FREEDOM STRUGGLES

Early American newspapers struggled with the question of control by colonial authorities, and that fight gave birth to freedom of the press. The first colonial newspaper, Benjamin Harris's *Publick Occurrences Both Forreign and Domestick* in 1690, contained stories that scandalized the British Crown and Puritan authorities; it was shut down after one issue. Boston postmaster John Campbell started the rather boring *Boston News-Letter* in 1704, published "by authority" of the royal governor, and it lasted 72 years.

James Franklin began an independent newspaper, the *New England Courant,* with no "by authority" approval. As a result of his unapproved, scandalous opinions, he was jailed and forbidden to publish. To evade further punishment, James registered his apprentice brother's name as editor. Benjamin Franklin had a flair for words and writing, and he soon moved to Philadelphia to start his successful publishing business with the *Pennsylvania Gazette.*

The question of editorial independence and criticism of authority was raised again in 1733 when John Peter Zenger published a newspaper openly critical of the British governor of New York and was jailed for criminal **libel**. Despite British legal precedent to the contrary, Zenger's lawyer, Andrew Hamilton, argued that the truth of a published piece was itself a defense against libel. Appealing to the American jury not to rely on British law and precedent, Zenger won the libel case, which established the important principle that true statements are not libelous. In the Zenger case and other events that followed, the British colonial authorities still tried to control the fledgling American press, particularly as calls for revolution increased. British domination left colonists, particularly journalists and printers, convinced that freedom of speech and of press were essential. They insisted that even radical statements, such as calling for the overthrow of an unjust government, be permitted. Benjamin Franklin drew the first American editorial cartoon in 1754, showing a snake chopped into eight pieces and the caption "Join or Die," which represented the colonies in a united stand, protesting France's power in America. It was used again to urge the colonies to unite against the British. The political press that emerged was very important in building support for the American Revolution (1776-1783) and in defining the role of the American free press. Partisan newspapers proliferated. Newspapers published key documents including the Declaration of Independence (1776) and the debates over the Constitution in 1787.

> **Libel** is harmful and untruthful written criticism from the media that intends to damage someone.

THE FIRST AMENDMENT

Freedom of the press was formally established in the United States at the Constitutional Convention. The desire to protect freedom of speech and freedom of the press resulted in the First Amendment to the Constitution. It says:

> Congress shall make no law respecting an establishment of religion, or prohibiting the free exercise thereof, or abridging the freedom of speech, or of the press; or the right of the people peaceably to assemble, and to petition the Government for a redress of grievances.

Seditious speech is aimed at overthrowing the government.

Despite this strong stand for freedom of the press, there was soon an attempt to limit **seditious** speech under the Alien and Sedition Acts, and several newspaper writers and editors were charged with sedition at the turn of the eighteenth century. When the acts expired in 1800, they were not renewed because a consensus had grown for freedom of the press.

DIVERSITY IN THE PRESS

Diverse viewpoints are essential to the functioning of the press in a free society. After the American Revolution, the politicization of newspapers continued, representing a wide diversity of political views, similar to what we see today with online newspapers. These publications took on more partisan leanings and were often openly involved in political campaigns, such as the abolition of slavery.

Advertising and commercial interests began to be important as well. Benjamin Franklin was successful in part because he was a clever writer and designer of advertising copy. In 1783 the first daily newspaper in the United States, the *Pennsylvania Evening Post and Daily Advertiser,* was begun. By 1800 most large cities had at least one daily, but circulations were limited because printing presses were slow, and readers had to be literate and relatively wealthy: one copy cost as much as a pint of whiskey, around five cents. Newspapers were one of the forces that drew people into thinking about themselves as Americans, forming an "imagined community" of people who had access to the same information and identified with each other (Anderson, 1983). However, real differences existed among Americans, and not everyone was welcomed into the larger community. Thus, in addition to the "mainstream" press, other newspapers were published to address the needs of diverse audiences.

Native American Press. The first Native American newspaper, the *Cherokee Phoenix,* was established by the Cherokee Nation in 1828. A year later, the Georgia legislature took away all the legal rights of Native Americans, including freedom of speech. In 1832 the editor of the *Cherokee Phoenix* resigned in protest, and its publication became erratic and eventually ended. It was not until 10 years later—after the Cherokee were removed from their lands—that a new Cherokee Nation newspaper was firmly established. Several other Native American groups published newspapers, and some of them suffered similar discrimination, such as suppression by state authorities to limit sympathy for Native American claims to retain their lands.

African-American Press. About 40 black newspapers were published before the Civil War. The first, *Freedom's Journal,* was established in 1827 in New York City. This newspaper had strong ties to the abolitionist press, and its goal was to encourage racial unity and the progress of African-Americans in the North.

LEADING STAR Frederick Douglass used the African-American paper, *The North Star,* to promote and push for the abolition of slavery.

Bettmann/Corbis

Another important African-American paper, the *North Star,* was founded in 1847 and edited by Frederick Douglass, an escaped slave and probably the best-known African-American at the time. It had the following prospectus:

> Frederick Douglass proposes to publish in Rochester, New York, a weekly anti-slavery paper with the above title. The objective of the *North Star* will be to attack slavery in all its forms and aspects; advocate universal emancipation; exact the standard of public morality; promote the moral and intellectual improvement of the colored people; and . . . hasten the day of freedom to our three million enslaved fellow-countrymen.

He called it the *North Star* because slaves escaping at night used the North Star as their guide. Along with others, Douglass helped push what abolitionists called "the War to Free the Slaves"—the U.S. Civil War.

THE PENNY PRESS

For democracy to function, ideas must be widely circulated as well as diverse. The early 1800s saw technological innovations in the field of printing (see Chapter 3), which in turn permitted lower-cost papers aimed at a broader audience. At the same time, social conditions favorable for the creation of the mass audience and mass newspapers were building. More people were learning to read via the expanding public education system, wages were increasing, more people were moving to the cities, and an urban middle class was growing. Whereas most newspapers had been aimed at an elite class and were expensive, innovative publishers responded to this new market by covering local news and selling cheaper newspapers. Thus, in both the United States and Britain, the mid-1800s brought forth the **Penny Press**. However, many people still could not read or afford newspapers, particularly among the waves of immigrants who arrived in the United States from the 1840s on.

In 1833, Benjamin Day launched the first low-cost daily mass newspaper. Called the *New York Sun,* the paper sold for a penny—hence the nickname Penny Press. To offer his paper at that price, Day not only had to rely on advertising and sales, but also had to reach out farther to the urban audience, using newsboys to sell papers in greater volume. Five years later, James Gordon Bennett Sr., publisher of the successful *New York Herald*, was the first to publish news promptly and give daily coverage to business, sports, and women's news. He also added a personals (classified) section and required advertisers to change their ads every day. The Penny Press was one of the first media to create a truly mass audience, big enough to attract advertisers and justify their investment. And with the advent of faster rotary presses in the early nineteenth century (see Chapter 3), costs decreased even further. As newspapers began to address larger, more diverse, and less clearly partisan

> **Penny Press** included daily newspapers that sold for one cent.

The Granger Collection, New York

ONLY A PENNY The *New York Sun* was the first low-cost daily mass newspaper, first published in 1833.

audiences, modern journalism also began to evolve. Although most newspapers had covered business and politics, the Penny Press reached across party lines and used common language to tell stories about the average person. This combination of factors spawned the modern daily newspaper.

Another boon to the mass newspaper was Samuel Morse's telegraph in 1844, which led to a marked improvement in speed and reach in news gathering. By the time of the Mexican-American War (1846–1848), telegraph technology enabled newspapers to get news of the war as soon as their reporters returned by ship from the front in Mexico City. (Ten years later, the first transatlantic cable was laid for the telegraph.)

Additionally in 1848, several New York newspapers started the New York Associated Press news service to share the cost of covering stories. Reporters employed by the service covered events and sold their stories to all the papers, so each newspaper saved money by hiring fewer of its own reporters. The service expanded with the ability to send stories over the telegraph, thus becoming the first **wire service**. This and other regional wire services joined in 1892 to become what is now called the Associated Press (AP). Wire services helped newspapers lower their costs, add more general-interest material, and appeal to a wider audience, with the side effect of news becoming more objective and less partisan in coverage.

[**Wire services** supply news to multiple publications; they were named originally for their use of telegraph wires.]

FOLLOWING THE FRONTIER

Newspapers expanded westward with the American population in the years before the Civil War. Mark Twain began his career as a frontier newspaper journalist and later became famous for his books and short stories. As presses were made lighter in weight with hollow legs and became transportable to the West, newspapers proliferated and diversified. For example, the second half of the 1800s saw more than 130 Spanish-language newspapers started in the Southwest (Huntzicker, 1993). Frontier newspapers were often blunt and antagonistic, and their editors were opinionated. Many chastised eastern liberals for sympathizing with the "Indians." Jane Grey Swisshelm, founder of the *St. Cloud Visiter*, criticized the politicians of St. Cloud, Minnesota. They retaliated by destroying her press, but they made her reputation, as she rebuilt her press and exposed the mob who had destroyed it (Huntzicker, 1993).

WAR COVERAGE

Although newspapers helped Americans build a nation, they also played a catalytic role in the conflict that tore it apart. A prime example is Harriet Beecher Stowe's *Uncle Tom's Cabin* (1852), which exposed the evils of slavery and was published in serial form in *The National Era*, the most popular abolitionist newspaper of the time. The story was then published in book form and sold more than a million copies in two years.

The debate over slavery and the events leading up to the Civil War were well covered by the Penny Press. The Civil War (1861–1865) expanded newspaper readership because people wanted immediate news of the conflict. That interest, fueled by reports telegraphed directly from the front, reinforced newspapers' focus on yesterday's events and headlines. Not surprisingly, northern and southern papers often saw things very differently.

THE NEW JOURNALISM

Newspapers plunged into the post–Civil War industrial expansion, flourishing in the cities where industries grew and people flocked to get jobs. Along with other industries, newspapers saw a chance to grow, and they more aggressively pursued advertising and newspaper sales.

Headlines were large, gossip was news, and pictures showed emotion. **New journalism** was lively, brash, self-conscious, impetuous, and sensational. It concentrated more on news, increasingly defined as the latest events of the day, and less on editorials and essay columns. *Scoops* that beat rival newspapers to press became more important, as were crusades against corruption.

For example, several big-city bosses tried to corrupt the press by paying for favorable coverage of stories, such as the Tweed Ring in New York, which also stole hundreds of millions of taxpayers' dollars (*New York Times*, 1901). Although most other newspapers were on the Tweed Ring's payroll in 1870, the *New York Times* rose to prominence partly as the result of its successful campaign against the Tweed Ring. *Harper's Weekly* magazine editorial cartoonist Thomas Nast supported the *Times* with strong visual statements against the Tweed Ring. The campaign eventually brought down the Ring, and subsequent investigations showed that, among other things, the politicians bought off many newspapers through $500,000 of advertising. Most of those 89 newspapers died afterward (Parton, 1874).

Furthering their appeal, newspapers of this era added a new visual element, the news photograph. During the Civil War, photographer Matthew Brady had popularized photographic images, but they could not be reproduced in newspapers or magazines (see Chapter 3 for Civil War illustrations). However, in 1880 a process for integrating photos and text on the same page was developed, and the first bona fide newspaper photos appeared.

Toward the end of the 1800s, newspapers reached broader audiences. In the largest cities of the day, large-circulation papers, such as *The National Police Gazette* tabloid, pursued a mass audience with sensational stories on sex, murder, scandal, popularized science, and medicine, and other human-interest events accompanied by large headlines and lurid illustrations. As European immigration increased, many immigrants published foreign-language newspapers.

North Wind Picture Archive

NAST'S FAMOUS CARTOON, "LET US PREY"

EFFECTIVE WIT *Harper's Weekly* magazine editorial cartoonist Thomas Nast was famous for cartoons denouncing corrupt politicians.

[**New journalism** was the investigative reporting of the nineteenth century.]

ELIZABETH COCHRAN
("NELLIE BLY") was one of the first investigative reporters and one of the first women recognized for serious reporting. She also was a champion for women's rights and social reform.

[**Yellow journalism** was the sensationalistic reporting of the nineteenth century.]

YELLOW JOURNALISM

Yellow journalism was a product of new journalism. It grew from the rivalry of two late-nineteenth-century media moguls, Joseph Pulitzer and William Randolph Hearst, and from changing newspaper economics. The term itself was an outgrowth of the first newspaper cartoon strip, called the "Yellow Kid," that depicted a clueless youth from the New York tenements who wore a yellow nightshirt. One of Hearst's stunts was to hire away Pulitzer's staff, including the artist of the Yellow Kid. Another artist filled his place and for a while, New York had two versions of the Yellow Kid, whose ridiculous adventures reminded people of the publishers' rivalry.

Hungarian immigrant Joseph Pulitzer came to the United States, joined the army, and turned to journalism after the war. In 1878 he pulled together enough money to merge two struggling St. Louis newspapers into one, the *St. Louis Post-Dispatch,* and he established himself as a nonpartisan social critic by conducting popular crusades against corruption and complacency. Pulitzer bought the *New York World,* intending to publish a newspaper for the underdogs in New York City. For example, he hired Elizabeth Cochrane, known as Nellie Bly, who became famous by feigning insanity to investigate the notorious Blackwell Island insane asylum. Her stories on the poor conditions and abuse of patients prompted official investigations and improvements (Everett, 1993). In another instance, *The World* championed her as she competed with Phileas Fogg by going around the world in less than 80 days. Because of its successful escapades and escalating circulation, *The World* became the paper that others imitated.

One of the imitators was William Randolph Hearst. Hearst inherited his family's fortune and came to New York City to buy the ailing *New York Journal.* There followed a dramatic war between Hearst's *Morning Journal* and Pulitzer's *World.* A legendary example of Hearst's yellow journalism was when he sent his best reporter and best artist to cover the Cuban unrest. After a week or so they cabled Hearst that there was no revolt and they were coming home. His purported response was, "Please remain. You furnish the pictures and I'll furnish the war."

Another myth reflecting the zeal of yellow journalism was Hearst's and Pulitzer's spectacular coverage of the 1898 explosion of the U.S. battleship *Maine* in the Havana harbor, which the *Journal* blamed on the Spanish, although the cause of the explosion was found in later years to be a spontaneous combustion in the battleship's ammunition magazine. Many historians credit the *Journal*'s frenzied coverage with helping to push the United States into war with Spain over Cuba and the Philippines (Sloan, Stovall, & Startt, 1993). So, in a sense, Hearst did furnish the war.

Yellow journalism was more than just a result of the competition between two men. During the 1880s and 1890s, papers were no longer read only by the elite but also by the general population. With this shift in the marketplace came a shift in the sources of income from circulation to advertising. The newspaper that survived sold its ads and subscriptions at the greatest profit, and these sales depended on the size of the paper's audience. The journalistic style that was used to amass a bigger audience emphasized sensational photos and story selections, large headlines, an abundance of personality and human-interest stories, and sometimes even hoaxes and fake interviews. The sensationalism and over-the-top stories were also a product of how journalists were paid. The longer the story, the better the quotes, and the more exclusive the interview, the bigger the pay rate. This caused journalists to forget ethics as they used flowery language, made up quotes, and hid sources from other newspapers. In other words, the lowering of journalistic quality was a combined result of change in the marketplace; Hearst and Pulitzer were simply responding to the change. But in the process, commercialism grew as a threat to the ideal of the press in a free society.

STOP&REVIEW

1. What case established the precedent for freedom of the press in colonial America?
2. What was the Penny Press? What led to it?
3. What are the differences between new journalism and yellow journalism?
4. What effect did the telegraph have on newspapers?
5. How did wire services influence a change in the newspaper business?

RESPONSIBLE JOURNALISM

Although yellow journalism may have gotten out of hand, both Hearst and Pulitzer contributed substantially to the development of the profession. Pulitzer created a new journalism that defined social responsibility for newspaper coverage. Hearst encouraged higher salaries, bylines, and other recognition for journalists. These innovations were important milestones in the evolution of journalism as a valued and respectable profession. Both Pulitzer and Hearst helped mentor and create a number of good journalists.

Publishers shifted formats to keep pace with changing social conditions. They focused on things that preoccupied city dwellers trying to make sense of their rapidly changing world, such as divorce, murder, and other crime. Newspapers adjusted direction to keep up with the changing times. For example, African-American papers shifted to a more urban focus as their audiences migrated north. Furthermore, immigrant ethnic press overall declined as readers assimilated into American society and as their children learned to read English.

Responsible journalism advanced when Adolph Ochs bought the *New York Times* in 1896. Ochs turned the nearly dead paper into an exceptional twentieth-century newspaper of record. He resisted sensationalism in photos, extravagant typefaces, fake stories, and stunts, of which many readers had tired. He stressed impartiality and independence—which today we call "**objectivity**." He made sure that advertising was clearly distinguishable from stories, unlike other papers that made money by allowing ads to masquerade as legitimate stories.

[**Objectivity** fosters news stories free of biases and opinions.]

The *Chicago Tribune* was also making headway as a serious newspaper. Whereas most newspapers pushed sensationalism to attract readers, the *Tribune* invested in color technologies that would print art on the front page for the public. It published comic strips in color in the early 1900s and was the first newspaper that printed four-color illustrations.

MUCKRAKING

The early 1900s, called the Progressive Era, was a time in which society wanted reform legislation for politicians, big business, and social ills. Then-President Theodore Roosevelt likened the passion of investigative reporters to that of someone who exposed filth and raked the muck away. Most of the muckraking exposés were published in the national magazines (discussed in Chapter 3), but many of the journalists who exposed corruption and helped achieve reform also wrote for newspapers.

THE EFFECT OF CHAIN OWNERSHIP AND CONGLOMERATES

Printed papers peaked as a mass medium between 1890 and 1920. Newspaper circulation increased twentyfold while the U.S. population tripled between 1850 and 1900 (McKearns, 1993). In 1900, there were 1,967 English-language dailies, and 562 American cities had competing dailies. New York City alone had 29 dailies.

By 1910 the newspaper industry had grown larger than its resources of advertising and circulation could support. Inevitably, mergers and consolidations began to trim the numbers back. Usually, stronger papers acquired weaker, profitable ones to get their circulation and advertising base. The new group owners were businessmen who bought and then closed down the competition or consolidated papers to maximize profits. The largest owners were the Hearst and the Scripps-Howard chains that closed more than 30 papers between them. The chain phenomenon continued into the 1930s, as Harry Chandler (the Times-Mirror group), Frank Gannett (the Gannett group), John Knight (Knight Ridder Publications), and others joined the chain ownership trend. By the end of the 1930s, six chains controlled about a quarter of newspaper circulation (Folkerts & Teeter, 1994).

Thus, the diversity in newspapers that marked the late-nineteenth-century press began to erode with group ownership. In addition, antitrust regulators became concerned about diversity in content as *monopolies* or *oligopolies* emerged, particularly among the news services that supplied the newspapers with much of their material: Associated Press, United Press, and the International News Service.

Critics worry that **conglomerates** have the same effect of narrowing diversity in content. Conglomerates might own several different types of companies, including news organizations. Thus, owners could discourage the publication of critical news on their other holdings. The opposite also could occur, with only good news about company holdings being published (see Chapter 3 for more discussion on conglomerates and Chapter 16 on media ethics).

PROFESSIONAL JOURNALISM

The excesses of yellow journalism and the rising tide of commercialism in newspaper operations sparked the further evolution of the journalistic profession from a free press to a **social responsibility model**. One of the key points was the evolution of journalists from anyone who could write and had a nose for news in the nineteenth century, to the college-educated professionals of the twentieth century. That depended on professional education and the rise of accredited journalism schools. Another key development was the rise of professional associations with well-structured codes of ethics (see Chapter 16 for ethics codes).

Daily newspapers helped shape the events of the late nineteenth and early twentieth centuries, so much so that attempts were made to make the press behave more responsibly in times of national crises. During the first half of the 1900s, newspapers crusaded both for and against government policies, such as entering World War I (1914–1918). For example, sensational newspaper coverage of the 1915 German sinking of the British ocean liner *Lusitania,* which killed more than 100 U.S. citizens, aroused public sentiment in favor of entering World War I against Germany.

Conglomerates are big businesses or corporations that own seemingly unrelated holdings. They are made up of diverse parts from across several media industries and are involved in multiple areas of business activity.

Social responsibility model calls on journalists to monitor the ethics of their own writing.

The government created the Office of War Information to ensure that official government decisions would be covered and publicized. They also closed German-language newspapers and censored news during World War I to make sure that no military secrets leaked out through the newspapers. U.S. government propaganda was more restrained during World War II, but was still presented to the public through newspapers, magazines, movie reels, and cartoons. Controls were still placed on newspaper coverage to avoid divulging military secrets. Censorship was abolished with the end of hostilities in 1945, but the give-and-take between the government and the press over the preceding decades of crises helped to entrench the social responsibility model, and the press assumed a rather uncritical stance toward national policy.

MOBILE JOURNALISTS Many journalists are skilled in writing, shooting photos and video, and uploading stories to a website without ever going into the newsroom.

NEWS MEDIA COMPETE FOR AUDIENCES AND ADVERTISERS

As the first mass medium to carry news, the newspaper has encountered competition from every new mass medium that has come along. And, the newspaper has survived as each new medium squared off, stretched, and grew into its niche. Along the way, content changed in its dance with other media.

Radio burst on the scene in the late 1920s and could offer current headlines. To set themselves apart, newspapers pursued deeper news analysis and interpretation. Newspapers could deal with complex government programs and economic crises, reporting various points of view in and out of government with in-depth investigative reporting, a technique not well suited to radio. They were also able to display pictures of products on sale—something that radio couldn't do.

But television could. In the early 1950s, television also ate into the national advertising base that newspapers had once dominated. However, local dailies continued to be important social and political institutions, so although newspapers continued to consolidate, at least one daily survived in most towns. The number of competing newspapers in major cities declined. By 2008, fewer than 40 cities boasted two newspapers; by 2009, several of those papers were published online only. Newspaper chains steadily grew in dominance as the number of dailies declined. Chains such as Gannett (owns 84 dailies), McClatchy (32 dailies), and Scripps-Howard (14 dailies) often owned the only daily newspaper in town.

Nonetheless, some new journalistic voices began appearing. Community weekly newspapers, often owned by chains, followed the middle class away from city centers into the suburbs. They have loyal, local advertisers and were not as affected by the recession as metropolitan newspapers. However, they compete with weekly "shoppers," alternative press publications, and city and regional magazines for advertising.

THE WATCHDOGS

Through their coverage of civil rights, the Vietnam War, and the emergence of advocacy movements championing the rights of other ethnic minorities, women, and gays, some crusading papers adopted a critical stance toward the status quo.

Since World War I, most media had supported the government out of a sense of patriotic duty. But with the Cuban Missile Crisis, the Vietnam War, and the Watergate scandal, journalists began to distrust the government's official announcements and to see themselves as "watchdogs"—outside critics with a primary responsibility to keep an eye on government mistakes and public deception.

Journalists had generally protected the reputation and decisions of presidents and, in turn, government officials usually trusted the press with information to be publicized later. But the Cuban Missile Crisis was a turning point as John F. Kennedy gave the press and the public inaccurate or incomplete information while recovering from the Bay of Pigs disaster (an aborted invasion of communist Cuba).

In another crucial test of press freedom, the *New York Times* published secret government documents, known as the Pentagon Papers, proving that the United States had been illegally bombing neutral Cambodia during the Vietnam War (1959-1975). Such coverage set the news media in conflict with government authorities (Braestrup, 1977).

Also during the Vietnam conflict, Carl Bernstein and Bob Woodward, two junior investigative reporters working for the *Washington Post,* broke the story of the Watergate scandal. In 1972, Republican Party operatives burglarized Democratic Party headquarters in the Washington, D.C., Watergate complex, looking for documents that might damage Democratic Party candidates. With the help of a confidential informant in the Nixon administration, Bernstein and Woodward exposed the foul play and the cover-up that followed. These revelations ultimately led to Richard Nixon's resignation from the presidency.

Many observers wonder who will watch the government if a free press diminishes. More recently, *Detroit Free Press* reporters Jim Schaefer and M. L. Elrick used the Freedom of Information Act (FOIA) to obtain text (and sexting) messages that led to the downfall of former Detroit Mayor Kwame Kilpatrick, who continuously lied to the public and spent taxpayers' money for personal use.

NEWS IN THE INFORMATION AGE

Throughout the years, newspapers have remained profitable, although revenues dipped during the recent recession. With no major newspaper closings since then, a hiring trend is on its way for journalists who report news stories well.

Newspaper's overall audience—print and digital together—is growing, up from the harrowing years of a bad economy that hit all businesses. Advertising revenue and circulation is cautiously on the upswing. Newspapers continue to

PAYING FOR EXPERTISE The *New York Times* is free to all light readers. It only charges for extensive reading.

operate successfully in the black as they always have, but with profits ratcheted down from what shareholders demanded 20 years ago.

Several influences are causing newspapers to transform themselves, according to the Pew Research Center's Project for Excellence in Journalism (http://stateofthemedia.org). Newspapers have a business model of being supported by advertising. In hard economic times, businesses don't advertise. Some businesses don't see an advantage to advertising online. To meet this challenge, news organizations are experimenting with alternatives to obtain revenue.

The *New York Times*, for example, has a "metered" model that lets users read 10 articles a month, but then charges for extensive reading. This keeps news available for light readers while charging those who are heavy readers. The number of readers remains attractive to advertisers. Over time, assessing a fee for news and information might work as people become increasingly accustomed to paying for news online (just as they are accustomed to paying for cable TV and satellite radio while broadcast is free).

Another influence causing newspapers to transform themselves is people's use of technology. As the number of consumers who get their news from a mobile device increases, newspapers are offering their news to be read on diverse

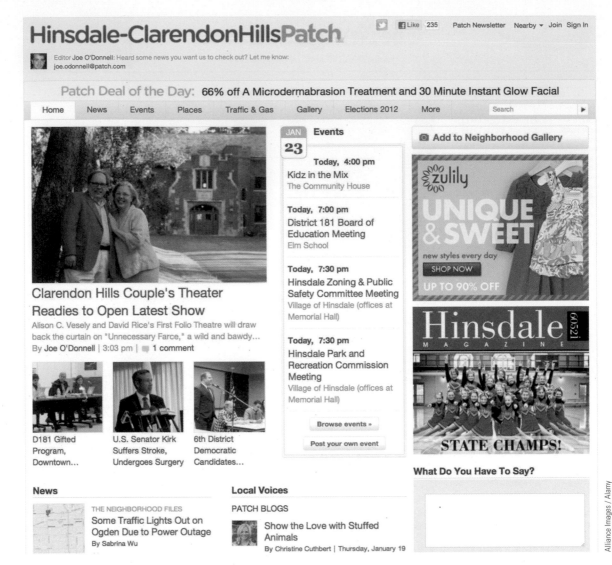

HYPERLOCAL NEWS Since 2010, Patch has launched more than 850 hyperlocal news sites in which reporters cover issues and events in their community that they feel are overlooked by the traditional news outlets.

platforms and developing apps—for iPods, iPads and other tablets, e-readers and handheld devices. Newspapers are jumping on board the social media trend by encouraging readers to comment on stories and to share news and comments with their followers and friends on Twitter and Facebook.

News organizations also are demanding compensation for their articles that are found elsewhere online and are collaborating on revenue. Most of the fact-based news appearing in media originates from traditional news organizations employing professional journalists. Their stories appear on Internet browsers or search engines, such as Yahoo!, Google, and Bing, and social networking sites (SNS), such as Facebook. These aggregates scrape news from newspapers (online and print), reformat it to attract readers to their sites, and place advertising around it. Thus, the search engine gets the traffic and advertising dollars that news attracts, whereas the online news organization that paid the reporter for the original story receives nothing for its efforts.

The Associated Press (AP) decreed that these websites now must obtain permission and share the revenue with them or face legal consequences. AP also announced that it will embed software in its stories, letting it track how the article is being used.

As the economy improves, local news with local reporters is making a comeback. Newspapers are gaining the resources to cover local news—hyperlocal news—that is unique to their communities. For instance, AOL Huffington Post Media Group owns Patch.com with 863 hyperlocal "citizen journalism" news websites. They hire professional journalists with news judgment who know how to write in different formats and shoot photos and video.

However, not all news websites are run by professional journalists, and there is a danger that the credibility of the news will be undermined by these amateur efforts. For example, Matt Drudge is not a professional journalist and is sometimes regarded as an activist, based on the tone of his writing. His popular news site, the Drudge Report, began as an e-mailed newsletter with gossip on personalities and activities in Hollywood and Washington D.C. The site today is sometimes considered simply an aggregate of links to news originated by professional media. However, it was also the first source to break the Bill Clinton-Monica Lewinsky scandal.

Another social media trend is the *citizen journalist* who provides commentary in a personal **blog**, posts comments to online publications, uploads news videos captured on cell phone cameras, or "reports" stories with varying degrees of editorial—and sometimes no—oversight to review the stories (Outing, 2011). Professional journalists are trained to research information and verify sources before writing a story. Many untrained citizens simply repeat what someone has said (gossip) without verifying tweets or quotes—and then call it "news."

> A **blog**, short for Web log, is commentary addressed to the Web audience. A blog is similar to an online opinion journal.

Newspaper owners worry that younger readers are not acquiring a regular and loyal news "paper" habit as they use various electronic media for their news. One response has been to focus on community news, issues, and services, whereas larger newspapers often accentuated the trend toward investigative reporting and critical analysis. Another response is to go where audiences are and put news online and on mobile devices, such as e-readers and tablets. In addition, most online news stories give the readers the opportunity to comment, using social media.

TECHNOLOGY TRENDS: ROLL THE PRESSES!

Advances in publishing technology were reviewed in Chapter 3. Here we will consider innovations that have shaped the newspaper industry, where speed is of the essence in all phases of gathering, presenting, publishing, and disseminating the news.

NEWSGATHERING TRENDS

Before the telegraph, the speed of news was the speed of transportation systems from the clipper ship to the pony express and even to carrier pigeons. A generation later, the telephone also improved the speed of news gathering, even though some late-nineteenth-century reporters disdained it as a "lazy" way to avoid honest footwork (Sloan, Stovall, & Startt, 1993).

In times past, journalists would do their reporting away from the office. Today, all the modern means of electronic communication are found in the newsroom. In addition to traditional methods, high-tech reporters scan radio,

BACKPACK JOURNALISM Some journalists enjoy doing it all while being in the thick of the action. They investigate and can present stories by writing and shooting photos and videos.

TV, and cable and satellite channels for news stories and ideas. They monitor police communication frequencies and use Twitter to get tips and confirm stories. They also check Internet news sites, blogs, chat rooms, and listservs (see Chapter 9) to turn up leads and track down rumors.

Computer-assisted reporting (CAR) is now a common term for using computers to access search engines and sift through mountains of raw data. By taking advantage of public and commercially available databases, reporters write stories about trends in crime and poverty and objectively compare areas or groups of people with one another without relying on self-serving handouts from politicians or lobbying groups. They use campaign finance databases to find financial connections between the way politicians vote and the businesses that support them. Some reporters use social science methods (see Chapter 14) by analyzing trends in voter behavior, finding correlations between crime and poverty rates and their possible causes, and producing detailed maps of poverty or crime in a region (Davenport, Fico, & DeFleur, 2002).

CONVERGENCE

News organizations are combining multiple media in the same newsroom or sharing their resources with other media in a trend called **convergence**. They can cut costs by sharing resources, such as video, audio, text, and photographs, and by editing those resources for several different media. Sharing resources may encourage story accuracy over speed, whereas news organizations once tried to "scoop" the competition (get it out and fix it later).

The convergence trend has led to a new form of multimedia journalism called **backpack journalism**, which is practiced by reporters who combine interactive text, graphics, photos, video, and sound to make a story with multiple versions—from straight text to podcasts—that will go on different media. In addition, reporters can interact with readers through social media, such as Twitter, blogs, chats, or e-mails. In the process, stories may become more

Convergence is the integration of mass media, computers, and telecommunications. It occurs when news organizations share different formats of information for multimedia news.

Backpack journalism is the term for reporters who carry a digital video camera (a mini DV; see Chapter 7), tape recorder, and notebook, often in a backpack.

reporter-driven and less editor-driven, a significant challenge to the traditional newsroom structure.

PRODUCTION TRENDS

In Chapter 3 we saw how innovations such as the rotary press, linotype, and phototypesetting greatly increased the number of pages printed in an hour's time. Newspaper pages went from a few to many, prices decreased, and circulation grew into the hundreds of thousands as a result.

Teletypesetting was a significant improvement in the 1950s. Stories were set in type by a highly skilled typesetter employed by a wire service, then punched out onto paper tape by the local newspaper, and then automatically fed into the newspaper's own typesetting machines to produce a near-perfect copy. By the late 1960s and the early 1970s, data contained on paper tapes were stored in computer memory, paving the way for the computerization of print production. Today, reporters compose and edit their stories and designers lay out the pages of newspapers on computers. The latest computer-to-plate processes generate the printing plates directly from computer images, using sophisticated cousins of the ink-jet and laser printers found in the home. This eliminates the expensive step of photographing the layouts and chemically processing them for the press run.

Satellite delivery of copy to remote printing plants also speeds the news to your door or device. Newspaper copy, complete with photo layouts, is sent by satellite from central editorial offices to remote printing plants in distant cities. The *New York Times,* the *Wall Street Journal,* and *USA Today* are printed in several different locations to make local same-day delivery possible almost anywhere in the country.

More geographically diverse news organizations are working with each other to produce local news. For example, the *Chicago News Cooperative*, an online news site with local news, recently partnered with the *New York Times* to produce two pages of news for the *Times* delivery in Chicago.

ONLINE AND MOBILE NEWS

Readers like news on the Web and mobile devices because they can check pieces of news quickly. For many news consumers, however, news on the Web looks too different and they are never truly comfortable with the layout and design and computer screen. For some, the ergonomics are all wrong for relaxing with casual reading from a desktop or even laptop computer that is often used for work. Many in the profession believe that e-readers and tablets will save the day. Now, readers can have the look of the traditional newspaper appear on an e-reader. People are spending more time with the news and they have more choices as to how they want to get their news. Some enjoy using their tablets or e-readers so much that they are reading more news, reading it for longer periods of time, and going to several mainstream media places to get that news (Pew Research Center, 2010).

Digital news makes sense because it cuts the costs of expensive ink, paper, and delivery methods (trucks and personnel). The idea of distributing news electronically is not new. Nineteenth-century financial barons had stock tickers in their homes. In the 1930s, newspapers

STOP&REVIEW

1. What was the impact of Watergate on American journalism?
2. What are the main recent trends in newspaper delivery technologies?
3. What are potential problems with citizen journalism news sites run by non-professional journalists?
4. Compare how news on the Web and e-readers, tablets and other mobile devices influence the news business.

experimented with "faxing" newspapers to special home radio receivers (Shefrin, 1993). In the 1980s, several newspapers invested millions in experiments to transmit news and information digitally over phone lines and by cable. Knight Ridder developed a **videotex** service called Viewtron, sending digitized news to the home over phone lines for display on television sets. Times Mirror did a similar experiment called Gateway, but used cable as the transmission line. These trials failed because of the cost to consumers and the idea of putting dense textual information on a television set capable of color and moving images, which people used for entertainment in their living rooms. More successful consumer online services, such as CompuServe and America Online, followed suit using early desktop computers. Meanwhile, other countries used **teletext** piggy-backed on broadcast signals to transmit news to the television set (Davenport, 1988).

A wide diversity of online news forms has grown to meet a large number of amateur writers and readers. Online newspapers range from the Web presence of major national newspapers to the growth of Web-only "newspapers" that include everything from blogs to neighborhood newsletters. It helps a news site to have a solid reputation based on a successful existing newspaper. Many online readers are drawn by the brand name and credibility of existing media, particularly the elite national newspapers. Readers also use online editions of community newspapers for news of former hometowns, universities, or other places that interest them.

Online newspapers have many features that their print versions lack: up-to-the-minute breaking news, sports scores, and stock prices; computer-searchable classified ads; interactive forums where readers exchange views; audio and video clips for major stories; and automatic news alerts to your iPhone or iPad.

Websites are becoming creative with news as they compete for audiences and advertisers. In an effort to improve on the conventional newspaper, portal websites like Yahoo! are building on the concept of the "Daily Me" first advanced by the former director of MIT's Media Lab, Nicholas Negroponte. You select the type of coverage, topics, and formats that fits your personal lifestyle. Potentially, this concept could be expanded to include software programs that develop a profile of what you like to read, listen to, or watch, and then interact with information providers on the Internet to find things that you might like. The only type of information that would come to you would be news automatically chosen for you by a computer. Critics of this system worry that we would become a fragmented audience, narrowing our fields of interest and have nothing in common with others. With newspapers, readers are attracted to headlines and read information they would not seek otherwise, and become more informed about what is happening in their communities or around the world. The serendipitous nature of reading a newspaper is beneficial, they argue.

News can be customized, and so can news delivery systems, from Kindle to cell

5,000 STORIES A DAY Bloomberg produces general and specialized news online and in newspapers, magazines, radio, TV, and apps for news bureaus and individuals across the globe. Its growing number of 2,500 news and multimedia professionals are in 146 bureaus in 192 locations in the world. http://www.bloomberg.com/pressroom/facts/

NetPhotos / Alamy

phones. Almost half of the 95 million mobile subscribers use their phones to go online (twice that of two years ago). And, newspaper content is the most popular stop after portal sites and e-mail (Nielsen Mobile, 2008). Verve Wireless is providing mobile versions of newspapers for 4,000 newspapers owned by 140 newspaper publishers.

More reporters now use Twitter to alert "followers" to breaking news or to news stories online. Whereas tweets are an alert, blogs are used mostly for opinion and insight about news events and issues. Blogs have morphed from electronic bulletin boards systems (BBSs) to newsgroups to weblogs. There are now more than 118 million blogs on the Web, written by anyone, from teenagers about their high school soccer team to political candidates on issues of the election. Some blogs are predominately text, whereas others incorporate digital photos, links to other sites, MP3 or audio download links, or podcasts.

INDUSTRY: THE NEWS LANDSCAPE

About 83 percent of Americans get their news on a daily basis in one form or another (Pew Research, 2010). With all of the new options on where and how to get news, people are spending more time with news than they have in about a decade. The time that was spent only with traditional news media (printed newspaper, radio, TV) is now also being spent on newspapers on the Web, mobile devices, tablets and e-readers. In addition, you can get news in other ways, including online citizen journalism sites, blogs, podcasts, and receive tweets and RSS feeds that fill specialized niches in the media landscape.

Mass audiences exist for traditional major metropolitan, national, and regional daily newspapers if we include online readership through computers and other various devices). As readership for printed newspapers declines, it increases for digital platforms.

While about 75 percent of Americans receive their news from traditional sources (printed newspapers, radio and TV), they are supplementing it with digital news. The Pew Research Center (2010) found that people spend about an hour with traditional media—the same as they did in 2000, but are now

Table 4.1 Number of Daily Newspapers & Total Newspaper Circulation

| | DAILY NEWSPAPERS | | SUNDAY | |
YEAR	TOTAL NEWSPAPERS	TOTAL CIRCULATION (IN THOUSANDS)	TOTAL NEWSPAPERS	TOTAL CIRCULATION (IN THOUSANDS)
1940	1,878	41,132	525	32,371
1950	1,772	53,829	549	46,582
1960	1,763	58,882	563	47,699
1970	1,748	62,108	586	49,217
1980	1,745	62,202	736	54,676
1990	1,611	62,328	863	62,635
2000	1,480	55,773	917	59,421
2009	1,397	46,278	919	46,850

Source: Editor and Publisher International Yearbook. http://www.naa.org/Trends-and-Numbers/Circulation/Newspaper-Circulation-Volume.aspx

adding more time with online news. This does not include the time spent getting news from cell phones, iPods or other mobile devices.

There is also a considerable, growing audience for mid-sized and small, community daily and weekly newspapers covering local and entertainment news, and **shoppers** filled with local advertising. The shoppers website and e-newspapers have the same content as their print counterpart. The different types of newspapers are explained next.

Dailies. Newspapers published at least five days a week are termed *dailies* and can be national, metropolitan, or suburban. Their numbers have declined slowly. Although 11 newspapers fell victim to the economic problems of 2008 and 2009, no major newspapers closed in the following years.

In 2012, daily print newspaper circulation was about 43 million, a 4 percent decrease from the 2011. This is separate from news appearing online or in mobile apps. (Pew Research, 2012). About 40 percent of all adults rely solely on traditional news outlets and don't access digital news. Those moving from the print to the digital include teenagers and early 20-somethings (including many of our readers).

Many people consider television to be their immediate news source, although better-educated audiences tend to rely more on newspapers and the Internet. They use the radio and television to hear about an event or issue and then turn to print or online newspapers for more in-depth information.

National Dailies. Most national dailies are metropolitan newspapers that are distributed via satellite to multiple locations. The *Wall Street Journal,* with the largest paid circulation for combined print and online—more than 2 million—is considered a specialized business paper but has a general readership as well. *USA Today*, with just under 2 million, began with the intent of covering the country.

Metropolitan and Suburban Dailies. Some of the larger metropolitan daily newspapers, like the *Chicago Tribune,* declined in print circulation during the recent recession. Others, such as the 150-year-old *Seattle Post-Intelligencer,* the 100-year-old *Christian Science Monitor*, and the 90-year-old *The Capital Times* of Madison, Wisconsin, moved from print to online-only. The *Detroit Free Press* and the *Detroit News*, a Joint Operating Agreement (JOA), developed a successful hybrid system: the newspaper is printed every day, but is home delivered three days a week and updates are posted 24 hours online. Eight other newspapers have followed the hybrid print/online model, including the New Orleans *Times Picayune* in 2012.

A recent trend is the growth of the Sunday print edition of many metropolitan newspapers. With focused marketing, Sunday edition deliveries and single copies have significantly increased circulation and revenue profits from advertising.

[**Shoppers** are free to readers and are supported by advertisers. Content sometimes includes news stories, but advertising is the main objective.]

Table 4.2 U.S. Largest Newspapers

NEWSPAPERS BY CIRCULATION SEPTEMBER 2011	TOTAL CIRCULATION
Wall Street Journal	2,069,169
USA Today	1,784,242
New York Times	1,150,589
New York Daily News*	605,677
Los Angeles Times	572,998
San Jose Mercury News*	527,568
New York Post	512,067
Washington Post	507,465
Chicago Tribune	425,370
Dallas Morning News*	409,642
Newsday [NY]	404,542
Chicago Sun-Times*	389,353
Houston Chronicie*	369,710
Denver Post*	353,115
Philadelphia Inquirer*	331,134
Minneapolis Star Tribune	298,147
Arizona Republic	292,838
Orange Country Register*	270,809
Cleveland Plain Dealer	243,299
Seattle Times	242,814
Oregonian	242,784
St. Petersburg Times	240,024
Detroit Free Press	234,579
San Francisco Chronicle	220,515
San Diego Union-Tribune	219,347

Source: http://stateofthemedia.org/2012/newspapers-building-digital-revenues-proves-painfully-slow/newspapers-by-the-numbers/ *Image location:* http://stateofthemedia.org/files/2012/01/17-Newspaper-Top-25-Circulating-Daily-Newspapers.png

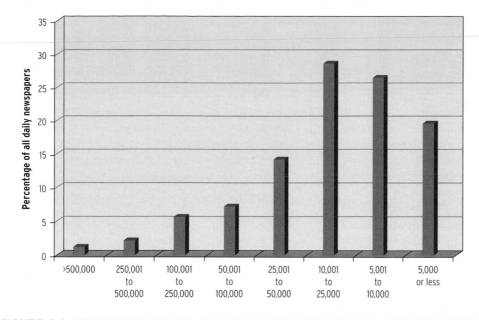

FIGURE 4.1 PERCENTAGE OF ALL DAILY NEWSPAPERS BY CIRCULATION CATEGORY.
Source: http://www.stateofthemedia.org/2009/chartland.php?id=1000&ct=col&dir=&sort=&c1=0&c2=0&c3=0&c4=0&c5=0&c6=0&c7=0&c8=0&c9=0&c10=0&d3=0&dd3=1

Usually when a single newspaper dominates a city, it tends to be sustainably profitable. On the one hand, local monopoly newspapers tend to be more profitable because they share content and management costs with other newspapers belonging to an ownership chain. On the other hand, instead of re-investing its profits to improve the local newspaper, the profits from one newspaper might go to a fledgling newspaper in another town also owned by the chain. Still another scenario is exemplified by the fact that when the *Seattle Post-Intelligencer* went completely online, its print competition, the *Seattle Times,* began turning a profit with a circulation increase of 30 percent.

Newspapers continue to operate in the black, even with reductions in circulation or advertising revenue. However, their stockholders are not happy with a reduced margin. The circulation of metro newspapers has declined in part because many readers have shifted to national dailies, newsweeklies or newsmagazines, television, radio, the Internet or other electronic devices. Additionally, many large cities, such as Detroit, have declined as centers of population, while suburban areas have increasingly grown with industry, business, and entertainment.

Consequently, suburban—or community—newspapers have risen in importance. The numbers of these newspapers have grown by over 50 percent since 1985. As many towns grow in economic importance, their local dailies gain in numbers and circulation. In response, many of the metropolitan dailies added suburban sections and publish regional editions, such as the San Fernando Valley and Orange County editions of the *Los Angeles Times.*

Local and Specialized Weeklies. Weeklies, shoppers, and specialized publications in the United States are supported by readers or advertisers or both.

Most weeklies—published fewer than four times a week—cover small-town or rural areas that are too small to support a daily. About a third of weekly papers also cover the suburbs.

The alternative press is another form of weekly paper whose numbers have grown in the past two decades. Different types appear in many areas,

OCCUPY WALL STREET: NEWS, THE INTERNET, AND SOCIAL MEDIA

Not quite 10 years ago, political campaigns discovered the Internet and social media. Blogs have fanned the flames of passion among activists, especially since the initially wildly successful Democratic primary campaign of Howard Dean in 2004 was driven in part by passionate young bloggers, who created a buzz of political excitement, raised millions of dollars, and organized a grassroots campaign of house parties, street canvassers, and phone callers.

The recent protest movement called Occupy Wall Street began as a small group of activists angry about the increase of greed in Wall Street and the decline of the middle class. Nobody noticed them, including the media, but when they used social media to publicize their cause, the movement caught on like wildfire.

Adbusters (a group against commercialism) registered a domain name called OccupyWallStreet.org, and called for a protest to occupy Wall Street. Publicity mounted as supporters posted photos and stories to a Tumblr page (*The Week*, 2010). About 1,000 people set up camp on Wall Street in New York as a form of protest. Over time, as more supporters posted more photos, videos, stories, and comments online,

the movement grew to include celebrities and protests across the country. Major media from traditional news sources to digital platforms to talk shows cover the activity that is ramping up again.

If you think the Internet and social media don't have a great impact on spreading news and information that affects society and culture within the global village, then consider these numbers about Internet and social media use, and perhaps think again:

Internet
- 2 billion Internet users
- 255 million websites
- 21.5 million websites added within the past year.
- 80 million domain names

Social media
- 107 trillion emails sent (89 percent are spam!)
- 152 million blogs
- 175 million people on Twitter
- 600 million on Facebook
- 2 billion videos watched per day on YouTube
- 3,000 photos uploaded per minute to Flickr
- 3 billion photos uploaded per month to Facebook

including entertainment-oriented alternative weeklies like the *Boston Phoenix* or the *Austin Chronicle* that are given away at music stores, bookstores, and other locations. These free weeklies are supported by advertising and cover dining out, movies, live concerts, and local events. Some cities also have political weeklies, and yet others have ethnic or minority group–oriented weeklies that focus on news and events within a particular community, and which add a great deal of diversity to news coverage.

Community weeklies survived the 2007–2009 recession better than the larger papers for several reasons. Local businesses run ads in the local paper because of the high circulation rates. And, they are less dependent on national advertising.

News Wire Services and Other Newspaper Sources. Many news service organizations—traditionally called *wire services* (see page 98)—contribute to newspaper content. International and national stories are taken directly from the news services or are combined with local reporting to put a unique local angle on international or national news.

As you read earlier, the Associated Press was the first wire service in America and it is still the leading national news service. For international news, the AP competes with Agence France-Presse (the oldest wire service in the world), Reuters, and the Interfax News Agency (headquartered in Moscow), and several other global news agencies.

Dozens of other news services, including those run by major newspaper chains, such as Gannett, or major metropolitan newspapers, such as the *Los Angeles Times–Washington Post* News Service, distribute stories written by their own reporters to other newspapers that subscribe to the service. Other news services not directly affiliated with newspapers, such as Bloomberg, gather news and write stories about specialized topics, such as finance or environment.

Other news syndicates supply subscribing news organizations with comics, crossword puzzles, and editorials by national columnists, all popular staples of newspapers. The King Features Syndicate, a subsidiary of the Hearst Corporation, is the largest. Syndicators employ the cartoonists and the editorial writers or make distribution arrangements with writers' "home" newspaper organizations. They then resell the funnies and commentaries to other newspapers on a contractual basis.

NEWS AGGREGATOR The stories in Yahoo News! come from other news organizations. Only recently has it begun to generate original news.

Gary Lucken/Alamy

CONTENT: TURNING THE PAGES

Most newspapers and their websites contain several distinct sections that serve different audiences: international news, national news, local news, editorial and commentary, sports, business, lifestyles, entertainment, comics, and classified advertising. Sections make it easier for newspaper readers to navigate to these specific interests. *USA Today* is widely credited with accelerating this trend with its sections: News, Sports, Money, and Life. Newspapers try to build overall circulation by providing something for everybody and to increase targeted audiences for advertising.

Print and online newspapers vary a great deal in the sections they emphasize, usually depending on the geographic area they cover and their news focus.

- *National newspapers* report on international news, national news, editorials and commentaries, business news, and lifestyle, and entertainment news of a general nature.
- *Metropolitan dailies* usually focus more on regional and local news, lifestyles, entertainment, sports, and comics. They have more local ads for such businesses as supermarkets, auto dealers, and real estate.
- *Local weekly newspapers* go even further toward local news, such as **hard news** and soft news or human interest (feature) stories that do not have immediacy, shopping information, and ads and sometimes are the town's number one booster.

Online newspapers narrow these headings further. For example, "sports" can be subheaded into college and high school teams. "Opinions" usually includes social media—editorials, columnists' blogs, letters to the editor, readers' blogs,

> **Hard news** is the coverage of recent events, such as accidents and crime.

THE FUNNIES King Features, of the Hearst Corporation, is one of the largest syndicates in the world, supplying news organizations with comics, crossword puzzles, editorials, and other nationally distributed features.

and readers' uploaded photos and videos. Some online newspapers program "top picks" of comments, photos and videos, based on reader's votes. Whereas at one time, reporters rarely heard from their readers, they now enjoy readers' immediate feedback on their stories and comments that sometimes add to the story, offer follow-up story ideas, or correct inaccuracies immediately.

[**Unique visitors** per month is the measure of how many different people visit the site within a month. A visitor can make many visits to the site, but is counted once. (It is the computer origination that is counted and not the person.)]

NEWS WEBSITES, CITIZEN NEWS & E-NEWSPAPERS

As the number of people going online and using a mobile device for their news has increased, the number of subscribers for printed newspapers has decreased.

News organizations now combine measurements of print and online readers to get a more accurate picture of who is accessing their news (no matter if it appears in print or online). It is easier to count subscribers for the newspapers that charge for both online and print subscriptions. However, others count print subscriptions and online unique visitors for their numbers.

Newspaper websites attract more than 110 million unique visitors per month and the numbers continue to climb (Sadowski, 2011).

In addition to newspaper websites, citizen journalism sites have emerged. Citizen journalism sites are the product of citizens who report and write on the local area, and give other interested citizens the opportunity to contribute news. They have emerged for two reasons: 1) The cost to begin an online news site is relatively cheap and 2) The citizen or professional journalists feel that their town is not being covered as well as it should be by other news sources. For example, Patch.com has more than 850 local news websites run by professional journalists covering neighborhoods; EveryBlock.com is operated by MS-NBC and routes news feeds to local areas; and Placeblogger.com collects blogs from different towns.

The Guardian is combining the resources of a traditional news organization with the resourcefulness of citizens. It is advocating what it calls "open journalism," encouraging bystanders to use their smartphones to begin or add to the story process. This approach is met with mixed feelings. While some like the idea, others criticize that "citizen journalists" are not qualified to recognize the elements of a good news story nor how to report it well. As critics are fond of repeating: "The fact that a guy has a scalpel doesn't make him a doctor any more than publishing on the Internet makes someone a journalist." Journalists are trained professionals.

NEWS SECTIONS News organizations group stories in topical sections to attract different audiences. *USA TODAY* newspaper and usatoday.com use the same section names, such as MONEY, which navigates readers to stories about business.

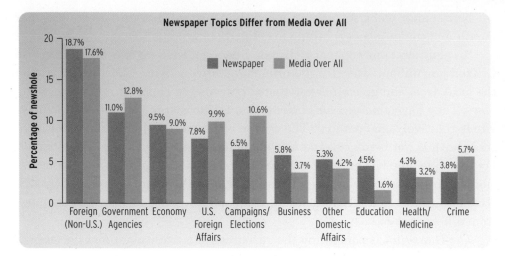

FIGURE 4.2 NEWSPAPER COVERAGE Compared to other news media, newspapers cover more news on health and medicine, education, business, and foreign and U.S. issues and events. (Newspaper Association of America, Pew Research Center's Project for Excellence in Journalism, 2012 State of the News Media http://state-ofthemedia.org/2012/newspapers-building-digital-revenues-proves-painfully-slow/newspapers-by-the-numbers/)

Table 4.3 Aggregated U.S. Newspaper Website Audiences (By Month)

2011	TOTAL UNIQUE VISITORS (000)	% REACH	AVERAGE DAILY VISITORS (000)	TOTAL MINUTES (IN MILLIONS)	TOTAL PAGES VIEWED (IN MILLIONS)	TOTAL VISITS (000)	AVERAGE MINUTES PER VISIT	AVERAGE VISITS PER VISITOR
December	111,639	63.9%	24,106	$3,649	4,047	1,048,679	3.5	9.4
November	110,302	62.7	25,325	3,809	4,048	1,064,940	3.6	9.7
October	112,196	63.7	24,671	4,129	4,452	1,090,319	3.8	9.7
September	112,006	64.2	24,535	3,674	4,442	1,045,036	3.5	9.3
August	112,299	65.1	25,300	3,947	4,678	1,121,340	3.5	10
July	107,040	62.4	22,640	3,420	4,235	1,000,188	3.4	9.3
June	108,151	63.2	23,699	3,457	4,115	1,000,504	3.5	9.3
May	112,649	65.5	24,196	3,740	4,314	1,048,024	3.5	9.3
April	111,646	65.2	23,547	3,534	4,162	985,420	3.6	8.8
March	113,183	66.6	24,725	4,217	4,545	1,075,466	3.9	9.5
February	103,872	61.5	23,390	3,387	4,037	942,274	3.6	9.1
January	107,713	63.5	22,768	3,639	4,409	1,016,428	3.6	9.4
2010								
December	103,903	61.3	21,457	3,496	4,126	949,897	3.7	9.1
November	106,720	62.9	22,373	3,416	4,180	962,474	3.5	9.0
October	105,250	61.8	20,744	3,238	3,992	915,282	3.5	8.7
September	102,843	60.6	20,328	3,307	4,052	869,195	3.8	8.5

Source: comScore via Newspaper Association of America, Pew Research Center's Project for Excellence in Journalism, 2012 State of the News Media

Some newspaper consumers just don't like getting their news online. They don't like the look of news on a website nor the idea of using their (work) computer to get it. They enjoy the experience of reading their news leisurely. They like the layout and design of a newspaper page and reading other stories that appear on the same page—stories they wouldn't ordinarily seek out. They also like the fact that news organizations have professional gatekeepers for their news, picking the news events and issues that are important to know. Guess what? It is not the new technology that is holding back some of these laggards, but the design and presentation of the news. Some of these same people who complained about news websites have become early adopters of tablets or e-readers because the newspaper page is replicated and they are not using a work device (such as a computer)—it's leisure reading.

Certainly, news apps are further changing the news landscape. The introduction of the iPod in 2001, the iPhone and Kindle in 2007, and the iPad and Kindle Fire in 2011 has had an impact on how people are getting their news. For regular news consumers, time that is spent reading news from a computer, mobile device, tablet or e-reader has taken away from some of the time that was spent with just the newspaper. More than half of the adults in America get their news and information from a mobile device. And, the new tablets and e-readers have attracted more newspaper readers who were uncomfortable getting news from a website or who simply enjoy their digital experience. They now spend even more time getting news and seeking it digitally from a variety of news agencies (Pew Research 2011).

CHAIN OWNERSHIP AND CONGLOMERATES

Newspapers have long been consolidating with other types of media outlets, including radio, television, cable, and Internet. Some mergers put newspapers into vertically integrated groups working directly with radio, television, cable and satellite channels, and Internet sites to share content. Other large chains, such as McClatchy and Scripps-Howard, tend to buy newspapers that already have a **local market monopoly**, pursuing national horizontal integration of newspapers across the United States. The *Columbia Journalism Review* website (cjr.org/resources) offers a guide on who owns the major media companies.

The economic downturn in the news industry put many newspaper chains in play for corporate buyouts, break-ups, acquisitions, and bankruptcies. In the process, family-owned chains that were once common in the industry—McClatchy and the Tribune were the last of that dying breed—have given way to conglomerates that have in turn given way to bankrupt media enterprises.

Companies that own many seemingly unrelated businesses are called *conglomerates*. For example, media conglomerate News Corporation, owned by Rupert Murdoch, bought the *Wall Street Journal's* publisher, Dow Jones. News Corporation has holdings in every type of media internationally, as well as restaurants, bars, recording technology, and other miscellaneous businesses. Media critics worry that news might become biased to further an owner's other interests.

Some businesses go under in a recession, and newspapers are not immune. A recent trend is for private equity owners to buy up newspapers as prices have lowered or bankruptcies occurred. Typically, they beef up the news organization to sell it at a higher price, thus profiting on their investment. Several owners are concentrating on producing local news to appear in digital initiatives first (online and apps) and in the printed paper second.

> **Local market monopoly** occurs when one company owns (controls) the media in that community.

TECHNOLOGY DEMYSTIFIED

WHO'S TWEETING NOW?

Twitter is not just for letting your friends know how you did on your mass comm test today. It is also a valued social media journalism—news and information—business tool.

- Kathy Hoffman, reporter for the Associate Press, uses Twitter to publicize her government and public affairs stories. She makes a short comment and then lists the URL where readers can locate the story to find out more (http://twitter.com/kathybhoffman).
- Joe Grimm, a Michigan State University professor and former *Detroit Free Press* recruiter, offers tweets with new advice appearing on his JobsPage website on career strategies for journalists (http://twitter.com/jobspage).
- Dave Poulson and student writers for *Great Lakes Echo* for the Knight Center for Environmental Journalism regularly tweet about stories on the environment and motivate people to become more aware of the effects of their actions (http://twitter.com/greatlakesecho).

Journalists and news organizations not only tweet to promote their brand and to alert readers to stories or new developments in follow-up stories, but also use Twitter to help write the stories.

Gathering the right information is a significant component of journalism. Reporters and opinion writers send tweets to find out what the public thinks, using this tool to replace the traditional "man-on-the-street" interviews used for finding out how the "average" person responds to a particular issue or subject. Questions can be flung out into the ether and answers arrive from more and different voices than ever before, adding a richness to stories that includes views from many different walks of life. Sometimes the question or topic is very narrow, but Twitter gives reporters the capability to cast a world-wide net and get in touch with the one person who might have the answer—immediately, from a mobile device or a computer.

Journalists are accustomed to writing tight, concise sentences; thus, the 140-word limit of a tweet is not a problem. What is challenging, however, is thinking of the many different ways that a reader might interpret a short phrase, since there is no room for words that create context, no facial expressions, and no voice inflections. Some helpful websites for journalists are listed below:

- Patrick Thornton's video ("screencast") on beatblogging.org is a fundamental how-to lesson for journalists who want to use Twitter for their reporting.
- David Brewer has written "Editorial Ethics for Twitter Journalists" on the Media to Media website that includes advice on how to regard information sent and received in tweets.
- And, a useful tool for journalists is Muck Rack, a website that aggregates journalists' tweets and sorts them into beats, helping other journalists know immediately what is happening in different parts of the world and enabling them to quickly get in touch with one another.

MEDIALITERACY

RESPONSIBLE REPORTING

POLITICAL ECONOMY: LOCAL MONOPOLIES ON THE NEWS

Most U.S. cities are served by one newspaper. The result is a local monopoly that has political, economic, and social effects. Politically, the one newspaper is likely to reflect a single editorial perspective, although other local media may reflect alternate viewpoints. Economically, newspaper choices available to both advertisers and readers are reduced, which can lead to higher subscription and advertising rates. Socially, readers are all depending on the one newspaper for accurate information to lead productive lives. Sometimes people won't ever know what the newspaper doesn't report.

Traditionally, owning more than one media organization within one market was prohibited because it did not produce a diversity of voices whose opinions could be heard. However, in the 1980s, the Reagan administration relaxed restrictions on horizontal integration in the belief that the role of government should be reduced so that competition could thrive. As a result, major newspaper group owners have steadily acquired more newspapers. In 2008, the Federal Communications Commission (FCC) decided to allow companies to own newspapers and broadcast outlets in the same city, as long as the company was able to show that local news coverage would improve as a result. The federal court overturned the decision, not because of its merits, but because not enough time was given for public comment before the ruling was made. Local cross-ownership is now back in court. Many people do not realize they are getting their news from the same parent company. For example, the largest newspaper group in the United States, Gannett, now owns 82 daily newspapers and about 850 non-daily publications, in addition to its 23 TV stations, websites, mobile apps and other media.

Joint operation agreements (JOAs) have been one solution to the problem of excessive concentration. When competing newspapers cannot survive economically, they can negotiate an agreement with each other to share facilities, production costs, administrative structure, and advertising while attempting to maintain editorial independence. That negotiated limit on competition was permitted by the Newspaper Preservation Act of 1970. Seven cities maintain two newspapers through JOAs.

In Detroit, for example, the liberal *Detroit Free Press* and the more conservative *Detroit News* have a JOA. They share facilities and keep their writers separate.

> **Joint operation agreements (JOAs)** allow competing newspapers to share resources while maintaining editorial independence.

FREEDOM OF SPEECH AND THE FIRST AMENDMENT

Newspapers have been far more protected in freedom of speech than have electronic media, such as radio and television. There have been few attempts in the United States to limit freedom of speech or of the press.

For example, during the 1950s, the anti-communist campaign of Senator Joseph McCarthy resulted in many authors being blacklisted (many were falsely accused of being Communist sympathizers), which prevented them from publishing books or writing for Hollywood films and television. However, McCarthy steered away from directly attacking newspapers, including how they covered Communism (perhaps because he needed press coverage).

Freedom of the press has enabled journalists to take unpopular stands. It tends to protect journalists in the United States from outside pressure to avoid certain stories. But in many other countries journalists face outright pressures—their stories are censored, they are fired, or are threatened or even killed. The International Federation of Journalists, composed of journalists from more than 100 countries, works to defend press freedom and social justice (ifj.org). The Committee to Protect Journalists (cpj.org) keeps a tally of the number of journalists killed in Iraq and other countries. About 42 journalists were killed in the first quarter of 2012. The deadliest countries were Pakistan, Iraq and Libya in 2011 and Syria in 2012. Another international organization, Reporters without Borders, tracks the degree of freedom and censorship of the press—through print or the Internet—in different countries (en.rsf.org).

ETHICS

About 90 percent of readers believe what they read in their local newspapers (Pulse of America, 2011)—a result of journalists' good judgment and ethics. Reporters know their stories are scrutinized by thousands of readers. They know their stories need to be accurate—from the correct spelling of peoples' names to placing the information in the appropriate context. Readers use the information from news outlets to make the good decisions that lead to productive lives—from paying taxes to voting to making real-estate purchases—so journalists need to get it right.

The accuracy and objectivity of information has long been the primary concern of most journalists and of their newspapers. Accuracy means fair and balanced information when gathering, organizing, and presenting the news. Journalists strive to be objective by reporting without favoritism or self-interest. It means avoiding stereotypes and unsubstantiated allegations. The ethical treatment of a news story is a question of credibility for media organizations that can affect their success at all levels from economic survival to perceived prestige. Accuracy and objectivity are professional obligations that are treated in more detail in Chapter 16.

Thousands of reporters do their jobs well. However, the nature of the news business exposes the reporter who is a "bad apple." Journalists who get it right are rarely named, but those who have become unethical are often publicized. In recent years, **plagiarism, fabrication,** and **anonymous sources** have

Plagiarism is using someone else's ideas and work without citation.

Fabrication is information that is made up instead of emerging from facts.

Anonymous sources are people who gives reporters information but do not allow the publication of their names.

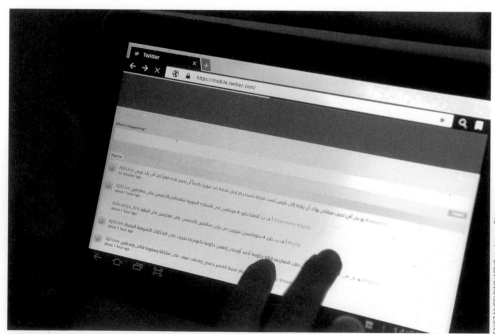

FAYEZ NURELDINE/AFP/Getty Images/Newscom

VERIFY! Twitter is a quick and easy way to get information. It is sometimes so quick that the information has yet to be verified—unless it is from a trained journalist.

gotten reporters in trouble. Sometimes, inexperienced journalists use quotes and wording from online sources or press releases and fail to attribute the sources. This is considered plagiarism. Reporters also try to avoid using anonymous sources because they place doubt in a reader's mind as to why the person can't stand up for what he or she is saying. When a person speaks to a reporter on the condition of anonymity, the journalist can use that as a lead to find someone who is willing to be named.

When newspapers make an error, they correct it immediately online or acknowledge it with a correction in print somewhere near where the error appeared or in a standard corrections box the next day. Substantial errors, particularly those that may have damaged the reputations or careers of the persons covered, are acknowledged in follow-up stories or in a letter to readers from the editor.

News organizations have a social responsibility to the public to present news accurately. In addition, ethical lapses are bad business. Numerous retractions are bad for business because readers go elsewhere for the news, and then there are fewer audience members to sell to advertisers.

Most news organizations have codes of ethics (see Chapter 16), which sets them apart from other news and information sources and sites. Journalistic ethics standards require very careful checking for accuracy. One of the reasons that websites for well-known newspapers are important news and information sources for Internet users is that they continue to offer a high level of accuracy compared with many other sites that are not so careful (see Chapter 16). But increasingly, blogs provide an important check on the accuracy of mainstream journalism.

PUBLIC'S RIGHT TO KNOW VERSUS INDIVIDUAL PRIVACY

Privacy issues revolve around a conflict between the public's right to know something and the right of private citizens to keep it to themselves. The media treat public figures differently than private citizens. However, many questions remain about just how closely public figures can be scrutinized before the boundary of ethical behavior is crossed. Some journalists disregard the adulterous affairs of a public official, whereas other critics reason that if a marital promise is broken then it points to personal character and potentially broken promises to constituents.

Libel. Press freedom is not absolute, even in the United States. The publication of libel, defamation, and the invasion of privacy is not protected by the First Amendment. Libel and slander refer, respectively, to printing and to making false statements about private citizens that might damage their reputations. Writing true things about someone is not libel (see Colonial and Revolutionary Freedom Struggles, page 95). Libel, however, is handled differently for private and public individuals. For example, bloggers who write nasty things about their private personal relationships may find themselves facing a libel suit from a "significant other," whereas similar nasty comments can be made about public figures, such as the president.

Laws against libel are supposed to protect the reputations, welfare, and dignity of private citizens. Public figures, such as media professionals, celebrities, and public officials, are not generally protected against libel on the theory

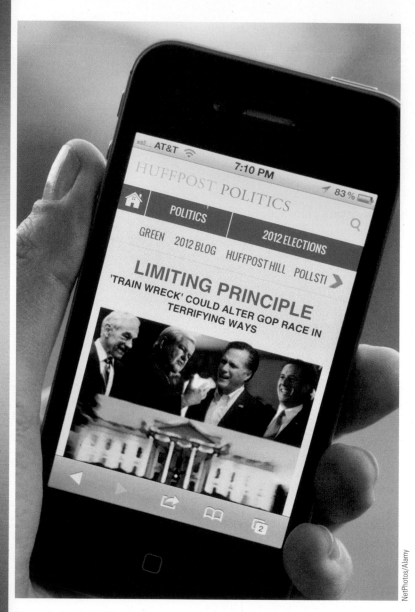

NEWS ANY WAY YOU WANT IT *The Huffington Post,* began in 2005 as a political weblog, was the first digital news medium to win a Pulitzer Prize (in 2012). It continues to grow and seek new employees: http://www. huffingtonpost.com/p/jobs-at-huffingtonpostcom.html

NetPhotos/Alamy

[**Tabloids** are newspapers focused on popular, sensational events.]

that they have chosen to act in the public sphere and not remain private citizens. This is because U.S. legal policy balances libel concerns against the watchdog role of the press, which is to expose corruption or incompetence on the part of officials or public figures. When people take a public position and seek publicity for their views, then libel against them is also harder to prove. They have become public figures.

Tabloid Journalism. Sensationalist **tabloids,** such as the *National Enquirer,* whose headlines you read as you stand in the grocery store checkout line have questionable methods and stories. Audiences for these publications are declining, and several publications, such as the previously popular *Star that folded, can now only dish it out online.* Contrary to journalism ethics codes, tabloids are known to pay their sources for information, and sources often will falsify information or exaggerate in order to be useful.

Celebrity blogs, such as Perez Hilton, and paparazzi are not considered journalists, mostly because they do not follow codes of ethics. Paparazzi usually are photographers who intentionally invade the privacy of celebrities, in an effort to snap a photo to sell to magazines, such as *ok!, Globe,* or *National Enquirer.*

BEING A GOOD WATCHDOG

Investigative reporting became a hallmark of the newspaper profession in the 1960s and 1970s with Vietnam and Watergate, and students flooded into journalism schools. Today, the watchdog role has spread from major national newspapers and websites to smaller local newspapers and community blogs. Investigative journalism is practiced in all corners of the globe. For example, as a result of a story called "Stock Option Abuses" by the *Wall Street Journal,* 130 companies and 60 top executives were under federal investigation for rewarding themselves illegally through stock options. Blogs have expanded the investigative role by adding to the number of watchdogs. Conservative bloggers closely scrutinized the memos obtained by Dan Rather of CBS News for a critical story about President Bush's service in the Air National Guard, and found them to be false. This forced an embarrassing retraction by CBS News and paved the way for Rather's early retirement. That incident showed two things about blogs as watchdogs: many of them are partisan and many are run by people driven by political passion.

Blogs are a part of a partisan media system that serves as both watchdog and agenda-setter for the less partisan press. Conservative bloggers often turn up material that then appears on conservative radio talk shows, then in cable talk shows, then Fox News, then perhaps the national press. Similar patterns can be seen on the liberal side.

DEFINING NEWS

"Man Bites Dog!" For years news has been defined for many as what is unusual, striking, even sensational. Remember, the Penny Press, new journalism, and yellow journalism all strove to capture people's attention with large, shouting headlines, photos, and sensational topics—even with muckraking and investigative reporting.

Editors look for news that has certain clear characteristics. It involves many people (magnitude), tends to be very recent, unusual, personal (human interest rather than institutional), critical of things that need to change (rather than supportive), linked to familiar places and cultures (rather than distant, unfamiliar ones), and often tragic in the sense of reporting disasters. These news elements were first observed in a study of Norwegian papers in the 1960s (Galtung & Ruge, 1965) and have been confirmed in many studies and in several countries.

Journalists argue that their "watchdog" role is to be critical, to hold people and institutions responsible for their actions, especially while other people, such as politicians, companies, and their public relations staff, are pushing only "good" news about their policies or institutions. Furthermore, reporters argue that watchdog journalism is in fact what sells news; the public wants to know what their local government is doing, how any wrongdoing affects them, and how the situation can be improved.

Today a variety of experiments are taking place that are testing our perception of news. Some newspapers are stressing community journalism focused on engaging community issues. Others promote public participation, interacting with news sites online. And of course, many other sources of news now exist from television to talk radio to social media on group websites to blogs to YouTube to Facebook to Twitter.

STOP&REVIEW

1. What are the main sections and content of newspapers?
2. Is there still a mass audience for newspapers?
3. What are the concerns about monopolies in the new industry?
4. Can social media counter these concerns about monopolies since more people can comment on stories and news events and issues?
5. What are the main ethical issues for newspaper reporters?

YOUR MEDIA CAREER

REPORTING THE NEWS THAT OTHERS USE

This is an exciting career, where something new happens every day. Journalists begin the day by hitting the ground running and learning about new issues and events. Their minds and bodies are continually at work, helping local and global communities.

People always want news and information. It is important to know about issues and events that affect our decisions on how to lead productive lives. And, we must be able to trust the journalists who do the reporting and writing.

Journalists come in all packages: as reporters, news analysts, correspondents, writers, editors, designers, information graphics experts, photographers, and videographers, to name a few. They use honed news judgment to discern what their audience needs to know and how to tell it best—to report the news. These journalists are experts in gathering, organizing, and presenting information in various formats (text, visual, auditory, multimedia) for distribution on different platforms (newspaper, magazine, radio, television, online and mobile devices).

Critical thinking, great news judgment, clear writing, and good visual communication skills are ingredients of successful journalists.

Journalists also have insatiable curiosity about the world around them and a desire to find answers. They might go to a scene to observe the situation, take pictures of it, record it on video, do background research on the people or topics involved, interview bystanders or relatives, and then put the different pieces of information together in such a way that best tells the story of what happened or why it happened. Reporters use qualitative research skills (observing, interviewing, studying documents) and quantitative social science research skills (analyzing databases or putting numbers into a spreadsheet) to give events and issues context and meaning to their audiences.

Most journalists learn reporting and writing skills by pursuing a major in journalism at a college or university. Students take journalism courses to gain critical-thinking, writing and reporting (or story telling). Students also take courses outside of journalism to learn about the world, because journalists report on life. In addition, journalism students should have several internships or part-time jobs in journalism to experience the work before they graduate and to make them more marketable to employers.

Journalists can be general reporters, covering all aspects of a community; or specialists in a particular area, such as science and health, sports, environment, medicine, government, fashion, or education; or foreign correspondents, traveling to report on events and issues in other countries.

Nationwide, there are more than 69,000 news analysts, reporters, and correspondents, about half of whom are employed in print media. Many more are employed writing news for new and different forms of digital news available to audiences through technologies, such as the Web, tablets, e-readers, and mobile devices. The best opportunities are expected to be in new media fields and in smaller print and electronic media markets (BLS, 2012).

Journalism students should train in all aspects of multimedia in order to be prepared to work in any news environment. The more knowledgeable the applicant, the better the chance at being hired. Furthermore, many journalists move around in the news industry; feature writers might switch from TV to print, editors become columnists or opinion writers, newspaper reporters become TV reporters, and radio journalists become podcast interviewers online.

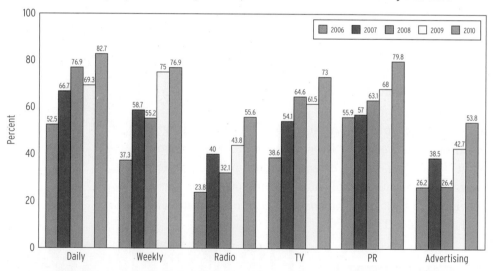

Employed Bachelor's Degree Recipients In Communications Doing This Work

Bureau of Labor Statistics BLS (2012). News analysts, reporters and correspondents.

Source: Vlad, T., Becker, L., Olin, D., Wilcox, D., & Hanisak, S. (2009). 2008 An-nual Survey of Journalism & Mass Communication Enrollments. Retrieved from http://www.grady.uga.edu/annualsurveys/.

NEWS EDITORS AND GATEKEEPING

Newspapers perform important functions for audiences. Some newspapers that focus on government policy, such as the *New York Times*, pride themselves on having an influential readership and on sometimes shaping policy debates with their articles. The *Wall Street Journal* focuses on reaching the business elite but aims at government policy makers too. The *Christian Science Monitor* (csmonitor.com) offers internationally oriented news. The *Los Angeles Times*, especially

its calendar section, serves the film, music, and television industries. Readers look to these newspapers in part to tell them what is important in these areas.

Editors do several things that require human intuition and creativity. First, they perform a **gatekeeping** function: they tell you about important issues and events happening in the world that you ought to know. Thus, you avoid the frustration of reading more of what you already know. Second, newspapers and magazines can make intelligent suggestions about new things that you may be interested in *beyond* what you already know. This helps you avoid the claustrophobic narrowness of interests implied by Negroponte's idea of a "Daily Me," that is, a newspaper customized exactly to our own specific interests.

By definition, however, gatekeepers must make choices about the issues and events covered. Not all of the infinite number of things that happen every day can be reported, nor all points of view: there simply isn't the space nor the resources. Some social media provide a check on the gatekeepers. For example, in 2012, major news organizations were slow to report the killing of Trayvon Martin by a neighborhood watchman and began to pay attention only after a major outcry in Facebook and Twitter.

Some readers respond positively to the way the Internet permits them to radically expand the information available to them, as well as focus and personalize their news. However, many others continue to prefer the classic editing and **gatekeeping** functions that a good newspaper provides. As the *New Yorker* magazine noted, "Newspapers are not just yesterday's news; the good ones are carefully prepared buffets, cooked up by skilled editors who sift the news and present it in a way that makes each edition unique. Computers, for all their strengths, are very poor at replicating human judgment and intuition, and those qualities are what editing newspapers is all about." Mark Willes, former chairman of the Times Mirror Company and publisher of the *Los Angeles Times*, said, "As we have this continued proliferation of news and information sources, we all need editors, and that is one of the things that newspapers provide. . . . The Internet is the epitome of an unedited information glut" (Auletta, 1997). That "glut" has increased multifold.

> **Gatekeeping** is deciding what will appear in the media.

SUMMARY&REVIEW

WHAT ESTABLISHED THE PRECEDENTS FOR PRESS FREEDOM IN COLONIAL AMERICA?

The colonial press was often critical of British governors. In a key case in 1733, John Peter Zenger published a newspaper critical of the British governor of New York. Zenger was jailed for criminal libel. Despite British legal precedent to the contrary, Zenger's lawyer, Andrew Hamilton, successfully argued that the truth of a published piece was a defense against libel.

WHAT WAS THE PENNY PRESS? WHAT LED TO IT?

By 1800 most large cities had at least one daily, but circulation was limited to the political and business elite. By 1830 new technological inventions made possible lower-cost papers aimed at a broader audience. More people were learning to read, public education was expanding, wages were increasing, and more people were gathering in cities. Benjamin Day launched the first low-cost daily, the *New York Sun,* in 1833. It sold for only a penny.

WHAT WAS MUCKRAKING?

In the early 1900s, crusading newspapers turned their attention to exposing scandals and corruption in government and among industry cartels. Muckraking contributed to several acts of legislation designed to reform various industries for the good of society.

WHAT ARE THE DIFFERENCES BETWEEN NEW JOURNALISM AND YELLOW JOURNALISM?

After the Civil War, the new journalism covered stories that would interest the average person: divorces, police news, scandals, disasters, and features about prominent personalities and social events, such as weddings, deaths, and parties. Sensationalism, with exciting illustrations, large headlines, elaborate descriptions, and exaggerated stories initially spiraled into the yellow journalism of Hearst, Pulitzer, and Bennett in the late 1800s, although some of it is still very much alive today.

WHEN DID NEWSPAPERS PEAK AS MASS AUDIENCE MEDIA?

The efficiency of newspaper printing increased rapidly and coincided with the peak of the newspapers' monopoly as a mass medium by about 1920. The newspaper industry had grown larger than its advertising and circulation could support. In addition to other print publications, motion pictures and the phonograph began to vie for people's attention and money. Newspapers' status would be challenged again by radio in 1927, by television in the 1950s, and by the Internet today.

WHAT WAS THE IMPACT OF WATERGATE ON AMERICAN JOURNALISM?

Woodward and Bernstein went against the tide and dug into a presidential cover-up story that ultimately led to Richard Nixon's resignation from the presidency. This story is pointed to as a test of courage and tenacity, exemplifying the watchdog role of the press and investigative reporting.

WHAT ARE THE MAIN RECENT TRENDS IN NEWSPAPER DELIVERY TECHNOLOGIES?

Newspapers were often delivered directly in cities and in bulk along railroads and shipping lines. In the 1990s, delivery by the World Wide Web became an alternative for "newspaper" delivery. Today, print news is increasingly delivered to e-readers, tablets and hand-held devices that replicate the look of a newspage.

WHAT IS THE IMPACT OF THE INTERNET ON NEWSPAPERS?

Newspapers can now reach more audiences through the World Wide Web. However, readers have more access to more news online. Newspapers must now compete for readers with a rapidly increasing variety of websites, such as other online newspapers, wire services, search engine news links, citizen journalism websites, and social media such as blogs, online commentary, Facebook, YouTube, and Twitter.

WHAT ARE THE MAIN NATIONAL DAILY NEWSPAPERS?

The *Wall Street Journal* is a specialized business paper with a broad general readership. The *New York Times* specializes in interpretation of the news and focuses on media and business. *USA Today* carries shorter news items and more entertainment. National dailies have responded to a public interest in national and international news and have been able to reach national audiences at an affordable price by using new technology for satellite delivery to primary plants. Almost all of them contain ads.

HOW DOES THE INTERNET AFFECT NEWSPAPER ADVERTISING?

Newspapers sell audiences to advertisers; the larger the audience, the more newspapers can attract and charge advertisers. However, advertisers want their ads where they will be noticed. As more people go online for their news, advertisers are also going online, which is taking business away from print newspapers.

WHAT ARE THE MAIN SECTIONS AND CONTENTS OF NEWSPAPERS?

The national newspapers stress international news, national news, editorials and commentaries, and business, with some lifestyle and entertainment news. Metropolitan dailies usually focus more on local and regional news including local lifestyles, entertainment, sports, and comics. Many weeklies focus almost exclusively on local events, shopping, and entertainment.

IS THERE STILL A MASS AUDIENCE FOR NEWSPAPERS?

What's the definition of a newspaper? Is it ink on newsprint? If so, then about 40 percent all American adults still read printed newspapers daily. However, as readership for the printed product decreases, readership for digital news increases. People spend more time with news, and they are doing so by supplementing the traditional news source with digital media, such as newspapers online, e-readers, tablets and mobile devices (Pew Research, 2010).

WHY ARE THERE CONCERNS ABOUT CONSOLIDATION IN THE NEWSPAPER INDUSTRY?

A number of formerly competitive newspapers have entered into joint operation agreements to share facilities, costs, administrative structure, and advertising while attempting to maintain editorial independence. However, the lack of competition and the nature of the joint operation may well reduce independence and diversity in editorial points of view. Chain ownership may similarly reduce local independence and standardize editorial and reporting approaches across the country. Cross-ownership at the local level between newspapers, radio, broadcast, cable, and satellite television is also a concern, particularly when newspapers owned by chains are also part of media cross-ownership.

SHOULD WE WORRY ABOUT CONGLOMERATES?

Large corporations that own many companies other than newspapers might have a tendency to make purely business decisions that affect journalistic ethical standards. A conglomerate that has entertainment holdings might use the newspaper to promote its other businesses.

WHAT FIRST AMENDMENT ISSUES AFFECT PRINT MEDIA?

Freedom of the press for newspapers has been limited at times by concerns about libel, defamation, and invasion of privacy (and pornography and obscene speech), but within the media and courts, freedom of speech has usually been the dominant principle.

WHAT ARE THE MAIN ETHICAL ISSUES FOR NEWSPAPERS?

The main ethical issues for newspapers revolve around accuracy, fairness, and balance. Journalists must also consider each case separately to help the most people while incurring the least harm, such as in weighing the public's right to know with individual privacy.

THINKING CRITICALLY
ABOUT THE MEDIA

1. What is the proper role of a free press in a democratic society?

2. Go through your local newspaper—in print, on the Internet, or digitally—and describe the objective of each section. How do local newspapers differ from national ones in content?

3. Why do most people prefer getting their news from a traditional news organization (whether in print or digitally) with an editor than searching online or reading a blog?

4. What does it mean for journalists to be the watchdogs?

5. What is news for you? And, what should be news?

KEY TERMS

anonymous source (p. 122)

backpack journalism (p. 108)

blog (p. 107)

corantos (p. 94)

convergence (p. 108)

conglomerate (p. 102)

dateline (p. 94)

fabrication (p. 122)

gatekeeping (p. 127)

hard news (p. 115)

joint operation agreement (JOA) (p. 121)

libel (p. 95)

local market monopoly (p. 119)

marketplace of ideas (p. 94)

new journalism (p. 99)

objectivity (p. 101)

Penny Press (p. 97)

plagiarism (p. 122)

seditious (p. 96)

social responsibility model (p. 102)

shopper (p. 112)

tabloid (p. 124)

teletext (p. 110)

unique visitors (p. 116)

videotex (p. 110)

wire service (p. 98)

yellow journalism (p. 100)

RECORDED MUSIC provides much of the soundtrack of our lives, both new sounds like Adele and classic sounds like The Beatles, as the music industry faces challenges from iTunes and Internet radio.

5

RECORDED MUSIC

HISTORY: FROM ROOTS TO RECORDS

The roots of today's popular music can be traced to earlier musical traditions. Hip-hop rhythms have roots in drumming in African religious ceremonies. African-American gospel music took root in the nineteenth century and is still performed today by groups like the Kingdom Heirs. White gospel spread from churches to country-and-western recordings with such songs as "Rock of Ages." Appalachian folk songs, such as "I'll Fly Away" on the *O Brother Where Art Thou?* soundtrack, are still often recorded, with many younger artists now recording similar music and calling it Americana. Delta blues songs, like Robert Johnson's "Crossroads," were recorded by 1960s-current blues guitarists like Eric Clapton. Cajun music is performed by the Cajun All-Stars. Mexican border *rancheras* (love songs) and *norteño* (border) music are recorded by Los Tigres del Norte.

Some of the earliest printed materials were lyrics and musical notations. In America, the sheet music industry dates back to the late nineteenth century. Back then, songwriters, not performers, had a more

1877	Thomas Edison introduces the speaking phonograph	1999	Napster introduces Internet file sharing
1940	Frank Sinatra becomes the first modern teen music and radio idol	2003	Apple introduces iTunes and iPod, and legal Internet sales of music take off
1951	"Rocket 88" is the first rock song	2011	Digital music sales are over half of U.S. music industry sales
1981	MTV music channel appears on cable TV	2012	Online community revolts against proposed anti-piracy laws
1982	CDs revolutionize "record" sales		

central role and were more widely recognized. Thus rather than waiting until a performer made the music popular, people flocked to buy the latest sheet music of well-known composers or lyricists, such as ragtime great Scott Joplin and march composer John Philip Sousa.

THE VICTROLA

During the late 1800s and early 1900s, in an attempt to reproduce music for the public, inventors created mechanical devices, such as music boxes and **nickelodeons**. Thomas Edison developed the first **acoustic** recording and playback technology in 1877, a "phono-graph." He imagined using the device to record dictation or to act as a telephone answering machine, but musical entertainment quickly became its main use. In 1906 the Victor Talking Machine Company introduced the home **Victrola**. People liked listening to recorded music in their homes, so the phonograph quickly became a widely used medium.

> **Nickelodeon** is a phonograph or player piano operated by inserting a coin, originally a nickel.
>
> **Acoustic** is a sound that is not electronically amplified.
>
> **Victrola** was the trade name for an early phonograph.

EARLY RECORDED MUSIC

The home Victrola introduced more people to new kinds of music more rapidly than ever before. The notion of popular music caught on, as writers and composers began to discover what kinds of music most appealed to a mass audience. Jazz, such as New Orleans Dixieland, became popular in the 1920s and 1930s. So did show tunes from talking movies, such as Al Jolson's songs from *The Jazz Singer* (see Chapter 7). Blues was popular among African-American audiences but did not cross over to other audiences much at that time (Romanowski & George-Warren, 1995).

BIG BAND AND THE RADIO DAYS

Radio had an immediate impact on recorded music, like the impact of television on cinema attendance later. When people could first hear live music at no cost on the radio, they bought fewer records. As radio took off in the late 1920s, record and phonograph sales dropped by almost half. That produced a panic in the record industry similar to the current reaction to Internet music downloads. Gradually, however, listeners bought their own recordings of music they had heard. In fact, the recording industry began to rely on radio to make people aware of recording artists, and the performers they heard on the radio began to be more important than the composers of the music.

Because early recording technology had not achieved very **high fidelity**, and because radio fees for recording artists had not yet been worked out, music was primarily broadcast live. Networks introduced the most popular groups and orchestras to the entire country. Radio stimulated a demand for a variety of musical genres, ranging from classical to country and western, making big stars out of singers like Bing Crosby and Hank Williams.

BIG BAND MUSIC AND THE WORLD WAR II GENERATION

The most popular music in the 1930s and 1940s was the "big band" sound. Developed from jazz, it was the pop music of its day. Band leaders Glenn Miller and Tommy Dorsey put together orchestras that introduced a number of singers, such as teen idol Frank Sinatra, who led pop music into the 1950s.

Record sales had dipped and some predicted the death of the phonograph, but one event that helped revive record sales was the appearance of Sinatra. Wherever he went, he was pursued by hordes of screaming teenage girls. Mass production had kept record prices down around a dollar, making records fairly affordable, and the fans began asking stores for the latest Sinatra record. The idea of stars and fans echoed the movies and built a powerful industry force that still exists today.

NEW MUSICAL GENRES

National radio networks featured the pop music of the day: big bands, light classical music, and movie and show tunes. However, important developments in musical genres were happening in regional recording companies and radio networks. A network of southern stations carried the Grand Ole Opry and bluegrass acts, such as the Carter Family, featured on recording labels that served largely southern audiences. These new music genres built on the main regional musical traditions of American music, such as southern **gospel**, **blues**, and **bluegrass**.

They also reflected the popularity of western music and singing cowboys in the movies, like Gene Autry, who began to sell enough records to interest major recording labels. Genres blended too. The combination of bluegrass, gospel, western, and western swing eventually became known as country and western, led by singers like Hank Williams. It followed southern migrants

NOW HEAR THIS The phonograph, pioneered in 1877 by Thomas Edison, helped create the technological base for the music recording industry.

High fidelity is accurate reproduction of natural sound.

Gospel music derives from white and black southern church hymns.

Blues came from music by black slaves in the South, which was characterized by specific chord progressions and moods.

Bluegrass came from white music in the South and Appalachia, building on Irish and Scottish instruments and traditions.

north as they looked for jobs in the industrial Midwest. A recording industry for this music grew up in Nashville, where the Grand Ole Opry was broadcast. National music labels like Capitol and RCA began to pick up country stars and project their music far beyond the South and Southwest.

The blues followed African-American migrants from the South to Chicago and New York, where a harder, electric blues developed in the 1940s and 1950s. Small, independent labels developed new artists and new audiences who had not been served by major record labels or network radio. Chess Records in Chicago, for example, carried a number of blues and rhythm-and-blues artists who were played only on what were called "black" stations back then. The movie *Cadillac Records* (2008) tells a fictionalized version of the Chess story.

Blues greatly influenced rock and roll. Rock bands of the 1960s Cream and the Rolling Stones, did versions of Chicago blues songs by Muddy Waters. (See Media & Culture: Black Music: Ripped Off or Revered?, page 135). Gradually, blues and gospel songs were blended with elements of pop music into new genres, such as rhythm and blues (R&B), which produced artists like Ray Charles. Black music was originally considered "race" music by the recording industry, which did not target it to white audiences for most of the 1930s, 40s, and 50s. R&B initially served a largely African-American audience in the early 1950s, but some of its artists, like rock and roll pioneer Little Richard, were playing music that white audiences saw as part of the rock and roll they liked. But even in the 1960s, guitar great Jimi Hendrix started on the black music circuit until he made his breakthrough with a white backup group in Britain.

ROCK AND POP HISTORY

People like to debate the origins of rock and roll in the early 1950s and what was the first real rock song. Rock built on a variety of roots, **hybridizing** them into a blend that gradually took on an identity that people could call a new genre. Rock's deepest roots were in blues, like Big Mama Thornton's version of "Hound Dog" (that Elvis later **covered**), but country, western swing, and rockabilly all fed in too.

A blend of jump-blues and western swing produced "Rock Around the Clock" in 1954 by Bill Haley and The Comets. It was the first rock record to become a hit and register loudly in the national consciousness. Elvis covered a song, "That's All Right, Mama," by blues singer Arthur "Big Boy" Crudup that some think was the most important song in getting widespread acceptance of rock. Elvis first emerged on Sun Records, one of the first labels that produced blues, country, and rock records.

The young "rock" radio-listening and record-buying audience gradually turned to R&B and soul music as it gave rise to the Motown sound of the Supremes and the Temptations, which was a major part of the pop music of the 1960s. Rock was still somewhat unified as a genre until the late 1960s, when the genre diverged with Motown, English groups including the Beatles and the Rolling Stones, and heavy rockers, such as Led Zeppelin and Jimi Hendrix, all known as "rock" (Limmer, 1981).

The recording industry began to rely on radio more than ever as a promotional device to make the public aware of new music and to help the recording industry sell records. The relationship got a little too close when record labels bribed **disc jockeys (DJs)** to play their records, a practice known as **payola**.

Hybridizing genres or music blends different traditions into a new form.

Covers are artists' performances of others' songs.

A **disc jockey (DJ)** is a radio station announcer who plays records and often emphasizes delivery and personality.

Payola occurs when record companies give bribes to DJs to get their records played.

MEDIA&CULTURE

BLACK MUSIC: RIPPED OFF OR REVERED?

What happens to cultures when one group "borrows" music from another? For some, like African-Americans, it seems that other people have long ripped off their musical traditions and ideas, even ridiculing them in the process. For example, many white Americans in the 1920s and 1930s enjoyed seeing Al Jolson, who performed in blackface, doing his versions of African-American jazz and blues, but they would not have listened to black singers doing their own songs. Many African-Americans felt insulted by the whole idea of a white man doing their music in blackface, and black musicians were restricted to performing their own music in media and venues aimed at African-Americans. Thus, white musicians appropriated the music of another group. Some black musicians did eventually benefit from the exposure given to their music, but many died in poverty and obscurity.

VICTIM OR IDOL? Blues musician and songwriter William James "Willie" Dixon wrote songs that were covered by many popular white artists including The Rolling Stones, Bob Dylan, and The Doors.

The tradition of white covers of black music continued in the 1950s and 1960s with Elvis, the Beatles, and the Rolling Stones doing covers of blues, rhythm and blues, or soul songs, often selling far more records than the original artists. Now black hip-hop and rap musicians are very popular. However, white artists like Eminem, who have borrowed black genres, still sometimes make more money. Critics like Herman Gray have argued that black music performed by white people lacks authenticity—a sense of the context in which it was created. Certainly a critical issue for an artist like Eminem, performing in a genre that came from and is still predominantly performed by African-Americans, is whether both black and white audiences consider his music and performance authentic enough to be worth listening to.

A largely positive interpretation of such trends would be that such musical "borrowing" is a natural part of an ongoing process of cultural hybridization. Examples might be Eminem, who was produced by an African-American rap artist, or a black fusion musician like Jamaican reggae singer Shaggy, who can blend rap, reggae, and white pop into a song like "Angel of the Morning." In this view, African-American and white American music have been mingling, to the long-run benefit of both, for hundreds of years.

Hybridization also applies to other cultures. For example, Matisyahu blends race and religion with his fusion of Orthodox Judaism and classic reggae music, even though it's highly unusual for an Orthodox Jew to achieve success singing reggae. But his revolutionary lyrics celebrating contemporary youth and his dynamic live performances made him popular with a wide variety of audience

THE RECORD BOOM AND POP MUSIC

The recording industry had slumped somewhat during World War II due to shortages of some components like the shellac used to make records and a musicians strike that lasted two years. Technological innovations revitalized the recording industry and had an impact on radio as well. In 1947, magnetic

WHAT I SAY Ray Charles blended gospel and R&B to create soul music and cross over into pop stardom.

tape improved sound fidelity, reduced costs, and made editing easier. This enabled the recorded music industry to produce the music of more artists less expensively and with better quality. In 1948 and 1949, Columbia introduced the large 33 1/3 rpm long-playing (LP) record and RCA introduced the smaller 45 rpm record (rpm stands for revolutions per minute). The 33 1/3 rpm LP albums prevailed for albums, whereas the faster-spinning 45 rpm records dominated releases of single songs (Sterling & Kittross, 1990).

For a while, the limits of the 45 rpm single had limited pop songs to under six minutes. Radio also preferred shorter songs. Some producers, like Phil Spector, managed to pour entire symphonies of densely layered production into a two- to three-minute single, like "River Deep, Mountain High" by Ike and Tina Turner, but by the mid- to late- 1960s, some groups were beginning to find the format very constraining. The Beatles, together with their producer, George Martin, were creating increasingly elaborate arrangements with multiple segments and layers of instruments, as on songs like "Penny Lane." The concept album, like *Sergeant Pepper's Lonely Hearts Club Band*, strung together a number of cuts that were still mostly short enough to fit standard two- to three-minute song radio formats. However, the Beatles and others steadily pushed toward longer songs that allowed more complex ideas and arrangements. Another strong new direction that expanded rock's horizons came from singer-songwriters like Bob Dylan, who scandalized folk purists by strapping on an electric guitar and doing rock albums like *Highway 61 Revisited* (1965).

THE ROCK REVOLUTION WILL BE SEGMENTED

After 1970, both recording companies and FM radio stations began to diversify into distinct rock formats, such as album-oriented rock (Bruce Springsteen), Top 40 (Michael Jackson), rock oldies (Chuck Berry), heavy metal (Led Zeppelin), adult contemporary (Linda Ronstadt), R&B/urban (Funkadelic), disco (KC & the Sunshine Band), and country and western (Tammy Wynette).

Rock's diverse roots fed further diversification into a number of branches or subgenres, which produced new radio formats, as can be seen in Figure 5.1. By the 1990s, dozens of subgenres had descended from 1960s rock, pop, and soul roots. Rap and hip-hop became favored genres for political and social commentary. Several early rap groups, like Public Enemy, did a number of songs clearly designed as political commentary to challenge ideas about the relations between black youth and the police. The continuing formation of smaller recording labels gave expression to musical subgenres and the subcultures that enjoyed them. Some musicians, like Dr. Dre, turned into producers and label owners. This was enabled by technological developments that lowered the price of recording tapes, records, and CDs.

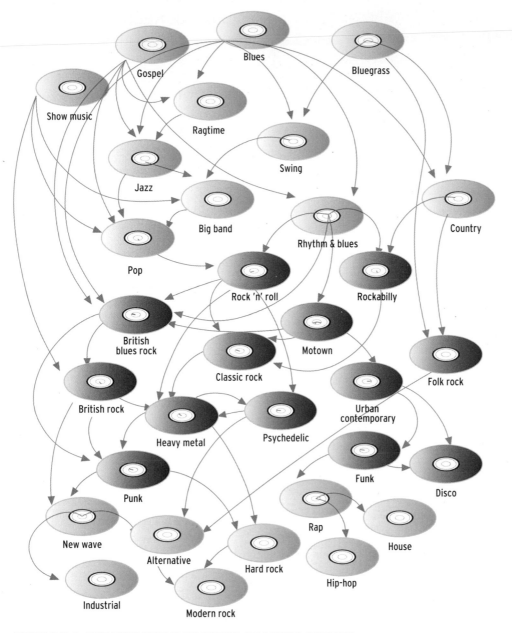

FIGURE 5.1 THE EVOLUTION OF POPULAR MUSIC GENRES

In 1982, a new round in the recording format wars began with the introduction of compact disc recording. Some were not very impressed with the shiny new discs at first, finding their sound rather harsh and brittle. But the recordings were more compact and relatively immune to dust and scratches compared to LP phonograph records.

By the late 1990s, CDs had pushed vinyl 33 1/3 record albums and cassettes off the record store racks (although some listeners persisted in their love of vinyl, spawning a comeback of sorts for LP records). Retail CD distribution also moved to the Internet, in online music stores and catalog sellers that sold recordings on websites for delivery through the mail. Radio stations joined the digital trend with hundreds of radio stations broadcasting on the Internet, using technologies such as RealAudio and MP3, although in 2002, **copyright** fees for music were imposed on Internet radio stations, cutting back the number of such stations.

> **Copyright** is the legal right to control intellectual property. With it comes the legal privilege to use, sell, or license creative works.

MUSIC TO GO Digital music players like the Apple iPod, or iPhone allow users to play AAC recordings and travel with tens of thousands of songs in their pockets.

Vicki Beaver

DIGITAL RECORDING

Increasingly, both musicians and music consumers are recording music in new digital forms. By the 1990s, some artists, like Fat Boy Slim, were essentially doing professional performance and recording on their own computers. The number of people recording music using low-cost digital equipment is skyrocketing as music recording equipment costs go down. What used to require specialized mixing and effects equipment can now be done on computers, including shooting music videos, producing surprise hits like "Friday" in 2011 on video channels. Like Moore's Law, which says that computing power will steadily double in power while its cost drops by half (see Chapter 9), it seems that digital audio and video recording similarly drops in price and grows in power.

MEDIA&CULTURE

MEDIA AND CULTURE: CEE LO GREEN AND THE HARD WORK OF MUSIC

Music is hard work. Like most media work, getting in, becoming full time, and staying on top is hypercompetitive. As the music business changes with technology and media industries, music careers have become more complex and multi-layered. It is not enough to get a record contract and make some hits. Even at its peak, few artists made a lot of money in music. Cee Lo Green is a good example of both hard work and the multiple ways musicians make money these days.

Cee Lo made $20 million in 2011. The sale of recordings was the smallest part. Music always involved touring to promote recordings. Now that is the main way that many musicians make money. A popular artist like Cee Lo Green logs hundreds of concerts and appearances in a year. Around Christmas in 2011, he appeared in New York, Alabama and Las Vegas in one long day.

Music careers tend to grow from niches. Cee Lo first produced and co-wrote the Pussycat Dolls' hit "Don't

Cha." Next he had a No. 1 around the world with "Crazy" with Gnarls Barkley. He rose to real stardom with the online hit "F**k You (the radio edit was named "Forget You,") which sold over 5 million downloads in the United States Cee Lo made about $700,000 on those downloads, both as artist and writer. So he still has to capitalize on his fame to make money with touring, TV appearances, and product endorsements. To stoke those up, he has become as much showman as singer, creating performances that build on humor as much as music. He stars as a regular judge on NBC's reality singing competition, "The Voice." He has a publishing company, which is one traditional way to make money, but has turned it into more of a marketing and branding company. He stepped on a number of older fans' sensibilities by rewording John Lennon's song "Imagine" but for a controversial lyricist whose own lines are often X-rated, he has managed to make himself into a remarkably mainstream personality.

So the music industry role as gatekeepers over who gets to record has diminished greatly. Many bands make money by touring and selling their own CDs and merchandise at concerts or over the Internet. Consumers also have many new options about how they obtain, buy, record, store, and mix music. In fact, the line between producers and consumers is blurring. People at home can now take elements or tracks of various pieces of music and remix them to create their own versions, even if they don't see themselves as musicians. DJ Dangermouse remixed Jay-Z's *The Black Album* and the Beatles' *White Album* into a new mix or mash-up, *The Gray Album*, which he received a court order not to distribute; but it was already loose on the Internet and impossible to completely recall.

These rapid decreases in cost permitted artists in many locales around the world to record their own local music. Austin (Texas), Salvador (Brazil), Shanghai (China), and many other places have local music markets in which a local artist can record, sell CDs, get on the radio, and promote their own concerts. Although musicians based locally would clearly like national or global success as well, increasingly musicians can get a good start and sometimes even survive economically with a local base, working with local labels, local concert venues, and local radio stations and promoting themselves through social media.

THE TALENT Lady Gaga has quickly become a sensation not only because of her musical ability but because of her avant-garde costumes and theatrical stage performances.

MUSIC ON THE INTERNET

The true potential of digital recording was unleashed as users began playing and recording music on CD drives built into personal computers, as well as sending and receiving music over the Internet. In 1999, Shawn Fanning started Napster, a file server that let people exchange songs as digital music files via the Internet. The term "social media" was not in wide use back then but that's what Napster and other file sharing sites to follow were in that they shared content uploaded by users, albeit illegally "shared" files that were not of the users' own making.

The recording industry preferred the term "stolen" to "shared" and so in 2000, the Recording Industry Association of America (RIAA) began to file lawsuits to force "free" music exchanges like Napster to shut down and followed with suits against individual users. Artists also went to court. Prince sued The Pirate Bay, a notorious download site based in Sweden, in an effort to stop free downloads of his recordings. However, Pirate Bay is still in operation today even after losing numerous court judgments. Another popular file sharing site, MegaUpload, was closed down in 2012 when government officials in several countries arrested its managers but tens of millions are still downloading music with through file sharing sites based on BitTorrent. Also, in 2012, RIAA worked with the film industry to get legislation passed through the U.S. Congress that would have required Internet service providers and search engines

STOP&REVIEW

1. How did music genres evolve from earlier music traditions?
2. What are the major genres and traditions that fed into rock and roll?
3. How did record/CD sales and radio affect each other over time?
4. What has led the segmentation of rock into sub-genres since the 1960s?
5. What has been the impact of MP3s and Internet music downloads on the recording industry?

to block sites that carried copyright protected material without permission. The online community rebelled, including a one-day shut down by Wikipedia, and forced the industry to rethink that plan.

The record industry very slowly moved to create a system for letting people get music online for a charge. In 2003, Apple broke ground by creating a pay download service, the iTunes Music Store and followed up with its popular iPod players. Steve Jobs of Apple was the first to present a convincing package of technology and price, and persuaded the music industry majors to go along. Apple initially charged $.99 per song but a downloaded song could be copied only onto a limited number of devices. Frustration with copy protection standards led to selling songs free of copyright protection. In 2008 Apple surpassed Walmart to become number one in all record sales, online or off. A number of companies, like Amazon, now are offering similar download stores, with comparable features and cooperation from the music industry. Download sales are still the main source of digital profits for the music industry.

Subscription music services offering unlimited downloads are now being packaged together with other services that customers are used to paying for, like mobile phone subscriptions. Others, like Spotify, are standalone services that are supported by a combination of advertising and monthly fee services. In 2011 both Google and Apple introduced options to let users store and stream their own music onto computers, portable players and smartphones from Internet servers in "the cloud." (See Technology Trends, page 141). Also gaining in popularity are ad-supported music streaming services. Some of these have pre-programmed services, like Internet radio. Some, like Pandora, let you create your own channels by suggesting music based on what you already like. Using computer algorithms that examine patterns among users to see that people who like Neko Case also like Gillian Welch, Pandora then makes suggestions for you.

CD sales continue to decline, but more slowly (5% in 2011), despite Walmart promotion of $5 CDs. Sales of digital tracks grew, but only at 9 percent, down from 28 percent in 2008. Digital album sales grew 20 percent, in part due to full album download promotions, like Amazon offering Lady Gaga's latest for 99 cents for two days in 2011. Overall album sales in the United States grew 1.3 percent, largely thanks to Adele, reflecting the continuing importance of blockbuster hits (Sisario, 2012). Overall, global sales declined 7 percent even though some emerging markets saw increases. Revenues from sales of digital single tracks; digital albums; managing live performances; Internet streaming; music subscription services and licensing music to television, film, and video games, like "Guitar Hero," are beginning to increase but so far haven't replaced CDs as the cash cow of the industry. The music industry is ahead of all others in making revenue from digital sources (29%) vs. newspapers (4%) and all others, except videogames (39%) (IFPI 2011; see Figure 5.2), but it has also lost more to unlicensed digital traffic, too—a 31 percent decline in the value of the global recorded music industry, 2004–2010.

Critics, such as Winseck (2011), argue that are several problems with only focusing on recorded music sales. It ignores the fact that there is considerable revenue growth in concerts and live performances, Internet and mobile phone services, global markets, and publishing (licensing, digital platform use, Internet radio, TV and film soundtracks). (See Figure 5.2 and Box on Cee Lo Green.)

Social media continue to impact the music industry in new ways. Facebook Music helps popularize new music by linking tunes from your friends' music services and hosting fan clubs and profiles of performers. Top acts like Lady Gaga communicate with their faithful fans through Facebook and Twitter. Aspiring stars are finding that they can launch careers and push album sales through social media without the backing of either a major label or extensive concert tours. For example, singer-songwriter Lana del Rey became a sensation in 2012 after a posting a music video on YouTube and generating buzz in Twitter and Facebook.

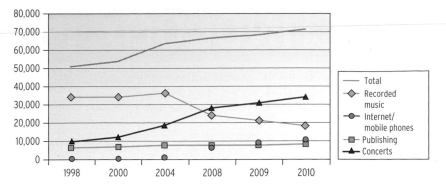

FIGURE 5.2 SOURCES OF REVENUE, GLOBALLY, FOR THE MUSIC INDUSTRY. As recorded music sales drop, the industry and musicians both rely more on concert ticket sales.

TECHNOLOGY TRENDS: LET'S MAKE MUSIC

The first music recordings were purely analog. With Thomas Edison's phonograph of 1877, sound waves were recorded as indentations on a spinning cylinder covered with malleable tinfoil. Analog records and tapes lasted almost 100 years (see Technology Demystified: From the Victrola to the CD). Digital CDs seemed revolutionary at first, but what really reshaped music are computer-based technologies, from GarageBand for cheap recording and remixing, to the Internet for distribution and iTunes and iPods for listening.

NEW DIGITAL FORMATS

Music recording technology and computer media converged rapidly. Recordable CDs and DVDs are equally at home in the CD bays of personal computers and stereo systems. But files of music data can also be stored on a computer's hard drive. So for many of our readers, your laptop, or smartphone is also now your stereo, with extensive selections of accessory speakers and headphones.

Another option is the personal digital stereo player, a product first introduced in 1998 but soon dominated by Apple's iPod product line. They store "near" CD-quality music downloaded from the Internet or "ripped" (copied) from CDs using the digital recording and storage formats known as **MP3** and AAC (the default for Apple products including the iPod, iPhone and iPad). We say "near" CD quality because this format uses digital compression that does not make perfect reproductions but sounds almost as good to the listener and takes up only a tenth of the space to store. Fidelity can be increased with higher bit rates. Apple raised the quality of iTunes by increasing their bit rate from 128 to 256 thousand bits per second in 2009. Services like Mog and Apple "lossless"

[**MP3** is a sound digitization and compression standard, short for MPEG-2 Layer 3.]

FROM THE VICTROLA TO AAC

The wax and foil cylinders used in early recordings were replaced by more durable flat gramophone disks first invented in 1882 by Emile Berliner (Brinkley, 1997). In the early twentieth century the hand cranks gave way to electric motors. In later electronic equipment, movements of the stylus, or "needle," generated an electric current that was amplified and sent to the speakers. There the current activated an electromagnet attached to a vibrating membrane inside the speakers that reproduced the original sound waves.

In the recording studio, modern microphones all employ a thin membrane that catches the sound waves. The "condenser mics" found in recording studios have a pair of thin, electrically charged flexible metallic plates inside. As the sound waves press against one of the plates, its vibrations push electrical charges back and forth between the plates, creating an electrical current that matches the sound.

Early records spun at a rate of 78 rpm and had one or two songs per side on a 10-inch disc. The high rpms gave reasonable sound quality but limited the length of the material. Beethoven's Ninth Symphony was sold on several 78 rpm disks inserted in paper sleeves and bound together in a cardboard-covered album.

In 1948 two new recording formats were introduced. The 33 1/3 rpm LP records held 23 minutes of music per side. The 45 rpm records held up to about six minutes to a side. Both new formats used better needles and amplification to achieve improved sound that was thought of in the 1950s as high fidelity. Magnetic tape came along at about the same time. In **electromagnetic recording**, flexible plastic tape passes over a recording head, an electromagnet that imparts a residual magnetic field to tiny magnetic particles stuck to the surface of the tape (see Figure 5.3).

Tape recording permitted a series of gradually improved recordings to be put onto a record. Initially, recordings were only a single monaural track, but recording equipment in studios gradually increased the number of tracks recorded to 2 (stereo), 4, then 8, then 32, even before the process was ultimately digitized. The listening experience improved dramatically in 1956 with the first **stereo** recordings. Stereo tricks us into hearing the musicians as though they were sitting in different chairs in front of us, whereas the previous monaural recordings made it seem that all the sounds were coming from the same point. Stereo adds the illusion of depth to the music. To accomplish the illusion, we divide the

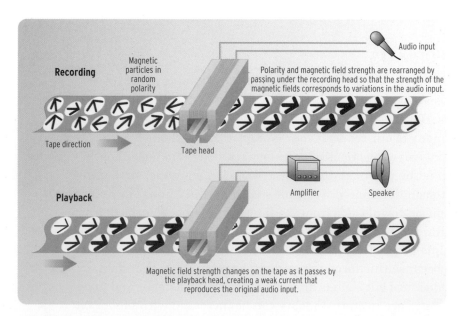

FIGURE 5.3 AUDIO RECORDING Music is stored in tiny magnetic particles on the surface of audio tapes.

music into two separate sources, or tracks, and replay them so that they are heard over different speakers.

CDs arrived in 1982. As we noted in Chapter 1, CD recorders convert sound waves into the 1s and 0s of computer data. During playback, another laser shines on the surface of the disc, but the light is scattered when it hits the pits, turning the laser's reflection off for a brief moment. This pattern of "lights on" and "lights off" regenerates the computer data and, eventually, the original sound (Benson & Whitaker, 1990). CDs faithfully reproduce the entire range of sound frequencies audible to the human ear and are less vulnerable to dust and scratches than earlier recording media. They also provide more capacity than the previous recording media. Now Beethoven's Ninth Symphony fits on one side of a CD. In fact, the size of the CD was set so that it could fit the 74-minute playing time of Beethoven's "greatest hit."

However, in devising the standards for CDs, certain compromises had to be made to limit the amount of digital information required to record a song, such as limiting the number of computer bits per sound sample. Online music file standards such as MP3 (short for Motion Picture Expert Group-2 audio layer III, and **AAC** (Advanced Audio Coding), WMA (Windows Media Audio) make further compromises in sound quality to reduce file sizes. Although the details vary, the basic trick they all use is some form audio compression, which removes redundant information that the listener does not perceive. For example, when you turn up the volume of your iPod to drown out background noise you "mask" (no longer perceive) the unwanted noise. That's because when two sounds of approximately the same pitch occur simultaneously we perceive only the louder of the two. Audio compression uses computer algorithms to filter out the sounds that we would not perceive anyway, so that the resulting music can be digitally encoded using fewer bits with acceptable (e.g. "near CD quality") results.

offer even higher quality recordings. Multichannel surround sound is also available. Windows Media Audio 9 has 7.1 surround sound built in.

Multichannel sound is also available in the form of Super Audio CDs and DVD Audio. But these also have built-in piracy protections that limit their popularity, as does the lack of interest by major record labels and popular performers. Also, the music listening experience has changed from sitting in front of a stereo with expensive speakers to portable players with ear buds. These days recording studios emphasize volume over fidelity, the better to blast the ears of iPod users. As a result the new formats are a niche product featuring classical music and the back catalogs of once-popular rock bands like Pink Floyd.

Electromagnetic recording is a method of storing information as magnetized areas on a tape or disk.

Stereo is splitting recorded sound into two separate channels.

AAC is Advanced Audio Coding.

ISALES Apple's iTunes store leads the way in legal music downloads and has surpassed Walmart to be music's main retailer.

SINKING THE PIRATES

Widespread "sharing" or "piracy" of MP3s online led to the development of the music industry's secure digital music initiative. This made it possible to encrypt (or scramble) the music so that only paying customers of industry-backed online music services can download it. Much to the dismay of users, the technology can also put an "expiration date" on the music if the subscriber doesn't keep paying and adding copy prevention to prevent users from ripping their own CDs from the songs they download or copying them onto the Internet. That was at the core of the business strategy for the industry's pay music services and for some CDs. For example, Apple's FairPlay digital rights management system originally only let users make a certain limited number of copies of a song downloaded from its iTunes Music Store. Consumer reaction was so poor that eventually Apple, Amazon, and others eliminated copy protection standards like FairPlay in 2008 and sold digital music downloads without restrictions.

Technology is also aiding the music industry trade association Recording Industry Association of America (RIAA) as it tracks music piracy online. The RIAA uses a library of digital fingerprints that it says can uniquely identify music files that have been traded online as far back as 2000. Such fingerprints can separate those who copied their own CD into MP3s on their computer from those who downloaded a fingerprinted version of a file that has been identified as in circulation on file-sharing Internet services. The industry hopes to use these fingerprints in their (so far unsuccessful) attempt to promote new laws that will make it possible to automatically block the transmission of pirated recordings over the Internet.

STREAMING AND CLOUD MUSIC SERVICES

Is it time to think about throwing your iPod onto the same trash heap as your old CD player? Now music fans can enjoy unlimited access to their music by storing it on a "cloud." That is the term used for storing (legally purchased) music on the Internet so that it can be downloaded or streamed to any device you wish, whenever you want. Apple's iCloud, Google Music, and Amazon Cloud Drive let users store music they purchase online plus music they upload from their own collections into what is called a cloud locker, a music archive on a remote server that lets you play your own music through a variety of devices.

Your next portable music player is possibly your cell phone. It began with downloading ring tones of favorite songs to "play" on cells. Advanced high-speed wireless networks (see Chapter 12) offer the capacity for speedy downloads and smooth streaming, including music stored on the new cloud services.

SOCIAL MUSIC MEDIA

Social media on the Internet, such as Facebook and YouTube, are changing music promotion. MySpace was originally a music-oriented site, where bands could include streaming music files on their pages for other people to check out. Now bands and distributors and independent musicians push music through YouTube, Facebook, Bandcamp, Soundcloud, and Twitter. Facebook users can link to groups, promote lists of what they like, and let their "friends" know what they are listening to. Music blogs let listeners find new music and musicians promote theirs.

INDUSTRY: THE SUITS

New digital technologies seem to allow many more new entrants in music recording, music production, and distribution. However, economic and regulatory changes have also encouraged unprecedented concentration of the ownership of most of the major players (in terms of hits, sales, and profits) all across the music industries. So the music that is such a part of our culture has largely been controlled by "the suits," the men and women in business suits who run the record industry. However, some former outsiders, like Dr. Dre or Timbaland, have forced their way into the inside by becoming successful producers and managers.

THE RECORDING INDUSTRY

The key elements of the recording industry are the talent (the singers and musicians), the producers, the recording studios, the recording companies and their various labels, the distributors, independent promoters, and the retailers. Also important to musicians' success are their songwriters, managers, and arrangers. Despite the fast-paced developments in digital music, most musicians still hope to get a contract from a record company to make money. Unfortunately, the road to riches is lined with traps set by the suits who charge the bands for marketing and concert promotions and retain the rights to the music. So more and more groups try to make it on their own.

The Talent. Groups form at a local level. There are tens of thousands of aspiring local groups and singers throughout the United States. For example, the college club scene in Chapel Hill, North Carolina, spawned Ben Folds Five and the local scene in Portland, Oregon produced the Decemberists. Such acts perform locally, try to get concert or dance bookings out of town, become better known, and make a recording to circulate to record companies or sell directly through the Internet. Many move to larger, more competitive locales more frequented by record company scouts, such as Los Angeles, Nashville, and New York. A number achieve regional status as traveling acts that circulate in a state or region. A few are discovered and make it big, but most break up, whereupon the more talented musicians form new groups and move on. Talent scouts from record companies are always looking around college towns, festivals like South by Southwest (Austin), and concert circuits for new acts, but competition is fierce. However, increasing numbers of groups avoid record contracts and sell or distribute their own music at concerts and over the Internet.

Recording Studios and Record Companies. It used to be that recording companies would bring promising acts into the recording studio, where engineers and arrangers could capture their music on tape for an album or single. Recording studios are now relatively cheap to create and can be found in most cities of even a few hundred thousand people. Aspiring groups can increasingly cut or record a CD locally for $500–$600. Others cut and edit their own

HIP HOP INNOVATOR Cee Lo Green is a prominent innovator in hip hop. Reflecting a current industry pattern, he has gone back and forth between groups like Gnarls Barkley and solo work.

CDs and online music files on personal computers. That CD won't reflect professional assistance with arrangements, but with it a group can look for more club dates and promote its recordings on the Internet as CDs or AAC music files. They can also promote their music to talent scouts from record companies or sell their tunes directly to the public.

However, recording companies are still gatekeepers; they often still decide who gets distributed and promoted nationally on the radio, in social media, in concerts, and in record stores. The most visible to musicians are Artists and Repertoire (A&R) executives, who search for, spot, recruit, and nurture talent. They travel to some likely music spots, particularly regional festivals like South by Southwest.

Four big companies dominated the music industry: Sony, EMI, Universal, and Warner Music Group. However, EMI declined and was broken up in 2011, with parts sold to Universal and Sony, so now there are three. Warner was sold to a new conglomerate (Access Industries). Music group ownership has been volatile in the face of declining CD sales, as the EMI breakup and Warner sale show. However, these companies still dominate distribution in the United States and the world. Industry figures worry that reducing four ownership groups to three may reduce competition in recording, distribution and music publishing in ways that are not good for consumers or artists (Billboard, Dec. 17, 2011).

Recorded music is very much an international industry. Sony is a Japanese company, which recently bought BMG, Arista, and RCA from the German BMG. The French company Vivendi bought the Universal Music Group. Foreign owners have not pursued different kinds of musical content from domestic owners. All the majors have operations in a number of countries where they develop local and promote global artists, much more than do global conglomerates in film or television.

Some of the major recording companies have a number of separate labels, each with a separate image and intended market segment. Sony Music Entertainment has the Columbia and Epic labels; Warner Music Group (now owned by Edgar Bronfman, Jr.) has Rhino, Elektra, Warner, Sire, and Atlantic.

Independent distributors had 12 percent of the U.S. market in 2011, compared to 35 percent for Universal and 29 percent for Sony (Billboard, Dec. 17, 2011, p. 57).

Recording companies decide which albums and songs to promote via radio, billboards, and newspaper and magazine ads. Recently, major labels, like the movie industry, rely on first-week sales to determine whether a new release will be a hit. The labels' first copy costs for new CDs are often high, starting with recording, mixing, and producers' costs, not to mention the huge salaries they pay "the suits." Labels also often have to pay an independent promoter to get a song on the radio, and they also have to pay producers, directors, and crews to do a music video that will make it onto cable music channels or be a hit on YouTube. All that can cost millions, so the labels are often tempted to slow or even stop promoting a group that is not an immediate big hit, and maybe even cancel the group's contract.

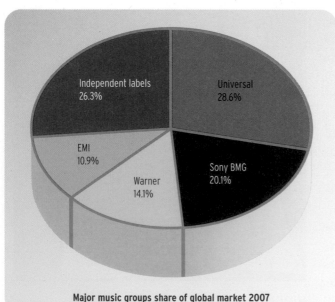

Independent labels
26.3%

Universal
28.6%

EMI
10.9%

Warner
14.1%

Sony BMG
20.1%

Major music groups share of global market 2007

FIGURE 5.4 BIG FOUR MUSIC GROUPS' SHARE OF GLOBAL MARKETS

Rather than going with majors, many groups increasingly go with independent labels, which came back strongly in the 1990s. An independent label is one owned by someone outside of the three majors and can vary in size from tiny (three or four employees) to medium size (50 or so employees). Some independent labels work on very low promotion and profit margins so that they and a group can make money after selling as few as 25,000 copies, compared to the millions required for a major label hit. So most tend to see the promotion of a band as a long-term project. And some see file sharing as an ally, a way for people to hear about new groups on their labels, who then often buy the CD or buy a legal download. As in the movie industry, there is an increasing synergy between indie labels and music producers. If a new group on an independent label does well, it may be picked up for distribution by one of the big three, either by striking a deal with the indie label or buying out its contract.

Social media are helping musicians and audiences find each other through, or sometimes around, labels. Related new forms of distribution, like net or digital labels are growing. They help musicians sell music either by download or CD, accepting payment via PayPal or credit card.

An important part of the promotion of the most promising groups with national potential used to be making a music video for MTV. When MTV came on the scene in 1981, it had great influence on which records become popular and even what gets played on radio stations. However, MTV has been supplanted by YouTube. Also still important are singer contests like *American Idol* and *The Voice*, which have launched several hit singers and strengthened the careers of others. Soundtracks to television shows, like *Grey's Anatomy*, turned Brandi Carlisle's song "The Story" into a hit.

Radio has become less central to music promotion now that the playlists on our iPods are at least as important as those on local radio stations. A controversial and expensive part of music promotion to radio stations is independent promoters. These promoters are hired by record companies to convince radio stations to play new records. There have been several scandals involving payola, or bribes, from promoters to station managers or program directors, to play records, which led to calls for reform of the business of promoting music to radio stations. One example was paying stations substantial "fees" for access to their playlists. All four then major music groups (EMI, Warner, Universal, and Sony) were investigated over payola. Sony, Warner, and Universal paid millions in legal settlements.

Music Distribution. The record companies distribute recordings in a variety of ways. Some stores, like Walmart, deal directly with record companies. Big-chain record stores, like Tower, once dominated this retail business, but Tower went bankrupt, and huge general retailers, such as Walmart and Best Buy, grew in importance. Now they have been bested by iTunes. The top five music retailers in 2011 were iTunes, Walmart, Best Buy, Amazon, and Target.

The conventional music store model is not the only way to distribute recordings. Record clubs that once sold music through direct mail are mostly a thing of the past thanks to competition from Amazon.com and other online retailers, although Columbia House is still around as of this writing. Recordings are also still pitched via TV commercials for phone ordering. The increasingly dominant form of distribution is the purchase and download of music over the Internet from online stores, such as the iTunes Music Store or Amazon. An

MUSICIANS, MOGULS, MUSIC IN EVERYTHING ELECTRONIC

As the music business changes with technology and media industries, new careers open as others close. There is as much room as ever for singers, musicians, arrangers, composers, and directors, but like most media work, getting in, becoming full time, and staying on top is hypercompetitive. There were about 240,000 jobs in 2008: 186,400 held by musicians and singers; 53,600 for music directors and composers. Around 43 percent worked part time; 50 percent were self-employed (U.S. Occupational Outlook Handbook, 2010).

Jobs for the recording industry are declining, as technology permits more people to record their own music at home. However, there is still a niche for high-end recording. There are also new jobs in applying music to film, television, games, websites, and all kinds of interactive media. Placing music in these venues is increasingly important to musicians and the music industry, so work in these interfaces is growing.

Music careers tend to show the importance of connections. Many people follow family or other connections into the industry. Some start in radio, then move to music promotion, producing, writing songs or recording. Work in college radio often pays off in experience and connections, as does work on music videos. Producing your music video and putting it on YouTube works for some, as it did for Rebecca Black with "Friday," in 2011, but her parents had deep enough pockets to pay for high quality recording, so connections still matter, even if the barriers to entry are a lot lower these days.

emerging business model treats music as a loss-leader as part of a scheme to sell hardware. Apple nets only a few pennies per iTunes song after paying the record label and credit card processing fees. But they profit enormously from their iPod, iPhone and iPad hardware sales, which are driven by iTunes sales. Amazon took a different approach when it started selling its Kindle Fire for slightly less than it cost to make in 2011, assuming the tablet, tightly integrated with its online store, would drive Amazon content sales and profits.

The combined effect of all these competing forms of distribution, plus the continued growth of illegal file sharing, has been a decrease in CD sales. So, the 10- to 12-track album as the dominant mode of music sales is declining even though digital album sales are now increasing, and the single, the forgotten champion of the 1950s and 1960s, is back, in digital download form instead of 45 rpm records.

While streaming services had been a fairly marginal part of overall music consumption until 2011, it has now begun to realize some of the industries' hopes for a substantial new revenue stream. Labels, performing artists, and writers get very small payments each time a song is played on Pandora, but those small sums add up quickly as such services become more popular. Similar small revenue streams come each time someone plays music that they have placed in a cloud-based music service, like iCloud, Google Music, or Amazon Cloud. Since these systems are now promoted heavily by three of the strongest technology firms, their use and importance to musicians and labels in likely to grow significantly.

Music Industry Associations. The RIAA and other trade associations function as the industry's lobbying and legal arm. The American Society of Composers, Authors and Publishers (ASCAP) represents more than 170,000 songwriters, lyricists, and music publishers. Broadcast Music Incorporated (BMI) has close to double that number of creative artists and publishers, with 300,000 affiliates. Both help artists collect royalties from live performances by others, radio plays of recorded music, Internet radio, elevator music, use in commercial sound channels for stores, and other ways in which music gets played. ASCAP and BMI both monitor play on media, collect royalties from media, and distribute them to artists. For songs covered by others, on every album with at least 10 tracks, the music publishers representing the authors of the songs earn 7.5 cents per track, which they distribute to the writers with whom they have agreements.

A number of alternative ways of looking at artists' rights to and benefits from their music are developing. Some artists, like Phish or the Grateful Dead, were very accepting of fans' recording and sharing concerts, assuming that people will buy tickets and CDs anyway. Others, like Dispatch, saw record companies as something to avoid and see Internet file sharing and music blogs with Internet downloads as good ways to market and sell their music. One recent idea was the Creative Commons, in which artists make their music available, not only for simple download and listening, but for sampling and mashing up. These artists' idea is that music is to be shared, sampled, and reworked to spur creativity, and they seem to assume that people will still buy their CDs or pay to go to their concerts and download their music anyway. Increasingly, they also sell music directly through net labels that often use Creative Commons licenses. Other artists, such as the Eagles, are trying to use the "termination rights" clause of the DMCA to recover ownership rights to their own compositions. However, other artists are unwilling to risk that and have lined up behind RIAA's efforts to restrain file sharing. (See "Sharing or Stealing?" on page 150.)

STOP&REVIEW

1. How has the digitization of recording formats affected the industry?
2. What is the relationship between recordings, labels, and major music companies?
3. What is the impact of record clubs and major retailers like Walmart on the music industry? What about online retailers like iTunes?
4. What copyright challenges are raised by Internet music technologies?

WORLD VIEW

HOW MUSIC CROSSES BORDERS

Music is one of the few instances in which American audiences are widely exposed to cultural products from outside the United States. English rock and pop have had a strong presence since the 1960s, so much so that many American listeners take it for granted, along with music from Canada and Australia. Some musicians, like Canadian Neil Young, moved to the USA and became part of the U.S. scene. Others, like the Beatles or Rolling Stones, toured the USA to promote their music but continued to live elsewhere. Musicians from other English-speaking countries have had an easier time breaking into the U.S. market, even when they sing in a notably different dialect, like that of Jamaica (calypso, reggae, ska, dance hall). A number of other musicians have also learned to sing in English to break into both U.S. and global markets. Scandinavian artists like Abba and Björk have become familiar this way. So music is a one of the best examples of how the USA is part of a transnational Anglosphere, or English-speaking world, in culture. (See more on transnational cultural-linguistic markets in Chapter 16.)

The broad genre of world music represents a relatively serious music industry effort to market singers and groups that are often extremely popular in their home markets, into the United States. Some examples have included bossa nova and samba from Brazil; Celtic music from Great Britain, Ireland, and France; various African genres; and other Latin American and Caribbean music, along with Balkan, Greek, and others.

WHO CONTROLS THE MUSIC?

One of the most important issues to understand, in order to be media savvy or literate, is who makes the decisions on music: who to record, distribute, and promote. The music industry seems large and diverse, with dozens of recording labels. However, how large and diverse is the group of people making content decisions? How is that changing with technology, industry, and other changes?

RECORDED MUSIC IN THE AGE OF THE NEW MEDIA GIANTS

The music business has never been regulated in the same way that broadcasting traditionally was. Most of the major film studios—Warner Bros., Disney, Columbia, and Universal—were once involved in the music recording and distribution business. However, the music business is now seen as less profitable than some other media businesses, so a number of sales and mergers have taken place, resulting in three giant companies: Sony, Universal, and Warner.

Antitrust concerns are also raised by two other segments of the music industry that have a direct impact on aspiring musicians as well as their fans: concert promotion and concert ticket sales. Both are dominated by Live Nation Entertainment, a spin-off of Clear Channel Communications. Live Nation owns over 100 top live music venues including the Fillmore theaters, operates dozens more, and manages top performers including Madonna, U2, Shakira, and Jay-Z. Ticket sales are also dominated by Live Nation as a result of a 2010 merger with Ticketmaster, although regulators insisted that the firm license its software and open up competition in concert ticket sales as a condition for approving the deal.

SHARING OR STEALING?

Reuse of copyrighted music has been a major issue for the recording industry. When artists record a piece of music written by someone else, whether for direct sale or for broadcast, they have to obtain permission and usually pay a royalty, a fee charged for use of the writer's intellectual property. Some well-known court cases have been fought over whether an artist used another's basic melody. This problem has been accentuated with the rise of sampling in hip-hop and rap music, music **mashups**, and multimedia, where artists record and reuse bits, or samples, of existing works. Courts decided in 2004 that any sampling requires getting permission and paying royalties.

Distribution of music over the Internet raises another copyright and intellectual property problem. Virtually flawless digital recordings can be transmitted over the Internet for recording on a hard drive, digital tape, disc, or recordable CD. Technical solutions were sought to prevent illegal copying and transmission, while permitting the legal sale of music over the Internet, but most copy protection was dropped by 2008. Internet sites, such as those using the BitTorrent protocol, allow users to swap high-quality digital files that contain music. Much of the music being swapped between computers is copyrighted, and swapping those songs can be considered piracy—violation of the copyright of the artists or recording companies who own it. So as a listener,

[
A **mashup** combines several audio and/or video segments or tracks into a new creation.
]

you have a legal dilemma when you turn to the Internet and MP3s to look for diversity of music. By looking for new talent on the Internet, you can help new bands get around the gatekeeping of the music and radio industries, but if you only listen to their MP3s and don't buy their CDs, they won't survive.

RIAA, representing the music industry, also began to sue individual downloaders—more than 20,000 by 2008—and settled suits with 3,900 of them, according to RIAA. This proved sufficiently controversial that RIAA discontinued their policy of prosecuting downloaders. Nonetheless, it appears that file sharing is beginning to decline in favor of other forms of free online music such as Internet radio. However, the industry was concerned enough about continuing piracy issue to press in 2011 for new laws, referred to as SOPA (Stop Online Piracy Act) or PIPA, to fight online trafficking of copyrighted material by targeting those who advertise on or sell access to sites that sold illegal downloads. Internet industry groups and users reacted strongly to potential restrictions placed by the act, to the point where the proposed laws were withdrawn in Congress. But the recording industry is still looking for ways to restrict what it considers to be piracy.

PITY THE POOR, STARVING ARTISTS

In their struggle against file sharing, a favorite tactic of the RIAA has been to call attention to the plight of poor, starving artists whose livelihoods have been ruined by illegal downloading. Some artists, notably Metallica and Prince, agree and have filed suits of their own. Other, less established artists see downloading as a way to break through the creative stranglehold that the industry has on new acts and reach the public on their own terms.

And, it is comical that the industry should accuse music fans of starving the musicians when the industry itself has been bleeding artists dry for years. Rock-and-roll bad girl Courtney Love "did the math" for the suits a few years back at an RIAA gathering. She pointed out that after paying for record manufacturing and promotion fees, a band with a hit record gets only a modest middle-class income, not the riches that aspiring musicians imagine.

What's more, you don't even own your own songs. Standard industry practice is to have the artist sign over the rights in their first recording contract. The Copyright Term Extension Act further empowers the media giants at the expense of the artist. Would your garage band like to record its own rendition of some song that would now be public domain under the old act? A hit from 1935, Depression-era hits like "The Good Ship Lollipop" might strike a resonant chord today. You can't use it under the current copyright laws.

Artists disagree on how to deal with record companies. Most just sign on and hope for the best. However, some are exploring their options. Many groups go to independent labels because no big label wanted to sign them. But some groups create their own label or go to a smaller one to keep more control or get a better deal in terms of revenue sharing. Independent labels, those that are not owned by the big conglomerates, are growing, although many get bought up by major labels. Many of these independent labels are actually distributed by major recording companies, but not all.

GETTING DISTRIBUTED MEANS GETTING CREATIVE

Both recording artists and record companies are grappling with the Internet, which has toppled established techniques for promoting talent and marketing music sales. One novel approach was Radiohead, which released *In Rainbows* for digital download on its own website, asking fans to pay what they thought it was worth. Although many downloaded it for free, it garnered so much publicity that *In Rainbows* doubled the sales of their previous two albums.

One new means to promote music to very specialized interests is Internet radio. Latino rappers, among others, use Internet radio to reach people who aren't necessarily concentrated into large, easily identified geographic areas for conventional radio coverage. As Internet radio slowly takes off, recording companies have demanded that webcasters pay royalties for recorded music they play. Two industry groups, the Digital Media Association (DMA) and the RIAA, agreed in 2003 to a proposal for royalty fees that Internet radio services must pay record companies for webcasting their songs. That is administered by the non-profit, SoundExchange. It collects royalties on the behalf of recording copyright owners and featured artists for non-interactive digital transmissions, including satellite and Internet radio (see Chapter 6).

Recording companies are finally beginning to get a bit more creative about distribution over the Internet. Warner Music is experimenting with some relatively unknown acts by signing them to a digital-only label. It will release their songs through services like iTunes and Rhapsody, where its digital sales have grown considerably. They hope signing acts with small but established audiences will earn the company a profit on digital sales alone. This also lets them avoid the costs of the conventional distribution model: making a music video, paying music promoters to push the songs to radio stations, and advertising.

Some new distribution groups, such as Netlabel, are springing up. EMusic started an online music service that will give independent musicians a new option. The site will sell music from over 3,000 independent labels, a total of a half-million tracks. It may help fans locate small, obscure, and eccentric music; help musicians find their fans; and grab a chunk of the more than $2 billion in revenues generated annually by independent music labels. Another kind of alternative is a company called ArtistShare. Bypassing labels, distributors, and retailers, ArtistShare sells discs over the Web and turns over all the proceeds (minus a small fee) to the artist.

Some have hoped that the Internet would provide a meaningful counterforce to the music industry giants. That is beginning to happen, with artists like Lana Del Rey, selling music and branded merchandise online on their own, through social networks, or through new net labels such as found at www.netlabels. org. At this moment, in online music, Apple enjoys a level of market dominance that attracted the attention of antitrust authorities in Europe.

MUSIC CENSORSHIP?

The record industry had some self-censorship up through the 1960s. To get on the Ed Sullivan Show in 1964, the Rolling Stones changed the lyric "let's spend

NOT FOR SALE IN PERSON Radiohead released their album, In Rainbows, on the Internet first, letting fans pay what they wished for it.

ZUMA Press, Inc. / Alamy

the night together" to "let's spend some time together." Even in the late 1960s, FCC rules against obscenity and indecency restrained many radio stations from playing songs with lyrics like Jefferson Airplane's "up against the wall, mother fxxker." But many major rock groups carried by big labels began to use graphic language and explicit themes. This spread from rock to rap and hip-hop, so that quite a bit of the most popular music by the 1980s had some explicit lyrics.

Congressional hearings in 1989 resulted in warning labels on record and CD covers, but their effectiveness has been questionable. In fact, many music sellers noted that music labeled with warning stickers sells faster, and sells at a higher volume, to both children and adults. In part, lyrics that might be considered problematic were very pervasive. In fact, even more challenging artists, like Cee Lo Green, whose big hit "Fxxk you" could not be said out loud on radio, are now widely distributed and played on the radio. However, the climate for acceptance of rough lyrics can change.

The concentration of power in top retailers was apparent when, starting in 1997, Walmart refused to carry certain recordings that it considered offensive, including all CDs with parental advisory stickers. Walmart has some reason for caution. It was sued by parents over a CD by rock group Evanescence that contains swear words (Freemuse, 2007). Some artists now change lyrics in order to ensure that major chains, like Walmart, will carry them.

GLOBAL IMPACT OF POP MUSIC GENRES

Rap and hip-hop have flowed quickly and widely out into the rest of the world, where many people are listening to U.S. hip-hop and rap artists like Kanye West. This type of music is popular in a wide variety of countries from China to Mozambique, so much so that some people are worried about musical homogenization as hip-hop and rap replace earlier imports, like U.S. rock and local music. Clearly, this wave is sinking in. The authors have heard people singing or humming along to hip-hop in Brazil, Denmark, France, Mexico, Mozambique, and Taiwan. U.S. hip-hop dominates among imported music in many countries.

For many, however, the big story is not Chinese kids listening to Lil Wayne, but Chinese kids and others doing their own hip-hop and rap. A remarkable number of countries are producing their own rap or hip-hop, and local versions tend to do much better on the local charts than the imports. Many musicians also see rap as an appropriate music of protest to use in their own circumstances. Moroccans living in France listen to rap from home to feel less culturally isolated or to protest their living conditions in France. A Brazilian documentary, *Little Prince's Rap Against the Wicked Souls* (2000), shows a local rap group cheering on a vigilante who takes on drug gangs when the police don't act.

Some critics insist that hip-hop and rap reflect a specific urban African-American culture and history, so other cultures' appropriations of them would be a new form of cultural imperialism, homogenization, or Americanization. For example, the original film *Black Orpheus* (1959) introduced Brazilian samba and bossa nova to the rest of the world, so many Brazilians were shocked when a remake, *Orfeu* (1999), featured as much Brazilian hip-hop as samba. Many others see hip-hop and rap as just another global musical genre to be appropriated and localized. For example, well-known Brazilian samba and pop musician Caetano Veloso defended the use of hip-hop in *Orfeu* as highly appropriate for dramatizing issues in Brazilian slums and a good fit for the adaptability of Brazilian culture (2002). Analyzing this as musical hybridity, it seems that cultures have never been static. They always take in new forms and ideas (Pieterse, 2004). Rap itself is a hybrid with many roots, particularly from Africa. So it fits well with the ongoing diaspora of African musical traditions across the globe, which previously nourished rock and samba, among many others.

SUMMARY&REVIEW

WHAT KIND OF MUSIC INDUSTRY EXISTED BEFORE THE PHONOGRAPH?

Music was performed live for audiences. It was also printed as sheet music and sold for home performance. The phonograph made casual listening easier and increased the sizes of audiences for music.

WHAT WERE THE MAIN ORIGINAL TRADITIONS IN POPULAR MUSIC?

Blues is an African-American musical tradition based primarily on guitar and distinctive plaintive lyrics. Gospel originated as southern Protestant religious music. Country music developed from English, Scottish, and Irish roots with similar instrumentation and ballad forms.

HOW DID RADIO CHANGE THE MUSIC INDUSTRY?

It further increased the reach of musical performances. It also increased the size of the audience to a truly mass audience and emphasized performers over composers. It created national audiences for music but also permitted regional genres—such as country and western and blues—to evolve.

HOW DID RADIO BROADCASTING AFFECT THE RECORDING INDUSTRY?

At first, the recording industry's sales fell off, as people moved to purchase radios instead. Over the long run, the recording industry came to rely on radio to make people aware of artists and recordings that they could purchase.

HOW HAVE THE MAIN MUSIC GENRES EVOLVED?

The most popular genres in the 1920s were probably big band music, jazz, country, blues, classical, Broadway tunes, and gospel. From those evolved rhythm and blues, soul, and rock and roll, which have fragmented and further evolved into contemporary genres like hip-hop, rap, metal, modern rock, alternative, etc.

HOW DO COMPACT DISCS WORK?

Whereas phonographs reproduce analog sound from grooves in records, CDs reproduce sound digitally, from 1s and 0s recorded as pits on the CD surface. The digital signal is then reconverted to analog form and sent as electrical impulses to the amplifier and then to the speakers.

HOW DOES MAGNETIC RECORDING ON TAPE WORK?

The tape passes over a recording head, an electromagnet that rearranges the magnetic fields on the tape according to an electric current produced by a microphone. When playing back, the tape runs over another electromagnetic head, which responds to the patterns stored on the tape and generates another modulated current that is sent to a loudspeaker.

HOW IS THE INTERNET AFFECTING MUSIC DISTRIBUTION?

Some artists are now releasing music over the Internet to increase their audience and promoting it through social media. Internet users are also exchanging copyrighted music files over services like LimeWire, leading record companies to fear that they are losing control over the business. Record companies and recording artists have sued both MP3 exchange services and Internet radio stations to get better compensation.

WHAT ARE THE KEY COMPONENTS OF THE RECORDING INDUSTRY ORGANIZATION?

They include the talent (the singers and musicians), the recording studios and technical producers, the recording company, the distributors, and retailers. Recording studios are diversifying, as cheap digital systems based in computers let small studios and even individuals record music too.

WHAT ARE RECORD LABELS?

Labels of record companies are particular names for a group of recordings, which usually represent a consistent type of music. One company may own several diverse labels.

HOW ARE RECORDS DISTRIBUTED AND SOLD?

Record companies decide which albums and songs to promote through radio, billboards, newspaper and magazine ads, and music videos. The record companies distribute recordings in a variety of ways, including rack jobbers, retail music stores, big-chain stores, Internet stores or catalogs, and record clubs. The big three are Sony, Universal, and Warner, which have over 80 percent of the U.S. market.

WHAT ARE THE LIMITS ON FREEDOM OF SPEECH IN RECORDINGS?

The record industry practiced some self-censorship up through the 1960s. But after that major rock groups carried by major labels began to use more graphic language and explicit themes. Congressional hearings in 1989 resulted in warning labels on record and CD covers, but their effectiveness has been questionable, since even more challenging artists, like Khia or Ludacris, are now widely distributed and played on the radio.

WHAT ARE THE MUSIC COPYRIGHT ISSUES?

Issues include making sure that artists get reimbursed for radio and Internet play and trying to forestall piracy of digital recordings over the Internet.

THINKING CRITICALLY
ABOUT THE MEDIA

1. How does the history of popular music help us understand where music is going as a business? As artistic statements? As politics?

2. What can other media industries learn from the challenge digital media created for the music industry?

3. Has large-scale listening to black music by white audiences helped race relations?

4. Does the drive by the music industry to discover the next big hit keep other interesting music from being discovered?

5. Is the American music scene too fragmented? Or is it a good thing that people listen to just what they want?

KEY TERMS

AAC (p. 143)

acoustic (p. 132)

bluegrass (p. 133)

blues (p. 133)

copyright (p. 137)

cover (p. 134)

disc jockey (DJ) (p. 134)

electromagnetic recording (p. 143)

gospel (p. 133)

high fidelity (p. 133)

hybrid (p. 134)

mashup (p. 150)

MP3 (p. 141)

nickelodeon (p. 132)

payola (p. 134)

stereo (p. 143)

Victrola (p. 132)

WILL SERVICES LIKE PANDORA, where individuals create their own customized channels, be the death of broadcast radio, or will popular local DJs like Cherry Martinez at Power 105.1 in New York hold their audiences?

6

RADIO

HISTORY: HOW RADIO BEGAN

SAVE THE *TITANIC*: WIRELESS TELEGRAPHY

In 1896, Italian inventor Guglielmo Marconi created a "wireless telegraph" that used **radio waves** to carry messages in Morse code. This was the first practical use of radio. Marconi employed his business flair to establish the Marconi Wireless Telegraph Company, setting up a series of shore-based radio stations to receive and retransmit telegraph signals to oceangoing ships, where telegraph wires could not reach. His company also manufactured and operated the radio equipment and dominated radio in Europe and the United States in an early example of global **vertical integration**.

In 1912, the wireless telegraph played a pivotal role in the *Titanic* disaster. The British ocean liner struck an iceberg and sank suddenly in the North Atlantic. It sent radio distress calls, tapped out in Morse code over the Marconi wireless system, relayed to radio operators in New York.

Not only was radio crucial to saving many passengers, it became central to reporting about the disaster, riveting people on both sides of the Atlantic. This attracted public attention to the fledgling technology—so much that the U.S. Congress took note and placed radio licensing under the supervision of the Department of Commerce in the **Radio Act of 1912,** beginning **regulation** of the airwaves.

Radio waves are composed of electromagnetic energy and rise and fall in regular cycles.

Vertical integration is when a company with the same owner handles different aspects of a business (within the same industry), such as film production and distribution.

Radio Act of 1912 first licensed radio transmitters.

Regulation is government restriction or supervision of privately owned activity.

157

1896	Marconi develops radio transmitter, goes into business	1970	FM stations increase, go stereo, target segmented audience
1906	De Forest invents vacuum tube	1996	Telecommunications Act sets off radio station merger frenzy
1920	Frank Conrad starts KDKA in Pittsburgh		
1926	RCA starts NBC Radio Network; AT&T pulls out of broadcasting	2000	Pandora and other Internet radio services take off
1949	DJ era of radio begins	2011	Over half of Americans tune into Internet radio each week

REGULATION OF RADIO

> A **patent** gives an inventor the exclusive right to make, use, or sell an invention for 20 years.
>
> **Frequency** is the number of cycles that radio waves complete in a second.
>
> **License** is a legal permission to operate a transmitter. Licenses grant legal permission to operate a radio transmitter.

During World War I, the U.S. Navy accelerated radio technology by intervening in **patent** disputes between Marconi and other early inventors, standardizing the technologies. After the war, Marconi tried to buy U.S. patents to consolidate a U.S.–European communications monopoly, but the U.S. government opposed foreign control of a technology so crucial for military purposes. The Navy still held temporary control over radio technology and assets. It proposed making radio a government operation. A negotiated settlement forced Marconi, an Italian citizen, to sell his American assets to General Electric (GE), which set up a new company, Radio Corporation of America (RCA), with American Telephone & Telegraph (AT&T) and Westinghouse to develop the radio business in the United States. GE, RCA, and AT&T set up a patent pool in 1920 because none of them owned all the patents to make completely functioning radio transmitters or receivers (Streeter, 1996).

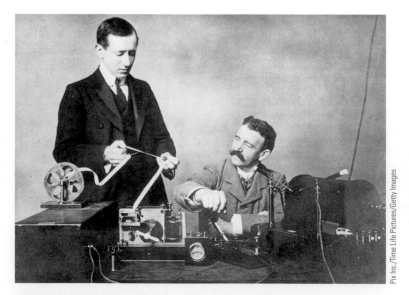

Pix Inc./Time Life Pictures/Getty Images

BEFORE CDS Early radio broadcasted Morse code, not music. Here Marconi, at left, receives the first transatlantic signal.

BROADCASTING BEGINS

Frank Conrad, a Westinghouse engineer, began the first regularly scheduled radio broadcasts in the United States in 1920, attracting interest and newspaper coverage. A Pittsburgh department store sold radios to pick up Conrad's broadcasts. Westinghouse realized that regular radio broadcasts could help sell radios, so it opened station KDKA in Pittsburgh. Retail stores started radio stations to promote their goods. Newspapers saw news potential; schools and churches saw educational possibilities. With so many rushing into radio, the Commerce Department was asked to combat **frequency** interference, so it issued hundreds of **licenses** in 1923.

Two visions of radio probably determined its future. In 1916, David Sarnoff, then commercial manager of American Marconi, wrote a prophetic memo to his boss. He proposed "a plan of development which would make radio a 'household utility' in the same sense as the piano or phonograph. The idea is to bring music into the house by wireless. . . . The Receiver can be designed in the form of a simple 'Radio Music Box' and arranged for several different wavelengths, which should be changeable with the throwing of a single switch or pressing of a single button." Sarnoff's memo was ignored, but he anticipated perfectly the physical form that radio would take within 10 years. Later, as head of RCA, he had a chance to help make this vision of radio and a similar vision of television a reality.

The second key vision for radio—entertainment supported by advertising—came from AT&T's station WEAF, started in 1922 in New Jersey. Following the model of the telephone industry, AT&T charged content providers a fee for the use of its radio stations, based on how much airtime they used. This evolved into letting manufacturers sponsor programs to advertise their goods, then into advertisers paying to have their ads carried on programs. WEAF broadcast the first "commercial." Advertisers immediately responded to the opportunity. Commercial broadcasting grew quickly.

By 1927, U.S. radio had attained a distinct shape. Privately owned stations were linked into networks that determined most of the program choices, focused on popular entertainment, heavily tilted toward music, and supported by commercial advertising—a model it retains today. This had an enormous impact on U.S. culture as people became more aware of how those in other parts of the country lived. It also increased awareness of national issues; the experience of being a national audience inspired a feeling of being more of a nation (Douglas, 2004).

A number of strong economic interests came together to set this pattern. RCA and other radio manufacturers wanted to sell radio sets. They wanted the most broadly appealing content broadcast to sell more radios. Radio stations, and soon radio networks, discovered a way to make a great deal of money selling advertising. Networks arose to supply stations with the most popular entertainment in a way that spread costs across a number of stations. Advertisers saw a way to create a mass consumer public, turning people first and foremost into consumers by promoting their goods on the airwaves. This changed how Americans thought about money, careers, credit, even where they wanted to live: country, small town, or city (Hilmes, 1997).

Radio offered advertisers direct access to the home. To increase the size of the audience for their ads, advertisers steered stations toward entertainment programs, which were more lucrative than news or education (Streeter, 1996). In the 1920s, regulators and the radio industry worried that audiences would reject radio if it carried too much advertising. However, people were so enthusiastic about the new medium that

SOS Distress signals from the *Titanic* called public attention to radio communication.

Bettmann/Corbis

they accepted the ads without much objection, and a commercial advertising-based model was soon firmly entrenched (Barnouw, 1966). This quick shaping of radio by commercial interests laid down a pattern that other media followed, both in the United States and abroad. The global shape of broadcasting today reflects this then-unique arrangement of radio in the United States.

BBC, LICENSE FEES, AND THE ROAD NOT TAKEN

In 1922–1923, the British sent a commission to the United States to study radio development. They observed a rush toward a radio industry dominated by musical entertainment and paid for by advertising. They saw that as a waste of the medium's cultural and educational potential. On returning home, they recommended a public radio monopoly oriented toward education and culture, financed by a license fee paid by listeners, and overseen by a board intended to keep it independent of both government and private interests, such as advertisers. This system, which became known as the British Broadcasting Corporation (BBC), was highly regarded for news, cultural, and educational broadcasting, although many find some of the programming elitist, dry, and stuffy. Globally it represents an alternative to the model chosen by the United States in the 1920s.

RADIO NETWORKS

AT&T became the first broadcast network, as it used its phone lines to link several of its stations. However, the U.S. government and major electronics companies opposed AT&T's domination of both broadcasting and telephony (Sterling & Kittross, 1990). Thus, to keep its telephone monopoly, AT&T sold out to RCA in 1926 and agreed to act as a transmission medium for all radio networks on an equal basis.

PAYING FOR PROGRAMMING: THE RISE OF RADIO NETWORKS

RCA set up its radio network, the National Broadcasting Corporation (NBC), in 1926. Networking, linking of stations together to share programming costs, made each station cheaper to operate by realizing economies of scale (see Chapter 2). Competition came when the Columbia Broadcasting System (CBS) quickly put together a network to rival NBC's. Both networks had their own stations, called owned-and-operated stations, or **O&Os**. Both also began to attract a number of **affiliated** stations, which they did not own but which carried their network programs as well (Sterling & Kittross, 2001).

Early network radio programming in the 1920s–1930s was focused on music but also included news, comedy, variety shows, soap operas, detective dramas, sports, suspense, and action adventures. Many radio performers came in from vaudeville-style theater, such as George Burns and Gracie Allen. Comic books lent heroes, such as Superman, to radio adventure shows. Pulp-fiction westerns like *Riders of the Purple Sage* fed into radio westerns, such as *Gunsmoke*.

Because recording technology had not achieved very high fidelity, music was primarily broadcast live. Recording artists and companies were also initially

O&O is a TV or radio station that is owned and operated by a network.

An **affiliate** is a station that contracts with networks to distribute their programming.

unwilling to let radio play their recorded and copyrighted music until a royalty system was devised to compensate them. Networks introduced the most popular groups and orchestras to the entire country, which reinforced their appeal and power. The major pop music of the day included big band, light classical music, and movie and show tunes. Eventually, however, radio also stimulated a demand for a variety of musical genres, ranging from classical to country and western.

RADIO NETWORK POWER

There was concern that the radio networks were abusing their power in one-sided dealings with their affiliated stations and with the on-air talent. The FCC's 1941 **chain broadcasting** ruling prohibited the networks from forcing programming on affiliates and put the networks out of the talent-booking business. The FCC also forced NBC to sell off its second network, which became the American Broadcasting Corporation (ABC).

Network radio remained strong through World War II. Money spent on radio ads doubled, surpassing expenditures on newspapers. Radio was the paramount information medium of the war. Internationally, the use of radio for propaganda purposes frightened many people and stimulated research into the power of mass media over their audiences (see Chapter 13).

CBS radio reporter Edward R. Murrow broadcast memorable live reports from London during World War II (1939–1945), dramatically covering the German bombing of London. His reports conveyed vivid, realistic, and often highly moving word pictures. He emerged as one of the most credible and admired newsmen in the CBS news organization (Edwards, 2004) and helped network radio achieve preeminence as a source of news.

COMPETITION FROM TELEVISION

After 1948, television exploded across the United States (see Chapter 8). Radio was quickly and adversely affected. Many non-musical broadcast programming genres, from news to soap operas, moved to television.

Radio networks saw their own parent corporations, such as RCA and CBS, refocus their energy on new television networks. They were entranced with both the audience and advertiser response to television, seeing it as an even more profitable medium than radio. So their radio networks were left to struggle to try to find new niches and functions.

NETWORKS FALL, DISC JOCKEYS RULE

As television's popularity skyrocketed and it became the main source of mass entertainment nationwide, network radio began to slip. Audience attention, especially during the prime evening hours, moved to television. Advertising followed popular programs and audiences to television. Stations began to

AND NOW, LIVE FROM NEW YORK! Early network radio like this early game show, Pot-O-Gold, was all live, but also very popular and eagerly supported by advertisers like Tums.

[**Chain broadcasting** is synonymous with a broadcasting network.]

THIS IS THE WOLFMAN HOWLIN' ATCHA! DJs like Wolfman Jack characterized radio from the 1950s to the 1980s.

leave the networks and network revenue dropped even more. Radio station management explored new ways to attract a more local audience.

Radio advertising shifted from a national to a local focus and began to rely on cheaper, more localized **formats,** such as recorded music, news, and talk. Success began to depend on the talent of each station's own announcers, on their ability to find the right music mix for their local market. Programming strategies organized around a **playlist** of music and focused on a particular genre or audience.

New radio formats featured rhythm and blues (R&B) and rock and roll. Disc jockeys (DJs) played records aimed at local audiences, so although many records became national hits, local music, such as bluegrass in the South, blues in Chicago, and country and western in rural areas, all saw stations thrive that catered to those local needs.

Todd Storz probably invented Contemporary Hit Radio (CHR), or **Top 40,** in 1949. He wondered why radio could not be more like a jukebox, playing the hit songs that people really wanted to hear the most, over and over. Top 40 was the dominant radio format from the 1950s until the early 1970s. It played a mix of rock and roll, pop, Motown, and some R&B.

Formats are radio label content aimed at a specific audience.

Playlists are the songs picked for air play.

Top 40 is a radio format that replays the top 40 songs heavily.

THE FM REVOLUTION

The growth of FM radio revived radio in the 1960s. FM has high-fidelity sound, but a short range—within the line of sight of the radio transmitter. That allows for more stations in each market by reducing interference with stations in nearby markets that use the same frequency. Since each market could have at least 15 FM stations, there was a tendency to focus on segmented audiences with more specific formulas and formats. AM licenses were difficult and expensive to obtain, whereas licenses for FM stations were much easier to get.

Radio continued to grow, along with the boom in pop music. Both FM and 33 1/3 rpm records moved into stereo sound (two separate, coordinated channels of music). By the late 1960s, many popular groups were recording songs much longer than the two- to three-minute cuts typical of Top 40 AM radio, but which were fine for new formats on FM.

In the 1970s, "rock" radio split into Top 40, new wave, heavy metal, punk, soul, and disco. The 1980s and 1990s added formats for alternative, industrial/techno, new age, ska, reggae, rap, and hip-hop. These stations gave expression to musical subgenres, the audiences that enjoyed them, and the advertisers that coveted those subcultures. Subcultures like punks, skaters, or hip-hop not only listened to different music but consumed very different clothes and shoes, so marketers targeted them via specific radio formats.

Some targeted FM radio formats, such as classical, jazz, or album-oriented rock, took advantage of the musical quality of FM's higher fidelity and new stereo capability. Much of the audience was also interested in improved sound quality, because high-fidelity stereo systems were becoming much more popular, and that had a decisive appeal for discerning listeners (Jones, 1992). FM came to dominate the radio industry. By 1979, FM stations drew over half of the audience, and their share was growing steadily.

LOCAL DJS DECLINE: A NEW GENERATION OF NETWORK RADIO

Though radio was characterized by local operations in the 1970s and 1980s, new forms of network radio began to emerge in the 1990s. Some stations bought into centrally produced program formats distributed via satellite. Large radio ownership groups began to act like the radio networks of old, looking for economies of scale from centralized program production.

To meet the demand for interesting music, news, and talk programs on dozens of FM and AM stations in each market, a number of outlets began to produce programs for **syndication.** Conservative pundit Rush Limbaugh developed a network of stations that carried his syndicated program. Other companies began to offer complete radio formats, such as "The Mix's" alternative rock format on syndicated distribution. Advertising, the DJ's patter, and even "local" traffic, and weather are increasingly broadcast from a distant location using local information. Regionalization is the dominant trend, with Clear Channel dismissing dozens of local DJs in its stations in small markets in 2011, replacing them with regional voice talent who voice "local" stations to reduce costs.

Changes in ownership limits established in the **1996 Telecommunications Act** permitted radio station groups to acquire many more stations and grow much larger. The new regulations lifted national caps on how many stations a group could own but limited ownership within local radio markets, depending on the size of the market. As a result, thousands of stations changed hands in a few short years and ownership consolidated.

Clear Channel Communications was the largest ownership group that emerged. In a number of local markets, stations belonging to just two or three

[**Syndication** is rental or licensing of media products.]

[The **Telecommunications Act of 1996** is federal legislation that deregulated radio ownership rules and the communications media. It opened the U.S. telecommunications industry to competition.]

groups controlled 80 to 90 percent of radio ad revenues. That peak of concentration raised both policy questions and internal management problems. Clear Channel never became as profitable as anticipated, so it sold off over 400 stations from a peak of 1,100. After declining in 2009, radio advertising sales rose 6 percent in 2010 (but only 1 percent in 2011).

With the return of advertising dollars, group owners are again on a buying spree. Clear Channel is adding stations again and is challenged by Cumulus Media. Cumulus is also challenging Clear Channel's talk show king Rush Limbaugh with new hosts including Geraldo Rivera and former presidential candidate Mike Huckabee. Internet and mobile phone music apps (see Chapter 12) revenues rose from 2009 to 2011, so Clear Channel and others have invested in new media as well.

NEW GENRES: ALTERNATIVE, RAP, AND HIP-HOP RADIO

Radio stations, particularly in FM, have continued to change or modify formats to follow the evolution of music genres and audience interests. For example, rap and hip-hop became prominent in the "urban" radio format. Rap emerged from New York street disc jockeys who used turntables as instruments to set up a beat to rap, and talk in improvised rhymes over music samples. Both African-Americans and Latinos have been involved in the development of rap since the early days, but black artists have been promoted more heavily by the music industry, so much that rap and hip-hop are perceived by many as black genres. Rap, hip-hop and the kind of contemporary R&B of artists like Beyonce have given African-American artists perhaps their highest visibility in pop music and Top 40 radio since Motown in the 1960s.

Neal Preston/Historical/CORBIS

ONLY ROCK N' ROLL The Rolling Stones are one of the bands that launched album-oriented FM radio in the 1960s.

Latino artists have created a strong rap and hip-hop tradition of their own, which has fed into new musical genres and radio formats like reggaeton, mixing elements of hip-hop, reggae, and various Latin genres. An increasing number of Spanish-language rap format radio stations are a good example of how music genres grow and subdivide, closely followed by radio formats. Some artists start in a smaller format, and then move to more widespread formats, as Latino artist Cypress Hill did when he moved from Latino to hip-hop stations and gained overall hip-hop radio popularity. Rap and hip-hop have also spread internationally, so raperos and reggaeton singers in Mexico now create music that flows back into the United States and vice versa. For example, a new radio format called "Spanish Contemporary" includes salsa and other Caribbean music, Mexican norteño, and Latin alternative.

RADIO IN THE DIGITAL AGE

Satellite radio offers hundreds more channels than terrestrial broadcasters, which are limited to, at most, 20 to 30 FM channels and a dozen or so AM channels in most American cities and towns. The two companies that dominated satellite radio, XM and Sirius, merged their operations in 2008. They hoped that by making exclusive deals with the likes of Howard Stern, they would pull listeners from conventional broadcasts. Broadcasters worried that satellite radio would lead to a decline in both number and variety of local radio stations, plus a concentration of programming decisions in the hands of fewer companies. However, after several tentative years, satellite radio is just now growing in the number of listeners and in revenue, finally turning a profit with 21 million subscribers in 2011.

Internet radio is also growing, and quickly. Web radio networks list thousands of Internet radio stations. They cover mainstream pop artists and include many of the familiar formats of commercial radio, like country and western or adult contemporary. Hundreds of radio stations feed their programming to the

MEDIA&CULTURE

SATELLITE RADIO—WITH FREEDOM COMES RESPONSIBILITY?

For radio personalities looking for the freedom to say and play what they want without restriction, subscription satellite radio seems like the answer. Just as network television and cable are regulated differently by the FCC (see Chapter 8), satellite radio is not subject to the same rules regarding content as is "terrestrial" radio.

In 2004, Janet Jackson's "wardrobe malfunction" during the Super Bowl halftime show set in motion a culture clash among lawmakers, regulators, broadcasters, and consumers about what content should and should not be allowed on radio and television. Ultimately, Congress increased fines on broadcasters who aired "indecent" content. That put a huge damper on explicit broadcasting content and hit shock jocks particularly hard—hence Howard Stern's jump to Sirius.

How satellite radio exercises its freedom remains to be seen—or heard. Will this new outlet provide ever more explicitly sexual and controversial material and will audiences still care? Or will it provide a stimulating diversity of content and more challenging journalism? Ultimately, it will be the public who will decide with their subscription dollars and consumption choices. Or should regulation be changed to treat satellite radio more like broadcast radio?

STOP&REVIEW

1. How did advertising come to dominate radio economics?
2. What kind of regulation was necessary for radio to develop technically?
3. What kinds of programming characterized radio networks in the 1930s–1940s? Why did they decline?
4. How did radio formats change after the decline of radio networks?
5. How did FM radio and 1960s–1970s music genres affect each other?
6. Why did radio station ownership concentrate in the 1990s?
7. How do new technologies like webcasts, smartphone apps, and podcasts affect broadcast radio?

[**Podcasting** is recorded messages or audio programs distributed through download to computers, iPods, or other portable digital music players.]

AP Photo/Michael Becker/PictureGroup

YOU'RE ALL WE NEED Despite changes in technology to play and deliver music, new genres like reggaeton and hit music by popular artists like Rihanna are still what draw people.

World Wide Web through sites such as Yahoo.com in an effort to reach out-of-town listeners and people at work. But there are many "Internet-only" channels that cannot be found on the air, playing things much too specific or offbeat to ever get on the air. According to Arbitron, the radio ratings company, 56 percent of Americans over 12 listen to online radio networks while 93 percent still listen to broadcast radio on a weekly basis (Arbitron, 2011).

When radio stations offer Internet streams it can boost the number of listeners they have, but any who tune in from outside the station's local broadcast market do not support the prevailing broadcast radio business model that depends on local ad sales. **Podcasting** is also a threat in that it lets almost any individual create audio programs that can be downloaded onto computers or iPods. The current digital trend is "radio" apps for smartphones and tablet computers, offered by groups from Clear Channel to Pandora and Spotify. A listener in rural Iowa who wants gospel-flavored Latino hip-hop probably won't find it on the local airwaves but can easily do so on Web-based stations, like DAR.fm, podcasts, or a perhaps even a smartphone app. However, podcast and app listeners, DAR.fm users, and subscribers to the new "cloud" music services (see Chapter 5) all threaten the traditional radio broadcast model in that they can subtract music fans from the radio advertising base in the local markets where their listeners live. Social media also pose a continuing threat to the conventional broadcast model. The music file-sharing craze that rocked the music industry (see Chapter 5) was an early social media phenomenon that pre-dated the rise of social networking services like MySpace and Facebook and continues today. Now music fans can share their favorite tunes with their Facebook friends, bypassing CD retailers and iTunes as well as their local radio stations. YouTube is another social media threat to radio broadcasters following a deal that was struck between its owner Google and music publishers that allows advertising to run along-side music videos on the site. Meanwhile, new artists like rapper Mac Miller are finding that they can promote their music through social media and can distribute it online without the benefit of radio airplay.

Nonetheless, broadcast radio continues as an enjoyable and even indispensible medium for millions of listeners, from those who want the hits to those who want the news from NPR. Although traditional AM/FM radio revenues increased in recent years, broadcast radio is challenged by competition from new digital media, and changes in listener interests. Another tactic is to hobble the competition, such as by lobbying the FCC for rules that prevent satellite radio from transmitting local traffic information and supporting extra copyright fees on Internet radio. At the other extreme, broadcasters lost their campaign to limit extremely local low-power radio stations, so the FCC will begin to license 100s more. But broadcasters are also banking on an innovative new digital offering of their own, high-definition radio and there are over 1500 HD radio stations already in operation, or about 10 percent of all radio stations (Arbitron, 2011). Stay tuned (to the next section) for more on that.

TECHNOLOGY TRENDS: INSIDE YOUR RADIO

FROM MARCONI'S RADIO TO YOUR RADIO

Radio was the first wireless communications medium but the others that followed, including broadcast television and cell phones, follow the same basic principles of electromagnetism that Marconi harnessed in the nineteenth century. If you are interested in how things work—or are curious about the radiation that pulses through your head when you hold your cell phone to your ear—then be sure to read Technology Demystified: Fun with Electromagnetism?

TECHNOLOGY DEMYSTIFIED

FUN WITH ELECTROMAGNETISM?

You may remember a demonstration by your fifth-grade teacher, we'll call her Mrs. McGiver. She showed you how you could make an ordinary iron nail into an electromagnet by winding a wire around it and connecting it to a battery, remember? Then Mrs. McGiver sprinkled some iron filings on a piece of cardboard, reconnected the electromagnet to the battery, and showed you that she could move the filings around the surface of the cardboard by passing the magnet under it. This proved that electromagnetic fields are invisible and act at a distance without any physical medium to convey them, just as a radio transmitter affects the antenna on your radio from miles away.

Then she hooked up a coil of wire to a meter that measured electric current and moved a magnet back and forth through the middle of the coil. As the magnet moved, the needle on the meter twitched, showing that a changing magnetic field made an electric current flow in the wire. This is what happens inside your radio antenna and also in the playback head of a tape recorder, converting a magnetic field back to electricity.

Like the waves of water, radio waves rise and fall in regular patterns, called cycles. The number of cycles that the waves complete in a second is their frequency and is measured in **Hertz (Hz)**. We refer to the height of the wave as its amplitude, and the phase refers to the point in the cycle at which we begin. In water, we can splash by either forcing our hand down on the water's surface, creating a "trough," or by bringing our hand up from below the surface, creating a "crest." The spectrum is a means of classifying electromagnetic radiation according to its frequency. The sounds made by our stereos and our iPods are between 20 and 20,000 Hz, the range of frequencies that can be heard by the human ear.

The radio frequencies used in our consumer electronics devices are organized into bands. For example, AM radio is in the High Frequency band; VHF television (channels 2–13, see Chapter 8) takes its name from the Very High Frequency band—that's also where FM radio is located. Similarly, UHF is the Ultra High Frequency band. Cell phones and satellites use yet higher-frequency bands.

Communication channels are assigned according to the frequency of their carrier waves. But additional frequencies clustering around the carrier are needed to encode the audio or video information, and the more space we have for each channel, the more information we can transmit. The total range of frequencies needed is the bandwidth of the channel. AM radio channels are 10,000

Hz, compared to 100,000 for FM radio and 6 million for television. Some parts of the spectrum are better than others. For example, the AM radio spectrum is highly desirable because waves can travel thousands of miles, whereas FM signals can barely peep over the horizon.

AM is short for **amplitude modulation**, which means that the sound information is carried in variations in the height, or amplitude, of the radio wave. In an AM radio system, the electric current that comes out of a microphone or an electronic recording device is combined with a high-frequency electromagnetic carrier wave that corresponds to the frequency of a particular radio channel that can be found between 535 and 1,705 kHz. For example, the carrier wave is 540,000 Hz if you have your radio tuned to 540 on the AM dial. The combined wave is amplified and fed into a radio transmitter, which is essentially a giant electromagnet. The combined electromagnetic wave induces a weak electric current inside your radio antenna. Then the carrier frequency is removed, and the original audio is recovered, amplified, and sent to the speakers (see Figure 6.1).

In **FM (frequency modulation)** radio, the sound information is carried by variations in the frequency of the radio wave around the central carrier frequency, which is 101,700,000 Hz if you are tuned to FM 101.7. Compared to AM, FM has a greater frequency range and less static, so stereo broadcasting was begun in the FM band (88–108 MHz). The FM channels are wide enough so that two slightly different versions of the broadcast can be carried. These are electronically combined inside your receiver to produce the two separate signals you hear in your left and right speaker.

Hertz (Hz) is a measure of the frequency of a radio wave in cycles per second.

AM, or **amplitude modulation**, carries information in the height, or amplitude, of the radio wave.

FM, or **frequency modulation**, carries information in variations in the frequency of the radio wave.

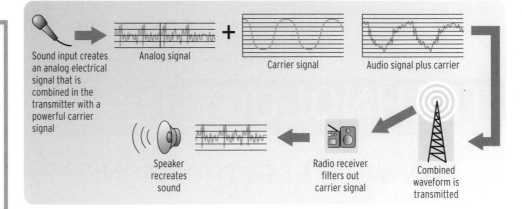

Sound input creates an analog electrical signal that is combined in the transmitter with a powerful carrier signal

Analog signal

Carrier signal

Audio signal plus carrier

Speaker recreates sound

Radio receiver filters out carrier signal

Combined waveform is transmitted

FIGURE 6.1 HOW AM RADIO BROADCASTING USES RADIO WAVES The announcer's voice is converted to electricity by the microphone. This electrical signal is then combined with a powerful, high-frequency carrier signal and transmitted to the home receiver. The receiver filters out the carrier and re-creates the original electrical analog signal, which the loudspeaker converts back to sound energy.

HIGH-DEFINITION RADIO

High-definition radio (formerly known as Digital Audio Broadcasting) transmits audio that has been converted to computer data, as in a CD recording, over the air from earthbound radio transmitters to special digital receivers. This increases the quality of the sound and makes radio signals less susceptible to fading. Near CD-quality sound is the result, leading to the "high-definition" label, borrowed from High Definition TV (see Chapter 8). The digital signal also includes information about the music so that listeners may set their radios to "seek hip-hop" if they so desire and see the name of the station and the tune they are listening to on their display. The digital signals can also pack additional channels of information, such as news updates and alerts about travel and weather conditions.

While HD radio has been on the air since 1997 in Europe, it is now finally catching on in the United States. To protect their vested interests, radio stations insisted that the new service be transmitted in the same frequency band and on the same channel (the approach is called "in band, on channel") as their current stations, while maintaining the conventional analog service, which took several years to perfect. Digital radio allows stations to broadcast several different channels. NPR stations have taken the lead in many areas, broadcasting a classical music channel in addition to their regular programming, for example.

SATELLITE RADIO TECHNOLOGY

Sirius transmits music via satellite to compact receivers via wafer-shaped antennas that can be placed on the roof of a car, bypassing earthbound radio stations entirely. Local repeaters mounted on the tops of buildings and hills operate in the same frequencies as the satellites and enable Sirius's signals to be available even if the view of the satellite is blocked by buildings or mountains. That is also what allows satellite radio to insert local traffic and weather reports—and potentially local ads—into their transmission.

INTERNET RADIO TECHNOLOGY

In 1995, hobbyists, ad agencies, and regular broadcast stations began to create full-time Internet radio stations. Near CD-quality stereo can be had if you have a fast enough network connection. Internet streaming technologies (see Chapter 9) make it possible to listen to programming in real time instead of downloading and saving prerecorded files. Podcasts are MP3 digital files (see Chapter 5) that can be downloaded to your cell phone, iPod, or mobile media player so you can listen to talk, news, music, or whatever someone with a computer, microphone, and software wants to create. A variety of radio stations now broadcast on the Internet, some through websites, some through apps on cell phones and tablets.

WEIGHING YOUR DIGITAL RADIO OPTIONS

HD radio stations are slowly becoming more available and may take off now that HD radios are being offered as original equipment in new cars. Home satellite radio receivers boasting hundreds of channels are already an option, although one that carries monthly subscription fees and which is not quite as portable as terrestrial radio. Many HD stations are also available now on Internet radio. Internet "appliances" that play online radio without a computer are already available, and the spread of Wi-Fi hotspots could make that another "free" option through which to access tens of thousands of stations. The latest iPods and iPads already have built-in Wi-Fi capabilities. Or, your cell phone/iPhone or tablet computer could be your digital radio (see Chapter 13). Several cell phone companies already offer music streams. Some of these impose monthly fees, depending on how much you listen, but cell phone providers are also experimenting with advertising-supported models. Branded streams through smartphone apps, like Pandora's or Clear Channel's iHeartRadio, are also growing, often at lower cost. Pandora became profitable in 2009 and had 700,000 songs in 2011. Services like Pandora and Spotify are also now working with social network programs like Facebook, so you can see what friends are listening to. So, unlike what they say in radio, don't stay tuned!

INDUSTRY: RADIO STATIONS AND GROUPS
RADIO IN THE AGE OF THE NEW MEDIA GIANTS

Radio lives in a contradictory time of countervailing trends. New digital technologies seem to allow many more new entrants in radio, broadly defined, although they have also led to the dominance of digital music by Apple. However, economic and regulatory changes also encouraged unprecedented concentration of the ownership of a few major players (in terms of hits, sales, and profits) all across the radio industry in the 1990s and early 2000s.

Radio stations were once owned by many kinds of individuals and small groups. After the 1996 Telecommunications Act deregulated ownership, concentration of station ownership in the hands of new, nonlocal groups increased dramatically (Table 6.1). The goal for these large groups has been to achieve national coverage. The largest of these, Clear Channel, boasts that it offers potential advertisers as much national coverage via its radio stations as do television networks. Groups can now own multiple radio stations in a single market, too, so they can offer a national advertiser exposure on several different formats, such as country, classic rock, and urban contemporary.

Regulations in the 1996 Telecommunication Act permitted increased **cross-ownership** across industries. So Cox (cable), Disney (film), and others acquired radio station groups, too. Most of the major film studios were involved in the music recording and distribution business. Regulations in effect until the 1980s prevented those studios from owning broadcast stations or networks, or vice versa. Now as studios like Disney acquire networks, such as ABC, they also get involved in the radio business, integrating broadcast distribution with their existing music production, an example of vertical integration. Some ownership groups, like Clear Channel, Entercom, Emmis, and Cumulus/Citadel, are based primarily in radio (*FreePress*, 2011), which reflects horizontal integration more than the kind of vertical integration represented by Time-Warner and CBS (see Chapter 2).

[**Cross-ownership** occurs when one firm owns different media outlets in the same area.]

INSIDE RADIO STATIONS

Radio stations vary greatly in the size and complexity of their staff. However, they all have to take care of certain basic functions: administrative (payroll, accounting, purchasing), technical (engineering, transmitter operation, maintenance of FCC logs), programming (local, news, music playlists, network or syndicated programs, promotion of programs), and sales (local sales, relations with national and regional sales firms). Traditionally, most of these were done locally with at least a small staff. However, with the growth of ownership groups, most of these functions are done by a centralized group staff, which covers a number of stations across a state or region. That has radically reduced the number of jobs available in radio.

In an independent station, the manager oversees planning, audience development, ratings, and sales. The program director supervises the

TABLE 6.1 Top Radio Industry Ownership Groups

RADIO GROUP	NUMBER OF STATIONS OWNED IN 2011
Clear Channel	850
Cumulus Broadcasting (purchased Citadel Communications)	579
Infinity Broadcasting	184
Entercom	104

Source: "Inside radio," WSJ Research; Broadcasting and Cable, corporate sites.

air sound, playlists, DJs, and announcers. A music director plans the playlists. Producers are usually required for talk shows and drive-time shows. Many stations also have a news director. Someone has to keep the station on the air, so there needs to be an engineer on duty. Commercial stations have a sales manager and an advertising sales staff. The advertising sales staff was crucial for selling local advertising. However, at network stations, most of these jobs have been consolidated on a regional basis. Even local weather is often remotely announced by someone hundreds of miles away.

When it comes to working with national advertisers who might want to sell national spot ads in the local market, that function is delegated to advertising representative firms. The representatives work on behalf of radio stations to sell ads to national advertisers, although large radio station groups are heavily involved in this as well. Advertising declined precipitously from 2008 to 2009, but local radio advertising revived from 2010 to 2011, particularly among growing Hispanic audiences.

Syndication (see Chapter 2) is an important factor in the radio industry. Syndicators produce programming for resale to other media outlets. For example, Sean Hannity, who started as a talk show host on WABC in 1997, was syndicated to other stations in other markets in 2001, and gained listeners rapidly as part of the wave of popular conservative talk show hosts in the early 2000s. In 2009, 530 stations carried his show, although some dropped it in 2011 amid controversy about conservative talk radio. Since 1996 he's also hosted television talk and politics shows on Fox News. There are 20 to 25 main syndicators.

NONCOMMERCIAL RADIO

Commercial radio dominates, but many stations are licensed for noncommercial formats and purposes. They tend to focus on education, classical music, jazz, independent rock, a variety of ethnic immigrant music, news, and public affairs. Many are owned by universities or other educational groups, although quite a few are owned by foundations, local nonprofit groups, churches, and others. More **low-power** licenses will now be offered by the FCC, so the diversity of ownership among noncommercial radio will probably increase greatly, as many community groups currently excluded from ownership would start broadcasting. (Some of those broadcast now as pirate stations, but FCC enforcement shuts down most unlicensed broadcasters relatively quickly. Others might move from Internet-only radio to broadcasting.) Most noncommercial broadcasters are FM stations, typically at the lower end of the dial. Most AM licenses were granted before the FCC started reserving a few licenses in each market for educational and noncommercial groups.

Public broadcasters are roughly one-third of all noncommercial stations, compared to a larger number of student-run stations at universities, and a smaller number of religious stations. Most depend on a mix of government, institutional, and listener support. Public stations tend to have more news, and more public affairs programs, than most commercial stations, although many AM stations and some FM stations now program a mix of news, syndicated talk shows (like Don Imus), sports talk, and local call-in talk shows.

Some public stations program music that is not commercially profitable, depending on the market. Over a third of public stations program a great deal

Low-power stations have more limited transmission power and cover smaller areas than regular FM stations.

Public broadcasters aim to serve public interests with information, culture, and news.

of classical music; others program jazz, and, on many college stations, folk, indie rock, noncommercial rap, and so forth. There are also a number of non-commercial stations that program to religious audiences or in languages spoken by too few local residents to support commercial broadcasting. Some large cities may have several noncommercial stations specializing in different formats and audiences.

The economics of noncommercial radio have always been difficult. Before 1990, public radio stations tended to depend quite a bit on program support from the Corporation for Public Broadcasting and financial support from federal and state governments. Since 1990, the funding for those national resources has been steadily cut back, so public stations have come to depend more on their sponsoring institutions (including many colleges and universities), other supportive local institutions, local sponsors, and direct contributions from listeners.

GENRES AROUND THE DIAL

RADIO FORMATS

[**Format clock** is an hourly radio programming schedule.]

Rigid musical programming formats dominate many stations. They focus on an hourly cycle of music, advertisements, station promotions, short news items, traffic reports, and weather reports. We can visualize this hourly cycle as a **format clock** in the shape of a record (see Figure 6.2). This hourly schedule shows the DJ when to play certain kinds of music; when to read a news item; when to play prerecorded ad spots or promotions (promos); when to read ad copy; and when to bring in another announcer for news, weather, sports, or traffic.

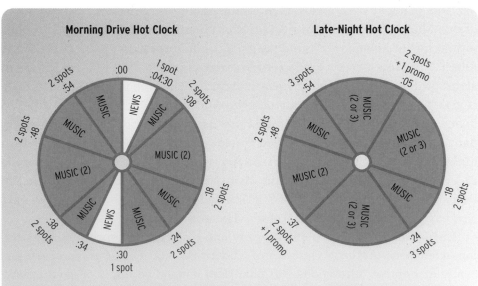

Source: Eastman and Ferguson, *Broadcast/cable programming: Strategies and practices*, 5th ed. Wadsworth Publishing, p. 364

FIGURE 6.2 CLOCK CONCEPT OF FORMATS Radio programmers and disc jockeys often use a clock concept to program what will be played in an hour: music from different lists, spots or ads, news and weather, and so on.

This hourly schedule often includes just enough news, sports, weather, and talk to meet the audience's general interests, but focuses on music. The key programmer, therefore, is the music director who selects the music that fits into the various parts of the hourly schedule to capture and hold the audience's attention. The music director creates a playlist of songs, organized by categories. A typical Contemporary Hit Radio (CHR) station has a playlist of a few top songs that might be repeated almost hourly at various points on the clock, interspersed with a few songs that are rising into popularity and a few others that are fading but still popular. Depending on the station, the DJ either plays exactly what the music director specifies or picks songs within a fairly narrow range. For stations that use syndicated program services or among stations owned by national groups, music selection is often centrally decided. Although the format clock is most associated with Top 40 radio (or CHR in contemporary terms), similar repetitive patterns may be found at country and western, urban contemporary, and even classical stations.

The format clock is no longer followed as religiously as it once was. For example, many stations have turned to a menu of talk and humor lightly interspersed with music during the morning drive-time hours, while focusing more on music later in the day. Others vary their music blocks to provide "Thirty continuous minutes of commercial-free music" or "Twelve in a row" in hopes of attracting audiences during commercial breaks at other stations.

These blocks may be commercial-free but not promotion-free, as radio stations seem to be constantly promoting themselves. The various on-air contests, station identifications, listener call-ins, dedication lines, and concert promotions are a vital part of radio programming, too, to build listener loyalty and get them to put that station on the preset buttons of their car radio, or the equivalent on their mobile apps or computer.

THE ROLE OF RADIO RATINGS

Inside the radio business, many professionals see their advertisers as the real customers. Clear Channel, for example, boldly states that it is in the business of selling audiences to advertisers. In order to persuade those advertisers to buy time on their stations, they rely on audience research to show how large their audience is and, more important for many advertisers, who the audience is. This kind of pragmatic audience research is called a **ratings** study. They estimate how many people are listening to a station at a certain time. Ratings also break down the audience by key demographics that are particularly important to advertisers, so they know whether the people their ad is reaching are older or younger, male or female, Anglo, Latino, or African-American, and so on.

Arbitron is the leading provider of radio ratings. In 50 of the largest radio markets Arbitron uses electronic meters that radio listeners carry with them, called portable people meters, that automatically record the stations they come in contact with during the day while working, playing, or driving. Eventually, the company hopes to replace paper diaries in all of the 303 markets it tracks nationwide. Through its electronic meters Arbitron now examines all manner of radio listening, broadcast, online, through apps, considers programs

> **Ratings** measure the proportion of television households that watch a specific show, or how many people are listening to a radio station.

such as Pandora as well as conventional radio stations, and plans to follow listening across many kinds of devices in different spaces and places. However, the electronic meters have dramatically lowered the ratings of stations that target minority groups, probably because Arbitron has a difficult time retaining African-Americans and Hispanics in their panels. Also, the meters show that listeners tend to tune out to disc jockey chatter between songs, leading to efforts to cut back on talking between records including announcements of the song that just played.

Ratings can be crucial for establishing the importance, or more specifically, the commercial attractiveness, of a new format or audience group. For example, whereas Latino audiences are virtual majorities in many cities, in others, it is not clear whether there are enough people interested in Latino music to attract advertisers and justify a commercial station focusing on them. In this kind of case, audience ratings research can help show whether a new station has a viable audience. Good ratings in one city for a new format, like "jammin' oldies" or "Jack," may lead other commercial broadcasters to try the format. Poor ratings may lead to long-standing stations or radio personalities undergoing radical changes. Many both inside and outside the industry are frustrated with the power of ratings.

MUSIC GENRES AND RADIO FORMATS

Increased competition for audience segments has also increased the importance of research. When deciding which music format to adopt, stations increasingly rely on consultants who poll local radio listeners to determine which new format or format variation is likely to draw the biggest audience. This is becoming increasingly true of large ownership groups who own up to half a dozen stations in a single market. They use research carefully to avoid overlap in the audiences that they reach and to ensure that they reach the audience segments that are the most attractive to their advertisers.

In fact, stations are frequently targeted to some audience groups that are smaller than others but sufficiently attractive to advertisers so that both advertisers and radio programmers prefer to focus on them. This is apparent in Table 6.2 (page 175), which shows dramatically that although Top 40, or Contemporary Hit Radio, draws the fourth-highest national share of radio listening, it has fewer stations than eight other formats, including news/talk, country, contemporary Christian, religious, variety, adult contemporary, sports, and classic rock, most of which have lower listening shares nationwide. Similarly, urban adult contemporary has the seventh-highest share, but fewer stations than 20 other formats. However, in specific local or even national advertising markets, the audiences for those other formats may well have greater purchasing power and be much more attractive to advertisers and, hence, to programmers. Some formats, like religion, are carried on commercial stations because of the personal interests of their owners rather than ratings.

Music genres evolve with their audiences, and many radio formats have changed quite a bit in the last decade. For example, starting in the late 1990s, many stations went to an "alternative rock" format, including some nationally

Table 6.2 Radio Formats' Popularity Versus Share of Stations Fall 2010

FORMAT	12+ SHARE	TOTAL	PRIMARY			HD RADIO					STREAMING				
			FM	AM	TOTAL	HF	HA	F2	F3	F4	IF	IA	G2	G3	G4
Country + New Country	13.3	2,728	1,421	323	1,744	136	0	36	1	0	712	86	13	0	0
News/Talk/Information	12.1	3,795	558	1,364	1,922	220	96	92	74	6	463	793	70	53	6
Adult Contemporary + SAC	9.4	1,435	738	118	856	117	0	11	0	0	408	37	6	0	0
Pop Contemporary Hit Radio	7.6	898	415	3	418	103	0	40	1	0	315	2	18	1	0
Classic Rock	4.9	929	509	11	520	78	0	38	1	0	277	3	12	0	0
Classic Hits	4.9	883	446	87	533	56	2	20	1	0	231	29	10	1	0
Urban Adult Contemporary	4.0	348	138	35	173	45	2	13	1	0	93	17	4	0	0
Hot Adult Contemporary	3.9	786	459	8	467	66	0	5	0	0	245	1	2	0	0
Rhythmic Contemporary Hit Radio	3.5	396	160	0	160	50	0	39	0	0	129	0	18	0	0
All Sports	3.4	1,200	119	574	693	19	48	19	30	1	82	288	6	13	1
Mexican Regional	3.0	509	196	143	339	25	3	6	0	0	79	52	5	0	0
Urban Contemporary	2.9	268	122	18	140	29	0	12	0	0	77	6	4	0	0
Contemporary Christian	2.8	1,618	843	41	884	19	1	18	6	0	652	21	13	4	0
Active Rock	2.3	404	196	1	197	32	0	27	0	0	140	1	7	0	0
Adult Hits + 80's Hits	2.2	428	209	15	224	39	1	20	3	0	127	5	8	1	0
Alternative	2.1	640	291	5	296	38	0	52	5	0	212	5	27	5	0
Album Oriented Rock	1.8	302	156	2	158	23	0	14	2	0	102	1	1	1	0
Oldies	1.6	871	290	307	597	12	3	27	4	0	112	104	9	3	0
Classical (see *Public Radio Today*)	1.6	781	248	2	250	122	0	94	9	0	217	2	78	9	0
All News	1.5	74	6	21	27	3	7	3	6	0	6	17	2	3	0
Spanish Contemporary	1.4	192	66	42	108	17	3	10	0	0	33	17	4	0	0
Religious	1.3	1,598	747	390	1,137	8	13	9	4	0	244	176	5	2	0
Album Adult Alternative	1.2	504	184	4	188	49	0	54	16	0	144	3	38	12	0
Spanish Adult Hits	1.1	114	44	8	52	16	1	5	0	0	32	4	4	0	0
Variety	0.9	1,455	693	112	805	106	3	23	7	0	438	51	18	4	0
Classic Country	0.9	475	105	209	314	6	3	34	1	0	39	67	11	0	0
Rhythmic AC	0.8	68	24	0	24	12	0	6	0	0	22	0	4	0	0
Contemporary Inspirational	0.7	237	119	19	138	10	2	6	1	0	65	9	5	1	0
Gospel	0.7	451	82	229	311	3	7	10	0	0	29	86	5	0	0

LEGEND

FM	FM Station
AM	AM Station
HF	Digital (HD Radio) FM Station
HA	Digital (HDRadio) AM Station
F2	HD Radio Multicast Station
F3	HD Radio Multicast Station
F4	HD Radio Multicast Station
IF	Internet Stream of FM Station
IA	Internet Stream of AM Station
G2	Internet Stream of HD Radio / Multicast F2
G3	Internet Stream of HD Radio / Multicast F3
G4	Internet Stream of HD Radio / Multicast F4

Source: Arbitron Marketing Communications, Radio Today 2011: How America Listens to Radio, p. 12.

distributed package formats like the Hot Adult Contemporary format "Mix 107" (or whatever the frequency of the local affiliate is). In the meantime, other formats were rising, like "Jack," a supposedly random mixture of 1970s through 1990s rock hits with no disc jockeys allowed. This format deliberately reached across a number of audiences for earlier, more targeted formats, like classic rock. "Jack" managed to bring in both younger and middle-aged audiences, thus reaching an interesting breadth of people for its advertisers.

This section has discussed mainly FM formats. Because of AM's broader signal reach, many stations in sparsely populated smaller towns adopt a format that is broad-based, middle-of-the-road, country-western, talk, religious, variety or oldies (e.g., classic rock, classic hits).

TALK RADIO

Music is not the only game on radio. All-news stations and news talk formats are on the rise. As stations specialize, news, talk, weather, and sports information grow in importance. A number of audiences are strongly attracted to news, sports, and talk, so station owners and advertisers who wish to pursue that audience tend to consider using this format. So the news and talk general area is subdivided into a number of niches. Some stations do 24-hour news and weather. Most of those are national network news stations, but very few do primarily local news. Many stations carry nationally syndicated talk shows, such as those of Rush Limbaugh, Laura Ingraham, Glenn Beck and others.

On the AM band, sound quality is not quite as high as on FM, so many AM stations emphasize news, talk, and sports. A mixture of talk and music has also proven very successful, particularly during morning commute hours. Morning shows on major stations increasingly reflect a more chatty drive-time format, both on AM and FM. As the syndicated talk formats gain more of an audience, many FM stations that had focused on music find themselves changing to talk formats because they draw a more lucrative audience.

NATIONAL PUBLIC RADIO

Many public stations get much of their programming from a few key national sources: National Public Radio (NPR), Public Radio International (PRI), American Public Radio, and, for a few, the Pacifica Network. NPR is a growing source of news and news talk radio to more than 27 million Americans, and provides an afternoon news program called *All Things Considered*, a morning news program called *Morning Edition*, and other programs to a large group of affiliated public stations. Government funding is the majority of support, but some foundations and corporations offer funding for the certain kinds of programming and news that interest them. For example, the William and Flora Hewlett Foundation gives grants to NPR (The William and Flora Hewlett Foundation).

RADIO PROGRAMMING SERVICES

The economics of radio programming have changed again to favor centralized, syndicated, or networked programming. A number of different sources exist

LOCAL DJS DECLINE BUT OTHER FORMS OF RADIO RISE

Jobs in the radio industry are strongly affected by the trends discussed in the chapter. DJ and announcer positions are reduced as broadcast stations use syndicated program services. Centralized sales and management also reduce the availability of some jobs; however, new jobs have been created by satellite and Internet radio in these areas and others. Changing news talk formats also create jobs.

Broadcasting provided about 316,000 wage and salary jobs in 2008. Around half are in radio. Many small stations (38 percent) employed less than five people, but most jobs are in companies of at least 50 employees (Occupational Outlook Handbook, 2012). There are jobs in program production, news, technical, sales, and management. At small stations, jobs are less specialized and employees often perform several functions. On-air positions are the most visible jobs in broadcasting, but the majority of employment opportunities are behind the scenes. Most managers start their careers in advertising and sales.

from which to choose. Many stations now subscribe to national, regional, or state networks for news and sports (including the regional networks on which college sports are broadcast).

Music-oriented stations also carry syndicated programs, such as concert specials or Top 40 hit countdowns. Many also switch away from music in drive-time hours when a mix of local weather, traffic, and news is most appealing.

For an increasing number of station owners, locally programmed stations are a risky venture. Many stations buy complete, packaged music services designed by outside experts who look at the prospective audience, consider the format options, and evaluate what has worked in similar markets. The 1960s-style DJ who picked his own records is almost extinct, eliminating quite a few entry-level jobs in radio.

A variety of radio programming services is available. The most complete are satellite-based networks that deliver news, music, and other entertainment and even sell national advertising. Those are the easiest options for an owner, who simply affiliates with a network and carries its programming, like old-fashioned network affiliates. Format syndicators provide a full music program but do not sell commercial ad time for the station or provide news or other information services. Full program-service companies, such as Global Digital, provide completely automated formats, such as "Jack-FM." Full-service automation became popular when a wave of mergers swept the radio industry in the 1990s. Nonlocal owners were less likely to feel that they knew the peculiarities of the market and more likely to rely on relatively safe, nationally standardized formats. Locally programmed automation systems became cheaper; for example, a fully programmable system that handles up to 300 CDs, as well as tape machines for commercial and announcement inserts, costs under $10,000.

MEDIALITERACY

THE IMPACT OF THE AIRWAVES

One of the most important issues to understand, in order to be media savvy or "literate," is who makes the decisions on radio content. Radio seems very diverse, with dozens of stations in most areas. However, how large and diverse is the group of people making key radio content decisions?

WHO CONTROLS THE AIRWAVES?

The FCC is supposed to use a "public interest" standard for reviewing and renewing licenses, but that has proven too vague to provide a basis for denying license renewal to misbehaving broadcasters. For example, Howard Stern's indecency violations did not result in the denial of license renewals for any stations, but it made them nervous, and he moved to satellite radio. In 2006 Congress passed a bill to increase radio and television indecency fines by ten times, up to $325,000 per incident per station, which may create more significant pressure on stations and networks. However, leadership change at the FCC has decreased its focus on enforcement of these rules.

In the past, the FCC created rules about ownership, **concentration** and cross-ownership, obscenity and indecency in radio content, and the role of networks and affiliates. The Telecommunications Act of 1996 eliminated the national limits regarding ownership. Under the 1996 Act, a single owner can own up to eight radio stations in a market with 45 or more commercial radio stations. However, such limits have been challenged in the courts. A definitive FCC ruling was expected in 2011, but had not been issued by press time (FCC, "Review of the Broadcast Ownership Rules," http://www.fcc.gov/guides/review-broadcast-ownership-rules, accessed June 8, 2012).

CONCENTRATING OWNERSHIP, REDUCING DIVERSITY?

Fewer radio station owners than ever are local residents of the areas their stations serve, which presumably limits their ability to understand local interests. Fewer owners are minorities or female. Fewer stations are programmed locally because **group owners** often supply programming from a central source. The local stations are automated and play just the prerecorded programming.

The counterargument is that concentrated ownership may actually provide more format diversity. When one group owns six to eight stations in a market, it will target each one at a different interest group.

What is more problematic is that news and information content lack genuine local input or diversity. This seems to go against the principle of maximizing localism that has, in theory, guided FCC licensing decisions since the 1934 Communications Act. A poignant case in point was a train accident in Minot, North Dakota, one night. Local residents tried to call the radio station to warn residents to evacuate, only to discover there was no one "there" at the remotely controlled "local" station.

Concentration of ownership occurs when several kinds of media or many outlets of the same kind of media are owned by a single owner.

Group owners own a number of broadcast stations.

From 2003 to 2004, an effort to increase the amount of concentration of ownership permitted by the FCC encountered an unexpected groundswell of public opposition. What many groups objected to was precisely the decrease in local control and local input that the growth of groups like Clear Channel seemed to imply. Enough individual citizens and groups complained to their congressional representatives that Congress instructed the FCC not to change the rules, and the FCC decided not to fight to change them. However, the FCC is still struggling to institute new cross-ownership rules as of this writing. On the other hand, the FCC did vote to permit increased cross-ownership of newspapers and television in the same cities. (See Chapter 15 for more information on how this process works.)

Extreme horizontal integration may not even be in the interest of the owners. At its peak in 2006, Clear Channel owned 10 percent of all stations, but it took in about 20 percent of the overall advertising revenue and attracted about 25 percent of total listeners nationwide, which seemed to give it considerable advantage. It also took a lot of flack from critics, took on debt, and saw profits stall. So Clear Channel spun off its concert promotion business and sold over 400 stations in smaller markets, to focus on its core business and markets. It still has over 850 stations. In 2011, the number-two radio ownership groups, Cumulus, purchased the third largest, Citadel and now has 572 stations. So extreme horizontal integration is still an issue regulators have to consider.

So, the bottom-line question amounts to this: Is there enough diversity on radio for YOU? If the answer is no, you can join the Media Reform campaign (www.freepress.net). And you do have options from satellite or the Internet. If those are still not enough, then start your own radio station on the Internet. Internet radio providers like Live365 will put your station on the net for a few dollars a month and tell you how to share in advertising revenues, although you will have to pay royalties on the songs you play (see the section that follows). Don't do it to get rich, though, because it won't happen. Do it for the love of your own unique genre of music and, just perhaps, the joy of hearing your own voice on the radio.

FROM FACEBOOK AND YOUTUBE TO MAINSTREAM Rebecca Black launched her musical career outside of the typical channels. Her parents connected her to Ark Music Factory, who supplied her a song, "Friday," and studio video recording for $4,000. She got her big break when comedian Michael Nelson tweeted that it was "the worst video ever made." The song then rode Facebook and YouTube networking to over 170 million views, and over 3 million dislikes. It reminds us a bit of legendary circus man P.T. Barnum who did not care what people said about him as long as they talked about him and spelled his name right.

YOU CAN'T SAY THAT ON THE RADIO

Freedom of speech continues to be a focus for radio broadcasting. In contrast, the recording industry has traditionally been lightly scrutinized. It has been considered analogous to publishing in that it doesn't involve use of a scarce public resource, such as the airwaves; it has a large degree of competition; and exposure to recorded music is, in principle, entirely voluntary.

Radio has been more closely scrutinized under the rationale that the air-waves are a scarce resource to be used in the public interest. The FCC has standards restricting **obscene** or **indecent speech.** Up through the 1970s, certain words could not be used, and broadcasters were held responsible even for call-in programs to make sure that prohibited language was not broadcast. The late comic George Carlin developed a comedy routine in that era about "Filthy Words," which featured words you couldn't say on public airwaves. Those prohibitions were challenged in court (see Chapter 15), but the FCC still restricts speech that is considered indecent—that is, that uses graphic language pertaining to sexual or excretory functions. The FCC prohibits such language during daytime and evening hours but has made the late-night hours between 10 p.m. and 6 a.m. a "safe harbor" for more explicit kinds of speech. Despite the prohibition, shock jocks, such as Don Imus, routinely violate the rule, are fined, and consider paying the fine a cost of doing business. Thousands of radio stations play music by stars whose lyrics probably also violate those rules, but music has been less scrutinized by the FCC than comedy or commentary. In 2004, due to congressional pressure, the FCC imposed stiffer fines and penalties for indecency. Some conservative activists suggested extending broadcast indecency rules to satellite radio and cable TV, but that has not been considered seriously, leading some in broadcasting to think that they are being treated unfairly.

Others wonder whether the definition of indecency should be expanded from talk about sex and excretory functions to racial slurs and sexism. In 2007 radio host Don Imus was suspended from his show after protests over his use of a racial slur against black players on a college women's basketball team. In 2012 Rush Limbaugh caused a national scandal, and lost several advertisers, for calling a birth control advocate "a slut" on his syndicated radio show.

BREAKING OR SAVING INTERNET RADIO

Reuse of **copyrighted** music, syndicated talk shows, and other intellectual property has been a major issue for the radio industry. The licensing of recorded music for play over the radio is complex. Copyright law requires payment for performance of work copyrighted by an artist, including the playing of a recording over the radio. Two main music-licensing groups—the American Society of Composers, Authors and Publishers (ASCAP), and Broadcast Music Incorporated (BMI)—serve as intermediaries between songwriters or other copyright holders, and radio stations (although not the recording artist, since they don't receive performance royalties from radio). These two traditional groups have been joined by the Radio Music License Committee, which represents radio stations in negotiations with ASCAP. Radio stations get licenses for the music listed by the music-licensing group in return for a fee, usually 1 to 2 percent of the station's gross income. ASCAP or BMI then pays the copyright holders according to how often each song is played.

Things are different for Internet radio, however. Internet radio stations are required to pay both

[**Obscene or indecent speech** depicts sexual conduct in a way that appeals to sexual interests in a manner that is "patently offensive" to community standards, and lacks serious artistic, political, or scientific value.]

[**Copyright** is the legal right to control intellectual property. With it comes the legal privilege to use, sell, or license creative works.]

STOP&REVIEW

1. What kinds of radio networks exist now?
2. How are radio formats related to music genres?
3. What are the target audiences for some of the main radio formats?
4. Why does the concentration of radio ownership cause concern?
5. What copyright challenges are raised by Internet radio and podcasting?

songwriters and performers, at a rate higher than satellite or terrestrial radio. Rules in 2007 called for the rate per play to more than double by 2010, by requiring a fee per song for each listener. It also required a separate fee of $500 a station, no matter how small the station. The recording industry sees this as a new revenue stream to replace declining CD sales (see Chapter 5), but webcasters were afraid that many of them would be driven out of business.

SoundExchange, an industry-backed organization that collects royalties for record labels and artists; Pandora; and other companies negotiated a compromise in 2009 that distinguishes between paid streaming services and large and small free services. All pay an initial streaming fee; then different-sized operations have choices between paying fees per song played or flat percentages of their revenue, after they have established profitable revenue streams.

SUMMARY&REVIEW

WHAT WERE THE KEY DEVELOPMENTS THAT LED TO RADIO BROADCASTING?

Marconi pioneered radio as a form of two-way communication. The development of the vacuum tube by de Forest was crucial. It permitted continuous sound-wave transmission and reception, beyond the on/off transmission that had sufficed for transmission of coded messages in wireless telegraph systems. Other crucial developments included better microphones, amplifiers, tuners, and more powerful transmitters.

WHAT CAUSED THE RISE AND FALL OF THE ORIGINAL RADIO NETWORKS?

The main radio networks were put together by David Sarnoff at RCA/NBC and William Paley at CBS, who saw potential to make and sell radios, as well as to sell advertising. During their high point, network radio relied largely on music but also carried news, sports, comedy, variety shows, soap operas, dramas, suspense, and action adventures as well. Many of those genres moved to television after 1948. After television coverage and audiences began to grow, around 1948, network radio also began to lose much of its audience to television. Some of the types of entertainment it had relied on worked better for the mass audience with a visual component on television. Radio came to rely more on music, which could be programmed locally by DJs playing records.

WHEN DID FM RADIO BEGIN TO INCREASE IN IMPORTANCE? AND WHY?

FM radio began to increase as more receivers became available in the 1960s. It also prospered as FM stereo became widely available and appreciation of music quality increased among the audience, making FM the main radio medium for music.

WHAT KINDS OF RADIO NETWORKS EXIST NOW?

New ownership and programming syndication groups, such as Global Digital and Clear Channel, created new networks around popular syndicated shows, such as Rush Limbaugh's. Large ownership groups like Clear Channel use a number of nationally programmed formats, such as "Jack-FM," which are the main new networks. National Public Radio also emerged as significant news and public affairs programming service, linking most of the nation's noncommercial, or public, radio stations.

HOW IS THE INTERNET AFFECTING RADIO?

Many radio stations are now transmitting their music, news, and other programs over the Internet to reach new audiences, both in their regular coverage areas as well as distant ones, but some stations may have to close because of an inability to pay royalties to record companies and recording artists. Internet-based services, like Pandora and Spotify, increasingly integrated with other services, like Facebook, now also compete with radio.

WHAT ARE RADIO FORMATS?

A format is a particular radio programming strategy oriented around a playlist of music and focused on a particular genre or audience. Common examples are Contemporary Hit Radio/Top 40, R&B, and modern rock. Radio formats have followed the segmentation of the audience and fragmentation of music genres.

Radio programming became decentralized as local stations pulled away from networks in the 1950s. DJ-driven formats like Top 40 or Contemporary Hit Radio dominated. New formats evolved on the increasing numbers of FM stations in the 1970s-80s. With the rise of large ownership groups and talk radio, centralized program service providers created a new form of network.

On FM, the main formats now are news/talk, country, contemporary Christian, religious, variety, adult contemporary, sports, classic rock, Contemporary Hit Radio, oldies, classical, hot adult contemporary, Spanish, alternative, and urban contemporary. AM stations tend to emphasize news, call-in talk shows, and talk and sports. AM stations also tend to serve smaller towns and rural areas, where the population is less dense.

WHAT ARE THE KEY COMPONENTS OF RADIO INDUSTRY ORGANIZATION?

The main elements of industry organization are national ownership groups, like Clear Channel; national music program services, like Digital Global; national business services, like ratings organizations; and local stations. Affiliates in broadcasting are stations that contract to use the programming of a network and to share advertising and advertising revenues with it. Networks also have owned-and-operated (O&O) stations. Group owners own a number of broadcast stations. Sometimes group owners provide these stations with common programming, as a traditional network would. New kinds of networks are emerging that provide programming for stations for a fee or for shared advertising. Companies can provide ready-made programming for dozens of formats.

WHAT WAS CHANGED BY THE COMMUNICATIONS ACT OF 1934?

The Communications Act of 1934 defined the broadcast band, standardized frequency designations, and created a more powerful regulatory body, the Federal Communications Commission (FCC). The FCC devised more systematic procedures for granting radio licenses and rules on transmitter power, height, and frequency use. The FCC imposed rules about ownership, concentration and cross-ownership, and the role of networks and affiliates.

WHAT WAS CHANGED BY THE TELECOMMUNICATIONS ACT OF 1996?

The Telecommunications Act of 1996 changed FCC rules about station ownership limits. It eliminated previous station ownership limits. For radio, there are no national limits, and local ownership caps increase with market size. This considerably increased concentration of ownership, which raises issues about content diversity, localism, and minority ownership.

WHAT ARE THE ISSUES INVOLVED IN CONCENTRATION OF RADIO OWNERSHIP?

A few large ownership groups now own as many as half of all stations in many cities. This clearly reduces the localism of ownership, which may then reduce responsiveness to local interests. Group stations are increasingly programmed at a distance, including programming of "local" news. Diversity of both music and news may well be reduced, although ownership groups claim that they actually increase the diversity of music formats available in a market.

WHAT ARE THE LIMITS ON FREEDOM OF SPEECH IN RADIO BROADCASTS?

Up through the 1960s, certain obscene words could not be used, and broadcasters were responsible for ensuring that they were not used. Those prohibitions were successfully challenged in court, but the FCC still restricts speech that is indecent. The FCC prohibits such language except during late-night spots that are a "safe harbor" for more explicit speech.

THINKING CRITICALLY
ABOUT THE MEDIA

1. How does the history of radio help us understand how Internet radio, podcasting, and other audio media are going to develop as commercial forms? As artistic forms?

2. The United States was the first country to turn radio into a commercial medium. What does that tell us about how new media will develop in the United States? How might they be different elsewhere?

3. Does obscenity on radio need to be more tightly controlled? Please justify your answer with examples from radio history.

4. What might justify new regulation to break up large radio groups and make radio a more local medium again?

5. Do you think broadcast radio still plays a positive role in helping people like you learn about new music? If not, what if anything should be done about it?

KEY TERMS

affiliate (p. 160)

AM (amplitude modification) (p. 168)

chain broadcasting (p. 161)

concentration of ownership (p. 178)

copyright (p. 180)

cross-ownership (p. 170)

FM (frequency modification) (p. 168)

format (p. 162)

format clock (p. 172)

frequency (p. 158)

group owners (p. 178)

Hertz (Hz) (p. 168)

indecent speech (p. 180)

license (p. 158)

low power (p. 171)

O&O (p. 160)

obscene speech (p. 180)

patent (p. 158)

playlist (p. 162)

podcast (p. 166)

public broadcaster (p. 171)

Radio Act of 1912 (p. 157)

radio waves (p. 157)

ratings (p. 173)

regulation (p. 157)

syndication (p. 163)

Telecommunications Act of 1996 (p. 163)

Top 40 (p. 162)

vertical integration (p. 157)

Lucasfilm/20th Century Fox/The Kobal Collection/Hamshere,Keith/Picture Desk

MOVIES LIKE STAR WARS that are powerful enough to frame how we think about ourselves now converge and cross over with books, music, and video games.

7

FILM AND HOME VIDEO

HISTORY: GOLDEN MOMENTS OF FILM

The early years of film were marked by experimentation with content and forms, major technological innovations, and disputes over who could use, control, and benefit from the inventions. The first challenge was to capture motion on film. The next trick was to find a useful way of recording and showing events in motion.

Thomas Edison invented the first functional motion picture camera in 1888 (see Technology Trends: Making Movie Magic, page 198). The French Lumière brothers came up with the idea of projecting movies on a screen. Most early films simply showed short black-and-white, silent depictions of actual events in motion, such as horse races. The Great Train Robbery, made by Edwin S. Porter in 1903, was the first story film and was very popular. At first, audiences ducked when the train robber's gun fired into the camera.

Edison and Biograph, which had somewhat superior camera and projector technologies, pooled patents to establish a single motion picture standard. They tried to collect a fee from every new film. Independent producers started to use bootleg equipment and moved their operations far away from

1888	Edison develops motion picture camera	1977	*Star Wars* highlights focus on big-budget blockbusters
1915	*Birth of a Nation* is first feature film	1995	*Toy Story* first major-release computer-generated film
1927	*The Jazz Singer* is first "talkie"		
1946	Peak of film box office—90 million attend weekly	1997	DVD introduced
1948	Television competes; major studios have to divest their theater chains	2007	Netflix streams films over Internet to increasing number of devices
1968	MPAA movie ratings introduced	2010	*Avatar* highest-grossing film of all time, breaks 3-D into the mainstream

the dominant companies in New York. They chose Hollywood, California, for its weather and space for studios. The industry became centered in Hollywood after 1915, and the old companies lost their control.

In 1915, film director D. W. Griffith took a major step forward in film form and technique with the controversial drama Birth of a Nation. He used well-produced outdoor battle scenes, close-ups, and cuts between different simultaneous sequences of action, such as the threat to an imperiled heroine and the rescuers riding to save her, to increase dramatic tension. It was the first full-length, over 90 minutes, **feature film**. It was the most popular film in the United States for more than 20 years. However, the film, set during and after the Civil War, featured anti-Black Ku Klux Klan members as its heroes and was used by the Klan as a recruiting film. Although the film was revolutionary in form, it was racist in content and was boycotted by the NAACP in its initial release. Concerned it would incite violence, several states banned the film, an early instance of film censorship. Soon after, in the 1920s, the industry started self-regulation. (See Violence, Sex, Profanity, and Film Ratings on page 208.)

[**Feature films** are story films, usually over one and a half hours.]

HOW TO USE IMAGES: SILENT FILMS SET THE PATTERNS

Hollywood has had several "booms" or "golden ages" of prosperity, artistic success, and widespread cultural impact. These periods have later been followed by "busts," when the film industry lost parts of its audience to newer media technologies. The first golden age was silent film, from 1903 to 1927.

Silent films established classic genre formulas for telling stories on film that are still followed today. Because producers of silent films had to rely on visuals, with only brief written dialogue added in still frames, these films were oriented toward action, dramatic visuals and lavish sets. *The Great Train Robbery* featured action and suspense, and *Birth of a Nation* showed battles, chases, and historical scenes. The genres they relied on are alive and well today in action-adventure (*Mission Impossible: Ghost Protocol*) and historical costume dramas (*A Dangerous Method*). Table 7.1 (see page 187) describes the major silent and early sound film genres.

TABLE 7.1 Early Film Genres

SILENT FILM GENRES	EARLY SOUND FILM GENRES
· Westerns, such as *The Great Train Robbery* (1903)	· Crime dramas, with cops, gangsters, and violence, such as *Little Caesar* (1930)
· War movies, with battles and character conflicts, such as Abel Gance's epic silent, *Napoleon* (1934)	· Animation, such as *Snow White and the Seven Dwarfs* (1937)
· Horror, including the original *Dracula*, *Nosferatu* (1922)	· Screwball comedies, with glamour and light humor, such as *It Happened One Night* (1934)
· Romances, love stories such as *The Sheik* (1921)	· Character studies, such as *Citizen Kane* (1941)
· Physical comedies, with car crashes and pratfalls (such as the *Keystone Cops* shorts) or facial expression and body language (such as Charlie Chaplin and Buster Keaton films)	· Detective movies, with complex heroes, such as *The Maltese Falcon* (1941)
· Historical costume dramas, with fictionalized plots, such as D. W. Griffith's *Intolerance* (1916)	· Suspense, such as Fritz Lang's *M* (1931)
	· Monster movies, such as *King Kong* (1933)
· Documentaries, such as *Nanook of the North* (1921)	· Horror movies, such as *Dracula* (1931)
· Action-adventure, such as Douglas Fairbanks' *Thief of Baghdad* (1921)	· Musicals, such as *Flying Down to Rio* (1933)
· Melodramas, such as *The Perils of Pauline* (1914)	· Film noir, "dark," skeptical films, such as *Double Indemnity* (1944)
	· Serials, such as *Buck Rogers* (1936–1940)

SETTING UP A SYSTEM: STARS AND STUDIOS

From their new base in California, several **major film studios** developed a strong industrial production capability, producing movies almost on an assembly line, leading critics to talk about cultural industries that mass-produced culture (Horkheimer & Adorno, 1972). Studios developed their own complete teams of actors, writers, directors, technicians, and equipment that enabled them to produce large numbers of successful feature films.

Film studios discovered that certain actors and actresses could attract viewers no matter what the movie was about. The **star system** was born. Rudolph Valentino (*The Sheik,* 1921), Lillian Gish (*Intolerance,* 1916), Mary Pickford (*Madame Butterfly,* 1915), and Charlie Chaplin (*The Gold Rush,* 1925) became such attractions that their names appeared above the title of the film on theater marquees.

Even silent, early movies were visually powerful enough to create both adoration and controversy. Some movies in the 1920s shocked audiences with sexual themes, partial nudity, and depiction of a fast urban life, as in *The Jazz Age* (1929), where both men and women "partied" hard. Stardom made the private lives of these early movie actors more visible, and some stars' lives were scandalous to many viewers. The industry decided to impose self-censorship before it was censored by outsiders. In 1922, the studios created the Motion Picture Producers and Distributors of America, known as the Hays Office. It created voluntary content guidelines, the **Motion Picture Code.** The Catholic Church, B'nai Brith, and National Education Association all pushed for a production code that forbade scenes that portrayed "crime, wrongdoing, evil, or sin" in a positive light. Hays soothed public complaints but imposed a tough internal censorship that bridled the creativity of industry writers, directors, and actors (Knight, 1979).

Major film studios like Fox or Disney integrate all aspects of production and distribution.

The **star system** was the film studios' use of stars' popularity to promote their movies.

Motion Picture Code of 1930 (Hays Code) was a self-regulation of sex on screen by the motion picture industry.

HOW TO USE SOUND: LOOK WHO'S TALKING

Attempts were made almost from the beginning to make the moving pictures talk. The studios and movie houses were initially reluctant to invest in sound technology because it was new and expensive. Eventually, Warner Brothers made the commitment to develop sound technology and created *The Jazz Singer* in 1927. It featured two sections of recorded music and included singing that was synchronized with the film so that the singer's lips moved when they were supposed to. It also had a little bit of recorded dialogue, which fascinated the audience. Unfortunately, *The Jazz Singer* also reflected American racism of the time: rather than featuring an African-American performer, the film used white singer Al Jolson playing the jazz singer in "blackface," dark makeup that made him look like a parody of an African-American.

[**Talkies** are motion pictures with synchronized sound for dialogue.]

"**Talkies**" ended the golden age of silent movies. Acting became less stylized, since plot could be carried by dialogue, not just by expression and gesture. Studios suddenly had to become skilled in the use of sound effects and music. Some actresses and actors did not have the vocal quality or more subtle acting skills to survive, as illustrated in the classic *Singing in the Rain* (1952). Talkies required an influx of new talent, such as Fred Astaire, from vaudeville and Broadway, who talked, sang, and sometimes danced. Because audiences liked talkies, they made even more money for the producers of the movies. In a few years nearly all films had sound.

New genres arose that emphasized the advantages of sound (see Table 7.1), showing one of the ways technology and culture interact. A new golden age of movies created extravagantly produced musicals, with lavish visuals, dancing, and singing. A series of films by the elegant dancing team Ginger Rogers and Fred Astaire, starting with *Flying Down to Rio* in 1933, put music and motion together.

Comedies became more verbal, with jokes and sophisticated bantering added to the silent repertoire of slapstick and sight gags. Several comedy subgenres were created to play with sound. The zany comedies of the Marx Brothers, such as *A Night at the Opera* (1935), poked fun at authority. Screwball comedies, such as *It Happened One Night* (1934), featured Clark Gable and other big stars in elegantly set and clever but silly stories.

Sound, dramatic visuals, and action were combined in increasingly complex genre formulas that often addressed concerns of the day. Crime stories, such as *Little Caesar* (1930), reflected a real-life increase in organized crime that grew with the prohibition of alcohol. Another genre was detective films, such as *The Maltese Falcon* (1941), directed by John

Bettmann/Corbis

FILM LEGENDS Stars were important to the success of the film medium. Douglas Fairbanks and Mary Pickford (bottom row) were so big that they started their own studio, United Artists (with Charlie Chaplin and D. W. Griffith).

Huston, which featured Humphrey Bogart. A key genre variation was the **film noir,** "the dark film," such as *Double Indemnity* (1944), which tended to be more skeptical, even cynical, and had antiheroes instead of the simpler heroes of earlier films. Suspense and mystery stories, such as Alfred Hitchcock's *The 39 Steps* (1935), constituted another major genre. Historical epics were another: *Gone with the Wind* (1939) continues to be a classic. Wars were such a pivotal experience for many Americans that World War II films like *Valkyrie* (2008) persisted as a genre long after the war was over. By the late 1960s and 1970s, the growing negative public reaction to the Vietnam War changed the nature of war films to a more critical view, with films like *Apocalypse Now* (1979).

Similarly, the western became another means for exploring the American myth and American character. Director John Ford created a number of classic westerns. They gradually changed from the optimistic, positive view of cowboys and cavalry soldiers exemplified by *She Wore a Yellow Ribbon* (1949) to films such as *Cheyenne Autumn* (1964), which began to consider the perspective of Native Americans as "good guys," with a different slant on the American conquest of the West.

Film noir comprised the "dark," moody American films of the 1940s, often focused on detectives or similar themes.

THE PEAK OF MOVIE IMPACT?

The cultural impact of movies in America, and the world, in the 1930s–1940s was extraordinary. Most people—especially children—went to the movies weekly if their families could afford it. One ticket got you into the movie house and you could stay all day, watching the double-feature films as many times as you'd like. Going to the movies meant watching a newsreel—visual news of the world before television news—serial dramas and cartoons sandwiched before and between the feature films. Audiences waited week to week to see what would happen next to Flash Gordon or other heroes of the serials. Although the Depression kept some people away, most tried hard to find a couple of dimes for the movies, and collectively bought about 70 million tickets a week. Hollywood provided a form of escapism that helped people forget their troubles. The pure fantasy of *The Wizard of Oz* (1939) and the antics of Shirley Temple and The Three Stooges are enduring examples of brilliant 1930s escapism.

American movies also went international. Other audiences were intrigued by the modern U.S. life they saw on-screen and studios pushed exports very hard. The studios had joined together as the Motion Picture Export Association of America (MPEAA) in the 1930s and had taken control of much of the international film distribution business.

BEYOND DISNEY Director Chuck Jones (1912–2002) added many innovations and a wry sense of humor to animation at Warner Bros. *One Froggy Evening* (1957) was one of many films he created.

LOONEY TUNES characters, names and all related indicia are trademarks of and © Warner Bros. (s03)

THE STUDIO SYSTEM: THE PROS AND CONS OF VERTICAL INTEGRATION

Movies made a lot of money. As profits went up and movies became a successful business, a merger wave took place. The Great Depression killed off many small producers and nearly 5,000 independent movie theaters (Gomery, 1991). This strengthened the economics and control of a few big studios, and it concentrated production decisions in the hands of very few studio executives, a reality that came to be known as the **studio system.**

By 1930, a fairly stable pattern of studio organization emerged. There were five major studios: Paramount, Loews/MGM, Warner Brothers, Fox, and RKO. These studios owned their own distribution chains of movie theaters, as well as extensive production facilities. They relied on teams of stars and directors who made movies together for them. They developed both prestigious feature films and **B movies,** which were cheaper and not as prestigious but made consistent profits as the second feature at local theaters. Control over production, distribution, and exhibition enabled studios to make sure that their movies were distributed and played widely, but it constituted a form of **vertical integration** that ultimately drew the attention of federal regulators to the concentration of power in the studios. The studios of that time provide an interesting parallel to our current system, where deregulation in the 1980s and 1990s has permitted extensive vertical integration to emerge again between film studios, TV, and cable channels.

Each studio also had its own distinctive style. Paramount was the most profitable and powerful studio, with over 1,000 theaters, employing proven directors such as Cecil B. DeMille (*The Ten Commandments,* 1956) and stars like crooner Bing Crosby and comedian Bob Hope. Loews/MGM sought prestige with new Technicolor musicals, but it also made a lot of money with B movies such as the *Tarzan* adventures. Twentieth Century Fox combined two studios, developed new stars such as Betty Grable, and also made money with documentaries including *March of Time* and *Movietone* newsreels. Warner Brothers promoted comedies; genre films such as Errol Flynn's *The Adventures of Robin Hood* (1938); and cartoons starring Bugs Bunny, Elmer Fudd, and Daffy Duck. RKO produced some quality films, notably *King Kong* (1933), Fred Astaire and Ginger Rogers musicals, and *Citizen Kane* (1941), but made most of its money from its movie houses and from cheaper, more predictably profitable B movies.

Several minor Hollywood studios of the 1930s and 1940s are now major players: Universal, Columbia, and United Artists. These studios struggled because they did not control their own distribution and exhibition networks. They also made most of their money with B movies. Another two studios were even smaller: Monogram and Republic. Republic was famous for a time for cowboy movies, launching John Wayne, and as a producer of action serials, whose cliffhangers and action sequences have been liberally borrowed by the likes of Steven Spielberg in his *Indiana Jones* movies.

The **studio system** in Hollywood emphasized key stars as a way to promote studio films.

B movies are cheaply and quickly made genre films.

Vertical integration occurs when a company with the same owner handles different aspects of a business (within the same industry), such as film production and distribution.

John Springer Collection/Historical/Corbis

BEST FILM EVER? Orson Welles' *Citizen Kane* popularized a number of filmmaking techniques, including new camera angles and types of shots.

The studio system peaked after World War II in 1946–1948. The war ended the economic limits imposed on movie production by the Great Depression. After the war, returning soldiers and sailors joined the masses of people attending the movies weekly. The year 1946 was the peak of audience exposure and financial success for **theatrical films** in the United States. Around 90 million Americans went to the movies every week to see features such as *It's a Wonderful Life* (1946). In 1947, the U.S. film industry **grossed** $2.4 billion, a figure that sank to $1.3 billion by 1962 (in 2010 dollars), reflecting competition from television (Mast & Kawin, 1996).

Theatrical films are those released for distribution in movie theaters.

Gross is the total box office revenue before expenses are deducted.

COPING WITH NEW TECHNOLOGY COMPETITION: FILM FACES TELEVISION, 1948–1960

As World War II veterans started families and moved to the new suburbs, far away from the downtown movie theaters, film attendance declined. Worse yet, after 1948, television quickly cut into Hollywood's theatrical box office receipts. The film industry suffered a severe, concurrent blow to its theater-based revenues. The government had become concerned with the **concentration of ownership** in the Hollywood system. In 1948, the government ordered studios to get out of at least one aspect of film business: production, distribution, or exhibition. Studios challenged the decision, but the U.S. Supreme Court confirmed it (*United States v. Paramount Pictures,* 1948).

Concentration of ownership, by integration of many aspects of media into one company, creates concerns about political control and loss of diversity.

The four biggest studios—MGM (Metro-Goldwyn-Mayer), Warner, Paramount, and Fox—struggled to readjust after selling off their theater chains. Ironically, this forced divestiture of theatrical distribution, which took place at a point when studios were losing their dominance. Almost every small town went through the shock described in *The Last Picture Show* (1971) as thousands of small-town theaters disappeared. Hollywood responded with suburban drive-in movies and then in the 1970s, shifted to new movie houses in shopping centers.

The film industry began to realize that if it couldn't beat television, it had better join it. Disney started producing programs specifically for television, such as *Disneyland*. Warner Brothers and Paramount made much of their money in the 1950s and 1960s by producing series and distributing movies for television (Gomery, 1991). The TV networks began to order most of their programs from film studios or independent producers since it was then cheaper to buy programming from companies that were already geared up to create it (Sterling & Kittross, 2002). Later, television networks were forced to buy most of their programs from the studios because of government rules that limited how much network programming the network itself could create or own (see Chapter 8).

After 1961, movies were more common on television, as *Saturday Night at the Movies* (NBC) topped the ratings. Television networks have been using movies strategically ever since to compete with each other. Airing movies became an even more important way for UHF, independent stations—even many PBS stations, and basic cable channels to compete with network TV programs.

As audiences got used to television, they demanded something different from movies in technological innovation. Although Technicolor had been invented in the silent era, it spread slowly with films such as *Gone with the Wind* and Disney cartoons. By the early 1960s, nearly all films were in color.

Another technology aimed at competing with TV was wide-screen film. Cinema-Scope had been developed in the 1920s, but it took hold only under encouragement from the head of the Fox studio in the early 1950s. Studios embraced the new wide-screen idea, but outfitting theaters with new screens proved expensive and time-consuming.

Hollywood tried to compete with TV by mounting lavish, big-budget spectacles such as *Ben Hur* (1959). It also capitalized on more controversial material than TV could offer: sex in the James Bond thriller *Goldfinger* (1964), or social issues like racial prejudice, in films like *Guess Who's Coming to Dinner* (1967).

By the 1960s, independent producers gained more of a role in producing movies for studios to distribute. Film studios began to spend much of their own time producing series for television. The studio system, which had flourished in its golden era, died due to changes in technology and the new industry competition that built on it.

STUDIOS IN DECLINE

Although movie studios suffered in the 1950s–1960s, only RKO went out of business. Most changed hands. Most struggled through lean years with few hits and fat years when a hit saved the day; *The Godfather* (1972), for example, made Paramount an unprecedented $1,000,000 a day for its first month.

Columbia and United Artists in some ways fared better than the larger studios by not having to adjust to the loss of theater businesses. Warner and Columbia Pictures made television series. Universal was acquired by MCA and also went into television production. United Artists capitalized on distributing movies, such as John Huston's *The African Queen* (1951), for talented independent producers. Disney moved into the studio ranks with animated films and its Buena Vista production and distribution company, which produced family fare epitomized by *Mary Poppins* (1964).

As independent producers gained more power, several things happened to American movies. Audiences changed, becoming younger, more cosmopolitan, and more interested in sensation and social observation. The values and

SPECTACLE Big-budget, big-screen historical epics such as *Ben Hur* were Hollywood's answer to competition from television in the 1950s. As the *Lord of the Rings* films showed, they still worked in 2004. Looking at all-time worldwide box office receipts, the big-budget fantasy epic spectacle, *Avatar* (2009), leads with $2.7 billion, followed by the historical epic, *Titanic* (1997) with $1.8 billion.

current interests of teenagers and college students began to dominate films (Mast & Kawin, 1996). New directors pushed into Hollywood, some from 1960s underground films, some straight from film school, and some from TV commercials. These new directors transformed traditional Hollywood genres, often by increasing the use of sex, violence, and social controversy, as did Francis Ford Coppola (*The Godfather,* 1972). Directors like Woody Allen (*Annie Hall,* 1976) tended to create much more offbeat, personal films, some of which turned out to be major commercial successes. Much of their innovation came from a new form of an old Hollywood practice, borrowing successful ideas from Europe, like the sexier, more personal, and artistic films of the French New Wave. These films experimented with cinematography and styles of storytelling, and pushed the edges of content.

GODFATHER REVIVES THE BOX OFFICE Coppola's *Godfather* films revived Hollywood audiences with violence, costume drama, and innovative production and editing.

Films became more political and topical. For instance, although *M*A*S*H* (1970) was set during the Korean War, it was filled with the antiwar sentiment many Americans harbored about the Vietnam War. Films such as *Taxi Driver* (1976) explored the underside of city life, whereas *The Graduate* (1967) explored the angst of growing up in the suburbs. Films reexamined American myths, such as the hard-bitten film noir detective, in movies like *Chinatown* (1974).

Rebellion against the strict morality that had inspired the Hays Office was part of the change American society underwent in the 1960s. The Hays Office itself closed down in 1945, although the code technically remained in force until 1966. Meanwhile, local censors were muzzled by free speech rulings from the U.S. Supreme Court. Movie producers continually pushed the limits of what was acceptable, which led to new calls from concerned parents that raised the specter of government censorship. Instead, the industry again opted for self-regulation, this time in the form of content ratings administered by the Motion Picture Association of America (see page 208).

Even as films seemed to turn inward to focus on American culture in the 1960s and 1970s, they were still selling very well abroad. Exports continued to help keep Hollywood profitable throughout the 1950s and 1960s.

Blockbusters. *Jaws* (1975) and *Star Wars* (1977) are usually regarded as the turning points in a return to spectacular, big-budget blockbuster filmmaking, which began a new golden age. Filmmakers such as Steven Spielberg (*ET,* 1982) rediscovered that film has a visual intensity well beyond that of television, especially in the darkened movie house with a big screen and thundering sound. Thus action sequences, striking landscapes, and special effects became competitive advantages for movies. As sophisticated Dolby and Surround Sound systems emerged, intense sound also characterized the movie theater experience. Thus film created new technological advantages that television only began to equal after 2000. Clever use of technology developments can reinvigorate existing industries as well as foment new ones.

STOP&REVIEW

1. What was the studio system?

2. Which were the main studios?

3. What were some of the main silent film genres?

4. What genres came in with talking films? Which were prominent in the 1930s and 1940s?

5. Why did studios want to own their own distributors and movie theater chains? Why did federal regulators force the studios to divest themselves of their movie theater chains in 1948?

6. How did the movie industry compete with television?

First-run distribution for film productions is made specifically for movie theaters.

For **first-run distribution** to movie theaters, most films were increasingly targeted at the 15- to 24-year-olds who still went out to film theaters. Still, blockbuster movies such as *Lord of the Rings* (2001) or *Forrest Gump* (1994) could ensure a studio's financial health for years by reaching a wide audience, even though they were more expensive. Filmmakers hurried to take advantage of the latest special effects, often raising costs. The star system also returned with a vengeance, which also raised film costs since stars such as Tom Cruise could get over $20 million for a film.

HOLLYWOOD MEETS HBO

By the late 1970s and early 1980s, the film industry took increasing advantage of cable TV and rented videotapes as new distribution channels. Home Box Office (HBO), launched in 1975 (see Chapter 8), initially relied almost exclusively on feature films for its content. The new superstations WGN, WOR, and WTBS concentrated on old films, as did independent TV stations, usually on UHF. These developments helped the film industry regain some of the revenue that it had lost to network television in the 1950s and 1960s.

Videocassette recorders (VCRs) and DVDs diffused very quickly to become the primary means of watching movies. The video rental business started with small independent rental shops. It later consolidated decisively, with independents shrinking, with some supermarkets and other stores renting videos as a sideline, and with massive video rental and sales chains like Blockbuster taking most of the business.

The spread of video rentals ultimately contributed both to the blockbuster phenomenon and to audience segmentation. Whereas many people rush to get the latest hit movie on DVD, others go straight for Japanese animation, old cowboy movies, old *Star Trek* episodes, or whatever else captures their attention. Similarly, many B movies now go straight to DVD or Netflix, where loyal fans are waiting for yet another raunchy guy buddy comedy or low-budget horror film.

By the 1970s, made-for-TV movies also became increasingly common. These movies could be turned into TV or cable TV series if they were popular, as was *Buffy the Vampire Slayer* (1997), and from TV series to movies, as in *Hannah Montana: One in a Million* (2008). Made-for-TV movies often did surprisingly well against other movies and series.

20th Century Fox/Photofest

TITANIC HIT *Titanic* became the biggest box office draw from 1997 to 2009, reviving Hollywood's faith in big-budget pictures, although its 2012 revival in 3-D brought fewer viewers than expected.

YOU OUGHT TO BE IN PICTURES

Unlike some media areas, the film industry is still growing. Film production continued to grow through the 2007–2009 recession, but film studios are finally cutting back what they produce directly and what they distribute for independent producers. However, film is still consumed through an increasing variety of media, opening new opportunities in the field. One of the first new apps for the 2010 iPad was a Netflix viewer, for example. So film production, distribution and related jobs should continue to grow as the economy regains growth.

Film employment is notoriously unstable. Everyone from camera operators, editors, special effects, and sound technicians to actors, producers, and directors are temporary workers on short-term production projects and do not hold steady jobs. Full-time employment in other fields, the proverbial "day job," may be necessary to support you at least in the early stages of a film career.

There are about 155,100 actors, producers, and directors, primarily in motion pictures, but also in performing arts and television, and the industry is centered in New York and Los Angeles, although thousands also work in regional production centers like Austin and New Orleans. Employment is expected to grow about 11 percent in these occupations over the next few years. Aspiring actors face especially keen competition and for low wages. The median wage is less than $17 an hour, which would work out to under $35,000 a year in the (unlikely) event of full-time employment. But few other occupations have $20 million per appearance at the top end of the pay scale! Directors and producers have median salaries of $64,000 a year. Most of those entering the film industry have university degrees in media-related fields or fine arts academy training, but many break into the business on the basis of talent, luck, or connections rather than formal training. There are a wide variety of entry points, including internships with production companies and employment in craft and service occupations involved in film production.

There are also a significant number of people who work for film production or distribution companies in other roles such as writers and marketers. Camera operators and editors are other possibilities (see Chapter 8). Yet others work for talent agencies and for a wide variety of service companies, from caterers to animal handlers, which film producers need.

Audiences and revenues for cable channels in the 1990s were so large that "made-for-cable" movies, like *High School Musical 2* (2007), also became increasingly common on channels such as HBO and TNT. Basic cable networks scheduled over 100 original films in 2009. In 2011, Hallmark's two channels alone produced 32 original cable films.

MOVIES GO DIGITAL

New technology and market forces continue to transform the movie industry. Home video had become a driving force, with revenues from rentals and direct sales of videos and DVDs outstripping box office receipts two to one, but that income has dropped sharply as new forms of digital distribution emerged and consumers tightened up their discretionary purchases after the 2008 recession. In 2011, DVD revenue fell by 3.4 percent compared with the previous year. At the same time, the cost of producing major films skyrockets as producers race to outdo each other with spectacular computer-generated special effects. In hopes of spreading those costs over larger audiences, the industry began to internationalize both its ownership—which now included foreign owners such as Sony Corporation and Rupert Murdoch—and its audiences. Moviemaking at the major studios began to gravitate more toward genres (for example, science fiction, action-adventure) that could translate and export well across cultures.

However, there was also a revival in the 1990s through the mid-2000s in independent filmmaking outside the major studios. Some directors, like the late John Cassavetes, had survived as independents for years. Many others followed in their footsteps. Computer technology for editing and high-quality, low-cost digital cameras drove down the cost of producing "small" or indie films and offered the prospect of a renaissance in filmmaking apart from the financial pressures of the blockbuster mentality that gripped Hollywood. It helped that some inexpensively made films, like *Once* (2006), also made considerable profits. Video rental chains promoted independent films with special packaging in many of its stores. But the idea of **independent film** is relative. The most successful recent indie film was *Juno*, 2007, which made over $143 million, but it was produced by Fox Searchlight. Some prefer to use the independent label for much smaller films.

About 400 independent feature films are made each year, often starting as film school projects and sometimes funded through relatives' credit cards. (One of the authors overheard one of his film students debating the wisdom of maxing out all his cards to make his movie just last week.) These films circulate at film festivals around the world, hoping to strike gold, like *Napoleon Dynamite* (2004), another of the most successful recent indies, produced by filmmakers who had recently been students in Utah. The trouble now is that financing for the kind of development money filmmakers got after their success at the Sundance Film Festival dried up after the 2008 economic recession. Studios are also picking up fewer indies for distribution. In 2010, only 40 of the 3,812 films submitted to Sundance were picked up for distribution. Most studios have closed their indie distribution divisions. But most independents still depend on studios for distribution. So indie filmmaking will inevitably decline, if both financial support and distribution possibilities continue to decline. Even well-backed new studios, like Dreamworks, are struggling in the current environment of increasing costs of production, promotion, and distribution.

Faced with mushrooming costs as well as competition from video games, the Internet, and digital television for the young movie-going audience, the motion picture industry confronts significant challenges in the digital age. The studios are battling with their stars, directors, and writers over the proceeds from digital rights to their productions. To battle piracy of first-run films, thought to cost the industry billions each year, in 2008 the industry began offering legal Internet downloads of some films on the same day as DVD releases. A 2010 court ruling allowed studios to activate copy protection codes embedded in video-on-demand movies distributed via cable, paving the way for a revolution in film distribution that could bring first-run movies in the living room. In the meantime, Netflix is bringing more movies into living rooms, even as some movies are being pulled back from its collection, since studios think they are not making enough money from new low cost distribution like Netflix and Redbox film rentals. That pushes Netflix toward increasing distribution of television shows and its own original productions, which may be counterproductive for the film industry, too.

To draw audiences into theaters, the studios rely more and more on "franchise films" such as *Twilight* or *Harry Potter*. They also increasingly rely on the revenue generated by higher priced ticket sales for 3D and IMAX screenings of popular films. Although the number of tickets sold in 2010 declined

Independent (indie) film refers to films not made by the major studios.

slightly, revenues actually increased due to the higher value of these more technology intensive screenings. So Hollywood majors rushed to produce more 3D and IMAX format films, as well reworking some existing new films to screen in 3D, like Disney with *Beauty and the Beast* in 3D in 2012. In 2010, 3D films were fighting for space in a limited number of theaters, which led to a rapid buildup of both 3D and IMAX theaters, both in the USA and abroad. However, in 2011, despite increased ticket prices for 3D and IMAX, box office receipts were down $500,000 from 2011, and attendance was down 5 percent in 2011, on top of a 6 percent decline in 2010. So as with many previous film technological developments, 3D helps some films but is not a permanent solution in film competition with other media. It may be a fad, but seems likely to

TECHNOLOGY DEMYSTIFIED

ENTERING THE THIRD DIMENSION

Stereopsis. That's the term for the magic behind 3-D movies like *Avatar*. It is an optical illusion, a trick that our eyes play on our brains that makes our brain think we are looking at a three-dimensional object when in fact we are looking at a two-dimensional picture. The trick is to send two, separate, flat image views of the same object to the brain at the same time. If the two views are taken from slightly different angles so that they appear to be about two and a half inches apart (the distance between our eyes), then our brain is fooled into thinking that it sees the object in three dimensions.

There are a variety of methods to induce the illusion and the trick has been used for amusement for quite a long time. A favorite parlor pastime in the 1800s was to peer at side-by-side still images taken from slightly different camera angles through a viewer that held the images at a fixed distance in front of the eyes. The early 1950s witnessed a 3-D movie craze that had audiences peering at cheesy horror flicks with names like *Bwana Devil* and *Creature from the Black Lagoon* through cardboard glasses with filters that sent different images to the left and right eyes. *Avatar* and other 3-D movies of the current day use high-tech active glasses with side-by-side liquid crystal displays (LCDs) in place of lenses. The two LCDs alternate between being open and closed and are synchronized with the images on the screen via radio transmitters in the theater. The images on the screen alternate between the left eye image and image as seen from the right eye but that happens so quickly that, thanks to persistence of vision, the two images

register on the brain at the same time and are blended into a three-dimensional illusion.

But there is a lot more film magic behind *Avatar* than the 3-D illusion moviegoers experience in the theater. Old-fashioned 3-D movies from the *Bwana Devil* era were shot with two synchronized cameras positioned side by side and two and a half inches apart. Both images were projected on the movie screen and integrated into a single image inside the viewer's brain. Save for a few sequences, there were no cameras in the studio when *Avatar* was made. The actors' movements were recorded by motion capture suits that recorded their body movements and facial expressions. This trick has been around for a while, for example, in making an animated Tom Hanks in *Polar Express*. *Avatar* producer James Cameron integrated the digital image of the characters with a 3-D image of the virtual environment of Pandora generated in real time so that he could see the 3-D world as he directed the movements of the actors. If he didn't like the way the scene came out, he could remake it from an entirely different angle after the actors were gone by moving the point of view around inside the virtual space. Generating the alternate left and right images for the 3-D version was a simple matter of shifting the point of view slightly, by about two and a half inches.

Source: Anne Thompson (2010, January). *How James Cameron's Innovative New 3D Tech Created Avatar*. Popular Mechanics, http://www.popularmechanics.com/technology/industry/4339455.html

continue to be important for certain kinds of movies. The industry also continues to internationalize with a Chinese theater exhibition group buying the U.S. theater chain AMC in 2012, in part to get better access to new exhibition technologies like IMAX and 3D.

TECHNOLOGY TRENDS: MAKING MOVIE MAGIC

Eadweard Muybridge's first motion picture of a galloping horse used a rather unwieldy recording system—the horse's hooves triggered trip wires on 700 still cameras to yield a mere 60 seconds of action. Edison's kinetograph in 1888 was a close relative to his phonograph (see Chapter 5), in that the pictures were recorded a frame at a time on a hand-turned revolving cylinder with a light-sensitive surface. Soon the cylindrical photographic plates gave way to strips of the newly invented Kodak film.

Edison's kinetoscope was the first playback mechanism for the masses—but for only one viewer at a time. The Lumière brothers originated the movie projector in 1895 by shining a light through the strip of picture transparencies and enlarging the pictures with an optical lens. If the frames were changed fast enough (20 frames per second was about right), the viewer had the sense of continuous motion. This was because the afterimage of each frame persisted just long enough for the next frame to appear.

Apart from some advances in film processing and developing, basic motion picture technology did not change much over the next 25 years. The actors' words appeared printed on the screen, not spoken, and a live organist played theme music in the theater.

MOVIE SOUND

The first successful talkie was *The Jazz Singer* (1927). AT&T Bell Labs scientists synchronized a record with the film. Soon a way was found to record the sound on an optical track right on the film. A photoreceptor picked up variations in the light shining through the sound track and reproduced them as weak electric currents that were fed into an amplifier and then the movie theater's speakers. The latest Digital Theater Sound (DTS) systems hearken back to the old AT&T system, except that digital CDs hold the sound and are synchronized with the images via digital codes printed on the film, yielding multidimensional digital surround sound. Surround sound systems have proliferated in home theaters to simulate the sound of the theater experience.

SPECIAL EFFECTS

Early audiences were easy to fool with simple stop-action effects. If you showed them a magician climbing into a box and closing the lid, stopped the camera long enough for the magician to exit, and then restarted the film to show an empty box, early moviegoers were convinced that the magician had magically escaped. (*Hugo* [2011] shows how some of these early effects were done.) Later, the actors were filmed against the backdrop of another film projected from behind. This technique, called **rear projection**, gave the impression that actors in the studio were really paddling a boat in the rapids or engaging in other dangerous stunts; many a model train and toy boat were sacrificed to simulate real-life cataclysms.

[**Rear-projection** effects have images projected behind performers who are in the foreground.]

Modern special effects are often traced back to the 1933 classic *King Kong*. The big ape was actually an 18-inch furry doll with movable limbs that were painstakingly moved one frame at a time. When Kong grabbed our heroine, Fay Wray, she was filmed in the clutches of a life-sized mock-up of a giant gorilla's arm. *King Kong* was the first film to use a technique called **front projection.** When our heroine appeared struggling on the top of the Empire State Building, a building model was shot with a miniature movie screen on its roof, onto which pictures of the real Fay struggling were projected. *King Kong* also relied heavily on the already-familiar rear projection, as well as a technique in which live actors were filmed against a neutral backdrop and then composited with a background shot of, say, a charging dinosaur. The background was matted, or blacked out, in the areas where the actors would appear so that the two images could be superimposed. Stop-action, **compositing**, **mattes**, and scale models are still the staples of many special-effects sequences today. For examples, look at the production documentaries that are included on DVDs such as *The Lord of the Rings* (2001), which has a particularly extensive set of "making of" documentaries.

Front projection lets actors be photographed in front of an image so that they appear as part of it.

Compositing is merging several layers of images that were shot separately.

THE DIGITAL REVOLUTION

The computer is taking over in special effects. *Star Wars* (1977) used computer-driven cameras to construct multilayered space battles. In an update of Muybridge's pioneering technique, computer-controlled still cameras shot the spectacular slow-motion action scenes in *The Matrix* (1999). In 1995, Pixar Animation's *Toy Story* became the first full-length computer-animated hit film. No one had to draw each frame, or cell, of animation as in all previous animated movies.

Mattes are background paintings or photographs that are combined with performers in the foreground.

Increasingly, computer-generated monsters and sets are filling in for scale models. Sometimes computer images stand in for real actors in dangerous action sequences, such as the "people" falling off the *Titanic* (1997) as it slipped beneath the waves. The waves were computer-generated too. "Green screen" techniques allow actors shot against green backgrounds to be digitally inserted in live-action scenes or computer-generated backgrounds. Computer effects are also what made it possible for makers of *The Lord of the Rings* to use the motion capture technique, in which motion sensors are attached to a live actor to create motion for the character Gollum, but then change his appearance to something much less human. James Cameron's film *Avatar* (2009) pushes computer special effects in another dimension. A number of major characters, particularly those of an alien race, exist only as computer animation, but seem real (see Technology Demystified: Entering the Third Dimension).

Special effects are glitzy, but the real computer revolution in Hollywood is taking place behind the scenes, during the **postproduction** process when films get their finishing touches. Film editing used to involve unspooling miles of raw film footage and manually cutting and splicing to make a master copy. Now the filmed sequences are transferred to computer media where they can be accessed at random and spliced with the click of a mouse—a process known as **nonlinear editing.** Not only is this faster, but it also allows the editor to be more creative in playing "what if" in the editing suite.

Postproduction includes editing, sound effects, and visual effects that are added after shooting the original footage.

Nonlinear editing uses digital equipment to re-arrange scenes to make the master copy.

Celluloid film itself is becoming obsolete with the advent of digital cameras that record high-quality images directly in digital formats—with no chemical film processing required. In fact, they don't call it "filming" anymore; now it's "image capture." George Lucas's *Attack of the Clones* (2002) was the first major

TECHNOLOGY DEMYSTIFIED

YOU OUGHT TO BE MAKING PICTURES

One of the biggest barriers to aspiring auteurs has always been the cost of producing a student film. Doing it the "old-fashioned way," using 16-mm photographic film, rented cameras and sound equipment, and traditional editing and film processing techniques, could set the young film artist and her family back $30,000 or more, even if her film school buddies wrote the scripts, performed, and directed for free pizza. No more.

What does it take now? The newer completely digital high-definition (HD) format or the older MiniDV format yields results comparable to 16-mm film in many settings, with twice the resolution of old-fashioned analog video cameras. A truly professional HD camera can cost $12,000 but cheaper versions cost $4–5,000 and mini-DV cameras can be had for less than a thousand dollars and use the same charge coupled device (CCD) technology in their image sensors (see Chapter 8) as high-end digital video cameras. Some have still image recording capabilities and use the same storage media (for example, Compact Flash or Memory Sticks) that digital still cameras do, so you can take your production stills with the same camera. The latest models boast "near broadcast quality" megapixel resolution (that is, millions of picture dots, or pixels, per frame), at least 20X optical zoom, and sufficient light sensitivity to film in total darkness—some in a device the size of a pack of cigarettes. For Mini-DV 60-minute cassettes are less than $5 apiece and, like any other videotape, can be erased and reused if the actors fluff their lines; however, for HD, you need to record on digital storage. MiniDVs were designed to be consumer electronics gadgets, so the production quantities and features are always going up and the prices going down. Although MiniDV is still common now, increasing numbers of would-be filmmakers will be advancing into the next stage of HDV, high-definition video. Those cameras record in a completely digital form on S cards, compact flash, or other digital storage media still emerging. Some upper-end digital cameras now take high-quality video as well.

Moving digital images create a lot of data, so it has to be compressed. DV cameras use a method based on the JPEG standard used for still photos you see on the Internet rather than the MPEG-2 standard found in other video applications, but the two can be converted. Or, you can download the compressed files to your computer for editing. Universal serial bus (USB) and IEEE 394 (more popularly known as FireWire) are standard connections on both MiniDV cameras and the latest personal computers. The multigigabit disc drives also found on most personal computers nowadays provide adequate storage for short films (an hour of film takes up 13 billion bytes), but you will need lots of RAM and a video graphics card too. For editing, home computers using Adobe Premier or Apple's Final Cut Pro will do. Home computer sound editing products also do an acceptable job on the soundtrack.

So, if you can borrow a MiniDV or HDV camera from a gadget-loving relative and get your friends to work for free pizza, your student film can now be produced for a few hundred dollars. For truly professional results, you could upgrade to the higher-resolution XDCAM (Sony) format, but those cameras cost 5–10 times as much.

To get it distributed, you may need to have your "film" transferred to film; that can cost thousands of dollars. However, many film festivals now project "films" in video, and many of the commercial outlets for short subjects (for example, European television and the Independent Film Channel on cable) are video venues. There are also sites on the Internet (for example, AtomFilms) that will distribute short works online, either as downloads or as streamed files (see Chapter 9). YouTube is now one of the main outlets that can get student works noticed. Students also use social networks like Facebook to drive traffic to short films on YouTube. If you fancy actually making money on your film in theaters, then you will have to pay for the film transfer, at least until the new digital projectors become more common.

production to use **digital video** for image capture. Now it is increasingly common in animated films like *Tintin* (2011).

Digital video is recorded, edited, and often transmitted in digital form as used by computers.

Now that computers have become involved in all aspects of moviemaking, "desktop" filmmaking is fast becoming a reality. Small groups of talented people can shoot films in video and edit them on personal computers with off-the-shelf software and without Hollywood actors, directors, cameras, sets, or key grips. Digital filmmaking lowers costs, opening the film industry to student filmmakers and diverse artistic visions. The Internet is beginning to serve as a distribution mechanism for digital filmmakers, removing the last analog stop in film production and perhaps also the last financial barrier to the solo film artist-auteur. In fact, we already have virtual film studios, such as Pixar Animation Studios, started by Steve Jobs, cofounder of Apple Computers. Pixar has become known for its various hit movies, like *Toy Story 3* (2010) produced entirely with digital animation inside computers, starting with the *Toy Story* series.

MOVIE VIEWING

Movie producers have always tried to stay a step ahead of the competition by offering an aesthetic experience that cannot be duplicated by its competitors, so look for bigger screens and ever more sophisticated digital sound systems.

The old movie projector is being replaced by new digital light processors (DLPs) that show digitized movies stored on compact discs. The digital light processors, or DLPs, have microchips with millions of tiny mirrors on their surfaces. The mirrors are adjusted thousands of times per second to reflect tiny dots, or pixels, of red, green, and blue light onto the movie screen. Digital cinema has been slow to catch on, in part because the projectors cost several times what conventional ones cost, and the DLPs have lower resolution, about 1,300 lines compared to 4,000 lines for conventional film. But that is changing fast. Some of the new digital films have 4,000 lines of resolution, 48 frames per second speed to improve the quality of images in motion, and increasingly clear surround sound. *The Hobbit* is an example of these new production image and sound standards.

There were almost 17,000 digital screens in North America in 2011, and that number is increasing rapidly. Many of those are also converting to 3-D. The number of IMAX theaters is also growing, including the conversion of traditional screens in multiplexes. They feature films shot in a special large image, high-resolution format, very large immersive screen technology, and very high-quality sounds. IMAX screens are also prized venues for 3-D movies, such as *Avatar*.

Although the movie theater may never die, movies are increasingly viewed in the home with digital technologies, including DVD and digital video recorders, or DVRs. Sony's Blu-Ray high-definition DVDs is the

CARS BACK AT PIXAR AND DISNEY *Cars 2* (2011) is one of the latest computer animations produced by the Pixar Studio as part of Disney. The studio, created by Steve Jobs, has specialized in creating entirely digital animated films.

STOP&REVIEW

1. Who developed the basics of film camera and projector technology?

2. How does movie sound work?

3. How was movie image quality improved?

4. How have special effects in film developed?

5. What will be the impact of high definition and 3-D on film technology and business?

latest home standard but has not fully displaced regular DVDs This means buying a new home video player that can store a full-length, high-definition movie and play it on one of the new wide-screen digital televisions. With the film screen success of 3-D, television manufacturers are promoting new 3-D televisions, as well (see Chapter 8).

On the Internet, a download movie battle is looming to rival the fracas over music downloads. BitTorrent scatters fragments of large, often illegal video files across multiple computers, making it faster to "share" the lengthy files. The industry has responded with pay services such as Netflix' streaming service and download services by Amazon and iTunes. With well two-thirds of all U.S. Internet homes now on broadband connections, movie streaming and downloads are driving out home video stores. The main success has been Netflix, using the U.S. mail as well as a rapidly growing Internet service that streams movies to your computer, a TV connection box or game system, or directly to your television itself. Another growing home video option is video-on-demand service offered by cable companies. Unlike conventional pay cable services, these allow viewers to start and stop—and rewind or fast forward—the movie as they please. The FCC's 2010 decision to activate the copy protection technology embedded in video-on-demand movies will make it impossible to copy movies during the first 90 days after their release, opening a new "window" during which first-run films might be distributed directly to the home earlier that the current 90 day window.

Another preferred industry option is to sell digital copies of films, which are placed in a cloud locker (a secure spot on a remote server), rather like the iTunes and Amazon cloud music services described in Chapter Five. From this server/cloud system, the owner of the film can access it from a number of different digital platforms, including their home theater as well as their iPad.

THE FILM INDUSTRY: MAKING MOVIES

THE PLAYERS

Today, the film industry is a high-volume mixture of large and small players that continue to shift and evolve. There are eight major film producers: the old-time studios—Columbia, Fox, MGM, Paramount, Universal, and Warner Brothers—along with Buena Vista (Disney) and TriStar (Sony). Most of these are part of vertically integrated **conglomerates** that dominate video and film production and distribution. Each has tended to produce 15 to 25 movies per year, combining for about one-fifth of the over 550 feature films released annually in the United States (MPAA, 2011). In contrast, at the height of Hollywood's fame in 1946, the major studios each produced 40 to 50 movies every year.

Today the major studios invest an average of about $66 million per film, plus an average of $36 million in advertising per film, and they spend a high overhead to keep the studio organizations running. Top actors and directors further drain profits by demanding a percentage of the profits. A big name like Johnny Depp can earn an additional $50 million on the "back end" of a

Conglomerates are big businesses or corporations that own seemingly unrelated holdings. They are made up of diverse parts from across several media industries and are involved in multiple areas of business activity.

successful film in addition to the $20 million he makes "up front" just to appear. So the stakes are high and the pressure to produce big hits is enormous.

One "new" studio, DreamWorks, started by Steven Spielberg in 1995, has been successful in animation, but struggled in other areas, leading to concerns about its survival. With the *Shrek* and the *Madagascar* series, DreamWorks has become the main competitor to Pixar Studios in popular animated films. Pixar had primarily worked as an animation production group distributed by Disney. It became part of Disney in 2006, with Pixar executives like John Lasseter taking the lead of the combined animation operation.

INDEPENDENT FILMMAKERS

Most films (81 percent in 2010) are now being produced outside the studios (MPAA, 2011). However, although many independent films are being produced, fewer are being distributed. Over 900 films were produced in the United States in 2011, but only about 550 were actually distributed to theaters (MPAA, 2011). Many films go directly to video distribution and many simply never get released at all. So for indie directors, particularly students, getting distribution is the primary goal. Furthermore, financing through studios and other sources has declined, so indie production is also declining.

Still, there are some independent film companies, like Tom Hanks's Playtone and Drew Barrymore's Flower Films. These are not to be confused with an extensive, much less formal network of independent filmmakers. These indies usually produce films for much less than the major studios or the major independent production companies, often only a few million dollars. A classic pattern is that new filmmakers eke out a hodgepodge of financing for their first film. Once new filmmakers have their first feature film, they can try to get it shown at a variety of festivals. There are both national festivals, such as the Sundance Festival in Park City, Utah, and regional festivals, such as South by Southwest in Austin, Texas. Various organizations run specialized film festivals, presenting film series focused on LGTB (lesbian, gay, transgender, and bisexual), Jewish, and Asian content, for example, or by filmmakers belonging to these cultural groups.

THE GUILDS

As the 2007–2008 Writers Guild and Screen Actors Guild strikes showed, the craft guilds in Hollywood still wield a great deal of power. Whereas television can shift programming to unscripted reality shows, films require writers. Editors, lighting, sound, and many other technical guilds are also important. However, one reason so many productions have fled to other countries is to get around guild rules and labor costs, so Hollywood has responded by offshoring many jobs too.

FILM FINANCE

Films are financed in a variety of ways. In the U.S., one of the ways Hollywood retains its power is in its control over finance. Nearly any film with a budget over a few million dollars tends to be at least partially financed by the major studios, which often sets them up for control over distribution and other decisions as well. Sometimes other kinds of investors are drawn into film projects, but the risk of expensive failure for any given film tends to scare away those who are not committed to the business long term. Outside the U.S., national governments, regional governments like the European Union, and sometimes even states and cities all help finance movies through direct investment, tax incentives, cooperation with production needs for locales, extras, etc. The rising costs of moviemaking and distribution have tended to keep Hollywood central, even to the financing of major film projects in other countries. However, now Hollywood studios themselves are looking for financial partners, both with governments in places like China and Europe, as well as with production and finance groups in places like India with their own thriving film industries.

FILM DISTRIBUTION

Windows are separate film release times for different channels or media.

Films have traditionally been distributed in a series of **windows** of time linked to specific channels. The classic distribution for a major film used to be theatrical distribution, international theatrical distribution, pay-per-view, pay cable, DVD rentals and sales, paid downloads through iTunes or similar stores, streaming through Netflix or similar operations, network exhibition, basic cable networks, and finally syndication. All the domestic steps have an international parallel.

All the windows are compressing to reduce effects of piracy. Films now tend to be released almost simultaneously in the United States and abroad. By 2011, some films were being released abroad first to limit piracy. In 2012, one of the biggest blockbusters of the year, *The Avengers*, was released first in several overseas markets for that reason. DVD, pay TV, online streaming, and other releases have also been moved forward in the United States, and online distribution is moving up to meet the DVD release dates to try to get legitimate copies into markets as soon as pirate copies arrive. Fights are looming between theaters, which want to keep a privileged first window, and studios and others who want to get the movies out into other channels or windows as soon as possible. In general, there are many more film distribution options now than in the heyday of studio control. Many films not seen as worth the promotional costs for theatrical release go straight to video for distribution in stores, on cable, and streaming on Netflix.

Revenue from theatrical distribution of films has grown in the late 1990s, after years of decline, and remains very profitable now, despite the recent recession. Over two-thirds of the U.S. and Canadian population went to the movies in 2010. U.S. moviegoers attend the movies an average of 4.1 times a year (MPAA, 2011). However, movie going has shifted to audiences under 40. They are particularly affected by word of mouth and electronic discussion, so some movies like *Green Lantern*(2011) now tank earlier after their openings, due to poor word of mouth. Audiences might wait to see the movie on DVD or Netflix.

However, movie theaters are still growing in number. There were fewer than 18,000 screens for films in the United States in 1980, but almost 40,000 in 2011, 80 percent in multiplexes. Over 16,000 of them have digital projection, half of those 3-D. The push toward 3-D has increased revenues by an average of about $3 per film, split between theaters and distributors. However, both production costs and theaters equipment costs have gone up with 3-D.

International audiences steadily became more important to the Hollywood bottom line. In 2010, international film distribution was 70 percent of total receipts, and growing. In contrast, home video was over 42 percent of film income in 2010, compared to 25 percent at the box office, according to the Video Software Dealers of America (http://www.vsda.org), but video was shrinking while 3D and international distribution were growing.

DVD sales declined 44 percent in 2010, even though 35 percent of people prefer to watch movies that way. Declining DVD sales worries studios, since that has been their largest source of revenue for years. They hope to replace it with a new form of digital sales, in which a customer purchases a film digitally, places it in a cloud locker (a secure spot on a remote server), from which they can access it from a number of different platforms.

Rentals are changing. Redbox and similar vendors in 2010 had 19 percent of the rental market. Studios are concerned about Redbox because its low $1 price puts downward pressure on rental income. Rent-by-mail services like Netflix had 36 percent of the market. Traditional stores had 45 percent, but that was declining. Streaming services by Netflix and others are increasing rapidly in popularity. In 2011, 16 percent preferred to watch movies via streaming. Among households with Netflix, it is the second most popular "TV" channel and the main way of watching movies.

Both rentals and sales of DVDs are now driven in part by additional scenes and extra features, such as documentaries about special effects and other aspects of the making of the film. The *Lord of the Rings* films managed to sell two or three different DVDs of each film to some buyers by releasing more extra scenes, extra features, extra merchandise, and longer previews of the next movie in the series with each successive DVD release.

STOP&REVIEW

1. How do independent filmmakers differ from studios?
2. What is currently the typical distribution cycle of a film?
3. What has been the effect of home video on the movie industry?
4. What is the current effect of streaming and other digital channels?

TELLING STORIES: FILM CONTENT

Film, more than any other medium other than perhaps printed novels, is centered around storytelling, the creation of striking and memorable narratives that draw people in to spend fairly high amounts of money to see them, often repeatedly.

TEAM EFFORT

Much more than in fiction writing for novels, songwriting, or even television production, creating film content or stories is an ensemble or group effort. Although audiences tend to think of movies in terms of which actors star in them, filmmaking is probably more driven by directors, producers, and writers, as well as visual designers, photography directors, music directors, film editors, special effects people, and casting directors. Even less obvious but just as critical are script readers, development executives, market researchers, focus group services that examine ideas and plots, studio finance people who package various sources of money together, marketing strategists who plan promotional campaigns, and release strategists who assemble theaters so that films can open "big," and gain momentum that carries them into DVD sales, streaming, etc.

Many people add to the substance of a film's contents. A memorable, award-winning film, like *Avatar* (2009), is based on strong performances, innovative

GROUP EFFORT Although it's the famous actors and directors who are glorified during awards shows, making a movie is an ensemble process involving the creative talents of many people.

use of special effects, and strong directors like James Cameron, who pushed and worked on the film for almost 20 years. But it also depends on the casting of less well-known actors, striking visual design, original cinematography, memorable music, sound effects, and the central role of the director in orchestrating all of these processes and the people who perform them. Although the number of Academy Awards may seem endless, it is interesting to think about how all these people contribute creative elements to the final film content. The complexity and organizational and financial demands of putting all these people and their roles together in a finished film is one reason that the Hollywood studios dominated film production for so long and are still central to the production of most major films, performing most of the business, finance, and marketing functions that give the artists budgets to work with.

Most often, the controlling hand on film production and storytelling is the director. Sometimes directors are simply hired to oversee a process envisioned by a producer, who typically lines up the financing, story developers, scriptwriters, director, and sometimes major stars. However, the most memorable films usually reflect the artistic vision of a director who selects and directs the people who actually act, shoot the film, create the special effects, and so on. The most strongly creative directors often write or co-write the scripts or story concepts for their films.

Many films start with a writer's draft film script, which is circulated among studios, producers, directors, and even leading actors, looking for interest. Thousands circulate, hundreds get optioned for a serious look, but few get made. Sometimes scripts emerge as films with remarkably little change. More often film scripts go through revisions, including the addition of other writers, and are often changed substantially by directors on the scene of production or in the final editing.

FINDING AUDIENCE SEGMENTS

The history section of this chapter describes the earlier genres that laid the foundation of current moviemaking formulas. These are still present, but an explosion of new film genres began in the 1950s and continues today as filmmakers experiment with new ways to attract audiences. Table 7.2 lists several more recently evolved film genres.

New genres proliferate in search of audience segments. However, the basic ones are the kinds of genre categories that you find labeling the aisles of video stores or Netflix' website: comedy, drama, action, horror, science fiction, classics, family, western, animation, documentary, and foreign. These genres continue to dominate, as filmmakers blend classic genres to reach very broad audiences both in the United States and abroad. The blockbusters favor genres in which big budgets and special effects can be used to best advantage: action-adventure, crime, horror, drama, and science fiction.

Film content has become more diverse in part because film audiences have become more diverse. However, films are often still made to maximize the box office earnings of the initial theatrical distribution (Table 7.3). The initial box office is what gives a film its "buzz," its momentum. Thus studios still tend

TABLE 7.2 Film Genres

- Youth rebellion movies, such as *The Wild One* (1954) or *Youth in Revolt* (2009)
- Spy stories, with gadgets and action, such as James Bond in *Goldfinger* (1964) or *Mission Impossible: Ghost Protocol* (2011)
- Romantic comedies, with varying degrees of sex, such as *Pillow Talk* (1959) or *No Strings Attached* (2011)
- Science fiction, such as *Forbidden Planet* (1956) or *Prometheus (2012)*
- Slasher movies, such as *Friday the 13th Part VII* (1998) or *Saw IV* (2007)
- Rock/pop music movies, such as *A Hard Day's Night* (1964) or *Shine a Light* (2008)
- "Black" movies, such as *Superfly* (1972) or *Hancock* (2008)
- Spanish-language movies, such as *El Mariachi* (1992) or *Pan's Labyrinth* (2006)
- Coming-of-age movies, in which teenagers discover things about themselves, such as *The Breakfast Club* (1985) or *Superbad* (2007)
- Antiwar movies, such as *Apocalypse Now* (1979) or *The Green Zone* (2009)
- Sword and sandal movies, with heroes and muscles, such as *Conan, the Barbarian* (1982) or *Robin Hood* (2010)
- Disaster movies, such as *The Towering Inferno* (1974) or *2012* (2009)

to make movies for people who go out to the movies. This makes the typical movie theatergoer, who is younger and more tolerant of sex and violence, disproportionately influential in decisions about what kinds of movies are made.

Increasingly, filmmakers are relying on social media to help them create buzz. Facebook "likes" and Twitter tweets quickly get the word out about a new release faster than conventional word of mouth ever could. Producers enlist their stars to tweet about new releases and post on their Facebook pages as well as creating Facebook pages for their movies that users can "like" and refer to their friends. These social media strategies build on the enthusiasm of teens and young adults for social media. Almost half of film viewing at theaters is by people aged 12 to 29, a third of whom go to movies at least once a month, compared to a fifth of all older adults (http://www.mpaa.org).

TABLE 7.3 Top 10 Worldwide Movie Earners of All Time

FILM	STUDIO. YEAR	DIRECTOR	BOX OFFICE GROSS (IN MILLIONS)
Avatar	Fox, 2009	James Cameron	2,781
Titanic	Paramount, 1997	James Cameron	1,835
Harry Potter and the Deathly Hallows: Part 2	Warner Bros., 2011	DavidYates	1,328
The Lord of the Rings: The Return of the King	New Line, 2003	Peter Jackson	1,129
Transformers: Dark of the Moon	Paramount, 2011	Michael Bay	1,114
Pirates of the Caribbean: Dead Man's Chest	Buena Vista, 2006	Gore Verbinski	1,065
Toy Story 3	Walt Disney Pictures/ Pixar Animation Studios 2010	Lee Unkrich	1,062
Pirates of the Caribbean: On Stranger Tides	Buena Vista, 2011	Gore Verbinski	1,041
Alice in Wonderland	Walt Disney Pictures, 2010	Tim Burton	1,023
The Dark Knight	Warner Brothers, 2008	Christopher Nolan	1,002

Source: www.IMDB.com/boxoffice/alltimegross?region=world-wide. Accessed January 12, 2012.

Films are now viewed in many ways: on television, cable, home video, and streaming. The average amount of time spent watching films on video has increased dramatically in the last decade. Over three-quarters of Americans rent videotapes or DVDs at least occasionally. The average household spends over $240 per year renting, streaming, and buying films. The interests of these Americans are more diverse than those who go to movie theaters. For example, young adults, especially those with young families, are among the heaviest renters, and children's videos are the most popular genre. Some sequels to popular animated features, like *The Land Before Time* (1988) or *Aladdin* (1992), were released on video only.

MEDIALITERACY

FILM AND YOUR SOCIETY

The film industries are embroiled in a number of policy and social issues that affect how they conduct business and the kinds of content they create.

VIOLENCE, SEX, PROFANITY, AND FILM RATINGS

For years, one of the most powerful forces in the entertainment industry has been the Motion Picture Association of America (**MPAA**). The MPAA, composed of the major film studios, has been a significant player in American culture and politics.

[**MPAA** (Motion Picture Association of America) is a trade organization that represents the major film studios.]

After years of debate and what seemed to be an increase in the number of movies with profanity, explicit sex, and violence in the 1960s, the Motion Picture Association of America instituted a rating system in 1968 to give people an idea of what they might encounter in a film, to avoid outside regulation by letting people make more informed choices. After some further modifications over the years, the **MPAA rating** categories are as follows:

[**MPAA ratings** are part of a movie rating system instituted in 1968.]

G—For all ages; no sex or nudity, minimal violence

PG—Parental guidance suggested; some portions perhaps not suitable for young children, mild profanity, non-"excessive" violence, only a glimpse of nudity

PG-13—Parents strongly cautioned to give guidance to children under 13; some material may be inappropriate for young children

R—Restricted; those under 17 must be accompanied by parent or guardian; may contain very rough violence, nudity, or lovemaking

NC-17—No one under 17 admitted; generally reserved for films that are openly pornographic, although some mainstream films receive this rating

Many people have debated the appropriateness and utility of these ratings. Some argue that as a form of industry self-censorship, the ratings violate freedom of speech for filmmakers. Others argue that, as with music lyric advisories, the ratings simply excite the interest of younger viewers. Many observe that the restrictions imposed on teenagers by R and NC-17 ratings are not enforced by theaters, whose managers are aware that teens are the

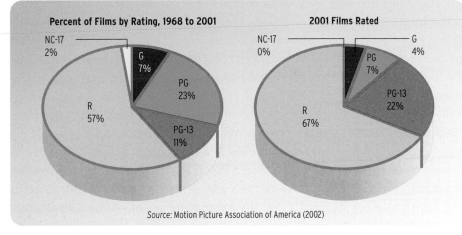

Percent of Films by Rating, 1968 to 2001

NC-17 2%
G 7%
PG 23%
PG-13 11%
R 57%

2001 Films Rated

NC-17 0%
G 4%
PG 7%
PG-13 22%
R 67%

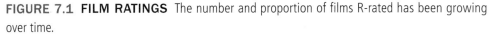

Source: Motion Picture Association of America (2002)

FIGURE 7.1 FILM RATINGS The number and proportion of films R-rated has been growing over time.

main moviegoers. Indeed, enforcing the rule would be hard; in multiplex movie theaters, people under 17 often buy a ticket for a PG movie, then go into an R-rated one. There is also category creep. Films that might once have been rated R now squeak through with a PG-13. Many people would like to distinguish what some call "hard R" movies, like *Saw IV* (2007), which feature gruesome violence or torture, from other R films. But NC-17 films don't tend to do well, so filmmakers resist accepting that rating and tend to change just as much as they have to get an R rating from MPAA reviewers.

The ratings system also allowed filmmakers to continue to produce films with sexually explicit and violent content, because they can argue that audiences are alerted to avoid such material. Ratings have not decreased the numbers of violent or sexual films. Since 1968, 58 percent of all films have been rated R, although most top-grossing films have been PG or PG-13 (mpaa.org). In 2010, 12 of the top 25 films were PG-13 and nine were PG (MPAA, 2011). Movies are usually rated R for profanity, nudity, or sex, whereas PG-13 movies are often by far the most violent in amount and intensity. Starting in 2007 MPAA also includes the incidence of on-screen smoking as a factor in the ratings. One study shows that parents care most about shielding their children from scary violence, whereas raters seem to care more about guarding against sex or profanity. Although many parents have expressed appreciation for the ratings, which give them something to work with in guiding children's viewing, they say the ratings are not dependable because they are not consistent from movie to movie.

We suspect that many of our readers are enjoying their newfound freedom to watch R-rated films, but in a few years many will be in the role of "concerned parents" themselves, wondering how to shield children from excessive sex and violence. The movie ratings are one option. Another is a technology called *ClearPlay* that automatically edits out sex and violence in DVDs as they are played back, by simply skipping over time codes on the disc that correspond to the offending material.

VIEWER ETHICS: FILM PIRACY

Illegal use of copyrighted intellectual property has been a serious issue for the film industry (also see Chapter 14). Film industry estimates of financial losses to studios and other film copyright holders resulting from illegal copying or piracy are in the hundreds of billions of dollars, both in the United States and abroad.

Films have been relatively easy for many people to copy ever since videotape technology came into wide use in the 1980s, and the introduction and early popularity of VCRs unnerved the movie industry, which feared that illegal copying or piracy would keep people from paying for either a movie ticket or a video rental. The MPAA initially tried to suppress the diffusion of videotape technology, fearing massive piracy. When that attempt failed, the MPAA put a great deal of energy into demanding the enforcement of laws against illegal video copying of movies, both in the United States and abroad. As the law enforcement crackdown began to reduce piracy, and as more people started renting legitimate copies from a rapidly expanding set of online video rental outlets, the MPAA studio producers began to realize that video was more of a gold mine than a threat.

The film industry hopes to discourage illegal film copying at the consumer level. Consumers may make a copy of a film that is being broadcast or cablecast for their own use. However, they may not sell or rent that copy to anyone else. A consumer may not copy a film from one computer, VCR, or DVD onto another. This is why all officially copied films have an FBI warning against illegal copying at the beginning of the tape or DVD. In most cases, both digital copies and DVDs of films have technological safeguards against copying. The MPAA is concerned about fast Internet download programs, like BitTorrent, that permit downloading of feature-length films, and has tried to put several similar networks, like LimeWire, out of business. However, the most recent MPAA effort to restrict online trading and down-loading, a proposed bill in the U.S. Congress called the **Stop Online Piracy Act** (**SOPA**), was seen as too intrusive into online freedom and was fought down in Congress by an online campaign that had been pushed hard by computer and Internet industry interests.

The big issue in piracy is illegal copying by people who intend to sell or rent the illegal copy. This practice defrauds copyright holders of rentals or sales that they might otherwise have from potential consumers who rent or

Stop Online Piracy Act (SOPA) was an anti-piracy initiative by the film and music industries, defeated in 2011 because it seemed to limit Internet rights.

Columbia Pictures/courtesy Everett Collection

THE AVENGERS VS. THE PIRATES The *Avengers* can whip any super villain but still loses money to pirates at home and abroad.

MEDIA&CULTURE

SAVING NATIONAL PRODUCTION OR THE NEW CULTURAL IMPERIALISM?

It worries many countries that Hollywood films tend to dominate their viewing screens. Hollywood films can take up to 90 percent or more of screen time in many countries, perhaps even more of video and DVD rentals and sales. So countries are increasingly anxious to find ways to increase national production. (For more on the history of why U.S. films dominate, see Chapter 17.)

One phenomenon that is blurring and perhaps also partially solving the issue is an increasing tendency for Hollywood to participate in complex co-productions with other countries—for example, *The Lord of the Rings films*. A UNESCO (2003) study cited co-productions as an example of how Hollywood films dominate, but are they in fact Hollywood films? The basis for the films is J.R.R. Tolkien's novel trilogy of the same name, which the author seems to have originally intended as a mythology for Great Britain, his home country (*The Letters of J.R.R. Tolkien*, 1981). Critics such as John Garth (2003) argue that the story and some of the characters come directly from Tolkien's experience in the British Army in World War I. The director, the main screen story adapters/writers, the special effects people, and a number of actors are from New Zealand. The films were shot and edited in New Zealand and the special effects created by a New Zealand company, Weta Workshop, which has become a major global special effects house. Most of the lead actors were British or American. Financing and distribution came from Hollywood. One can argue whether the sensibility is essentially that of a Hollywood blockbuster. Fans of the books have scrutinized the films closely to see if the original story has been overwhelmed, and opinion from them is mixed.

The films have helped create a burgeoning film industry in New Zealand. Other films like *The Adventures of Tintin* (2011) and British novels like C.S. Lewis's *Narnia* books have been made into films there.

A number of other current examples abound. After the recent success of a number of Mexican films, directors, and writers, Hollywood is actively looking in Mexico for scripts, directors, and actors for co-production. The same is true with Hong Kong, India, and Brazil. Critics in those countries are wondering whether some of their best and brightest are being seduced into making films that are directly co-produced using Hollywood money and formulas, or less directly borrowing Hollywood formulas to eventually gain global distribution by Hollywood distributors, who control global distribution (see Chapter 16). However, other critics and viewers are happy that Hollywood money, distribution, and formulas are facilitating the revival of filmmaking by national directors.

One way of looking at this is as a new wave of U.S. cultural imperialism (see Chapter 17), with U.S. ways, if not literally U.S. movies, continuing to dominate the world (Miller et al., 2005). Or one can view it as a complex globalization where the United States and other countries interact with each other, even though the United States still tends to dominate the overall output and flow of films.

Source: The Letters of J.R.R. Tolkien, edited by Humphrey Carpenter. Boston: Houghton-Mifflin, 1981, p. 144. John Garth. *Tolkien and the Great War: The Threshold of Middle-Earth*. Boston: Houghton-Mifflin, 2003. Toby Miller et al., *Global Hollywood* 2. London: BFI, 2005. UNESCO. (2003). Convention for the Safeguarding of the Intangible Cultural Heritage. Paris: UNESCO.

---

buy the illegal copy instead of the legal one. Only legal copies provide royalties to the copyright holders, compensating them for the expense and work that went into the movie. Thus the film industry, via the MPAA, has pushed law enforcement officials both in the United States and abroad to enforce copyright laws by pursuing large-scale, commercially oriented pirates. Those who are illegally copying tapes on a large industrial scale are the ones principally targeted by enforcement efforts.

The MPAA has had remarkable success in getting many governments to crack down on film piracy abroad. The U.S. government has helped apply

STOP&REVIEW

1. What movie genres are most dominant now?
2. How are films targeted to audience segments now?
3. Why were film ratings developed? What are the pros and cons of ratings?
4. How has audience segmentation changed film production?
5. What copyright and piracy problems does the film industry face?

pressure on other governments to enforce the existing international copyright agreements. Nearly all governments have signed the Berne Copyright Convention, which covers video piracy.

New issues arise in protecting intellectual property that exists in digital form since it is easier to pirate digital material because a computer can be used as the main copying tool. Internet hackers crack discs' copyright protection and "share" movie sites over the Internet. The movie theater is another front in the anti-piracy war. Films now include flashing colored dots that carry identifying information about the print so that the studios can track down pirates who surreptitiously tape first-run movies at the multiplex. Other technologies, including night vision goggles, are used to look for hidden cameras in the audience on premier nights. Google is also perfecting a "video fingerprinting" technology that makes it possible for computers to spot copyrighted material. Avast, movie pirates!

SUMMARY&REVIEW

HOW HAS MOTION PICTURE TECHNOLOGY DEVELOPED?

Thomas Edison invented most of the major components of the camera, whereas the Lumière brothers in France discovered the principle of projecting light through transparent filmstrips. Film has been improved by increasing the number of frames or images per second, making the image wider, and adding color. Special effects developed from mechanical models, as in the classic 1933 *King Kong*, have become more sophisticated and ultimately replaced by computer-generated images. The superimposing of images and the use of background mattes has also been made more sophisticated by computers. Digitization changed not only effects, but image capture (cinematography), editing, and, increasingly, projection.

WHAT WERE THE STAR SYSTEM AND STUDIO SYSTEMS?

Rudolph Valentino, Lillian Gish, and Charlie Chaplin were such attractions that their names appeared above the name of the film on movie marquees. The studios rose on the basis of this star system, using the stars' popularity to promote their movies.

The studio system consisted of production companies that employed the complete set of facilities and people required to make and distribute movies. The major movie studios grew by developing a stable of actors, writers, and directors who worked for them over a period of years. The main Hollywood studios were United Artists, Paramount, MGM (Metro-Goldwyn-Mayer), Fox, Warner Brothers, Universal, Columbia, and RKO. The major film producers are still the old-time studios—Columbia, Fox, MGM, Paramount, Universal, and Warner Brothers—along with Buena Vista (Disney) and TriStar (Sony). Independent film companies work alone or with majors. Individual independent filmmakers, or "indies," usually produce more films but for much less money than the majors—often a few million dollars. Indie films are still primarily distributed by the majors.

WHAT WERE SOME OF THE MAIN DEVELOPMENTS IN FILM FORMS AND GENRES?

D. W. Griffith pioneered using a large screen, well-produced outdoor battle scenes, moving shots, feature-length films, and close-ups. The silent film genres included westerns, war movies, science fiction, romances, physical comedies, and historical costume dramas.

Talking pictures created a sudden change, starting with *The Jazz Singer* in 1927. Acting became less overstated and stylized. The actors' voices and the use of sound effects, as well as music, became important. Talkies required an influx of new talent, which came mostly from vaudeville and Broadway. A number of new genres, such as musicals, film noir, and others, took advantage of both technology and studio system possibilities. The basic current genres are the categories you would find in video stores or on Netflix: comedy, drama, action, horror, science fiction, classic, family, western, animation, and foreign.

HOW DID HOLLYWOOD AND ITS FILMS CHANGE AFTER THE ADVENT OF TELEVISION?

The film industry was closely tied to theatrical chains, and television quickly cut into their revenues. As small theaters closed all over America in the 1950s, the film industry began to realize that it couldn't beat television. Disney started producing programs for television in 1954, and other studios followed. All began to license films for showing on television, and many eventually produced made-for-TV movies. By the 1960s, the power of the movie studios was declining. Independent producers

gained more of a role in producing movies, and film studios began to spend much of their time producing TV series. Movie channels like HBO provided an important new distribution channel for films, and cable channels began to commission new made-for-cable films.

WHY WERE FILM RATINGS DEVELOPED? WHAT ARE THEIR PROS AND CONS?

After years of debate and what seemed to be an increase in movies with explicit language, sex, and violence in the 1960s, the MPAA instituted a ratings system to give people an idea of what they might encounter in a film. Some critics argue that as a form of industry self-censorship, ratings violate freedom of speech for filmmakers. Others argue that the ratings simply draw the interest of younger viewers. The restrictions on teenage viewing of films rated R and NC-17 are often not enforced by theaters, because teens are the main moviegoers.

THINKING CRITICALLY
ABOUT THE MEDIA

1. How does the history of film help us understand how movies will develop as they interact or converge with parts of the Internet, like iTunes distribution or Netflix?

2. How does learning the forms and history of film help us understand how other visual, narrative forms, like video games, are going to develop as commercial forms? As artistic forms?

3. What would be the most effective response by the film industry to keep it from being hurt by piracy in the way that the music industry has been?

4. Does violence in film need to be more tightly controlled? Please justify your answer with examples from film history and from controversial films like the *Saw* series.

5. Do you think that the impact of special effects and other technology on films is positive? Do the new tools help or harm storytelling in film?

KEY TERMS

B movies (p. 190)

compositing (p. 199)

concentration of ownership (p. 191)

conglomerates (p. 202)

digital video (p. 201)

feature film (p. 186)

film noir (p. 189)

first-run distribution (p. 194)

front projection (p. 199)

gross (p. 191)

independent film (p. 196)

major film studios (p. 187)

mattes (p. 199)

Motion Picture Code (p. 187)

MPAA (p. 208)

MPAA ratings (p. 208)

nonlinear editing (p. 199)

postproduction (p. 199)

rear projection (p. 198)

star system (p. 187)

Stop Online Piracy Act (SOPA) (p. 210)

studio system (p. 190)

talkies (p. 188)

theatrical films (p. 191)

vertical integration (p. 190)

windows (p. 204)

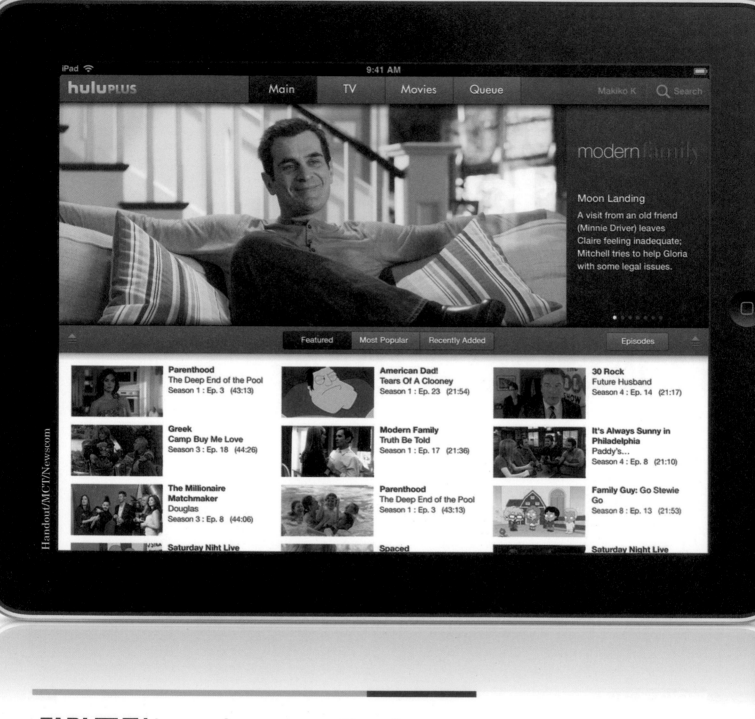

Handout/MCT/Newscom

TABLET TV is one of many new options for viewing discussed in this chapter that change and challenge conventional television networks.

8

TELEVISION

HISTORY: TV MILESTONES

TELEVISION IS BORN

Early television experiments sparked public interest in "radio with pictures" throughout the 1920s and 1930s, and the technical standards that would define television for decades to come were put in place in 1941. However, the medium did not begin to flourish until after World War II when wartime shortages of electronic components ended and new technologies developed for the war effort made television networks possible.

Network television's first big star was comedian Milton Berle. Legend has it that people bought televisions—and stopped going to movie theaters on the night he was on—just so they could see him. Demand for TV channels grew so fast that the FCC put a "temporary" freeze on new stations in 1948 while it came up with a plan that it hoped would ensure plenty of viewing choices for everyone. However, the technical issues surrounding the introduction of color television complicated the plan, and the freeze dragged on until 1952 (Sterling & Kittross, 1990). In the interim, cable television systems sprang up to distribute signals from distant cities to the residents of small cities and towns without stations of their own.

The 1952 FCC rules, the Sixth Report and Order, expanded the **VHF** (very high frequency) television band (channels 2 to 13), opened the new **UHF**

1952	TV freeze ends with FCC's Sixth Report and Order	1996	Telecommunications Act triggers merger wave
1961	Newton Minow calls TV a "vast wasteland"	1998	Broadcast networks lose dominance
1975	HBO goes on satellite	2009	Transition to digital TV in the United States
1987	Fox network challenges the Big Three		

VHF is the very high frequency television band, channels 2 to 13.

UHF stands for ultra-high frequency, channels 14 to 69.

(ultra-high frequency) band (channels 14 to 83, later reduced to 14 to 69), and set aside channels for educational broadcasting. Only VHF stations prospered, though, because those signals are stronger and because the FCC did not require UHF tuners in all new TV sets until 12 years later. The FCC's decision effectively limited the number of national television networks to the Big Three (ABC, CBS, and NBC) because most cities had only three VHF channels available. So, instead of a bounty of viewing choices for all, the freeze ultimately had the effect of limiting almost everyone's choices to three for decades to come.

The cultural and economic impacts of television were quick to arrive, thanks to radio pioneers (see Chapter 6) David Sarnoff at NBC and William Paley at CBS who put the talent and sponsors developed by their radio networks at the disposal of early television producers. In those days television was a "social medium" of sorts, as television owners invited their family and friends over to share the novel viewing experience and relived moments from top rated shows in conversations the next day. In the early years, ABC was led by Leonard Goldenson, a former movie executive who was the first to bring Hollywood production values to the small screen. Advertisers flocked to a medium that could display moving pictures of their products to a national audience and sponsored entire shows that they named after themselves (e.g., *The Kraft Television Theater*) and filled with plugs for their brands. By the mid-1950s television was the leading advertising medium in the United States, ahead of radio, newspapers, and magazines. Meanwhile, movie attendance dropped to half its peak of 1946.

CBS-TV / THE KOBAL COLLECTION/Picture Desk

LUUUUUUCY! Comedienne Lucille Ball was a popular star in the TV's Golden Age and a pioneer female executive behind the scenes.

THE GOLDEN AGE

The late 1940s and early 1950s are called television's "Golden Age," largely as a tribute to live drama anthologies. Unlike today's predictable episodic dramas, the anthologies had a different storyline and characters each week and often dealt with thought-provoking subject matter. Rod Serling's *Twilight Zone* series is a good example of the Golden Age style. (Samples of suspenseful *Twilight Zone* episodes in black and white and other Golden Age favorites can be found at YouTube.com by key-wording TV series titles from the "early examples" in Table 8.5.)

News and public affairs programs were also hallmarks of the Golden Age. *Meet the Press* went on the air in 1947 and continues today. The first regularly scheduled TV news program was a 10-minute newscast on NBC in 1948. In one of television's finest moments, CBS news correspondent Edward R. Murrow exposed Wisconsin Senator Eugene McCarthy's anticommunist "crusade" of the early 1950s as a campaign of innuendo and half-truths, establishing TV's ability to impact the nation's affairs.

INTO THE WASTELAND

The Golden Age died as audiences shifted and **ratings** ruled (see Figure 8.1 and Media&Culture: Going by the Numbers, page 217). By 1956 TVs were in two-thirds of American homes and 95 percent of all stations were affiliates who carried the network feeds of the Big Three. The broader audience didn't appreciate the highbrow drama anthologies as much as the well-educated, urban, East Coast early adopters had. Sponsors wished for more upbeat lead-ins to their snappy commercial jingles. Advertising practices changed so that sponsors could purchase minute-long (and later 30-second or 15-second) "spots" rather than entire programs. This focused attention on "buying" audiences by the thousand (the **cost per thousand**), and programs that appealed to refined, but uncommon, tastes had prohibitively high costs on that basis.

> **Ratings** measure the proportion of television households that watch a specific show, or how many people are listening to a radio station.

> **Cost per thousand** is how much a commercial costs in relation to the number of viewers that see it, in thousands.

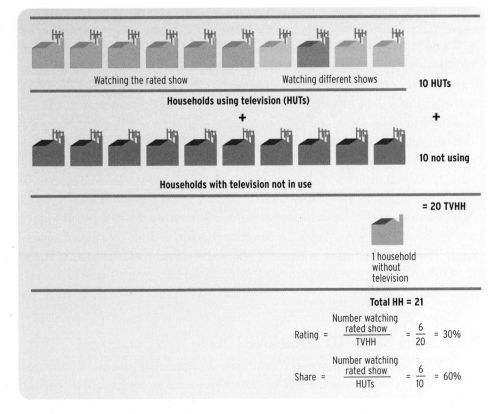

Watching the rated show   Watching different shows   **10 HUTs**

Households using television (HUTs)

\+   \+

10 not using

Households with television not in use

= 20 TVHH

1 household without television

Total HH = 21

$$\text{Rating} = \frac{\text{Number watching rated show}}{\text{TVHH}} = \frac{6}{20} = 30\%$$

$$\text{Share} = \frac{\text{Number watching rated show}}{\text{HUTs}} = \frac{6}{10} = 60\%$$

FIGURE 8.1 HOW RATINGS ARE COMPUTED Ratings are computed by dividing the number of homes watching a show by the total number of TV households. Shares are computed by dividing by the number of households using TV at a particular time.

THE NATION WATCHED The first ever televised presidential debates between Kennedy and Nixon demonstrated television's power to inform the public and impact the nation's culture.

Paul Schutzer/Time Life Pictures/Getty Images

Ratings are one-half of the formula for economic success in television; low production costs are the other half. Situation comedies, or sitcoms, cost less than drama or variety shows, and the 1951 hit *I Love Lucy* proved their appeal. Cheaper still were quiz shows that eliminated scripts and professional actors—we call them reality shows today—and those shot to the top of the ratings in the mid-1950s. Television executives also turned to Hollywood for more efficient productions. ABC ordered the first series from a film studio, *Disneyland*, in 1954. Western movies were popular then, and ABC recycled sets and unemployed actors from westerns to produce shows like *Maverick* on the cheap. By the end of the decade nearly all entertainment production had moved west leaving behind in New York only network news and soap operas like *Days of Our Lives*.

As television's influence grew, its power to offend audiences and degrade culture as well as to entertain and enlighten became evident. The children of the early 1950s suffered an epidemic of broken limbs as they jumped from garage roofs while attempting to imitate TV's Superman, incidents that helped lead to the first congressional hearings about the effects of television on children. A few years later greedy sponsors rigged popular TV quiz shows to improve their ratings, causing a national scandal. In 1961, FCC Chairman Newton Minow called American television a "vast wasteland" of mediocre, uninformative programs.

Television continued to have golden moments. The whole nation seemed to watch together as events like the Kennedy-Nixon presidential debates, Kennedy's funeral, the Vietnam War, and the moon landing unfolded in the nation's living rooms. Entertainment programs from that era also left their mark. *All in the Family* focused on the clash between generations and exposed racial bigotry, whereas the *Mary Tyler Moore Show* offered positive images of professional women. *Roots,* a blockbuster miniseries about the passage of African-Americans in the United States, sparked renewed pride in African origins and interracial dialogue.

TELEVISION GOES TO WASHINGTON

So the question for regulators in Washington became how to balance the good that television could do against the cultural damage it could inflict. Perhaps the Big Three's oligopoly (see Chapter 2) had to be broken, beginning with their stranglehold on television production. The FCC imposed the Financial Interest in Syndication Rules (known as Fin-Syn for short) in 1970 to push the networks out of the **syndication** business through which they profited

Syndication is the rental or licensing of media products.

MEDIA&CULTURE

GOING BY THE NUMBERS

Since 1950, the Nielsen Company has been a force in television audience measurement with technology that automatically records when the television set is on and the channel to which it is tuned. The households that participate in ratings studies are randomly selected so that every home has an equal chance of being included. This makes the sample statistically representative of the population from which it is drawn—all U.S. television households. The same basic techniques are employed in the public opinion polls that are used to predict election outcomes.

Figure 8.1 (page 217) shows how television ratings are calculated. A television household is any home with a (working) television set, and there are about 115 million in the United States. An HUT is a Household Using Television; about 60 percent of all TV households are usually HUTs during prime time. A rating is the percentage of all television households tuned in to a particular program. Each rating point thus represents 1 percent of the total, or about 1,150,000 households. A share is the percentage of HUTs watching a program: thus, it is based on only the homes actually watching television at a particular time.

Advertisers perform an additional computation to arrive at the cost per thousand (or CPM, as it is known). They multiply the rating by the number of households each rating point represents and divide that into the cost of buying a commercial spot in the corresponding program. So, if *60 Minutes* has a 10 rating, that translates into 11.5 million television households, or 11,500 lots of 1,000 homes each. If a 30-second spot on *60 Minutes* costs $94,000, we divide that by 11,500 and arrive at a CPM of $8.17. Generally, advertisers select the programs that have the lowest CPM.

The old-style meters that recorded only household-level viewing have given way to People Meters that record individual viewing for national rating reports, called the *National Television Index (NTI)*. The 21,000 People Meter families are prompted by a flashing red light to push buttons on a box to indicate who is in the room at that moment. Conventional meters have been phased out in 56 local markets that Nielsen monitors continuously and have been replaced with Local People Meters that are included in the national sample. Meanwhile, paper diaries to record viewership are still mailed out in some 150 smaller local markets in the months of November, February, May, and July, about 500,000 diaries in each of these months. You may have noticed that the programs are a little better and the local news stories are a little more sensational during those "sweeps months" as broadcasters compete for attention in the Nielsen homes.

The accuracy and validity of ratings is a growing concern. Only about a third of all the homes contacted participate in diary studies and many "fudge" their answers by writing in programs they would like Nielsen to think they watch, but don't actually tune in to. Nielsen hopes to eliminate diary studies entirely in favor of people meters. However, viewers in People Meter homes, especially young children, tire of pushing buttons during the two years they remain in the sample and are often undercounted. The ratings of shows starring minority characters also do poorly in People Meter homes compared to diary surveys, even though the proportion of African-American and Hispanic households in the people-metered sample closely matches the national percentages of these groups.

Nielsen is striving to keep up with the new media environment. It now provides ratings of individual commercials as well as the TV shows they appear in and includes delayed DVR playbacks in its data. Its "anytime anywhere media measurement" initiative aims to integrate data across television, Internet, and mobile phone screens. Starting in 2010, the company measures online viewing in 7,500 of the homes in its national metered sample. DVR playbacks are included in national television rating reports but online viewing is kept in a separate Extended Screen report. At present advertising rates are set according to the number who view programs on their televisions, but not their computers cell phones or tablets, within three days of their original broadcast. Nielsen also tracks video game consumption and has developed new panels to measure viewing in bars, sports clubs, and college dorm rooms. Wireless people meters that can be sent through the mail or worn by individuals are also under development. Still, some of Nielsen's biggest customers in the advertising, broadcast, and cable industry are less than pleased, and they have formed the Consortium for Innovative Media Measurement to speed up innovation.

from reruns of popular shows. The 1970 Prime Time Access Rule closed the 7 to 8 P.M. time slot to network programming to increase the diversity of programming. And, in 1975, the Justice Department put limits on the number of hours of entertainment programming the networks could make in-house. These moves stimulated competition in production as television units associated with major film studios began to profit from syndication and the early evening filled with cheap-to-produce **first-run syndication** shows like *Wheel of Fortune*. By the mid-1970s, most homes finally had UHF tuners, and many UHFs turned into successful independent stations that competed against network affiliates with a mix of *Star Trek* reruns, first-run syndication, live sports, and old movies.

Another approach to breaking the Big Three's oligopoly was to provide a noncommercial alternative. The FCC's Sixth Report and Order allocated hundreds of channels nationwide for noncommercial educational TV. The first such station, KUHT in Houston, signed on in 1953. But no mechanism for public funding was provided and public stations struggled. The Public Broadcasting Act of 1967 established the Corporation for Public Broadcasting (CPB) to finance programming from federal tax funds, followed in 1969 by the Public Broadcasting Service (PBS) to distribute programs to public stations. Major PBS stations, such as WGBH in Boston, emerged as program producers. PBS added some new viewing choices, notably children's programming like *Sesame Street* and British imports like *Upstairs, Downstairs*.

Television's content as well as its structure was on the policy agenda. As the nation's inner cities and college campuses erupted in violence in the late 1960s and early 1970s, critics and researchers (see Chapter 14) pointed the finger of blame at the thousands of hours of violent programs served up by the Big Three each year. Critics claimed that the young viewers of these violent program were those rioting in the streets. In response, in 1975 the FCC pressured the networks to institute a Family Viewing Hour from 8 to 9 P.M. That policy collided with the First Amendment rights of broadcasters and was soon struck down by the courts (see Chapter 15).

THE RISE OF CABLE

New distribution technologies offered another means to break the Big Three's oligopoly. **Cable television** spread as cable operators built networks of microwave antennas that picked up broadcasts from major market TV stations and relayed their signals to smaller communities. However, these distant signals threatened local independent UHF stations since they often carried the same types of programs. To protect UHFs, the FCC ruled that cable systems **must carry** all nearby broadcast signals and banned cable from the 100 largest major markets in 1966.

The FCC reversed its ban on urban cable systems in 1972 and mandated that new systems have at least

First-run syndication is the rental or licensing for original productions made specifically for the syndication market.

Cable television transmits television programs via coaxial cable or fiber.

Must carry is the policy that requires cable companies to carry local broadcast signals.

Everett Collection

BROADCAST KNOCKOUT The big fight between Muhammad Ali and Joe Frazier was the first national pay event from HBO. Cable TV changed the industry in much the same way that Internet television is changing it today.

20 channels. That decision, along with the development of satellite distribution, made it possible for Home Box Office (HBO) to create the first national **pay TV** network. HBO's carriage of the Ali–Frazier boxing match was the first pay program distributed by satellite to home viewers, in 1975. **Basic cable** channels filled with local TV stations and with new distant signals, such as WTBS from Atlanta, were distributed nationally via satellite while others like ESPN were available only on cable. With new channels and the lure of pay cable revenues, large cable companies that owned multiple cable systems—**multiple system operators (MSOs)**—contended for cable franchise rights in the top 100 cities.

Surely, 50 channels should provide enough variety to silence TV critics, but "fifty channels and nothing on" soon became their refrain. Rather than exiting the wasteland, cable TV seemed to expand it by amplifying old program formulas (i.e., drama, movies, sports, news) to entire channels and further recycling old reruns of the Big Three. And, free of the indecency rules that broadcasters had to live by, original cable programming featured steamy music videos, nudity, and profanity that raised new concerns about the effects of television on children.

The first home videocassette recorders, or VCRs, appeared in 1975, and video stores spread like wildfire in the 1980s. It was feared that home video would lure people away from cable, but many viewers just added rented videos to their existing entertainment options.

Bettmann/Corbis

TOP RATED The Roots miniseries was one of the top-rated TV shows of all time and pioneered a new genre, the mini-series. Top rated shows like the Superbowl attract larger audiences today but reach a lower percentage of TV households than top shows of the 1980s.

Pay TV charges cable customers an extra monthly fee to receive a specific channel.

Basic cable is the lowest level of cable service that includes local broadcast stations.

Multiple system operators (MSOs) are cable companies that operate systems in two or more communities.

THE BIG THREE IN DECLINE

Some 25 years after television was first declared a "vast wasteland" of repetitive programming from the Big Three, the conditions were at last right for competition to emerge in the realm of network television. The Big Three weakened as they changed owners in the mid-1980s and the new bosses slashed staff to improve profitability (Auletta, 1991). Cable TV extended the audience coverage and economic viability of UHF stations, and the FCC increased the number of TV stations one corporation could own from 7 to 12. That made it feasible to create a national television network built around a collection of major market UHF stations. In 1987, Australian media magnate Rupert Murdoch did just that when he started the Fox television network, using his Twentieth Century Fox film studios as a base, which started a trend toward *vertical integration* of networks and studios. The Fin-Syn rules were lifted so that networks were once again allowed to produce and syndicate their own entertainment programs. That encouraged more new networks. Warner started the WB network and Viacom built UPN around stations it owned (these were merged into The CW in 2006). For Spanish-speaking viewers there was Univision. They were joined in 1998 by Pax TV (later calling itself Ion Television). However, the wasteland was still apparent. The new networks largely imitated the Big Three, even further pushing the bounds of good taste with offbeat family comedies like *The Simpsons* and sexy youth-oriented shows.

Danny Feld/ABC-TV / The Kobal Collection/Picture Desk

WHAT'S NEW? Network TV continues to recycle old ideas and familiar faces, as in *Private Practice*, a spin-off from *Grey's Anatomy*.

> **Direct broadcast satellite (DBS)** is a television or radio satellite service that transmits television signals from satellites to compact home receivers.

Next, Washington reined in the Big Three's biggest competitor. The 1992 Cable Act forced cable programmers to offer their services on an equitable basis to competing distribution systems and within four years **direct broadcast satellite (DBS)** operators DIRECTV and the Dish Network emerged as alternative television delivery systems that transmitted satellite signals directly to the home for a monthly fee. That made cable channels available to satellite TV subscribers as well. The cable act also changed the must-carry rules so that broadcasters could demand compensation from cable operators who carried their stations.

But still, broadcast ratings declined. The list of top-rated shows of all time, exclusive of sports, has not had a new addition since the early 1980s (see Table 8.1). In 1998, for the first time, the Big Three attracted less of the daily viewing audience than ad-supported cable networks (Figure 8.2). Only profits from the networks' owned-and-operated (O&O) kept them afloat.

The Telecommunications Act of 1996 further relaxed media ownership rules and triggered a merger binge that married broadcast networks to cable television, music and print publishing, Internet enterprises, and movie studios. Some of the wheeling and dealing went sour. Viacom Corporation divided its operations between slow-growing "old media" properties like CBS Television and faster-growing new media like MTV to pump up its stock value. Time Warner spun off its cable television business in 2009. In 2006, CBS folded its UPN network together with Time Warner's equally marginal WB to form The CW network, with MyNetworkTV splitting off in the process.

Table 8.1 The Top 10 TV Shows of All Time (excluding sports)

RANK	PROGRAM	NETWORK	RATING	SHARE	DATE
1	*M*A*S*H Special* (Last Episode)	CBS	60.2	77	2-28-83
2	*Dallas* (Who Shot J.R.?)	CBS	53.3	76	11-21-80
3	*Roots Part VIII*	ABC	51.1	71	1-30-77
4	*Gone with the Wind–Part 1*	NBC	47.7	65	11-7-76
5	*Gone with the Wind–Part 2*	NBC	47.4	64	11-8-76
6	*Bob Hope Christmas Show*	NBC	46.6	64	1-15-70
7	*The Day After* (Sun. Night Movie)	ABC	46.0	62	11-20-83
8	*Roots Part VI*	ABC	45.9	66	1-28-77
9	*The Fugitive* (Last Episode)	ABC	45.9	72	8-29-67
10	*Roots Part V*	ABC	45.7	71	1-27-77

Source: Nielsen Media Research-NTI. Retrieved from **http://fbibler.chez.com/tvstats/misc/all_time.html**.

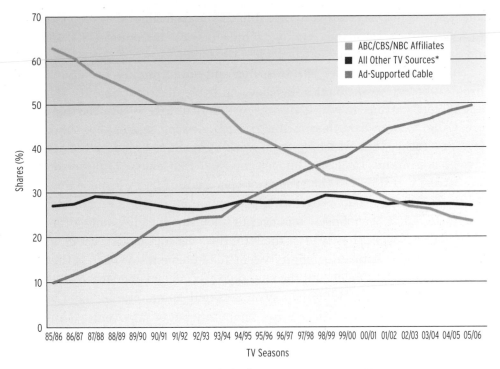

*All Other TV includes independents, Pay Cable, FOX/WB/UPN/PAX Affiliates, PBS, and all other cable.

Note: NHI Quarterly NTAR. All shares are based on the sum of total U.S. HH delivery (not HUT) for total day.

FIGURE 8.2 **THE BIG THREE IN DECLINE** Audience viewing shares for the Big Three are half of what they were in the mid-1980s

TELEVISION IN THE INFORMATION AGE

Inter-related changes in technology, audience behavior, industry structure, and economics are transforming the television medium. The spread of digital video recorders (DVRs) and iPads, streaming video sites like Netflix and Hulu, video games, and new social media options have freed audiences, especially young adults, from the tyranny of broadcast TV schedules. Shows like *Modern Family,* whose ratings grow substantially after delayed DVR playbacks are counted, have gotten a lift from new technology. However, traditional late night comedians like Dave Letterman are an endangered species since playbacks of prime time shows in late night hours subtract young viewers from their audiences while other young adults prefer the political humor of *The Daily Show* and *The Colbert Report* on cable. The 2012 Super Bowl broadcast set a record for the largest television audience of all time, but it did so with a rating of only 48 percent compared to 60 percent for the final episode of M*A*S*H, a former record holder from 1983. Thus, the record audience ironically provided further evidence of the decline of network television in a new media environment with many home entertainment options that were not available 30 years ago.

The 2007–2009 recession and the economic instability that followed strained the broadcast TV business model. Production costs for scripted entertainment programs continued to skyrocket and basic cable shows like *Jersey Shore* attracted audiences rivaling the top 10 shows on broadcast networks. Meanwhile, Internet ads replaced the TV spot as the staple of advertising.

In 2011, Comcast, the largest cable television operator in the United States, closed a deal to gain control of NBC Universal from General Electric.

Comcast was not especially interested in the unprofitable NBC television network but did desire money-making cable channels including USA, MSNBC, and SyFy that came along in the deal.

Streaming video over the Internet and smartphones is beginning to threaten both conventional broadcast and cable distribution with the prospect of "cord cutting" in which viewers switch to online sources for their video fare. Other viewers run their own marathon viewing sessions for their favorite shows rather than watching them week-by-week as broadcasters and their advertisers intend. To close a budget gap in 2012, Congress approved a plan to cluster TV stations in the broadcast spectrum to free up space for smartphone data transmission, a growing proportion of which is streaming video. Lately, there has been a decline in overall television viewing among the under 35 audience as well. Shortly after the NBC deal closed, Comcast established its own online video distributor, xfinitytv.com, to implement its vision of the future of television. In this model, all the channels carried on cable are available online through the Internet for display on personal computers, Internet-enabled television sets, smartphones, or tablet computers but only to Comcast subscribers. Anticipating the streaming video trend, a host of new players are entering the television business with their own plans for Internet video and video "apps" for tablets and smartphones. These include firms with financial resources that dwarf those of conventional broadcasters such as Apple, Google, Microsoft, and Verizon. Meanwhile, Netflix is starting to produce original programming in an effort to take on HBO as the leading provider of premium video. Hulu is producing original content, too, and began selling ads for upcoming seasons of its new shows in direct competition with broadcast networks in 2012.

Given these changes, is there a future for ad-supported "free" network television as we have known it in the past? It remains to be seen whether the

IDOLATRY American Idol succeeds because it is popular with audiences, but also because it is cheap to produce, and despite a shifting cast of judges. High ratings and low production costs continue to be a formula for economic success in the television business.

likes of YouTube and Neflix will be able to produce appealing content that can compete with network TV fare. Rights fees paid to CBS Television by streaming video sites for classic shows like *Star Trek* have also become a bright spot in their financial statements. Also, the network television advertising business is rebounding for networks like CBS that have top-rated shows, although not for those like NBC that do not. There is a potential upside for advertising revenues when networks begin charging advertisers for the extra audiences attracted through DVR playbacks over a week's time following initial broadcast, which they have thus far refrained from doing. Network television could get a further ratings boost when Internet streaming videos of their shows are added to the ratings, especially if they can prevent ad skipping online. The networks have their eyes on new revenue sources that could leave the conventional model intact. Local broadcasters are pressuring cable operators to pay **retransmission fees** for the right to carry their channels, often threatening to remove their stations from local cable systems on the eve of major sporting events as a bargaining tactic. Television networks are reversing the long-honored practice of compensating their affiliates for carrying network programs. Now they are demanding that the affiliates pay fees to the network or a share of the retransmission fees for the privilege of carrying network programs. However, a future in which all TV is pay TV is also possible. Stay tuned for further developments.

> **Retransmission fees** are monthly per-subscriber fees that local broadcasters charge cable companies for the right to carry their programs.

TECHNOLOGY TRENDS: FROM A SINGLE POINT OF LIGHT

All television pictures are formed by a single point of light that races back and forth and up and down the television screen so fast that it fools the eye into seeing a full moving image. This approach was originally designed for analog TV sets but digital receivers use it, too, with some refinements (see Technology Demystified: Inside HDTV, page 227).

Whether analog or digital, TV thus uses the same optical illusion exploited by motion pictures (see Chapter 7): persistence of vision. In 1884, Paul Nipkow of Germany first had the idea of scanning an image by breaking it up into a series of light spots that moved in a linear progression across the field of vision— what we would call *pixels* (short for picture elements) today. Idaho native Philo Farnsworth translated that notion into an electronic scanning system in the 1920s and he is often credited, at least in American textbooks, with inventing television. In 1941 the National Television Systems Committee (NTSC) set the technical standards that defined the analog television service in the United States and much of the rest of the world for the next seven decades. By today's standards, NTSC video was low resolution, with the equivalent of only 525 vertical lines of vertical resolution, and also rather "square-ish" with a ratio of screen width to screen height of only 4 to 3, the aspect ratio.

DIGITAL TELEVISION IS HERE

The original goal of digital television was to improve the viewing experience by making the picture seem clearer and wider and sound better. Broadcasters hoped that these improvements would revive their profits by drawing more viewers, much as color television had when its use became widespread in the 1960s. However, digital television is having a much wider impact than its original advocates may have bargained for.

Digital video that matches NTSC's quality and aspect ratio is now called *standard-definition TV (SDTV)*, whereas **high-definition television (HDTV)** provides pictures suitable for large-screen home theater systems. Both forms are called *digital television*. Satellite television, digital cable services, video discs, and digital video recorders all use digital forms for transmission or storage as well. HDTV more than doubles (to 1080) the number of vertical scan lines, widens the picture to match the 16 to 9 aspect ratio of movie screens, and adds six-channel "surround sound." Digital television also brings with it multicasting—that is, transmitting up to four standard-definition signals simultaneously on a single channel. These are designated as subchannels. For example, WNBC Channel 4 in New York City transmits an all-news service on Channel 4.2, whereas Channel 4.1 is the designation for its primary broadcast service. The digital television transition completed in 2009 forced viewers to buy either a digital television set or a digital converter for their old analog sets.

Digital television has also produced new viewing options in the form of on-demand video—that is when cable or satellite television subscribers request streams of video that are stored as digital files by their providers. The content is delivered on one of several digital channels reserved for on demand offerings so that each subscriber can receive a different program and fast-forward, pause, or rewind as they please.

However, your next digital TV provider may not be a broadcaster, cable operator, or satellite TV company. Telephone companies are up and running in many cities with fiber-optic systems (FiOS) that offer expanded channel capacity along with high-speed Internet connections that make cable seem old and slow. The cable industry is responding with a new high-speed technology called *DOCIS* (Data Over Cable Service Interface Specifications) 3.0 that will make it possible to receive multiple HDTV video streams simultaneously. Internet service providers, including both wireline and wireless broadband Internet providers (see Chapter 9), cell phone companies, or Apple or Google can also be your television company. Many have plans to offer their own channels of original video content (see Chapter 12). More and more television is being delivered as Internet data streams through high-speed connections, especially so for young adults whom advertisers especially value.

Mario Tama/Staff/Getty Images News/Getty Images

INTERNET TV. Apple is among the several computer and Internet companies that want to offer video distribution systems that will compete with broadcasters and cable companies.

TECHNOLOGY DEMYSTIFIED

INSIDE HDTV

Television pictures are an optical illusion generated from a single point of light racing back and forth across your TV screen. In old-fashioned sets with cathode ray tube (CRT) screens, the light is produced by a beam of electrical charges that are "shot" from an electron gun at the rear of the picture tube. When they hit the inner surface of the tube, they cause the coating on the inside of the tube to give off a glow. The more electrons that hit the surface at a given instant, the brighter the glow. The electron beam sweeps back and forth in successive rows to create each full-screen picture from top to bottom, one pixel, or picture element, and one horizontal line at a time. That feat was duplicated 30 times per second. Each frame of the picture was made up of 525 lines, but that is divided up into two sets (or fields) of 262 and a half lines, and the two halves of the picture are combined, or interlaced, to complete the picture.

CRT sets are becoming rare now, but standard-definition digital sets replicate the same picture creation process with new flat-screen display technologies, whereas high-definition sets improve the clarity of the picture by increasing the vertical resolution to 1,080 lines. Digital televisions employ two different scanning methods, 1080i (the "i" is for "interlaced") or 1080p ("p" is for "progressive"). The latter is the scanning method used in computer monitors and is said to produce a better picture and works better with high-definition DVDs.

There are several digital TV technologies from which to choose. Liquid crystal display (LCD) screens have three tiny, lightweight solid-state devices at each pixel that control the flow of light through miniature red, green, and blue filters. Flat-screen plasma displays have three miniature fluorescent lights located at each pixel that are activated by grids of invisible wires running across the screen. For the home theater crowd, Digital Light Processing (DLP; see Chapter 7) technology has made its way into consumer video projection systems. Another projection system option is LCOS (liquid crystal on silicon). OLED (organic light emitting diode) screens are the latest; they are a fraction of an inch thick and have low power consumption and high-contrast pictures and so will be found in portable devices as well as in home TV receivers that you can hang on the wall like a picture frame.

Behind the wider and clearer picture lies a complete change in the way television programs are made and transmitted to the home compared to analog TV. The output of the camera is digitized using the same basic techniques of sampling and quantizing we learned about in relation to music CDs, in Chapter 1. (You might wish to review that discussion, on page 7). But video contains a lot more information than audio, so the information is sampled much more often than for musical recordings. Our eyes are less sensitive to color information than they are to light and dark (luminance), so the color components are sampled less frequently.

Next, the signal must be cut down to a size that can be transmitted over a standard TV channel. This is done by removing redundant information within and between frames of the television picture. The compression uses a process called *MPEG-2*, after the Motion Picture Expert Group that developed it. (The MP3 music files on the Internet reflect the audio portion of this standard.) The picture comes out of the MPEG encoder chopped up into hundreds of chunks, or packets, that make up each frame of the picture.

The next step actually adds to the length of each packet by appending data that helps to detect and correct errors that may occur during transmission. The data stream modulates a carrier signal in much the same way that a modem sends data over a phone line (see Chapter 12, page 361). However, there is more bandwidth, or capacity, in the TV channel, so data can be transmitted at much higher speeds.

Back in the studio, early TV cameras used the image orthicon picture tube ("immy" for short, the origin of the "Emmy" designation for awards in television excellence, incidentally). Modern TV cameras use solid-state components called *charged coupled devices (CCDs)* to make pictures, instead of glass tubes. In CCD cameras, each pixel is represented by a miniature solid-state component that converts light to electricity. The electrical voltages associated with individual pixels are transmitted one at a time according to a fixed scanning pattern. Color cameras separate the incoming light from the scene into three separate color components, each with its own CCD.

VIDEO RECORDING

Magnetic audiotape was introduced in the late 1940s, but television contained so much more information than audio that mountains of tape would have to move across the recording head at impossible speeds. The key development that paved the way for the home VCR was *helical scanning*. It stores video tracks on a slant (imagine cutting up tape into short segments and pasting them together slantwise), so the length of the tape can shrink to manageable proportions.

DVD players store compressed digitized video on higher-capacity versions of the familiar audio compact disc (see Chapter 5). HDTV recording requires improved laser and video compression technologies to put movie-length high-definition features on a single disc, up to 50 GB in all. In 2008, the "format war" between Blu-Ray and the competing HD DVD standard ended with Blu-Ray the winner.

DVR systems cross a VCR with a computer hard drive, continuously storing compressed digital video as it is transmitted. The TiVo brand name is often associated with these, but most of them are now being rented by cable TV and direct broadcast satellite companies rather than sold. Although few people ever mastered the intricacies of programming their VCRs, the DVR interfaces are easy to learn and the machines can "remember" the shows you want saved. The technology also makes it possible to skip the commercials, a feature that threatens the existence of both commercial broadcasters and basic cable or satellite channels. Not surprisingly, new models of the DVRs distributed by cable companies lack the commercial-skipping feature.

What's next in home video recording? Perhaps its death. Video-on-demand services offered by cable and satellite companies and streaming video Internet services like Netflix and Hulu aim to make home recording technologies obsolete.

VIDEO PRODUCTION TRENDS

Over the years, cameras have steadily shrunk in size for easy portability. Rugged portable cameras (and, increasingly, videos shot by viewers on digital cameras and cell phones) have greatly expanded coverage of live events from the studio, to floors of political conventions, to the helmets of football players. Electronic news gathering (ENG) systems transmit the news footage back to the studio via remote microwave antennas mounted on mobile vans. Other footage arrives in the newsroom via satellite, and the incoming digital video files are stored on video servers, which are massive computer disc drives. Reporters and news editors view the files and compose and edit stories while sitting at computer workstations that are linked to the video server through high-speed local area networks that interconnect all the computers in the newsroom.

These systems take advantage of digital film production techniques (see Chapter 7) that have been adapted to television. Nonlinear editing had a great impact on video production by speeding up postproduction and lowering costs. Digital graphics, special effects, and computer animation are also becoming routine. For example, many TV stations have virtual news studios in which the reporters perform on an empty stage and computer graphics fill in the set. Digital production techniques are migrating from specialized studio equipment to personal computers so that what once required a professional editing suite can migrate to an ordinary desktop.

INTERACTIVE TV

The idea of "talking back" to your TV and having it respond is nothing new. In the 1970s Time Warner experimented, and failed, with an interactive cable system called "Qube" and tried and failed again in the early 1990s. Conceptions of interactive programming have had a certain sameness over the years: interactive quiz shows, audience participation gimmicks, selectable alternative endings to dramas, alternative camera angles or in-depth statistics for football games, and ordering products by "clicking" on their on-screen images. Today, the DVR offers limited forms of modifying the content (essential to the definition of interactivity presented in Chapter 1) such as "skipping" commercials and getting instant replays. Another limited form of interactive is video-on-demand that stores video on huge computer hard drives back at the cable company.

INTERNET TV

Emerging interactive TV ideas combine television with the Internet. One new option is the ability to make TV commercials "clickable" by moving a cursor over objects that appear on the screen so that viewers can call up information or order free samples for the products they see. Social media are proving to be a way to attract and hold a highly involved audience, such as the dedicated Twitter users who tweeted while watching *The Game* on BET and made that show a hit on basic cable. Social media users also follow their friends' links to play video clips and TV episodes. Video chatting while viewing could be the next craze, with set-top boxes and DVD players coming out that have video chat applications built in.

Internet-capable television sets with built in WiFi connections are being introduced to take better advantage of the growing selection of movies and videos that can be viewed through websites like Hulu, Amazon, Netflix, and xfinity. Video is also being repackaged for consumption on tablet computers like the iPad and for smartphones. However, anyone with a broadband connection can experience **Internet television** (sometimes called IP TV, after the Internet Protocol (IP) that sets the rules for data transfers on the Internet, see Chapter 9) by surfing over to those sites and downloading the software that plays the videos. But who wants to hover over a keyboard to watch *Modern Family*? At a modest cost you can add a wireless mouse and a flat-screen color monitor and connect the computer headphone jack to your stereo system to get the full "couch potato" experience. Or, prop your tablet up on your stomach as you kick back on the couch.

[**Internet Television** is a television program viewed over the Internet.]

The integration of computer and television technology may also make the TV remote obsolete. Cell phone and iPad apps are available that take the place of conventional remotes. Device-free channel surfing is another possibility. Video game manufacturers are licensing their motion sensing controllers, like Microsoft's Kinect, to TV manufacturers so that gestures or facial expressions might be used to change the channel. Voice recognition technologies, such as the Siri iPhone application, are another possibility. That will bring channel changing technology full circle back to the 1950s when voice commands were first used in early TV homes, "Junior, go over and switch the channel to Ed Sullivan."

STOP&REVIEW

1. What was TV like in its Golden Age?
2. How did cable television develop?
3. Why is network television in decline?
4. How has digital technology impacted television?

3-D TV

The success of the 3-D blockbuster *Avatar* at the movie box office revived interest in 3-D TV. Three-dimensional consumer electronic products and program services first appeared in the United States in 2010. As with 3-D film technology (see Chapter 7), 3-D TV relies on tricking the brain into thinking it sees a three-dimensional object on a flat screen by flashing slightly different views of the picture to the left and right eyes. Active shutter glasses, like the ones used in movie theaters, are synchronized to home TV sets to produce the image but the cost of extra pairs of glasses is a barrier to those who like to watch college sports with their friends. Three-dimensional viewing without glasses is also possible by placing a layer of miniature lenses on the TV screen that direct separate "left" and "right" images to the eyes. However, those systems require the viewer to sit directly in front of the screen and so are perhaps better suited to the computer than the home TV set. And they seem especially likely to make viewers feel nauseous, a problem with all 3-D systems. Other approaches to 3-D TV without glasses are being developed but are still a few years away from consumers.

INDUSTRY: WHO RUNS THE SHOW?

Once-clear separations between the companies that produce, distribute, and exhibit television programs locally have been erased by industry deregulation, converging technologies, and a wave of mergers and buyouts. Here we will concentrate on the pieces of those conglomerates that absorbed the conventional television business. However, standing in the wings are Apple, Microsoft, Netflix, Google, Amazon, and Verizon. They might like to repeat Apple's wreckage of the music business and Amazon's demolition of the book business in the online television arena, including (at least in the case of Google's YouTube and Netflix) the production as well as the distribution of video content.

INSIDE THE BIG FIVE

The Big Five that dominate television today are Time Warner, Disney, National Amusements (Viacom/CBS), News Corp, and Comcast. These top companies are vertically integrated conglomerates that combine film and video production, national and local distribution, and other media properties under a single corporate umbrella (see Table 8.2). Their top managers come from the field of finance rather than entertainment.

There are other major players that participate only in one or two aspects of the television industry. For example, Sony Corporation produces TV shows through its Sony Pictures division, has international satellite TV channels, and manufactures television and video equipment. Discovery Networks owns a stable of cable channels including Discovery Channel and Animal Planet. A+E Networks runs the Lifetime, A&E, and History cable channels, among others, and is a joint venture of the Hearst Corporation, Disney, and NBC Universal.

The force behind the urge to merge is *synergy*, getting multiple benefits from integrating production and various forms of distribution. For example, by

TABLE 8.2 The Big Five Television Companies

NAME	BROADCAST TV	PRODUCTION STUDIOS	CABLE TV	OTHER
Time Warner	The CW	Warner Brothers, Warner Brothers Animation, New Line Cinema	HBO, Cinemax, CNN, Headline News, TNT, Turner Classic Movies, TBS, Cartoon Network, Adult Swim, truTV	134 magazines, DC Comics
The Walt Disney Company	ABC Television, 10 O&Os	Walt Disney Pictures Miramax Touchstone Pixar ABC Studios	ESPN, Disney Channel, ABC Family, SoapNet, Classic Sports Network, pieces of Lifetime, History, A&E	Theme parks, ESPN radio, 32 radio stations, Hyperion Books, Disney Music Group, Disney Cruise Line, The Muppets
National Entertainment/ CBS & Viacom	CBS Television, The CW, 28 O&Os	Paramount Pictures	MTV, Nickelodeon, BET, Nick at Nite, TV Land, VH1, Spike TV, CMT, Comedy Central, Showtime, The Movie Channel, Flix	CBS records, 124 radio stations, Simon & Shuster Publishing, 23 Web properties
News Corp	Fox, 27 O&Os, MyNetworkTV	Twentieth Century Fox Shine Group	Fox Movie Channel, FX, Fox News Channel, Fox Regional Sports Networks, Fox College sportsSPEED Channel, FUEL, Pieces of National Geographic Channel, Big Ten Network	46 newspapers, BSkyB, Harper Collins Publishers, The *Wall Street Journal*, 19 Web properties
Comcast/ XTINITY	NBC, Telemundo, part of PAX, 10 NBC O&Os, 16 Telemundo O&Os	Universal Pictures, Universal Media Stuios	MSNBC, CNBC, Bravo, Mun2, USA, SyFy, E! Entertainment, Golf Channel, Style,G4, Versus, Oxygen, Sleuth, Chiller, Weather Channel, Sprout, 9 regional sports networks	5 theme parks, 6 Web properties, Philadelphia 76ers and Flyers

Source: *Columbia Journalism Review. Who owns what,* Retrieved from **http://www.cjr.org/tools/owners/Accessed January 3, 2012**

ordering TV shows from their own production companies, the conglomerates save on production costs for their first-run television programs and profit directly from subsequent off-network syndication. Syndicating productions from their studios to their own cable channels and the TV stations they own and operate (their O&Os) is far more lucrative than licensing programs from others, because the profits from both sides of the business stay "in the family." In buying NBC Universal in 2009, Comcast gained control of popular television programming that it can distribute both through its cable television systems and through broadband Internet connections.

VIDEO PRODUCTION

The way that television programs are produced varies somewhat according to genre. Each reflects a slightly different economic model.

Entertainment. Production companies hire the directors, actors, and technicians, and shoot and edit television entertainment programs. However, most of the talent, both behind the camera and in front of it, are not full-time employees of either the networks or the production companies. Rather, they are hired on a project-by-project basis. Actors, directors, screenwriters, and the other creative minds in the television business belong to labor unions, called *guilds* (e.g., the Writers Guild and the Screen Actors Guild), which negotiate the basic terms of employment with the production companies.

The networks contract with production companies for the rights to first runs of the shows, and typically pay fees that cover two-thirds to three-fourths of the initial production costs. The production companies may profit from the syndication rights by selling them in off-network syndication. For example, each episode of *The Simpsons* is worth about $4 million in syndication fees when rerun on local stations. However, with the abolition of the Fin-Syn rules in 1993 and the recent merger craze, most network entertainment programs are now either produced in-house or co-owned by the networks. The rest are usually purchased from production companies associated with other members of the Big Five. Many independent producers have been forced out of business or have been gobbled up by the Big Five. This kind of vertical integration may limit the diversity of content, which the Fin-Syn rules originally tried to expand.

Reality shows represent a different economic model. By using amateur actors and doing away with scripts and elaborate sets, reality shows can be produced at far lower cost than scripted dramas or situation comedies. Reality shows also economize by using nonunion labor and paying production staff members about half the salaries they might command if they worked on unionized, scripted programs.

Not all the new program ideas go to network television, though. First-run syndication programs are rented to network O&Os, network affiliates, cable networks, and independent stations. Each of the Big Five has subsidiaries that produce programs for first-run syndication, but others are associated with movie studios (e.g., Sony Pictures, producers of *Wheel of Fortune*) or major television group owners. A new niche is opening for programs produced for digital television subchannels; for example, Live Well HD, a channel dedicated to health and lifestyle programs.

Network News. News programs are journalistic endeavors, and we refer the reader to Chapters 4 and 16 for a discussion of those aspects of news production. We should point out that television journalism differs from print journalism in several important respects. Due to the nature of the medium, television news stories are often reduced to "sound bites" and short video clips that lack the in-depth reporting found in leading newspapers. The visual nature of the medium introduces a serious bias toward prioritizing stories that contain a gripping visual element: "If it bleeds, it leads," as the saying goes. Critics argue that the ratings-driven nature of the television business also causes television news to avoid controversial stories that may alienate viewers and to pander to the interests of sponsors.

Here we consider the news in the context of other types of television programming. News programs have little value in syndication, so their producers have to make all the money during their first run. The Big Three produce the evening news and magazine shows like *60 Minutes* through their own in-house

VIDEO PRODUCTION

The producers and directors described in Chapter 7 often complain about the interference of "the suits," the studio and network television executives who oversee their projects. "We have some notes," they say as they hand the producer a tattered script covered with yellow stickies (or these days, Microsoft Word comment boxes). "You mutilated my work" is one often-heard complaint from the producer. Perhaps you would rather be one of the suits? Actors, producers and directors account for only about one-third of the professional employment in the industry. Here we will go a little further behind the scenes to look at some of the more plentiful occupations we can find there.

There are more suits, people employed in the industry as business and financial managers, than as actors, producers, and directors combined, reflecting the "bottom line" focus of the industry. These are occupations that students prepare for by majoring (or double majoring) in business, finance, accounting, marketing, or public relations.

There are also more film and video editors and camera operators than actors (employed ones, at least). There are about 25,000 film and video editors and an equal number of camera operators nationwide. Picture yourself working under a deadline to get the latest film clips from a revolution in the Middle East or a protest in your home town edited in time for the evening news. Most of these jobs are in large metro areas, including New York and L.A., although many of the entry-level television jobs are in much smaller markets. Median annual wages are about $51,000 a year for editors and about $11,000 less for camera operators. College training in film and video production courses can help land an entry-level job. However, competition is keen due to the large number of students who wish to enter the industry. Only slow growth in these occupations is expected over the next decade due to automation and a trend toward combining reporting and editing roles in broadcasting. So, personal connections and internships are essential when starting out. And image capture and editing are rapidly becoming all digital, so computer savvy is increasingly important.

Another option is to be one of the creators who puts the computer "magic" into movies and film. The fastest growing occupations in the video and motion picture industries are in the high-tech ranks of computer specialists, multimedia artists, and animators. As film and video rely more on digital animation and special effects, people with these skills are essential to making video magic, so much so that they make more on an hourly basis than either actors or film and video editors.

Sources: Bureau of Labor Statistics. (2011). Career guide to *industries, 2010–11 edition, motion picture and video industries.* Retrieved from http://www.bls.gov/oco/cg/cgs038.htm#related; Bureau of Labor Statistics. (2011). *Occupational Outlook Handbook, 2012 edition, television, video, and motion picture camera operators and editors.* Retrieved from http://www.bls.gov/oco/ocos091.htm.

news divisions. The networks cut many of their correspondents, and cut back on investigative reporting to reduce costs during the rounds of mergers and acquisitions that brought them into the orbit of the Big Five. They continued to economize by laying off news staff in the wake of the great recession of 2007-2009. Only NBC News has been somewhat immune to cuts since it shares revenue from its cable TV operation MSNBC. Now they rely more on footage supplied by local network affiliates, foreign television networks, independent "stringers," and even amateur video caught on cell phone cameras. CNN has replaced the Big Three (and specifically

Adam Rose/CBS/Landov

PRODUCTION COSTS. Leading actors for top rated scripted series like *Two and a Half Men* bid up their salaries over time and can make them unprofitable to continue producing.

CBS) as the network of record by building its own international news operation, and Fox News now draws bigger audiences than CNN by targeting a political niche audience—a strategy copied by MSNBC.

Local News. Most programs produced by local television stations are either newscasts or magazine-format shows. Local news is a major profit center, accounting for nearly half of all station revenues on average, so much so that local stations run an average of 5 hours of news a day (Waldman, 2011). Stations profit from the news because it is popular both with local audiences and local advertisers and the revenues go directly to the local station—they are not shared with the network or a program syndicator. The news expansion has also been fueled by the ready availability of news footage, including that obtained from networks via satellite, as well as what comes from the station's own local electronic news-gathering capacity (Live! From Newschopper Five!) and cell phone footage submitted by viewers. Production costs have declined over the years as equipment has become cheaper and news staffs have contracted, although those cost savings are easily erased by the purchase of news helicopters, weather radars, and HDTV camera equipment.

Sports. Who produces the Super Bowl? Is it the NFL? No, but the networks can't just walk into the stadium and set up their cameras; they have to buy the rights to the broadcasts from the sports leagues and pay dearly for the privilege. For example, ESPN pays the National Football League $1.1 billion a year just for the rights to *Monday Night Football*. ESPN can still profit by further increasing the affiliate fees paid by cable operators, already the highest in the business. The same was not true for ABC Television, which had only advertising fees—and declining ratings—for the broadcasts. That's why *Monday Night Football* moved to ESPN in 2006.

Public TV. Most PBS programs are produced by PBS stations in Boston, San Francisco, Los Angeles, New York, and Washington, D.C. Independent producers, notably Sesame Workshop (the producers of *Sesame Street*, formerly known as Children's Television Workshop) and the British Broadcasting Corporation (*Masterpiece Theater*), account for the rest, some through co-production agreements with PBS stations. The Corporation for Public Broadcasting (CPB) funnels taxpayers' money to fund PBS programming. PBS now follows a centralized programming decision-making model, not unlike the commercial networks, under which programming executives in Washington decide which series to develop and air nationally on PBS stations. Producers depend on a mix of funding from CPB, PBS member station contributions, corporate **underwriting**, public contributions, and foreign network co-sponsorship. Contributing corporations and foundations are acknowledged in underwriting credits, those on-air announcements that express appreciation for financial support and describe what the donors do, but aren't commercials—not really.

> **Underwriting** is corporate financial support of public television programs in return for a mention of the donor on the air.

Mark Richards / PhotoEdit

AFFILIATE PROGRAMMING Local affiliates of major TV networks also produce their own programming—most notable are the local news shows. Local news is a major revenue source for local TV stations.

Cable Production. National cable networks follow the same content acquisition strategies as the national broadcast networks, but local production is rather limited. Many cable systems produce their own **local origination** programming. The most elaborate operations resemble television stations, producing local news and sports for advertising-supported channels that are programmed by the cable operator. These are sometimes organized at a regional level to spread production costs across multiple cable systems. Most cable systems also maintain **community access** channels over which the operator has no direct control. Employees of the local educational or governmental institutions create the programs, or they are sometimes made by individuals who want their own cable show staff their productions. Community groups subsidize these local productions, whereas franchise fees paid by the cable operator to the municipal franchise authority finance the facilities used to produce them. However, several states, such as Texas, have now eliminated local public access by restricting the right of municipal franchise authorities to require operators to pay for them.

Local origination means created within the community by the cable operator.

Community access means created by community residents without the involvement of the cable operator.

NATIONAL TELEVISION DISTRIBUTION

Television programs are distributed nationally by either networks or syndicators. Broadcast and cable networks differ somewhat in the ways they finance national distribution.

Commercial Networks. CBS, NBC, and ABC have been joined by Fox, The CW, MyNetworkTV, Ion, and Univision. These eight commercial broadcast networks all develop and schedule programs for national audiences, distribute them to their local affiliates via satellite, and profit from the sale of spots to national advertisers.

Profits are hard to come by in network television. The Big Three and Fox each generate several billion dollars in network advertising revenues per year, but profits are drained by huge payments for sports rights, production fees for entertainment shows, and multimillion-dollar salaries for on-air talent, plus the same taxes and routine operating expenses that all media firms incur (see Chapter 2). Television network operations often incur huge net losses, some soaring into the hundreds of millions of dollars. The network TV losses are offset by profits from other lines of business, including their cable networks and their locally owned and operated (O&O) stations. Shares of the retransmission fees that local affiliates of the networks charge cable operators and rights fees from online networks like Hulu are growing sources of revenue. However, the profits from their O&O stations are declining as more advertising moves to the Internet, leading to a sell-off of smaller market stations owned by the networks in recent years.

Basic Cable Networks. Over 300 basic cable TV networks are delivered via satellite, either to local cable systems that redistribute them to their customers or directly to the home via direct broadcast satellite operators Dish and DirecTV. The Big Five media conglomerates control many of the leading cable channels. Basic networks derive their revenues from national advertising sales and affiliate fees. The **affiliate fees** are paid by cable operators, on a per-subscriber basis (these range from five dollars per month per subscriber for ESPN to a few cents per month for C-SPAN). Many basic networks also make

Affiliate fees are monthly per-subscriber fees that cable programming services charge local cable operators.

TABLE 8.3 Top 10 Cable Networks

NETWORK	WEEKLY VIEWERS (000)
USA	2,999
Disney Channel	2,485
FOX	2,366
ESPN	2,321
Family Network	2,116
TBS	1,925
A&E	1,873
TNT	1,718
History	1,669
FX	1,584

Note: Total day live plus seven-day viewing for the week of December 18, 2011.

Source: Nielsen TV Ratings.

local advertising spots available that local cable systems sell to local advertisers. The largest basic cable networks (Table 8.3) are found on virtually all cable systems where they are usually part of basic cable offerings purchased by all customers. There are about six dozen regional basic cable networks (e.g., Madison Square Garden Network, New England Cable News). Superstations like WGN and WWOR are special cases in that they are also local television stations in their home markets but sell ads primarily to national advertisers.

Premium Services. Home Box Office is the largest premium cable TV network. Along with its companion network, Cinemax, it reaches over 28 million subscribers. Showtime and Starz/Encore are the other leading pay networks. Pay TV networks derive their revenues exclusively from affiliate fees. With only one revenue stream, these fees are substantially higher than for basic services. A small cable operator might charge subscribers $10 per month for HBO and pay half of that back to HBO. Large cable multiple system operators (MSOs) have the market power to negotiate discounts, so they may pay HBO only about half of what the small cable company does and keep the rest of the subscriber fee as profit.

Pay-per-view programming is also delivered by satellite and financed by affiliate fees, predicated on the number of pay-per-view orders. The spread of digital cable has brought with it many new pay-per-view options, with some systems offering dozens of movies each night. Video-on-demand systems expand choices to include classic movies as well as recent movie releases.

Public Broadcasting. PBS is careful not to call itself a network, but it performs many of the same functions, notably developing and distributing a lineup of programs nationally via satellite. There are no advertising sales, but PBS does funnel money to national program development.

Syndication. Local stations fill out their schedules with syndicated programming, particularly during the daytime and the 7–8 P.M. time slot set aside by the Prime Time Access Rules. These include first-run syndication programs, licensed directly to local stations, and off-network syndication, reruns of programs that previously aired on network television.

Syndicators obtain the rights for programming and then license the programs to local stations. Syndication is increasingly dominated by the Big Five (e.g., *The Ellen DeGeneres Show* is distributed by

THE KOBAL COLLECTION/Picture Desk

SYNDICATED Longtime syndicated hit *Wheel of Fortune* is licensed directly to local TV stations. It is an example of first run syndication in that its episodes were not previously seen on network television.

Warner Brothers), but affiliates of lesser media conglomerates, such as Hearst Entertainment Distribution, and independent companies also play a role. Stations may pay for the programs outright (cash), pay a reduced price and show some advertisements or commercial spots arranged by the syndicator (cash plus barter), or pay nothing but give the syndicator more commercial minutes to sell to national advertisers (barter). Syndication contracts have an exclusivity clause so that only one station per market will have the right to show a particular program. Many of these deals are made at the annual convention of the National Association of Television Program Executives (NATPE), which functions as a bazaar for syndicated programming.

LOCAL TELEVISION DISTRIBUTION

Local distribution of television was once the exclusive province of the local TV station. Now, cable television and satellite systems also play a role. A television station is an organization that holds a federal license to create or organize programs for a specific community and transmit them on its assigned channel. There are currently about 1,400 local commercial TV stations nationwide, and they may be categorized according to their ownership arrangements and relationships to national networks.

Group-Owned Stations. Many stations are operated by companies with multiple broadcast properties, called *group owners*. Group owners benefit from economies of scale in management, programming, and advertising sales. To prevent monopolization, limits were set on the number of stations one group could own. Currently, no ownership group may own stations that reach more than 39 percent of the television audience among them. That's according to the way that the FCC counts coverage, in which UHF station coverage is cut in half; but when UHFs are fully counted the Ion Media group reaches over three-fifths of U.S. households (McAvoy, 2011). Duopoly, that is, ownership of two stations in the same market, is permitted in large markets but not in smaller ones, and triopolies are prohibited. Local management agreements also allow group owners to manage local stations they do not own on a contractual basis. Cross-ownership rules that would allow one company to own both a newspaper and a television station in the same market are under revision as of this writing.

The Big Five (with the exception of Time Warner) are also group owners. Their O&O stations are concentrated in major markets where they are major profit centers for their parent. The largest group owners in terms of the number of stations are Ion Media, with 60 stations, and the Sinclair Broadcast Group, with 58.

Network Affiliates. A common misconception is that the TV networks own all their local outlets. However, aside from the network O&Os which currently represent about 100 stations in all, local distribution of network programs is carried out by affiliates. These are individually owned or group-owned stations that have contractual arrangements with a network to show its programs locally.

Network affiliation is desirable because of the ratings draw of network prime-time shows. Local stations profit from the sale of local ad spots that run during network programs. A little over half of station revenue comes from local ads, including those placed in locally produced or syndicated programs as well as the local ad availabilities in network shows. The other half of the revenue comes from ads placed through the station by national and regional advertisers. These are arranged through *rep firms* that act as intermediaries between local stations and advertisers based in other cities.

Network affiliation has been especially profitable over the years because the Big Three paid their affiliates to take their shows, a practice called *affiliate compensation*. Now the networks are starting to charge the affiliates for programming, either as a flat fee or as a percentage of the retransmission fees that local stations collect from cable TV operators, and bidding wars have erupted among group owners for the right to represent the Big Three in major markets. Local stations also hope to profit from selling ads on their new digital subchannels that are part of the HDTV transition.

Independent Stations. Independent stations are not affiliated with any network. Independents buy most of their programming from syndication services and sell their advertising in the local, regional, and national spot markets. Relatively few independents remain now that there are eight networks in operation.

Down at the Local Station. Local stations vary in size from a couple of dozen employees to several hundred, depending on the size of the market they serve. Regardless of size, all commercial television stations have a common set of key roles (Table 8.4) organized around the basic tasks of obtaining and transmitting programs that will attract audiences and, with them, advertisers.

The program director arranges contracts with networks and syndicators and is responsible for filling the overall broadcast schedule. Local news programs are an important source of profits and so account for most of the local programming resources. Stations employ news directors, assignment editors, news writers, on-air personalities, and remote camera crews to produce their

TABLE 8.4 Local Television: Key Personnel

JOB TITLE	JOB DESCRIPTION	HELPERS
Station Manager	Overall responsibility for management, financial performance, planning, community relations	All other managers, front-office staff of secretaries
Chief Engineer	Keeps station on the air, monitors FCC standards	Transmitter engineer, studio technicians
Program Director	Selects and schedules programs, negotiates for syndicated programs	Syndicators
Promotion Director	Plans and directs on-air and off-air community promotions	Graphic artist, copywriter
News Director	Responsible for local news programs	Assignment editor, writers, announcers
Production Director	Produces the station's programs	Producers, directors, production crew
Sales Manager	Sells advertising time	Account executives, national rep firm
Director of Finance	Controls the station's finances, monitors the budget	Accountants and bookkeepers
Research Director	Analyzes and compiles reports on ratings, commissions local research	Ratings services
Traffic Manager	Schedules commercials	Advertising agencies

Source: Telecommunications Management: Broadcasting Cable and the New Technologies by Barry L. Sherman, NY: McGraw Hill, 1994.

news shows. Promotion managers draw audiences with on-air promotions ("Plane crash coverage, live at 11!") and use advertising, public relations, and their websites to make the station more visible in the community.

Advertising sales are the lifeblood of every commercial television station. The sales director manages a staff of account executives who make sales calls to local advertisers. They carry rate cards that list the charges for advertising according to the time of day and length of the commercial spot. The sales director also contracts with a rep firm to sell blocks of commercials through national and regional advertising agencies. The traffic manager makes sure the commercials air at the proper times. Stations contract with Nielsen Media Research to provide ratings data that they use in their sales presentations. Large stations employ their own research directors who analyze the ratings and conduct local market studies, such as evaluations of local news anchors.

Stations also employ engineers to keep the station on the air and maintain the transmitter and studio equipment. The finance department keeps track of revenues and expenses for the benefit of the station manager, who has overall responsibility for the profitable operation of the enterprise.

NONCOMMERCIAL STATIONS

There are over 350 public television stations. There are community stations that rely on individual and corporate contributions and educational stations, usually affiliated with local colleges or universities that also receive funding from state or local governments. PBS stations must pay for the programming they receive from PBS and also for any syndicated programs. In place of the advertising sales force found in commercial stations, public stations have managers in charge of staging on-air membership and auction drives and soliciting contributions from private individuals and local foundations. They also seek corporate underwriting of local and national programs.

TELEVISION ADVERTISERS

Advertisers spend about $13 billion a year on television network advertising and another $19 billion on cable networks. Cable surpassed broadcast in network ad revenues for the first time in 2006. There are several basic types of TV advertisers with differing needs. National advertisers sell general-consumption items, such as soft drinks. They buy blocks of advertising time from national broadcast networks during the *up-front* season. That's the time each spring when the networks sell time on the next season's shows. Time that is not sold then goes into the *spot* market and later into the *scatter* market, for last-minute ad sales. National spot advertisers and regional advertisers sell products with more limited geographic appeal, such as snow tires. They buy spots through advertising rep firms from both network affiliates and independent stations. Local advertisers, such as automobile dealers and supermarkets, buy slots in locally produced shows or those allocated by the networks to their local affiliates during network programs.

STOP&REVIEW

1. What are the Big Five media conglomerates?
2. Why is it hard to make a profit from network television? How do networks stay in business?
3. What is the relationship between television networks and their affiliates?
4. How do the economics of broadcast television production differ from those of cable channels?

GENRES: WHAT'S ON TV?

As we know from chapter 2, genres reflect a negotiation between the artist and the audience as to what is engaging or entertaining. In television, advertisers and network accountants are very much parties to that negotiation, however. We saw throughout the history of television that genres evolved to pursue audiences that interest advertisers and also in response to the changing economics of production.

BROADCAST NETWORK GENRES

Until recently, reality shows proliferated on broadcast networks but now scripted comedies like *New Girl* are making a comeback. But almost anything that appeals to 18- to 49-year-olds who are especially beloved by advertisers stays on the air, whereas shows with older audiences are canceled.

Examples of each of the main television genres, along with their early television ancestors and predecessors in other media, are shown in Table 8.5. The table also shows some of the major genre variations. For example, dramas may be subdivided into medical, legal, and police dramas. Other variations hinge upon the interplay of plot and character development. In many sitcoms, the characters are static and only the situations change from week to week (e.g., *Modern Family*), whereas in others the characters continually develop and stories revolve around their interactions (Mad Men). In yet others, the weekly stories are woven into continuing plot lines (e.g., *Grey's Anatomy*).

Television genres continue to develop over time in response to changes in audience tastes and original creative ideas. Now television is becoming increasingly globalized as television networks look for creative formats from around the world that can be adapted in many countries. For example, *The Biggest Loser* was developed by The Shine Group, a British company recently acquired by Fox.

TABLE 8.5 Prime-Time Television Genres

GENRE	ORIGINS	EARLY EXAMPLE	CURRENT EXAMPLE	GENRE VARIATIONS
Situation Comedy	Radio comedy skits, "screwball" movie comedies	*I Love Lucy*	*Modern Family*	Family, workplace, buddy
Drama	Live theater, radio and movie dramas	*The Twilight Zone*	*Grey's Anatomy*	Crime, medical, law, romance, soap opera
Action-Adventure	Radio serials, westerns, gangster movies	*The Lone Ranger*	*Hell on Wheels*	Detective, science fiction, western, police
Reality	Radio quiz shows, movie documentaries	*Queen for a Day*	*Dancing with the Stars*	Talk shows, home video, police footage
Movies	Live theater, vaudeville	*Monday Night at the Movies*	*American Movie Classics*	TV movies, miniseries
Game Shows	Radio quiz shows	*21*	*Jeopardy*	Quiz, celebrity guessing games
Newsmagazine	Newspapers, radio news, movie newsreels	*See It Now*	*60 Minutes*	Newsmaker interviews

WHAT'S ON CABLE?

Cable networks elevated counterprogramming to an art form by chipping away at the network prime-time audience with specialized target audience programs. Headline News and the Weather Channel follow the programming clock model found in radio, scheduling recurring segments at the same time each hour. General audience cable channels such as USA Network maintain a balance of programming intended to attract a broad audience throughout the day, translating the broadcast television daypart strategy to cable, in which genres vary over the course of the day to match the audiences that are available at different hours.

Cable is well known for niche channels dedicated to particular interests or groups of viewers, or narrowcasting. Narrowcasting works for cable but not for broadcasters because advertising-supported cable networks supplement their income from affiliate fees paid by local cable systems. And advertisers will pay a premium if the audience includes a high proportion of viewers interested in their products. For example, a computer company may find a higher concentration of potential customers viewing a cable TV show about computers than among viewers of a broadcast situation comedy. Genre channels extend particular genres to occupy entire full-time channels, for instance, CNN (all news) and ESPN (all sports). As the channel capacity of cable systems climbs, the genre channels diversify into subgenres. For example, the "news" category includes channels dedicated to regional news (Northwest Cable News), local news (NY1 News), sports news (ESPNEWS), entertainment news (E! Entertainment Television), and business news (CNBC).

Other channels are built around audience characteristics; they are target audience channels. For instance, Black Entertainment Television schedules music videos, black college sports, and public affairs programming for African-American viewers. Women (WE), children (Nickelodeon), and Hispanics (Univision) are among the other demographic target audiences. Others might better be described as lifestyle channels. Their programs are aimed at people who share a common interest or way of life, on channels for people who enjoy the outdoors (the Outdoor Channel) as well as for homebodies (HGTV).

Cable channels are quick to spin off genre variations around hot themes. For example, there is the "treasure TV" genre built around the lost treasures in people's attics and backyards, following on the success of *Pawn Stars* about a family-owned pawn shop in Las Vegas. Now we have *American Pickers* (rolling treasure hunters), *Storage Wars* (competing treasure hunters who frequent storage locker auctions in Southern California), *Auction Kings* (treasure hunting for high end antiques), and *Auction Hunters* (expert storage locker

MONTY BRINTON/CBS /Landov

LOOKS LIKE A NEW GENRE Combine a cop show with a hospital show and you get a forensic investigation show, like *CSI*. New shows often combine elements from previous hits in an effort to define new winning program formulas.

plunderers who tour the country), to name but a few. All of these are arguably variations on *Antiques Roadshow* on PBS, itself a copy of a British TV show by the same name. Cable network programs can now compete head to head with broadcast networks. The ratings for cable-originated shows like *The Closer* and *Rizzoli & Isles* match those of top 20 shows on the broadcast networks. Scripted dramas such as *Boardwalk Empire* and *Mad Men* win critical acclaim for dealing with subject matter that broadcast networks avoid.

PBS PROGRAMMING

PBS stations are not as ratings-driven as commercial television, but they still need audiences to attract donations, corporate underwriters, and voter support for continuing government subsidies. PBS stations focus on cumulative (or "cume") ratings that reflect program viewership over a week or a month. This gives PBS the freedom to specialize in different genres from commercial broadcasters. Documentaries, highbrow cultural programming, and drama anthologies could not survive on network television but pull in enough occasional viewers to keep public broadcasting viable.

PROGRAMMING STRATEGIES

The underlying assumption of program scheduling has long been that television viewing is a deeply ingrained habit and that most people, most of the time, sit (or lie) down to watch television as opposed to specific programs. Thus, the key to ratings success is to be the least objectionable choice among the many programs offered at a particular time of the day.

Program executives build ratings by maintaining a consistent flow of viewers from one program to the next, and the tactics they use fill a colorful vocabulary—*hammocking, stripping, tent-poling*, and so on (Eastman, 1993). They may schedule programs in blocks of the same genre (e.g., edgy cartoon family comedies *The Simpsons* and *Family Guy* back to back) that appeal to the same audience segment. They will lead off a time block or lead into a promising new show with a proven show like *CSI* in hopes that the weaker that follow will inherit the audience. A new show's chances can also be improved by following it with a highly rated, established show like *Grey's Anatomy* as a *lead out*, or by inserting it between two strong shows, which is called *hammocking*. If there aren't enough established programs for that, a strong show may be placed between weaker ones, which is called *tent-poling*. Local stations rely on *stripping*, running the same program in the same time slot every day of the week, and *checkerboarding*, rotating programs in a particular time slot.

The competitors try to disrupt audience flows. *Stunting* includes changing the time slot or length of a program, adding high-profile guest stars, running intensive promotions, or scheduling specials to make some of the viewers "flow" away from their usual programs and disrupt established viewing habits. Programmers may go *head to head* with the competition by scheduling a program in the same genre as the competition's, such as running a police drama opposite *CSI*. Or they may *counterprogram* with an offering from a completely different genre that caters to a different audience, such as going against *Monday Night Football* with a sensitive drama. In this light, PBS might be seen as a counterprogramming network.

However, in the new media environment these techniques are losing their effectiveness, in part because of changes in the way ratings are gathered. With the acceptance of the "broadcast plus three" ratings method that allows broadcasters to count viewers who watch through their digital video recorders within three days of the original broadcast, the flow of audiences is perhaps losing its relevance. Time-honored programming customs like fall preview week, summer rerun season, and sweeps months (when the rating services conduct studies in all TV markets) are also eroding as more markets are monitored continuously throughout the year.

MEDIA&CULTURE

DIVERSITY IN TELEVISION

On-screen and behind the screen diversity are logically related. It takes diverse people to make diverse images. So we ask: How diverse is television ownership and television employment?

Females and minorities are drastically underrepresented in the ranks of TV station owners and board memberships, and minority television station ownership is declining. The FCC once had rules to encourage minority ownership, but these were abolished by federal courts as imposing racial quotas. According to FCC data, minorities own only 3.2 percent of the nation's TV stations, even though they comprise one-third of the total U.S. population. Women own 5 percent of all TV stations even though they make up 51 percent of the population (Turner & Cooper, 2007). And, minority and female ownership is declining over time. The merger wave in the television industry left women and minorities behind, since they do not enjoy equal access to financing for station acquisitions, and every time the limits on broadcast ownership are raised, that threatens minority ownership.

The FCC's current equal opportunity rules require only monitoring of minority employment and outreach efforts for minority applicants, and minority groups complain that the FCC has not applied the rules when evaluating TV station license renewals. In 2010, the FCC revisited the issue with new commissioners appointed by the Obama administration as part of a review of media ownership rules it is required to make every four years.

Minorities have been historically underrepresented in front of the camera, sometimes leading to threats of boycotts by minority groups like the NAACP and La Raza. Most minority actors are found in roles in racially segregated programs that are shown in blocks targeted primarily to minority audiences, and this trend is increasing (Children Now, 2002). The good news is that this trend has increased the overall level of representation of Hispanic and African-American characters to match and even exceed their numbers in the general population (Glascock, 2003). However, other groups, including Asian Americans and Native Americans, are almost invisible on television.

Females are also underrepresented, although this, too, is improving over time (Glascock, 2001). Female actors still play traditional female roles in television programs and their commercials. For example, women who appear in computer commercials on television tend to be clerical workers rather than business professionals or managers (White & Kinnick, 2000).

Diversity in television matters. First, all of society benefits from diverse points of view and one of the best ways to guarantee that is to have owners, managers, producers, and performers drawn from all segments of society. Second, children take their cues from television. Seeing a predominance of white males in powerful TV roles may give minority and female children the mistaken impression that it is their "place" in society to be subservient and submissive. Broadcasters respond that they are in the business of entertainment and making money, that it's not their job to cure all of society's ills. However, this ignores the prominence of television and also, perhaps, the broadcasters' obligation to operate in the public interest.

OUT OF THE WASTELAND?

Today there are hundreds of viewing options—hundreds of thousands if we count the Internet—where once there were only three. But have we really left the "vast wasteland" that Newton Minow described 50 years ago? What can we as viewers, consumers, and voters do to improve television?

THE NEW TELEVISION HEGEMONY

The influence of the Big Five is limited by a law that prevents any entity from owning TV stations that reach more than 39 percent of all TV households. The restrictions are to prevent excessive **horizontal integration** that might limit the diversity of content, especially the news. Even so, the Big Three (and now CNN) all cover basically the same stories, in about the same order, with similar footage, and with a similar slant. The Fox News Channel and MSNBC are alternatives, supporting the "diversity through abundance" argument. But the objectivity of the news is undermined by corporate interests and the commercialization of news content

As major producers of entertainment programs, the Big Five influence culture as well as public affairs. The television industry is trying to avoid the mistakes of the music industry (see Chapter 5) that allowed online distribution to ruin its business and made Apple into a dominant force in music distribution. Broadcasters have been building on their proven advertising-supported model by offering downloads of popular programs from websites like Hulu and their own in-house websites.

How to guarantee diversity? We could require television to cover controversial issues or give advocates of opposing views the right to reply. The Fairness Doctrine once required it, but in 2000, the Supreme Court struck it down. Diversity in entertainment might be improved through rules assuring more diverse ownership of television stations (see Media&Culture: Diversity in Television, page 243), but those rules also have been eliminated. We can hope that the Internet will foster diversity: Google is distributing $150 million in seed money to start up 100 new channels for YouTube. But that might drive us into the arms of a new Big Media colossus.

How can we break free of the smothering embrace of the Big Media? Political economists tell us that the problem is with the capitalist system that promotes "bigness" in media corporations and "sameness" in programming, but changing the system is a tall order. We can try writing Congress. We can do a Google search for the House Subcommittee on Telecommunications and the Internet, but our message will probably get through only if we live in the congressional district of one of the subcommittee members and contributed to his or her last campaign. And the policies governing television are the subject of intense lobbying by powerful industry groups like the National Association of Broadcasters that will drown us out.

So to make our voices heard we might support advocacy groups like Fairness and Accuracy in Reporting (on the left) or the Media Research Center (on the right). Another strategy is to "vote with our dials," choosing sources of news and entertainment that are not dominated by Big Media. Or, we could

Horizontal integration is the concentration of ownership by acquiring companies that are all in the same business.

switch off our TVs and amuse ourselves with the social media of the Internet. That revolution will not be televised.

IS TELEVISION DECENT?

Janet Jackson's "wardrobe malfunction" during the 2004 Super Bowl halftime show sent a shock wave through the executive suites of the broadcast networks. In the wake of the public outrage that the incident caused, CBS was forced to pay a half million dollars in fines. Congress raised the fines so that a 2004 episode of *Without a Trace* featuring a teen sex orgy cost CBS $3.3 million. However, in 2012 the Supreme Court overturned fines for the Superbowl incident and other examples of "fleeting" indecency on the grounds that the FCC had not properly notified broadcasters of its rules governing fleeting indecency (see Chapter 15).

Broadcasters complain that it's not fair that they are subject to decency restraints but cable is not. The rationale for that policy is that broadcasts enter the household unbidden, over the public airwaves, whereas viewers must pay to receive cable. So, if anyone finds cable indecent they can either choose not to subscribe or buy lock-out devices that will screen out indecent channels. With either cable or satellite subscriptions now in 90 percent of U.S. homes, this argument is getting a bit shabby.

This is one of the few instances where the average viewer can take direct action that could have an impact. If we see something on television that offends us, we can file a complaint with the FCC electronically (at www.fcc.gov/cgb/complaints_obscene.html) and they will investigate, although there is currently a backlog of over 1 million complaints pending the recent resolution of the indecency cases. Of course, if our concern is that there is already too much censorship on television, there is no easy way to register that sort of complaint with the FCC. For that we might lend our support to free speech advocacy groups such as the American Civil Liberties Union.

CHILDREN AND TELEVISION

How to keep TV sex and violence away from children? Usually, regulatory efforts run up against the First Amendment and its protection of free speech, so industry self-regulation has been the inevitable outcome. However, self-regulation has never been effective in the long run. Broadcasters question the validity of research about the effects of television (see Chapter 14) and insist that it is up to the parents to mind their own children. To help parents do their part, the Telecommunications Act of 1996 required a V-chip that enables viewers to block programming, via an electronically encoded system that works off voluntary content ratings supplied by the networks. However, less than 20 percent of parents actually use the V-chip, and only about half consult TV ratings to decide what children can watch (Rideout, 2007).

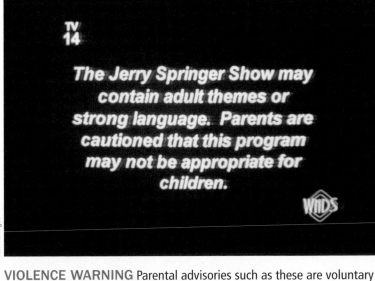

VIOLENCE WARNING Parental advisories such as these are voluntary ratings supplied by the networks to help parents control children's viewing. They also help to stave off criticism about excessive violence on television. TVY—All Children; TVY7—Directed to Older Children; TVG—General Audiences; TVPG—Parental Guidance Suggested; TV14—Parents Strongly Cautioned, TVMA—Mature Audiences Only.

MEDIA & CULTURE

TELEVISION AND THE DAYS OF OUR LIVES?

If films are larger than life, television seems more intimate, the very stuff of our daily life. Television seems to influence our daily routine more than any other medium. In the 1950s, people began to eat their dinners off TV trays so they could watch the tube during dinner. Now students schedule their studying around *Gossip Girls*, and *American Idol* got families to reschedule vacations.

Anthropologists observe how people see television as an essential part of their daily lives, and television programmers have tried hard to see that this continues. Some of the more successful "new" television genres, talk and reality shows, play up this connection to daily life, looking in on the daily lives captured on the screen of MTV's *Jersey Shore*.

This focus on daily life in television studies corresponds to changes in social theory. Social and cultural theorists, from Fernand Braudel to Anthony Giddens, have focused our attention on how people live their daily lives and how it reflects the choices they make. Scholars like David Morley look at the patterns of daily life to see how television is affecting us and whether we are accepting or rejecting its messages. Feminist scholars, like Charlotte Brunsdon, look at how women watch soap operas to resist and cope with the pressures on women in society.

Television is often the source of some of the main narratives of our lives, the topics we talk about with our friends, family, and co-workers. Horace Newcomb called television a cultural forum, one of the places where important forces like race and gender, and issues like fear of terrorism or crime, get discussed in very broad ways.

TV DINNER Television has had a profound influence on our daily routines since the 1950s.

At another level, Raymond Williams talked about the flow of television—that television is not just a series of discrete programs, but more of a continuous flow of experience. Both academic and industry researchers try to understand how television holds the audience over from one program to another (Williams, 1989). Since the 1950s, television programmers have been pushing the message: "Don't touch that dial." They hope that if we really like *CSI*, we will also stick around to watch what comes next. But the early natural flow of television declined with the remote control, ended with the enormous multiplication of channels brought by cable and satellite television, and is now totally defeated by the DVR.

An alternative to censorship is to ensure a supply of educational children's programming; this was the objective of the Children's Television Act in 1990. However, the FCC wrote rules broad enough to allow *The Flintstones* to be counted as educational. After years of quibbling over what was "educational" and what was "specifically designed for children," a quantitative standard of three hours per week of children's programming was set (Kunkel, 1998). However, industry follow-through has been unenthusiastic and has not met the spirit of the rules, and perhaps not even the letter of the requirements.

The track record of advocacy groups in "cleaning up" television for children is disappointing given the supremacy of the First Amendment, but still they try. The Parents Television Council (www.parentstv.org) is one such group trying to reform television. At this point, the most effective action is to take advantage of the self- regulatory tools that Congress put in place. The FCC has a guide to using the V-chip and parental lock-out devices on its website (www.fcc.gov/parents). For the civic-minded, there is also a grade-school curriculum, Student Media Awareness to Reduce Television, aimed at reducing exposure to television (notv.stanford.edu).

WILL PUBLIC TELEVISION SURVIVE?

The fate of public television hangs in the balance every year when Congress approves the annual appropriation for the Corporation for Public Broadcasting, currently $430 million. Critics question the need for federal funding of public broadcasting amid the abundant sources of educational, children's, and cultural programming provided by the marketplace through cable television and the Internet. Defenders suspect the real target may be the public affairs programming on PBS that conservative pundits claim has an excessive liberal bias even though many observers agree that diversity in the points of view presented there has increased in recent years. These are time-worn arguments, but a wave of budget-cutters entered Congress in 2011 who lent them new urgency. State governments chip in about the same amount that the Federal government does but that source is already drying up, with state governors slashing appropriations to cope with their own budget deficits. Public donations that account for about a quarter of the funding for public broadcasting are also declining (Waldman, 2011). Other woes come from within the PBS community. KCET in Los Angeles defected from the national programming pool after finding that it could no longer afford to pay its dues and other stations are considering their own withdrawals or closing down completely. On the plus side, popular shows like *Downton Abbey* could win over a new generation of PBS supporters.

TELEVISION NEEDS YOU!

If you think television is still a vast wasteland, why don't you do something about it? Why not make your own TV show and post it on YouTube or one of the dozens of other websites that welcome user-made video? The basic steps are a snap: sign up for a YouTube account and click the video upload button. Using either your cell phone's camera or a webcam (now selling for under $20), you can upload the videos without any special software. Just turn on the camera and start talking, dancing, or doing something mildly disgusting. Then you can be a YouTube star like LonelyGirl15, whose serial postings were seen by millions and attracted the attention of Hollywood talent agents!

Or maybe not. It turns out that LonelyGirl15 was an aspiring professional actress by the name of Jessica Rose and her lines were written by a script writer. Many popular YouTube videos have professionals and many hours of preparation and post-production behind them. Still, that makes them an excellent way for aspiring video stars, producers, and directors to showcase themselves.

YouTubers do need to be careful about stepping on the toes of the Big Five as they go about their business. Including snippets of video from copyrighted

STOP&REVIEW

1. Why are there so many reality shows on TV these days?
2. What strategies do networks use to maintain the flow of audiences between programs?
3. What are the current rules governing television station ownership?
4. How can we clean up violence and sex on television?
5. How diverse is television ownership?

television shows or movies is unlawful and YouTube makes an effort to remove submissions that include such material. How diligent they are in this is the subject of dispute, resulting in lawsuits between the copyright owners and Google, the owners of YouTube. Google is working on image recognition software that it hopes will automatically detect copyrighted content and filter it out immediately upon uploading.

SUMMARY&REVIEW

HOW DID THE BIG THREE NETWORKS DOMINATE TV?

NBC, CBS, and ABC brought their programs, stars, audiences, and advertisers with them from radio. During the FCC freeze, most cities had only one or two stations, and NBC and CBS were the top affiliation choices. ABC rebounded when it ordered programs produced by Hollywood studios.

WHAT WAS THE GOLDEN AGE?

Early network television featured variety shows, drama anthologies, and quality public-affairs programming seldom seen today. Top actors and writers based in New York tackled serious dramas. Shifting audiences, creeping commercialism, Hollywood production values, and quiz show scandals spelled the end of the Golden Age.

HOW DID VIEWING CHOICES EXPAND BEYOND THE BIG THREE?

FCC Chairman Newton Minow called television a "vast wasteland" of bland programming in 1961. The Corporation for Public Broadcasting and the Public Broadcasting Service were established to provide an alternative source of programming. The Fin-Syn rules and other regulatory measures limited the amount of television programming that the networks could produce and own. Independent UHF stations began to prosper after UHF tuners were required in new television sets and the FCC opened up the major cities to cable television. That paved the way for pay services like HBO and advertising-supported basic channels like WTBS.

HOW DID NEW TELEVISION NETWORKS DEVELOP?

In 1987, Rupert Murdoch started the Fox television network. Cable TV helped Fox, since most Fox affiliates were independent UHF stations, which cable brought to most homes with excellent picture quality. Fox also pursued younger viewers beloved by advertisers. The WB, UPN (later combined into the CW), and Ion networks followed.

WHAT IS THE IMPACT OF CABLE ON BROADCAST TV?

The proportion of viewers who tune in to prime-time broadcasts from ABC, CBS, and NBC has declined dramatically in recent years. Cable households are heavy viewers of television, and over half of viewing in cable households is now devoted to channels available only on cable.

HOW IS NETWORK TELEVISION CHANGING?

Now, broadcast networks are part of vertically integrated media conglomerates that also include movie studios, cable networks, and other media assets. The Big Five media conglomerates (Time Warner, Viacom/CBS, Disney, NBC Universal/Comcast, and Fox) have replaced the Big Three as the dominant players in the television industry. Old program formulas are proving too expensive to sustain, so the networks are searching for new financial and programming models involving digital distribution technologies.

WHAT IS DIGITAL TELEVISION?

Television completed the transition to digital broadcasting in 2009. High-definition television (HDTV) sets display sharper, wider pictures. Broadcasters also transmit standard-definition television (SDTV) pictures on digital subchannels. New digital options are appearing, including DVRs, video-on-demand systems, and television distribution through the Internet and cell phones.

WHERE DO COMMERCIAL PROGRAMS COME FROM?

Companies owned by the Big Five dominate the production of network television and cable programs, the production and distribution of first-run syndicated programming, and the syndication of off-network reruns of network programs. Lesser media conglomerates and a dwindling number of independent producers and syndicators account for the rest. National broadcast, cable, and satellite networks transmit programs to the public. The broadcast networks own their own stations (O&Os) in major markets and rely on affiliates to broadcast them elsewhere. Cable channels reach the home through local cable television systems.

WHAT ARE THE MAIN TELEVISION GENRES?

Sitcoms, dramas, action-adventures, movies, news, and reality shows are the main genres in network prime time today. Genres that appeal to 18- to 34-year-olds predominate, as that group is highly valued by advertisers.

WHAT ENCOURAGES DIVERSITY IN TELEVISION?

Horizontal and vertical integration in the television industry threaten the diversity of ideas. Limits on television station ownership and on cross-ownership of media have been relaxed over the years. Companies can now also own or manage more than one station in a single market. Policies that encourage minority and female ownership and employment in the television industry, or that mandate fairness in the coverage of important issues, can also increase diversity. Marketplace forces might produce diversity on their own by providing many competing alternatives. However, the dominance of the Big Media conglomerates calls this policy into question.

WHY CAN'T THEY CLEAN UP TV?

The First Amendment frustrates efforts to censor violent or sexual content, so industry self-regulation is ultimately the only option. Cable has even fewer restrictions than broadcast TV on the premise that parents can simply discontinue their subscriptions or purchase lock-out devices if they find its content objectionable.

THINKING CRITICALLY
ABOUT THE MEDIA

1. Are we coming out of the TV wasteland at last or getting lost in it more deeply than ever before? Explain your opinion.

2. How do you assess your options for future TV viewing? If you had to buy a TV right now that would meet your needs in 2015, what would you buy?

3. If the conventional network TV model is in fact dying, what do you think should replace it?

4. How does television fit into your entertainment diet? What do you rely on it for?

5. Pitch your idea for a YouTube video. Think about what would make it appeal to 18- to 24-year-olds since that is a group that advertisers prize. Make it good if you want to be discovered by Hollywood!

KEY TERMS

affiliate fees (p. 235)

basic cable (p. 221)

cable television (p. 220)

community access (p. 235)

cost per thousand (p. 217)

direct broadcast satellites (DBS) (p. 222)

first-run syndication (p. 220)

high-definition television (HDTV) (p. 226)

horizontal integration (p. 244)

Internet television (p. 229)

local origination (p. 235)

multiple system operators (MSOs) (p. 221)

must carry (p. 220)

pay TV (p. 221)

ratings (p. 217)

syndication (p. 218)

retransmission fees (p. 225)

UHF (p. 216)

underwriting (p. 234)

VHF (p. 216)

ANNOYING OR TRANSFORMING?

Google is giving the Annoying Orange his own channel on YouTube in an effort to transform video viewing habits through the Internet.

THE INTERNET

HISTORY: SPINNING THE WEB

Many think of the Internet as a relatively recent development, but electronic computers and computer networks date back to the hot and cold wars of the last century. John Vincent Atanasoff of Iowa State University is generally credited with inventing the electronic computer on the eve of World War II, although he never assembled a complete working model. During World War II the British secret service invented an all-electronic digital computer (named *Colossus*), conceived by computer pioneer Alan Turing, to crack Nazi secret codes. The original general-purpose computer, the electronic numerical integrator and calculator (ENIAC), was enlisted in the Cold War that followed, running calculations for the first hydrogen bomb.

Early computer networks were also electronic warriors. The SAGE air defense system, dating from the early 1950s, introduced **modems** to feed warnings of approaching Russian bombers (which never came) into the first **wide area network (WAN).** The first **local area network (LAN)** linked computers at the Livermore, California, atomic weapons laboratory.

1972	The Internet is invented		2000	Dot-com bust
1991	The Internet opens to commercial users; HTML developed; the World Wide Web is born		2007	Web 2.0
1995	Amazon.com popularizes e-commerce		2011	Social media used in democracy movements world-wide

Modems(modulator–demodulators) convert digital data to analog signals and vice versa.

Wide area networks (WANs) connect computers that are miles apart.

Local area networks (LANs) link computers within a department, building, or campus.

The Internet itself was originally developed to continue weapons research at Livermore and other labs even if civilization was wiped out in a nuclear war. It was then called *ARPANET*, the Advanced Research Projects Agency Network, and was funded by the U.S. Department of Defense. Anyone who has ever struggled with an Internet connection will appreciate its famous first words, in 1969. The operator typed "L. . . O. . ." (trying to tell the person at the other end to *LOG* IN), but the system crashed before the message could be completed!

THE WEB IS BORN

The reinvention of the Internet for you and me involved bringing computer technology to the desktops of average users. The experimental Alto computer, developed by the Xerox Corporation in the early 1970s, was the first personal computer. It boasted a mouse, a graphical user interface, and a high-speed local area network connection called *Ethernet*, invented by Bob Metcalfe.

The first commercially available personal computer, the Altair, inspired a young computer hacker from Seattle by the name of William Gates to write a programming language for it, called BASIC, and to found Microsoft Corporation. It also inspired young Steve Jobs to build the first Apple II in 1977. In 1984, Apple's Macintosh introduced high-resolution graphics and multimedia to personal computers. Apple's HyperCard software popularized the *hypertext* concept, the "linking" function that makes it possible to navigate by "mouse clicking" on keywords or icons in a non-linear method, made familiar by links on the Web.

With computers entering the home, networks were developed for—and sometimes by—home users. Early systems used television sets as their display units (hence the "video" part of the name) and were limited to text (the "tex" part) and crude graphics. The world's first commercial *videotex* service, Prestel, was launched in Great Britain in 1979 (Bouwman&Christofferson, 1992). America Online (AOL) started out as a user-friendly videotex service in 1985.Today's social media trace back to the first *Bulletin Board Systems* (BBSs) of 1978, many

GOOD JOB Apple pioneered the personal computer in 1977 with the Apple II, which featured a floppy disk drive.

THE FATHER OF THE WEB Tim Berners-Lee originated HTML and gave us the Web.

operating from closets of computer enthusiasts, to exchange e-mail, post opinions online, and upload and download information (Rafaeli & LaRose, 1993) that soon migrated to the Internet.

The year that stands out for the "birth" of the Internet is 1972, for several reasons: ARPANET, a project funded by the Defense Advanced Research Project Agency (DARPA) had its first public demonstration, e-mail was first introduced, and the network acquired its name and essential character (Cringely, 1998; Leiner et al., 2002). The term *internetting* was introduced that year to describe the idea of a "network of networks" that still characterizes the Internet today. The basic rules, or protocols, for communication between networks were also laid out at that time, and these evolved into the **transmission-control protocol/Internetworking protocol (TCP/IP).** Internet pioneer Jon Postel contributed the system of naming and numbering addresses on the Internet.

> [**Transmission-control protocol/Internet protocol (TCP/IP)** is the basic protocol used by the Internet.]

A widening user base of college professors helped push the Internet out of the embrace of the Department of Defense as connections to major universities were added. A number of other "closed" networks grew in parallel, including an e-mail system for university professors (BITNET) and a popular discussion group system (USENET). These networks were merged under the National Science Foundation in 1986 to form NSFNET.

The Internet was reinvented again in 1991 to open it to commercial users and the general public, as NSF started withdrawing its financial support. Now college students and other users of the network, rather than big government-funded labs, began to push further innovations. Programmers at the University of Minnesota came out with Gopher, a word play on their school mascot, which first brought hypertext online, although it could link text files only. Also in 1991, Tim Berners-Lee of the CERN laboratory in Switzerland wrote the **hypertext markup language (HTML)** and the first Web browser to solve the problem of transporting text documents across different computer systems. That was the basis of the World Wide Web.

[**Hypertext markup language (HTML)** is used to format pages on the Web.]

THE DOT-COM BOOM

Many of the Internet properties and pioneers that have since become household names got their start in the mid-1990s as entrepreneurs realized there was money to be made from the rapidly growing online population. A group of students at the University of Illinois led by Marc Andreesen designed the first graphical Internet **browser**, Mosaic, so that the average computer user could surf the Web. Their university wasn't interested in commercializing the product so Andreessen and his colleagues rewrote it for their own private company as Netscape. By 1995, Netscape had over 50 million users, the operation of the Net was turned over to commercial providers, and online services like America Online (AOL) began offering Internet access to all. The Internet craze was in full swing, fostering a cultural and economic phenomenon that became known as the *dot-com boom*.

[**Browsers** are computer programs that display information found on the Web.]

Amazon.com started that year as an electronic bookstore before it evolved into an online mega-mall. Internet auction house eBay also made its mark that year as a marketplace for oddball collectibles, such as the Pez candy dispensers sought by the wife of its founder. Yahoo!, the brainchild of two grad students from Stanford, began a year earlier as an online search engine before being supplanted by Google (the work of two other Stanford grad students, Sergey Brin and Larry Page) and evolving into an advertising-supported portal.

Other Internet pioneers did not fare so well. America Online (AOL) introduced tens of millions of homes to the Web, but it faded into the background when it merged with the Time Warner media conglomerate at the turn of the century. Netscape was soon supplanted by Internet Explorer on the strength of Microsoft Corporation's dominance of the home computer market. In 2000, the dot-com boom gave way to the dot-com bust as investors soured on Internet stocks, online consumers tired of the novelty of clicking on banner ads, and the general economy weakened.

REINING IN THE NET

The cultural impact of the Internet was also changing shape. On the positive side, many found the Internet to be a venue for making new friends, reconnecting with old friends, staying in touch with family members, engaging in public debate, learning about political candidates, gathering information, finding a good deal on products and services, and exploring pleasant diversions. The Internet did not always live up to the promises of "Internet evangelists," however, who touted it as the cure for isolation, poverty, ignorance, political oppression, and boredom. The governments of the world began to consider how to control an international medium that evaded their laws and challenged national media systems.

Content restrictions became an issue as the Internet collided with the cultures of diverse nations. A portion of the Telecommunications Act of 1996, the Communications Decency Act, was written to ban "indecent" material, such as images of naked female breasts, from the Internet. That law was ruled to be unconstitutional, but efforts continue to restrict sexually explicit material in the United States (see Media Literacy: Getting the Most Out of the Internet, page 276). Tales of child molesters stalking children (cyberstalking), teens harassing one another (cyberbullying), online gamers destroying their families (Internet gaming addiction), and identity thieves trolling for private information in online venues raised further concerns. Parents came to regard the Internet, rather than television, as the number one media threat to children (Common Sense Media, 2006).

Political communication across borders is also problematic. France apparently has no problem with breasts but tried to ban material considered politically obscene, such as souvenirs from Nazi Germany. China bans online criticism of its government and pro-Tibetan websites by blocking dissident Web pages and monitoring public Internet cafes. North Korea prohibits Internet access to prevent its citizens from learning of the world beyond their borders. In the wake of the 9/11 attacks it became evident that the terrorists used the Internet to coordinate the plot, to raise funds, and to help recruit new members to their cause.

Intellectual property (see Chapter 15) also became an issue. Countries such as the United States, with strict copyright protections, were alarmed to find that other countries with more lenient statutes became havens for file-sharing services that supported massive copyright piracy. Thousands of U.S. college students were threatened with lawsuits from the recording industry as a result.

Access to the Internet, as well as its content, has an impact. Instead of curing poverty, ignorance, and isolation, some believe the Internet perpetuates them. People can run companies and communicate with others without ever having to be seen, but there are gaps in access for minority, low-income, or rural families persist (NTIA, 2011). Developing countries in Africa, Asia, and South America have been left further behind in the development of a global information economy (Castells, 2004).

Frustrated by the difficulty of enforcing their own laws and customs beyond their borders, governments are calling for international oversight and an end to U.S. control. The ruling bodies of the Internet, notably the Internet Architecture Board and the Internet Engineering Task Force (see Internet Organizations, page 266), have gradually expanded to include international representatives. ICANN (Internet Corporation for Assigned Names and Numbers) was formed as a nonprofit private corporation to oversee the assignment of the .com, .net, and .org Internet addresses (called *domain names*) and to develop new ones. However, the U.S. government maintains control over ICANN, a sticking point with all the other nations of the world.

Efforts continue to internationalize control of the Web. The United Nations established the Internet Governance Forum to further diversity, security, and education in the information society and convened the World Summit on the Information Society in 2003 and 2005 to address ICANN control, the digital divide, and other issues (http://www.itu.int/wsis/index.html). Significant

IS THAT A COMPUTER IN YOUR GAME COLSOLE?
Video game consoles like Microsoft's Xbox 360 include Internet connections and enough computer power to double as personal computers.

Vicki Beaver

progress was made in 2009 when ICANN authorized the use of the characters from many of the world's leading non-Western alphabets in Internet addresses.

OLD MEDIA IN THE INTERNET AGE

Now that nearly three-fourths of American adults use the Internet (NTIA, 2011), the Web offers serious competition for conventional media. Google is the new king of the media, surpassing television and cable networks, newspaper chains, and magazines as the number one vehicle for advertising. Craig's List is siphoning off classified ads that were once the life's blood of print newspapers. Music file sharing ravaged the business plans of the music industry and paved the way for Apple's iTunes to become a powerful new force in music distribution. The iPad is a rapidly growing personal media channel that threatens to drain revenues from print magazine publishers and video producers who find that they have to cut a deal with Apple to get their products seen. Netflix competes head-to-head with Home Box Office to be the leading pay TV service.

Many old media outlets are adopting the philosophy of "if you can't beat them, join them." Some troubled newspapers have transformed to online-only publications, for example. Nearly a million books are available for Amazon's Kindle e-book. Legal music services supported by ad sales or subscription fees are starting to appear with the blessings of major record labels. Thousands of television programs and Hollywood movies are available for streaming online, so many that video traffic now far outpaces more conventional Web traffic on the Internet (Anderson & Wolff, 2010). The broadband connections that reach 64 percent of U.S. homes (NTIA, 2010) make it possible to add Internet options to TVs, stereos, VCRs, game consoles, and DVD players as sources for home entertainment.

THE RISE OF SOCIAL MEDIA

Although MySpace and Facebook are the leading names in social networking today they were not the first. As previously mentioned, BBS and videotex systems of the 1970s also shared content and messages originated by their users. GeoCities began hosting personal web pages in the mid 1990s, many of which resembled the social network profiles of today, and SixDegrees.com users could create profiles and lists of friends. The advent of blogging (in 1997) and Wikipedia (2001) were other milestones in the evolution of **social media** (Curtis, 2011).

The creators of Facebook, Twitter, YouTube, Flickr, and Wikipedia are pursuing the **Web 2.0** model for news and entertainment in which we, the audience, provide much of the content. Advertising and public relations practitioners hope to "go viral," meaning that their pitches will be picked up by users of social media and spread like a virus through the Internet. Affordable and easy-to-use audio and video production technologies lower the barriers to entry (see Chapter 2) to the point that anyone with a computer and a digital camera can aspire to be a media star. Facebook is fast becoming the new king of the media, with three-quarters of a billion users worldwide, by acting as a portal to news and entertainment as well as social interaction for its users, and by becoming a major force in online advertising,

Social Media are media whose content is created and distributed through social interaction.

Web 2.0 is a new way of using the Internet for collaboration and sharing of data among individual users.

The impact of social media is boiling over into the real world as political movements across the globe use them to organize protests against repressive governments. Facebook and Twitter played key roles in the rebellions that swept through North Africa in 2011 and in the Occupy Wall Street movement in the United States. Repressive governments are fighting back; for example, the Egyptian government effectively turned off the Internet in an effort to suppress a democracy movement, and Iran tracked down dissidents who used the Internet to organize anti-government demonstrations. In response, the U.S. State Department is funding technologies that will help protestors circumvent the dictators. However, this raises the specter of cyberwarfare that could cripple the Internet and the global economy that relies on it. Sadly, this could bring the Internet full cycle back to its origins as a weapon of war.

Much like the dictators' efforts to dominate the offline lives of their citizens, social media have the potential to dominate our online lives. Social media "apps" like Facebook snatch eyeballs away from conventional media and the Web alike. Although the front door to Facebook is reached through the Web, once inside users are in a "walled garden." Content is still delivered over the Internet, but not through our Web browsers and it is "off limits" to search engines like Google. We are a captive audience subject to the whims of the owner of the garden.

TECHNOLOGY TRENDS: FOLLOWING MOORE'S LAW

The continual reinvention of the Internet is influenced by advances in computers and their networks. According to Moore's Law, processing capacity in computer chips has doubled about every 18 months since the late 1960s (Moore, 1996). That is why new personal computers are obsolete as soon as they come out of the box. And according to Metcalfe's Law (after Bob Metcalfe, one of the founders of the Internet), the value of the Internet increases rapidly with the number of users. This drives continual Internet technology growth and also explains the sometimes explosive popularity of new Internet applications like Facebook.

COMPUTER TECHNOLOGY TRENDS

Increasingly, the same technologies that we find in our computers are migrating to entertainment media and mobile devices. The iPod is basically a computer hard drive or flash memory with a small computer display and a data connection, whereas TiVo and other DVRs are computer hard drives with connections for your TV. Blu-Ray disks capable of storing high-definition video are on the latest personal computers. Convergence came to display technologies long ago. The cathode ray tube (CRT) display is a relic of the 1960s. The LCD displays and other "flat-screen" technologies (see Chapter 8) that we now use for TV were originally developed for laptop computers.

As you may have learned in your high school computer class, the evolution of computers is traced through their central processing units (CPUs), where all the actual data processing takes place. Today's personal computers are fourth-generation computers with very large-scale integrated (VLSI) circuits with millions of components each.

Future reinventions of the Internet are inextricably intertwined with new developments in the computers connected to it. The prevailing trend has been to continually make computers more powerful, but now there is a countervailing movement to make them simpler and more compact.

The lightweight netbooks popping up in college lecture halls are part of the "less is more" scenario, as are iPhones and iPads. As more applications and data move onto the Internet, the amount of processing power and storage capacity needed in your personal computers may decrease. Continuing the trend, special-purpose computers might take over your office, living room, and even your kitchen—all connected through the "Internet of Things." Everyday objects from clothing to furniture to the products on your pantry shelf will have miniature sensors, identification tags, transmitters, and data processors that will connect them to the Internet or send text messages to your cell phone ("Dear Dale: The milk is sour and your jeans are, too!").

In the "more is better" case, multimedia computers will add new sound and video processing capabilities until they become home entertainment servers sitting in the middle of a high-speed computer network that distributes entertainment and information throughout your home. A capacious hard drive will let you store all of your MP3s and video downloads and retransmit them to all the rooms in your home. If you want your new smartphone (or your digital camera) to "talk" to your PC without a wire, there is Bluetooth for wireless connections across your tabletop. Advanced video game machines, like the latest PlayStation or Xbox 360, also compete to fill a similar niche, playing movies on DVD and connecting to the Internet.

NETWORK TECHNOLOGY TRENDS

At only 56,000 bits per second, the "high-speed" computer modem of just a few years ago is an obsolete slowpoke. Digital subscriber line (DSL) connections have caught up to cable modems in the race to wire the country for broadband connections capable of millions of bits per second. To keep up with all the music and digital video files that broadband users download, the connections in the Internet backbone are also being upgraded to fiber-optic cables that carry billions of bits per second. Telephone companies are connecting individual homes to fiber in many parts of the country that will transmit billions of bits per second, too. These companies hope that will give them the edge over cable companies in the long run.

Why not use the third wire you have coming into your home, your electrical power line, for data transmission? That is the promise of broadband over power lines (BPL). Until recently, electrical interference from power transmission posed serious problems, but the technical barriers have been overcome. By taking advantage of a network that is already installed—in the walls of your home as well as the streets of your neighborhood—BPL could mean low-cost broadband connections for everyone, and competition for telephone and cable companies.

The other network trend is wireless. Third-generation (3G) and fourth-generation (4G) cell phones (see Chapter 12) make it possible to check your e-mail and surf Web pages with your phone faster than current networks and, coming soon, to run two-way video conferences and watch high-definition television on your cell phone.

TECHNOLOGY DEMYSTIFIED

INSIDE THE INTERNET

To understand trends in Internet technology, we need to recall that there are many varying patterns of communication, or **protocols**, that are the basic building blocks of Internet applications. There are over 100 protocols associated with the Internet, known collectively as TCP/IP (transmission-control protocol/Internet protocol). Some of the protocols that are readily apparent to Internet users include:

- Mail. The simplified mail transfer protocol (SMTP) is for sending e-mail between host computers on the Internet. The Post Office Protocol (POP) connects users to their mail servers. The listserv protocol governs electronic mailing lists (listservs) that "broadcast" e-mail to special-interest groups.

- File Transfers. The file transfer protocol (FTP) governs how electronic documents and computer programs are transmitted across the Internet, such as when Web pages are uploaded to a Web server. The **hypertext transfer protocol (http)** handles file transfers over the Web.

- Locators. The domain name service (DNS) translates Web addresses that people use (such as http://www.msu.edu) into the addresses that the Internet uses (such as 35.9.7.102).

- Document Display. The hypertext markup language (HTML) governs the display of Web pages on the screen.

Several of these protocols work together when you go surfing on the Web. Web pages are stored as files on Web servers connected to the Internet. The servers may be ordinary personal computers running special software that lets remote users access the data, but that makes for very slow downloads. Large commercial sites use high-powered computers connected to high-speed lines so that they can store gigabytes of data and serve thousands of users at once. The Web page files include HTML tags that your browser software (for example, Internet Explorer) uses to display the text and graphics on-screen (see Figure 9.1 on page 260).

When you request a Web page by typing its Uniform Resource Locator (URL) into your browser or by clicking on a hyperlink, the DNS protocol translates the address of the Web page you ordered into the numerical form of the address and sends the request out to the Internet through connections supplied by your Internet service provider (ISP). The request is formatted using the hypertext transfer protocol (http).

Your request is a short message, but the Web page you receive in return may be quite lengthy, and that could tie up both the server and the network connection. So, before sending your requested page to you, the server breaks it up into a number of packets of about 1,500 characters (or about 12,000 bits) each. (This paragraph has about three-quarters of that many characters, including the spaces.) If you are downloading a music or video file, the computer data for those are also broken up into packets. One second's worth of music for your iPod takes up about six packets' worth of data, for example. The server appends a header with dozens of bits of information that indicate how many packets are in the message and the sequence number of each packet, along with the result of a mathematical calculation that is used to check each packet for errors that might occur during transmission. The rules for doing all that are called the transmission-control protocol, or TCP.

The packet of data and the TCP information are then placed in a digital "envelope" that has your Internet address (known as your IP address), the address of the server, and instructions about what to do about packets that get delayed for some reason. That is done according to the Internet protocol (IP). Taken together, these two sets of rules are referred to as TCP/IP.

Then the TCP/IP packet is sent to a network switching device called a *router*. Routers are like postal clerks. They check the IP address on each packet and select the best path for it through the Internet backbone network. Along the way, the packets pass through several routers, and some packets may be diverted to alternate routes depending upon which path is the least congested at a given moment. The TCP/IP packet containing the requested Web page is ultimately directed to your ISP's router, then into the ISP's network , then to your local phone or cable connection, and finally into your own computer. You may need a router, too, if you have multiple Internet users in your home who all want to be online at the same time.

Your computer reassembles the packets according to the sequencing information (the TCP part), checks for errors, and requests replacements for any corrupted packets. Then all the addressing and sequencing information is stripped away, and the parts of the original HTML file are merged together and sent to your browser. The browser displays the page for you according to the instructions it finds in the HTML file. Then you see the Web page.

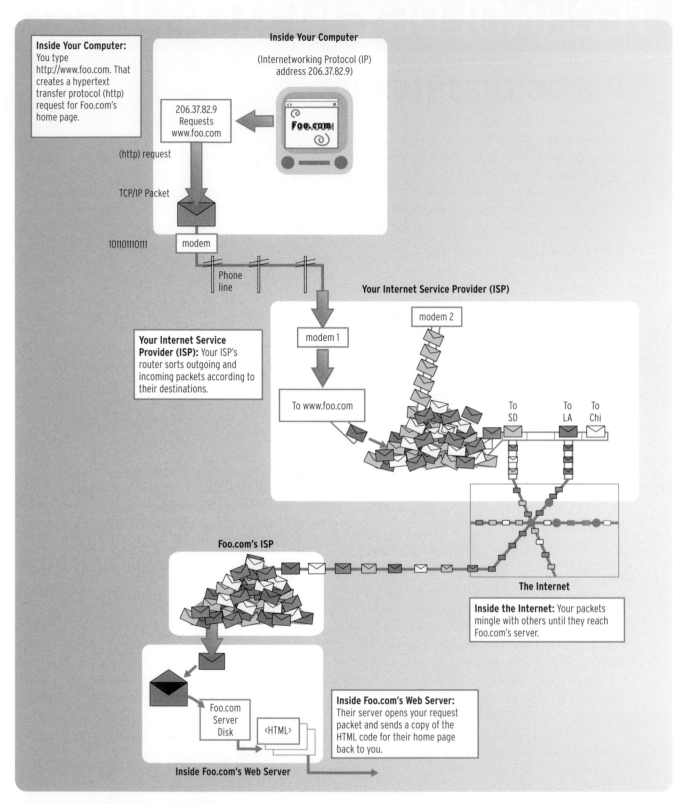

Inside Your Computer: You type http://www.foo.com. That creates a hypertext transfer protocol (http) request for Foo.com's home page.

Inside Your Computer

(Internetworking Protocol (IP) address 206.37.82.9)

206.37.82.9 Requests www.foo.com

Foo.com

(http) request

TCP/IP Packet

101101110111 modem

Phone line

Your Internet Service Provider (ISP): Your ISP's router sorts outgoing and incoming packets according to their destinations.

Your Internet Service Provider (ISP)

modem 1

modem 2

To www.foo.com

To SD   To LA   To Chi

The Internet

Inside the Internet: Your packets mingle with others until they reach Foo.com's server.

Foo.com's ISP

Foo.com Server Disk

<HTML>

Inside Foo.com's Web Server: Their server opens your request packet and sends a copy of the HTML code for their home page back to you.

Inside Foo.com's Web Server

FIGURE 9.1: INSIDE THE INTERNET Information is sent over the Internet using the TCP/IP protocol. The addressing and sorting functions are analogous to the Post Office's.

WiFi (more formally known as IEEE802.11) offers wireless broadband access from "hotspots" covering a growing number of college campuses, airports, Internet cafés, and homes. Newer versions of WiFi offer speeds over 100 times faster than cable modems and make it possible to move around town without losing your connection. If the limited range of WiFi hotspots frustrates you, watch for new WiMAX and EV-DO services that will cover entire cities. Now you can become your own mobile hotspot through a device connected to your computer that will let your iTouch, cell phone, and other WiFi-capable gear share a wireless connection.

Further in the future, **Internet2** (not to be confused with Web 2.0) is a project involving more than 200 universities that conduct experiments with the next generation of Internet technology and give us a preview of more things to come at speeds of 100 billion bits (or gigabits) per second. In 2011 a consortium of 29 universities announced the Gig.Uproject, that aims to extend gigabit networks to neighboring communities. High-resolution medical imaging and instant downloads of high-definition movies are possible applications.

INTERNET TRENDS

The future of the Internet is shaped by changes in network transmission technology that move those packets at ever-higher speeds, and by the software that runs Internet applications and by changes in the rules, or protocols, that are used in Internet transactions. Everything from music (MP3s, see Chapter 5) to telephone calls (Voice over Internet Protocol or VoIP, see Chapter 12) to video (see the sections that follow) is being transmitted over the Internet, and more is to come.

IP Version 6. An update to the basic Internet protocol, *IPversion 6*, is beginning to appear. It will extend the length of Internet addresses so that more can be made. The current system will run out of addresses after "only" about four billion have been issued, sometime in 2012. If we issue addresses in all of the world's languages, that could soak up billions more. And what happens when your car, your TV set, and your toaster need their own IP addresses? Version 6 (we currently use version 4) will have the capacity for trillions of addresses and should provide smoother streaming of audio and video in the bargain. Internet providers and popular websites are hard at work to minimize the impact on consumers from their end. If your computer runs Widows XP or Mac OS 10.0 or a newer operating system there should be no problem on your end, either. However, problems may occur with home networking equipment, such as the WiFi router that many people use to connect the devices in their homes, so an equipment upgrade may be in your future there.

Cloud Computing. Google, Microsoft, and many other Internet companies are expanding their Internet software businesses. Their free, Internet-based e-mail programs are only the beginning of a movement that is revolutionizing the way we buy and use computer software. For example, Google Docs and Spreadsheets are available on an as-needed basis through the Internet and lets you store your documents on the Internet instead of on your computer's hard drive. Apple's iCloud service is another example. You may no longer need a hard drive, just a simple computer with a screen, keyboard, and an Internet connection. This is sometimes called *cloud computing*. The business models are still developing. We might make "micro-payments" to use the software by the minute or the hour, pay per usage, pay a flat monthly fee, or get the software free in return for viewing advertisements.

> **Protocols** are technical rules governing data communication.
>
> **Hypertext transfer protocol (http)** is the Internet protocol used to transfer files over the Web.
>
> **Internet2** is a new, faster version of the Internet.

MARC MUELLER/EPA/Newscom

FLASH GAME FarmVille uses the Flash plug-in to manage in-game interactions on personal computers but Flash is a failure on smartphones. HTML5 will likely replace Flash in the near future.

Plug-ins. These are "helper programs" that work with browser software to perform a number of functions including playing audio and video (for example, Windows Media Player and QuickTime), activating animations (Flash), or displaying documents (Acrobat). Some plug-ins are large programs that must be downloaded and installed before the features will work, but the more popular (and less proprietary) ones eventually get built into new versions of Web browsers.

Among the most popular is Flash 11 (from Adobe). It turns your computer into a multimedia machine that can display high-definition streaming video in the same wide-screen format as HDTV (see Chapter 8). However, the late Steve Jobs never liked Flash and banned it from Apple's mobile hardware, so HTML5 (described in the sections that follow) will likely replace Flash on both desktop and mobile hardware.

Scripts. When you see a gray box that says "application loading," that means a Java program is downloading to your computer. Java Scripts are written with a subset of the Java language. They also can change the appearance of buttons as your mouse "rolls over" them and perform other interactive tricks. At **e-commerce** sites, your credit card and order information is funneled to the Web store's computer with another type of interactive program, Common Gateway Interface (CGI) scripts.

New Markup Languages. Also adding much "coolness" to the Web are variations on the basic HTML. XHTML ("X" for eXtensible) lets programmers define their own tags. Tags are the commands that tell your browser how to display the document, for example, where to locate a picture on the screen and how big it should be. XML is a "meta language" from which tags for specific applications can be made. For example, NewsML-G2 is an XHTML variation that standardizes the presentation of audio and video clips and interactive features alongside Internet news stories. RSS (Really Simple Syndication) is another form of XHTML that posts frequent updates from other websites (such as the current *New York Times* headlines) to a personalized reader page, like iGoogle.

XHTML is part of the development of "the semantic Web." This development is designed to attach useful indexing labels to the content of the Web. For example, if we were composing a story in NewsML, we might have a tag that indicates that the content that follows is a video. We could also add tags identifying the location and nature of the story and indicating that the headline is about a hurricane hitting the Central American country of Belize. Then it would become easier to organize information about Belize, or hurricanes, and incorporate

E-commerce (electronic commerce) completes online purchases and financial transactions on the Web.

that in compiling databases about Central American countries or global climate change even if we didn't use the search terms "Belize" or "hurricane."

HTML5. HTML5 combines semantic Web features with multimedia players. For the user, that means this new version of HTML will play videos and music files without having to download and launch plug-ins, making media consumption on the Web as convenient as tuning a stereo or a TV set with a remote control. New types of interactions with Web pages will become possible, including the ability to drag and drop elements within a page, to draw objects on a page, to work offline with interactive applications, and to interact with forms in new ways, such as using slider bars. HTML5 is also for smartphones, with geo-location capabilities built in. Browser software is still catching up with the full range of HTML5 capabilities, but many of the basic features like audio and video players are already standard. To test the capabilities of your browser, you can visit http://html5test.com/.

Tracking. Some other Web technologies aren't so cool if you are concerned about your privacy. **Cookies** are the files that some websites deposit on visitors' hard drives. That's how sites recognize visitors and greet them by name without making them log in every time. But cookies can also track and collate information between sites without the user's knowledge, and third-party cookies placed by companies that monitor Web advertising may also do so without the user's knowledge.

> **Cookies** are small files that websites leave on their visitors' computers.

Web bugs are tiny (one-pixel) or invisible (for example, matching the background color of the Web page) images that are embedded in HTML code. When your browser pulls them up, the server that stores the invisible images receives a notification. These bugs can follow your tracks inside a website and also track you to other Web pages. They can also extract codes from cookies stored on your computer that identify you uniquely at the sites you have registered. And your e-mail can be bugged too, letting the sender know when you open it and also if you forward it to someone else!

YOUR SECURITY IS A LOCK Look for the https (at the beginning of the URL) and the lock icon next to the URL window to be sure that you are on a secure Internet connection.

STOP&REVIEW

1. What were the early origins of the Internet?
2. How was the World Wide Web born? Who were its pioneers?
3. What impact is the Internet having on conventional media?
4. What are some new Web technologies?

[**Spyware** is malicious software that secretly sends information about your online activities.]

However, even when there are no cookies or Web bugs present, your privacy is not ensured. That's because the basic operation of the Internet protocol routinely uses your Internet address to route information. When you switch from one website to another, the site you leave receives information about where you are going, and the next one you visit also "knows" where you were last. The fonts you use and the version numbers of the plug-ins you use create electronic "fingerprints" that make it possible to uniquely identify each web user.

Yet another privacy threat is **spyware** (sometimes also called *adware*). These are programs that are downloaded to your computer when you install other applications from the Internet, such as music file-sharing programs. The spyware not only monitors your surfing behavior, but in some cases also causes ads to pop up on your screen in the hopes of directing you to e-commerce sites.

Your online safety is also threatened by security "holes" in your browser or operating system software. These allow hackers to get access to personal information stored on your computer or to use your computer to launch spam or viruses at other users using robotic programs, or bots, for short.

INDUSTRY: DAVID VS. GOLIATH

The Internet industry has several major sectors. Each industry sector has giant firms but also many innovative small ones that sometimes overturn the Goliaths with bold new ideas.

Google is the current Goliath, having dethroned Yahoo! and Microsoft. It is most visible as a search engine company, of course, but nearly all of its revenue comes from serving up ads on the Internet. That includes the ads that appear alongside their search results, the AdSense service that places clickable ads on other websites, and the display ads that are distributed across the Web through Google's DoubleClick subsidiary (see Chapter 11). Google is also, among other things, a Web portal (Google News), a software publisher (e.g., Picassa photo editor, Chrome Internet browser, Android operating system for smartphones), a cell phone distributor (Nexus One), a social networking site (Buzz), an e-mail service (Gmail), and an online video distributor (YouTube). In 2011 Google also made a bid to acquire Motorola, a major cell phone manufacturer. But watch out, Google. Facebook is gaining on you and somewhere out there a group of college students is working on The Next Big Thing.

COMPUTER TOY MAKERS

The hardware sector includes makers of computers (further subdivided into supercomputers, mainframes, minicomputers, workstations, and personal computers), computer storage devices (such as disk drives), and their peripherals (such as printers and modems). The Internet also relies on specialized network gear that directs packets of Internet data to their proper destinations. In the personal computer market, Dell and Hewlett-Packard are the leaders. The two companies that started the personal computer trend, Apple and IBM, are now lesser players, and IBM's personal computer operation was sold to a Chinese company, Lenovo. Cisco Systems is the leading maker of network gear for the Internet.

WHERE MICROSOFT RULES

Software manufacturers develop applications for personal computers, an industry several times the size of another well-known "software" industry, motion pictures. Microsoft dominates personal computer operating system software (that is, Windows) and many application categories, including word processing (Microsoft Word) and Web browsers (Internet Explorer). Software manufacturers resemble book publishers, in that sales are made through retail outlets that offer titles from many different publishers. Much of the software that winds up in the hands of consumers is bundled with computer hardware at the time of purchase. Increasingly, though, software is bought and downloaded over the Internet, an important component of electronic commerce.

A great deal of software is *freeware* or *shareware*. This is software, such as the Linux operating system, for which the authors do not claim copyright protection or whose developers lack a sophisticated distribution network. They hope that users pay voluntarily. That means users can often download the software for free (from sites like download.com) and pay on the "honor system" later if they

WHERE'S THE COFFEE? Internet cafés offer temporary ISP service and computer access for a fee. They are a poor substitute for home Internet access for solving the problem of the digital divide.

like it. In other cases the software is free but the user may be asked to pay for documentation, enhanced features, or updates. Linux users can run Microsoft Office programs or opt for alternative "productivity suites" including word processing, spreadsheet, and presentation programs. As for Internet browsers and plug-ins distributed for "free," they are still part of a moneymaking scheme. Their creators profit from the sale of other programs that make new content and the specialized software that runs the servers on the Internet. As we mentioned previously (see Cloud Computing, page 261), another trend in freeware is to offer free online versions of popular applications, such as word processing and e-mail that operate and store files over Internet connections.

INTERNET SERVICE PROVIDERS

Internet service providers (ISPs) connect users to the Internet and provide e-mail accounts. Telecommunications giant AT&T and cable TV giant Comcast (which now operates under the XFINITY brand) are the industry leaders and account for nearly half of all U.S. Internet subscriptions between them. Some

[**Internet service providers (ISPs)** provide connections to the Internet]

ISPs, such as America Online and Microsoft Network (MSN), create original content and so combine the roles of ISP and content provider (as described in the next section). Others, such as EarthLink (and thousands of small local providers across the country), are purely ISPs, in that they provide access but little in the way of content aside from portal pages that welcome their users with the news of the hour when they log on. ISPs usually lease high-speed connections to the Internet backbone from telecommunications carriers or local phone companies or are affiliated with companies that provide network connections of their own. Currently there are more than 400 ISPs in the United States with national coverage and many more that cover local communities (http://www.thelist.com). Although many are still small local operations, giant telephone and cable companies dominate.

CONTENT PROVIDERS

Web pages are often made by in-house design departments. Some of the largest are the multimedia design departments at old media titans, such as Disney. But new media companies, such as Google and Amazon, have in-house staffs, as do thousands of companies large and small that are not directly connected to the media business. Another model is to reformat content produced for the old media side of the business, as they do at the *New York Times*, but even that requires dozens of employees with Web design skills. Many newspapers or other old media firms create new or extended content for the Web and provide ways for readers to contribute both stories and commentary.

There are also thousands of independent design firms and Web developers (see http://www.1234-find-web-designers.org/) who blend the creative talents of graphic design professionals with the technical skills of webmasters (see Your Media Career: Web Designer, page 267) and computer programmers. Interactive ad agencies are another source of Web creation expertise. Web design firms once congregated in a few locations around the country, including the "south of Market Street" (SOMA) neighborhood in San Francisco, Silicon Alley in New York City, and in the Los Angeles area. However, the dot-com "bust" of the early 2000s nearly emptied out those areas, and since then Web design has cropped up nearly everywhere. Traditional graphic design, advertising, and public relations firms have entered the market, as have Web hosting companies that provide server space for clients and will design and maintain the site itself for an additional fee.

We also need to include the many sources, ranging from the National Weather Service to the author of the local elementary school lunch menu, who create the raw information that others shape into information services. If you have ever posted your own "home page" on the World Wide Web or created a Facebook profile, then you are a content provider.

INTERNET ORGANIZATIONS

Who runs the Internet backbone (officially known as the very high-speed Backbone Network Service, or *vBNS*), the network that connects ISPs, Web servers, and individual computers around the world? It is a not-for-profit, cooperative enterprise of major regional networks, such as the MERIT network in Michigan. The Internet is made up of high-speed digital lines that are leased by the regional networks from long-distance telephone companies. At the local level, the ISPs lease or own high-speed lines that connect their local users to the Internet.

The larger national ISPs maintain their own high-speed networks, interconnecting with the rest of the Internet only at regional *Network Access Points* (NAPs).

One of the most important issues is the assignment of addresses and domain names. ICANN was entrusted with this task. ICANN ultimately decides who gets the rights to domain names and charges an annual fee to the domain owners for the privilege. However, if you want the rights to www.Iluvhiphop.com, you don't deal directly with ICANN. Instead, you contact one of the hundreds of domain name registries (DomainsPricedRight.com in this case) that ICANN authorizes around the globe.

ISOC (the Internet Society) is a nongovernmental international membership society that promotes the orderly use and development of the Internet. It is modeled after the professional associations that college professors belong to—a throwback to when the Internet was a research network run by major universities. The World Wide Web Consortium (W3C) is an international membership organization that formulates and approves standards for the Web, such as the new HTML5. The Internet Architecture Board (IAB) is a committee within the Internet Society

——————YOUR MEDIA CAREER

WEB DESIGNER

The Internet is fast replacing television and film as the new "glamour medium." In Chapter 8 we noted that some of the fastest-growing occupations in the television and movie industries are computer-related. Here we will explore other computer-related jobs in the new media industry. Many programs in mass communication and journalism now offer courses in Web design. You can be the one who "saves the business" by creating or redesigning a Web page that drives a significant increase in visitors or "click throughs" to the online shopping cart. Unlike conventional media where the results are often weeks or months in the future, Web designers experience the excitement of getting instant feedback on their designs and have the capability of quickly responding to consumer reactions.

Web skills courses open the door to some of the largest, fast-growing, and best-paying professional occupations in the U.S. economy, namely, software developers (900,000 employees currently, expected to grow 30 percent over the next 10 years), Network and Computer System Administrators (347,000—28 percent), and Information Security Analysts, Web Developers, and Computer Network Architects (300,000— 22 percent). By comparison, less than 200,000 professionals are employed in broadcasting, with slower than average growth expected, and 250,000 in publishing, with a future decline in employment anticipated there. And computer "stars" like Bill Gates make much more money than media stars and similar wage differentials apply at all levels of employment.

There is a big BUT coming: but, many of these jobs require technical degrees in computer science or information systems.

Now for the HOWEVER: however, there are many niches that graduates of mass communication and journalism programs can fill if they acquire Web skills. Web developers, sometimes also called Web designers, create Web pages from software applications like Dreamweaver and gather user feedback to refine the aesthetics and functionality of the Web pages they design. A background in photography, video, or graphic design can give our readers an advantage over computer science grads. With a little more technical savvy, Web developers can assume the responsibility of Web masters who monitor and troubleshoot the performance of the Web servers that distribute the content to users. With a little bit of programming skill—but not necessarily a computer science degree—Web developers can learn to program interactive applications using Java scripts or HTML5. Having learned the basics in college classes, Web designers can upgrade their Web skills through on-the-job training, free online computer programming courses, workshops, and community college computer programming classes that stress problem solving and logical thinking rather than math. Web skills can also be the door opener for internships and entry-level jobs across all media fields, and indeed across the entire information economy.

Sources: Bureau of Labor Statistics. (2012). Occupational Outlook HandbookAvailable: http://www.bls.gov/ooh/

that makes important policy decisions about operations and future developments. Its members are, for the most part, employees of large corporations (such as Microsoft) that have important financial stakes in the Internet. Technical matters are overseen by the Internet Engineering Task Force (IETF) through its various working-group committees. The concentration of such activities in the United States makes other nations, companies, and users nervous, so international organizations like the International Telecommunications Union have tried to assert more control over Internet directions, so far with little success.

CONTENT: WHAT'S ON THE INTERNET?

The Internet has some characteristic forms of content that we have called *genres* in previous chapters. However, these concepts are still couched in the technical terms of protocols and domains.

[**Uniform resource locators (URLs)** are the addresses of Web pages.]

The World Wide Web's content can be characterized according to the various domains that are appended to **uniform resource locators (URLs)**. URLs are the jumbles of letters, "slashes," and "dots" that indicate the network addresses of content stored on Web servers. The last set of letters, such as the .edu at the end of your school's home page, indicate the top-level domain. Each country also has a top-level domain of its own (e.g., .us for the United States). Others, such as .edu and .org, reflect the basic types of institutions that own the addresses. Recently, ICANN opened up the top level domain system to include domains names that use non-Latin letters, such as Arabic and Chinese. After years of controversy, the xxx domain was approved in 2011 as the home for "adult" content on the Internet. Beginning in 2012 proposals for a wide range of new top level domain names will be considered, so we might soon see .kids or .comedy but also possibly .beer and .whatever.

Each of the top-level domains has its own characteristic types of content, but.com is still where most of the "sizzle" is found (see Table 9.1). We'll begin by considering types of content that fit well with the conventional mass media functions of surveillance and entertainment introduced in Chapter 2, and then go on to consider some of the newer forms.

TABLE 9.1 Top 10 Web Properties

RANK	PROPERTY	UNIQUE VISITORS (000)
1	Google	186,659
2	Microsoft	175,489
3	Yahoo!	173,481
4	Facebook	166,007
5	Amazon	112,878
6	AOL	106,209
7	Ask Network	89,935
8	Turner Digital	87,336
9	Wikimedia Foundation	84,637
10	Glam Media	83,901

Source: http://www.comscore.com/Press_Events/Press_Releases/2011/12/comScore_Media_Metrix_Ranks_Top_50_U.S._Web_Properties_for_November_2011

ELECTRONIC PUBLISHING

Electronic publishing includes online versions of conventional print publications, as well as information published only on the Internet, but with a difference. Even formal "old media," such as the *New York Times* (http://www.nytimes.com), reorganize content for the Internet crowd (such as the online *Times*' blog section, with comments by reporters and their readers) and add links to other sites, searchable indices of past articles, online forums, and multimedia extensions. The multimedia extensions include audio and video files and computer simulations. The online *Times* has additional links to local television listings not included in the printed version.

Magazine publishers (see Chapter 3) place full electronic copies on the Web, especially those who want to appeal to college students who are hard to reach through conventional magazine subscriptions. Others are using the Web to extend their brand names in hopes of enticing new readers and advertisers. For example, *Vogue* magazine has a broadband "channel" on the Internet (style.com) that features fashion show videos, episodic television shows, and fashion shots uploaded by visitors as well as articles and ads from the print magazine. Now many magazines are introducing apps of themselves for tablet computers that enhance the conventional print experience with video and personalized content. Similar to Facebook, these are "walled gardens" that are not freely accessible through the Web and search engines like Google. Online magazines are not limited to Big Media companies, however. There are thousands of amateur magazines, many covering aspects of popular culture. These used to be called *'zines* (see Chapter 3) but now most prefer to call themselves *blogs*.

Corporate sites run by large companies (for example, http://www.ibm .com) usually confine themselves to publishing information about themselves, their products, and their services that were once published in paper product brochures, annual reports, and press guides. But many, including Hewlett-Packard (http://www.hp.com), offer useful information to consumers and professionals in their fields of interest. Others, notably Cisco Systems (http://www .cisco.com), a manufacturer of network gear for the Internet, include electronic commerce storefronts to sell their wares to consumers or to other businesses.

Government information is growing in importance, with U.S. government Web pages among the most popular (http://www.usa.gov). For example, to see what is going on at the Federal Communications Commission, there is www .fcc.gov. All levels of government have a trend toward e-government, so that citizens can find public information about everything, from where the fish are biting to how to file for unemployment. An increasing number of applications and transactions with government agencies can be completed online.

ENTERTAINMENT

The music file-sharing craze introduced millions of people to the concept of getting their entertainment through the Internet. The practice has spread to print, video, and video games with two important differences: the content is increasingly "shared" by commercial enterprises and much of it is no longer free. Once-popular file-sharing services like Napster and Limewire have knuckled under to legal pressure from the music industry and have either gone out of business or transformed into legal pay music services. Although file sharing (the entertainment industry prefers the term *copyright piracy*) continues, the question becomes not if we will pay for online entertainment but how.

Advertising-supported online entertainment at least preserves the illusion of being "free." Online entertainment attracts audiences in numbers that appeal to advertisers, with 189 million tuning in to online video each month(Comscore, 2011) and 57 million to online radio each week (Arbitron, 2011). YouTube is perhaps the best known with a mix of original amateur video and professional video clips that can draw more viewers than prime-time television shows. Google has allocated $150 million to seed professionally produced channels for YouTube featuring celebrities like Ashton Kutcher and Shaquille O'Neal as well as not-ready-for-prime-time (television, that is) productions such as *Machinima* (videos of video games), KickTV (for soccer fans), and Red Bull (for action sports). Other sites like Hulu.com specialize in TV series from Big Media companies such as NBC Universal. There are thousands of ad-supported streaming radio stations in cyberspace. LAUNCHcast (Yahoo!), AOL Radio Network, and Clear Channel are among the leaders, each offering links to hundreds of streaming music channels. Other services like Pandora and Slacker Radio customize music channels for individual listeners.

However, pay entertainment services are beginning to dominate. Some, following the iTunes model, require a payment for the purchase of music and videos that the users "own," although often with limits on making copies and reselling the product. Netflix is a well known example, with a base of paying subscribers that equals that of popular pay cable channels and it has ambitious plans to produce its own original content. The xfinitytv.com service from cable television giant Comcast (see Chapter 8) has a unique twist: the videos are "free" if the user subscribes to the level of cable television service on which the channel is carried. The "app" model is also becoming popular, in which the user pays a fee for the use of a downloadable application with a limited shelf life, similar to yearly magazine subscription. Others, including Pandora and Hulu, lure users with the promise of free service but also charge premium services with advanced features.

ONLINE GAMES

Online games are a form of entertainment, but their intense interactivity puts them in a category of their own. The staple of online gaming, originally known as *Multi-User Dungeons* (MUDs, or role-playing games), evolved from text-based fantasy games ("Now the dungeon master enters the room and sees the magic key, now he turns to the princess and. . .") and have developed into multiuser graphical interfaces. As their name suggests, Massively Multiplayer Online (MMO) games engage large numbers of users in online play. *Massively Multiplayer Online Role-Playing Games* (MMORPGs) are the most popular genre, with elaborate multiuser communities inhabited by players who adopt roles in an online virtual environment. One, "World of Warcraft," has 10 million players worldwide, and tens of thousands may be playing online at one time.

You can choose from more than 200 multiplayer games. Sorcery and magic fantasy themes are the most common. A variety of other themes are also popular, including action-packed "shooters," sports fantasy, and flight and race car simulator games. Social interaction games like "Second Life" focus on social life among avatars representing our real selves in an online environment, combining the appeal of online play and social networking. Game developers openly brag about the "addictive" quality of MMOs, with many players choosing to live several hours a day as their virtual selves.

So-called casual games are also part of the social networking phenomenon. "Scrabulous" (now known as "Lexulous"), the online version of Scrabble, became a major craze for early Facebook users. More recently, the FarmVille farm simulation game has become a sensation and is played with such intensity by some that "casual" is perhaps not an appropriate term for it.

Online casino and poker games that allow real-world bets to be made were once the rage, but U.S. players were cut off when law enforcement cracked down on credit card payments to poker websites made through American banks. However, in 2011 the Justice Department ruled that online poker was legal if kept within state borders, so online poker is returning.

PORTALS

Portals combine directories, interpersonal communication, and information into an all-purpose, customizable "launch pad" that users will visit first whenever they go on the Internet. Portals greet registered visitors by name and keep track of their favorite types of content.

Portal content is organized around familiar categories, such as news, entertainment, travel, computing, health, and personal finance. Interpersonal communication features include e-mail services, chat rooms, and discussion groups. Portals compete with one another with new customer services; some will keep track of appointments or remind you of anniversaries. In that respect, they fill the surveillance function (see Chapter 2), once the province of newspaper headlines and television news broadcasts, with a new personal twist. Advertisers see them as the Web's equivalent to the electronic mass media. Leading portal sites include Yahoo! and those of Internet service providers, such as AOL and MSN. Many portals scrape the news from traditional news sites without paying for the information (see Chapter 4). However, social networking sites now compete with conventional portals by offering news and sports updates of their own.

SEARCH ENGINES

Search engines match the words you type into the "search window" to seek information based on matches to the keywords supplied by website owners, the content on the website, and the behavior of other searchers who have looked for an item in the past. Google has emerged as the giant among search engines, with Yahoo! and Bing trailing far behind. Google is consistently one of the top 10 Web properties (see Table 9.1), so much so that turning up near the top of its search results is the key to success for many websites. The same queries posed to other search engines may have different results because of the different ways in which the engines search for keywords. Search engines also differ in how they look for keywords in various locations on a web page—such as in the title of the Web page, how high it appears on the page, or the frequency in which the keyword appears. It also depends on how often the search engine's software or "bot" searches the Internet. Students everywhere especially appreciate search engines of databases, such as Lexis-Nexis, Web of Science, and ProQuest, which connect them directly to articles they can cite in their term papers, without a trip to the library. There are also specialized search engines for academic publications that can help college students with their term papers (Google Scholar), for still images (Google Images), and for moving images(YouTube). The most revolutionary innovation is arguably the "sponsored links." Those are the links that appear to the right and top of the Google page, where advertisers bid for primacy of place in auctions. Those humble print blurbs for products and services are displacing newspapers and television as the premier advertising medium. The latest development is real-time search engines that will sift through online postings in micro blogs like Twitter (as described in the sections that follow).

MEDIA, THE INTERNET, AND THE STORIES WE TELL ABOUT OURSELVES

Not long after the Internet started being used by mass numbers of people in the United States, Jon Katz wrote in *Wired* magazine about the impact of the Internet on the presidential election of 1996. The main impact then, he wrote, was that the Internet had enabled all the fringe groups to find and reinforce each other.

In that regard, many thought that the Internet was the very essence of a new postmodern society. One of the main points of postmodernism is that society is gradually losing its big stories that almost everyone knows— its meta-narratives. For example, most people until at least the 1960s were familiar with a variety of biblical ideas and expressions, even if they were non-believing Christians or Jews. Now writers or speakers cannot really assume that people in their audiences will be familiar with those once-common sayings and concepts. Similarly, most people going through the educational system until the 1970s or 1980s had read a good deal of Shakespeare, so that many of his lines had become common phrases. Those are now also less widely familiar in the United States. Both of these sources contained much of what was considered common wisdom about life's essentials and how to live. Many of those meta-narratives were taught by parents, schools, and churches, but many of their specific elements and references had also been carried across society by traditional mass media, like newspapers, magazines, and the Big Three television networks that almost everyone watched until the 1980s. Many people had common topics to discuss because most were exposed to the same few channels.

Postmodern theorists like Jean-Francois Lyotard observed that one of the primary reasons for the breakdown in consensus over the main stories guiding our society was the fragmentation of people's experience with media. As media proliferated, people had more choices, so fewer shared common sources of ideas. People listened to different music, listened to talk shows of very different opinions, read different novels, and watched television shows with different spins and focuses. Within universities and high schools, people argued furiously over what ought to be read and taught,

Raymond Depardon/Magnum Photos

CULTURAL DIVERSITY OR FRAGMENTATION?
Michel Foucault, pictured here in West Berlin in 1978, is one of the originators of the postmodern school.

so no one could assume that people had read the same things in their freshman English courses or their introductions to literature. So overall, even before the Internet, people were receiving increasingly wildly diverse ideas from fragmented media. Many of the postmodernists consider this rather liberating. With less uniformity of media, it will be harder for anyone to exercise hegemony over ideas, to create and enforce an ideological consensus that limits freedom of thought. However, some sociologists, like Todd Gitlin in *The Twilight of Common Dreams*, worry that the consensus necessary for addressing social problems is breaking down into factionalism.

Other scholars are wondering whether this supposed fragmentation is taking place. Looking at the Internet, for example, Edward Herman and Robert McChesney argue that since so much of the Web traffic goes to the same large corporate media sites, the Internet does not have much potential for really breaking down the hold of the main media on the audience. They see news and information on the Web dominated by the same faces with the same hegemonic intent (see Chapter 2).

SOCIAL MEDIA

Social media are currently the most popular online genre of all, accounting for about a quarter of leisure time spent online in the U.S. (Nielsen, 2011). The phrase has become almost synonymous with Facebook and other social networking sites that replaced published albums of pictures of incoming college freshmen (known in the olden days as "face books") with interactive online profiles. Since just about all college students belong to Facebook, there is little point in describing it further here. However, because our definition of social media (from

Chris Hondros/Getty Images

SOCIAL NETWORKING Initially considered a waste of time, Facebook is an ideal medium to spur needed social change. In 2011, many Egyptians communicated through Facebook pages to collectively stand up to their oppressors.

Chapter 1) specifies content generated through social interaction, more of what appears on Facebook is not social media as the application evolves into a general-purpose platform to deliver news, entertainment, and advertising to its users. Still, many familiar Facebook functions including friending, tagging, wall posting, and liking as well as participating in discussion groups and social games like CityVille are social media activities under our definition.

Twitter, Flickr, YouTube, Google+, and Wikipedia are other popular social media applications. The social media craze has reached such heights that it seems every major website is going "social." Online newspaper stories invite commentary from readers, while websites connected to popular TV shows solicit real-time user comments to stimulate viewer engagement. Links to Facebook and Twitter are popping up seemingly everywhere so that Web surfers can instantly react to what they are seeing. Social media versions of familiar online forms are also appearing. Digg creates lists of top news stories and entertainment offerings based on the votes of visitors. Kaboodle is a "shopping community" for dedicated shopaholics. Groupon provides discounts to groups of consumers who self-organize through social interaction at that website. Now marketers can track the success of brands and celebrities by counting the numbers of Facebook friends, Twitter followers, and YouTube views they receive or by monitoring the words that are used in Twitter.

BLOGS

Weblogs, or blogs for short, are an older but still influential form of social media that are organized around special themes such as technology (TechCrunch) and celebrity gossip (TMZ) with the hope of attracting like-minded contributors. Although they are being somewhat upstaged by more recent forms such as Facebook discussion groups, commentary in the "blogosphere" has a growing impact on public discourse. Many are written by professional journalists in their off-hours. Among the most popular is *The AOL Huffington Post*, with political chatter and original stories organized by political gadfly Ariana Huffington. In 2011, the Huff Post, as it is often known, was acquired by AOL as part of an effort to revitalize its online journalism. Millions of Web surfers have their own blog, far too many to keep up with, but there are websites (like technorati.com) that index the latest postings from thousands of blogs. Tumblr and Blogger are popular social media sites that make it easy for you to start your own customized blog.

ELECTRONIC COMMERCE

E-commerce businesses that make sales directly to consumers are known as *b to c* (business to consumer). They follow the familiar catalog shopping model, except that the product information and order blank are online. These sites are what the retail trade calls *category killers*: they specialize in one line of products, such as children's toys (for example, eToys). Others, like Amazon, imitate shopping malls by carrying many different types of products. Some are pure e-tailers that exist only online. Many, like Walmart, are online offshoots of brick-and-mortar retailers that are called *clicks-and-mortar operations*. In the aftermath of a giant meltdown in Internet stocks in 2001, many e-tailers (like the original eToys operation) closed up shop, but more conventional retailers are going online to incorporate the Web in their overall marketing effort. Some customers shop for products on the Web before going into their real-world stores to actually buy them. Other customers shop in the real-world stores and return home to make their purchases online, hoping to undercut the prices of local retailers.

Other sites depart from the catalog shopping model. Services as well as products are sold online, with the Internet taking the place of the travel agent (for example, Expedia) and the hotel clerk (hotels.com). Auctions such as eBay (sometimes called *c to c*, for consumer to consumer) let visitors bid on antiques and yard-sale items offered by other visitors. Reverse auctions like priceline. com let shoppers name the price, and sellers bid to meet it. Or, shoppers can buy things from other people by tuning into newsgroups that specialize in buying and selling goods. There are e-commerce sites that don't actually sell anything, but act as clearinghouses for comparative shopping information (for example, for automobiles at http://www.autobytel.com). Others have product directories, coupons, and buyer incentive programs.

By far the biggest category of e-commerce is one that doesn't want your business, unless you *are* a business. Business to business (or *b to b*) sites sell products to firms. Network equipment manufacturer Cisco Systems became one of the largest corporations in the world with that business model. There are also online shopping malls for business supplies and services, and some of the biggest corporations are organizing online bazaars for their suppliers and customers. The watchword is *disintermediation*, eliminating distributors that serve as intermediaries between manufacturers and their customers.

WHAT MAKES A GOOD WEB PAGE?

Over 2 billion people worldwide actively use the Internet. E-mail is the most common activity (see Table 9.2). The amount of time we spend each day on the Internet is slowly catching up to the amount of time spent on television, largely due to the long hours spent on social networking sites. Yet, most Web pages are viewed for less than a minute, so the question of what makes a good Web page that surfers will want to spend time with is still an important question.

Some of the techniques thought to increase user engagement are borrowed from old media, including contests and giveaways (borrowed from radio), continual updates of content (à la the news-breaks on network radio and television), and episodic storytelling (from television). Graphic designers adapt eye-catching colors and attractive layouts from magazine pages. Content counts, too, with Web surfers preferring short items (about a screenful) to lengthy articles. Portal sites borrow their basic "everything you need to start the day" strategy from newspapers. Other inducements to stick to e-commerce sites are drawn from retail promotions, including coupons, sales, and celebrity appearances. And if we can't beat TV, why not *be* TV? That's the premise of the various radio and TV services, to lengthen visits by streaming video and music videos.

There are other strategies unique to the Web such as interactivity. Many an Internet user has gotten hooked by playing online games, social networking, or even compulsively answering e-mail. Another strategy is personalization of content to individual users. In a sense, the website gets to know its visitors, responding to and even anticipating their needs. If you have bought much from Amazon, when you log on it frequently suggests book or record ideas, based on your previous purchases. Amazon follows up by sending you e-mail to tell you it has found something it thinks you will like. After establishing a personal relationship, visitors linger longer and return more often. Abandoning the site would incur the cost of reentering detailed personal information at a new portal, selecting from its content options, and waiting for it to learn our innermost desires by tracking our surfing behavior.

TABLE 9.2 Most Common Daily Internet Activities

ACTIVITY	PERCENTAGE INTERNET USERS
E-mail	94
Using Search Engines	87
Looking up Health Info	83
Checking the News	75
Using Government Websites	67
Watching Videos	66
Buying a Product	66
Making Travel Reservations	66
Social Networking	61

Source: Based on adult Internet users, Pew Internet. Retrieved from **http://pewinternet.org/Reports/2010/Generations-2010.aspx**

WHAT'S COOL? Although it's hard to determine what makes a good website, Web developers agree that Apple's home page (www.apple.com) is a "cool" site. This doesn't mean that it's a high-quality, user-friendly one.

STOP&REVIEW

1. List the major types of content on the Web.
2. What makes a good Web page design?
3. Who are the leading makers of computer hardware and software?
4. What is the difference between a content provider and an Internet service provider?
5. Who runs the Internet?

But perhaps the amount of time users spend at a site should not be the primary criterion for a "good" Web page. That reflects "old media" thinking tied to the need to deliver eyeballs to advertisers. What about good design as reflected by the winners of Webby awards (www.webbyawards.com) selected by Web design professionals? From that perspective, the key to having a good Web page is lots of empty dark space (or blank white space or gray space) with small print, intriguing animations, and large graphic design spaces. Among media-related websites the 2011 winners were NPR (news and radio categories), *The New Yorker* (best magazine), Pandora (music), Vido (social media), and Boardwalk Empire (television).

Another school of thought is that the amount of time spent on a page is an indication of *bad* design. Usability researchers hold stopwatches on users and train cameras on them as they surf Web pages. They try to identify and correct confusing features that slow users down. Designing Web pages around tasks, giving all the pages in a site a consistent look and feel, supplying site navigation aids, and minimizing download times are key design considerations. In this approach, "cool" Web pages with artistic designs, unreadable text, and slow-loading animations that don't help users complete a well-defined task are bad designs. For example, the Harvard University website was criticized for, among other things, having text that was difficult to read against a dark background. Some of the very same sites that win good design awards also show up on webpagesthatsuck.com, where the usability researchers have their say. But "uncool" designs with lots of text and buttons all over the place also tend to flunk their usability tests, so at least the designers and the usability engineers can agree on that.

MEDIALITERACY

GETTING THE MOST OUT OF THE INTERNET

As we have seen, the Internet has been continually reinvented by its users. But that won't always be the case unless we all do our part. Big business, governments, thieves, and hackers could determine the Net's future course if we don't.

DOES INFORMATION WANT TO BE FREE?

We hear a lot about the problem of Internet piracy: how ordinary Internet users are stealing free content from the corporations that own it and the steps that should be taken to prevent it. We don't hear so much about how Internet corporations take advantage of their market power and hardball tactics to enrich themselves at our expense. Who are the real Internet pirates?

Aside from their sheer economic might, **copyrights** and **patents** (see Chapter 14) are the most important tools that corporations have to control the Internet. The Digital Millennium Copyright Act of 1998 is a key weapon. It added an "anti-circumvention" provision that made it a crime to engage in activities like copying a music CD to a computer hard drive. New legislation is being considered in Congress that would give copyright holders the right to shut down websites that violate their copyrights and to prevent search engines from linking to them.

The entertainment industry would prefer to limit distribution to secure sites like iTunes that can charge users for each copy. Another tactic is to cut off free access. Media giant News Corporation and the Associated Press, among others, are putting forward plans that would require those who post their news articles to pay a fee. Others would like to follow the iTunes model, perhaps using the new Apple iPad as their technology platform, and require news readers to pay for the articles they read. Yet others like cable and broadband Internet giant Comcast would like to see the cable television model in which content fees are bundled into a monthly service charge.

The Internet service provider industry of which Comcast as well as telecom giant AT&T are part is another lair for would-be corporate pirates. Many of them oppose the **net neutrality** policy that treats every Internet packet with equal priority. The industry argues that it is only fair to block file-sharing applications when they slow network connections, noting that many of the "shared" files are in fact acts of piracy. For example, the BitTorrent file-sharing service was a target of a network management effort by cable giant Comcast to block file transfers that clogged its networks. The FCC ordered Comcast to cease that practice and imposed a fine. However, "reasonable" network management practices are permissible, and Comcast responded with a new plan to assign packets from file-sharing services a lower priority than others when local networks are congested. And it caps monthly usage at 250 billion bytes of information per user per month, the equivalent of about 125 feature-length movies.

Net neutrality advocates fear that the Internet service providers will use their power to jack up rates for content providers that will be passed along to all Internet users and will also be tempted to control the development of content and new technologies to their advantage. In 2011 the FCC issued rules that mandate transparency in network management practices and prohibit blocking or discriminating against lawful content. However, the rules do not apply to mobile Internet services.

Will information continue to be free on the Internet in the future or will it follow the pay TV or iTunes models? You the reader can be part of the solution by joining (that is, by doing a Google search for) a movement called *Creative Commons*. Creative Commons advocates that authors opt into, or opt out of, specific copyright protections for their work. For example, you might allow all noncommercial use of your original work that you post on your Web page, or let others modify or sample from it—rights that are reserved by holders of conventional copyrights. The net neutrality issue is also a good one to explore in the blogosphere: www.savetheinternet.com if you favor net neutrality; www.freedomproject.org if you don't.

> **Copyright** is the legal right to control intellectual property. With it comes the legal privilege to use, sell, or license creative works.

> **A patent** gives an inventor the exclusive right to make, use, or sell an invention for 20 years.

> **Net neutrality** means users are not discriminated against based on the amount or nature of the data they transfer on the Internet.

CLOSING THE DIGITAL DIVIDE

There continues to be a digital divide. For example, Caucasians are much more likely have home broadband connections (66 percent) than African-Americans (46 percent) or Hispanics (40 percent) (NTIA, 2010). The income gap is even wider. Broadband is in 89 percent of homes with annual incomes of $150,000 or more compared to 29 percent of those with incomes under $15,000. The ability to use the Internet effectively once you have it is also an issue; some call it the second digital divide, whereas others refer to it as the knowledge gap (see Chapter 14).

The Obama administration has made closing the gap a priority, pledging billions of dollars to put broadband in 90 percent of U.S. homes by 2020. To help bring that about, $7 billion was allocated through the American Recovery and Reinvestment Act of 2009 to upgrade broadband Internet networks and community computing facilities in schools and libraries. The FCC plans to redirect universal service funds (see chapter 12) that formerly subsidized telephone connections in low income households to subsidies for Internet access. The FCC encouraged cable companies to institute the Connect2Compete program that offers low cost computers, $9.99 a month broadband connections, and free computer training to families with children who participate in the free lunch program at school.

Unfortunately, the federal government's broadband stimulus program won't provide the funds needed to keep the libraries open longer hours. So it's too early to conclude that the digital divide is going away. The danger is that as public institutions and political activism move online, the poor will be disenfranchised. In the long run, inferior Internet access will also mean inferior access to employment and educational opportunity, deepening the cycle of poverty that costs all citizens dearly, both in this country and worldwide.

By some standards all U.S. citizens are on the wrong side of a broadband gap. In terms of overall broadband penetration, the United States ranks a dismal 15th among 30 leading developed countries, such as Finland and Canada (OECD, 2011). By international standards U.S. broadband service is also slow and expensive. Another international scorecard gave the United States top grades, though, after factoring in the productive uses and skills of American users (Waverman&Dasgupta, 2009).

Our readers can take direct action to close the digital divide themselves by helping classmates and relatives use the Internet more effectively. If helping others interests you and you have good computer skills, check out Geeks for America or the Intel Computer Clubhouse Network, volunteer organizations that provide computer support for nonprofit organizations and low-income communities, respectively. Or do a Google search for "computer volunteers" to find opportunities to help people in your area learn how to use computers.

Loren Santow/Stone/Getty Images

CLOSING THE GAP Before the digital gap can close, more minority households will have to see scenes like this one, where families have personal computers in their homes (and tech-savvy children can teach their parents how to use them).

GOVERNMENT: HANDS OFF OR HANDS ON?

Government intervention is one answer to threats of corporate abuse or class conflict. However, too much government control could destroy our Internet freedoms.

Governments like to tax what they control, which could retard the growth of the Internet. The taxation urge is strong at the state level, where e-commerce sales cut into sales taxes, which are the states' primary source of revenue, creating critical budget shortfalls in difficult economic times. Online stores are required to collect sales taxes on purchases made by customers in the same state, but that applies only to the state in which the Internet subsidiary is located. If you buy a product from an out-of-state website, you, the customer, are supposed to pay the appropriate sales tax to your own state. However, few people are that mindful, and thus far states have only gone after purchasers of big-ticket items. The Streamlined Sales Tax Project is an ongoing effort that would simplify tax collection by retailers, but without federal legislation retailer participation is voluntary.

It is tempting to look to the government for solutions to some of the social problems of the Web. For example, the Communications Decency Act was an attempt (although an unconstitutional one; see Chapter 15) to ban pornography sites on the Internet, while the Children's Internet Protection Act requires libraries and schools to filter out inappropriate content. The Child Online Privacy Protection Act restrains sites that obtain personal information from children. The CANSPAM law makes it a crime to send spam that does not have a legitimate return address. New laws are in the works to crack down on child molesters who prowl social networking sites.

However, too much government involvement could have frightening implications for our civil liberties. What preserves one person's sense of privacy, safety, or morality limits the freedoms of others. The USA PATRIOT Act, passed in the immediate aftermath of the 9/11 terror attacks, enlists Internet ISPs as government informers. The Homeland Security Act empowers government agents to sift through e-mail and Internet traffic logs to detect "patterns of terrorist activity." Another issue is how long ISPs and search engines should keep files detailing our online activities. The U.S. government wants to keep them for years; the European Union, in contrast, limits the record keeping to a month or two. The leading U.S. search engines keep data for 12 to 18 months.

And how will governments resolve conflicts that cross their borders? Efforts to stamp out smut on the Internet in America could undermine free-speech rights in other countries with more liberal mores. The Chinese government demands that search engines block searches related to that country's pro-democracy movement, a practice that Google backed away from in 2010, threatening the company's ability to do business there. U.S. copyright protections are stronger (some might say excessive) compared to other countries. Stronger European Union privacy laws are becoming a standard that U.S. companies have to meet if they want to do business there. Online gambling is another example. The World Trade Organization sided with Antigua, where online betting is legal, and accused the United States of unfair trade practices in attempts to cut off American gamblers.

A new role for governments is protecting their nations against cyberwarfare. When Google and several other major websites were attacked by hackers based in China in 2009, it set off alarms in national defense circles. That is because the nation's economy is heavily dependent on the Internet and critical infrastructure systems, including the telephone network and the national energy grid, which are susceptible to attack. There have been periodic outbreaks of politically motivated attacks involving hackers in Russia and former satellite nations including Estonia and Georgia. The United States stands accused of unleashing computer viruses aimed at disabling uranium enrichment equipment in Iran and spying on foreign governments. There is concern that further attacks will be coordinated by sovereign states or terror organizations and that due to the uncontrolled nature of the Internet they will be impossible to stop.

Global issues are even more intractable than national ones when it comes to "doing something," but remembering that "all politics are local," this is a case where campus activism might have an impact. Colleges and universities are ISPs and staunch defenders of freedom. So interested students might read their institutions' "acceptable uses" policies to see if issues are covered, such as who can snoop through your e-mail and the length of time records are kept. Some discussion in a Facebook forum might generate ideas for calling attention to gaps in the existing policies and proposals for change.

ONLINE SAFETY

Crime and fraud run rampant on the Internet. Many of us have fallen victim to **phishing** scams, also known as *social engineering*. The obvious scams are the e-mails purportedly from former officials of countries seeking our assistance in getting money out of their country. Others are harder to spot, such as when you get a legitimate-looking request from, say, someone who claims to be from the campus computer center who needs your password to investigate a security breach. More sinister are scams involving personal information snatched from the social networking sites, such as an e-mail requesting that you wire money to bail out a friend who has landed in jail while on vacation. Online thieves are waiting to plunder your account. Just visiting the links in phish mail could lead you to a Web page that downloads spyware or a virus. Or the "phishcatchers" may turn your computer into a zombie machine that attacks others or sends spam to everyone in your e-mail directory. Spreading viruses over the Internet, soliciting sex from minors on MySpace, and pitching fraudulent stock market schemes via e-mail are other popular Internet crimes.

Our privacy is also at risk from intrusive commercial activities, such as from **spamming** and spyware. Many Internet users still do not realize that they place themselves in the crosshairs of direct marketers who employ harvesting programs when they expose their e-mail addresses in chat rooms or social networking sites. The software we download may also contain spyware that will report our online behavior and, in some cases, expose private information stored on our computers. Keyloggers are a growing threat. They are software programs that record all of your keystrokes (including your passwords and credit card numbers) and send them to criminals. Internet cafés

[**Phishing** is an online scam in which criminals pretend to be someone you trust in an effort to obtain money or sensitive information.]

[**Spamming** is unsolicited commercial e-mailing.]

and other public terminals are popular sites of infection, but keyloggers can also be introduced on your home computer by opening an e-mail attachment or visiting a website. Routine Web searching and surfing can put your privacy at risk, as well. The search terms you use and the cookies deposited on your computer by commercial websites can be linked in the service of online advertisers. And we hope you realize that anything you post on Facebook also makes you more vulnerable to hackers and marketers.

But let's not blame too much the evildoers or the government. We, the users of the Internet, also have a personal responsibility to make the Internet safer. We each need at least three basic protections: a virus scanner, a spam filter, and a spyware eraser. So if you don't have all three, you are part of the problem. Most ISPs, including your college or university, offer these protections free of charge, but it is up to you to install them, use them, and update them. Your browser and operating system should also be set to receive automatic updates to plug security holes. Internet browsers have many options that will help you block online safety threats but some of them may also block content you want to receive. It's advisable to experiment to find the highest security and privacy settings you can use that will still pass your favorite content. The latest browsers have the option of temporarily overriding the settings you have on a case-by-case basis.

Beware of downloading protections from unknown sources, however. Some purported anti-spyware protections are spyware themselves! *Rogue anti-spyware* programs are the ones that pop up out of nowhere informing you that they have scanned your computer and found numerous serious infections, problems that they will fix if you just send them your credit card number to start a subscription. Some of them block the legitimate protections you already have and keep you from accessing websites where you can download software that will erase the rogues. So, always Google for reviews of any protective software before you download it, and from multiple sources.

The easy-to-remember passwords you use also pose a risk. There are log-in **encryption** (just Google those keywords) products available that will automatically generate and manage complex passwords for you. Another emerging technology is biometric verification systems that, for example, scan your fingerprints or facial features to make sure it's "really you" logging into your bank account.

Here are some other safety tips: never open e-mail attachments from unknown correspondents, click on Web links sent to you in e-mail (even those seemingly sent by an institution you trust), or respond to requests to verify the receipt of an e-mail from an unknown party. Always read user and privacy agreements to check for spyware before you download software, especially file-sharing software. Read the privacy policy before you supply personal information to register at a website and avoid those that reserve the right to share your information with third parties (unfortunately websites using this practice include most of the biggest names on the Internet). Always look for the "https" at the top of the page and the lock icon in the browser frame before you send credit card information. If you have a broadband connection of any type, you must activate the *firewall* (that's software that filters out unwelcome intruders) or ask your installer or personal computer expert to do it for you. Don't post your birth date or reveal your travel plans in Facebook since those

[**Encryption** is used when a message is written in a secret code.]

1. What are the main public policies governing the Internet?
2. What is the digital divide?
3. What does net neutrality mean?
4. What are some of the major threats to privacy on the Internet?
5. How can you keep yourself safe online?

lead to identity theft and "bail me out of this Turkish prison" scams. Think twice about posting pictures of your last keg party anywhere on the Internet, especially on Facebook. We can see you; so can online scam artists, and someday, prospective employers and your own children may see you, too. And, by using cheap facial recognition software we can take a picture of the real you participating in, say, a postgame college riot and match it to your Facebook you.

SUMMARY&REVIEW

WHAT ARE THE ORIGINS OF THE WEB?

The first electronic computers were developed during World War II and forerunners of the Internet were developed to support nuclear weapons research. Today's Internet began in 1972 as ARPANET, a computer network using the TCP/IP protocol to transmit messages among defense-related research labs. It slowly evolved to serve wider groups of academic and organizational users before being opened up to all computer users in 1991. Early videotex and online services connected personal computer users to send e-mail and exchange files. The World Wide Web represents one of the most successful protocols used on the Internet, the hypertext transfer protocol (http). It was the culmination of developments in computer graphics, hypertext, and consumer videotex services that crystallized with the creation of the HTML language in 1991.

HOW HAS THE INTERNET IMPACTED SOCIETY?

On the plus side, the Internet can contribute to meaningful social interaction and public debate. On the downside, it can be accused of replacing human interaction with superficial online chatter and cultivating hate. As an international medium, content and user behavior acceptable in one country may not be permissible in others. Pornography, intellectual property rights, political speech, and social inequality are among the issues raised by the spread of the Internet.

HOW HAS THE INTERNET IMPACTED CONVENTIONAL MEDIA?

The advertising, newspaper, and music industries have seen their conventional ways of doing business threatened. Old media firms are scrambling to create new revenue sources by either selling content online or developing new ad-supported outlets like the Hulu video service. The popularity of social media like Facebook and Twitter poses a fundamentally new way of creating content that challenges old media models at their core—by having the audience create the content.

WHAT ARE SOME FUTURE DIRECTIONS FOR THE INTERNET?

One is to make personal computers simpler, perhaps yielding "a network of things" that will be found in many everyday devices such as TV sets and household appliances. The other direction is the design of more sophisticated multimedia computers that will replace all of the other communications media found in the home today. Both scenarios foretell the evolution of the Web into a multimedia network that will carry radio, TV, and phone conversations. HTML5 will integrate today's plug-ins and make information more accessible. IP version 6 will expand the number of people and devices connected to the Internet. Broadband speeds are increasing as new wireless and fiber-optic technologies become available.

HOW IS THE INTERNET INDUSTRY ORGANIZED?

Google has become the giant of the Internet through its search and ad-serving businesses, but is expanding into software publishing, hardware, and video. Computer hardware companies such as Dell and Apple make the computers. Software companies such as Microsoft manufacture common computer applications. Content providers are the companies that create information for the Web and multimedia applications, whereas Internet service providers make the actual physical connections to the Internet.

WHAT'S ON THE INTERNET?

Internet content can be defined in terms of the major varieties of protocols that are used, which include e-mail, file transfers, and document display. The Web is an example of the latter. Web pages may be categorized by their top-level domain names (such as .com and .edu) or by the nature of their content. Social media, online games, e-commerce, and entertainment sites are the leading categories today, but new genres are continually emerging.

WHO RUNS THE INTERNET?

No one entity owns or controls the Internet or the Web. They are run by a patchwork of voluntary organizations, including the Internet Corporation for Assigned Names and Numbers (ICANN), the Internet Engineering Task Force, the World Wide Web Consortium, and the Internet Society. The high-capacity backbone that interconnects major Internet nodes is operated by long-distance carriers, and local connections to those nodes are handled by Internet service providers (ISPs) and local telephone companies. ISPs provide basic Internet connections and sometimes also provide content (as in the case of America Online), but most content providers are independent.

WHAT SOCIAL ISSUES SHAPE THE INTERNET?

Most issues revolve around the control of the Internet. Some proposed policies are aimed at keeping the Internet open and diverse, such as by protecting individual privacy, preventing monopolization by corporate interests, providing equal access for all, and keeping it free of taxation or direct control by national governments. Net neutrality is the concept that users should not be discriminated against based on the amount or nature of the data they transfer on the Internet. Others would clamp down on cyberspace by restricting pornography, encryption, and hate speech or by strictly enforcing the intellectual property rights of copyright and patent holders.

THINKING CRITICALLY
ABOUT THE MEDIA

1. Explain who deserves the most credit for "inventing" the Internet as we know it today.

2. Try watching your favorite TV program online and discuss the advantages and disadvantages of IPTV versus broadcast television. Refer to "Diffusion of Innovations" (see Chapter 2).

3. What would be the best way to govern the Internet in the future? Why?

4. How do you explain the popularity of social media among college students?

5. Analyze your online privacy and security practices and outline a plan for making yourself safer online.

KEY TERMS

browser (p. 254)

cookies (p. 263)

copyright (p. 277)

e-commerce (p. 262)

encryption (p. 281)

hypertext markup language (HTML) (p. 254)

hypertext transfer protocol (http) (p. 261)

Internet service provider (ISP) (p. 265)

Internet2 (p. 261)

local area network (LAN) (p. 252)

modem (p. 252)

net neutrality (p. 277)

patent (p. 277)

phishing (p. 280)

portal (p. 271)

protocol (p. 261)

social media (p. 256)

spamming (p. 280)

spyware (p. 264)

transmission-control protocol/ Internet protocol (TCP/IP) (p. 253)

uniform resource locator (URL) (p. 268)

Web 2.0 (p. 256)

wide area network (WAN) (p. 252)

GOVERNMENTS, COMPANIES, INSTITUTIONS, POLITICIANS, AND CELEBRITIES all strive to gain the goodwill of their audiences. It is the job of public relations professionals to craft their images for clients, from Breeder's Cup horse racing to British Petroleum through the media of mass communication.

10

PUBLIC RELATIONS

HISTORY: FROM PRESS AGENTRY TO PUBLIC RELATIONS

According to Edward Bernays (1961), who penned the first book and taught the first college course on public relations, the three main elements of public relations—informing people, persuading people, and integrating people with other people—are practically as old as society itself. Of course, the means and methods of accomplishing these ends have changed as society has changed, but a mutually beneficial relationship with audiences, appropriate skills and tools, and maintaining an ethical profession are still the necessary components for successful practitioners.

1900 The Publicity Bureau of Boston is founded as first public relations firm

1913 Ludlow Massacre establishes value of corporate public relations

1917 Creel Commission formed to motivate public support for World War I

1923 Edward L. Bernays publishes *CrystallizingPublic Opinion*, first book on professional public relations

1929 Bernays and Fleischman stage Torches of Freedom march to promote women and smoking for Lucky Strike cigarettes

1948 Public Relations Society of America (PRSA) founded

1989 *Exxon Valdez* crisis becomes PR nightmare

2009 Federal Trade Commission (FTC) regulates viral campaigns

2010 Toyota recalls and British Petroleum's oil spill in the Gulf Coast: the new PR nightmares

2012 PRSA replaces the 1982 definition of public relations to emphasize "mutually beneficial relationships"

CIVILIZATION AND ITS PUBLIC RELATIONS

[**Public relations** are organized activities intended to favorably influence the public.]

For Bernays and historians of the practice, professional **public relations** has always gone hand in hand with civilization. Kings and warriors of ancient civilizations, such as Sumeria, Babylonia, Assyria, and Persia, were memorialized in storytellings, songs, poems, and other communications to promote their prowess in battle and politics. In Egypt, much of the art and architecture (statues, temples, tombs) was used to impress on the public the greatness of nobles, priests, and scribes. In ancient Rome, Julius Caesar carefully prepared the Romans for his crossing of the Rubicon in 49 BCE by sending reports, such as "Caesar's Gallic Wars" (52 BCE), on his epic achievements as governor of Gaul.

Augustus, who succeeded Julius Caesar, is historically renowned for being a master at communicating with the public. He used money, among other communication devices, to spread information. On one side of a coin was his picture and on the other side was news, such as his military conquests, public works, and governing triumphs. The coins and news spread as his citizens and soldiers traveled and traded throughout Europe, Asia, and Africa.

Later, the teachings of Jesus and his apostles took center stage in the battle for religious dominance in the public mind. Once the Christian church took shape, it relied on eloquent speeches and letters, such as Paul's epistle to the Romans, to guide the faithful and win converts.

[**Propaganda** is the intentional influence of attitudes and opinions.]

In the fifteenth century new knowledge spread in new forms—such as translations of the Bible from Latin into everyday languages, mass-printed books, and newspapers. This created an explosion of public communications. By 1792, the National Assembly of France created the first government-run **propaganda** ministry. It was part of the Ministry of the Interior, and it was called the *Bureau d'Esprit*, or "Bureau of the Spirit." It subsidized editors and sent agents to various parts of the country to win public support for the French Revolution.

THE AMERICAN WAY

Great documents of liberty crystallized the power of **public opinion**, including the *Magna Carta*—the thirteenth-century English charter of human rights and liberties that inspired the U.S. Constitution. England's rebellious American colonies produced a host of public relations experts for fashioning the machinery of political change. Three of these influential statesmen, Alexander Hamilton, James Madison, and John Jay, are credited with winning public approval of the ratification of the Constitution by publishing letters they had written to the press in 1787 and 1788. These letters became known as the *Federalist Papers*. Other great documents produced by the founders of the United States—the Declaration of Independence, the Constitution, and the Bill of Rights—may all be seen as masterworks of public relations in addition to being masterworks of political philosophy and democratic governance.

No history of public relations is complete without mentioning the master of all nineteenth-century press agents and publicists, Phineas T. Barnum. Showman par excellence, Barnum created waves of publicity stunts and coverage that made his circus, "The Greatest Show on Earth," an irresistible draw in every city and town it visited after its inception in 1871. Barnum sent anonymous controversial articles to local editors to drum up curiosity about his traveling shows. He also used his creativity and imagination to write articles and illustrative ads about his intriguing American museum in New York. His successful publicity for a midget named "Gen. Tom Thumb" (Charles S. Stratton) and his wife (Lavinia Warren Stratton) sent all of them to England, where the Queen met them, artists painted the "Little General's" portrait, and composers wrote songs about him. Barnum also made the "The Swedish Nightingale," Jenny Lind, popular in the United States.

THE TIMING WAS RIGHT

The rise of the Industrial Age was a terrific force, propelling the need for public relations practitioners. Then after World War I, other factors came into play that cemented the public relations profession: America was building a consumer culture, people were more engaged in leisure activities, and public opinion was a common topic—thanks to influential communication theorists, such as Walter Lippmann, John Dewey, and Harold Lasswell. Advertising and publicity became a mainstay in newspapers and magazines, but also appeared in radio and movies. For example, efforts to influence public opinion about World War I appeared in films,

> [**Public opinion** is the aggregate view of the general population.]

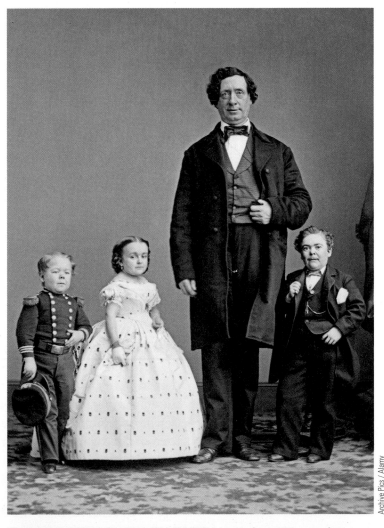

Archive Pics / Alamy

THE GREATEST SHOW ON EARTH More than 150 years later, P.T. Barnum is still celebrated for pioneering successful public relations practices.

newsreels, and cartoons at movie houses. From 1920, when the first commercial radio station went on the air, to the end of the decade, sponsored programming and advertising streamed into more than 10 million households.

Entrepreneurs came to recognize and need the skills of public relations practitioners. Many industrialists were arrogant, and their dispassionate attitudes toward the public were epitomized in 1892 by the cold-blooded methods of Henry Clay Frick in his attempt to crush a labor union in the Carnegie-Frick Steel Company's plant in Homestead, Pennsylvania. The employees' strike was ultimately broken and the union destroyed, with the help of the state militia. Physical force won the battle for immediate control, but public opinion, framed in the struggle of the workers, won the war (Cutlip, Center, & Broom, 1985). Industrialists quickly learned the value of combating hostility and courting public favor through professional public relations.

Corporate leaders also soon learned the value of practitioners who could drum up publicity in attracting customers and investors. Companies across America established press bureaus to manage the dissemination of news favorable to themselves and unfavorable to their competitors. The "battle of the currents" between Westinghouse (advocate of alternating current, or AC, power transmission) and Thomas A. Edison's General Electric (advocate of direct current, or DC, transmission) is one of the earliest examples of how public relations was first conducted in the United States by powerful economic interests. Using former newspapermen as their publicists, the companies competed for media attention, political influence, and marketing advantage.

Trade associations were quick to catch the public relations fever in the late 1800s. The Association of American Railroads is thought to be the first organization to use the term *public relations* in its 1897 *Year Book of Railway Literature*. Certainly, the railroad barons used public relations tools of the trade to expand the railroads across towns and countrysides.

By the early 1900s, charities saw the emergence of public relations departments within their local, national, and international offices, and soon, most nonprofit enterprises of any significance had in-house PR departments and/or outside PR agency counsel. These operations were much smaller than those in the corporate world, but their role was equally important. They helped to communicate their organizations' purposes, practices, and performance with the goals of building public awareness, raising money, influencing legislation, recruiting volunteers, and otherwise currying public support for their interests.

Whether in-house or acting as an independent agency, public relations in the early 1900s had evolved from being individual press agents and publicists to counseling firms that offered their services as experts in the field. The nation's first publicity firm, the Publicity Bureau, was founded in Boston at the turn of the twentieth century, and the PR industry continues to experience robust growth more than a century later.

PR PIONEERS IN THE MODERN WORLD

Ivy Ledbetter Lee was a well-known forerunner of today's public relations practitioner. He convinced companies to be open to the public and to the media, whether the news was good or bad. He believed that business had to tell its story honestly, accurately, and openly in order to win public understanding and support. He developed a publicity policy of "the public be informed" in contrast to the infamous statement of financier William Vanderbilt, "the public be damned." Sometimes, however, Lee helped his clients to appear more sympathetic than they were. For example, John D. Rockefeller, Jr., asked for Lee's advice in handling the so-called Ludlow Massacre that began in 1913 in southern Colorado when some 9,000 miners tried to form a union to protest their substandard living and working conditions. In response, the Rockefellers hired a private police militia who set fire to the miners' tent city and, in a skirmish, killed several of the miners, two women, and 11 children. With the family name being pilloried across the land, the Rockefeller family turned to Ivy Lee for help. One of Lee's strategies was to have Rockefeller, Jr., visit the camps after the strike and stage photographs of him talking with miners. Rockefeller would appear in newspapers and magazines as a concerned owner who cared about the miners' quality of life. At another time, Lee advised the senior Rockefeller, whose questionable business ethics were being attacked by muckrakers such as Ida Tarbell (see Chapter 3), to publicize his charitable contributions. Sometimes the allegiance to his clients took precedence over other "publics." (Lee was being investigated before his death in 1934 for his involvement with Nazi-owned businesses.) However, his efforts with the Red Cross in World War I were highly praised. He raised $400 million in donations, recruited thousands of volunteers, and catapulted the Red Cross's image as a relief organization.

Competing with Ivy Lee was Edward L. Bernays and his associate and wife, Doris Fleischman. Bernays is credited with coining the term *public relations counsel* in his first book on the subject, *Crystallizing Public Opinion*, published in 1923. Bernays and Fleischman viewed public relations as an art applied to a science. They would find out what the public thought and liked about their clients and then go about highlighting those attributes. They went well beyond publicity in their roles as consultants to business, government, and not-for-profit enterprises. During World War I, Bernays—who was a theatrical press agent at the time—joined the U.S. Committee on Public Information, also known as the Creel Committee, which was successful in selling war bonds and generally promoting the war effort. George Creel was a remarkable practitioner who was able to form public opinion through information vehicles such as movies, cartoons, photographs, newsreels, and other media. The famous Uncle Sam "I Want You" poster was commissioned under Creel's direction.

One of Bernays and Fleischman's classic campaigns was the 1929 Torches of Freedom in which they chose 10 women to walk down Fifth Avenue smoking cigarettes, symbolizing torches of equality with men during a time when women were only "allowed" to smoke in their homes. With the press already alerted, the coverage helped to advance feminism while setting the stage for a surge in

"I WANT YOU!" SAYS UNCLE SAM America's most famous poster is a prime example of a successful PR campaign for the war effort. The poster was illustrated by James Montgomery Flagg for the Creel Commission during WWI.

A NEW AUDIENCE Public relations pioneers Bernays and Fleischman started a PR campaign to attract women to smoking. If Amelia Earhart smokes Lucky Strikes, then all women should!

smoking by women. What the public and the press didn't know, however, was that Bernays was a consultant to the American Tobacco Company, whose director realized that profits could be doubled with women smokers. All the news reports showed women smoking his Lucky Strike cigarettes. Bernays and Fleischman continued to contribute to women's equality. They were members of the Lucy Stone League (an equal rights, suffragist group), and Fleischman was the first married woman to be issued a passport with her maiden name.

Whereas Lee, Bernays, and Fleischman were consultants with their own public relations agencies, Arthur Page was a public relations pioneer in corporate communications. American Telegraph and Telephone (AT&T) hired Page as vice president of public relations, and he advised executives on how to respond to public opinion and the media. He believed that public relations was publicity, but it included what managers said and how they acted with the public. Further, he said that the PR staff's job was to ensure that company promises to the public were kept.

PUBLIC RELATIONS MATURES

In the 1930s and 1940s, several organizations were founded to represent the interests of public relations practitioners, culminating in 1948 in the formation of the Public Relations Society of America (PRSA). Today, the PRSA remains the world's largest public relations membership association with more than 21,000 members, primarily in the United States.

By the late 1960s, public relations had matured into a professionally recognized enterprise, comprising in the United States several hundred public relations agencies and more than 100,000 individual practitioners in business, government, and nonprofit enterprises. Part of the driving force for this growth was the great burst of political turbulence that engulfed the world. Another part was the burgeoning consumer movement that sought to protect the average person against unsafe products, unhealthy working conditions, unfair pricing, and other breaches, real and alleged, of the expanding social contract that said, in effect, "the customer is king." Corporations found themselves crafting "Bills of Rights" for their customers, recasting their credit agreements, and instituting numerous other reforms to guarantee consumer satisfaction. Colleges and universities were particularly affected, as their campuses became hotbeds of social action, and they, too, had to pay attention to their publics.

In the 1980s and 1990s, business and government became the primary targets for initiatives aimed at curbing air pollution, water pollution, deforestation, and the general threat of ecological disaster caused by global warming and the destruction of the world's natural habitats. When the *Exxon Valdez* tanker ran aground, spilling 11 million gallons of oil off the coast of Alaska, the environmental catastrophe sparked a public relations calamity for the entire industry. Even now, ExxonMobil faces complaints of harm from thousands of Alaskans whose livelihoods still are affected. This disaster showed the need for, and set into motion, crisis communication management planning among corporations. ExxonMobil continues to work on its image by publicizing its efforts at making the world more environmentally friendly.

This period also witnessed the growth and extension of consumer activism around issues such as unfair labor practices and unrestrained corporate expansion and market control. By 2000, these issues became lightning rods for public concern about the almost unbridled success and globalization of such megabrands as McDonald's and Walmart.

THE NEW MILLENNIUM MELTDOWN

Good public relations practices are needed in reaction to national events. There was the boom and bust of the dot-com bubble in the late 1990s; followed by the 9/11 terrorist attacks in 2001; and by the meltdown of ethics and governance in companies in 2002, such as Enron and WorldCom, whose executives embezzled investors' money and destroyed public trust, which led to bankruptcy. And, more recently, the CEOs of the Big Three automakers flew in private jets to Washington, D.C., to ask Congress for a $25 billion bailout in federal aid. (What were they thinking?) Even Apple has its PR crises as people found out about the deplorable conditions for workers in China's Foxconn supplier factory where its iDevices are assembled. PR practitioners have their work cut out for them with the barrage of pet food recalls, toy recalls, Toyota recalls, British Petroleum's massive oil spill in the Gulf of Mexico, and NewsCorp's phone hacking scandal in the United Kingdom. On the one hand, PR practitioners are chastised for not doing enough to persuade companies to come clean sooner about their deceptions. On the other hand, many have received praise for all they did during and after 9/11 to help corporations, government agencies, and nonprofit organizations communicate with the American public and the world about what happened and what to expect in the near future. In today's world, public relations faces a complex scenario in which audiences spread their opinions by social media instantaneously, and international bad guys, such as al-Qaida, also have much greater access to use social media to influence both national and world opinion.

PR PERSONIFIED The president of the United States performs a public relations function whenever he addresses the nation.

Jason Reed-Pool/Getty Images News/Getty Images

What began as mainly a U.S. enterprise in the early 1900s has grown to become a global enterprise with about 310,000 PR managers and specialists in the United States, scores of national PR associations, and more than 100,000 additional practitioners worldwide.

GLOBAL PUBLIC RELATIONS

With the transformation of larger PR firms into global entities, particularly firms from the United States, there has been a corresponding increase in promotion and publicity campaigns across national and regional borders. These global entities now manage publicity that not many years ago would have been handled by local firms in the target countries because of their familiarity with the local language and culture.

Since English has increasingly become the default language for international business, cultural and linguistic barriers seem to have become less critical when dealing with the business publics. However, if you can communicate in the local language, you can promote and publicize much more effectively to the local market.

The classic example of Harry Potter publicity from U.S.-based Ketchum PR exemplifies this trend. A few months after the release of *Harry Potter and the Sorcerer's Stone*, Ketchum PR handled the global launch of the film's DVD and VHS versions. The core event featured the Hogwarts' Express steam train from the film. Platform 1 was transformed into Platform 9 3⁄4, as in the film, complete with a Hogwarts'-themed enclosure, which became the venue for the launch party. A select number of 50 media from around the world were given group interviews with the cast.

In the end, the campaign generated more than 1,150 print articles, 21 website features, 37 radio features, and 6 TV features. The cumulative audience in the United Kingdom alone was about 37,981,000 for TV; about 389,585,100 circulation for print (with a potential readership of about 1,246,672,400); and about 81,423,600 for radio. Most important, 1.2 million units of the video versions were sold the first day, breaking all records for such sales.

In many ways, the trend toward more frequent cross-border and global PR initiatives is an important step forward in the evolution of cultural cooperation between and among different countries. But it is also a trend that could inflame national passions and create public and private tensions about issues such as cultural imperialism and world domination, particularly by the United States. Social media could be the battleground for these developments. On the one hand, the U.S. government has pledged to keep social media channels open to foster pro-democracy movements such as those that emerged in the Middle East in 2011. On the other hand, countries sometimes regard these efforts as unwanted intrusions in their internal affairs and prefer to expand control over the social media. For example, in China government censors monitor social media chatrooms and in Iran state security used online postings to track down protesters. In the decades ahead countries such as China or those of the European Union could find themselves similarly challenged as they grow in global power.

TECHNOLOGY TRENDS: TOOLS FOR GETTING THE JOB DONE

Welcome to the new world of public relations! Although public relations practitioners promote goodwill and communications between clients and the public, some also promote publicity for an organization's image, product, or service. PR methods have grown from the traditional tools of print publications and publicity stunts to sophisticated strategies, such as viral Web campaigns for movies and other products. Viral campaigns include online video clips, games, text, verbal messages, and social media such as Facebook, YouTube, and blogs that are easily passed along to others. For example, in an effort to publicize its Xperia X1, Sony Ericsson used a viral campaign with YouTube to create an aura of mystery about a character named Johnny X. Target used Facebook to get people to vote in its Bullseye Gives campaign.

Certainly since the early 1900s, the dominant PR tools have been news releases, pitch letters, and press kits that are sent to traditional media. The desire is for the information to get to the public as objective news content (instead of expensive advertising). The printed and electronic formats are still very effective today but are employed among an array of new technology tools that bypass traditional media to go straight to the public (see Table 10.1, page 294. Although this section discusses a practitioner's tools, their most important skills are still excellent writing (for a variety of media and audiences) and research to understand their audiences, clients, and the communication process.

THE VOICE Many television shows with similar formats compete with each other. PR practitioners find the right combination of tools and media, such as Facebook, Twitter, YouTube, websites, and blogs, to reach their audiences.

Table 10.1 Public Relations Tools

Advertorials	Meetings	Seminars
Annual reports	e-Newsletters	Social media
Audiotapes	News releases	Speakers' bureaus
Audiovisual presentations	Novelties	Special events
Blogs	Open houses	Speeches
Brochures, flyers, circulars	Opinion polls	Sponsorships
Compact discs	Paid advertisements	Streaming video
Computer demonstrations	Photographs	Surveys
Conventions	Plant tours	Teleconferences
Editorials	Podcasts	Tweets
Electronic press kits	PowerPoint presentations	Video conferences
Event sponsorships	Press conferences	Video news releases
Exhibits and displays	Press kits	VIP visits
Feature articles	Product placements	Webcasts
Interactive news releases	Public demonstrations	Web logs
Legislative alerts	Public service advertisements	Websites
Legislative testimony	Radio news releases	Workshops
Letters to editors	Satellite broadcast media tours	

TRADITIONAL TOOLS

News releases (print, digital, or electronic) are news stories with up-to-date information (about a client's product, service, campaign, or event) sent to newsrooms in the hope that the story will be published. They are written in broadcast or print style and contain news elements. Some releases are used as a news lead for reporters to investigate further and write their own stories on the topic. From the PR point of view, the best news releases are published with no changes. From the news organization point of view, however, using press releases verbatim reflects badly on them because the story is not unique and their readers or viewers can find the exact same story in a competitor's medium.

Pitch letters (print or digital) offer story ideas to particular reporters and include contacts, websites, and other resources that the reporters could use.

Media or press kits are a collection of materials about the client and include a cover letter, news release, publishable photos, brochures, biographies, business cards, and other information in different formats for media use. All of this might be sent to news organizations on CD-ROMs or found with links that appear in information online.

Digital or multimedia press kits contain all of the bells and whistles associated with Internet activity. This may be a Web page that lists links to media materials, including videos, PowerPoint, or audio files for iPod downloads. E-kits are often found on major corporate websites.

NEW TOOLS

Video news releases (VNRs) are the video equivalent of print or digital news releases. They are professional, ready-to-air television news stories sent to news organizations as potential content for news broadcasts. When a VNR is added to the news lineup or incorporated into news websites, it will appear to

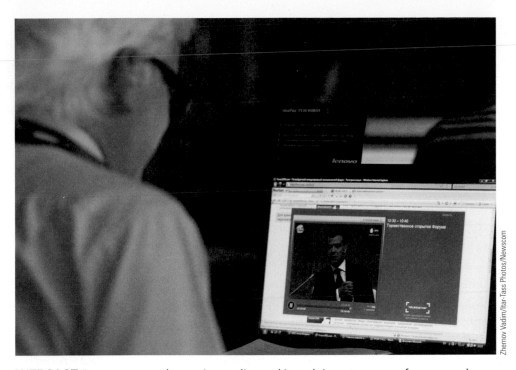

WEBCAST Reporters can ask questions online and in real time at press conferences and use the footage in their newscasts.

the audience as though it came from an objective reporter and not a public relations practitioner representing a client. Many VNR news stories cover health care, consumer, technology, travel, and business stories that would appeal to viewers. The publicity that VNRs generate in airtime and attention within markets is usually well worth the high cost of making the video. (Nielsen Media Research's SIGMA system has been a boon to VNR producers, allowing them to electronically track what stations aired the VNR and report this information to clients.) VNRs are distributed by satellite and tape and benefit from the Internet and digital transmission. By using their own digital video servers, news producers can call up VNRs—along with related stories from their networks and other news sources—then incorporate what they want into their news broadcasts and websites.

Webcasts are a form of Web-based broadcast production that incorporates streaming video and audio, such as press conferences. Reporters or producers view video, text, and photos from their desktops; participate in interviews if they are part of the package; then download the satellite or Internet feed to get excerpts for their on-air coverage.

> A **webcast** is a real-time event transmitted over the Internet.

Webcasts are a supplement to VNRs and SMTs (described in the sections that follow). However, their use and impact are increasing as the Internet expands as a direct, first source of news and information for both individuals and media personnel. Webcasts also respond to "on-demand" requests by people who may have missed the original broadcast or by producers who may want to use some of the content later for other purposes. Increasing numbers of sites, such as Google Video or YouTube, offer easy downloads of short videos.

> **Podcasts** are recorded messages or audio programs distributed through downloads to computers, iPods, or other portable digital music players.

Podcasts are audio interviews with industry representatives or executives that are placed online. Anyone is welcome to download and store the podcasts or listen to them online at any time.

Satellite media tours (SMTs) differ from podcasts because they are a video of a spokesperson being interviewed that is distributed via satellite. Unlike a VNR, SMTs are pitched to the media weeks ahead so that bookings are secured in advance. The PR practitioner has control of the message and has previewed the questions from the media. The stations can run the interview live, tape it for later use, or edit excerpts into a news program. As part of the SMT, a video of the product or service can also be transmitted as B-Roll (background video) for a package or rolled as background during the interviews.

E-SMTs, or satellite media tours via the Internet, have little to do with satellites and a whole lot to do with computers. Like webcasts, they provide an easy way for public relations clients to allow the media and others "virtual attendance" and participation in press conferences, where they can watch the event in progress and e-mail questions before, during, and after the event.

E-mail has been a boon to all practitioners, who can reach out to their audience with information, calls to action, and requests to volunteer. However, PR by e-mail has become a bane for many journalists who consider it to be spam that fills their inboxes with unwanted communications.

E-mail has given way to texting for immediate communication. For instance, the press secretary of a governor might text a particular reporter across a crowded room, asking if she would like to stay afterward for an interview. Online communication, such as blogs, tweets, and other social media can spread news, rumors, attacks, and opinions so fast that they demand nearly impossible reaction times from PR practitioners. For example, users of social media posted thousands of messages within one weekend complaining that Amazon.com had removed gay and lesbian books from its listings and rank sales searches. Amazon finally responded on Monday that there had been a "glitch." Critics protested that Amazon reacted way too slowly to users in this day and age of 24/7 brand monitoring. They complained that even if Amazon didn't have a good answer, it should have at least responded that it was looking into the situation. Besides monitoring social media better, companies also need to practice due diligence during the weekends. The public never sleeps.

SOCIAL MEDIA

Social networking sites are becoming major tools for PR research data gathering and as vehicles for getting a message out. Facebook has been on the hot seat with its users about privacy because it can track members' actions—such as what areas they visit and what products and services they buy—and hand that information over to their client company's PR departments and to other members. Companies also have Facebook groups and advertising that users can visit.

GE Global Research

BLOGGING: IT'S THE NEW PR GE's blog, called From Edison's Desk, has essays and commentary on science and technology global research.

MEDIA&CULTURE

SOCIAL MEDIA: THE NEW PR TOOLBOX

Just as playing games has moved from the neighborhood sand lot to the digital ether, public relations is shifting from print to online tools and techniques. And the neighborhood is now the global village.

In order to know how to reach their publics, PR practitioners research where their different audiences get their information: It used to be that audiences were easy to reach with radio and three broadcast TV channels, local and national newspapers and magazines. Now, about 2 billion people are online, visiting millions of different websites. And about 800 million users read and trade information on Facebook, Twitter, and YouTube social media. Practitioners also know that e-reader, tablet, and handheld device apps are becoming more popular daily.

What does this mean to a PR professional? You know the answer: You must get your message digital to be seen and heard. It doesn't matter if your company or client is local, national, or international.

The traditional tools (print, broadcast, events, conferences) are fast becoming the add-ons to the Internet for getting information noticed and communicating with others for relationship building. Traffic is in high gear for website content, social media, blogs, and interactive games, for instance.

Blogs and Facebook are especially big. PR agencies have their own blogs and Facebook pages, advise their clients and companies to develop blogs, and court other bloggers for publicity. Side by side with text and photo blogs are podcasts and video blogs. Websites such as General Electric's Edison's Desk use blogs to cover global news of their own and other scientific works (and the complimentary reader comments look as if they also come from GE

PR practitioners). They also have a Twitter component. Other companies, such as Microsoft with Xbox 360 gaming, communicate with bloggers, participate in blogs, or tweet about a new product or service. Universities use Twitter and Pinterest to announce awards or discuss research to drum up interest in their departments.

Edelman, a PR firm that also does "reputational management" was hired to help Walmart, America's largest employer, with its image problems stemming from employee low wages and long hours, nonexistent health care benefits, sex discrimination issues, and the fallout from indirectly jacking up jobs overseas while leaving "made in America" behind. Edelman consultants for Walmart include former bloggers who know the ropes.

However, Edelman almost had to hire itself to get out of trouble. One of its PR stunts, called *Walmarting Across America*, had two people traveling across the country in an RV and blogging about how great the Walmarts were along the way. Edelman soon made a public apology because (surprise!) it was a fake blog or "flog," with the intention to deceive their audiences. The techniques of Edelman caused ethical debates. Should PR practitioners who feed company information to bloggers identify themselves and their objectives, or is it all right to be regarded as just another blogger? And do blog owners need to attribute where they get their information if it is copied directly from a PR person's e-mail and appears verbatim in other blogs? The Federal Trade Commission clamped down on this type of activity with regulation that would make bloggers cough up the real reason they were promoting a product or company—that they were being paid to do so.

Two billion videos are watched on YouTube each day, many uploaded by companies trying to sell an image, service, or product. All 2012 presidential candidates ran part of their campaign on YouTube. What a wonderful way to communicate with potentially 20 million viewers who pass clever videos along to friends, who pass them along to their friends.... This snowballing effect removes the worry of having to get to a particular demographic; viewers do that for them. And it's free!

A recent example of a company's effective use of social media is British Petroleum's (BP) belated communication efforts about its Deepwater Horizon oil explosion and debacle. Anxious to try to turn the tide (no pun intended) in a situation that was quickly going from bad to worse, BP infused social media everywhere—on Facebook, YouTube, and Twitter—in which people voiced their anger to BP and the company showed the problems it faced and gave updates and corrections. However, BP's PR challenges continue.

PR DATABASES

PR databases help public relations practitioners gather and disseminate information.

Online media databases are loaded with information on the tens of thousands of reporters and editors in the United States and around the world. PR practitioners use these databases to research individual records; print address labels; and send "blast" faxes, e-mails, and tweets. Among the largest online databases—with more than 300,000 contacts by name and editorial "beat"—are Cision and BurrellesLuce, a PR business that is more than 120 years old. Vocus, a company that specializes in PR software and cloud marketing (social media and other marketing that takes place on the Internet), offers its database of 1.4 million media contacts and outlets, bloggers, and analysts.

Reporters scanning for news tips go online to PR Newswire, Business Wire, and Media Distribution Services (MDS). In addition, there are scores of smaller databases targeted to specific media and audiences, such as Hispanic Americans and African-Americans.

Journalists use these databases to make requests for information or assistance concerning stories they are covering, and PR practitioners and others can respond accordingly. Trade and professional associations offer their own online connections to their members as well as related news and information.

Online tracking and monitoring systems help PR practitioners examine what the media, competitors, and the public are saying about their employers or clients. Many PR practitioners hire companies that employ sophisticated tracking software. BurrellesLuce and CyberAlert, for example, monitor tweets, blogs, and media coverage throughout the World Wide Web and deliver summaries of the stories they find to their clients' desktops. CyberAlert monitors more than 55,000 news sources in 50 languages and delivers them daily.

Online press rooms are often a menu item on the home page of corporations or nonprofit organizations. Even Girl Scouts of America has a news center: www.girlscouts.org/news/ to make it easy for editors and reporters to access news announcements and find staff contacts when they are seeking information or comment. Most online press rooms also have archives of earlier releases, photos, fact sheets, and related supporting materials. In addition, some companies and their public relations firms have established "dark" sites that can be uploaded at a moment's notice to serve as specialized press rooms should a crisis occur that requires an immediate response. For example, if a car manufacturer suddenly had to recall some of its vehicles, it could use one of these "dark" sites to launch its version of the story within minutes of hearing about the recall. Being proactive, it is able to reach the media and other audiences in almost real time and thereby minimize media inquiries for basic facts about the situation. These crisis preventive sites are also used to quell or otherwise control rumors. Of course, if manufacturers were confident about their products, they might not think a "dark" site was needed.

INDUSTRY: INSIDE THE PUBLIC RELATIONS PROFESSION

Public relations practitioners have a great many responsibilities and employ advertising, direct marketing, and related tools and techniques in representing their employers' or clients' interests, but these are not central to the PR function, per se. These have different purposes and are professions that in and of themselves require specialized expertise and knowledge for their execution. Understanding the difference helps to keep the public relations function in perspective and avoid client misunderstandings about what to expect from PR practitioners, their skills, and services. Given the complexity of public relations and the vast array of skills and technology used in communications between organizations and the public, it's not surprising that definitions of the practice of public relations abound.

In 2012, the Public Relations Society of America (PRSA) established a new definition of public relations: "Public relations is a strategic communication process that builds mutually beneficial relationships between organizations and their publics." (prsa.org) This replaces the prior definition from 1982, and reflects the changes in society and technology that both public relations practitioners and their publics use.

PR AGENCIES AND CORPORATE COMMUNICATIONS

PR practitioners usually work in a PR agency or within a business company. PR agencies range in size from one person who freelances to gigantic global companies employing thousands of experts. Agencies contract with different clients to perform distinct roles for varying amounts of time—whatever the client needs—such as putting out a monthly e-newsletter or annual report, to handling special events, such as company anniversaries or celebrations or the introduction of a new product or service. The needs of the client or "account" will determine which PR experts are wanted—those who are skilled in new technologies or those who can write speeches.

PR practitioners who work in a PR department within a corporation do corporate communications. In small companies, the PR department does media relations and represents the company to the public. In large companies, the in-house PR department might have two jobs: (1) media relations and (2) internal communications. For example, a national jewelry company would want to keep all of its employees who work within its several hundred stores across the country networked together and feeling as if they are a vital part of the company. So internal communications might include writing and designing employee newsletters, sending out birthday cards, visiting stores, shooting videos, holding contests, and maintaining an employee website.

ELEMENTS OF SUCCESSFUL PUBLIC RELATIONS

The practice of public relations is based on research, including public opinion polls, surveys, questionnaires, interviews, focus groups, and literature searches. Although it is a continuous process, PR research is conducted in three basic phases: (1) preparation, (2) implementation, and (3) impact (Broom, 2009). Successful public relations begins with a serious assessment of public attitudes. Without adequate background on the people you are trying to reach and how they think, it is difficult, if not impossible, to communicate effectively. More specifically, without research and evaluation, you cannot identify public attitudes for your client or design programs that will achieve your communication objectives.

Second, public relations is a detailed strategy, not a hit-or-miss proposition. And it must be managed well. You must oversee the many small tasks that taken altogether achieve the overall organizational objectives. A strategic plan begins with a written action chart that allows for changes and contingencies along the way, and it must have the seal of approval from top management. Timetables and deadlines are scheduled for needed media communications and publications, such as newsletters and reports (print and digital), VNRs, blogs, electronic and print press releases, and speeches and presentations at special events.

Third, public relations has the goal of fostering public support. The public might support a for-profit organization by purchasing products, investing in stock, or voting for or against specific trade regulations. Public support for a nonprofit organization might take the form of donations of money or materials, volunteer assistance, or paid memberships. For a government agency, it might mean legislative influence, taxpayer cooperation, or public participation.

An evaluation of the campaign is always the last step in a strategy: What worked? What didn't? Where did we miss? Metrics are needed: How many more volunteers/money/publicity pieces do we have now when compared to the start of the campaign? What was the cost, and how have we profited? Were the results worth the investment? You can see the process of a PR campaign in Figure 10.1 on page 301.

Over time, the public relations unit makes use of all communication modes available in our society—digital, electronic, print, and personal appearances. These are the tools and techniques that help organizations reach their publics. They are the vehicles that carry information back and forth between private and public interests.

PROFESSIONAL RESOURCES

An ever-expanding list of websites covering public relations continues to help practitioners with their skills, tools, and strategies. Included among these are www.online-pr.com (hundreds of listings and hyperlinks to PR, marketing, and advertising sites worldwide), www.prsa.org's Silver Anvil Awards (PR case studies), and www.iabc.com (networking internationally). Other websites encourage particular practitioners, such as www.womcom.org, whose membership is made up of women in communication (AWC). Still more online resources can be found for PR: entertainment, technology, hospitality, health care, event planning, press releases, software, education and training, and job consulting. You need it; the Web has it.

PR professionals can be characterized in terms of the organizations they belong to and the publications they read. Although the Public Relations Society of America (PRSA) with its 21,000 members has dominated the public relations industry for most of its history, competing organizations have formed

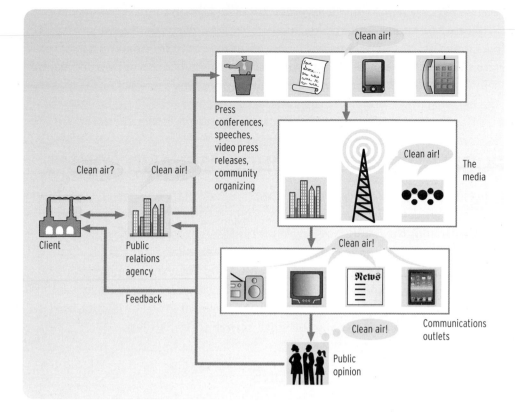

FIGURE 10.1 PR CAMPAIGN Public relations agencies organize communications events such as press conferences, speeches, and telemarketing campaigns to alert communications media organizations to important issues so that the subsequent media coverage will sway public opinion in favor of the client. Opinion polls and direct responses from the public provide feedback to the client and the agency.

to serve particular specialties or power groups within the profession. Chief among these groups are the International Association of Business Communicators (IABC), the National Investor Relations Institute (NIRI), and the Association of Women in Communications (AWC). There are also several invitation-only organizations for senior practitioners, such as the Arthur Page Society and Women Executives in Public Relations (WEPR). The Council of Public Relations Firms was established to represent the business and professional interests of the PR agencies in the United States. And there has been a comparable growth in professional societies worldwide. Besides the European-based International Public Relations Association (IPRA), which acts as a kind of clearinghouse for practitioners outside the United States, there are membership associations along the lines of the PRSA, although significantly smaller, in most of the major countries of the world. All are devoted to improving the practice of public relations and helping members succeed in their careers. The IPRA website lists more than 80 of these organizations.

The growing power and professionalism of public relations are also reflected in the development, over the past 30 or so years, of several respected publications that cover the field. There are weekly newsletters and tweets, such as *Jack O'Dwyer's Newsletter*, *Bulldog Reporter*, and *PR News*; magazines such as *PR Strategist* and *Communication World*; online publications such as *PR Week*; and research journals, such as *Public Relations Review* and *Public Relations Quarterly*. Newsletters such as *Interactive Public Relations Report* were developed to serve the interests of the growing ranks of new media and technology specialists. And some publications are trade journals sent to members of particular PR organizations.

PUBLIC RELATIONS FUNCTIONS AND FORMS

In previous chapters we discussed genres of content as a negotiation between audiences and media producers. There is a parallel process in public relations, although the "audience" includes all the various publics that the public relations professionals communicate with, including their clients and the media, as well as the general public. Some of the forms of public relations are defined by the tools of the trade (see Table 10.1, page 294). Others are defined by the functions that those in the profession perform for their clients, needs of their various publics, and the relationship with those publics.

PUBLIC RELATIONS FUNCTIONS

Media relations focus on establishing and maintaining good relations with the media.

Public relations practitioners advise and counsel the organization's management on communications questions affecting its publics, they serve as an early warning system on emerging issues related to its success, and they respond to crises. PR departments and agencies also provide technical support for other management functions with an emphasis on publicity, promotion, and **media relations**. In addition, they act as gatekeepers with the press, legislators, and government officials. Most managers prefer their PR person to represent the organization to the public. Other important PR functions and their descriptions are noted in Table 10.2. Many of these functions also represent specialty areas for public relations professionals.

THE PUBLICS OF PUBLIC RELATIONS

Publics are the different audiences that PR practitioners communicate with as part of their daily work.

Public relations activities are addressed to one or more of the many **publics** that can influence an organization's success: customers, employees, shareholders, donors, the press and the media they might use, such as Facebook and Pinterest (see Table 10.3). Depending on the needs and interests of the institutions they represent, a particular list of publics could be extensive. Multinational corporations deal with many publics, whereas the average nonprofit organization may deal with only a few.

Normally, the publics are targeted with a mix of PR tools and techniques, many of which are used in conjunction with related, but independently developed, marketing, advertising, and human resources initiatives.

Table 10.2 Functions of Public Relations

FUNCTION	DESCRIPTION
Publicity or media relations	Gaining press coverage through news releases, press conferences, and other materials
Promotion or selling	Developing and disseminating print and audiovisual materials, arranging exhibits and displays, and providing promotional giveaways
Community relations	Working with community groups and other key community interests that can influence public attitudes and public policies
Government relations	Assisting or influencing state, local, or federal government action on problems involving legislation, regulation, and related activity
Public information	Developing and disseminating print and audiovisual materials whose purpose is to inform, educate, and assist
Special events	Planning and managing internal and external events, such as ground breakings, ribbon-cutting ceremonies, tours, and open houses aimed at attracting public attention
Employee relations	Assisting management in informing staff at all levels about personnel policies and practices, labor relations, contracts, benefits, and other issues that involve the health and welfare of the labor force
Issues management, reputation management, crisis communications	Identifying and helping to manage the big issues that affect institutional success, such as air and water pollution (the environment), foreign competition, ethnic diversity, plant closings or relocations, public censure, and corporate malfeasance
Lobbying	Working with legislators and their legislative aides to influence the content and course of legislative action that affects institutional practices through contributions to political action committees (PACs), campaign contributions, and other direct assistance not included as part of more conventional government relations efforts

Table 10.3 Examples of Public Relations Publics

FOR BUSINESSES	FOR NOT-FOR-PROFIT ENTERPRISES	FOR GOVERNMENT AGENCIES
Shareholders/investors	Contributors/donors	Taxpayers/voters
Customers/consumers	Clients/consumers	Legislators
Employees	Volunteers	Lobbyists
Suppliers	Employees	Related government agencies
Financial institutions	Members	Employees
Legislators	Suppliers	Community activists
Community activists	Legislators	
Educational institutions	Community activists	
Print/broadcast media	Print/broadcast media	

TABLE 10.4 Four Models of Public Relations   Public relations expert and professor James E. Grunig identified four models of public relations that also represent its evolution.

MODEL	TYPE OF COMMUNICATION	PURPOSE
Press agentry/publicity	One-way	To manipulate public opinion and behavior
Public information/journalism	One-way	To disseminate information to the public
Two-way asymmetric	Two-way	To persuade and find out how the public reacted
Two-way symmetric	Two-way	To gain mutual understanding and find a win–win common ground

STOP&REVIEW

1. How did big business and muckraking figure into the evolution of public relations?
2. What PR tools go beyond the traditional press releases, pitch letters, and staged events?
3. What are some of the specialties or functions of PR?
4. What are the key elements to successful public relations?

FOUR MODELS OF PUBLIC RELATIONS

Public relations expert and professor James E. Grunig identified four models of public relations that define the relationship between public relations practitioners and their publics. They also represent its evolution in the development of the profession (see Table 10.4).

The model of early press agentry is most commonly associated with P. T. Barnum's style of publicity. He used creativity and almost any means to attract audiences to his enterprises. The public information model is what you often see in newspapers, TV, or online—it is sending news and information about a company, product, or service out to the public. Although Ivy Lee is associated with this model, many PR practitioners work along these lines still today. The third model is likened to Bernays and Fleischman. They used various methods to influence public opinion and then tested to see if the methods worked. If not, they tinkered with the message or their methods and tested it again. Bernays and Fleischman are also linked to the fourth model. They used social scientific methods to foster a mutual understanding of organizations and their publics. They wanted to know what audiences thought and how their clients could make improvements or help the public. No doubt, Bernays and Fleischman today would appreciate social media as an immediate and ideal way to communicate to, and receive feedback from, audiences. You can guess which is the ideal model.

MEDIALITERACY

MAKING PUBLIC RELATIONS ETHICAL AND EFFECTIVE

Throughout history public relations professionals have faced the difficult challenge of performing their functions ethically while still meeting the needs of their clients. Here we examine some of the issues and case studies involved in keeping that balance.

PERSONAL ETHICS IN THE PROFESSION

Everyone thinks they are ethical. You have morals; your friends have morals. You know, however, that many people differ in the level of their principles because there were some pranks last year that you or your friends would or wouldn't join in on. So not everyone has a high sense of ethical decisions and behaviors or the guts to differ from group mentality.

Most public relations practitioners use good judgment and make ethical decisions. However, when a few disregard their inner conscience and do not think about the social consequences of their actions, then the public, their client, the PR image, and they themselves lose out. Their poor decisions attract media attention because of the massive domino effect that can occur; for example, employees may lose their jobs, stockholders may lose their hard-earned investments, or people may lose their lives.

A classic example was the failure of Bridgestone/Firestone and Ford Motor Company to warn the public and their customers about structural weaknesses in tires installed in the Ford Explorer. The companies remained silent or seemingly uncaring for many weeks after the failures became public knowledge. More than 140 deaths and 500 injuries were attributed to accidents in the vehicles equipped with the faulty tires. The public relations practitioners who worked for these companies didn't initiate the actions that led to the fiascoes, but they certainly played a major role in perpetuating the pattern of deception by promoting the companies' actions and then playing down the consequences when the damage was done and became public.

Toyota faced a similar situation when sudden acceleration in its popular Prius may have contributed to about 35 deaths and 245 injuries since 2000. Toyota recalled 3.8 million vehicles (to replace gas pedals and braking systems) in 2010 alone, and with the announcement came more than 1,000 complaints within the week to the National Highway Traffic Safety Administration (NHTSA) website. It is the PR person's job to see potential problems that may result from a client's decision. Ethical PR practitioners counsel management to take the high road in an effort to prevent a potential need for crisis management. Ethical practitioners also make commonsense decisions for the good of society.

Although there are accepted codes of ethics that guide the practice of public relations (see Chapter 16), the pressure on many practitioners to give unequivocal support to their employers' actions, even when those actions may be unethical and possibly illegal, remains a critical challenge for the profession. Other issues affecting public relations include personal and professional ethics, public interest, conflicts between private and public interests, professional development, and use of research and evaluation.

Public relations practitioners are ethical professionals. However, ever-evolving social media cause additional challenges for these professionals. On the one hand, the public uses Facebook, YouTube, Twitter, and blogs to tell companies what they think, firing off thousands of messages before the company can react. On the other hand, public relations professionals use these same social media sites to spread the word to the public about issues, events, and new products. Marketers spend billions of dollars on word-of-mouth campaigns. They hire celebrity bloggers to promote products, and pay endorsers to roam from one site to another, posting comments from a seemingly objective viewpoint, which many regard as unethical behavior. Thus, the Federal Trade

Commission (FTC) in 2009 proposed to regulate viral campaigns and blogs in a way similar to the regulation of paid advertising and infomercials. Bloggers who do not state that they are compensated for their endorsements will be held liable—and so will the paying company.

CRISIS COMMUNICATIONS MANAGEMENT

Good public relations has many benefits: greater sensitivity to public needs, increased credibility and accountability, stronger public identity, more favorable press coverage, improved employee morale, larger market share, increased sales, and better internal management, among other things. Bad public relations can exist as well, often because the PR people in charge do their jobs poorly or because they choose to work with companies or clients who do not see the public interest as a priority. In these cases, the relationship between the company and the public is not mutually beneficial.

Perhaps management allowed the production of faulty products, permitted pollution of the environment, or illegally manipulated the price of the company's stock. In these instances, a PR practitioner has a hard job because he or she is called in afterward to clean up the mess, to soften the fallout (negative press coverage, public outrage, or regulatory punishment). Only a change in management policy or practice will truly make a difference. Using PR professionals to counsel management, help set company policy, and being proactive instead of reactive would prevent many problems from happening. If one cliché dominates public relations thinking, it is this, "You can't undo something once it has happened."

One of the classic examples of "what not to do" PR was Exxon's Valdez 750,000-barrel oil spill in Alaska in 1989. It damaged 11,000 square miles of ocean, ruined 1,300 miles of coastline, and killed thousands of animals. Yet, the chairman did not visit the site nor comment for a week. He also established headquarters far away in New York. Exxon spent $2.5 billion cleaning up their mess(es).

This case study is now replaced by British Petroleum's Deepwater Horizon oil explosion that killed 11 people and wounded 17 more. It emptied 5 million barrels of oil into 4,200 square miles of the Gulf of Mexico and onto 320 miles of Louisiana coastline, threatening wildlife, fisheries, and tourism. It is still spending billions on cleanup.

The company's response? "There's no one who wants this thing over more than I do. You know, I'd like my life back," complained the CEO. BP gave no apologies, denied responsibility, and pointed fingers at the makers of the rig, the foundation, and the government, for starters. In

BAD PR The Deepwater Horizon explosion and BP's poor reaction is a pertinent example of how bad publicity can hurt major corporations.

a fine show of concern, BP wanted $11.8 billion in tax write-offs, claiming the cleanup as an ordinary business expense. This meant U.S. taxpayers would pay about 30 percent of the cleanup costs.

In crisis communication, people want to hear acceptance of responsibility, concern, and plans for rectifying the situation. After its gaffs, BP mounted PR campaigns that included social media and ads in newspapers and TV, telling Americans that BP would recapture the oil, clean up the ocean and land, and pay for the cleanup.

Sometimes public relations can cause a crisis instead of control it. That's what happened when PR firm Burson-Marsteller was caught planting negative stories about Google on behalf of its client Facebook. Failing to reveal its involvement was a serious ethical breach of public relations practice that reflected back on the client, Facebook.

PRIVATE INTERESTS VS. THE PUBLIC INTEREST

There is often a natural tension between corporate interests and the public interest. This tension can be seen and heard daily in the press when corporations are charged with corruption, environmental pollution, undue political influence, and restraint of trade—in sum, with using their money, power, or influence in ways that compromise or undermine the public interest. In recent years, the agenda of issues has expanded to include critical social issues.

Simply by writing a story and putting a name in the news, the press gives coverage that can advance corporate interests—strong company earnings, successful government initiatives, noteworthy charitable events. Much of the background for these and related stories, particularly in the business press, comes from PR representatives with a journalism background who send news releases and pitch letters to editors and reporters suggesting angles that they and their publications or stations might take. These representatives also make countless phone calls to the media. They organize press briefings, press luncheons, and other "contacts" to stay in touch with editors and reporters for offensive as well as defensive purposes.

And if public opinion isn't enough to win the day, lobbyists attempt to directly influence votes on legislation affecting major corporations by making donations to the campaigns of politicians who enact the legislation. For example, the communications and electronics industry, led by Microsoft and AT&T, donated nearly $130 million to political campaigns. A number of media commentators speculated that such donations to the George Bush campaign, coupled with a generally less aggressive overall approach to antitrust enforcement, helped win Microsoft more favorable treatment by the former administration. Others wonder if Bush's corporate backers influenced his negative stand on environmental policies.

Public relations practitioners have to worry about what the public wants as much as what their employers want. Consequently, some live with a divided sense of self, whereas others choose clients with goals they appreciate. PR practitioners are both makers of messages and messengers. But most practitioners seem to relish their role despite its inherent difficulties. They understand the importance of the role that public relations plays in society, and they are willing to tolerate criticism in order to accomplish their goal.

The Public Relations Society of America (PRSA) awards PR practitioners who've shown excellent judgment and skill on behalf of business, government, and nonprofit associations in a variety of categories including crisis management, community relations, issues management, public service, internal communications, and multicultural public relations. Winners of the Silver Anvil Awards can be found online at www.prsa.org/awards/silverAnvil.

PROFESSIONAL DEVELOPMENT

Practitioners are continually retooling; their professional development and personal growth are always evolving. Clearly, there is a need for practitioners to become more sophisticated about how to use new technology for communications purposes. They also have to learn more about the basics of business, how it is structured, and how it is managed. Since many practitioners enter the field after majoring in journalism, communication, or a related field or after having worked in journalism and publishing, they should learn how corporations and small businesses operate. To communicate profit-and-loss issues for their clients, they need to get up to speed as quickly as possible.

YOUR MEDIA CAREER

PR JOBS ARE IN THE FAST LANE

Although *public relations* is the preferred term in most corporations, other designations that may appear in an organizational chart or in the titles of practitioners are public affairs, corporate communications, and corporate relations. In specific industries, such as public utilities, you might find the terms *consumer affairs* or *community relations*; in nonprofit and government organizations, it might be *public information* or *marketing communications*. In addition, the function may be subdivided further to reflect specific areas, such as investor relations, financial relations, fundraising, charitable contributions, and media relations. Sometimes the subdivision may reflect specific skills, such as writers, videographers, or bloggers.

Today, all leading corporations have public relations departments of one sort or another. The same goes for major nonprofit organizations such as colleges, hospitals, and national charities. Government has similar operations, although they are usually called *public affairs offices* or *public information offices*.

To assist these entities, there are more than 4,000 public relations firms, most with a relative handful of employees, but many with 50 or more. The top PR firm in the world and in the United States by far is Edelman with about 4,200 employees in more than 63 offices internationally. The PR counseling industry generates revenue in excess of $8 billion worldwide, $4 billion in the United States alone. O'Dwyerpr.com annually ranks the PR firms in the United States.

According to the Bureau of Labor Statistics (www.bls.gov), public relations is expected to grow faster than most occupations through 2018. Most public relations practitioners major in journalism, public relations or communications and have some experience, such as an internship while in school. Excellent writing for all media is expected, as well as the ability to organize PR campaigns.

There are about 310,000 PR managers and specialists in the United States. Some public relations experts are in corporate communications, others are in agencies, and still more are independent. Most in the industry are concentrated in areas where press services and other communications facilities are readily available and many businesses and trade associations have their headquarters, particularly New York and Washington, D.C.

Beginning practitioners start in the area of publicity and media relations, learning online tools, writing and editing news releases, mastering desktop publishing for layout and design of brochures, contacting reporters and editors, shooting photos and video, and generating press coverage. Seasoned practitioners are more involved with audience research; setting company policy, planning, and management; training executives to communicate with media; and other sophisticated issues, such as government relations and crisis communications. When these practitioners write, it is most often speeches, proposals, and presentations for themselves or for top management.

There is also a great concern in the field about maintaining the high standards in writing and critical thinking that have been the foundations of the practice's success over the years. Senior practitioners, in particular, complain about how difficult it is to find employees who are strong, journalistically oriented writers.

There has also been tremendous growth in the numbers of local, national, and international public relations conferences, seminars, and workshops sponsored by professional associations, universities, and for-profit enterprises. These meetings cover everything from the basics of public relations to trends and issues driving the management of organizational communications. PRSA developed a Universal Accreditation program to judge an individual practitioner's understanding and knowledge. It also has a Fellows program to recognize long-term involvement in, and major contributions to, the practice of public relations.

The Accreditation and Fellows programs are viewed as measures of professional integrity and success. In this sense, they open doors to jobs, promotions, and industry leadership. More generally, they underscore the public relations field's interest in improving the value of what practitioners do as communicators in the information society.

USE OF RESEARCH AND EVALUATION

A general criticism often leveled against the industry is that practitioners need to conduct more research on their audiences and increase their evaluation of the impact and effectiveness of their PR efforts. Although both activities are included in the traditional public relations planning process, research and evaluation are still used scantily in helping define the goals of programs and activities and later in measuring their effectiveness.

Part of the reason for limited assessment is money. Most public relations budgets allocate little money for anything beyond the essentials. These budgets focus largely on tactical, not strategic, thinking. To move forward in this area, practitioners integrate research and evaluation into their plans and budgets. They also educate top management on the value of research and development in designing and delivering more effective messages and programs.

Major research techniques in public relations include environmental monitoring (assessing the corporate climate), audits (evaluating an organization's standing with its publics), and readability studies (analyzing a publication's effectiveness).

In the absence of research and evaluation, public relations' effectiveness is compromised and the practitioner's credibility and accountability suffer. Unless you have the expectation of results and measure them, you will never really know whether you have succeeded. Clients or employers cannot rely on promises and recommendations, so you need to point to hard data substantiating the impact of your programs.

STOP&REVIEW

1. What are four models of public relations?

2. Why is ethical behavior important in public relations?

3. What does it mean to be a public relations professional?

4. What is the role of research and evaluation in public relations?

SUMMARY&REVIEW

HOW DID BIG BUSINESS AND MUCKRAKING FIGURE INTO THE EVOLUTION OF MODERN PUBLIC RELATIONS?

Muckrakers sought to improve society with their stories as they investigated and uncovered corrupt and unethical business practices. Modern public relations evolved in the late nineteenth century as large corporations sought to defend their interests in the arena of public opinion. The first independent public relations counsel was established in the early 1900s. Ivy Lee was an early practitioner who worked to improve the image of the industrialists and German dictators of the late nineteenth century. Arthur Page worked to engage AT&T and the public in a mutually beneficial relationship, and Edward Bernays and Doris Fleischman are widely regarded as the originators of the current professional practice. Mass-persuasion propaganda campaigns during both world wars were also influential in expanding the scope and effectiveness of public relations.

WHAT PR TOOLS GO BEYOND THE TRADITIONAL PRESS RELEASES, PITCH LETTERS, AND EVENTS?

Expansion in the number of media outlets, especially online and using social media, has increased the opportunities for public relations professionals to present their message to the public. Practitioners use video news releases (VNRs) to place public relations stories in newscasts. Satellite networks and videoconferences afford new opportunities to deliver highly targeted press briefings. Electronic mail, mass calling, Web pages, blogs, podcasts, and tweets are also being applied in modern public relations practice. Interactive news releases and digital press kits are popular. The use of computers can automate routine PR tasks and gain access to relational databases and online information services that offer public relations information. PR techniques used in political campaigns take advantage of advances in computer and telecommunications technology, giving politicians new opportunities to circumvent mass-media channels and state their case directly to the public on websites and on social networking sites (SNS).

WHAT ARE THE KEY ELEMENTS OF SUCCESSFUL PUBLIC RELATIONS?

Public relations campaigns succeed to the extent that they promote mutual understanding between the organization that sponsors the campaigns and one or more of the publics on which the organization depends to achieve its goals. Although it is a distinct function, public relations often relies on the successful execution of related pursuits, such as using social media, advertising, and marketing, for its campaigns to succeed. Evaluation and attention to ethical standards are two other key elements.

WHAT ARE SOME OF THE SPECIALTIES OR FUNCTIONS OF PUBLIC RELATIONS?

Most large organizations have their own public relations departments, although they go by various names, including public affairs and public information. Other corporate communicators (PR) use their skills to connect employees and upper management. There are also thousands of independent public relations agencies that supplement corporate PR departments or perform these services for smaller firms. Public relations may also be categorized in terms of functions, including media relations, promotion, community relations, government relations, public information, special events, employee relations, issues management, and lobbying. Public relations professionals are often members of such organizations as the Public Relations Society of America and the International Public Relations Association.

WHAT ARE THE FOUR MODELS OF PUBLIC RELATIONS?

There are many models of public relations. Grunig's four primary models describe the evolution of PR practices through the years, all of which are still used today: (1) The press agentry/publicity model is the practice of one-way communication, telling the public almost anything to get them to act in a prescribed manner. (2) Public information/journalism operates by simply sending out information you want to convey to the public, through various media channels. You don't even check to see if they got the information. So this is also one-way, and not really communication. (3) Two-way asymmetric is sending out information and then doing research to see if the public understands it in the way you intended. If not, then you might refine your methods. (4) Two-way symmetric is the most conducive for optimum mutual benefit. It involves researching the audience and finding out what is important to them and how they get their information, as well as evaluating how the public and the company see their relationship as mutually beneficial.

WHY ARE ETHICS IMPORTANT IN PUBLIC RELATIONS?

Ethical behavior—having high standards of principles and morals—is important in a person's private and social life. Because the nature of the PR profession is to communicate with different publics, the actions and decisions of a practitioner and his or her client affect the public. Ethical practitioners make commonsense decisions. If you have to think twice about a decision, then your answer is probably evident, and you should go with what your gut tells you. Remember that there will be those who want you to explain your decision. When you disregard your inner voice of truth, then someone loses out and a domino effect occurs; eventual losses can be felt by the public, the company, perhaps its industry, the PR industry, and you. It will be hard finding a new job when the word is out about your bad judgment. And word *will* get out because a major component of PR is media relations. It is the media's job to tell the news.

WHAT DOES IT MEAN TO BE A PUBLIC RELATIONS PROFESSIONAL?

Today's public relations professionals hold college degrees in fields such as journalism, marketing, and mass communication. Also, more than 200 colleges offer pro-grams in the field of public relations. Practitioners seek accreditation from professional societies, such as the Public Relations Society of America, and follow the society's voluntary ethical standards. They keep up to date by reading professional publications aimed at the public relations field. They also participate in continuing education programs to develop their abilities throughout their careers.

WHAT IS THE ROLE OF RESEARCH AND EVALUATION IN PUBLIC RELATIONS?

Research helps public relations practitioners improve the effectiveness of their activities, and evaluation helps them determine how effective they have been. Environmental monitoring, audits, readability studies, trend analysis, and evaluation activities, such as soliciting feedback from public relations clients and publics, are examples of research and evaluation methods.

THINKING CRITICALLY
ABOUT THE MEDIA

1. Why and how has PR become a profession over the years?

2. Imagine that you are a PR practitioner hired to promote a new line of clothing to college-age students. What steps and tools would you use and why?

3. Let's say a client wants to hire your agency. The only problem is that you don't agree with their ethics. What would you do and why?

4. What should you avoid that might rub news reporters the wrong way and they eventually ignore your messages and efforts? On the flip side, how can the relationship between PR and news organizations be mutually beneficial?

5. Will there be a continued need for public relations? Explain your position.

 **KEY TERMS**

media relations (p. 302)

podcast (p. 295)

propaganda (p. 286)

public opinion (p. 287)

public relations (p. 286)

publics (p. 302)

webcast (p. 295)

WITH ITS FIERCE COMPETITION for the attention of consumers—and for the purse strings of the advertisers who want to reach them—advertising is an exciting field. Ads impact images of ourselves and our society.

Come to where the flavour is.
Come to Marlboro Country.

FILTER C

Ma

11

ADVERTISING

by Teresa Mastin, Ph.D.
College of Communication, DePaul University

HISTORY: FROM HANDBILLS TO WEB LINKS

The history of advertising is the story of advertising professionals' creative insights. Advertising professionals excel in taking advantage of the new media of the day to craft new forms of messages to entice consumers and to innovate with business models that serve advertisers better. **Advertising** is often thought of as a twentieth-century phenomenon, but it is a creative art form that has existed for centuries. Signage on the walls of ancient cities of Greece and Rome marketed food and wine. Centuries later, town criers filled the streets of Europe to tell the citizenry about the "good deal" to be found "just around the corner."

The printing press was the hot new technology of its day when it was introduced in Europe in 1455. It soon spawned a new form of advertising, the *handbill*. With this new medium, the message could be copied efficiently and distributed to many people in a relatively short time, and the content could be expanded to include detailed product descriptions and "special offers" to induce sales. Printing also enabled the first newspaper advertisements, which began around 1625. Fast forward to 2012: with global adoption approaching

1704	First classified ads in an American newspaper	2003	Social networking sites emerge as advertising gold mine
1833	Penny Press originated	2006	Google is the number one advertising vehicle
1849	First formal ad agency		
1926	First radio network	2007	Users rebel against Facebook advertising methods
1960s	30- and 60-second TV commercials dominate advertising	2010	Viral marketing is a new advertising technique
1994	Internet banner advertising		

> **Advertising** is communication that is paid for and is usually persuasive in nature.

30 percent, smartphones such as the iPhone, Blackberry, and Android continue to be the hot advertising venue. Mobile is projected to account for 15.2 percent, or $22.4 billion, of global online ad spending in 2016.

ADVERTISING IN AMERICA

The earliest newspaper ads in America were classified ads published in the *Boston News-Letter* in 1704 (see Chapter 4) (Sandage, Fryburger, & Rotzoll, 1989). An example of advertising from the colonial period is the following ad, which appeared in Benjamin Franklin's newspaper, the *Pennsylvania Gazette*.

> To be SOLD A Plantation containing 300 acres of good Land, 30 cleared, 10 or 12 Meadows and in good English Grass, a house and barn lying in Nantmel Township, upon French Creek, about 30 miles from Philadelphia, Enquire of Simon Merideith.

Benjamin Day's *New York Sun* originated the concept of the mass circulation newspaper, or Penny Press, in 1833 (see Chapter 4). From that point on, we see advertising emerging both as a form of persuasive communication, bought and paid for by the advertiser, and later as an economic engine with the potential to support the media enterprise financially.

THE RISE OF THE ADVERTISING PROFESSION

The business relationships between advertisers and media evolved as mass production expanded from local to regional to national markets and as the number and scope of advertising-supported publications expanded. The complexity of the then-new print media gave rise to a profession of "go-betweens," the predecessors of today's advertising professionals.

The earliest advertising professionals were essentially advertising agents, who wholesaled advertising space on behalf of publishers. The best-known advertising agent from

The Granger Collection, NY

EARLY PRINT ADVERTISING This ad for Cook's Virginia tobacco appeared around 1720. It is an early example of enhancing print ads with illustrations.

this era was Volney B. Palmer, who started in the advertising business in 1842 and coined the term *advertising agency* in 1849. Palmer represented some 1,300 newspapers and originated the commission system, under which publishers paid a fee on completion of an advertising sale. Palmer also offered a wider range of services than other agents. He not only sold advertising space but also produced the ads, delivered them to the publishers, and verified their placement—all important functions of advertising agencies today.

In 1865, George P. Rowell, considered to be the founder of the advertising agency as we know it today, began contracting with local newspapers for a set amount of space and then brokered the space to clients. This arrangement made Rowell something of an independent "middleperson" who had to cater to both publishers and advertising clients. Rowell advised his clients on which newspapers to select for their needs.

Political propaganda also played an important role in the evolution of modern advertising. During World War I, advertising found its voice directed away from the materialistic needs of the average citizen and toward the good of the country as a whole. This campaign—in which Albert Lasker, an advertising pioneer and managerial genius, played an important role—included activities designed to build public sentiment for the war effort as well as appeals to the homefront to curtail unnecessary consumption and to "buy war bonds" instead. The success of the war bond drives convinced many of the power of advertising.

ADVERTISING GOES TO WAR During World War I, advertising turned from promoting consumption of goods to getting citizens involved in the war effort by buying war bonds. After the war, ad agencies applied techniques perfected during the war to mass market consumer goods.

THE RISE OF BROADCAST ADVERTISERS

Radio, the new technology of the early twentieth century, came of age as an advertising medium in 1926 when RCA purchased a chain of radio stations from AT&T, including WEAF in New Jersey, and established the National Broadcasting Company (NBC). The Columbia Broadcasting System (CBS) soon followed. The creation of the radio networks gave national advertisers an unprecedented means of distributing messages to prospects across the nation simultaneously (Fox, 1984). The new medium was designed to bring news, information, and entertainment to the public at large and depended exclusively on revenues received from advertisers (see Chapter 6).

Radio had two important limitations: it could not show pictures of the products and did not lend itself to detailed product descriptions. That created an opportunity for the growth of magazine advertising between the two world wars, a period that saw the birth and growth of mass-circulation magazines like *Time* and *Life*.

The years following World War II saw the explosive expansion of television as a new advertising medium, especially after the establishment of national television networks in 1948. Television quickly grew to compete with other forms of mass communication as the key creative medium for national advertisers. The combination of sight and sound gave advertisers the ability to demonstrate products to millions of viewers in a dramatic way.

HARD SELL VS. SOFT SELL

The story of advertising is also the story of innovation with new advertising forms. At the turn of the nineteenth century, advertising copy was usually brief and hyperbolic, and most ads sought a direct, mail-in response from the reader. New approaches were needed to rise above the clutter of screechy direct-response ads. A defining moment in advertising occurred in 1905 when John E. Kennedy, a copywriter working in partnership with Albert Lasker at the Lord & Thomas advertising agency in New York, redefined advertising as "salesmanship in print." This *hard-sell* approach to advertising as a mediated sales tool used persuasive techniques and introduced the "reason why" philosophy to copy preparation (Wells, Burnett, & Moriarty, 1995). Ads turned into lengthy arguments on behalf of the advertiser that were expected to prompt a delayed response that kicked in the next time the reader visited the store. The hard sell lent itself to print media and so declined as radio and TV became popular.

The *soft-sell* approach was pioneered at about the same time by Stanley Resor and his copywriter Helen Lansdowne at the J. Walter Thompson agency. Their approach took advantage of the newfound ability to print photographs and color illustrations (as opposed to labor-intensive hand engravings) of products. That made it possible to feature enticing and entertaining images of the product. This approach tended toward an emotional rather than a rational appeal. The soft-sell approach became so prevalent by the 1980s that this period is often referred to as the **era of creativity**. Advertising continues to be as much about entertainment as it is about marketing as can be seen in *Life's Too Short for the Wrong Job* ads that promote the German company Jobsintown.de.

> In the **era of creativity** advertisers emphasized entertainment as well as information.

SOFT SELL iPod ads like this one stress the excitement of using the product rather than rational arguments for buying it. A hard sell approach would list the specifications and price of the device and present verbal arguments for making the purchase.

THE ERA OF INTEGRATED MARKETING COMMUNICATION (IMC)

Although traditional advertising has long been the most common form of marketing communication, it no longer dominates the way it once did. For example, the 30-second prime-time network television advertising spot, which was the ideal vehicle for reaching a national mass audience for nearly 50 years, is in deep decline in the eyes of advertisers. The broadcast television audience has been fragmented by cable TV and drawn away by the Internet and video games while viewers freely skip ads with digital video recorders (DVRs) such as TiVo. This has led to a new television advertising form—or rather a return to one that was prevalent in the late 40s and early 1950s (see Chapter 8)—in which products are featured, or "placed," in the entertainment portion of the program. For example, during an episode of *Glee* Matthew Morrison makes a comment about first class American Airlines tickets. When programs are produced in this manner, featured companies share the costs of making the program and they agree to purchase advertising. These programs are likely to continue proliferating as two-thirds of audiences tests do not perceive of the programs as ads.

Today, advertisers choose from a wide array of media—from ads delivered to smartphones to movie trailers on DVDs. This situation has created a phenomenon known as **integrated marketing communication (IMC)**, which encourages the use of virtually all communication channels available to the advertiser. For example, in recent years the ready-to-eat cereal industry has done more **sales promotion** (coupons, sweepstakes, sampling, and so on) than advertising. In the era of IMC, traditional media are not the only options, and the media used ultimately depend on the needs of the advertiser. Today, companies do not restrict themselves to advertising but instead try to find that combination of advertising, direct marketing, public relations, and sales promotions that best achieves their goals (Elliott, 2001).

ADVERTISING NOW

What makes advertising more exciting than ever now is the proliferation of new advertising media. Technological innovations, from "ad servers" that call up personalized advertisements to blogs and to smartphone alerts of new products and special offers, have ushered in a new phase of Integrated Marketing Communication in which advertisers seek to communicate and engage with consumers on an individual and ongoing basis. The Internet also provides the first global communications medium for advertisers. In the next section we examine some of the technology trends that lend new sizzle to advertising, but there are two that stand above the rest: social media and the humble-looking sponsored links that appear at the top and sides of Google's search engine results.

Display ads appearing in social media are a fast-growing, multi-billion dollar business, with Facebook racking up revenues in 2011 that rival those of some broadcast television networks. Advertisers are also taking advantage of new ways to attract customers through social media that don't rely on the conventional ad agency model, such as the Pepsi Refresh campaign that generates online buzz by doling out $20 million in grants to charitable causes. Other social media campaigns rely on relatively low-cost promotional activities, such as creating fan pages in Facebook and organizing celebrity plugs in Twitter (Kim Kardashian gets $10,000 per tweet). Many local retailers find that they can get free advertising from "word of mouse" generated by

> **Integrated marketing communications (IMC)** assures that the use of all commercial media and messages is clear, consistent, and influential.
>
> **Sales promotions** are specific features like coupons that directly spur sales.

Table 11.1 2010 Worldwide Revenue For World's Top Five Largest Agency Companies.

ORGANIZATION	HEADQUARTERS	2010 WORLDWIDE REVENUE*
WPP Group	London	$14.4
Omnicom Group	New York	$12.5
Publicis Groupe	Paris	$7.2
Interpublic Group of Cos.	New York	$6.5
Dentsu	Tokyo	$3.6

Source: Advertising Age. Retrieved February 7, 2012, **http://adage.com/article/agency-news/agency-report-u-s-agency-revenue-jumped-7-7-2010/227162/**

*Dollars in billions.

STOP&REVIEW

1. How would you describe advertising as a form of communication?

2. What role did the Industrial Revolution play in ushering in the era of modern advertising?

3. Which advertising techniques were influenced by war propaganda?

4. How does Colonial advertising of the late 1700s differ from advertising today?

5. What has been the effect of integrated marketing communication (IMC)?

6. What are some current advertising innovations?

consumers in online chatrooms. Groupon and Living Social deliver coupons to groups of customers who are driven by social media interactions to sign up for deals with local retailers.

Sponsored links helped Google become the number one advertising vehicle back in 2006 and to propel the entire online advertising industry to double-digit annual growth at the expense of the Big Five traditional advertising media, notably network radio and local television. Behind the sponsored links is a revolution in the way that advertising is bought, sold, and evaluated: advertisers bid against one another in an auction for prime locations near the top of the results, paying anywhere from a few pennies to over $100 per click for their favorite search words. Search-based ads are changing the way that advertisers think about advertising and their ad agencies by making it possible to precisely target ads to consumers who are actively engaged in seeking information about products they might like to buy. Leading global ad agencies (see Table 11.1) have had to add disciplines like *search engine optimization*, the art of getting their clients' websites near the top of Google's search results, to their skill sets. Search ads also give advertisers the ability to precisely measure response to their ads though the analytic data that Google provides them. Here is a quote often attributed to department store magnate John Wannamaker, one of the "fathers" of advertising, "Half the money I spend on advertising is wasted; the trouble is I don't know which half." If he were alive today he could tell which half that was.

TECHNOLOGY: NEW ADVERTISING MEDIA

The technology of advertising has developed side by side with the technology of the mass media. We will not recount these developments here since they are covered in Chapters 3 through 9, but will instead focus on the ways in which information technologies are starting to transform conventional advertising forms.

ADVERTISING IN CYBERSPACE

No development in the last decade has drawn more headline news in the advertising industry than the Internet. New technologies have made possible a high-definition media and marketing ecosystems, which combine to form an environment in which consumers are continually approached both online and in the real world. The banner ads that initially attracted the attention of advertisers to the Internet took advantage of the basic hypertext linking capability of the Internet (see Chapter 9). By clicking on the narrow horizontal *banner* that appeared across the top of the page consumers were immediately connected to the website of the advertiser, where they could find more information, tempting product images, and, in some cases, the advertiser's own e-commerce site at which they could complete a sale.

MEDIA&CULTURE

THE POWER OF THE FEW: HOW COLLEGE STUDENTS RULE THE MARKETPLACE

The 18- to 24-year-old college student crowd is "advertisers' favorite consumer base." They set trends. For example, in 2007 one of their most anticipated new products was the Apple iPhone. They have discretionary income, both theirs and their parents. Although this group is one of the smallest U.S. demographics, 18 million compared with the 80 million Baby Boomers, they are vastly influential. Their favorite books are *Harry Potter* and *The DaVinci Code*; their favorite magazines are *Cosmopolitan* and *People*; and their favorite television programs are *Grey's Anatomy* and *The Office*.

Nonetheless, until recently college students were significantly overlooked by the advertising industry: they were not included in television ratings studies. Nielsen Media Research has added college students to their TV samples, so programs that appeal to the college crowd, including daytime soap operas, will get a ratings boost.

However, as the **click-through rates** for banner ads plummeted, advertisers found that the hidden gold of the Internet was buried deeper, in the internetwork protocol (IP), which tells website owners the Internet addresses of visitors and also where they surfed from and where they go next. Together with the cookies and Web bugs (see Chapter 9) that websites use to track their visitors, this gave advertisers an unprecedented ability to identify and probe the media and consumption habits of individual consumers on a massive scale.

Advertisers can now reach consumers efficiently through a system of online ad networks, also known as *ad servers*, such as Atlas Solutions and DoubleClick, purchased by Google. They partner with thousands of websites to display Internet ads that reach millions of users collectively, but that also target each individual user. By collating information from IP addresses, cookies, and Web bugs, the DoubleClick program can identify website visitors who are likely prospects for buying a new car; for example, Web users who divulged their age (say, 21) and annual incomes ($35,000) when they registered at a website and who recently read a new-car review in the *New York Times*. Ad servers collate the demographic information (deposited in a cookie on the user's hard drive that can be opened and read by the ad server) with the surfing patterns collected by the *Times*. The next time the user opens the *Times* home page, he or she might see an ad for a new Honda Civic inserted in the home page, whereas prospective sofa buyers will see an ad for furniture. The ad servers are also responsible for many of the pop-up ads that we find annoying when they open on top of (or underneath) a Web page we are trying to reach. As of 2011, the top five most visited sites on the Web were:facebook.com; youtube.com; yahoo.com; live.com; and msn.com.

Google's sponsored links show advertisements that are specific to the keywords typed into its search engine. If you subscribe to Google's Gmail service you may also see sponsored links appear next to the e-mail messages, like the one Mom sends explaining that she can't send you money because she ran

> **Click-through rate** is the percentage of readers who click on the ad to visit the advertiser's page.

out of checks. Google analyzes keywords in the e-mail so that you might, in this fictitious example, see a sponsored link to a money-wiring service that accepts credit cards. Similarly, Google analyzes the discussions of participating blogs, posts relevant advertisements in them, and shares the revenues with the bloggers. For example, a forum about college football might attract a beer advertisement. Some blogs have been extremely successful in generating advertising revenue. TechCrunch, a blog about Internet start-ups, boasts 12 million unique visitors and 37 million page views monthly. The blog generates more than $200,000 monthly from ad revenue.

Advertisements are popping up everywhere in cyberspace. The Internet Advertising Bureau introduced new size options so that Internet ads now fill more of the Web page and may appear in the middle of pages instead of at the top and bottom margins. Animated ads play audio and video clips or feature graphics that sometimes literally leap across the page. *Intermercials* (ads appearing before the ISP connects to the Internet) and *buttons* (miniature banner ads) are other recent developments. Floaters are similar to pop-ups, but they use Flash animations (see Chapter 9) and are immune to the pop-up blockers many Internet users have to evade pop-up ads. Ads also appear in RSS (Really Simple Syndication) feeds, text messages that crawl at the bottom of popular websites with updates of the latest news, weather, and sports.

Another form of advertising at which the Internet excels is **viral marketing**. The advertisers' strategy is to stimulate brand-related discussion and hope that others will carry it on, spreading word of the product like a virus to new customers. For example, Blendtec, a blender company, asks: Will it Blend? To demonstrate the power of their blenders, the company blends unusual items, for example, a soft air gun, golf balls, marbles, or an iPhone. Their YouTube clip demonstration that featured blending an iPhone attracted approximately six million viewers and increased sales about 800 percent.

SOCIAL NETWORKING SITES: ADVERTISERS' NEW FRONTIER

On Facebook and Google+, users develop pages about themselves, post pictures, and create discussions (see Chapter 9). Because Facebook users provide demographic information, such as age, sex, geographic location, and religion, the social networking site is an advertiser's dream. Facebook is described as a "Net within the Net" because it allows advertisers to reach their target audiences with precision. In 2011, Facebook boasted 500 million users or one in every 13 people on earth, with over half of them logging in every day. The 35-years-of-age and older group continues to grow rapidly, now 30 percent of the user base; however, the 18–24 year-old-segment is growing the fastest, 74% year on year.

Attempting to capitalize on advertising opportunities, Twitter allows a group of celebrities, bloggers, and regular Internet users to send advertisers' commercial messages to their personal contact. Ad.ly is the social-media advertorial clearinghouse company most celebrities use to get paid to Tweet. YouTube, a video-sharing website and a subsidiary of Google, although extremely popular, has not become the phenomenal advertising revenue generator envisioned by Google. The website places advertisements with and around partner videos and splits the revenues with the creators. The website definitely

With **viral marketing** ideas are spread about products through chat rooms, blogs, social networking sites, or other Internet-based avenues.

generates revenue; however, costs outpace earnings. For example, YouTube was projected to earn $1.7 billion in 2012 but only made $1.1 billion in 2012 with its partners.

Facebook Ads were introduced in 2007, providing advertisers with a means to use targeted ads to connect with users, which is particularly important when one considers that a vast number of individuals who use social networking media no longer engage with traditional media. Facebook Ads has been labeled "a new way of advertising" by presenting ads to users based on their "profiles, social connections and their friends' recent activities" (Morrissey, 2007). Facebook also makes it easy for small-time advertisers to make and place their own targeted ads. Not to be left behind, MySpace announced its development of an "influencer" option that pinpoints users who have "large, active friend networks and interests in specific categories, such as music." Bono and Bobby Shriver's (Product)RED initiative, which encourages private companies to raise awareness and donations for The Global Fund for the purpose of combating AIDS in Africa, has done an excellent job of tapping social media to further their cause.

In 2011, Facebook introduced a series of new metrics that provide advertisers a word-of-mouth dashboard, "People Are Talking About This." The dashboard counts the number of people who have liked a page, shared a post, or taken some action involving the brand in the past week. Advertisers can see both potential and actual reach.

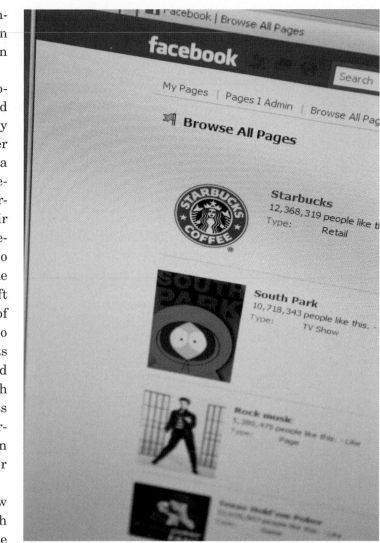

SOCIAL MEDIA ADVERTISING Companies like Starbucks have embraced social networking sites like Facebook, where they can freely invite users to become "fans," and the information gets published on their pages. When an advertisement shows up on a page, it will also indicate which of your friends are "fans."

THEY HAVE OUR NUMBER

The Internet is only one aspect of information technology that creates new ways of building relationships between consumers and brands. **Database marketing** makes this possible on a grand scale. One need not look further than a local grocery store for a starting point of database marketing. When we apply for discount cards or check-cashing privileges, we customers fill out a questionnaire giving personal information (address, occupation, income, product preferences, and so on) that is stored in a database along with a record of our purchases. The information is aggregated into national databases and then sold to advertisers, who in turn store the information in their databases and match it to personally identifiable data generated by their consumer "hot lines" and websites. If a consumer regularly buys chocolate chip cookies but does not purchase the cookies during a grocery shopping trip, the checkout counter transaction might generate a coupon for the cookies.

Database marketing is used when advertisers store information about consumers so that they can personalize messages.

Database marketing relies on a process known as *data mining,* or the on-going compilation and analysis of pertinent data for the purpose of updating marketing strategies as consumer needs evolve. Data mining enables much more targeted advertising, perhaps individual targeting, based on the compilation of information such as purchasing habits, online reading preferences, subscription information, product registration information, online movements across pages or click patterns, and personal credit histories.

Lands' End, Inc., which sells clothing and related merchandise via catalogs, has a highly developed database system in place. Customers create a 3-D model of themselves by providing critical measurements so they can "try on" items to see how they will look. When an order is phoned in, the operator is able to "call up" the individual from the database by using a variation of the Caller ID feature found on consumer telephones.

E-COMMERCE

At e-commerce websites you can find comparative product and pricing information, ask questions, read reviews from other consumers, and even complete your purchases. It is both an impulse and a directional technology. The impulse potential arises from when you are surfing the Net and decide to respond to a commercial message on a whim. For example, a reader of a book review in the online version of the *New York Times* may impulsively decide to click on the Barnes and Noble ad to order a copy. The Net becomes a directional medium when consumers decide to purchase a particular product and then go to a company's website to do so.

Some e-commerce proprietors still rely heavily on spam, or unsolicited commercial e-mail, to direct traffic to their sites. Spammers, as they are known, automatically "harvest" e-mail addresses by the millions from unsuspecting consumers who frequent chat rooms or discussion groups or post them on their personal Web pages. The more aggressive spammers send their messages through multiple servers, or disguise their true origins to defeat filtering by consumers' own e-mail programs. However, these actions are illegal under the **CANSPAM Law** (see Chapter 15). Nonetheless, spamming survives, often including Web bugs (see Chapter 9) in the e-mails that automatically notify the sender if the message has been opened. Spammers use eye-tracking technology to identify the "hot zones" of messages that people actually read so they can perfect their messages. Legitimate spammers (yes, they do exist) use *permission marketing techniques* in which the consumer consents to receive e-mail when registering at a website or activating a product warranty. In contrast, illegitimate spammers send their messages from countries that don't have anti-spam laws. Spam persists because it is free to send, so that a response rate of a few one hundredths of 1 percent—"male enhancement" spam for men and fashion spam for women are among the most effective—are enough to make spamming profitable.

> **CANSPAM Law** regulates commercial e-mail.

SMARTPHONE ADVERTISING

Smartphone ads are currently making a significant splash in the advertising world. Google owns AdMob, a leader in advertising on smartphone platforms such as Apple's iPhone and Google's Android. Like DoubleClick (also owned by

Google), AdMob is an ad server that inserts ads in Web pages and apps seen on smartphones that stimulate "click through" to the advertiser's website. In 2011 AT&T introduced a new service called ShopAlerts that notifies smartphone users when they are near participating retailers and provides them with information about special offers and downloads coupons to their phones. These two providers are examples of differing strategies for mobile advertising: AdMob clients try to pull customers into their websites and stores through conventional display and banner advertisements, whereas the AT&T model pushes geo-targeted ads to the individual consumer. ShopAlerts follows an "opt in" model in which consumers give permission to receive the location-based ads but in so doing provide demographic information that helps advertisers to further target their pitches. In both cases, the result is highly targeted and measurable advertising that helps advertisers determine the cost effectiveness of their investments. Foursquare lures smartphone users with the ability to locate their Facebook friends and Twitter followers in the real world while generating awareness of special offers from local merchants and national brands connected to the places where their social media relations "check in." Ads delivered via the Internet to personal computers have similar capabilities but smartphone ads achieve much higher response rates, at least while the novelty lasts. Advertisers are able to reach consumers through their smartphones and their tablet computers both of which appear to be inseparable appendages for most of their owners.

Bar codes are another fast-growing facet of mobile advertising. Smartphone apps use the devices' built-in cameras to scan barcodes to automatically display product information, download electronic coupons, show videos, or dial a phone number without having to type or search for information. One application of the technology makes conventional print ads interactive by printing small blocks of black and white squares called a QR (Quick Response) code next to each featured item. They can also be embedded in outdoor billboards and in-store advertising displays to make them into interactive, location-based advertising tools. Ralph Lauren uses mobile apps and a mobile website to bridge online commerce with in-store experiences.

MORE NEW ADVERTISING

Other new technologies offer alternatives to conventional broadcast media. Satellite radio is also extending the reach of advertisers—and cutting into the ad revenues of conventional national radio networks that link terrestrial stations. Consumers also listen to advertising-supported radio on the Internet and download videos of popular TV programs like *The Office* for their iPods, with the ads targeted to the trendy young iPod users included. Television advertisers are experimenting with two-way systems to make interactive ads to compete with Google's search term ads. For example, viewers of a Mercedes TV spot can use their satellite TV remote to "click through" to a website where they can schedule a test-drive.

The oldest form of advertising, the outdoor sign, is also undergoing a high-tech makeover. Digital imaging technology imposes signage onto stadium and arena walls that does not exist outside of the television screen, the same basic technique that superimposes a visible first-down line on the screen for football fans. These virtual ads reach large audiences and can be changed quickly and efficiently. Other developments in the outdoor industry include application of electronic message boards, which enable the placement of billboard-like ads in malls and other indoor venues. Tri-face or revolving signs give more advertisers the chance to promote themselves in sports arenas. For example, the sign next to the basketball floor at a major arena revolves to reveal a new advertiser every few minutes or so. Recent advancements have also made it possible to tailor ads to the tastes of individuals standing in front of a given billboard. Quividi, an automated audience measurement company, mounts tiny cameras to billboards. A simple video sensor enables the company to count actual viewers standing in front of a billboard, measure attention and dwell time, and the age distribution of the audience. Based on information transmitted to a central database ads are tailored for the individuals passing by a given billboard.

Digital video recorders (DVRs) are another technology forcing new approaches for advertisers. Their ability to circumvent commercials has led to a revival of forms of product placement not seen since the 1950s, in which products are written into the program's script. Oprah Winfrey, for example, gave away 276 Pontiac G6s to her studio audience during the normal course of the show. However, that also is really nothing new, but a throwback to the time in the 1950s when most TV shows had a single sponsor and were liberally sprinkled with "plugs" for the sponsors' products. Product placements are also going high tech. The same technology that makes it possible to project ads onto sports arena billboards during telecasts also makes it possible to project images onto dummy boxes of cereals posing on the breakfast tables in family sitcoms. Some day your DVR might insert ads customized for the viewers: boxes of Grape Nuts for seniors, Cocoa Puffs for young families. The point is, if people aren't watching the commercials, the advertising must appear where they are watching.

The same logic drives advertising in entertainment venues. Many moviegoers object to seeing commercials after they have paid $10 or more for admission, to the point that some municipalities have outlawed them. Still, theater advertising has expanded from conventional preshow trailers for upcoming new releases, to commercials only slightly modified from their original television forms, to "talking" popcorn bags and advertiser-sponsored text messaging. Some live theatrical performances now also come with equally live commercials.

New digital technologies make ads pop up in unexpected places. A program called fusion.runtime, developed by Double Fusion, an in-game advertising network, allows advertisers to place products in games late in the development cycle making it possible, for example, to place an advertisement for Pepsi in a game. The cost of computer chips that can synthesize the human voice is dropping quickly, raising the specter of the "talking cereal box" shouting advertising slogans at us as we walk down the supermarket aisle or reminding us (or our smartphone) to stock up when the box is half empty.

DVRs are also pushing an audience measurement innovation long desired by advertisers: TV ratings for commercials rather than television shows. Traditionally, the Nielsen ratings provided ratings only for 15-minute segments, and advertisers were forced to assume that those equated with the size of the audience delivered to the commercials running in those segments. However, high-tech commercial skipping has made a mockery of that assumption. Nielsen collects viewer data in 2.5-second measurement intervals for its electronic meter systems, which make it possible to track the viewership of individual commercials—and record when viewers leave the television viewing room for the bathroom. Nielsen also plans to go to automatic measurement in all of the nation's local TV markets over the next few years, replacing inaccurate paper diaries with wireless television set meters and personal meters that viewers will carry with them outside the home (see Chapter 8).

Advertising knows no limits. Our smartphones, video games, Kindles, iPods and favorite TV programs are all fair game for advertisers. Geo-targeted ads can reach us anywhere and if we turn them off we still may encounter ads in supermarket check out lines, doctors' office waiting rooms, and the back seats of taxi cabs. But not all new advertising media are high tech. In 2006, CBS television advertised its new fall line-up by printing ads on 48 million eggs!

STOP&REVIEW

1. What is database marketing, and how is it changing advertising today?
2. How might new technologies affect the practice of advertising in the future?
3. What is permission marketing?
4. Why is data mining so important in advertising?
5. What is a product placement?

INDUSTRY: INSIDE THE ADVERTISING INDUSTRY

Someone must identify the need for an advertising message—and foot the bill for the campaign that results. This initiator is the advertiser. Then the message must be created. Here the responsibility may either be retained by the advertiser or be subcontracted to an advertising agency. Next, the message must be placed in one or more of the **advertising media**, each of which has its own organizational form and structure. **Research organizations** then help all concerned evaluate and measure the target group, the message content, and the media vehicles under consideration. You can follow the development of an advertising campaign from the moment of its conception by an advertiser to its presentation to the public by examining Figure 11.1.

What makes the advertising industry so exciting is the dramatic interactions among these players and the competition between ad agencies and media outlets. The agency's creative staff may work for months on a concept for a new advertising campaign, only to have it shot down in a client meeting. Advertisers periodically fire agencies, even those who have been with them for decades, when their ad campaigns no longer produce the desired level of sales. Then competitions are held among agencies, sometimes ending in a "shoot-out" in which finished commercials are pitted against one another. Increasingly, advertisers and their agencies make dramatic changes in their purchases of advertising time based on audience trends revealed by media researchers, such as moving spending away from local TV and toward the Internet and mobile. Market research periodically chimes in with findings that seem to shout "This changes everything!" and force advertisers and agencies to rethink their approach.

Advertising media are the communication channels that carry messages to consumers.

Research organizations compile statistics about consumers and their media habits and evaluate advertising messages.

ADVERTISERS

The top categories of advertising expenditures are retail, telecommunications, automotive, financial services, and medicine and remedies. It is projected that in 2011, $157.4 billion were spent on advertising in the United States. Leading

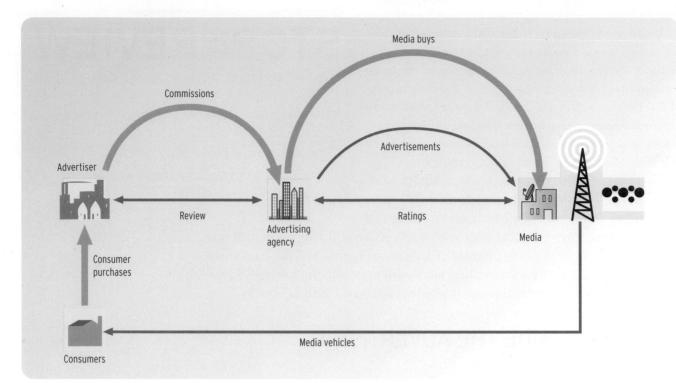

FIGURE 11.1 HOW ADVERTISING WORKS Advertisers pay commissions to agencies to create ads, and then review their work. Advertising agencies buy time on media and place ads according to ratings data. The media reach the public with the ad, and they buy the advertisers' product (or not). Consumer purchases resulting from the ads finance the next round of ad buys.

national companies such as Procter & Gamble and AT&T lead the list of major advertisers (Table 11.2).

All dimensions of a product that give it value, both tangible and intangible, constitute the **brand** of that product. Although the product may be something physical, such as salad dressing, the brand, "Newman's Own" for example, evokes loyalties and affiliations among certain consumers that cannot be explained simply by knowing the product's ingredients. How the advertising industry is structured and organized, then, centers around the goal of communicating the brand as clearly as possible to consumers.

In the past, it was not unusual to find a company's chief executive officer involved in decision-making about how to advertise the brand. This is less common in today's age of product segmentation. To cope with the myriad duties involved in getting a brand to market, companies typically assign the advertising, budgeting, and execution responsibilities to a *marketing manager* in charge of a family of brands, who in turn delegates the advertising duties for a specific family of products to a *brand manager*. Although the brand manager normally handles the day-to-day advertising operation, ultimate approval of the advertising budget is typically handed down from the marketing manager level or higher.

In a large company that sells a product for a national audience, the advertising process begins when the marketing manager calls for a meeting with the advertising

> A **brand** consists of all the dimensions that identify and give unique value to a product or company.

Table 11.2 Top Four Advertisers

ADVERTISER	REVENUE (IN MILLIONS)
PROCTER & GAMBLE CO.	$1,382.8
AT&T	$1,129.5
GENERAL MOTORS CORP.	$ 924.6
COMCAST CORP.	$ 884.5

NOTE: *All figures for first half of 2011.*

Source: *kantar media.* Press information. Retrieved February 7, 2012, from **http://kantarmediana.com/insight-center/news/ us-advertising-expenditures-increased-32-first-half-2011**

manager of the firm to discuss advertising goals, deadlines, and expectations for the coming year. The creation of the advertising message is generally not performed by the company itself but instead is delegated to an advertising agency (see Figure 11.1). An advertising agency can provide an outside, objective perspective that companies can't get internally. The advertising manager invites a number of agencies to make presentations and, when one is selected, acts as a liaison between the firm and the agency.

For a local retailer, the process is much simpler. Typically, the owner determines approximately how much to spend on advertising in the coming year, writes the ads, and arranges to have them placed in local newspapers, on local websites, or in other local media. This is not to say, however, that the selection of the target for the ad or the development of the message is any less important. It is just that the process unfolds on a somewhat lesser scale than in a national program.

Local retailers also take advantage of *co-op advertising support* from national companies. For example, a retail store that buys a product such as Colgate toothpaste gets an allowance for advertising from the Colgate-Palmolive Company. Ready-made print ads are also provided for the retailer to use. In other words, a good share of local advertising is actually paid for by national advertisers.

Although the positions of brand manager and advertising manager remain important in most companies, there is a growing necessity for all marketing employees to know something about advertising. As business consultant Regis McKenna puts it, "Marketing is becoming an integrated part of the whole organization, rather than a specific function" (Kuchinskas, 2000, p. 136). For this reason, in some companies the vice president of marketing is often a person skilled in *marketing communication,* as are the marketing managers and brand managers.

INSIDE THE ADVERTISING AGENCY

Most major companies do not want to plan and produce advertising campaigns themselves. Their business is to produce and sell a product, be it tennis shoes, soft drinks, or dog food. Therefore, a variety of advertising agencies have grown up at local, national, and international levels to plan and produce ad campaigns for them.

Agencies are organizations of businesspeople and talented individuals who create and place **advertising plans** (see Table 11.3) for their clients. Today, full-service agencies complete virtually all elements of an advertising campaign including research, strategic planning, and generation of creative ideas for ads.

The **advertising plan** is a written document outlining the objectives and strategies for a product's advertising.

Examples of major full-service advertising agencies include Ogilvy & Mather (now a subsidiary of the WPP Group), which produced many memorable campaigns and slogans, such as "At 60 miles an hour, the loudest noise in this new Rolls-Royce comes from the electric clock." These companies employ **account executives**, who act as liaisons between the agency and the client. They mobilize and coordinate all of the agency's work on the advertising campaign and are one of the entry points for careers in advertising (see Your Media Career on next page).

Account executives are the liaisons between the agency and the client.

Table 11.3 Elements of an Advertising Plan

ELEMENT	PURPOSE
Situation analysis	Explains where the company is, how it got there, and where it wants to be in the future. It identifies relevant problems that must be addressed by advertising and gives a detailed description of the consumer and the product.
Objectives	The goals we want the advertising campaign to achieve. Most advertising plans include both business objectives ("Increase unit sales by 25,000 during the next year") and communication objectives ("Achieve 65 percent awareness of the product within the target market"). Objectives differ according to the nature of the product, competition, consumer demand, and available budget.
Target market profile	A description of those individuals most likely to purchase the product. The target profile usually includes demographics (the target's age, sex, ethnicity, and income) and psychographics. Psychographics are lifestyle descriptions of the consumer's attitudes, interests, and opinions.
Positioning statement	A short paragraph explaining how the company wants the consumer to perceive the product. Much can be communicated (price, quality, convenience), but what is the most important thing the advertising has to convey? A recent campaign for Southwest Airlines positions the product as a friendly airline whose discounted fares offer "freedom to move about the country." The advertising is light and humorous and consistently conveys this theme.
Creative strategy	Describes the specific theme and approach of the advertising. In other words, the creative strategy is a description of what the advertising will actually look like. In national campaigns, the strategy contains a big idea or a fresh and interesting way to make a point about the product. The big idea for Little Caesar's Pizza is an animated Caesar character in a Roman toga who utters, "Pizza, Pizza!" in all ads to communicate that you always get two pizzas for the right price.
Media plan	Lists the communication vehicles that will carry the advertising. Should television be used? Why or why not? If Internet advertising is rejected, why? A good media plan ensures that a sufficient target audience is reached at an efficient price.

——YOUR MEDIA CAREER

BECOMING A MADPERSON

The popular TV series *Mad Men* offers an inside view of the advertising world of the 1960s that is still somewhat relevant today. Agencies still make high-stakes pitches to advertisers and compete for their business. Creatives still work through the night to come up with just the right slant for a new campaign. Researchers still sometimes inspire the creative process and at other times smother it. Although the large firms have gotten even larger and more globalized, there are still many smaller agencies like the one we see in *Mad Men*. Other things have changed: Smoking, boozing, and philandering in the office are no longer acceptable. Women and minorities play a much more prominent role in all aspects of the industry than they did back then, digital production techniques and social media have been added to the marketing mix that agencies manage for their clients.

For the purpose of analyzing career opportunities the Bureau of Labor Statistics (BLS, 2011) combines advertising with public relations (see also chapter 10). There are over 460,000 people employed in the industry and most jobs require a college education. The exception is in the creative department, where a two-year design degree is an option. As it was in the days of the *Mad men* on TV, advertising is a glamorous industry and so there is keen competition at the entry level. Account management and media buying are common points of entry and an internship is a definite plus.

Employment growth in the industry over the next decade is projected to be a little bit less than the average across the entire economy. The prospect of further regulation of alcohol, tobacco, and food advertising adds uncertainty to the prospects. Layoffs are common in response to downturns in the overall market for advertising and the loss of major accounts by individual agencies. The fastest growing areas of the field are projected to be market research, advertising sales (including media buyers), graphic design, and writing.

Agencies are experiencing considerable change stimulated by both new technology and the trend toward efficiency. A decade ago, agencies handled advertising in traditional media such as newspapers, magazines, television, and radio. Today, clients insist that they have expertise in direct marketing, online advertising, sales promotion, and public relations. Here are the major departments within a typical ad agency:

The Creative Department. A key element in the advertising plan is the creative strategy, or what the advertising will say in order to achieve the objectives of the campaign. Using the research data as a foundation, copywriters and graphic designers in the creative department begin work on a creative concept or "big idea." *Concepting* is the act of saying something in a unique way but at the same time ensuring that the message is "on strategy" with what needs to be communicated for the product to sell. A classic example is the campaign for Energizer Batteries featuring the battery-powered Bunny, whose power supply is so much better than competing brands that the toy seems to work endlessly. The creative concept is to show what appears to be a normal commercial for another product, and then the mechanical bunny rolls across the screen, interrupting the ad in an unexpected and humorous way. This campaign is a classic example of concepting in that it is both attention-getting and informative in terms of a unique product feature. More recent examples of great concepts include Capital One's "What's in your wallet?" campaign as well as the "priceless" ads by MasterCard.

A variety of creative professionals may be involved in the ad's execution: writers, artists, art directors, musicians, graphic designers, content or subject experts, and researchers. What emerges after a period of creative incubation is not a single clear-cut solution to all of the client's problems, but rather several executions, one of which will be able to survive the critical client review process. Once an execution gets approval from the client, the assignment is given back to the creative department for final production.

The Media Department. Meanwhile, the agency's **media department** is hard at work selecting media to carry the client's message, given the budget available. The account executive works constantly to keep all parties up to

LOW TO MIDDLE TAR As defined by H.M. Government.
EVERY PACKET CARRIES A GOVERNMENT HEALTH WARNING.

CREATIVE CONCEPT Memorable images like this classic ad for Marlboro cigarettes engage the audience. Successful ads help consumers remember the brand names but also may affect consumption behavior among vulnerable audiences, such as children.

[**Media departments**
negotiate on behalf of the advertiser to buy space from media companies.]

date on one another's progress. After the client and the media buyer approve creative and media recommendations, a specialist within the media department initiates negotiations with media suppliers for the purchase of specific media vehicles to carry the advertising message. In some agencies, the staff not only place the ads but also write them in the style needed by the media. It used to be that the media department dealt only with traditional media (for example, television, radio, newspapers, magazines, and billboards). Today, however, ads are placed in a wide range of nontraditional media as well, from ads stamped on fresh eggs to messages delivered through a smartphone based on a potential consumer's current location. New technologies are forcing media departments to consider new options, especially on the Internet. Another trend is better communication between the media and creative departments. The best media placements occur when media buyers understand the overall strategy and creative concept.

ADVERTISING MEDIA

The main economic base of many American media is advertising. For commercial radio and television stations, it is by far their most important source of revenue, whereas newspapers and magazines depend on a combination of newsstand sales, subscriptions, and advertising. In selecting media, advertisers consider whom they want to reach, what kind of message or information they want to communicate, and the costs of various media.

Advertisers try to reach the largest number of people in the target audience at the lowest possible price. The costs of various media depend on several factors: the size of the audience, the composition of the audience (age, wealth, education, and so on), and the prestige of the medium. In general, media with larger audiences can charge more for accepting and carrying advertisements. However, a smaller, more specifically focused audience can sometimes be even more valuable to an advertiser than a larger, more heterogeneous one. Comparisons among vehicles are made on a cost per thousand impressions (CPM) basis—that is, on the basis of the cost of reaching a thousand members of the target audience for the ad. This efficiency comparison is determined by dividing the cost of each ad by the size of the audience it delivers, in thousands (see Chapter 8).

Magazines continue to generate massive advertising revenue. Paid circulation numbers determine how much magazines can charge for advertising. Three of the most popular magazines for the college group, *People*, *Sports Illustrated*, and *Cosmopolitan,* command a high premium for four-color full-page ads, $305,000 each in the case of *People*.

The general goal is to try to reach the largest number of people in the target audience for the lowest dollar investment (Martin & Coons, 1998a), but many other factors may also be considered, including the inherent characteristics of different media. Table 11.4 lists some of the strengths and weaknesses of various advertising media. The nature of the target audience also affects media selection. Often media advertisers want to reach a broad general audience. Some advertisers want to sell products, such as soap or soft drinks that might interest virtually everyone in a mass audience. Other advertisers might use a general-audience medium if it has a high impact on

Table 11.4 Strengths and Weaknesses of Advertising Media

MEDIUM	STRENGTHS	WEAKNESSES
Newspapers (printed)	Intense coverage Flexibility Prestige Dealer or advertiser coordination Permanent message	Short life Hasty reading Moderate to poor reproduction
Magazines	Market selectivity Long life High reproduction quality Prestige Extra services Permanent message	Inflexible to coverage/time Inflexible to copy changes Low overall market penetration Wide distribution
Television	Mass coverage High impact Flexibility Prestige	Fleeting message Commercial wearout Lack of selectivity High cost
Radio	Audience selectivity Immediacy Flexibility Mobility	Fragmentation Transient quality of listenership Limited sensory input Fleeting message
Internet	Cost-efficient Personal Interactive	Loss of privacy Computer required

a particular group they want to reach. For example, although a very broad audience watches prime-time network television, ads are often placed there for products aimed primarily at seniors, such as denture adhesive cream. Television may reach a larger proportion of older people than any other audience segment. An advertiser that wants to sell athletic shoes to teenagers will pick the television shows and radio stations that appeal selectively to teenagers.

RESEARCH

Many people have the misconception that advertising is extremely powerful, but many campaigns are ineffective and even successful ones typically produce increases in sales of only a few percent. Few ads can penetrate the clutter to the point that consumers can remember them the day after seeing them, let alone be motivated to leave their homes or use their Smartphone or iPad to make a purchase. That's where research comes in, to measure the effectiveness of advertisements and to evaluate their potential impact before expensive investments in advertising space are made.

The Nielsen Company

ARE YOU WATCHING? Nielsen Media Research compiles local and national television ratings via PeopleMeters like this one. Viewers in Nielsen homes are expected to press buttons on the meter to indicate when they leave or enter the room in which the TV is running.

Market researchers collect and analyze data about product sales and factors that affect consumer opinions about products. In the advertising agency, account executives depend on research analysts and account planners to provide in-depth consumer profiles and key information about the competition. In other words, they try to get into your head to obtain a deeper, more thorough understanding of what drives you to buy products, such as the latest Abercrombie t-shirt instead of an American Eagle.

Media research experts work for both the media industry and the media departments of the advertising agencies to give them information about patterns of exposure to the mass media. Nielsen Media Research, supplier of TV ratings, is the best-known name in this field (see Chapter 8). Media research encompasses:

- Ratings for radio and television broadcasts
- Tracking online behavior
- Circulation figures for magazines and newspapers
- Profiles of the users of consumer products
- Media usage habits
- Qualitative studies that gauge audience reactions to specific media vehicles
- Reports on annual advertising expenditure levels of the leading national brands
- Copy tests that evaluate the effectiveness of ads under development

Examples of research companies and the audience information they provide are listed in Table 11.5.

Audience measurement studies are sufficient to tell us whether the advertising message is being exposed to a target group and roughly what numbers are involved, but it does not provide insights into how or why the advertising communicates successfully. For this purpose, we need a second dimension of audience research, one that enables the advertiser to talk directly with the target group. Because this research focuses on individuals and what "drives" them, it is often referred to as *motivational research*. Examples of this form of audience research include focus groups and mall intercepts.

[**Copy testing** evaluates the effectiveness of advertisements.]

Another form of advertising-related research, **copy testing**, is used to assess the effectiveness of advertisements while they are still under development. For example, a test ad might be inserted in television programs in selected markets, and researchers might contact respondents by phone on the

Table 11.5 Research Services and the Audience Data They Provide

MEDIUM	COMPANY	AUDIENCE REPORT CONTENT
National television	Nielsen Media Research	Ratings for programs on the national TV networks
Local television	Nielsen Media Research	Ratings for programs broadcast by local TV stations
Internet	Nielsen/Netratings	Assesses online audiences
National radio	Arbitron	Ratings for network programs by national radio stations
Local radio	Arbitron	Ratings for stations broadcasting in the local market
Newspapers	Audit Bureau of Circulation	The number of newspaper copies sold
Magazines	Simmons/MRI Research	Ratings for the top magazines in the United States

day after it appears to determine whether they can recall seeing the ad. More sophisticated methods allow direct comparisons of ads by doing "split runs" of magazines in which alternative versions of the same ad are sent to different households. Cable television systems can also be used in this way to provide comparisons of alternative treatments for television commercials.

Advertisers and their agencies are beginning to abandon traditional forms of audience research that focus on representative samples of consumers in favor of databases containing information about actual consumption and media behavior. For example, log information from advertisers' websites can tell them where visitors came from and where they go after their visits and record their activity, including purchases, while on the website. When combined with demographic information obtained when the consumer registers at the site, these data provide a more reliable and valid picture of the effects of advertising than conventional research.

CONTENT: ADVERTISING'S FORMS OF PERSUASION

Advertising must communicate important information about products (such as price, features, channel of distribution, and the like), but it also requires a creative way of stating these facts that cuts through the clutter of competing advertisements and gets the attention of consumers. As shown in Figure 11.2, all messages have an informational dimension and an emotional dimension. Because advertising has to get the attention of audience members who are usually not interested in the message, how the message is conveyed is just as important as what is said. In this section we look at advertising as a form of communication in terms of both its style and its content.

MINING POP CULTURE

One way in which advertisers align themselves with consumers is through the art and entertainment of popular culture. By borrowing familiar symbols in the culture, advertisers promote consumer identification with the product. Busta Rhymes and P Diddy began an explosive trend of alcohol in rap song with the phrase "pass the Courvoisier." A recent "Do it eBay" theme was featured in ads with on-stage music and dancing comparable to elaborate contemporary Broadway theater productions. Ultimately, advertising turns out to be a reflection of social and cultural norms due to a tendency and the necessity to communicate in the language of the familiar.

CONSUMER-GENERATED CONTENT

The rush toward online video advertisements is a result of broadband penetration and consumer demand, which drives advertisers to produce them so as not to be left behind. As a result video ads, roll-open banner ads, and stand-alone video ads, designed to show and tell more about products are becoming commonplace. To stay ahead of the pack in providing high-quality video, some advertisers and marketers encourage consumers to shoot video that is then uploaded to their sites where material that has potential is pulled out and edited together with the materials created by professional staff.

Similarly, in an effort to continue innovative ways of connecting with consumers, some advertisers are getting help from the very people they attempt to attract by using consumer-generated content (CGC) as a source for advertising ideas. More specifically, Tribal DDB a South Africa based digitally centric global advertising agency produced the world's first ever user-generated 3-D projection mapping event for Wrigley's 5 Gum. Internet users were able to manipulate the live projections through their iPads in real time. This is an example of how interactivity can add an element of excitement to the user experience.

Labeled the first social media Super Bowl, the 2012 game generated 11.2 million social media comments on sites such as Facebook and Twitter. The going rate for a 30-second TV ad was $3.5 million; however, a social media ad that was widely remembered likely cost the advertiser, Doritos, a mere $20. The ad emerged as a winner in the snack food's "Crash the Super Bowl Contest."

RELATIONSHIP MARKETING

With **relationship marketing** consumers develop a strong preference for brand through one-to-one communication.

In **relationship marketing**, advertisers and consumers communicate one-to-one through personalized media such as the Internet, direct mail, or the telephone. Companies use databases to personalize messages, with an emphasis on talking with consumers and "growing" them rather than sending out the same message to everyone.

Credit card companies, such as American Express, often study the demographic characteristics and buying habits of each individual cardholder in order to identify specific products that fit specific lifestyles (such as life insurance, special hotel accommodations, luxury gift items, and the like). Relationship marketing is successful when brand loyalty is achieved. This is the goal of automobile dealers who create a relationship time line for each car purchased. For example, at the point of purchase, GM takes a photo of the proud owners with their new car. A week later, the owners are sent a calendar with the photo inset. About two weeks later, a phone call is made, asking about purchase satisfaction and about a month later, a survey is sent, also asking about satisfaction. Then, about three months after the initial purchase, a letter or e-mail is fired off reminding the new owner that it is time for a tune-up. As the car gets older, additional letters are sent, offering a wide variety of discount services, up to and including special offers on a new car purchase.

DIRECT MARKETING

Direct marketing is a form of advertising that requests an immediate consumer response.

Direct marketing differs from conventional advertising in that it concentrates the marketer's resources on the most likely prospects, rather than sending a message to a wide audience in the hope that at least some of the prospects will receive it. Direct marketing also has a quality of immediacy, because recipients of the message are asked to take direct action, such as placing an order over the phone or returning a printed order blank by mail. Although direct marketing messages do not have the same glitz as mass-media advertising, they do have two major advantages over other forms of advertising: (1) they can be customized to individual consumers, using personal forms of address and bits of personal information gleaned from computer databases, and (2) their effectiveness can be measured so that they can be continually fine-tuned.

Direct marketing encompasses a wide variety of communications media and includes e-commerce. It has long been popular with book publishers, record clubs, and magazines, but now it is coming into favor with a full range of advertisers. Direct-mail (junk mail) solicitations, catalog sales, and telemarketing are perhaps the most obvious forms of direct marketing activities. However, anyone who has ever called a toll-free number to order the "the greatest hits of the sixties" or redeemed a coupon clipped from the newspaper has also responded to a direct marketing appeal.

Infomercials are a form of broadcast direct marketing. These are program-length, made-for-television presentations whose sole purpose is selling the featured product or service. The infomercial concept has been taken to its logical conclusion in the form of entire cable networks devoted to hawking products through toll-free numbers—the home shopping channels, such as QVC.

The direct marketing industry relies on many of the same creative and media professions that advertising does, but it has some unique disciplines of its own as well. For example, there are firms that specialize in compiling and matching computerized telephone and mailing lists, others that specialize in assembling direct-mail packages, others that receive only toll-free calls, and others that just open return mail and complete (or fulfill) the orders.

INFOMERCIAL. Advertisers of products such as the Flavorwave Oven, shown here being demonstrated by media personality Mr. T, to promote direct sales of products through program-length TV commercials.

Research also takes on a distinctive character in direct marketing campaigns. Direct marketers are able to gauge the results of their advertising appeal, as well as the appropriateness of the media chosen, by counting the dollars in the cash register at the end of the day. This direct cause-effect measure allows the advertiser to try out various approaches and see their results immediately without resorting to the various media research services.

[**Infomercials** are paid television programs that promote a product.]

TARGETING THE MARKET

Here are some ways in which advertising influences your actions, if you are in the target market:

Give new information. This includes announcements by advertisers regarding new products or product improvements, sweepstakes or contests, and other items of a newsworthy nature. The government-funded advertising campaign on the use of condoms to help prevent the spread of the AIDS virus is an example.

Reinforce a current practice. Advertisers who currently enjoy a dominant position in a product category and need to make consumers less receptive to competitive appeals are the primary users of this type of message. This is one of the most efficient uses of advertising, because it addresses the frequent users of the product who do not need to be convinced of its merits. In this case, the advertiser tries to increase **brand loyalty**, the propensity to make a repeat purchase of the product. A recent example would be the "The One and Only Cheerios" slogan that simply reminds consumers of the reliability of the product's quality.

Change a predisposition. This approach is exemplified by the often annoying ads that take on a competing product head-to-head. It is also the most difficult type of ad to execute successfully because it needs both to address and to change the purchasing habits of those who regularly use a competitor's product. (Furthermore, the competitors often answer with their own campaign.) Advertisers tend to be satisfied when they succeed in raising brand awareness, or the consumer's ability to identify the product. An example is a Kleenex bath tissue campaign using data from "touch tests" to argue that its Cottonelle brand was "softer than the leading premium brand."

> **Brand loyalty** is the consumer's propensity to make repeat purchases of a specific brand of product.

> The **buying motive** explains the consumer's desire to purchase particular products.

UNDERSTANDING CONSUMER NEEDS

Whatever communication approach is used, all advertising must appeal to a **buying motive** to be successful. Table 11.6 lists 15 consumer needs, or motives, to which most advertising appeals. The copywriter selects a creative approach that is unique and addresses some consumer need. For example, Dove is positioned as a cosmetic, not a soap, and Southwest Airlines is presented as the carrier that "frees" the economically minded flyer to "move about the country." The Internet site Yahoo.com markets itself not as a search engine, but as a "life engine," providing several services quickly and conveniently. The most effective advertising communicates the need clearly and repetitively.

Given all the advertising industry knows about you, your needs, your consumption patterns, your media behavior, and the forms of persuasion you are susceptible to, you might think it was a cinch to make an effective ad. However, there is no sure-fire formula for success. There is not even any agreement on what constitutes success: Is it sales, market share, brand loyalty, brand attitudes, emotional impact, brand recognition, advertising recall, or top awards in industry competitions?

Different metrics provide differing assessments of success. The CLIO Awards, which celebrated its 50th Anniversary in 2009, provide insight in this

Table 11.6 Consumer Needs Appealed to by Advertising

APPEAL	CONSUMER NEED
Achievement	Accomplish difficult tasks
Exhibition	Win the attention of others
Dominance	Hold a position of influence
Diversion	Have fun
Understanding	Teach and instruct
Nurturance	Support and care for others
Sexuality	Establish sexual identity
Security	Be free from threat of harm
Independence	Make one's own choices
Recognition	Receive notoriety
Stimulation	Stimulate the senses
Novelty	Do new tasks or activities
Affiliation	Belong or win acceptance
Succorance	Receive help and support
Consistency	Achieve order

Source: Adapted from Settle, R., and Alreck, P. (1986). *Why they buy*. New York: Wiley, 26–28.

who would have thought that getting tanned could be good for your skin.

New Dove Summer Glow Body Lotion combines rich Dove moisturisers and a hint of self-tanning agents. So it leaves your skin silky smooth and moisturised while gradually building a beautiful light summer tan.

Good for your skin – great for your look.

new

Body Lotion with
Self-Tanning Agents

campaignforrealbeauty.co.uk ❦ Dove

Advertising Archives

ADVERTISE GRACEFULLY This ad for Dove skin care products promoting "real beauty" wins awards. Including models of diverse races (and shapes) may help to counter the racial and gender stereotypes that have long been associated with mass-media advertisements.

arena. A 2011 CLIO Special Award, Facebook Integrated Marketing, focused on social media. The True Blood Season 2 DVD/Blu-Ray Integrated Campaign won for its success in providing fans with a brand experience that encouraged marathon viewing. The campaign promoted fan interactivity through interactive Web banners, Facebook tabs, and social media built into the Blu-Ray experience. So, depending upon the measure of effectiveness we choose, we might conclude that finding ways to capture audiences' attention for serious issues or humor is the key to making a successful commercial. Well-liked and memorable commercials are not always successful by other measures, however. A famous example from the 1980s featured a cantankerous senior citizen demanding to know "where's the beef?" in a nightmarish fast-food franchise's giant hamburger bun, spawning a catchphrase still in use today. Unfortunately, few consumers could associate the commercial with the sponsor, Wendy's.

What is more, popular advertisement campaigns do not always produce the desired end result—increased sales. Dove's Campaign for Real Beauty has been wildly popular receiving numerous awards and heaps of praise from a range of sectors. The message in the Campaign for Real Beauty is that the Pro-Age products are for women who choose not to worry about fighting the aging process. Yet, Procter & Gamble's Olay Definity line of anti-aging skin creams have posted more sales than all Pro-Age products combined. The different messages sent by the two products can be seen in ads for the products.

Rediscover luminous skin with Definity

DEFINITY

Goes beyond lines and wrinkles to diminish the look of discolourations

78% of women who tried it, said it was the best skincare product they've ever used.
For your free sample go to www.olay.co.uk

OLAY
love the skin you're in™

ADVERTISE SUCCESSFULLY This ad for Olay skin care products wins customers. Advertisers hope that consumers with characteristics similar to those of their models will be motivated to purchase products shown in the ads.

THE CHANGING NATURE OF THE CONSUMER

How are consumers changing? This is the question that drives **demographic segmentation**, which categorizes people on the basis of the personal and household characteristics that the U.S. Census Bureau tabulates, such as age, sex, ethnicity, and income. Trends in these areas are very important to advertisers. For most advertisers of consumer products, women between the ages of 18 and 49 are the primary target group; they make the most purchases in supermarkets and department stores.

Of all demographic variables, age and ethnicity are of considerable importance to marketers at the present time. Census data, for example, reveal a growing senior market. Children (5–12) and teenagers (13–17) total about 22 million in North America, making them important segments for advertisers. Males between 18 and 24 are also highly prized in part because they are so difficult to reach. College-age males are abandoning the traditional mass media in droves for the Internet and video games. Advertisers generally pursue young consumers in the hope that their ads will trigger lifelong brand loyalty.

In addition, advertisers are studying ethnicity as a demographic category. About 30 percent of the population belongs to an ethnic minority group. According to the Census Bureau, non-Latino whites will no longer be the majority population by 2042. The Latino-American population is the fastest growing, followed by Asian-Americans and African-Americans. These developments remind advertisers that consumer markets are not homogenous and that messages must be sensitive to the needs of emerging segments.

> **Demographic segmentation** is based on social or personal characteristics, such as age, sex, education, or income.

IMPORTANCE OF DIVERSITY

Taking into account the diversity of consumer groups, some companies have an ethnic plan so that advertising is inclusive and relevant to all consumers. There is inevitable diversity within target markets, and they shouldn't be thought of as a single homogeneous group. Consumers of Peruvian descent have different buying habits than those from Mexico, for instance. And, contrary to popular perception, not all Latinos prefer advertising in Spanish.

Prior to 1980, African-Americans were rarely featured in television commercials (Dates & Barloe, 1997). Although black celebrities such as Bill Cosby began appearing in commercials by the 1980s, it remained evident that advertisers were using "black celebrities, but few black faces" (p. 93). In other words, despite the fact that African-Americans are found in all professions from technical to managerial, advertising tends to reflect the stereotype that successful African-Americans are often portrayed as athletes or popular music stars.

How advertisers portray women has also been controversial. Women are consistently underrepresented and are less likely to be depicted in professional occupations. Women also tend to be portrayed as taller and thinner than average, a practice that raises the question of whether advertising encourages a feeling of dissatisfaction with one's own body. Researchers disagree, however, about whether these images actually create unrealistic expectations for young women and cause body dissatisfaction.

GLOBAL ADVERTISING

Technology and political change have given rise to a new business environment where international marketing opportunities abound. The Internet, in particular, makes it possible for businesses to reach foreign markets inexpensively; advertising is conducted online without high overhead costs. The global business climate is also the result of political initiatives such as the North American Free Trade Agreement (NAFTA), the General Agreement on Tariffs and Trade (GATT), and the World Trade Organization (see Chapter 17), which create new opportunities for international trade.

International advertising is expanding due to more aggressive competition from foreign businesses that create pressure on U.S. companies to explore international markets. Although international advertising requires knowledge of other cultures, many global campaigns are not clearly translated into various languages.

MEDIALITERACY

ANALYZING ADVERTISING

Media literacy for advertising leads us to ask critical questions about the medium. How can consumers protect themselves and their families from harmful and deceitful messages? How can we avoid being drawn into a false set of values based on the consumption of mass-marketed goods?

HIDDEN MESSAGES

More than 50 years have passed since advertising critic Vance Packard published *The Hidden Persuaders* (1957), in which he called attention to some of the more underhanded tactics advertisers and their agencies used to sell their wares, including embedding hidden subliminal messages that supposedly unconsciously stimulated buying. Some claim that when American Express placed pop-up ads in recent movies, the company was engaging in a subliminal strategy.

Advertising does more than just sell products; it also encourages a materialistic way of life. That is, the long-term impact of advertising has been to reinforce a market economy and create a consumer culture in which the acquisition of goods and services is the foundation of values, pleasures, and goals in a capitalist society. Lifestyle advertising for alcoholic beverages, which often situates products in luxurious settings, is an example. That reinforces the legitimacy of the capitalist system by sending the message that wealth is the top priority, ignoring the inequities and environmental damages caused by the system. It also leads people to think of themselves primarily as consumers rather than politically aware citizens.

It is estimated that the average consumer is exposed to some 5,000 advertisements each day (Pappas, 2000, p. 1). Some scholars express concern that this volume of advertising encourages false needs in consumers. Social critic

Stewart Ewen (1976) argues that advertising creates an ideology of consumption by promoting a materialistic way of life. When advertising trades in the core function of a product (a shoe's comfort and durability) for a lifestyle appeal (shoe as symbol of power or an affluent lifestyle), it promotes a culture of consumption in which consumers subscribe to the idea that problems can be solved by simply acquiring products (Featherstone, 1990; see Chapter 14). However, other observers have questioned whether advertising creates a consumer culture or is, rather, simply a by-product of our consumer impulses.

Black Friday and Cyber Monday exemplify consumerism and materialism. Black Friday, the day after Thanksgiving, is associated with traditional brick-and-mortar stores and is heralded as the ceremonial kick-off to the holiday shopping season between Thanksgiving and Christmas. It represents businesses moving from the red (loss) to the black (profit). Cyber Monday is the first Monday after Thanksgiving and has become the defining day of the holiday season for e-commerce sites. Cyber Monday was created by the National Retailer Federation because it has become synonymous with the first day consumers return to work and do not work but shop online.

In stark contrast to Black Friday and Cyber Monday, *Buy Nothing Day* is a day of protest against consumerism observed the day after Thanksgiving. The day was promoted by the Canadian *Adbusters* magazine (which helped launch the Occupy Wall Street movement in 2011). Never heard of it? That's not surprising, since the major television networks refuse to run advertisements paid for by the event's promoters. This is a case where you can take a

COUNTERADVERTISING Adbusters tries to counter the effects of consumer culture—but TV networks won't accept their ads. Long-term exposure to commercial advertising may make consumers believe that material goods are essential for their happiness.

stand by doing nothing, by staying home (and avoiding online shopping) the day after Thanksgiving. You may also have pop-up blockers on your computer and a fast-forward button on your DVR at your disposal. However, if you enjoy advertising-supported media, then it is your *duty* to watch the ads and buy the products you see advertised on the day after Thanksgiving!

PRIVACY

Citizens are often outraged about the sale of personal data to other companies, resulting in a mountain of unwanted mail and e-mail. For this reason, responsible companies engage in permission marketing, informing website visitors about how the information will be used. TRW, for example, spent $30 million in recent years updating their website and computer systems to address consumer concerns about privacy.

The Internet raises database marketing to a new level that many consumers find deeply troubling. Over time, information can be matched across sites and identified with individual consumers, even those who are careful to avoid revealing personal information on the Web. Personal information can then be matched to offline databases of commercially available public information, such as auto registrations, marriages, births, and home sales. From the advertiser's perspective this has the advantage of greater efficiency, limiting ad exposure to the most likely prospects, and reducing duplicate exposures. Consumers could benefit, too, by receiving useful information about products and special price offers when they are actually in the market for an item. However, personalized advertising can also mean discriminatory pricing: charging some people more than others for the same product. Amazon.com has done that.

Nevertheless, much to the excitement of advertisers and the chagrin of privacy advocates, innovation in the area continues to proliferate. For example, unbeknownst to some individuals, applications that use GPS (e.g., Yelp, Urbanspoon) have the capacity to capture information on your physical location and personal habits. Facebook advertisers have access to the user's profile information unless great care is taken in selecting among the site's many privacy options. Google now shares personal information across all of its websites, including search, YouTube, Gmail, and the Google+ social networking site.

Internet users are not the only ones giving up detailed personal information to advertisers. Digital video recorders also record detailed viewing information and upload the information as part of the subscription service that comes with the devices. Consumers can fight back by fast-forwarding through the commercials, but that fact is also recorded, perhaps targeting the consumers for a direct marketing pitch through another medium. Many models of DVRs no longer permit fast-forwarding, and newer TiVo units display advertiser logos while they are in fast-forward mode.

Online marketers assure your privacy by voluntarily subscribing to privacy seal authorities BBBonline and TRUSTe. However, these programs merely assure that the practices set forth in the website's privacy policy—including practices that invade consumer privacy such as selling information to third parties—are being followed.

If you don't wish to rely on the advertising industry to police itself, many of the online safety tips listed at the end of Chapter 9 will also protect you against the prying eyes of advertisers, especially spam blockers, spyware erasers, browser privacy settings, and social networking options. If you don't like to bother with reading the privacy policies at the websites you visit, you might consider maintaining a separate e-mail account for online shopping and website registrations, one you can dispose of when it becomes choked with spam. There are also anonymizers that will disguise your e-mail address. And when asked to "opt in" to e-mail alerts for new products, don't do it. Protests also work. Facebook modified its plans to share the list of products you had bought recently with all of your online friends, following a storm of protest from its users. Following an agreement between Internet browser software companies and the FTC in 2012, new browser versions will have a "do not track" option that the user can activate.

In the offline world, beware of sending in product warranty cards, applying for supermarket discount cards, and entering contests or promotions. Those put you in advertisers' databases. When you print new checks, leave your phone number off, since that is the primary way marketers match information between databases. And refuse to write your phone number on your checks when retailers request it. (They can track you down through your bank if your check bounces; they don't really need your number.) If you really want to avoid leaving tracks, pay cash whenever possible. All your credit card purchases go into commercial databases, too. To avoid telemarketers, put yourself on the FCC's Do Not Call list (see Chapter 12) and do a Google search for the Mail Preference Service offered by the Direct Marketing Association if you want to cut down on junk mail.

DECEPTION

To preserve their good names, most advertisers go to great lengths to avoid deceptive advertising. However, advertisers sometimes push their claims too far. For example, in 2010, the Federal Trade Commission (FTC) found that POM Wonderful made false claims about the health benefits of its pomegranate juice. Sometimes, however, deception is less obvious. The term *puffery* refers to the advertisers' practice of making exaggerated claims that can't be proven, such as "Best pizza on the planet." At which point should an advertiser be required to substantiate such claims? From the perspective of social responsibility, advertisers must also ask whether particular consumer groups are vulnerable to puffery (for example, children and seniors) and assure that groups are not taken advantage of. If you have been deceived, the FTC has an online complaint form (http://www.ftc.gov/ftc/contact.shtm). Or, you might start with your state's attorney general's or consumer affairs office. How can you decide if an ad is deceptive? One criterion is that it could mislead a reasonable consumer, such as you!

GRAPHIC WARNING. The Food and Drug Administration proposed horrifying graphic images such as these for cigarette packaging to counter the effects of cigarette advertising.

ADVERTISING HARMFUL PRODUCTS

If claims about ineffective products are prohibited, what about ads for products that are harmful to their users, such as tobacco and alcohol? How can the industry get away with advertising them? And if their ads are legal, why don't we see ads for cocaine? The short answer is that alcohol and tobacco, unlike other harmful drugs, are legal products and businesses have a free speech right to advertise them in the United States.

However, those rights have limits. Cigarette ads have been banned on television and radio since 1971. Cigarette ads moved to magazines after that but are required to include warnings about health effects. A new law took effect in 2010 that prohibits tobacco companies from sponsoring events and from displaying their logos on clothing, such as T-shirts. However, a court ruled that further restrictions that would have limited cigarette ads to plain black text would infringe on the free speech rights of advertisers and that issue is still making its way through the legal system. The U.S. Food and Drug Administration mandated graphic warnings for cigarette packages, such as a picture of a cancerous lung, that were to take effect in 2012. However, as of this writing a court blocked implementation on the grounds that the labels infringed the free speech rights of cigarette companies.

Alcohol advertising has followed a different path emphasizing industry self-regulation rather than legislation. Thus, for many years ads for hard liquor were not seen on television but that was because distillers voluntarily withheld them, a self-imposed prohibition that ended in 2002. Beer ads have long been abundant and remain so today, but the industry voluntarily follows some guidelines about their content. For example, cartoon characters that might appeal to underage drinkers should not be used, the pleasurable effects of alcohol should not be emphasized, and irresponsible drinking should not be encouraged. Another voluntary standard prohibits marketing liquor to minors. The Federal Trade Commission (FTC) guideline is that alcohol ads should only appear in outlets where at least 70 percent of the readers or viewers are 21 or older. To that end, publications like *ESPN The Magazine*, with significant younger audiences, have made an effort to create separate editions for subscribers under 21 that do not carry liquor ads. In 2011 the FTC launched a new investigation into alcohol promotions that use social media.

Potato chips and soda can also be harmful, especially to children. In an effort to curb an epidemic of childhood obesity, the FTC is working on food voluntary marketing guidelines that would urge advertisers whose products have unhealthful levels of fat, sugar, and sodium to cease targeting children between the ages of 2 and 11. The guidelines would cover subtle advertising pitches in video games and social media as well as conventional advertising venues.

CHILDREN AND ADVERTISING

Advertising for children can be harmful because children are a vulnerable audience who lack sufficient resources to make informed decisions about advertising appeals (Schudson, 1984). Complaints about children's advertising should go to the Children's Advertising Review Unit (CARU). It is made up of industry professionals who promote responsible children's advertising and respond to concerns raised by consumers. Among the guidelines on the www.caru.org website you will find injunctions against using children's program personalities and showing toys larger than life size as well as mandates for caveats such as "batteries not included," "some assembly required," and "part of a nutritious, balanced diet." Policy makers are particularly concerned with how well preschool children can explain the purpose of commercials and differentiate them from the entertainment portion of the programs. Recently, Disney was fined by the Federal Communication Commission (FCC) for running commercials for toys related to shows in the same time period on its ABC Family Channel. The number of commercials per hour that advertisers can include in children's programs is also limited. The FCC fined Nickelodeon for that offense.

Organizations such as the Center for Media Literacy and Citizens for Media Literacy encourage audience members to develop critical skills to analyze media at a young age. Although the effects are not fully understood, several studies explore whether (1) preschool-age children have difficulty explaining the intent of commercials, (2) children exposed to advertising make frequent requests for products to their parents, and (3) parental discussions of advertising increase children's comprehension of commercials (see John, 1999).

For their part, advertisers remind us that children have always had a desire for information about products available to them. Parental supervision also plays an important role in how children come to use advertising in everyday life.

STOP&REVIEW

1. What are the steps involved in making an ad campaign, and who implements each step?
2. What are the criteria for judging an effective ad?
3. What are some of the main social criticisms of advertising?
4. What aspects of advertising should parents review with their children?
5. What service does Nielsen Media Research provide that can be used by advertisers to monitor audiences that are viewing their ads?

SUMMARY&REVIEW

WHAT ARE THE MAIN EVENTS IN THE HISTORY OF ADVERTISING?

Advertising has been around in some form since ancient times. The Industrial Revolution and the rise of new information technologies are the most influential events ushering in the modern era of advertising. With the Industrial Revolution came a competitive environment that required advertising to be persuasive as well as informative in order to break through the clutter of competing messages. Radio, television, and computers have played major roles in commercial communication. Today, advertising is a meta-industry that penetrates virtually all sectors of society from medicine to religion.

WHAT HAS BEEN THE IMPACT OF THE COMPUTER ON ADVERTISING?

Computers allow advertisers to build databases and store information, so that personalized messages can be sent via the Internet. Database marketing helps build deeper relationships with consumers. Data captured from users of the Internet supplies detailed profiles of media usage as well as consumer behavior, providing an unprecedented opportunity to target advertising efficiently, but also threatening the privacy of users.

HOW ARE ADVERTISING CAMPAIGNS COORDINATED?

Marketing managers and brand managers who work for major advertisers budget and plan advertising strategies that will help them introduce new products or increase the sales of existing products. They work with an advertising manager to coordinate their companies' overall advertising efforts. Once a campaign is planned, they might contact one or more advertising agencies to execute the plan.

HOW ARE CAMPAIGNS ORGANIZED INSIDE AN ADVERTISING AGENCY?

The account executive is the liaison between the advertiser and the advertising agency staff. The account executive coordinates the activities of the creative department, which creates the ads, and the media department, which determines where the ads will be placed. Copywriters conceive of creative ideas and write the ads. The agency's media buyer negotiates with the media.

WHAT IS THE ROLE OF RESEARCH IN THE ADVERTISING PROCESS?

Advertisers rely on market research to help them understand the target market. In the agency, account planners ensure that there is a strong connection between research findings and the final advertising message. Researchers use data about who watches or reads media, but also use sophisticated breakdowns by audience segment and psychographics to target advertising. The Internet permits new, even more detailed forms of research and data gathering, but also raises potential privacy issues.

WHAT DIFFERENT TYPES OF COMMUNICATION DOES ADVERTISING USE?

Advertising is generally designed to achieve one of three basic goals: to provide new information (brand awareness), to reinforce a current practice (brand loyalty), or to change an existing predisposition. Advertising genres are further categorized according to the type of buying motive they appeal to. Advertisers have identified 15 needs, or buying motives, to which most messages appeal.

WHAT IS DIRECT MARKETING?

With direct marketing, the recipient of the advertising message is asked to make a direct and immediate response to the ad, such as by mailing in a printed order blank or dialing a toll-free number to place an order. Telemarketing, home shopping channels, infomercials, and catalog sales are other common examples. The popularity of direct marketing is likely to increase in the future as the spread of interactive technologies such as the Internet makes it easier to place orders in direct response to advertising.

HOW ARE ADVERTISING AUDIENCES CHANGING?

The number of seniors is growing, as are several ethnic groups. Advertisers in the future must have a thorough knowledge of diverse markets. The Hispanic market will be the largest ethnic group in the United States, in terms of both population and buying power. The African-American population is younger and growing faster than Anglo-Americans.

IN TERMS OF ADVERTISING, WHAT DOES IT MEAN TO BE MEDIA LITERATE?

There are professional and consumer levels of media literacy. Professionals must communicate in a way that gets the attention of the consumer, maintains interest, and motivates purchase. Consumers must be aware of implicit messages, teach children critical thinking skills, and understand the distinction between the world presented by advertising and actual society.

THINKING CRITICALLY
ABOUT THE MEDIA

1. What were the most important developments that led to the advertising industry of today?

2. What target markets do you belong to, and what media should advertisers use to reach you?

3. Debate the following proposition: Google will make advertising agencies obsolete.

4. Advertising receives substantial criticism, so let's accentuate the positive: What are the good things that advertising does for you and for society?

KEY TERMS

account executive (p. 327)

advertising (p. 314)

advertising media (p. 325)

advertising plan (p. 327)

brand (p. 326)

brand loyalty (p. 336)

buying motive (p. 336)

CANSPAM Law (p. 322)

click-through rate (p. 319)

copy testing (p. 332)

database marketing (p. 321)

demographic segmentation (p. 339)

direct marketing (p. 334)

era of creativity (p. 316)

infomercial (p. 335)

integrated marketing communication (IMC) (p. 317)

media department (p. 329)

relationship marketing (p. 334)

research organizations (p. 325)

sales promotion (p. 317)

viral marketing (p. 320)

THE "THIRD SCREEN" With TV and computer screens as the first and second screens in our lives, the third screen comprises the handheld screens that keep us in contact with our friends and relatives, bringing us a growing array of mobile entertainment and information options.

THE THIRD SCREEN:

SMART PHONES AND TABLETS

12

HISTORY: BETTER LIVING THROUGH TELECOMMUNICATIONS

If you asked the average college student what the most exciting and life-transforming development in new media was today, you might well hear that it's their smartphone (see Media&Culture: What My Cell Phone Means to Me, page 348). Perhaps that should not be surprising, though, since advances in the communication infrastructure that enables our smartphones and tablets today often have had astounding effects on the lives of individuals and societies in the past. Today, smartphones and tablet computers are ushering in a new phase of our relationships with telecommunications networks.

1876	Bell invents the telephone	1996	Telecommunications Act opens up competition
1934	Communications Act regulates telecommunications	2005	SBC becomes the new AT&T
1983	First commercial cell phone service in the United States	2007	The iPhone is introduced
		2010	The iPad is born

THE NEW MEDIA OF YESTERYEAR

> The **infrastructure** is the underlying physical structure of communication networks.

The story of the **infrastructure** is the story of how great civilizations create the means to communicate at a distance—the essence of telecommunication. The ancient Greeks and Romans had fire towers to carry messages from distant outposts of their civilizations. The Yorubas of eastern Africa had a network of drummers. The Anasazi people of the American Southwest "broadcast" fire signals from atop high plateaus in the twelfth century. In Napoleon's day, mechanical semaphore signal towers sent dispatches across France (Holzmann & Pherson, 1994).

All of the history-making networks mentioned in the previous paragraph are what we might now call "wireless." However, the early history of electronic telecommunications was dominated by wireline communication, before coming full cycle back to wireless in the current century. A review of that history is in order to help us understand the technological and legal frameworks in which our smartphones operate today.

Samuel F. B. Morse's telegraph was an early forerunner of the Internet in 1844. Historian Daniel Czitrom (1982) called the telegraph wires "lightning lines" both for their speed of transmission and for their transforming effects. Together with the railroads, the telegraph made national economies and a national culture possible.

The story of telecommunication in the United States is intertwined with the history of telecom giant AT&T. The story began one day in 1876 when Alexander Graham Bell called out for his assistant, "Mr. Watson, come here! I want to see you!" and the apparatus on his table relayed his words over wires to his assistant in the next room. A few years later Bell would invent an early, if initially impractical, ancestor of the cell phone he called the *photophone*. It transmitted voice wirelessly through the air over beams of light.

Library of Congress

LIGHTNING LINES The telegraph transformed communications in the business world in the late 1880s. Here telegraph wires span a busy New York City street.

MEDIA&CULTURE

WHAT MY CELL PHONE MEANS TO ME

Throughout history, telecommunications have had transforming effects on the people who use them and the societies they live in. What impact do cell phones have on us and our culture? Why not ask college students about that? They are members of the first cell phone generation. Accordingly, we convened small groups of students to discuss the meaning of cell phones in their lives.

Many restated the obvious benefits that cell phone companies stress in their marketing campaigns: convenience, safety, and staying in touch anytime, anyplace. However, some of these take a unique twist in the lives of college students: being able to make calls when roommates tie up the (wireline) phone, and coordinating pit stops between cars while on road trips. The positive effects center on increasing social interaction and the ability to participate in more social activities. On the negative side, students were annoyed by repeated calls from people they didn't want to hear from, the increased pace of their social lives, and a loss of spontaneity due

to over-planning. Some also found that their social interactions tended to become limited to the people they texted frequently.

Comments like these resonate with concerns about the effects of communication technology on society. One point of view is that Americans are becoming less involved in organized social activities; that they too often go "bowling alone" in the words of one social critic (Putnam, 2000). To the extent that cell phones stimulate and coordinate social activity, they could help reverse that trend. However, other critics fear that new media offer us too much choice in the content we consume and the associates we seek out, breaking our sense of living in a shared culture. If we limit our social contacts only to others with cell phones or those on our text messaging buddy list, that trend could accelerate. Whether cell phones ultimately improve or destroy social contact will, of course, depend upon which of these opposing tendencies becomes the dominant one.

These nineteenth-century "new media" foretold those of today. With its combination of interpersonal communication and information services, wasn't the telegraph the Internet of the nineteenth century (Standage, 1998)? Radio, in the sense of audio mass communication, might be traced back to an early telephone demonstration in which Mr. Watson delivered a speech from Boston to an audience in Salem. Much early speculation about the telephone centered on multichannel mass-media functions like conveying news and music to the home (LaRose & Atkin, 1992). Early phones often had party lines shared by multiple users who occasionally joined in on the conversations, a forerunner of today's social media.

THE RISE OF MA BELL

Soon after the Bell Telephone Company was established in 1877, it acquired Western Electric, an electrical equipment manufacturing firm, the third cornerstone of a **vertically integrated** monopoly that also included its local and long-distance networks. In its early years, the Bell Company ruthlessly used its **patent** rights to undercut its competitors and refused to interconnect competitors with its long-distance network. In 1910, the company, by then named American Telephone and Telegraph (AT&T), acquired the Western Union Telegraph Company, raising the specter of a national telecommunications monopoly.

Vertical integration occurs when a company with the same owner handles different aspects of a business within the same industry, such as phone manufacturing and phone service.

A **patent** gives an inventor the exclusive right to make, use, or sell an invention for 20 years.

Under threat of an antitrust suit, AT&T canceled the deal, promised to mend its ruthless ways, and offered to provide quality service for all, the principle of **universal service**. This agreement, the so-called *Kingsbury Commitment*, was formally enacted into law by Congress in the Graham Act of 1921 and still defines the philosophy behind telecommunications regulation today. That exempted AT&T from the Sherman Antitrust Act and validated the notion of a "natural monopoly"—that is, it only made economic sense to have a single phone company serving an area.

THE TELEPHONE AND SOCIETY

The telephone slowly expanded from the circles of wealthy tradespeople and professionals who owned them at the turn of the twentieth century (Fischer, 1992). It became a lifeline to rural families who felt less isolated and, along with the automobile, helped spur migration from the cities to the suburbs. It was something of a mixed blessing for women because while it connected them to family and friends it also confined them to their homes more than when they went out on social visits in person (Rakow, 1992).

AT&T began to impact national politics, perhaps more than it wanted. During the Great Depression (1929–1939), telephone subscriptions declined, but the company paid dividends to stockholders (mostly Republicans) while laying off thousands of workers (mostly Democrats). This placed communications policy on the agenda of Democratic President Franklin Roosevelt. The Communications Act of 1934 defined AT&T as a **common carrier**. This required AT&T and other telephone companies to offer service on an equal basis to all paying customers and prohibited them from having any financial interest in the content. AT&T also had to submit financial reports and rate notifications with the new **Federal Communications Commission (FCC)**.

The FCC soon launched an antitrust investigation that dragged on for almost 50 years. The basic problem was that it was virtually impossible for competing equipment manufacturers to make sales within the Bell System, and it appeared that its Western Electric prices were too high, fattening local telephone rates for consumers. The antitrust proceedings ultimately ended in the Modified Final Judgment (MFJ) in 1984, which forced AT&T to sell off, or divest, its local phone companies. The local exchanges were parceled into seven **Regional Bell operating companies (RBOCs)** that retained the right to the Bell trademark. Ma Bell was dead.

CUTTING THE WIRES

With AT&T's empire built on wires, wireless communication offered a different vision of the infrastructure. Practical wireless telecommunication dates back to Marconi's wireless telegraph in 1896 (see Chapter 6). As we

Universal service is the principle that everyone should have basic access to telecommunication services.

Common carriers provide service to all on an equal basis.

The **Federal Communications Commission (FCC)** regulates communication in the United States.

Regional Bell operating companies (RBOCs) are the local telephone operating companies that AT&T divested in 1984.

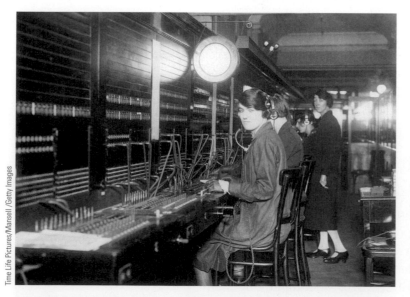

Time Life Pictures/Mansell /Getty Images

NUMBER, PLEASE Before automatic switching, live operators completed all calls by moving plugs around their switchboard. They were replaced by electromechanical devices that automated the process.

saw in that chapter, radio was primarily a two-way communications medium for the first 25 years of its existence, before radio broadcasting dominated the airwaves.

Although radio communication was wireless in those years, it wasn't very mobile. Because such bulky equipment and lengthy antennas were required, only large oceangoing vessels, like the *Titanic*, had mobile radios. The first land-based mobile radios in the United States were two-way radios installed in Detroit police cars in the early 1920s. Mobile radios advanced rapidly during World War II as they became commonplace in tanks and airplanes. The first handheld personal communication devices also appeared on WWII battlefields, in the form of the walkie-talkie. They were the work of Canadian inventor Al Gross, who went on to pioneer citizens' band (CB) radio and the telephone pager (Bellis, 2000).

However, AT&T swiftly co-opted wireless communication, too. After World War II, wireless **microwave** systems replaced telephone cables on highly trafficked routes between major cities. These systems were fixed in place, not mobile, anchored to tall towers. They carried thousands of simultaneous telephone calls between cities rather than between individual mobile handsets. Microwave technology also inspired science fiction writer Arthur C. Clarke to come up with the idea for **satellites**. They are essentially microwave transmitters launched into space, beginning with AT&T's Telstar satellite in 1962.

> **Microwave** systems transmit information between relay towers on highly focused beams of radio waves.
>
> **Satellite** systems send information back and forth to relays in orbit around the earth.

Mobile telephones for personal use have been around since 1947, but early systems had limited capacity owing to the FCC's unwillingness to allocate additional channels beyond the original 23, despite continuing requests from AT&T and technical improvements from the company's Bell Labs. That meant years-long waiting lists for new customers and busy signals for subscribers. Paging systems were introduced in the 1960s to relieve some of the pent-up demand. Primitive pagers could only notify the users that somebody was trying to call; later innovations automatically transmitted the caller's number and a short message. They are the forerunners of today's text-messaging services.

In 1975, CB radio service opened up to general use and quickly became the first wireless communication craze. Movies like *Smokey and the Bandit* and hit songs on the radio popularized the new medium. The CB airwaves were soon clogged with "good buddies" imitating the patter of

NOT FOR MY POCKET PHONE The first U.S. cell phone weighed 2 pounds, cost $4,000, and was known as "the brick." That's Martin Cooper, "the father of the cell phone," showing it off. Despite its weight and cost it caught on with businesspeople on the move and became a status symbol that encouraged further adoption.

Jupiterimages/Workbook Stock/Getty Images

BREAKER, BREAKER CB radios introduced the average citizen to mobile communications before cell phones were available. Early mobile phones only reached a handful of elite users.

long-distance truck drivers. The general public thus acquired firsthand experience with the potential of wireless communication but also with the frustrating limitations of CB radio, in that it did not allow private conversations, had limited range, and had insufficient channels for millions of users. Still, many enjoyed sharing information about the activities of traffic police and doings at the local truck stop, contributing to this early form of social media.

More CB channels were added at just about the time the craze died out. However, the demand for mobile communications still mounted, prompting the FCC to reallocate TV channels 70 to 83 for a new type of mobile telephone service that gave cell phones their name, analog cellular radio. The FCC was slow to authorize the new cellular service, which wasn't commercially available in the United States until 1983.

A second generation of digital wireless phones came along in 1995. Although wide-scale competition was planned, AT&T and its Bell Operating Company offspring soon dominated. The FCC declined to select a technical standard. Meanwhile the rest of the world settled on a European standard (*GSM*, short for Global System for Mobile communications) and enjoyed lower prices, wider availability, and more rapid innovation. This left the United States lagging behind the world in telecommunications for perhaps the first time since the invention of the telegraph.

THE GOVERNMENT STEPS ASIDE

Perhaps deregulation would help the U.S. catch up to the world. Under the **Telecommunications Act of 1996**, restrictions that prevented telecommunications companies in one industry (e.g., wireline telephone) from entering other telecom industries (e.g. cable television) were relaxed.

The **Telecommunications Act of 1996** is federal legislation that deregulated the communications media. It opened the U.S. telecommunications industry to competition.

The Telecommunications Act triggered a merger frenzy among infrastructure companies intent on offering "one-stop shopping" for conventional phone service as well as cell phones, cable TV, and Internet, and making themselves big enough to compete globally. For example, Bell Atlantic and NYNEX, two of the seven RBOCs divested by AT&T in 1984, combined to control local phone service from Maine to Virginia, then gobbled up the largest remaining independent telephone company, General Telephone (GTE), and renamed themselves Verizon. Southwestern Bell (covering Texas, Missouri, Kansas, Arkansas, and Oklahoma) bought up Pacific Telesis (California and Nevada), Ameritech (the upper Midwest), and BellSouth (the southeastern United States). In 2005, Southwestern Bell merged with the remnants of AT&T, which had dwindled down to a long distance and cell phone company, and reclaimed the AT&T name. Those moves left Qwest (formerly U.S. West, stretching from Minnesota to Washington State) as the sole survivor of the original seven "baby Bells" until it was purchased by CenturyLink in 2010. The Telecommunications Act also promoted competition in both the local and long-distance markets, expanding consumer options.

THE THIRD SCREEN ARRIVES

New technology is shaping the future of the telecommunications industry perhaps even more than government regulation. Cell phones have completely replaced landline phones in about a quarter of U.S. homes as they acquire exciting capabilities, including the capacity to take pictures, play music and video from the Internet, and keep up to date with our social networks. Number portability made it possible for consumers to switch from wireline to cell phone service while retaining their old telephone numbers, making the transition easier. The introduction of Apple's iPhone in 2007 and the iPad in 2010 foretells a future in which much of the content we now see on our computers, televisions, game consoles, and home video screens will instead appear on the screens of our cell phones and tablets.

However, Steve Jobs did not invent the **smartphone** even though it may sometimes seem that way. The idea of adding visual displays to phones dates back to AT&T's pioneering experiments with television in the 1920s—what we might call a *video conferencing system* today. AT&T periodically announced from the mid-1960s onward that video phones were going to be "the next big thing," but consumers were less than impressed because the audio and video were not well synchronized. Instead, the display screens for caller ID information began appearing on consumer telephones in the United States in the late 1980s and were successful.

[**Smartphones** are cell phones that can also access the Internet.]

The first cell phone that we might recognize as a smartphone today was IBM's Simon, first introduced in 1992 with a touch screen, data and voice capabilities and built-in "apps" including calendar, calculator, email, and games. Simon was aimed at business users and was too heavy and bulky to catch on with consumers, though. Handheld personal organizers known as Personal Data Assistants (PDAs) were introduced at about the same time and some could be purchased with cell phone add-ons as extra-cost (and extra-bulky) options. Finnish phone manufacturer Nokia came out with a line of cell phones that added e-mail and address book functions in 1996 that we might also call the first smartphone. The Blackberry, first sold in 1999, deserves special mention as the handheld telecommunications device that made mobile messaging a popular cultural phenomenon—and a personal obsession for many of its users (Reed, 2010).

Apple could claim to have developed the first modern tablet computer but it might be embarrassed to do so. A pen-based handheld computer called the *Apple Newton*, introduced in 1993, was a flop with consumers owing in part to a flawed handwriting recognition system. Microsoft's Tablet PC preceded the iPad by a decade, but was designed for business users rather than consumers.

The social impacts of the cell phone are becoming evident (Ling, 2004). On the plus side, cell phones can convey a sense of security in emergency situations on the road and intensify the nature of our social interactions particularly among teens (and among college students; see Media&Culture: What My Cell Phone Means to Me, page 368). Cell phones also allow users to "micro-manage" their appointments. The downsides are that using the cell phone to talk or text while driving is a safety hazard; it is an annoyance to those who have to listen to our conversations in public places; and it can be a way of withdrawing from face-to-face interaction with those closest to us (e.g., parents and teens). There are also concerns about "addictive" qualities of cell phone use, especially text messaging, and the health hazards of the electromagnetic radiation that leaks from them (see Chapter 14). However, cell phones aren't just for talking any more, with nearly two-thirds of mobile phone time spent on apps (Nielsen, 2012a). As the third screen carries more entertainment content, the negative effects associated with television, popular music, and video games (also see Chapter 14) are likely to be visited upon their users as well.

MEDIA ON THE THIRD SCREEN

The advent of the iPad, even more so than the iPod, iPhone and Kindle before it, made media executives rethink the future of mobile distribution. The iPad screen is large enough to make it a viable video player and game device, as well as a music player for iTunes and a passable e-book reader. Many of the hundreds of thousands of "apps" made for the iPhone also play on the iPad.

There is great interest in the media industry in iPad apps that deliver versions of print publications to the device. Unlike web publications that are open to anyone, apps create "walled gardens" that discourage users from surfing away as they read and make it difficult to hotlink into articles without viewing the ads that go with them. Also, Apple's App Store gives publishers a convenient way of selling online subscriptions without erecting their own online newsstands. In 2011 Apple introduced a plan that would give it 30 percent of the revenues from subscribers that they attract, which many publishers found to be too steep a price to pay. At the same time, Google introduced its OnePass system that would take a more reasonable 10 percent cut for apps running on its Android mobile operating system. However, while Google's platform has edged out Apple and Blackberry among smartphone users (Nielsen, 2012b), it is available on far fewer tablets than Apple's.

The market for smartphone video is also promising. Nielsen Media Research estimates that mobile phone users were watching almost four and a half hours of video a month on their phones by the end of 2011, about equal to online video consumption, although still dwarfed by the 147 hours a month spent on conventional television (Nielsen 2012a). Television providers are beginning to integrate tablet computers with TV viewing, including using iPads as TV remote controls, program guides, and for viewing streaming video from sites like YouTube and VEVO. Local television stations also plan to distribute their broadcasts via cell phone networks. The transition to digital television in 2009 (see Chapter 8) opened up new territory in the communications spectrum for advanced mobile services such as these. In 2012 the U.S. Congress adopted a plan to auction off some of the spectrum currently occupied by broadcast television to make even more space available for mobiles.

Telecom executives also see mobile content and fees collected from electronic shopping transactions completed with cell phones, sometimes called **m-commerce**, as the next big thing. They hope these will replace the dwindling revenues from conventional wireline telephone businesses and reinvigorate slacking cell phone profits. Mobile commerce is indeed growing fast but Internet companies rather than telecom companies are leading the trend. By the end of 2011, 14 million persons a day were visiting mobile commerce sites Groupon and LivingSocial to check out the deals (Nielsen 2012a).

STOP&REVIEW

1. Why did the government want to break up AT&T?
2. How has the structure of the telephone industry changed over the years?
3. What led to the development of smartphones?
4. What mobile services are emerging today?
5. What do we mean by "the third screen?"

m-commerce means electronic shopping transactions completed with a cell phone.

TECHNOLOGY TRENDS: DIGITAL WIRELESS WORLD

Wireless technologies account for much of the "sizzle" in future telecommunications networks. However, it helps to trace today's technology back to its analog roots, so we can better understand tomorrow's technology (see Technology Demystified: How Telephones Work).

FROM ANALOG TO DIGITAL

The basic way to transmit computer data is to turn on a tiny electrical voltage to represent a 1 and to turn off the voltage to represent a 0. Unfortunately, conventional analog telephone systems must reject certain electrical pulses to avoid confusion with the pulses that old-fashioned rotary phones use to dial numbers and to work within other technical limitations of this nineteenth-century invention.

For those few who still rely on dial-up Internet access, the **modem**, or **modulator-demodulator**, converts digital pulses to signals that can be accepted and processed by the phone system as if they were sound. However, **digital subscriber line (DSL)** transmits digital video as well as data and voice at millions of bits per second over standard telephone lines. Unlike

Modems (modulator-demodulators) convert digital data to analog signals and vice versa.

Digital subscriber line (DSL) sends high-speed data over existing phone lines.

HOW TELEPHONES WORK

An appreciation of Morse's telegraph—and all of the electronic media that followed—begins by harking back to an experiment popular in many elementary schools. The teacher wraps wire around a big iron nail and hooks the wire up to a battery. Then she flips a switch that sends electricity flowing through the wire and the nail instantly turns into a magnet that can pick up other nails. When she flips the switch off, the nails drop dramatically back to the table. Morse's telegraph operated on the same principle, except that the telegraph key acted like the teacher's switch, turning the flow of electricity on or off, and the magnet caused a thin strip of metal to click up and down many miles away as it became magnetized and demagnetized. The pattern of clicks spells out the letters of the alphabet in Morse code. For example, the letter A is a short click (called a *dot*) followed by a long click (called a *dash*).

Now we can understand what happened when Alexander Graham Bell called out to Mr. Watson. The air pressure waves from his voice hit a flexible membrane. A short wire was attached to the membrane, and as Bell shouted, the wire bobbed up and down in a beaker of acid, varying the electrical resistance in the circuit in response to Bell's voice. That was the *variable resistance transmitter* that was the basis for Bell's patent. The wire was connected to an electromagnet in the next room, which tugged at a flexible steel reed in response to the varying current. As it vibrated, the steel reed generated air pressure waves that sounded like Bell's voice. The acid was banished after it ruined Bell's trousers, but varying an electrical current in response to sound pressure waves is still the basic function of all microphones.

For the first 40 years after Bell's invention long-distance callers had to shout to make themselves heard, but no one could shout all the way from New York to San Francisco! One of the first inventions to emerge from AT&T's labs was the repeater amplifier that made it possible to complete transcontinental calls. It used the audion tube, an invention by Lee de Forest, that also was a key development in radio broadcasting (see Chapter 6).

Another challenge was to reopen the skies above major cities whose skylines had become blocked by dozens of wires dangling from telephone poles, a technical trick called *multiplexing*. Early multiplexing systems combined telephone conversations with high-frequency carrier waves to be sent over telephone wires, just as multiple radio channels are transmitted simultaneously through the air (see Chapter 6). Coaxial cable has a single, long wire running down its central axis and a second electrical conductor that is wrapped around it like a long metal tube. This arrangement keeps unwanted signals from entering the cable and also prevents the cable signals from leaking out and interfering with other communications. The very first telephone lines were dedicated wires that connected two locations. Later, human operators manually completed calls by plugging patch cords to interconnect callers. Early automatic switches were close relatives of the jukebox. Mechanical arms rotated and jiggled up and down, touching tiny electrical contacts connected to subscribers' telephone wires. Now *intelligent networks* use a separate data network that "checks ahead" for a busy signal, so you no longer have to hang on the line while intermediate connections are established as we once did in the "olden days" of the 1980s. Conventional telephone networks are still "circuit switched" as they were a century ago, however. That means a telephone circuit spanning the continent is dedicated to your New York to Los Angeles call while it is in progress, even if you are momentarily at a loss for words. That's the type of inefficiency that digital networks are designed to eliminate.

conventional modems, DSL requires a change in the connections inside the telephone company's central office switch and, sometimes, modifications in local telephone network cabling as well. Although it's called a digital service, DSL is really a close relative of the humble dial-up modem. DSL is a **broadband** technology, meaning that it transmits data at speeds of over 768 thousand bits per second.

[**Broadband** refers to high speed Internet connections.]

DIGITAL NETWORKS

If we could redesign the telephone network from scratch today, then we could make it all digital. Digital telecommunication began back in the 1960s with the introduction of a digital carrier system, known as a *T1*. It converted voices to digital pulses and back again (see Chapter 1) and reconstructed a simulated voice for the listener on the other end. By taking turns transmitting short digital voice samples from multiple calls, 24 simultaneous conversations were combined on a single copper wire circuit. When used for data instead of phone calls, T1 lines carry 1.5 million bits per second.

However, that isn't fast enough for locations with large numbers of highly active Internet users, like college campuses. In Alexander Graham Bell's photophone, electrical signals from a telephone made a light flicker, and as the blinking light fell on a photoreceptor that converted light to electricity, the original signal was recovered. Long strands, or fibers, of glass were found to conduct light over longer distances, but still the light faded too rapidly. The laser, invented at Bell Labs, ultimately held the key to practical fiber-optic systems by producing intense beams of pure, concentrated light. **Fiber-optic** carriers are ideal for computer data since they are immune to the electrical interference that plagues copper wire systems and thus are relatively error free. Their method for sending information, turning the light source on and off, is well suited to the 1s and 0s of data communication. Optical fiber signals travel hundreds of miles before they fade and have to be regenerated, further reducing errors.

Optical carrier (OC) systems in the Internet backbone reach speeds of billions of bits per second. Many colleges and universities find they need OC connections to cope with the volume of music and video files that their students are accessing over the Internet. The speed of optical networks, including those already installed, doubles about every 18 months as engineers devise new ways to combine multiple light sources (and thus multiple data streams) in a single strand of glass. Now telephone companies are installing fiber-optic system (*FiOS*, for short) connections directly to the home, offering data transmission speeds of up to 1 billion bits per second to home users.

Cable TV companies are also installing fiber optics in their networks and making the transition to digital transmission. However, they prefer to make the final connection to subscribers with a copper-based medium, the **coaxial cable** (see Figure 12.1). All the homes in a neighborhood share the same physical cable, and that's what sometimes causes **cable modems** to slow down when the line is congested.

Packet switching divides data streams into chunks, or packets, and mixes the data from many users together into a shared, high-speed channel rather than dedicate a separate channel to each pair of users. In other words, the messages are switched around instead of the circuits. Each chunk of data carries an address so the packets can be reassembled (see Chapter 9). This approach is used in the TCP/IP Internet protocol.

Fiber-optic systems use light instead of electricity to transmit information

Coaxial cable is the high-capacity wire used for cable television transmission.

Cable modems connect personal computers to cable TV systems.

Packet switching breaks up digital information into individually addressed chunks, or packets.

Rob Casey/Stone/Getty Images

BLINKING LIGHTS Fiber-optic systems carry information at gigabit speeds with few errors. They are replacing coaxial cable and conventional copper phone lines in most wireline networks.

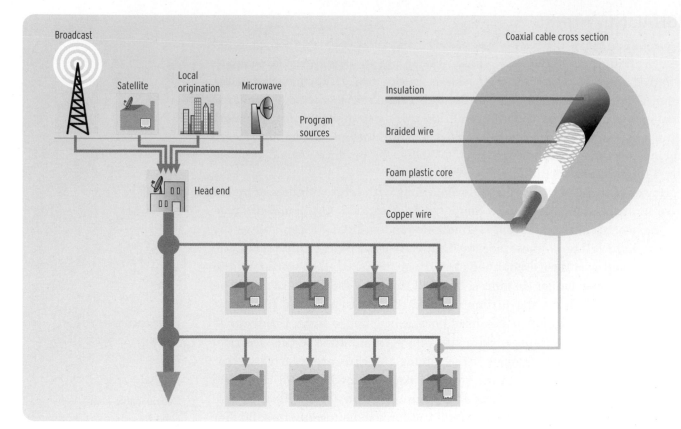

FIGURE 12.1 CABLE TV The cable head end feeds broadcast, satellite, microwave, and local origination signals into a coaxial cable distribution network of trunks, feeders, and drops in individual homes.

Packet switching is also found in the internal data networks that organizations run for themselves: local area networks (LAN see Figure 12.2). *Ethernet* is a common standard for networks for college computer labs and dormitories as well as businesses. LANs that use fiber-optic, or "fat" telephone cables (the ones with extra-wide connectors, known as RJ-45), and now wireless connections, have data transmission speeds of up to billions of bits (gigabits) per second.

Voice calls can also be digitized and divided into packets. Such calls may be terminated to conventional phone lines, or they can be completed between computers connected to the Internet, allowing for free long-distance calls. Internet telephony is revolutionizing the technology and the economics of the telecommunications industry. Since Internet protocols (IP) are used, Internet telephony also goes by the name voice over IP, or *VoIP* for short.

By integrating voice communication and Internet access in the same network, it will soon be possible to replace expensive telephone switches with cheap, generic packet switching equipment. In the United States, cable TV operators like Comcast are leading the way with local telephone service based on the same technology. Skype and Vonage as well as conventional phone companies like Verizon are among the many companies offering telephone service over Internet connections. The latest VoIP phones have the Internet connection built in so that your computer doesn't have to be turned on to make a call.

TECHNOLOGY DEMYSTIFIED

WHISTLING YOUR COMPUTER'S TUNE, OR HOW DSL WORKS

To understand how today's digital phone lines work we will backtrack to the old-fashioned modems. Modems had to use the same sound frequencies that we use to talk. Or whistle. We humans can transmit data, just not as fast. For example, to send a 1, whistle a high note (wheet). To send a 0, whistle a low-pitched note (whoot). Or, we could make a loud whistle (WHOOT) a 1 and soft whistle (whoot) for a 0. (Try it! 1000001 = WHOOT, whoot, whoot, whoot, whoot, whoot, WHOOT—that's the letter A in computer talk!). If you whistle very quickly, you might reach five bits per second, although no human listener could keep up.

The trick is to transmit more than one digit each time we whistle. For example, we could make a loud, high-pitched note (WHEET) correspond to 00, whereas a soft, low note (whoot) would be 11 (and wheet=01, WHOOT=10). Now we could whistle up the letter A as follows: WHOOT-WHEET-WHEET-whoot (we added an extra 1 at the right to fill out an eight-bit character, or byte).

Digital subscriber lines use the same old phone wires, but the phone company installs a new computer card for your line in its central office. By transmitting multiple digits every time we change the signal, we attain speeds of up to 18 million bits per second, enough for several digital television channels. Cable modems work much the same, except that the frequencies they use are farther up in the electromagnetic spectrum, well beyond the range of our hearing. The cable operator packs the data into unused television channel slots so that it travels to your home right alongside HBO.

Chris Cooley/Terry Wild Stock

NEED FOR SPEED Cable modems offer fast Internet access, but you have to share the connection with your neighbors. DSL connections can be faster but only if users are near the telephone company's central office.

MOBILE NETWORKS

Mobile communication uses techniques very similar to radio broadcasting (see Chapter 6) except that mobile services operate in different portions of the **communications spectrum** than broadcasters do and use far less powerful transmitters.

Mobile Evolution. Wireless telecommunications as we know them today are an outgrowth of World War II radar detection systems. Initially, wireless communications were *microwave* systems found at the center of the telecommunications network rather than at the periphery. They were used to carry bulk quantities of calls between cities rather than to connect Grandma and Granddad directly to each other. In 1945 Science fiction writer Arthur C. Clarke proposed that three microwave transmitters circling the planet could cover the

> The **communications spectrum** includes the range of electromagnetic radiation frequencies that are used in wireless communication systems.

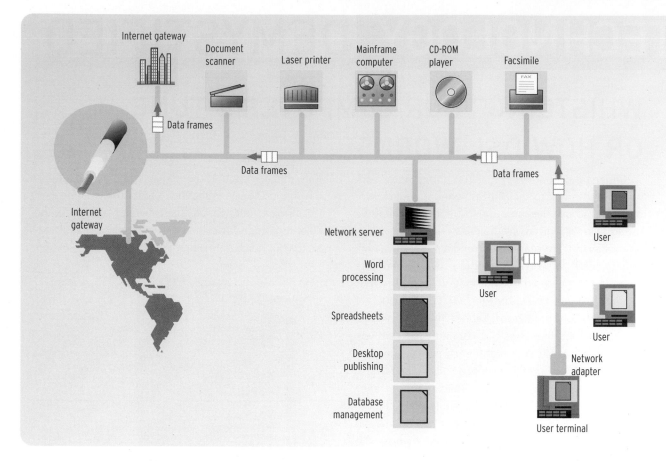

FIGURE 12.2 LAN Local area networks allow multiple users to share peripheral devices, such as printers, and to access software stored on a shared file server. Wireline LANs connect the offices on college campuses. Wireless LANs are a popular means of connecting multiple home computers to a single Internet outlet.

globe if their orbits (geosynchronous orbits 22,300 miles high) were such that their rotation speed matched that of the earth. However, the same principles would apply if we put the transmitters atop tall buildings.

The original mobile telephone service operated from a single central antenna and handled only 46 simultaneous conversations in any one city. This meant that the 47th caller did not receive a dial tone, which happened often as the subscriber base grew and multiple users contended for the limited number of channels. What was needed was a more efficient way to use scarce channel space.

First Generation. Cellular takes its name from dividing large service areas into clusters of small zones, or cells, each only a few miles across (see Technology Demystified: How Your Cell Phone Works, page 363). The transmitters in each cell are relatively weak, so it is possible to reuse their frequencies in nearby cells without causing interference. As the user moves, the call is handed off to the next cell in the network and automatically reassigned to a new channel. The first-generation cell phones, the Advanced Mobile Phone System (AMPS), use analog transmission. Some are still in use today, although cell phone companies are converting their customers to digital technology as fast as they can.

Second Generation. Second-generation cell phones are digital. They use smaller cells—some only a few hundred yards across. Digital compression is used to shrink the streams of digits and save network capacity. Digital transmission techniques make it possible for several users to share each channel,

TECHNOLOGY DEMYSTIFIED

HOW YOUR CELL PHONE WORKS

To imagine the structure of a cellular phone network, think of a honeycomb. It is made up of six-sided geometrical shapes (hexagons) arranged in neat rows. The hexagons are the cells, and in the center of each cell is a radio transmitter that "broadcasts" in the frequency range set aside for cellular radio service. The next time you ride an interstate highway, look for elongated pyramids alongside the road made out of metal tubing (they look a little like the Eiffel Tower) topped by triangular antenna arrays that look a lot like a wedge of cheese. Those are the cellular radio towers, and they are connected by wires with the rest of the public phone network through a mobile telephone switching office. Each tower has many different channels to carry calls, and those same channels can be reused at other towers that are one row of cells removed in the hexagonal pattern—that's what makes cellular radio much more efficient than the old mobile phone systems.

When you turn on your cell phone, it lets the nearest antenna know you are there. Then, when a call comes in for you, the system pages your cell phone, it rings, and if you answer your cell phone it negotiates with the nearest cell site to determine which channel to put you on. Similarly, when you place a call, your cell phone requests a channel for you and transmits the number you send.

Each cell is only a few miles across, and in a speeding automobile you may cross a cell boundary every few minutes. When that happens, the cell you are leaving automatically "hands off" your call to the next cell, which assigns you a new channel so you can continue talking.

Digital cell phones use digital compression to reduce the size of the channels that are required. They also take advantage of multiplexing to further expand capacity, but two different approaches used in the United States (and a third in Europe and most of the rest of the world) that make digital phones from competing systems incompatible. One approach assigns each caller to a designated time slot on a particular channel and then makes callers "take turns" transmitting brief streams of data on the same channel. The other approach (invented by 1940s movie star Hedy Lamarr) scatters the digital fragments of your conversation over many channels but attaches an identification code to each one so that they may be snatched from the air and reassembled into a phone conversation. Newer 4G systems break up our voice and data into packets and send them out on multiple, closely spaced channels, with the number of channels adapted to the type of transmission (e.g., voice or video).

---

expanding capacity and lowering costs. Most of the countries of the world adopted a common standard for second-generation phones called *GSM* (short for Global System for Mobile Communications), but U.S. operators built networks using two other competing standards as well that were incompatible with each other and also with GSM. GSM phones introduced the world to text messaging, more formally known as the *Short Message Service* (*SMS*) and have relatively slow (9,600 bits per second) data transmission speeds.

Third Generation. Third-generation (3G) phones were the first to cross a telephone and a handheld computer, with a built-in Web browser and e-mail service. 3G networks boast broadband transmission speeds of 1–3 million bits per second, enough to send full-color motion pictures through your cell phone, to download your favorite music and video files, and to effortlessly surf the Web on handheld computers. With data transmission speeds in the millions of bits per second, near-broadcast quality video is possible.

Not all phones with these capabilities are 3G, however, and only about half the cell phones in the United States are from that generation. So-called *2.5G phones* also have these features. They use a variation of packet switching that

> **Third-generation (3G)** cell phones have high-speed data transmission capacity for video and Internet.

IMAGINE THAT Multimedia cell phones like Apple's iPhone play music and videos as well as make phone calls. They foretell a future in which mobile Internet devices may replace conventional broadcast and print media.

TOWER OF TALK   Our smartphones connect through antennas like this one that are at the center of each of the "cells" in cellular telephone networks.

sends tiny chunks of information through the air with the address of the receiver's cell phone on each one. The 2.5G phones can surf stripped-down Web pages or can be connected to laptop computers to Net-surf at up to 100,000 bits per second. The 2.5G phones are also well suited for SMS (short message service) messages, and these phones initially launched the texting craze in the United States, where GSM networks were scarce.

If you are not an engineering student, you may wonder why it matters what generation your cell phone is and what standard it uses. It matters because of the way that many cell phone companies lock you into multiyear contracts when you buy a cell phone. Unfortunately, the lack of cell phone standards in the United States makes the selection of a carrier a risky proposition from the point of view of obsolescence.

Fourth Generation. In 2010, *fourth-generation (4G)* phones started becoming available. The profusion of incompatible cell phone standards may at last come to an end since telecom carriers around the world are adopting the *LTE* (short for Long Term Evolution) standard. The 4G phones treat both voice and data streams as packets of data like those on the Internet (see Chapter 9). They have download speeds of up to 100 million bits per second in a speeding car and up to 1 billion bits per second standing still. That is enough to support high-definition television shows and even high-definition video conferencing with our friends.

Wi-Fi. The **Wi-Fi (Wireless Fidelity)** hotspots that are cropping up everywhere are formally known as *IEEE802.11* (after the standard from the Institute for Electrical and Electronic Engineers that defines the service). Wi-Fi sends the Internet's TCP/IP packets through the air to wireless receivers at speeds of 100 million bits per second, so it is a broadband system. New Wi-Fi varieties are entering the market, some boasting the ability to move from one hotspot to another hotspot without losing the connection. Cell phones that use Wi-Fi networks, including the Wi-Fi network you may have in your home, allow you to make "free" telephone calls through your home computer connection or anywhere you happen to find a Wi-Fi connection without password protection. Some cities were planning to build Wi-Fi "clouds" to cover wider areas to offer low-cost broadband access, but these proved more difficult and expensive to build than originally thought.

Bluetooth. The desktop version of wireless networking is called *Bluetooth* (it's named after a tenth-century Danish king with dental issues). It links your digital cell phone to your personal computer, or to wireless printers, scanners, and digital cameras. It has a range of only about 300 feet and a top speed of 1/2 million bits per second, but even so, it is not limited to use around the house or the office. Bluetooth also connects your smartphone to the information systems that are quickly becoming standard on new automobiles.

customers and is now the third-ranking co[...]
well as the second-largest cell phone compa[...]

International record carriers (IRCs) hand[...]
tries. Once, every nation had a single inter[...]
was AT&T in the United States, but now the[...]
other countries have also instituted competit[...]

Interexchange carriers (IXCs in telepho[...]
long-distance telephone calls. Long-distance[...]
between area codes (such as between Grand[...]
area code 313) and those completed within a[...]
transport area (LATA) boundaries. These bo[...]
divestiture to demark local from long-dista[...]
and Sprint are now the leading IXCs. The re[...]
vided among hundreds of smaller long-dista[...]
complete calls over the Internet instead of u[...]

Local telephone service is the domain of[...]
The 1984 AT&T divestiture established seve[...]
nies (RBOCs), also known as "baby Bells" or[...]
to three: Verizon (Bell Atlantic plus NYNE[...]
soon to become CenturyLink), AT&T (forme[...]
Pacific Telesis, and BellSouth). These three [...]
pendent phone companies that served custo[...]
are now called *incumbent LECs*, or *ILECs.*[...]
ber of competitive local exchange carriers ([...]
all phone lines nationwide (FCC, 2010). So[...]
are operated by large cable companies like[...]
that now offer local and long-distance servi[...]

THE WIRELESS INDUSTRY

There are four competitors with national ce[...]
Cingular) and Verizon are the largest, follo[...]
There about 100 other cell phone compani[...]
network within local or regional markets[...]
other 50 are "virtual" cellular carriers wh[...]
but rather lease space from the major ca[...]
Virtual Network Operators (MVNOs). [...]
viders work through this arrangement as d[...]
youth market and leases network connectic[...]

Cell phone manufacturers are part of t[...]
sung and LG from South Korea are the wor[...]
mobile phones in use (FCC, 2011), althoug[...]
Google acquired Motorola, the fourth-leadir[...]
cell phones have their features programme[...]
the hardware but smartphones require soft[...]
becoming an important part of the wireless[...]
ing systems just as computers do. Nokia, A[...]
the Blackberry), Google, and Microsoft have[...]

The analogy to computer software ext[...]
grams, or **apps**, that are being develope[...]

Satellite. Voice calls using geostationary satellites like the ones used by satellite TV companies aren't feasible because callers have to wait for the signal to make a 45,000-mile round-trip to the satellite and back. However, wireless voice and data service can also be provided by satellites that fly in Low Earth Orbit (LEO), a couple of hundred miles up. The lower orbits mean smaller and cheaper receivers with a small whip antenna instead of a dish. Low-flying satellites constantly change their position so dozens are needed to ensure coverage. Satellite phones have never been an economical option and so are mainly used by foreign correspondents and arctic explorers whose travels take them to places not served by terrestrial cell phone networks.

Satellite-based broadband Internet services also have been slow to develop. The largest of these, HughesNet (formerly known as DirecWay), offers a 2 Mbps service for about the same cost of a cable modem, mainly to rural residents. Many rural areas have wireless terrestrial services offering broadband Internet speeds.

Another popular satellite technology is the *GPS* (geo-positioning satellite) system that locates lost boaters, drivers, and hikers by comparing the strength of signals received from three or more satellites turning overhead. It's becoming a standard feature in new cars to help the driver with navigation.

Smartphone gadgetry. GPS features are also in smartphones to power turn-by-turn directions and to help you locate your social networking partners. The multi-touch screen interfaces popularized by Apple's iPhone and iPad are also becoming standard. In addition, *NFC* (Near Field Communication) capabilities are being built into smartphones. These are short-range radio transmitters that allow you to send information, such as authorizing a credit card charge, by "bumping phones" with another NFC-equipped device. Other gadgets coming to your smartphone soon include altimeters (to keep track of what floor you are on in a building) and bio sensors that will monitor your health and your moods.

For now, Apple has an exclusive lock on combining voice recognition with artificial intelligence to produce a life-like electronic personal assistant it calls Siri. Siri is an example of "cloud computing" (see Chapter 9) in that requests are automatically relayed from a smartphone to a remote computer that processes the request. Similarly, Google's Goggles application triggers searches matching images that you snap with your smartphone camera. More of these are on the way, perhaps including instant facial recognition searches to help you pull up the Facebook pages of strangers you run into on the street.

New plans include head mounted display accessories for your 4G smartphone that will project information from the Internet onto eyeglasses. Google is planning one such device, a pair of geeky glasses that will superimpose information downloaded from the Internet onto your views of the real world. Directions to your destination, the price of products you are ogling, and the names of people you meet in the real world may magically appear before your eyes.

New sensors will be added to smartphones so that you can monitor the environment around you or your own internal states. Your smartphone might alert you when it smells smoke. It might monitor your heart rate as you jog or notify you that you have "sweaty palms," indicating that you are feeling anxious about the text message you just received from a significant other.

[**Wi-Fi** is short for wireless fidelity, a standard for wireless data.]

INDUST

The telephon
not unlike th
conventional
communicati
frastructure
types of busi

THE WIRE

Telephone co
the scope of t
long distance
ragged becau
nate them. Fe
after the AT&

Apps (short for applications) are software applications for use on smartphones.

Direct broadcast satellite (DBS) is a television or radio satellite service that transmits signals from satellites to compact home receivers.

makers of the operating systems make their own, the apps craze has also spawned a cottage industry of more than 100,000 independent developers. App developer is one of the possible niches in the realm of the third screen that might be filled by our readers, especially now that a variety of old media outlets in publishing and broadcasting are bringing their products to mobile platforms (see Your Media Career: Mobile Media Star).

SATELLITE CARRIERS

Most of the leading broadcast and cable networks are distributed by two dominant carriers, Intelsat and SES Americom. They build, launch, and maintain the satellites and lease transponders to the likes of CBS, CNN, and PBS. **Direct broadcast satellite (DBS)** operator DirecTV contracts with Hughes Satellite, and the Dish Network uses EchoStar for its satellite networks. Together, DirecTV and EchoStar count a fifth of the homes in the United States as subscribers. INMARSAT, Iridium, Globalstar, MSV, and Orbcomm offer mobile satellite services in the United States.

YOUR MEDIA CAREER

MOBILE MEDIA STAR

At first glance, the telecommunications industry that runs the third screen is not the best place for our readers to look for a career. Although it is one of the larger industries in the United States with over 1 million jobs, overall employment is shrinking. Many of the careers offered are in low-level customer service, installer, and sales positions whereas the upper ranks are filled with engineers and computer specialists (BLS, 2012).

However, there are a variety of interesting niches opening up that offer ground-floor opportunities not unlike those in the Internet realm a decade ago. For example, students with advanced Web design skills might consider designing apps for smartphones and iPads. Magazine publishers are getting into the app business to repackage content for the mobile user. So even if you can't write computer code there will be openings for those who can design a readable graphic layout. For those interested in video, producing and editing video content for mobile video channels is cited in the Occupational Outlook as a growth area for directors and producers. Advertising and public relations careers are another entry point. To prove our point, consider the example of Paul Scanlan, president and co-founder of MobiTV—a provider of video services to leading mobile carriers—who graduated with a BA in communication from the University of Wisconsin and started out in telecommunication sales.

Source: BLS. (2010). *Telecommunications*. http://www.bls.gov/oco/cg/cgs020.htm; http://www.mobitv.com/about/corporate-overview/management-team/

MOBILE TV MAN Paul Scanlan majored in communication at the University of Wisconsin and went on to head a mobile television company.

LATA 6

LATA 1

LATA 5

Area c

LATA 2

LAT

FIGURE 12.3 LATA Calls within an LATA are compl
long-distance carriers, whether or not both parties are in

Satellite. Voice calls using geostationary satellites like the ones used by satellite TV companies aren't feasible because callers have to wait for the signal to make a 45,000-mile round-trip to the satellite and back. However, wireless voice and data service can also be provided by satellites that fly in Low Earth Orbit (LEO), a couple of hundred miles up. The lower orbits mean smaller and cheaper receivers with a small whip antenna instead of a dish. Low-flying satellites constantly change their position so dozens are needed to ensure coverage. Satellite phones have never been an economical option and so are mainly used by foreign correspondents and arctic explorers whose travels take them to places not served by terrestrial cell phone networks.

Wi-Fi is short for wireless fidelity, a standard for wireless data.

Satellite-based broadband Internet services also have been slow to develop. The largest of these, HughesNet (formerly known as DirecWay), offers a 2 Mbps service for about the same cost of a cable modem, mainly to rural residents. Many rural areas have wireless terrestrial services offering broadband Internet speeds.

Another popular satellite technology is the *GPS* (geo-positioning satellite) system that locates lost boaters, drivers, and hikers by comparing the strength of signals received from three or more satellites turning overhead. It's becoming a standard feature in new cars to help the driver with navigation.

Smartphone gadgetry. GPS features are also in smartphones to power turn-by-turn directions and to help you locate your social networking partners. The multi-touch screen interfaces popularized by Apple's iPhone and iPad are also becoming standard. In addition, *NFC* (Near Field Communication) capabilities are being built into smartphones. These are short-range radio transmitters that allow you to send information, such as authorizing a credit card charge, by "bumping phones" with another NFC-equipped device. Other gadgets coming to your smartphone soon include altimeters (to keep track of what floor you are on in a building) and bio sensors that will monitor your health and your moods.

For now, Apple has an exclusive lock on combining voice recognition with artificial intelligence to produce a life-like electronic personal assistant it calls Siri. Siri is an example of "cloud computing" (see Chapter 9) in that requests are automatically relayed from a smartphone to a remote computer that processes the request. Similarly, Google's Goggles application triggers searches matching images that you snap with your smartphone camera. More of these are on the way, perhaps including instant facial recognition searches to help you pull up the Facebook pages of strangers you run into on the street.

New plans include head mounted display accessories for your 4G smartphone that will project information from the Internet onto eyeglasses. Google is planning one such device, a pair of geeky glasses that will superimpose information downloaded from the Internet onto your views of the real world. Directions to your destination, the price of products you are ogling, and the names of people you meet in the real world may magically appear before your eyes.

New sensors will be added to smartphones so that you can monitor the environment around you or your own internal states. Your smartphone might alert you when it smells smoke. It might monitor your heart rate as you jog or notify you that you have "sweaty palms," indicating that you are feeling anxious about the text message you just received from a significant other.

INDUSTRY: THE TELECOM MOSAIC

The telephone industry has an old media—new media transition in progress not unlike that found in the publishing and broadcasting industries. Here, the conventional wireline telephone industry is making a transition to a mobile communications industry as it converges with Internet technology. The infrastructure industry is a complex one, thanks to historic restrictions on the types of businesses that could enter.

THE WIRELINE INDUSTRY

Telephone companies can be divided roughly into three categories based on the scope of the calls they were traditionally allowed to carry: international, long distance, and local (see Figure 12.3). The distinctions are becoming quite ragged because the Telecommunications Act of 1996 was intended to eliminate them. For example, Verizon, formerly a regional local telephone company after the AT&T divestiture, now provides long-distance service to many of its

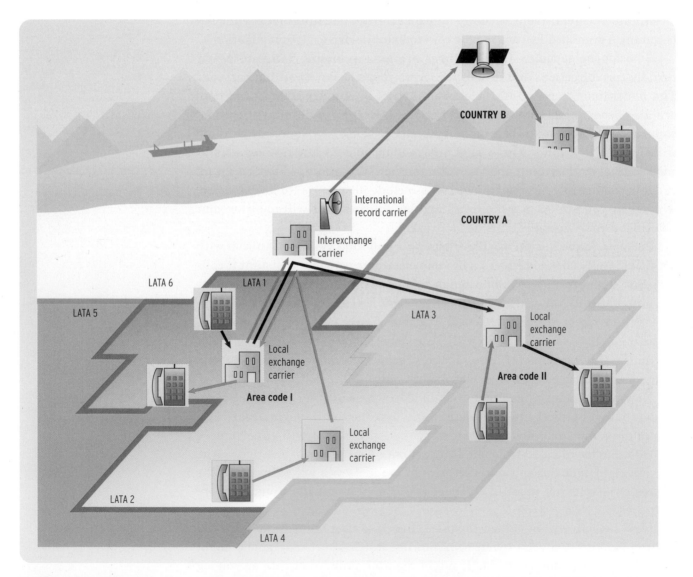

FIGURE 12.3 LATA Calls within an LATA are completed by a local exchange carrier. Calls between LATAs are handled by interexchange or long-distance carriers, whether or not both parties are in the same area code. International calls are handed off to international record carriers.

customers and is now the third-ranking consumer long-distance company as well as the second-largest cell phone company nationwide.

International record carriers (IRCs) handle long-distance calls between countries. Once, every nation had a single international long-distance carrier. This was AT&T in the United States, but now there are dozens of options, and many other countries have also instituted competition in international long distance.

Interexchange carriers (IXCs in telephone industry jargon) carry domestic long-distance telephone calls. Long-distance calls include those that are made between area codes (such as between Grand Rapids, area code 616, and Detroit, area code 313) and those completed within area codes that cross *local access and transport area* (LATA) boundaries. These boundaries were set during the AT&T divestiture to demark local from long-distance calls. Verizon, the "new" AT&T, and Sprint are now the leading IXCs. The remaining long-distance market is divided among hundreds of smaller long-distance companies, including many that complete calls over the Internet instead of using conventional phone technology.

Local telephone service is the domain of the local exchange carriers (*LECs*). The 1984 AT&T divestiture established seven Regional Bell Operating Companies (RBOCs), also known as "baby Bells" or telcos for short, which have merged to three: Verizon (Bell Atlantic plus NYNEX), Qwest (formerly U.S. West and soon to become CenturyLink), AT&T (formerly SBC, which bought Ameritech, Pacific Telesis, and BellSouth). These three and more than 750 other local independent phone companies that served customers before the AT&T divestiture are now called *incumbent LECs*, or *ILECs*. They compete with a similar number of competitive local exchange carriers (*CLECs*) that serve about a third of all phone lines nationwide (FCC, 2010). Some of the more successful CLECs are operated by large cable companies like Comcast and Time Warner Cable that now offer local and long-distance service over their cable networks.

THE WIRELESS INDUSTRY

There are four competitors with national cell phone networks. AT&T (formerly Cingular) and Verizon are the largest, followed by Sprint Nextel and T-Mobile There about 100 other cell phone companies that own and operate their own network within local or regional markets such as Leap and MetroPCS. Another 50 are "virtual" cellular carriers who don't have networks of their own but rather lease space from the major carriers and resell it, called **Mobile Virtual Network Operators (MVNOs)**. Many of the prepaid cell phone providers work through this arrangement as does Boost Mobile, which targets the youth market and leases network connections from Sprint Nextel (FCC, 2011).

Cell phone manufacturers are part of the wireless picture, of course. Samsung and LG from South Korea are the world leaders in terms of the number of mobile phones in use (FCC, 2011), although Apple is catching up fast. In 2011 Google acquired Motorola, the fourth-leading cell phone manufacturer. "Dumb" cell phones have their features programmed on the computer chips built into the hardware but smartphones require software, and supplying that software is becoming an important part of the wireless industry. Smartphones have operating systems just as computers do. Nokia, Apple, Research in Motion (makers of the Blackberry), Google, and Microsoft have competing systems.

The analogy to computer software extends to the many application programs, or **apps**, that are being developed for smartphones. Although the

[**Mobile Virtual Network Operators (MVNOs)** offer mobile services by leasing capacity from network owners.]

Ted Thai/Time Life Pictures/Getty Images

PLACING YOUR CALL Long-distance networks are monitored at network control centers like this one. Network engineers can intervene to redirect traffic when routes become overcrowded or damaged.

makers of the operating systems make their own, the apps craze has also spawned a cottage industry of more than 100,000 independent developers. App developer is one of the possible niches in the realm of the third screen that might be filled by our readers, especially now that a variety of old media outlets in publishing and broadcasting are bringing their products to mobile platforms (see Your Media Career: Mobile Media Star).

[**Apps** (short for applications) are software applications for use on smartphones.]

[**Direct broadcast satellite (DBS)** is a television or radio satellite service that transmits signals from satellites to compact home receivers.]

SATELLITE CARRIERS

Most of the leading broadcast and cable networks are distributed by two dominant carriers, Intelsat and SES Americom. They build, launch, and maintain the satellites and lease transponders to the likes of CBS, CNN, and PBS. **Direct broadcast satellite (DBS)** operator DirecTV contracts with Hughes Satellite, and the Dish Network uses EchoStar for its satellite networks. Together, DirecTV and EchoStar count a fifth of the homes in the United States as subscribers. INMARSAT, Iridium, Globalstar, MSV, and Orbcomm offer mobile satellite services in the United States.

————YOUR MEDIA CAREER

MOBILE MEDIA STAR

At first glance, the telecommunications industry that runs the third screen is not the best place for our readers to look for a career. Although it is one of the larger industries in the United States with over 1 million jobs, overall employment is shrinking. Many of the careers offered are in low-level customer service, installer, and sales positions whereas the upper ranks are filled with engineers and computer specialists (BLS, 2012).

However, there are a variety of interesting niches opening up that offer ground-floor opportunities not unlike those in the Internet realm a decade ago. For example, students with advanced Web design skills might consider designing apps for smartphones and iPads. Magazine publishers are getting into the app business to repackage content for the mobile user. So even if you can't write computer code there will be openings for those who can design a readable graphic layout. For those interested in video, producing and editing video content for mobile video channels is cited in the Occupational Outlook as a growth area for directors and producers. Advertising and public relations careers are another entry point. To prove our point, consider the example of Paul Scanlan, president and co-founder of MobiTV— a provider of video services to leading mobile carriers— who graduated with a BA in communication from the University of Wisconsin and started out in telecommunication sales.

Source: BLS. (2010). *Telecommunications.* http://www. bls.gov/oco/cg/cgs020.htm; http://www.mobitv.com/about/corporate-overview/management-team/

MOBILE TV MAN Paul Scanlan majored in communication at the University of Wisconsin and went on to head a mobile television company.

CONTENT: THERE'S AN APP FOR US

No one has yet defined genres of smartphone apps, but some broad categories are beginning to emerge. Apps, in the sense of programmed features, also exist for conventional wireline phones and mobile "dumbphones," although we are not used to thinking of them that way.

WIRELESS APPS

Visits to the "app stores" were our starting point in an effort to define app genres. Some of the app categories at Apple fit neatly into the functions of the mass media that we discovered in Chapter 2. The surveillance (apps for keeping current), values transmission (apps for students), and entertainment (music, fun, and games) functions are well represented. There is no obvious category that matches the interpretation function, but social networking and book apps might fill that niche. Conventional mass media such as newspapers and television were never ideally suited for some other vital functions that we have apps for, including making money, staying fit, and being productive at work, but we can find many apps for them. Other categories are defined by who you are (e.g., students, parents), whereas others are based on where you are (e.g., outdoors, travelling) or what you are doing (e.g., cooking, working out).

Table 12.1 is a list of the most popular app categories in terms of the number of active applications at the Apple app store, some 750,000 in all at the time of this writing. The iPad has about 140,000. Amazon, Google, Blackberry, and Microsoft have app stores of their own. Games are the top genre by number of apps. The biggest hit in appdom is the "Angry Birds" game with 100 million downloads and counting, although "Temple Run" is moving up the list fast. Video games account for half of the most downloaded apps across all platforms. Free versions of Facebook, Twitter, Skype, Google Maps, and Apple's iBook reader round out the list (Distimo, 2011).

One genre you won't find for the iPhone is pornography. Apple censors apps featuring nudity and explicit sex. Apple app developers also can't publish apps that incorporate the popular Flash program because Apple's review guidelines prohibit that as well, a restriction that many developers chafe at. The Android Market and Blackberry App World are less restrictive, a difference that might matter in the race to catch up with Apple.

LOCATION-BASED SERVICES

As the name implies, **location-based services** vary their content according to where we are and add some interesting new dimensions to our favorite online activities. For example, location-based social networking apps like Foursquare can create a map of where our online "friends" are in the real world in case we should want to talk to them face-to-face. They can also provide helpful directions if we get lost or want to find the nearest restaurant in a strange city. Advertisers

STOP & REVIEW

1. What are the major types of digital data networks?
2. What are the important trends in mobile communications?
3. What is the difference between 3G and 4G mobile services?
4. Define and distinguish the following terms: *IXC, LEC, CLEC, RBOC, IRC.*
5. What does an MVNO do?

[**Location-based services** use information about the location of mobile phone users to tailor content to specific locations.]

Table 12.1 Top 10 App Categories

CATEGORY	NUMBER OF APPS (PERCENT)
Games	99,795 (17.37%)
Books	61,175 (10.65%)
Entertainment	58,962 (10.26%)
Education	55,772 (9.71%)
Lifestyle	47,351 (8.24%)
Utilities	34,643 (6.03%)
Travel	29,636 (5.16%)
Business	25,875 (4.50%)
Music	22,990 (4.00%)
Reference	20,134 (3.50%)

Source: http://148apps.biz, based on active applications at the Apple App Store March 1, 2012.

are excited about the prospect of location-based advertising and smartphones that can scan barcodes from billboards and in-store displays (see Chapter 11).

M-commerce is just starting to catch on in the United States, although it has been common in Europe and the Far East for years now. The many shoppers who bring their cell phones into stores to search the Web for deals at other retailers or to order out-of-stock sale items online represent one aspect of this trend. Smartphone apps that use their built-in cameras to scan barcodes make this an efficient shopping strategy. Also coming are electronic wallets that will let us pay for our fast-food meal by pointing and clicking our cell phone at the cash register. There are also text-payment services that will let you transfer cash to those who don't accept credit cards—no more "Sorry, fella, I'm out of change."

WIRELINE APPS

The oldest app of all, although apparently one going out of style, is the ability to talk to a real person. Basic local telephone service has the acronym *POTS*, for plain old telephone service. The POTS functions—dial tone, transmission, and switching—are unchanged since the 1890s. Computerized switching added options like touch-tone dialing, call waiting, speed dialing, three-way calling, and call forwarding in the 1970s.

Many interactive features are available on cell phones and wireline phones alike. In the wireline world these are known as *Custom local area signaling services* (*CLASS*) if they are implemented as value-added services rather than in the telephone's hardware. They include caller ID, voice mail, automatic redialing of the last party we called, or the last party who called us. Wireline phone companies are beginning to imitate cell phone features, too. For example, some offer text messaging services that use a computerized voice to read the messages for those who don't have a display on their phone.

Long-distance calls on wireline phones are still often placed by a different company from the one that provides your local service: a specialized long-distance carrier. When customers sign up for local telephone service, they can designate one company as their primary long-distance carrier. Dial-around long-distance services, the ones that make you dial "ten-ten" or an 800 number, bypass the designated carrier.

Toll-free calls are also provided by long-distance carriers. These are so popular that the original block of 800 numbers is exhausted, so now 888, 866, and 877 prefixes are also used. These are not really free calls. The charges are reversed and callers ultimately pay for them in the price of the products they order.

MEDIALITERACY

SERVICE FOR EVERYONE?

The main issues confronting society regarding the infrastructure industry still revolve around fulfilling the Kingsbury Commitment (see page 352): how to provide affordable service to all. What does that commitment mean in an era of wireless, digital telecommunications?

SET MY CELL PHONE FREE!

In choosing a cell phone, an important consideration is whether or not the phone is "locked"; that is, whether it can be used only on the network of the carrier that you buy it from. Carriers lock their phones in an attempt to recoup the cost of the phone that is offered for free or for a deep discount at the time you initiate a service contract. But that means you may have to buy a new cell phone (and reenter all the addresses and phone numbers you have stored) to switch to a new cell phone company unless your carrier unlocks it at the end of the contract. The "lock" is not a physical lock but software that is loaded onto the SIM (Subscriber Identification Module) card that activates your phone on your company's network. Some carriers, and also some shady characters you can find on the Internet, may offer to unlock a phone for a fee but it still may not work correctly and could void your warrantee.

Until recently, buying your own phone at the full retail price or a cheap pre-paid phone were the only options, but a growing number of carriers offer un-locked options, so it is a good idea to check. The 2008 spectrum auction prompted an opening of cell phone networks. At the urging of Google, which has since come out with a cell phone of its own, the FCC agreed that some of the frequencies will be open and that winning bidders will have to offer unlocked phones.

CONSUMER ISSUES IN TELECOMMUNICATIONS

The Telecommunications Act of 1996 was intended to untangle ownership rules and line-of-business restrictions and let free market forces prevail for the benefit of consumers. The hope was that industry structure would remain fluid and that com-petition and continuing technological change would drive down prices. Whether it was policy or technology that was responsible, consumers do have many more op-tions these days that might save them money than before the Telecom Act.

There are hundreds of long-distance carriers to choose from but for the Internet-savvy, the "rock bottom" prices are found through VoIP providers like Skype and Vonage. VoIP providers can pick up the call from your local tele-phone company and switch it through the Internet, where it rings through to a conventional phone on the other end. For totally free long-distance calling on the Internet you have to arrange in advance with your calling partner and use their Internet (IP) address, rather than their telephone number.

No one should be paying more than a dime a minute these days, and some rates go as low as two cents a minute. Local toll calls, those that stay within the same area code but are still billed by the minute, are also competitive now. Consumers must designate a separate carrier for these calls as well. The same company that provides local service can carry the calls, but competing compa-nies may offer lower rates.

To sort through your cell phone options there are online comparisons of services available in your area (e.g., http://www.getconnected.com). When sign-ing up for a new plan, beware the practice known as "cramming." That is when the customer service rep you place the order with signs you up for extra-cost services. Now, unlocked options are being offered by many carriers and in the long run they can save users money despite the steep up-front purchase price of the phone itself. Thanks to an agreement between the FCC and cell phone companies, getting an unpleasant surprise when your bill arrives should not happen anymore. Carriers are supposed to notify you when you are getting near your monthly limit. You can also slash your phone bill by sending text messages and voice calls through data networks instead of the phone networks, by using services such as Skype or Apple's iMessage service. And, if you are worried about "maxing out" your minutes, you can also wait until you have a Wi-Fi connection to stream videos or music.

Cell phones are quickly making pay phones obsolete, but the ones that are left may have a nasty surprise in store if you are not careful. Pay phones charge as much as two dollars a minute and tend to be located where there are vulnerable populations, such as college students away from home for the first time.

WHOSE SUBSIDIES ARE UNFAIR?

It has long been the practice to subsidize some phone uses at the expense of others. Before it was broken up in 1984, the "old" AT&T diverted revenues from long distance to subsidize local telephone service with the regulators' blessings. Now surcharges of 7 to 12 percent are tacked onto your long-distance bill to support local exchanges.

Some users are subsidized as a matter of social policy. Low-income households get special low phone rates and homeless persons are being provided with cell phones to help them connect to employment and housing. In 2011 the FCC re-shaped universal service policy for the information age by re-directing some of the funds to improve broadband Internet access (see Chapter 15). Rural subscribers pay the same rates as city residents even though it costs much more to serve them.

Now there is a move to "de-average" telephone rates so that they will match the true cost of service. That sounds fair, doesn't it? But it may drive many rural residents off the network. And all residential phone subscribers are subsidized by businesses. Should that subsidy be eliminated, too? Ouch. Subsidies always seem unfair until it is *our* subsidy that is taken away.

UNIVERSAL SERVICE? The promise of affordable telephone services for all Americans has not been kept for everyone. Many people still have to rely on pay phones to make their calls, but the number of pay phones has dwindled and pay phone users are still susceptible to excessive per-minute charges.

WHO CONTROLS THE AIRWAVES?

Historically, licenses to use communication frequencies were awarded in competitive proceedings by the FCC to the companies that were best qualified to operate in the public interest (see Chapter 15). But now free markets are "in" and regulation is "out," and auctions have replaced competitive licensing. Less government bureaucracy is needed to monitor that system, and the proceeds from the auctions go into the public treasury, so theoretically they reduce the tax burden for all. However, the auction proceeds have been unpredictable and subject to speculation. Some "winning" bidders have been bankrupted by the exorbitant sums they paid, whereas other auctions have seen valuable spectrum space go for bargain-basement prices.

Auctions have also meant less government influence in achieving important social goals. Now the regulatory pendulum is beginning to swing back in the direction of government intervention. The economic stimulus plan enacted by Congress in 2009 to revitalize the American economy required the FCC to formulate a national broadband strategy. The FCC wants to make the speed and cost of the U.S. infrastructure more competitive with that of other developed nations. The United States has dropped behind fifteen other nations, making this more urgent (OECD 2011.) With the rapid increase in cell phone-only households and the growing use of cell phones for texting, Web surfing, and video, even the new allocations may not be enough to satisfy demand. A radical proposal is to take spectrum away from television broadcasters. In 2012, Congress enacted a law that will auction off broadcast television channels to wireless providers.

Television occupies some prime spectrum space where signals easily penetrate buildings. Also, the current channel allocations waste valuable space by leaving channels blank to prevent interference. However, the television stations we depend on for local news won't disappear. Rather, the channel allocations will be reorganized to move them closer together to free up space for wireless, and broadcasters will be compensated for their trouble.

ALL OF OUR CIRCUITS ARE . . . DESTROYED

An information society is inherently dependent on the functioning of its communications infrastructure. The September 11, 2001 terrorist attacks and Hurricane Katrina in 2005 demonstrated both the vulnerability and the resiliency of the telecommunications infrastructure.

The World Trade Center was a major hub for telecommunications. The falling towers destroyed telephone switching equipment serving 175,000 customers in lower Manhattan, cell phone and broadcast antennas atop the Twin Towers, and fiber-optic links in the Trade Center's basement that carried Internet traffic as far away as Washington, D.C. Still, emergency 911 phone service never went down, and portable cell phone towers were quickly trucked in to restore service near Ground Zero. AT&T technicians were able to open lines for outgoing long-distance calls with a few taps on their keyboards, and Verizon was able to quickly reroute local lines for use by government and emergency officials (Guernsey, 2001).

New Orleans residents were not so fortunate after Katrina hit. The floodwaters immediately knocked out the electronics for millions of customers, and more lines, including cell phone towers, continued to fail as their emergency backup power supplies ran out of gas. The Department of Defense was able to restore emergency communication links via satellite, but no one thought to stock extra batteries for the satellite phones that were supposed to provide coordination among emergency agencies. The result was chaos and a pointed reminder of how vital telecommunications infrastructure is to our civilization.

You and I can make these disasters even worse by immediately jumping on the phone to call our relatives, which just further overloads the networks. A helpful suggestion: next time use text messaging to let your family and friends know you

MAJOR HUB The 9/11 terror attacks disrupted phone service throughout the Northeast. Service was quickly restored but the telecommunications infrastructure remains vulnerable to disasters and hacker attacks.

survived. Texting puts far less strain on the networks we all rely on in emergencies. You will also start receiving emergency text messages about terror attacks, natural disasters, and child abductions from the president and local authorities as part of a new nationwide alerting system.

BIG BROTHER IS LISTENING

The 9/11 attacks also produced some changes in telecommunications surveillance laws. As any devotee of TV cop shows knows, law enforcement can listen in on phone conversations and read your e-mail only if they have a warrant from a local judge that establishes a probable cause for their search (that is, probable evidence that a crime will be discovered). About 1,300 wiretaps a year are authorized in the United States for criminal investigations, mostly for drug-related crimes. However, information about the time and destination of calls (sometimes called *trap-and-trace information*) is considered less private and is easier to obtain—law enforcement merely has to certify that it is needed for an investigation, with no hearing or probable cause required. This turned into a national scandal when it was revealed that phone companies had been supplying the government with the records of billions of domestic calls from ordinary citizens so that "patterns" of communication that might reveal terrorist activities could be discovered. Congress legalized that in 2008.

Digital technology complicated telephone surveillance. If the police tap an Internet connection, all they hear is computer noise, not "I'll send you the plans for the nuclear power plant next Tuesday." Copper wires are easy to tap since they radiate electromagnetic energy that can be readily intercepted, but fiber-optic lines are untappable without physically cutting into them. This led law enforcement officials to request—and receive—special access ports to digital networks in the telephone central offices. Under the Communications Assistance for Law Enforcement Act, they have special access to Internet provider networks, too, including those operated by colleges and universities. In the aftermath of the September 11 attacks, Congress passed the USA PATRIOT Act (see also Chapter 15), which significantly expanded the scope of surveillance. Trap-and-trace authority is extended to the Internet so that now law officers without a warrant can demand to see records of the websites you visited. The FBI and the CIA can conduct nationwide roving wiretaps without going through local courts or even naming specific suspects. The law seems to contain loopholes that would allow domestic law enforcement agencies to circumvent restrictions placed on them by claiming the search is covered by the Foreign Intelligence Surveillance Act, under which warrants are issued in secret. Similarly, national security agencies might circumvent the limits on them by obtaining information from domestic law enforcement agencies. Although we all hope these measures will help crack down on terrorists, civil libertarians fear this legislation could usher in a future society, patterned after George Orwell's *1984*, that will routinely monitor the movements and words of all citizens.

PRIVACY ON THE LINE

So we can't be sure the government isn't listening in on our conversations, but can our nosy neighbors hear us? The Electronic Communication Privacy Act

(ECPA) generally assures us that our wireline conversations cannot be tapped or recorded without our permission or legal authorization.

However, the issue of telephone privacy is a complex one, depending upon the technology we use and where we use it. If we use a cordless phone, we lose our legal right to privacy. That's because the frequencies that cordless phones use are in the easily accessible FM radio spectrum and are readily intercepted.

If we use a cell phone, the electronic transmission is protected even though older-model scanners can tune in. By law, newer scanners can't access the cell phone frequencies. That law was enacted precisely to preserve the expectation of cell privacy. But if we carry on our cell phone conversations in a public space we may lose that expectation. In addition to being rude, we are making public utterances that can be intercepted and recorded, and a sensitive microphone might also pick up the voice of the person we are talking to through our handset.

A new privacy threat comes from cell phone locator services. Cell phone providers have been required to deploy technology that makes it possible to identify the location of cell phones within about 1,000 feet. That's so emergency 911 calls can be traced back to their origin. New GPS-enabled phones will pin down your location even more precisely and in 2011 it came to light that Apple was quietly storing location information in hidden files on iPhones and iPads. Smartphone companies are eager to turn that information into cash by selling it to parents of wayward teens and to marketers. However, cell phone (and also e-mail) records have also become common items of discovery in divorce proceedings and civil suits. So, it's a good idea to erase your cell phone memory when you turn in your phone, by following the reset procedure in your user's manual (or download instructions from www.recellular.com).

On the plus side, the Federal Trade Commission has a Do-Not-Call list under the Telephone Consumer Protection Act, passed back in 1991. Now you can sign up online (just do a Google search for "Do Not Call" to find it) to have your phone number protected from telemarketing calls. Violators face fines of $11,000 per call. However, nonprofit organizations, pollsters, market researchers, and companies that you have a prior relationship with (such as your college's or university's alumni fund raisers) are exempt. And if you respond to a mail solicitation to request "further information" about a product or service, that establishes enough of a prior relationship to invite telemarketers to call. Cell phones get special protection from an especially annoying privacy invasion, so-called "robo calls" containing pre-recorded messages from politicians and marketers. There is also a new law, the Truth in Caller ID Act that prohibits the use of phony caller IDs by telemarketers. However, telemarketers have learned to disguise their true identities by forwarding calls through foreign countries over the Internet, making it difficult for both consumers and the FTC to track down the offenders.

Another privacy option is to encrypt your calls. Digital cell phone calls are scrambled and some of them scatter pieces of your conversation across a wide range of channels, making them difficult to intercept. Add-on encryption systems (Google "cell phone encryption") are available. But anything that can be scrambled can also be unscrambled with a powerful enough computer. What do you have to hide?

STOP&REVIEW

1. What are some major categories of apps?

2. What has been the impact of the Telecommunications Act on consumers?

3. What are the main issues in spectrum allocation?

4. Who receives subsidized telephone service in the United States?

5. What are the threats to phone privacy?

SUMMARY &REVIEW

WHAT WERE THE ORIGINS OF TODAY'S TELECOMMUNICATIONS INDUSTRY?

Morse's telegraph and Bell's telephone were the first electronic communications networks. Bell founded the company that was to become American Telephone and Telegraph (AT&T). AT&T's effort to monopolize the infrastructure by buying the Western Union Telegraph Company led to government regulation that shaped the entire telecommunications industry for decades. Important interventions included the Communications Act of 1934 and the Modified Final Judgment (MFJ) of 1984 that forced AT&T to divest itself of the companies (Regional Bell operating companies, RBOCs) that provided local telephone service, while retaining its long-distance network.

HOW DID MOBILE PHONES DEVELOP?

Before radio broadcasting began, the medium was used primarily for mobile wireless communication with ocean-going vessels. Although mobile telephone service dates back to 1946, early systems were plagued by insufficient capacity. CB radio and pagers were developed to fill the gap. In 1983 cellular radio service was introduced in the United States, expanding the capacity of mobile telephone networks. Consumer smartphones originated in the late 1990s, representing the convergence of cell phones and personal data assistants.

WHAT ARE THE IMPACTS OF MOBILE COMMUNICATIONS?

Mobile communication devices like the Blackberry, iPhone, and iPad are the third screen which, in addition to television and computer screens, offer a wide variety of entertainment and information services to their users. They are rapidly replacing conventional wireline phones and converging with Internet services to enable new forms of mobile e-commerce transactions. Mobile media offer both threats and opportunities to the business models of conventional mass media. At the individual level, mobiles can improve personal safety and interpersonal relationships but also pose threats to health and highway safety.

WHAT ARE THE TRENDS IN DIGITAL NETWORKS?

High-speed digital subscriber line (DSL), coaxial cable, and fiber-optic systems are replacing the pokey telephone modems of yesterday. Virtually all types of communication, including our daily phone conversations, are being converted to digital formats that can be transmitted as Internet data through packet switching.

HOW ARE WIRELESS DATA SERVICES EVOLVING?

Third-generation (3G) cell phones and other broadband systems are making wireless Internet access commonplace. Wi-Fi is the location-specific wireless Internet technology found in coffee shops and home offices. Bluetooth is the short-range wireless option for cell phone ear pieces and wireless printers. Fourth-generation (4G) cell phone networks becoming available offer high-quality video including two-way video services. Handheld devices are becoming conduits for radio, television, games, and movies.

HOW IS THE INFRASTRUCTURE INDUSTRY ORGANIZED?

Local exchange carriers (LECs) can carry local calls, interexchange carriers (IXCs) carry domestic long-distance calls, and international record carriers (IRCs) carry international calls. Competitive local exchange carriers (CLECs) are a new type of telephone carrier permitted to carry local telephone calls in competition with an established local exchange carrier. Both national and regional mobile phone companies can own and operate their own networks. Mobile Virtual Network Operators (MVNOs) resell discount cell phone services. Companies that provide software and apps for smartphones are a fast-growing segment of the telecommunications industry.

WHAT ARE THE TRENDS IN TELEPHONE SERVICES?

Local telephone service extends beyond plain old telephone service. Custom calling features made possible by the intelligent network, such as caller ID, give users a large measure of control over their communications. Music downloads and television services are extra-cost options that are being popularized by smartphones connected to advanced 3G and 4G networks. Smartphone apps fill a wide variety of entertainment, information, and personal productivity needs. Location-based services are a new category of interactive applications unique to the third screen.

HOW DO TELECOMMUNICATION POLICIES AFFECT CONSUMERS?

A recent policy change encourages cell phone operators to unlock cell phones. Other efforts to increase competition in telecommunications services have increased the number of options available to consumers and have driven down prices in some instances. Government regulations subsidize basic telephone and Internet service for low-income families, rural residents, and residential telephone subscribers. A long-term trend toward freeing up telecommunications markets in the United States is beginning to reverse amid efforts to assure universal service and international competitiveness.

WHAT CHALLENGES DO TELECOMMUNICATIONS NETWORKS POSE FOR SOCIETY?

Society must decide how to allocate scarce resources, such as the communications spectrum, to competing interests. The growing reliance on the information infrastructure makes society increasingly vulnerable to technical disruption of telecommunications providers. Advanced digital technology also poses barriers to the legitimate electronic surveillance needs of law enforcement officials while at the same time raising the specter of excessive snooping on ordinary citizens.

THINKING CRITICALLY
ABOUT THE MEDIA

1. How are mobile devices affecting the mass media?

2. How has your smartphone changed your life for better? For worse?

3. Pretty soon you will be able to have a two-way wrist TV. What would you do with that?

4. Describe how a cell phone works so that a 12-year-old child could understand it.

5. What will your mobile phone be like in 2020?

6. What is the justification for taking spectrum away from television and giving it to mobile providers?

7. Now that you know your cell phone is a threat to your privacy, what will you do?

KEY TERMS

apps (p. 368)

broadband (p. 358)

cable modem (p. 359)

coaxial cable (p. 359)

common carrier (p. 352)

communications spectrum (p. 361)

digital subscriber line (DSL) (p. 357)

direct broadcast satellite (DBS) (p. 368)

Federal Communications Commission (FCC) (p. 352)

fiber-optic (p. 359)

infrastructure (p. 350)

location-based service (p. 369)

m-commerce (p. 357)

microwave (p. 353)

Mobile Virtual Network Operators (MVNOs) (p. 367)

modem (modulator-demodulator) (p. 357)

packet switching (p. 359)

patent (p. 351)

Regional Bell Operating Companies (RBOCs) (p. 352)

satellite (p. 353)

smartphone (p. 355)

Telecommunications Act of 1996 (p. 354)

third generation (3G) (p. 363)

universal service (p. 352)

vertical integration (p. 351)

Wi-Fi (Wireless Fidelity) (p. 365)

VIDEO GAMES are the fastest-growing entertainment medium today, but did you know they can trace their roots to prehistoric times? From ancient Egypt to Xbox, we examine their controversial impact on society.

13

VIDEO GAMES

HISTORY: GETTING GAME
OPENING PLAY

Games are as old as civilization itself. Senet dates back nearly 5,000 years to ancient Egypt and its game boards engraved in stone have been found among the ruins of the pyramids. "Senet" involved a race to a finish line while overcoming various barriers and setbacks and so shares key play elements with video games in the "Mario Brothers" and "Sonic the Hedgehog" series. Chess, a forerunner of strategy and role-playing games of our day, emerged in its present form in Europe about 1,000 years ago after evolving from earlier games in India and the Middle East (Parlett, 1999). Early nineteenth-century war simulations played by Prussian army officers as well as family game room staples like "Monopoly" and penny arcade pinball machines were also forerunners of today's video games (Egenfeldt-Nielsen et al., 2008; Kent, 2001).

If we consider a **video game** to be one played on a television screen, then the first was "Chase," developed by inventor Ralph Baer in 1967. However, if we define video games to be **digital games** played on a visual display created by a digital computer, then the honors might go (there are competing claims) to the "Spacewar!" game created by Steve Russell and two other MIT students in 1962 (Kirriemuir, 2006).

Video game uses a television or similar screen to display the game play.

Digital game is a game in which a digital computer facilitates the game play.

1972	"Pong" is an arcade hit, Odyssey the first game console	1985	Nintendo Entertainment System introduced
1977	Video game market crashes, cartridge games introduced	2011	"Call of Duty Modern Warfare 3" achieves movie blockbuster sales
1983	Video game market crashes again		

Nolan Bushnell created an arcade version of "Spacewar!" called "Computer Space" that used a television as its display device, making it the first widely available arcade video game. However, in a world full of gaming novices it proved too difficult to play in its time. The first turning point for video games was the release of a second arcade game made by Bushnell in 1972, an electronic version of table tennis called "Pong." Bushnell founded Atari to manufacture and distribute the coin-operated version, and the company became a dominant force in the first golden age of video games that followed (Kirriemuir, 2006). Coin-operated arcade games like "Space Invaders," "Asteroids," and "Pac-Man" popped up in bars and shopping malls everywhere over the next decade.

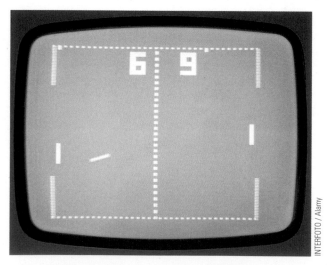

INTERFOTO / Alamy

YOUR TURN "Pong" was the first hit arcade video game. Together with versions made for home consoles, it launched the development of video games.

HOME GAME

Games entered the home to capitalize on the arcade game craze. Baer's invention evolved into the first home video game console, "Odyssey," that went on sale the same year "Pong" hit the arcades. A glut of "Pong" imitations and the introduction of second-generation consoles led to the first great crash in the video game market in 1977.

The second generation included consoles from Atari that accepted cartridges that stored the games; that enabled consoles to play many different games, and players could add new titles as they pleased, the same basic model that continues with consoles today. This innovation also encouraged independent software developers like Activision to begin making cartridges for the best-selling consoles. Popular home games built on arcade hits of the day and introduced titles such as "Mario Brothers" that have become mainstays across multiple generations of consoles.

A popular arcade game, "Donkey Kong," also marked the debut of Nintendo in the American home market. Japanese game artist Shigeru Miyamoto created the original Mario character (originally called "Jumpman") for that game. However, a glut of consoles, a price war among console makers, competition from personal computers and independent developers, and hastily designed and unoriginal games led to a second great crash in the video game market in 1983. Notable among the failures was "E.T. The Extraterrestrial" which, despite its tie-in to a block-buster movie, was so hastily developed that it is sometimes cited as the worst video game ever made. The crash eventually forced all of the console makers of that era to sell out or go bankrupt (Kent, 2001). Many thought that video games were dead.

PERSONAL COMPUTERS GET IN THE GAME

The integration of video games with personal computers was a turning point in the development of both. The Commodore 64 was an early personal computer that had "plenty of game" for its time and it played a major role in introducing video games in the home. It featured color graphics and

MARIO MAKER Japanese video game designer Shigeru Miyamoto created the original Mario video game character. The "Mario Brothers" series is one of the best-selling games of all time.

the same game controllers as the popular Atari game console. The Commodore inspired former Apple employee Trip Hawkins to found video game software maker Electronic Arts that would go on to be the largest video game publisher.

Other early computers were not as playful as the Commodore. The first IBM-compatible PCs had only four-color graphics, and the first Apple Macintosh had black-and-white images. However, by the end of the 1980s personal computers had colorful displays and sound and graphics options were available to make them viable game machines. Computer games became one of the main reasons for buying home computers.

Even before the Internet reached the home, online services were connecting their users to multiplayer games. The first online game was a 1969 version of "Spacewar!" that could be played on PLATO, an online system developed to deliver interactive school lessons. The system required specialized terminals and network connections that were quite rare at the time, but over the course of several years early versions of various multiplayer genres were developed for it, including role-playing, shooter, strategy, adventure, computer bridge, and flight simulator games (Koster, 2002).

"Dungeons & Dragons," a role-playing game developed in the early 1970s and initially played on paper with miniature figurines, inspired computerized versions like the one player interactive text game "Adventure," played on both the Internet and single computers, and multi-player games called *MUDs* (multi-user dungeon). Roy Trubshaw and Richard Bartle are often credited with developing the first one. A version was placed on ARPANet, the forerunner of today's Internet (see Chapter 9) in 1980, giving it a claim to be the first multiplayer game on the Internet (Koster, 2002; Mulligan, 2000).

"MegaWars I" was something of a hit in the pre-Internet era. It was hosted by an early online service called *CompuServe*. Present-day online game players who fret about the monthly fees, take note: early online services charged several dollars *per hour* for achingly slow connections of 300 bps (Koster,

2002). Given the crude displays of early home computers and the slow transmission speeds, early online games were either purely text-based or managed only crude images made from standard keyboard (ASCII) characters. Offline games were also making an appearance on home computer screens, with the puzzle game "Tetris" an early hit in 1986 (Gamespot, 2010).

Despite the crude graphics, the first reports of financial and family ruin related to excessive online gaming began to emerge. In 1993 the social impact of online games was also registered through an incident in the lambdaMOO (*MOO* stands for MUD, Object Oriented, another term used for early role-playing games). A virtual "rape" was committed, drawing wide attention to the online gaming community phenomenon (Dibbel, 1993). "Quake" was launched in 1996 at just the time that the Internet was becoming a social phenomenon, and the ability to shoot other players from a first-person perspective proved to be a major thrill for many. But "Quake" was soon topped by "EverQuest" that opened for business in 1999 and quickly came to define the category known as **Massively Multiplayer Online Role-Playing Games (MMORPGs)** (Koster, 2002).

GEAR WARS

Two years after the great crash of 1983 the third generation of home console systems kicked off continuing rounds of technological "one-upmanship" among console manufacturers to improve the speed and graphical richness of play that continue to this day. The Nintendo Entertainment System (NES), was itself a personal computer in the sense that it packed the same computer chip that was used in early home computers. Video game sales were still in a slump, but the NES included a Zapper gun that made "Duck Hunt" the first shooter game to cause a sensation in the home market. It also had a control pad in place of joysticks which many found less stressful for hours of continuous play. The NES also introduced a revolutionary new business model to the video game industry: Nintendo sold the game system at a loss but made profits on the software. "Super Mario Brothers" and "The Legend of Zelda" were among the other top titles of the third generation (Kent, 2001).

Fourth-generation consoles debuted in the mid-1980s with built-in CD players to add video action to games, although the original versions were too expensive to catch on. Sega briefly took the lead in the video game market by virtue of a more expansive library of games and superior hardware compared to Nintendo (Kent, 2001).

Fifth-generation machines with still faster processors initially disappointed due to expensive hardware and more hype than gaming excitement, and so the console game industry hit another slump in the early 1990s. Again observers pronounced the death of video games but 3-D graphics revived play. The Sony PlayStation became the overall winner in the console wars of the day by appealing to a broader, older market. However, Nintendo scored a hit with "Legend of Zelda Ocarina of Time," recognized by some as one of the best video games of all time (IGN Entertainment, 2010).

Sega responded by introducing its Dreamcast system in the United States in 1999 to kick off the sixth round of play. Sony continued to exploit the older end of the market and pushed gaming further out of the child's playroom and into the adult mainstream with titles like "Grand Theft Auto San Andreas." Software

Massively Multiplayer Online Role-Playing Games (MMORPGs) are online games that thousands play at the same time in a virtual world.

giant Microsoft's Xbox joined the fray by building on hardware and software components perfected in the personal computer market. "Halo" was such a hit on the Xbox that it pushed Nintendo into third place in North America.

Game consoles generally stayed a step ahead of most personal computers by incorporating advanced graphics and processor components. Still, PCs remained viable game machines with the addition of improved audio and CD-ROMs for games like "Myst" and "Wolfenstein 3D." "Doom" was a PC game that first popularized the first-person shooter (Kent, 2001). By the mid-1990s computers were able to keep up with game consoles and, with the addition of sound and graphics enhancements and suitable controllers, could emulate the console game experience.

Handheld games also evolved over the years. They were pioneered by Mattel in 1976 and portable games like "Simon" (an electronic version of the childhood favorite Simon Says) became big sellers (Kent, 2001). The category took off with the release of the Nintendo Game Boy in 1989 that caused a sensation with "Tetris" and went on to sell over 100 million units worldwide (Edwards, 2009) despite having a black-and-white display.

GAMES AND SOCIETY: WE WERE NOT AMUSED

Are games a threat to society? If so, the threat is nothing new. In twelfth-century Britain chess was so popular that it was considered a moral hazard that undermined the development of youth and there were efforts to ban it (Riddler & Denison, 1998). Similar concerns emerged in the early 1980s as tales of marathon games starting during school hours led to local bans on arcade play during school time (Kent, 2001).

Another concern about video games has been the possible effects that the violent and sexual behavior they contain may have on children (see More Harmful Than TV?, page 398). The first public outcry against video games was heard in 1976 with the release of "Death Race 2000," a racing game in which players earned points by running over people (Gamespot, 2010). Improved graphics in third-generation machines led to more graphic violence, notably in "Mortal Kombat." The gorier version of the game developed for the Sega Genesis outsold the toned-down Nintendo version, demonstrating the commercial appeal of graphic violence. Concerns about the impact of violence on children led to congressional hearings (Jenkins, 1999) and a rating system for video games that later evolved into the Electronic Software Review Board (Anderson et al., 2007).

WRITE TO CONGRESS "Mortal Kombat" was a hit title for third-generation machines. The gory violence led to congressional hearings about the effects of video games on children and to the establishment of the Electronic Software Review Board.

For a while the game industry was praised for its efforts to police itself. However, calls for content restriction were renewed after the 1999 Columbine High School massacre in Littleton, Colorado; in the incident, two teens, reportedly obsessed with "Doom," gunned down 12 of their classmates (Kent, 2001). Each new release in the popular "Grand Theft Auto" series also provokes criticism for increasingly graphic displays of violent crimes and other antisocial behavior found in the games. The media seemed to reflexively assign blame to games for every outbreak of violence, even in cases (such as the Virginia Tech massacre in 2007) where no evidence of game play was found.

Another recurring theme of game critics is the lack of games for girls and the sexual stereotypes that portray females as either victims or sex objects. Early video games were almost exclusively a male domain, raising concerns that girls would lag behind in an increasingly computer-oriented society. In 1996 "Barbie Fashion Designer" was the most successful game of the year, demonstrating that there was a female market, although the stereotypical female pursuit featured in the game (i.e., fashion design) raised further concerns about the effects on the life aspirations of young girls (Cassell & Jenkins, 1998). However, games continue to be populated by female sex objects and victims and designed mainly by males (Kafai et al., 2008).

THE NEW STATE OF PLAY

Game software is a $16 billion annual industry in the United States (NPD Group, 2012). That's more than either the domestic network television or film industries. Gaming reaches deeply into society: nearly three-fourths of all U.S. households play console or computer games, and the average age of gamers is now 37, and 42 percent are female (ESA, 2011).

The gear wars continue, with the latest seventh-generation consoles like the Xbox 360 and PS3 packing multiple processors running in parallel, capacious hard drives, broadband Internet connections, and high-definition graphics. Nintendo opted for lower-end performance but scored a hit with its wireless Wii controller that was popular in the family market as was Microsoft's new controller-less Kinect.

However, the conventional console game business model is under stress. Console game fans have rising expectations about production values, some of which might be described as interactive films with characters that seem like real actors. The latest "Modern Warfare 3" installment in the "Call of Duty" series registered more sales in its first week than most blockbuster Hollywood films do in their entire run. As a result game development budgets are soaring into the tens of millions and top game designers are being treated like Hollywood producers. A blockbuster mentality is starting to emerge on the console side of the business that may mean fewer, more expensive games in the future. Although Wii and Kinect are popularizing console games for the whole family, this also diminishes the industry's focus on producing new "core" games for hardcore players.

The history of video games has thus been one of boom and bust, invention and re-invention. The pattern continues. Console games are also being threatened by new distribution methods as sales through retail game outlets decline and new home console and handheld hardware fails to inspire avid gamers. Smartphone game apps like "Angry Birds" are a serious threat to conventional business patterns since they do not require the purchase of a packaged software product and could replace handheld game players. Games for tablets, like iPads, which use the whole tablet as both screen and controller also seem likely to challenge older gaming platforms. Downloadable games and social media games such as "FarmVille" are yet other new distribution channels that threaten both console makers Nintendo and game publisher Electronic Arts (NPD Group, 2012). Game apps are growing fast and drawing potential developers toward apps for phones and tablets. The game apps, downloads, and social media games all reflect a growing trend toward relatively simple **casual games** that can be played to conclusion in short periods of time. MMORPGs have been suffering from subscriber losses.

BUY THE FARM Casual Facebook games like "Farmville" are catching on. They threaten the dominance of conventional console games but also broaden the market for video games to new groups of players.

This has led many, including long-running favorite "World of Warcraft" as well as upstarts like "FarmVille," to adopt a free-to-play model in which game publishers profit from selling enhanced features or advanced levels of play from inside games without monthly subscription fees. Ads placed in games, such as Zynga's social networking games, represent another emerging business model. So even as gaming gains in popularity, its future direction is in doubt as rival gaming paradigms compete for screen time. Game on!

[**Casual games** are informal games that can be completed in short periods of time.]

TECHNOLOGY TRENDS: THE NEXT LEVEL

GENERATIONS

First-generation games like the home version of "Pong" had their programs hardwired into the consoles. The second generation was cartridge machines so that consoles could play a wider variety of games. Still, the games were hardwired inside the cartridges and therefore relatively expensive to produce, and the cartridges were not interchangeable between consoles. Graphics were limited to crude shapes and a narrow range of colors, whereas sound effects were mainly buzzes and beeps.

The gear wars that have played out over the last 25 years were largely defined by the number of computer bits that the central processing units of the game consoles could process simultaneously. For example, the

SECOND GENERATION The Atari 2600 was the leading console of the second generation of video games. The slot at the upper middle accepted game cartridges so that players could build libraries of games.

third-generation NES was an 8-bit machine, whereas its fourth-generation successor, the Super NES, was 16 bit, the fifth-generation machines like the PlayStation sported 32- and 64-bit processors, and sixth-generation products like the Xbox upped the ante to 128. Seventh-generation consoles use multiple parallel processors that work in tandem. The number of bits is important because it determines the resolution of the graphics and the speed with which new images can be projected on the player's screen. Seventh-generation machines create high-definition images and so need to be especially powerful since both the size and vertical resolution of the images have increased dramatically over early games designed for old-fashioned analog TV sets. Also important is the speed at which the game's central processing unit can move the bits in and out (the "clock speed" in computer technology terms) of the processor while implementing instructions from the game software's **game engine** (see Technology Demystified: A Look Under the Hood at Game Engines).

> **Game engine** refers to the software components that govern the physical properties of the game world, interact with the user, and render images for the player.

TECHNOLOGY DEMYSTIFIED

A LOOK UNDER THE HOOD AT GAME ENGINES

There's nothing magical about video game consoles; they are really just personal computers with high-end components. The video game magic that animates characters performing impossible feats in exotic settings in response to our every command comes from a collection of elements in the game's software generally described as the *game engine*.

The game engine is a development tool for game designers. It handles the basic functions that make the game operate, such as receiving user commands from the controller to record pulls on the trigger and running the graphical displays that keep track of the number of monsters killed. After computing and displaying your score, the game engine loads the image of the next monster and the dungeon it lives in and makes the monster move through the virtual environment. The physics engine makes the elements obey the rules of the physical world. It wouldn't be realistic if the monster walked through the torture rack in the middle of the dungeon (unless of course that is the monster's magical power), and the game engine governs interactions between objects to prevent collisions and overlaps. After you shoot the monster you expect it to fall to the floor under the force of gravity (unless of course the monster lives in outer space) so the physical properties of the in-game environment are also determined by the game engine using parameters set by the game designer. Finally, the game engine renders the images and sounds so you can see the impact of your silver bullets on the monster, watch him fall, hear him scream, and watch him bleed. The artificial intelligence of games like "Grand Theft Auto" is also built into the engine. So if the dying monster turns to you and says, "Argh, couldn't we start by shaking hands," that's the game engine talking.

Game engines are thus somewhat analogous to personal computer applications like PowerPoint. They enable a range of basic functions (e.g., slide transitions) that are selectable (e.g., fade) and modifiable (e.g., slow fade) by the designer. However, the content (e.g., final project presentation) comes from the mind of the designer herself. In the case of video games, the content includes the characters and the environments they live in, and the shapes, lighting, colors, and textures that are used to construct them. These are created in separate programs such as Maya and 3DS Max and then imported as "assets" that can be summoned by the game engine.

Video game engines are reusable. As games become more complex and expensive to create developers rely more on commercially available engines like "Unreal" that they can buy off the shelf rather than start from scratch with their own game engine. For the beginner, there are point-and-click game engines like "Torque Game Builder" and "Unity 3D" that require little computer programming.

Other game components have progressed over time as well. Graphics accelerators speed up the rendering of images so that games can instantly generate new images, including high-definition images in the latest gear, in response to controller input. Likewise, sound cards have advanced to provide stereo surround sound. The game storage medium is another defining characteristic, progressing from cartridges, to built-in computer memory, to CDs, DVDs, and Blu-Ray high-definition DVDs. The latest consoles include high-capacity hard drives so that they can store not only games but also movies and other multimedia downloads so that they can function as home entertainment centers. Later generations of consoles also feature Internet connections, beginning with the Sega Dreamcast in 2001 (Gamespot, 2010).

Personal computers can be made into game machines as well. To do so, game fans either start with the most advanced personal computers on the market or else upgrade standard computers with high-end components, including the computer's central processing unit, graphics, and sound cards. Add a custom controller, a Blu-Ray drive, headphones, and a big-screen HDTV and it might be possible to top the performance of the latest video game consoles. But that could cost several thousand dollars. Since console manufacturers sell their products for a few hundred dollars and hope to make money on the software, most gamers are content to enjoy the relative "bargains" offered by Microsoft, Sony, and Nintendo.

The security measures used by console manufacturers are another crucial component of the technology, although not one that game fans especially appreciate. Console makers include them so that games manufactured by outside developers won't play unless the game designer has signed a licensing agreement with the console maker that allows the latter to share in the revenues. Engineers for companies that make unauthorized game titles can eventually defeat the security codes, but that takes time, a time in which the console makers reap the profits of their latest release. However, courts have repeatedly ruled that this is their right under patent and copyright laws (Kent, 2001). The latest console units have modified CD-ROM and DVD units that enable security codes on the discs that cannot be read by standard home CD or DVD players.

NO MORE CONSOLES?

Why not just stream video games the same way we stream videos from YouTube and get rid of the consoles? OnLive will help you do that. An outgrowth of the cloud computing trend on the Internet (see Chapter 9), OnLive, GameTap and other services allow players to get in the game without a console, streaming games through a browser plug-in or downloading them for a modest monthly fee. Smartphones, tablet computers, and Internet-connected TV sets are other potential console killers as more and more games are downloaded as apps rather than sold as game software in a box. The Sony Playstation Vita poses another alternative to the conventional console. It is a handheld with high-resolution 3-D graphics that puts the power of a console machine in your pocket.

NO MORE BUTTON PUSHING?

Joysticks were the popular controllers for first- and second-generation games, but players had to hold the base in one hand and push the joystick with the other, which felt unnatural. The Nintendo Entertainment System's controller featured a cross-shaped pad that made it much more comfortable to navigate the game environment, although avid gamers sometimes developed calluses on their fingertips from using them. An astonishing variety of controller options are available. Some are built around specific games including steering wheels, throttles, and brake pedals for auto racing games and dwarf musical instruments for music games like "Rock Band." Dance pads and light guns are other popular controller accessories that transmit player actions to game software.

The latest is to make your body the controller. Nintendo's wireless Wii controller was a significant innovation, sensing the natural gestures of the player and converting them to actions inside the game. Infrared transmitters, similar to those in TV remote controls, track the position of the controller and another sensor keeps track of how fast the controller is changing its speed. A Bluetooth connection similar to those that connect "hands-free" cell phone ear pieces relays signals from the handheld "numchuck" to the game console. The EyeToy for the Sony PlayStation can respond to natural gestures without forcing the user to hold a controller.

Microsoft's Kinect system was an instant hit. It uses cameras to track the player's motions and to embed the user's "character" in three-dimensional environments. Rather than tracking a single motion with a device held by the player (e.g., waving the Wii wireless controller back and forth), a range of body motions are automatically translated into the game environment. Kinect qualifies as a form of **virtual reality** technology that places an avatar of the player inside the game world. It also reads lips and can recognize spoken commands. The Nintendo 3DS and Playstation Vita portable perform a similar trick, placing real world objects in the playing field via a built-in camera. Avatar Kinect uses facial recognition technology to add facial expressions to the game-playing version of you. The next generation Kinect will not only read lips but also detect the emotional responses of players by analyzing their facial expressions. Further down the line, brain wave and eye tracking controllers are under development.

Touch screens are another new controller trend, found in the Playstation 3DS, Playstation Vita, and the Wii U controller. Tablet computers that use the entire screen as a controller are other examples. Wii U will also be equipped for Near Field Communication, a technology that will allow gamers to interact with figurines and real world toys equipped with miniature radio transmitters.

[**Virtual reality** is a computer-generated environment that immerses the user in make-believe world.]

ZUMA Press/Newscom

ONE LESS REMOTE CONTROL Microsoft's Kinect for the Xbox 360 uses a camera and pattern recognition software to detect the motions of natural boxing movements with no physical controller.

NO MORE SCREENS?

Video games were originally developed as TV accessories and have made the transition to high definition, sometimes played across three screens simultaneously to enhance the experience. 3-D games are also catching on, beginning with a 3DS Gameboy from Nintendo. We examined 3-D technologies in Chapters 7 and 8, but video games are the first entertainment medium to make them possible without wearing glasses. That's possible by putting thin layers of lenses over the screen that direct images as viewed from slightly different angles to each eye, creating a 3-D effect. To make that work the viewer has to sit directly in front of the screen, as many video game players in fact do.

But soon players may not need (or want) either TV sets or computer monitors to play them. **Augmented reality** technology allows the game world to invade the real world. Google is developing glasses that will superimpose images from the game world on the real world.

NO MORE RULES?

Part of the fun of gaming is to master the tricks and traps of a new title. Having mastered them, the repetition is no longer as much fun and we begin to look forward to the new version. Wouldn't it be everlasting fun if the game continued to change by introducing new events and characters and never became entirely predictable? That is the promise of bringing **artificial intelligence (AI)** into the game. In the video game sphere that means features that make the virtual characters operated by the game act as if they were human. The most basic form of AI is found in any game that gets progressively more difficult as

STOP & REVIEW

1. What is the difference between a video game and a computer game?
2. Why did the video game market crash in the 1970s and again in the 1980s?
3. How have video games affected society?
4. What distinguishes the different generations of video game consoles?
5. What technological and market trends are shaping video games today?

> **Augmented reality** superimposes game objects on a real-world environment.

> **Artificial intelligence (AI)** is the property of an interactive medium that convinces users that they are interacting with a real person.

AP Photo/Bethesda Softworks

SMART DRAGON. Artificial intelligence features make game play less predictable and more engaging for players.

you play. If the enemies in a first-person shooter game are "smart" enough to sense you are aiming at them and they move out of the way, that is another basic form of game AI. Even if they have a limited number of moves in their repertoire, such as running away, ducking, rolling, or dropping to the ground, they seem more like humans if they vary their responses rather than just standing there waiting to be cut down. More advanced forms add new events to the game and the story evolves as you progress. "The Elder Scrolls V: Skyrim" is among the current leader in AI gaming.

Ultimately, game characters might respond to your actions or spoken words with improvised actions of their own. If the characters learn from your behavior and make decisions that are not simply preprogrammed paths through the game then they would achieve the status of "true" AI that is the goal of computer scientists. If you were confronting the artificially intelligent characters in an augmented reality environment, you might mistake them for real people, at least until you tried to shake their hands to introduce yourself.

INDUSTRY: THE GAME PLAYERS

The video game industry surpasses the music, network television, and movie industries in terms of total revenues and so is a significant entertainment industry in its own right. The major segments of the game industry include consumer electronics companies who make game gear, developers who design the games, publishers who manufacture the game software, and retailers who sell the games to the public. The relationships among these industry "players" vary according to the type of game **platform** involved: console game system, handheld, personal computer game, online game, or casual game (Kerr, 2006). To these we might add apps for smartphones and tablet computers like "Temple Run" and social media games like "FarmVille."

[**Platform** is a basic type or brand of game system.]

GEAR MAKERS

Nintendo (makers of the Wii and handheld Game Boy systems) is the world leader in manufacturing console games, followed by Sony (PlayStation and PlayStation Portable), and Microsoft (Xbox 360). Gear makers also include third-party manufacturers of custom controllers like Mad Catz Interactive and high-end game desktops like Dell Gaming's Alienware that speed up personal computer games.

Arcade games have been fading in popularity since the mid-1990s when home game consoles surpassed them in graphics quality. Namco Bandai Games ("Pac-Man") and Konami ("Dance, Dance Revolution"), and Sega ("Bass Fishing Challenge") are among the surviving manufacturers of the arcade games found in shopping malls and bowling alleys.

GAME PUBLISHERS

Game publishers are analogous to movie studios and record companies. However, unlike in other media industries that we have examined, hardware manufacturers continue to have a central role in software manufacturing by retaining their own in-house game publishers. For example, Nintendo acts as its own publisher for its most popular titles such as "Wii Sports" and "New

Super Mario Brothers" and is the leading game publisher overall. Sony Computer Entertainment and Microsoft are also top publishers. The top independent publisher is Electronic Arts. In addition to developing its own games, such as "Need for Speed" and "Madden Football," it also distributes games made by third-party developers that it does not own, such as MTV Games' "Rock Band." Social network games like "FarmVille" are becoming a significant presence in the game sphere and Zynga is the leading company in that realm.

The publishers make copies of games and historically have distributed them to consumers through one of three basic channels. The top selling games of all time are those that came bundled with game consoles. Other console titles and personal computer games are sold (or rented) through retail outlets. Online games are purchased online directly from the publisher or through retail stores. New distribution channels are emerging that threaten the console game market structure, however. These include games that can be streamed over the Internet, game apps that are downloaded onto smartphones and tablets, and free casual games found on Facebook. The placement of ads inside games and the sale of virtual goods within online games are emerging as a significant new sources of revenue for game publishers.

There is an important category of game software that every player uses indirectly, but that is not marketed to the general public: game engines. These are the programs that make the characters and objects in games move on the player's screen and do what they are supposed to, such as keep out of each other's way, fall to the ground when they are "killed," and cast shadows where they should (see Technology Demystified, p. 386). For example, the "Unreal Engine" by Epic Games of North Carolina is a popular engine that has been used in over 200 games, including multiple titles in the "Star Trek," "Medal of Honor," and "Tom Clancy" series. Epic licenses its engine to developers, which means that it collects fees—sometimes in the millions of dollars per title—for its use. Game developers also license tools that assist with specific game and graphics features, such as music, lighting, and textures. A growing segment is *middleware* that packages a variety of tools needed for game development. However, there are also dozens of engines that can be used free, such as "OGRE," a rendering engine that is found in several adventure and online role-playing games. "Unity" is a popular game authoring system among students since it has a free version as well as tutorials and user forums.

GAME DEVELOPERS

Game developers create game software by combining the skills of graphic artists and computer programmers (see Your Media Career: Getting Paid to Play?, page 392). Like the movie studios of old, leading game publishers have their own in-house design studios. For example, Electronic Arts has game development studios at its headquarters near San Francisco in Redwood City, California, and some two dozen other locations around the world. EA, as it is known, has absorbed a number of other game developers such as Maxis (makers of "The Sims"). Like the movie studios of today, game publishers also distribute the productions of third-party developers who have varying degrees of autonomy from the publisher, ranging from wholly owned subsidiaries (like Maxis at Electronic Arts) to recurring informal partnerships.

GETTING PAID TO PLAY?

Video game designer is one of the most exciting media professions today. What could be more thrilling than helping to create the entertainment industry of tomorrow, the games that everyone will be talking about? The opportunities are there. The industry employs over 100,000 people overall, and game designers account for about 60,000 of those. That is about three times the number of those employed as film and video directors and producers (see Chapter 7).

Computer programming and graphic design are the two skill sets that get you into game design and those who possess both skill sets are especially prized. Undergraduate degrees in computer science, art, or graphic design can be helpful, and a growing number of college media departments are offering specialties in game design. Although computer science degrees are not required, some computer programming background is essential. Unfortunately, most universities have erected barriers around their entry-level computer science courses by requiring daunting math and science prerequisites. For their part, journalism and mass-media departments don't usually offer computer programming. Some game design aspirants pick up computer programming on their own or seek out community college, technical school, or free online courses to get up to speed. Some colleges are starting to offer game programs that combine design and programming.

Designers are prized for their talent in creating inviting game play regardless of their degrees, however. One entry route is to start as a play tester whose jobs are more formally known as a *quality assurance* or *usability research*. In other words, you get paid for playing games and giving feedback to designers. Another entry path is to design informal games on platforms like Flash, the video game equivalent of the student film, to show off your design skills. Or, you might get started by writing design documents or routine computer code. Creative writing skills can also get you in on the ground floor of complex role playing games.

Designers progress through the ranks by adding to their portfolio, beginning with creating specific components for a new game (e.g., a more realistic explosion or a creepier monster), progressing to a "mission leader" for a specific level of a game, and finally assuming responsibility for the overall look and feel of a new game. To advance through the ranks designers must also be team players with excellent writing and project management skills. Designers who make it to the top can command six-figure salaries and stock options that make them millionaires while still young enough to enjoy it.

The game industry is not all fun and games. The industry has been criticized for exploiting young programmers and artists. When the ship date for a new game looms, 60- or 80-hour workweeks are expected without overtime pay. A never-ending succession of "crunch times" can lead to rapid burnout. The good news is that frequent burnouts open up more opportunities at the entry level for the aspiring designer to get in the game. But, like so many other media careers, the video game field is euphemistically said to be "highly competitive," meaning that there are many more college graduates trying to get into it than there are positions available for them.

If your talents lie neither in computer programming nor in graphic design or if you cringe at the thought of 80-hour workweeks there are many other roles to fill in this exciting industry. Sound design is another creative niche, one that coursework in audio production might help you fill. Video games are a big business, so just as in any other media field, there are plenty of openings for those with advertising, marketing, accounting, and management backgrounds.

Sources: Taylor, 2007; BLS, 2010. *Motion picture and video industries.* http://www.bls.gov/oco/cg/cgs038.htm

There are also thousands of independent game developers. Like independent filmmakers or "garage bands," these are individual programmers or small teams that develop games that they hope will be picked up by major publishers. The Independent Games Festival (www.igf.com) is the showcase for top independent game developers. For example, "Joe Danger" was one of the finalists for the top independent video game of 2010. It was the creation of Hello Games, a team of four artists and programmers who had previously worked for major game developers. Some developers specialize in making assets that are assembled in games developed by others, such as characters or the settings in which the characters move. Both amateur and professional developers also show off their skills by crafting game **mods** that change game features, ranging from adding new weapons into first-person shooter games to complete makeovers that change the basic nature of the game play. With smartphones appearing as appealing game platforms, the market for relatively simple game "apps" has radically expanded the market for game creators and lowered their barriers to entry.

Mods are modifications to game play or game environments made by users and amateur game developers.

SELLING THE GAME

Video games were originally distributed to users through coin-operated arcade machines and toy stores. Currently, game retailing resembles the home video market, with specialized outlets like GameStop competing with "big box" retailers like Walmart and game rental operations such as GameFly. Many players also buy used games from the likes of GameStop or online from eBay and Amazon.com. Currently, mainstream games require too much computer memory to stream them over the Internet, but that is changing (see The Next Level: Technology Trends, page 385) and pose a threat both to retail stores and to console manufacturers.

Online distribution is already an important outlet for independent game developers. There are online distribution channels for independent games sponsored by each of the major game hardware manufacturers, the Xbox game market place, WiiWare, or the PlayStation Network. Other indies, as they are called, develop informal games (e.g., using Flash) that they distribute as freeware over the Internet or sell on eBay. App stores run by Apple, Google, Amazon and others are revolutionizing how games are distributed and sold to smartphones and other portable wireless devices.

VIDEO GAME GENRES: RULES OF THE GAME

Although a big part of the fun of gaming is trying out the technology in the latest game consoles, there is more to it than that. What makes a game appealing to its players? In previous chapters we examined media **genres** when trying to understand their appeal to their audiences. The same type of analysis can be made for video games.

Genres are distinctive styles of creative works. The term is also used to represent different types or formats of media content.

The list of the all-time best-selling video games (Table 13.1) offers few clues beyond the obvious fact that Nintendo is the number-one game console maker. These figures include games that were distributed free with game systems, fattening the sales totals. The five Wii titles in the top 10 are arguably little more than demonstration programs for capabilities of the Wii console. Working with genre categories commonly used in the industry, we have a puzzle game, two sports games, a role-playing game, a racing game, three platform games, and a shooter game rounding out the list.

Beyond the top 10, a wider range of genres may be found but there is not much agreement about what the main genres are and how many variations, or subgenres, should be recognized. Since video games are often described as interactive movies (see below, Media&Culture: Video Game as Interactive Film?) it is tempting to draw on literary or movie genres, and indeed we can readily identify science fiction, horror, and action video games. However, many popular video games are so abstract that they have no plot, or narrative structure, and

Table 13.1 Top Ten Best-Selling Video Games of All Time

RANK	GAME	CONSOLE	YEAR	GENRE	WORLD SALES*
1	Wii Sports	Wii	2006	Sports	78.68
2	Super Mario Bros.	NES	1985	Platform	40.24
3	Mario Kart Wii	Wii	2008	Racing	31.62
4	Pokémon Red / Green / Blue Version	Game Boy	1996	Role-Playing	31.37
5	Tetris	Game Boy	1989	Puzzle	30.26
6	Wii Sports Resort	Wii	2009	Sports	29.43
7	Wii Play	Wii	2006	Misc	28.51
8	Duck Hunt	NES	1984	Shooter	28.31
9	New Super Mario Bros.	DS	2006	Platform	28.07
10	New Super Mario Bros. Wii	Wii	2009	Platform	25.03

Source: http://www.vgchartz.com/gamedb/ Retrieved March 4, 2012

even games that use the settings, symbols, and themes found in popular film genres usually lack a plot in the conventional sense. But game genres borrowing from film or literature merely re-cycle the conventions of old media. Genre analysis should give us insight into the underlying appeal of the interactive medium rather than focusing on superficial aspects of themes and settings.

One possibility is to adopt the genres of two-dimensional board games; for example, race, space, chase, place, and theme games (Parlett, 1999). Race games proceed in a linear fashion from start to finish with the object of being the first (or quickest) to reach the end. Games in the "Mario Brothers"

MEDIA&CULTURE

VIDEO GAME AS INTERACTIVE FILM?

There is a curiously close relationship emerging between video or computer games and movies. Both are very visual media that provide an intense experience for their fans. Both media employ the latest visual and auditory technologies to deliver ever more intense experiences. And, as the success of the "Call of Duty" game series attests, a blockbuster game generates as much revenue as a blockbuster movie.

Filmmakers and scholars have become interested in the narrative qualities of games, which some call "cyberdrama." So they might look at the image and character of Lara Croft in the "Tomb Raider" game the same way they look at her character in the movie and draw similar inferences about stereotypical attributes of females from both (Bryce, Rutter, & Sullivan, 2006). Other video game narratives resonate with those of popular films, telling stories that reinforce the hegemony of the dominant economic and cultural groups in society; for example, by reinforcing consumerism in "The Sims" or furthering the dominance of commercial media symbols while playing games spun off from "X-Men" or "Star Trek" (Crawford & Rutter, 2006) or reinforcing conventional sex-roles (Cox, 2011).

Movie-style story telling is beginning to find its way into games. "Heavy Rain" and "L.A. Noire" are often cited as examples of advanced story telling techniques. Artificial intelligence and the ability to interact through dialog (captured through game consoles that recognize spoken words or read lips) might make for compelling interactions with game plot lines. Perhaps video games will yet meet the challenge posed by famed film producer Steven Spielberg, to create a video game whose story will make us cry.

and "Sonic the Hedgehog" series fall into that category. In this context, space games aren't games set in outer space but rather involve aligning game pieces in a particular pattern; for example, "Tetris." Chase games are asymmetrical contests in which the goal of the player is to avoid capture, as in the "Metal Gear" series. In displace games the aim is to annihilate the opponent, also the goal of first-person shooter games like "Halo." Theme games engage players in a simulation of a real-world activity, like "The Sims," for example.

Another widely cited list of game genres is given in Table 13.2 (after Wolf, 2001). It focuses on the types of interactions (e.g., capturing, fighting, driving, shooting) that users engage in while playing. Early games were often built around single types of interactions but the complex games of today typically combine multiple genres of interaction. Also, is it important that the game simulates the cockpit of a racecar rather than the cockpit of a fighter plane? We might also distinguish genres from other characteristics of games such as their hardware platform (e.g., PlayStation or Wii; console, handheld, or PC), mode (e.g., single player or multiplayer, first-person or third-person perspective), level of involvement (e.g., hardcore or casual), and visual setting (e.g., science fiction or horror). We could also focus on the player's role in making the version of the game that he or she creates through intricate feedback with

Table 13.2 Selected Video Game Genres

GENRE	DESCRIPTION	EXAMPLE
Abstract	Nonrepresentational graphics, non-narrative; fill, empty, or visit the entire screen	"Tetris"
Sports/Game/ Activity/Gambling Adaptations	Games adapted from another medium or play activity	"Pong"
Adventure	Players wander through a "world" of multiple connected locations in pursuit of complex goals	"World of Warcraft"
Capturing/Catching/ Collecting/Dodging	Capture-Catch-Collect-Dodge objects	"Pac-Man"
Combat/Fighting/ Shoot 'em ups/Target	Shoot at opponents	"Battletech"
Demo	Games that demonstrate game systems	"Wii Play"
Driving/Flying/Racing	Skillful operation of conveyances	"Pole Position"
Educational	Games that teach a lesson	"Oregon Trail"
Escape	Escape pursuers or prisons	"Doom"
Interactive Movie	Branching between video clips with alternate endings	"Grand Theft Auto"
Simulation	Resource allocation to build or maintain an entity	"Sim City"
Obstacle Course	Traverse an obstacle course	"Tomb Raider"
Platform	Guide character movement through a series of levels	"Mario Brothers"
Puzzle/Maze	Figure out a solution to a puzzle	"Tetris"
Quiz	Find the right answer	"Jeopardy"
Role Playing	Create a character and play with other characters	"Diablo"
Rhythm and Dance	Play music or dance along	"Guitar Hero"
Strategy	Strategy, not fast action, counts	"Alone in the Dark"

Source: Wolf, 2010.

the game system rather than specific actions (e.g., dodging or shooting). For example, playing a racing game like "Project Gotham Racing 2" requires players to keep their eyes glued to the screen and to continually manipulate the controller in an intense performance feedback loop. In contrast, "Sim City" requires the player to make well-considered interventions based on the integration of information gathered over several screens as the player's virtual world evolves. Distinctions like these can also define different genres of interaction (Apperley, 2006).

MEDIALITERACY

SPOILING THE FUN: VIDEO GAME LITERACY

Now that video games are a significant medium in their own right, it is time to ask about their larger impact on society. The answers may not always be fun to think about.

BEYOND BARBIE

One of the enduring challenges to video game designers has been to develop games that appeal to females. In the early days, games attracted a largely male audience. An exception was "Centipede," an arcade game from the early 1980s that was the first to be popular among female players. Some attributed that to the female-friendly pastel colors, but the fact that it was designed by Dona Bailey, the only female programmer at Atari at the time, may have had something to do with it (Kent, 2001). Another notable exception was "Barbie Fashion Designer," released in 1996 that was a hit among girls and surged to the top of the sales charts that year.

However, in the United States and many (but not all) other countries, male gamers continue to be the majority of console game players, although online games and casual games appear to be more popular among females (Kafai et al., 2008). Games are designed to appeal to straight white male players on both a superficial and also a very profound level. On the surface, many female game characters are excessively buxom, scantily dressed, and overly submissive. At a deeper level, the action of first person shooters, the worlds game designers create, and the way characters are framed and carry themselves also reflect a male perspective on the world (Cox, 2011).

MORE ADDICTIVE THAN DRUGS?

Game developers sometimes brag that their new game is "more addictive than drugs." We might write that off to harmless boasting were it not for the fact that there have been cases of people literally dying to play. In South Korea there have been multiple cases of online game players dying from cardiac arrest after days-long sessions without breaks for food or water. In China the government has set up hundreds of boot camps to wean game addicts from their habits. Less dire effects also concern parents. Excessive amounts of sedentary game play may increase the risk of childhood obesity (HHS, 2010), a major health problem of American youth. "Play station palms" is a form of repetitive stress injury that can result from manipulating game controllers for hours on end. Effects on the social development of children have received the most attention in the United States. It has been estimated that 1 child in 12 in the United States suffers psycho-social impairment such as withdrawing from real-world social activities as a result of video game play (Gentile et al., 2004).

Internet addictions and video game addictions are often lumped together for the purposes of discussions like these, in part because online games seem especially problematic both as genres of video games and types of Internet content. Whether or not these are truly "addictions" in the same sense of an addiction to drugs (more properly known as substance abuse) or a pathological gambling problem is a highly controversial issue (Petry, 2011). Studies of video game addictions are often surveys in which college students or school children are asked to identify symptoms (e.g., Lemmens et al., 2009) that might not pass the scrutiny of a trained psychologist examining the participants in person. And, the criteria used to identify problem cases does not always require the presence of dire life consequences that make the condition truly serious, such as losing an important relationship or dropping out of school. The problem cases found in the few clinical studies that have been published may be the result of another underlying pathology. Consequently, the American Psychiatric Association decided not to classify video game and Internet addiction as a mental disease, and the matter is under study as of this writing.

Meanwhile, readers out there who may be wondering if they are game addicts should first note that having an intense desire for any activity is not the same as being addicted to it, even if the two are sometimes equated in everyday terms, as in "Yeah, I'm a game addict, I can't get enough of 'Call of Duty.'" Another common misconception is that the sheer amount of game play indicates addiction when the question is really how much it interferes with other aspects of your life. So, if you can honestly say that playing "World of Warcraft" 40 hours a week is not putting you in danger of flunking the class you are reading this for (honestly, now) then you are not an addict. On the other hand, if 3 hours a week (about the time the average family spends) is making you fail your classes or neglect your real-world friends, you might have a problem. If that is the case, chances are your "addiction" is just a temporary infatuation. In a recent study (van Rooij, et al., 2011) it was found that most of those who were categorized as

FAMILY FUN? Or Family Wrecker? Excessive involvement in video games can take time away from school, work, family, and friends. In extreme cases that could be termed an addiction. For most, games are just lots of fun, but some lose control of their gaming and for them it can be a life-endangering obsession.

addicted to games in one year were no longer addicted a year later. To get your gaming under control you should think about ways you might spend more time in the real world, or use an in-game tool that helps you keep track of the time you spend and begin rewarding yourself for cutting down on the time you spend playing from one week to the next. If you can't bring yourself to do even that, think about seeing a psychologist. Remember, it is only in the game world that you get "extra lives."

MORE HARMFUL THAN TV?

Other concerns about video games arise from content that is heavily laced with violence, sex, and traditional sex roles. The ability of television violence, sex, and sex-roles to have negative effects on children has been documented (but is also controversial, see Chapter 14), so seeing the same things in video games might also have harmful effects, might it not? Certain violent video games might be even worse than television, where there is usually a plot line that includes punishment for evil doers, whereas in many video games violence is an end in itself, leading to higher scores and new "lives."

There have been many studies linking exposure to violent video games to aggressive thoughts among children (Gentile et al., 2004) and college students (Anderson & Dill, 2000). As we will see in Chapter 14, reviews of the research have been contradictory, but according to one recent study (Anderson et al., 2010) the negative effects of video game violence are indeed significant. The magnitude of the effect is comparable to other risk factors for violence, including substance abuse, abusive parents, and poverty.

Recognizing the possible link between game play and antisocial behavior, the Entertainment Software Review Board (ESRB) provides helpful content ratings to assist parents when selecting games for their children. Like similar content rating systems that have been developed in the movie, music, and television industries, these are examples of industry self-regulation in which video game developers voluntarily submit their games to ESRB for review. The ratings initially developed in response to a public outcry following the introduction of fourth-generation games like "Mortal Kombat" in the early 1990s that featured extremely gory graphics. Critics contend that the Adults Only (AO) rating is only given for sexual content, whereas extreme violence should perhaps also be limited to adults. As with movie ratings, the game ratings are only effective if retailers faithfully check the IDs of game purchasers, but studies by the Federal Trade Commission indicate that enforcement is lax. Video game consoles come with parental lock-out options keyed to the ESRB ratings, but we suspect that the children are often the only ones who know how to use them.

It might help if a rating system was developed that specified the risk of violence effects ("playing this game may result in playground fights") and if the same rating system was used for television and films or laws were passed to prohibit sales of M-rated games to minors (Anderson et al., 2007). However, a California law banning violent video game sales to minors was struck down by the Supreme Court in 2012 on the grounds that game developers have free speech rights that include the right to make violent computer software. Also, the court did not find the studies proclaiming a link between video games and violence to be credible.

SERIOUS GAMES?

"Serious games" might seem like a contradiction in terms. However, there is mounting evidence that video games have positive effects on their players and that there could be a considerable upside to exploring their educational benefits. Perhaps you would rather play "Media Now," the game, rather than read *Media Now*, the textbook?

Until now, the greatest interest—and greatest source of funding—for serious games has come from defense departments around the world. The generals have found that battle tank simulators are an effective way of teaching recruits how to operate complex weapons systems at far less cost than running (and occasionally running into) the real thing. The generals appreciate "silly" video games, too, since the interfaces of computerized weapons systems in-

DANGER TO SOCIETY? Playing violent video games can stimulate aggression but the extent of the effects continues to be a controversial topic.

creasingly resemble video game controllers and there is evidence that playing action games like "Medal of Honor" can improve visual attention (Barlett et al., 2009), a useful skill for warriors. Also, if video game violence indeed does cause violent behavior, that might produce more effective killers for the military, a possibility that the Marine Corps explored by developing "First To Fight," a first-person shooter game used to train Marine recruits and sold as a commercial video game (Anderson et al., 2007).

Serious games are proving themselves in more socially beneficial applications, however. Serious games can produce situated learning that immerses the player in personalized simulations of the real-world environments in which they will ultimately be expected to perform (Gee, 2003). For example, simulation games can help doctors master the art of saving lives (Rosser et al., 2007)and encourage asthmatic children to use their inhalers more effectively (Lieberman, 1997). However, the effectiveness of games in formal educational settings has yet to be established and more research is needed (Vandercruysse et al., 2012). Others (e.g. Bogost, 2007) prefer the term "persuasive games," maintaining that the procedures players follow in games have an ability comparable to verbal arguments to convince people to change their ways. In this view, any game can have a persuasive impact, even if it is not primarily designed to meet an educational objective. Calling certain games "serious" doesn't give proper credit to other games that may be equally powerful. For example, might "saving the princess" repeatedly in the game world persuade players to come to the aid of others in the real world (or convince them that women are unable to help themselves)?

STOP&REVIEW

1. What are the major segments of the video game industry?
2. What do video game publishers do?
3. What are some of the genres of video games?
4. How can you tell if you have a video game addiction?
5. What are some possible negative effects of video games?
6. What are serious video games?

Educational games are a tiny segment of the commercial gaming market, and perhaps with good reason. Children soon tire of predictable educational game play, such as awarding points for each country correctly located on a map, issuing in-game awards, and promoting players to new levels. However, if we blend the geography lessons with the adventures of a cute child like "Dora the Explorer," we might teach something while having fun, an instance of incidental learning (see Chapter 14).

As for replacing traditional classroom instruction with video games, a major stumbling block is their considerable first copy costs (see Chapter 2). If educators tried to match the production qualities of "silly" games like "Call of Duty," then each video game "text" would cost tens of millions of dollars to produce. Those sums might be recouped across millions of students and dozens of years for a course like introductory algebra that is widely taught and relatively slow to change. However, even that would depend upon school districts everywhere adopting the same course, an unlikely prospect. For introductory college courses in rapidly changing fields like the media, the frequent updates required of the material would yield games that would cost several times the price of a print textbook.

So, any savings resulting from employing serious games in schools might have to come from eliminating the teachers, the buildings the students gather in, the campuses the buildings stand on, or even the football stadiums that the alumni fill. Failing that, serious games might become economically viable by adopting lower levels of technology than popular commercial titles. But, gee, what fun would that be?

SUMMARY&REVIEW

HOW DID VIDEO GAMES DEVELOP?

Games date back to the ancient Egyptians. Today's games evolved from classic board, arcade, and war games. The first popular arcade video game was "Pong," and Odyssey was the first console for home games, both from 1972. The video game industry survived major busts in the late 1970s and the early 1980s. Game consoles have evolved over seven generations of games, each adding to the quality of images and game play and extending the market for games. Early online games were text-based and have evolved into Massively Multiplayer Online Role-Playing Games of today.

HOW HAVE VIDEO GAMES IMPACTED SOCIETY?

Video game play now extends deeply into society, broadening its initial appeal to teenage boys to include female and adult players today. Excessive video game play can interfere with important life activities and may cause violent behavior and strengthen sex-role stereotypes. Alarming outbreaks of youth violence, such as the 1999 Columbine High murders, have been attributed to video games, although the link is impossible to prove conclusively.

WHAT IS THE STATUS OF VIDEO GAMES TODAY?

The video game industry is evolving. The console game industry is beginning to resemble the film industry with respect to the production values of games, their rapidly rising development costs, and their ability to make blockbuster profits for their publishers. However, console games compete with increasingly popular online games including inexpensive casual games available on social media sites. Games distributed over the Internet and through smartphones and tablets pose further competition to the console game market.

WHAT ARE THE IMPORTANT TRENDS IN GAME TECHNOLOGY?

The progression of game gear through seven generations of console games has been marked by the power of the central processing units built into the consoles, the technologies used to store the software, and the controllers that let users interact with the games. Seventh-generation games pack parallel processors, high-capacity disk drives, and high-definition video discs. Motion sensing technologies like the Nintendo Wii are revolutionizing the gaming experience. Some 3-D displays and portable displays completely immerse gamers in game environments.

HOW IS THE VIDEO GAME INDUSTRY ORGANIZED?

Sony, Nintendo, and Microsoft are the dominant console manufacturers. The manufacturers publish their own games, but independent game publishers including industry giant Electronic Arts as well as hundreds of smaller publishers are also in the game. Game development companies make the games and distribute them through major publishers, through developer exchanges run by the console makers, or online via the Internet. Online multiplayer game publishers and social networking sites are alternative distribution channels for video games.

WHAT ARE THE GENRES OF VIDEO GAMES?

Conventional movie genres such as action-adventure and science fiction can be applied to video games as can the genres of two-dimensional board games. The game industry uses its own categories, including role-playing, sports, and shooter games. Other attempts to define video game genres focus on the types of user interactions involved.

HOW DO VIDEO GAMES AFFECT THEIR PLAYERS?

Some players become so deeply involved in playing their favorite game that they might fairly be termed addicts, and psychiatrists are debating whether or not to classify game addiction as a mental illness. However, that applies only in extreme cases when severe life consequences, such as flunking out of school are involved. Playing violent video games is a possible cause of aggressive behavior, although the research is controversial. Military commanders for whom aggression is a desirable behavior are using video games to train the troops. Serious video games have also proven effective in encouraging healthy behaviors and have the potential to improve upon conventional classroom instruction.

THINKING CRITICALLY
ABOUT THE MEDIA

1. Have developments in video games been driven by technology or by their users? Explain.

2. What impact has video game play had in your life?

3. Have you ever felt "addicted" to a video game? What made you feel that way?

4. How would you go about getting a job in the video game industry?

5. Debate the following statement: Violent video games should be banned for children.

KEY TERMS

artificial intelligence (AI) (p. 389)

augmented reality (p. 389)

casual games (p. 385)

digital game (p. 379)

game engine (p. 386)

genres (p. 393)

Massively Multiplayer Online Role-Playing Games (MMORPGs) (p. 382)

mods (p. 393)

platform (p. 390)

video game (p. 379)

virtual reality (p. 388)

VIDEO GAMES ARE FUN, BUT ARE THEY BAD FOR YOU? Why do we spend thousands of hours every year with the media, and what is the cumulative impact on us as individuals and our society at large?

14

MEDIA USES AND IMPACTS

BASHING THE MEDIA

"Media bashing" is a recurring ritual. On the one hand, critics point to new evidence of harmful effects in the endless stream of violence, sex, and hate that they see pouring forth from the media. The talk shows and editorial columns buzz, and congressional hearings are held. On the other hand, the media criticize the research, blame the parents, say it's not their job to fix society, retreat behind the First Amendment (see Chapter 15), and promise to regulate themselves better. Then the debate simmers down until the next study comes out or the next outrage occurs. What does the research really tell us, and how much can we rely on it?

Violent video games are a case in point. It seems every time we hear about a new shooting or a bullying incident in our schools, the media run stories about violent video games the perpetrator was thought to have played. As noted further on in this chapter, when researchers have found evidence linking violent game play to real world aggression, Congress has held hearings. The industry responded with voluntary content ratings, but the ratings focused on sex, not violence, and anyway video game stores were lax about prohibiting sales to underage customers. California passed a law to prohibit the sale of violent games to minors but an industry group sued to overturn the law on the grounds that it infringed on their free speech rights. In 2012 the Supreme Court agreed, in part because the justices were skeptical about the research. Meanwhile, children still play violence-packed games with titles like "Call of Duty" and the shooting and bullying continue.

So, when the next school shooting happens or when we hear about bullying at schools in our own community. we are again likely to hear about the video games the perpetrators played and the social media they used. But how should we regard these stories? Is the problem widespread, or have isolated incidents been magnified by sensational media coverage? Research might tell us if the incidents indicate a serious national problem or if they are merely anecdotal and help us to understand if it is the media content or other factors that provoke them. For example, how many bullies or acts of copycat aggression would there be if violent video games were kept from the eyes of children? Are parents, or poverty, more to blame than the game publishers?

Media effects are changes in cognitions, attitudes, emotions, or behavior that result from exposure to the mass media. The term is often used to denote changes in individuals that are caused by exposure to the media. However, broader impacts on society, as opposed to individual effects, are also of concern to us. And, some scholars do not see a cause-and-effect relationship between media use and human behavior. We will use the term *media impacts* in the broader sense to encompass these varying aspects of the complex relationship between media and society. In this discussion, exposure to the media may itself be considered an impact, since the time we spend with the media affects our daily lives as a decision to engage in media consumption behavior at the expense of time that might be spent on other activities. Indeed, one of the main impacts of television on children found by previous generations of research was simply that children spent less time socializing, playing, and reading because of the time they spent with television (Schramm, Lyle, & Parker, 1961).

> **Media effects** are changes in knowledge, attitudes, or behaviors resulting from media exposure.

STUDYING MEDIA IMPACTS

Media impact can be studied in a variety of ways. All the methods have strengths and weaknesses that we need to understand to evaluate their contributions to the debate over media and society. First, we will consider some of the contrasting general approaches to understanding media impacts; then we will consider four systematic methods for obtaining evidence of those impacts: content analyses, experiments, surveys, and ethnographies.

CONTRASTING APPROACHES

There are several widely varying basic approaches to interpreting media impacts. These include deductive versus inductive reasoning, critical versus administrative research, and qualitative versus quantitative research.

Many social scientists begin with a theory based on the law of cause and effect. They derive, or deduce, predictions about media impacts from their theories of human behavior and culture and then test these predictions through observation. Their results either support the theory or refute it, which leads to new theoretical paradigms. Thus, they follow the scientific method. Mass media exposure is usually viewed as the "cause," or **independent variable**. Exposure to media content is seen as the trigger for mental processes and behaviors that are the "effects," or consequences of what people see and hear in the media. These effects—such as antisocial (e.g., violent) or prosocial (e.g., cooperative) behaviors—are called **dependent variables** (Wimmer & Dominick, 2011). Of course, if we are interested in the prior question of what causes media use or exposure, then media use becomes the dependent variable and the factors that may cause that use or exposure, such as gender, personality, and beliefs about the benefits of media exposure, become the independent variables.

> **Independent variables** are the causes of media effects.

> **Dependent variables** are the consequences, or effects, of media exposure.

Another paradigm is more inductive. Other scholars observe people's real-life interactions with media and with each other and then induce, or infer, theories about those interactions. These include most ethnographers and also many critical theorists. Ethnographers worry about existing theories blinding them to seeing peoples' behavior as they see it themselves. They prefer to create theories close to the explanations people give for their own behavior, or at least based on their own careful observation. Paul Lazarsfeld (1941), one of the pioneers in communications research, was the first to point out the difference between what he called *administrative research*, which takes existing media institutions for granted and documents their use and effects, and *critical research*, which criticizes media institutions themselves from the perspective of the ways they serve dominant social groups. Most of the research described elsewhere in this chapter, even that which results in "criticism" of the media for excessive sex or violence, falls into the administrative research category because it fails to critique the basic foundations of existing media institutions. Instead, critical theorists favor interpretive and inductive methods of inquiry drawn from such fields as history, feminist studies, cultural anthropology, Marxist political economic theory, and literary criticism (see Chapter 2).

Some social scientists use quantitative methods to enumerate their findings and analyze statistical relationships between independent and dependent variables. Other scholars infer the relationships from qualitative methods, such as by studying the symbols in media content or observing behavior in natural settings. Yet others believe it is important to combine both sets of methods and look for insights offered by both approaches and points of agreement between them.

CONTENT ANALYSIS

Content analysis is a quantitative description of the content of the media.

Content analysis characterizes the content of the media. Researchers begin with systematic samples of media content and apply objective definitions to classify its words, images, and themes. For example, what if researchers want to find out if television has become more violent over the years? They might select a composite week of prime-time programming by drawing programs from different weeks of the year to represent each of the shows in the prime-time schedule. They would develop objective definitions of violence, such as "sequences in which characters are depicted as targets of physical force initiated by another character." Trained observers would then classify each of the scenes in the sample of shows and compare notes to make sure that their definitions were consistent. Then the researchers would record the number of violent acts per hour and compare the results to those of studies in previous years (Gerbner et al., 1994).

Content analyses create detailed profiles of media content and identify trends in content over time. However, they cannot be used to draw conclusions about the effects of the media because the audience often perceives media in a different way than the researchers—or the producers of the content.

Content analysis is a time-consuming task, so researchers sometimes take only a limited sample (such as one week's worth of prime-time television shows) from major media outlets. That obviously doesn't reflect the full range of content that the audience sees. The definitions can be problematic, too. For example, if a character in a situation comedy slaps another character on the back (which might be a sequence in which a character is the target of physical force initiated by another character) and they begin laughing, is that violence? What if a character is hurt by a hurricane instead of another person? What about a football tackle? According to some definitions these are violent acts; according to others they are not. One type of content

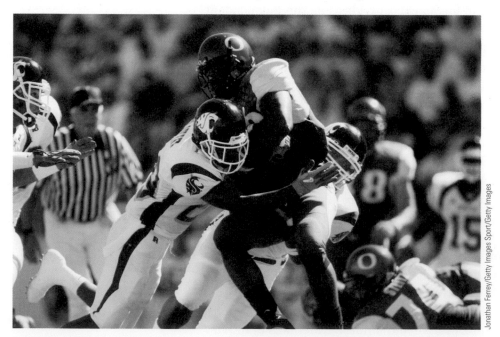

Jonathan Ferrey/Getty Images Sport/Getty Images

NONVIOLENT? Despite many sequences in which players are targets of force initiated by other players, football games don't "count" in studies of TV violence. But, if the same action was shown in a prime-time drama it would count. This exposes a limitation of the samples used in content analyses of TV violence.

analysis (quantitative) counts the acts and another type of content analysis (qualitative) examines how the acts should be regarded. Others draw even further back from the details of content to look at overall themes and narratives, trying to see the big picture that detailed content analysis might miss.

One landmark content analysis of television violence (Federman, 1998) overcame many of these problems. With multimillion-dollar funding provided by the cable television industry, the researchers examined three entire television seasons, rather than a single composite week, and included 23 different cable television and broadcast networks. They also were very sophisticated in their definitions of violence, examining the context of violent acts—for example, whether the violent behavior was rewarded or punished—rather than simply counting the number of gunshots and body blows.

The researchers found that television was very violent. In all three TV seasons, three-fifths of all prime-time programs contained violence, and they averaged over six violent incidents per program per hour. They estimated that preschoolers who watch two hours of television daily witness 10,000 violent acts each year. Most of these involved "high-risk" portrayals that children are likely to imitate, such as violent acts committed by attractive characters in realistic settings in which no harmful consequences are shown. In contrast, only one in 20 programs had antiviolence themes. Those numbers stand true today. By the time you graduated from high school, you saw about 200,000 acts of violence on television, including 20,000 murders by a handgun. Most of the time, the bad guys still are not punished.

EXPERIMENTAL RESEARCH

Experimental research studies media effects under carefully controlled conditions. Typically, a small group sees a media presentation that emphasizes one particular type of content. For example, preschool children are shown violent cartoon shows, and their responses are compared with those of preschoolers exposed to media that lack the "active ingredient," for example, nonviolent cartoons.

> **Experimental research** studies the effects of media in carefully controlled situations that manipulate media exposure and content.

Experimental subjects must be randomly divided between these groups—such as by flipping a coin—to minimize the impact of individual differences among subjects. If they were not assigned randomly—if the children were simply asked to pick which kind of cartoon they would like to see—the aggressive children might volunteer for the violent ones, and the results would therefore reflect the nature of the children rather than any effect of the media content. The same goes for sex, age, social status, and other variables that might affect the outcome. The randomization process cancels out their effects by putting equal numbers of boys and girls, rich and poor, in each group.

Perhaps the most influential media effects experiments were conducted by Albert Bandura (1965) and his colleagues at Stanford University. They showed preschoolers a short film in which an actor behaved aggressively toward a Bobo doll, an inflatable doll the size of a small child with the image of a clown printed on its front and sand in its base so that it rocked back and forth when hit (today's children sometimes call them "bop dolls"). The actor in the film, whom Bandura called the model, punched the doll in the nose, hit it with a mallet, kicked it around the room, and threw rubber balls at it. This aggressive sequence was repeated twice in the film.

Albert Bandura/Department of Psychology/Stanford University

TAKE THAT, BOBO In Bandura's classic experiment, children were shown a movie (top four frames) of a model hitting a Bobo doll. If children saw the model being rewarded for this behavior, they treated the doll similarly (middle and bottom rows). However, children who were neither rewarded nor punished still imitated the aggressive behavior.

All of the children saw that part of the action. However, there were three different endings to the film, and the children were randomly divided into groups that each viewed a different one. Children in the "model-rewarded condition" saw an adult actor reward the aggressor with verbal praise, soda, and snack food. In the "model-punished condition," the adult scolded the model and spanked him. A third group of children, those in the "no-consequences condition," saw only the opening sequence.

After the show, which the children were told was a TV program, subjects were led to a playroom equipped with a Bobo doll, a mallet, some rubber balls, and assorted other toys. As adult observers watched, many of the children in the model-rewarded and no-consequences conditions imitated the aggressive acts they had seen; those in the model-punished condition tended not to do so. However, even the children in the model-punished condition had learned how to perform the behaviors. When adults offered them candy to imitate what they had seen, they started beating up the Bobo doll, too.

The researchers concluded that the punishment the children experienced vicariously in the model-punished condition inhibited their aggressive behavior. However, the most important finding of the study was that the no-consequences condition also produced imitation. This suggested that mere exposure to television violence—whether or not the violence was visibly rewarded on-screen—could spur aggressive responses in young children.

The value of such a carefully controlled design is that it rules out competing explanations for the results (such as the possibility that subjects who

408 PART 3 | MEDIA ISSUES

saw the violent endings were more violent children to begin with). Only the endings of the film (also known as the *experimental treatments*) were varied among groups, so that any subsequent differences among them (such as the beatings the subjects inflicted on their own Bobo dolls) could be attributed to the differences in the media content.

However, the small and unrepresentative samples used in experimental studies, which often consist of college students in introductory classes or the small children of university professors, raise questions about **generalizability**, the degree to which the results apply to other populations and settings. The measures that are used (written responses to a questionnaire or highly structured experimental tasks) and the conditions under which the experiments are conducted do not reflect the real-world situations of ultimate interest, such as behavior in an actual child's playroom or on a school playground. This is the issue of *ecological validity*. More generally, **validity** is the degree to which research findings and methods reflect the true phenomena under study, without distortion. For example, college entrance exams are valid predictors of future performance in college only if those who score high on the exams also perform well in college later on. Or, to assess the validity of a paper and pencil measure of aggression, we might compare the results with observations of aggression on the playground.

A related concept is **reliability**, the degree to which our methods produce stable, consistent results. For example, if we re-administered a college entrance exam or the aggression measure to the same group of students a week after the first administration, we would expect that the individuals with high scores at the time of the first assessment would also have high scores the second time around. Researchers have to provide evidence of both validity and reliability when reporting their results.

The experimental treatments may also be unrealistic in that (1) they often involve much more intense sequences of content than are likely to be encountered in the real world and (2) they are often presented as disjointed segments that do not show the context of the actions. For example, in studies of pornography effects, excerpts from several pornographic films are edited onto a single tape. The edited sequences may have more "action" than the original films, which sometimes intersperse the sex scenes with some token plot and character development. Moreover, experimental subjects, often recruited from first-year college courses, may be exposed to content that they might not normally see, and that may exaggerate the effects. One of the arguments in favor of inductive, observational methods is that they analyze people in their natural contexts and are perhaps more likely to catch the nuances of actual behavior with media.

> **Generalizability** is the degree to which research procedures and samples may be generalized to the real world.

> **Validity** is the degree to which we are actually measuring what we intend to measure.

> **Reliability** is the extent to which a result is stable and consistent.

SURVEY RESEARCH

Survey methods also play an important role in media research. For example, researchers interested in the effects of violent video games might administer a questionnaire to a random sample of U.S. schoolchildren (see Technology Demystified: The Science of Sampling, page 410). Media effects are inferred by statistically relating the independent measures of media exposure ("How many violent video games have you played in the last week?") to the dependent

TECHNOLOGY DEMYSTIFIED

THE SCIENCE OF SAMPLING

Headline: Survey finds 10 percent hooked on the Web. "How can that be?" you ask yourself, "all the people I know are Facebook junkies." The answer to this riddle is the key to the science of sampling. Clearly, one's circle of friends does not adequately represent the opinions of the entire country. Survey researchers could talk to absolutely everyone while conducting a census, but that would be prohibitively expensive. By using probability sampling, researchers can get accurate results with far fewer respondents. Telephone interviews are a popular way to conduct surveys, so let's see how sampling is done for them.

The ideal is to start from a complete sampling frame, a list that includes all members of the population under study. The other important point is to sample the list randomly, so that everyone on the list has an equal chance of being selected. We could cut up all of the phone books in the country, cull the duplicate listings, pack the individual listings in a giant revolving metal drum, and start picking numbers. That would take a drum the size of a cement mixer and would overlook the many homes with unpublished numbers, including a large proportion of city dwellers. It also leaves out people who moved since the last phone book came out, and they tend to be young, low-income, and minorities. Researchers, therefore, use random-digit dialing in which a computer generates random telephone numbers so that all telephone subscribers have an equal chance of getting a call. To do so, they start with listed telephone numbers and replace the last two digits selected from tables of random numbers.

By following this procedure, researchers can get an accurate response by contacting a relatively small sample, and they can estimate the precision of their findings and also the probability that they are in error. For example, a sample of 400 homes yields a 3 percent margin of error (or standard error as it is more properly known) for a question that 10 percent of the respondents say "yes" to. For example, "Are you addicted to the Internet?"). That means the "true" proportion is likely to be somewhere between 7 percent and 13 percent, 10 plus or minus 3. If researchers replicated the survey many times to check its accuracy, the odds are that the results would fall within the range of sampling error 95 percent of the time. The beauty of this approach is its efficiency. A few hundred respondents can represent the opinions of the entire country. However, to cut the margin for error in half in our example (to 1.5 percent), surveyors must quadruple the sample size.

These neat calculations overlook a messy problem with surveys; however, the growing number of people who refuse to cooperate with them, or the problem of nonresponse bias. Cooperation rates have plummeted from 80 percent in early phone survey studies to 15 percent recently, and telephone technology trends (for example, caller ID and cell-phone-only homes) point toward further problems with nonresponse bias.

Some researchers are turning to mail surveys, door-to-door interviews, and Web surveys instead. However, these techniques have their own sampling problems. Well-designed mail surveys can achieve superior response rates compared to phone interviews, but only by paying respondents monetary incentives that may bias the results. And, the sad fact is that 20 percent of the adult population is functionally illiterate and can't read them. There is no comprehensive list of Web users and no efficient way to randomly generate e-mail addresses, so probability sampling is impossible there. Door-to-door interviewing still yields high response rates but cost 10 times as much as phone interviews. So, researchers have to economize by cutting their sample sizes, and that increases their sampling error.

---

variable of interest (such as self-reports of violent behavior: "How many fights did you have last week?"). If those who play a lot of video games also get in a lot of fights, and those who do not play many video games are relatively nonviolent, we would say that the two variables are **correlated**.

> [**Correlated** means that there is a statistical measure of association between two variables.]

Survey studies are often more generalizable than experimental studies because their samples may represent larger populations, such as all U.S.

schoolchildren in our example. Even if the samples are not strictly representative of a larger population in a statistical sense, they may still add to our understanding of media effects. For example, instead of randomly sampling all U.S. schoolchildren, a very expensive undertaking, we might conduct our survey in several school districts chosen to include children from diverse backgrounds. By extending research to more realistic settings and more diverse populations than in experimental studies, surveys can increase our confidence in the generalizability of the findings. They can also account for a wider range of factors than just media exposure, such as peer pressure to play violent games and religious beliefs that discourage them.

JUST A FEW MORE QUESTIONS Phone interviews are completed from computerized phone rooms like this one. The increasingly low response rates obtained in phone surveys call their ability to validly represent public opinion into question.

[**Survey studies** make generalizations about a population of people by addressing questions to a sample of that population.]

However, survey research provides ambiguous evidence about cause and effect. In our example, it is possible that aggressive children like to play violent video games. In other words, a tendency toward violence causes the playing of video games instead of the other way around. It is also possible that both violent behavior and video game use are caused by some unexamined third variable, such as lax parental supervision. This is the sort of situation in which experimental studies or ethnographic research might help to sort out the ambiguities. (This is discussed more fully later in the chapter.)

In media effects research, the most valid surveys are longitudinal studies that survey the same subjects repeatedly over a number of years. Huesmann et al. (2003) asked the parents of 8-year-olds to identify their children's favorite TV programs and asked the children's playmates to rate the children on their antisocial behavior. They recontacted the same families 5 and 10 years later and re-administered the survey. If the youngsters who watched a lot of television are more violent as teens than those who watched relatively little television as children, then we can conclude that childhood television exposure does indeed encourage violent behavior later in life. If some of the teens in the follow-up surveys have subsequently reduced their television viewing but remain violent, we can rule out the competing explanation that, "violent people like violent television." In other words, we can be fairly certain that television causes violent behavior, and rule out the competing explanation that violent people like to watch violence.

However, very few survey studies are repeated over time; most are just "one-shot" studies that compare media exposure and behavior but ignore the direction of any causal relationship. Even longitudinal studies cannot account for the influence of all the possible variables the researchers might leave out, such as parental supervision, which might explain both violence and television viewing. We should also note that other longitudinal studies of TV violence have found no effects (Milavsky et al., 1982). Still others have yielded rather puzzling results, including one by Huessmann and his associates (Huesmann & Eron, 1986) that showed a violence effect for girls but not for boys, just the reverse of earlier findings. Furthermore, a pattern of inconsistent findings emerged from similar studies in Poland, Finland, Israel, and Australia. This raises the likelihood that media effects may not be generalizable across cultures, since social values as well as media content patterns vary between countries.

ETHNOGRAPHIC RESEARCH

Ethnography is a naturalistic way of looking at the impacts of communications media. It adapts the techniques anthropologists use—participant observation and interviewing—to look at cultures in a holistic way. Ethnography places media in a broad context of media users' lives and cultures. It emphasizes observation over time, usually at least six months, so that researchers can see how people respond to changes in their environment, like the media they use. Sherry Turkle (2011) combined observations of people using social media in natural settings like Internet cafés with in-depth interviews conducted in her own office. She assembled a picture of how people use the medium to control and avoid human contact as well as extend it. Other researchers join online communities like "Second Life" as participant observers to examine social life in cyberspace. Nokia employs ethnographers to find out what people really want in their cell phones. They employ a variety of techniques, such as observing cell phone use in a variety of natural settings, or asking people to draw their ideal cell phone.

Focus groups are another way of capturing people "in their own words" through guided group interactions. A group of 6 to 12 people is gathered in a conference room and led by a skilled moderator as they explore a topic of interest to the researcher. Behind a two-way mirror sit researchers equipped with microphones and TV cameras taking in every word. These are free-flowing but guided discussions that produce long transcripts rather than neat statistical tables. Social scientists use them to explore new research topics and to help generate questions for surveys. Ethnographers also use them to produce the raw data needed to formulate inductive theories of media processes; for example, to understand the information needs of minority and low-income Internet users. Media developers use them to see how people react to new programs or new media proto-types.

Like all types of research, focus groups have their flaws and cannot offer a comprehensive answer to every question. With focus groups, it is sometimes hard to find participants, even when recruiters target members of a particular group and offer substantial monetary

> **Ethnography** is a naturalistic research method in which the observer obtains detailed information from personal observation or interviews over extended periods of time.

Spencer Grant / Photo Edit

A HOUSE OF MIRRORS Focus groups are conducted in front of two-way mirrors that let researchers observe and film the proceedings. Groups are a common tool of both ethnographic and market research where they are valued for letting participants respond in their own words. Their limited samples and group dynamics may produce misleading results.

incentives. The members of the targeted group, for example, fathers with teenage daughters, who show up for the interview in no way represent the general public, but do give some idea about the opinions or behaviors of fathers with teenage daughters. The other problem is group dynamics. A good moderator can generate profound insights and must skillfully steer away from individual participants' unique concerns that ordinary people would never reach on their own. Sometimes a strongly opinionated individual will dominate a group. Focus groups on the same topic are repeated until the researcher hears the same general comments from the different groups.

Ethnographers use unstructured or semi-structured interviews as an alternative to survey research. Surveys make it possible to compare many people through standardized questions, but they may impose response categories (e.g., multiple-choice answers) on the respondents. That approach yields standardized responses that are easier to tally, but ethnographers value letting people speak in their own words, using their own concepts and categories. Surveys force people to choose among predetermined responses, which raises the issue of validity. Does the forced choice reflect what the respondent really meant to say? Ethnographers let the participants respond in their own words and then they can ask follow-up, in-depth questions of the participants. Sometimes an in-depth interview will draw unexpected causal connections in that one person's life. All researchers have to select what to report and they interpret what the subjects' words in an interview or the numbers in survey research mean.

Ethnographies can yield in-depth information about a particular place at a particular time, but they do not permit much generalization. Although ethnographers try to record information so thoroughly and accurately that others would reach the same conclusions from their data, such reliability, or reproducibility, may be hard to achieve.

Looking for patterns of human behavior amid huge databases, referred to variously as *Big Data* or *predictive analytics*, is a new twist on ethnography. For example, statisticians might sift through millions of comments about new music in social media spaces to identify commenters who were talking about today's hot groups several months ago. By analyzing what those same forums are chattering about today they might predict what bands will be popular several months from now. The computer programs that make recommendations for you in Netflix and Pandora are other examples. These programs compare you with others with similar tastes to see what they like and calculate whether you might like it, too. Social science researchers have begun to examine server data in depth to discover, for example, exactly which forms of Facebook most affect our psychological wellbeing (Burke et al., 2010).

Thus, the different types of research methods tell us different things. Content analyses often show that the media are filled with violence and sex, for example, but tell us nothing about the actual effects on the audience. Experimental studies often find evidence of effects, even from extremely short exposures of 15 minutes or less, but cannot assess how other factors may reduce or enhance those effects in the real world. Survey studies use larger, more

STOP&REVIEW

1. What are some of the concerns about the impact of media on society that lead to "media bashing"?

2. Contrast the inductive and deductive approaches to studying the effects of the media.

3. What is a *media effect*?

4. What is the purpose of content analysis?

5. In what ways are experimental studies superior to survey studies? In what ways are they inferior?

6. What do ethnographers do?

representative samples than experimental research but seldom reach unambiguous conclusions about the effects of media exposure. Ethnographic studies provide deep insights, but the results are sometimes too subjective and particularistic to duplicate. It is important to explore these issues with a variety of different methods to find "what" happens, but also to find or describe the "how" and "why." A concept from ethnography might be made useful, by triangulating across different forms of evidence we can see if consistent patterns emerge. Triangulation might give us a more valid sense of how people behave with media and why.

THEORIES OF MEDIA USAGE

What medium will I choose today? A video game, an iPod, or a textbook? *Media Now* or *Introduction to Calculus*? You obviously picked *Media Now*, but why? To understand media impacts, we need to understand how the media work their way into our lives. Are we uncritical consumers of everything big media companies send our way, or do we actively select content? Theories of media exposure and use attempt to explain the processes we use to make our daily media consumption decisions.

USES AND GRATIFICATIONS

Uses and gratifications is the theory that media are actively selected to satisfy our needs.

The **uses and gratifications** perspective dominates thinking about media consumption behavior. This theory assumes an active audience (see Media&Culture: The Active Audience, page 415): Users actively seek out media that meet their needs for knowledge, social interaction, and diversion.

The various media satisfy differing needs. For example, interpersonal communication is one of the important gratifications that people seek from the Internet (Papacharissi & Rubin, 2000). Websites like Facebook that fulfill these expectations are thus likely to earn longer visits and repeat viewings. Entertainment needs are more likely to be addressed by Hollywood films or television situation comedies.

Uses and gratifications theory (Palmgreen & Rayburn, 1985) focuses on the match between the gratifications we seek and those we actually obtain from the media. For example, if we surf over to Facebook seeking to gratify a need for social interaction and find friendly wall postings from our online friends, we have obtained the gratification we sought and we are likely to visit Facebook again. If instead we are met by caustic comments from one of our online "frenemies" we might seek out other means to gratify our social interaction need, such as a face-to-face meeting with a real world friend. According to this theory, we arrive at our media consumption decisions by performing a mental calculation in which we compare the gratifications we obtain with those we seek from all of the media alternatives available to us, taking into account all of the needs (for example, for diversion, information, companionship) that are relevant to us at a given moment.

Cultural studies is a branch of scholarship that argues that media and audiences work together to define culture.

Our media behavior changes all the time because the gratifications we seek from the media are in a constant state of flux. We encounter new media that address new or different needs. Our life situation may change and with it the criteria we use to select media. We also may seek out media to adjust

MEDIA&CULTURE

THE ACTIVE AUDIENCE

Just how powerful are the media relative to their audiences? Some believe that the media have an enormous influence on audiences. For example, Adorno and Horkheimer (1972) saw powerful media propaganda as an explanation for the Holocaust and other brutal acts during World War II. And today, some see the media as powerful carriers of ideology that impose the interests of ruling groups on vulnerable audiences (Chomsky & Herman, 1988), such as by convincing young children that shiny toys are the key to happiness.

However, other scholars think the power of the media is limited by processes of selective exposure, selective attention, and selective perception that have been well studied by social scientists. However, this idea of a selective audience parallels a popular notion in **cultural studies** that media and audiences are both powerful. The communication process is a reciprocal activity involving the joint creation of meaning between the author or producer and the person who receives the message and makes sense of it (Hoynes 2002). Stuart Hall (1980) redefined encoding as creating a message with verbal, visual, or written codes or symbols that someone else decodes with her or his own understanding of those codes. From this perspective, communication involves the exchange of meaning through the language and images that compose the shared culture of participants. The receiver of the communication plays an active role, filtering messages through the lens of his or her own social class, culture, significant groups, and personal experiences (Morley, 1992).

One view of the audience reception process builds on the idea of reading. Media producers create texts. Here, "texts" includes radio programs, music, television shows, and films, as well as printed texts. In this context, reading is not literally the reading of words but our interpretations of the media. Creators of media content have a preferred reading that they would like the audience to take out of the text. However, the audience might reject it, or negotiate some compromise interpretation between what they think and what the text is saying, or contest what the text says with an alternative interpretation (Morley, 1992). The audience response depends on what they, their family, and their friends already think about things. For example, a Republican Party member watching a Republican political ad will agree with it, a Democrat will disagree with it, and an independent might agree with part and reject part.

---

our moods (Zillmann & Bryant, 1985) or to fulfill aesthetic urges to appreciate works of media art (Bartsch & Oliver, 2010). At some stages of our lives we may seek media that entertain; at other times information may be more of a priority. And, the different media vary with respect to the gratifications they provide us. For example, television is associated with entertainment, whereas the Internet is more related to information seeking (see Table 14.1).

> **Social learning theory** explains media consumption in terms of its expected outcomes.

LEARNING MEDIA BEHAVIOR

Uses and gratifications theory parallels two general theories of human behavior, **social learning theory** (Bandura, 1986) and the *Theory of Planned Behavior* (Ouellette & Wood, 1998) to some extent, except that our expectations of the media are said to form around outcomes of media consumption behavior rather than the gratification of needs. The outcome could be the feeling of joy we experience after seeing the latest

TABLE 14.1 Uses and Gratifications of Television and the Internet

I WATCH TV . . .	I USE THE INTERNET . . .
Because it entertains me	Because it's easier
Because it's enjoyable	To look for information
Because it relaxes me	To get information for free
Because it is a pleasant rest	Because it is a new way to do research
Because it allows me to unwind	Because it is enjoyable
When I have nothing better to do	Because it is entertaining

Source: Rubin, 1983; Papacharissi & Rubin, 2000.

George Clooney movie. The next George Clooney movie that comes along may attract us, too, because we expect a similar outcome. Likewise, if we find his new movie upsetting, we may pass up the one after that altogether. Uses and gratifications theory would call that enjoyment a gratification; social learning theory calls it an outcome expectation. In social learning theory our observations of the experiences of others are also important. For example, if we hear "positive buzz" from people who've seen a George Clooney movie, we may want to see it too. We also learn by listening to what others have to say about the media, including people in our daily lives and media critics.

Social learning theory adds to the uses and gratifications theory in many other ways. It explains the avoidance of media, as in "I'd better not let Mom catch me playing another video game, or I'll be grounded." Here, the expectation of a negative consequence dictates usage. Media behavior is also determined by our own inner self-regulation (LaRose & Eastin, 2004): "I'm not watching *Survivor* tonight because I am disgusted with how much of a couch potato I am." Much media behavior is governed by habit, in which we suspend active observation of our own media consumption and just automatically turn to the sports page or begin our day by checking our e-mail. In the extreme, self-control may fail those who repeatedly rely on media to relieve negative feelings. This type of reliance results in what some have called *media addictions*, such as overindulgence in music downloads (LaRose, 2010) or becoming a virtual resident of "Second Life."

Another factor is our perception of our own competency to consume the media, or our *self-efficacy*. If you've ever put down a book thinking, "That's too deep for me," self-efficacy influenced your media behavior. Self-efficacy strongly influences how computer media are used, especially by new users. What computer user has not had an attack of computer anxiety, or a fear of using computers, after a disastrous attack by a computer virus? Issues of self-efficacy can pre-empt certain kinds of media use, as when older people say they are too old to learn to use a computer.

Media Addiction. Is it possible to become so deeply involved with our favorite media activity that it acts like an addictive drug? Interactive media are especially enticing since they respond to our every move. Sometimes they do what we wish, but other times not, and the results are highly variable. That keeps us coming back for more—the same pattern of reinforcement that prompts pathological gambling. At times they even transport us to an ecstatic state called *flow* where time seems to disappear (Sherry, 2004). There have been cases of people who were literally dying to play, who suffered heart attacks during marathon sessions with online games. The addictive qualities are sometimes openly touted by game developers who promise a "better high than drugs" and by Webmasters who brag about making their creations more "sticky." Most of us have probably been late to dinner or missed a social engagement at one time or another while absorbed in an online pastime, a possible symptom of a life-wrecking problem, if it happens consistently.

Internet and video game addiction have been proposed as a new form of mental illness that might be termed Problematic Technology Use (Sim et al., 2011), so might you have a case of it? Some of the "symptoms" of this affliction, such as a preoccupation with your Facebook profile, are merely indications of the formation of media habits and most people regain control of them most of the time before spiraling into pathology (LaRose, 2010).

However, many college students do in fact encounter problems as a result of excessive time spent on the Internet, such as dropping a grade in a class because they spent too much time in Facebook, when they perhaps should have been reading *Media Now*. If that is true of you we recommend thinking about ways of restoring self-control. We will make you a deal: if you spend an extra hour reading *Media Now* that you would normally spend in Facebook, then you can treat yourself to an extra desert tomorrow. Deal?

WHERE DID THE TIME GO? Deep engagement in video games may induce a flow state in which time seems to disappear. Excessive game play can also steal time from important real life activities.

COMPUTER-MEDIATED COMMUNICATION

A great deal of the research on mediated interpersonal communication originated in organizational settings, where computer networks were used for all forms of electronic communication long before today's social media were invented. Hence, this field of study is known as *computer-mediated communication* and includes media that we may not immediately associate with computer networks, such as video teleconferencing, as well as others that are obviously mediated by computers, such as e-mail.

An important concept in computer-mediated communication is presence, "a psychological state in which virtual [that is, computer-generated] objects are experienced as actual objects" (Lee, 2004, p. 37). Social presence refers to the experience of social actors through the social cues provided in various communication media. E-mails that consist only of printed words are said to have low social presence, which theoretically makes them suited only for routine exchanges of information. Two-way videoconferences have high social presence since they convey important social cues in voice intonations and facial expressions and live interactions flow in both directions. These features supposedly make them suitable for more sensitive tasks like negotiating business deals and firing employees. However, e-mail is used for just about everything today despite its low social presence. How can that be? Even a "lean" medium like e-mail can be used effectively in tasks requiring social cues as parties learn about each other through repeated exchanges. Might social media like Facebook be even richer than real life, a form of *hyperpersonal* interaction (Walther, 1996)?

THEORIES OF MEDIA IMPACTS

Now that we have considered some theories about why people use the media, we can examine theories of the consequences of media usage for the individual (see Figure 14.1).

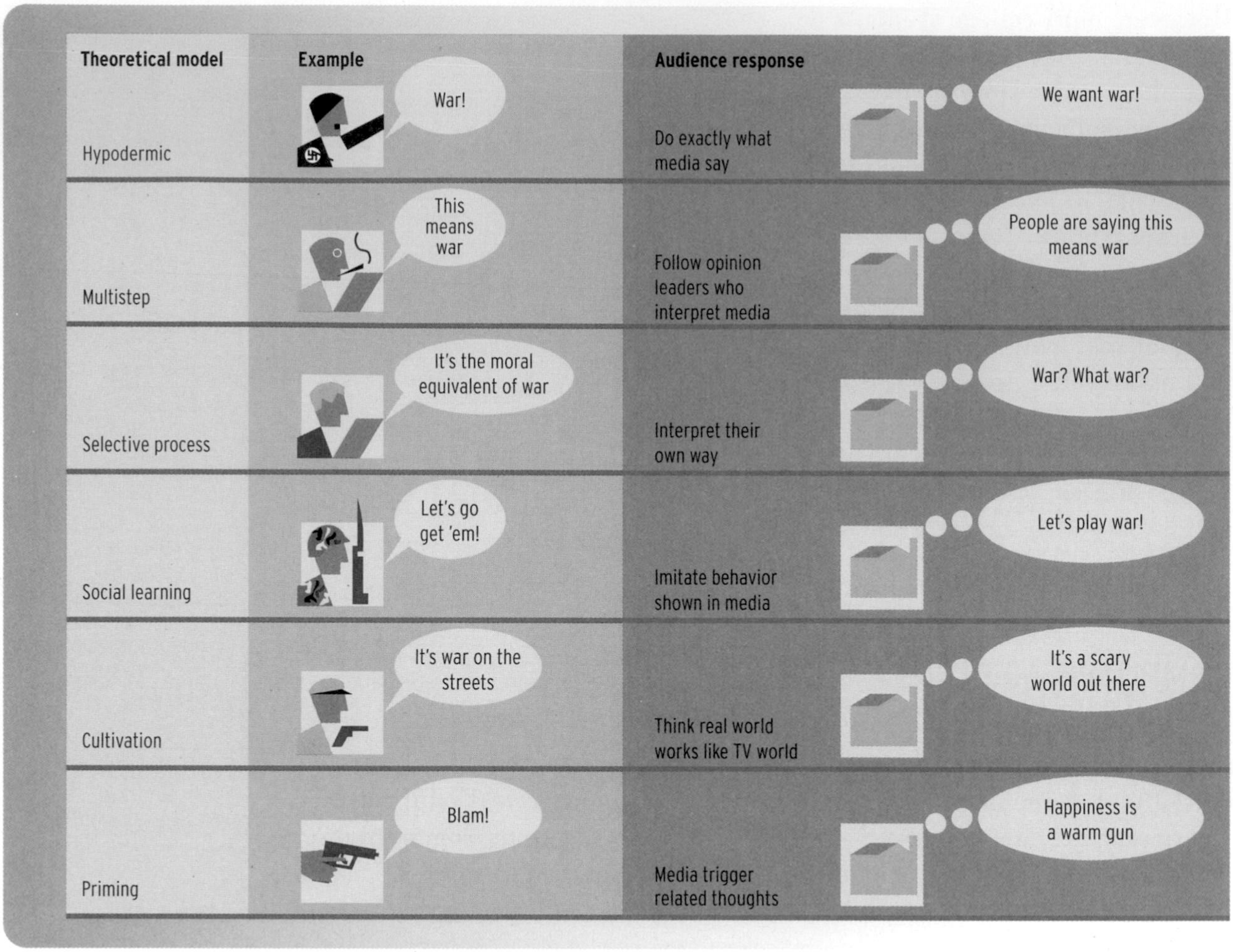

FIGURE 14.1 THEORIES OF MEDIA EFFECTS There are a number of alternative theories about how to understand mass-media effects. Over the years theories of strong effects have contended with theories positing weak effects. Currently we are in a "strong effects" period.

MEDIA AS HYPODERMIC NEEDLE

The United States was seemingly driven into war with Spain in 1898 by sensational coverage concocted by newspaper publisher William Randolph Hearst (see Chapter 4). His papers trumpeted so loudly the sinking of the U.S. battleship *Maine* in the Havana harbor and alleged atrocities by Spanish soldiers that the thirst for war became unquenchable (the *Maine*'s sinking was later found not to be the work of Spanish saboteurs as Hearst's papers implied).

This event made the mass media seem extremely powerful—capable of swaying minds with the impact of a speeding **bullet** or a *hypodermic* injection—images that led to theoretical models of the same names. Later, radio speeches by Nazi leader Adolf Hitler seemed to play a vital role in sparking the Holocaust of World War II. American film propagandists began the systematic study of the most convincing propaganda techniques. Experimental studies of **persuasion** begun during World War II identified the types of verbal arguments (one-sided versus two-sided appeals, and fear appeals versus reasoned arguments) that are the most convincing (Hovland, Lumsdane, & Sheffield, 1949).

The **bullet** model, or hypodermic model, posits powerful, direct effects of the mass media.

Persuasion is the use of convincing arguments to change people's beliefs, attitudes, or behaviors.

THE MULTISTEP FLOW

Survey studies of social influence conducted in the late 1940s presented a very different model from that of a hypodermic needle in which limited effects were instead perceived. For example, a **multistep flow** of media effects was evident. That is, most people receive much of their information and are influenced by the media secondhand, through the personal influence of *opinion leaders* (Katz & Lazarsfeld, 1955). The opinion leaders themselves are influenced by more elite media rather than everyday mass-media channels. For example, political opinion leaders might take their cue from the *Huffington Post*, a blog devoted to political commentary for an elite audience. In the second step, the opinion leaders share their opinions with members of their immediate social circles—say, the "Friday night regulars at the country club"—but only after some modification and adaptation to the norms of that circle. The club members belong to other social groupings (including their families, co-workers, and members of other clubs to which they belong) that are influenced in turn by them, and so on. Eventually, social influence radiates outward in society to people who never heard of the *Huffington Post*. But at every step in the process, social influence is modified by the norms of each new social circle it enters and by conflicting views that originate from other elite sources as well as popular mass-media sources, such as CNN. The point is that although the media have some influence, the process of actual persuasion is primarily a social one. Social media may amplify this impact now that three-quarters of Internet users get news forwarded to them through e-mail or social networking sites (Purcell et al., 2010) and the features of these sites make it easy to recommend content to others. So more of us may be opinion-leaders now if we forward or recommend things that others actually view and find interesting.

> The **multistep flow** model assumes that media effects are indirect and are mediated by opinion leaders.

SELECTIVE PROCESSES

Another theme of the media effects studies that followed World War II was that the selective reception reduces media impact. Audiences exercise *selective exposure*: they avoid messages that are at odds with their existing beliefs. Thus, those who take the "pro-war" position in the Iraq war debate are not likely to read a newspaper editorial advocating peace. Even when people expose themselves to discordant content, they distort it with *selective perception*. Thus, pro-war supporters who watch a TV interview with an anti-war advocate are more likely to find additional "proof" that their position is correct than to be converted to the cause of peace. *Selective retention* means that people's memories are also distorted, so that months later someone may remember that her side won a war debate when in fact her side was humiliated (Sears & Freedman, 1972).

In 1960, Joseph Klapper published an influential review of postwar research on the effects of the mass media. Klapper concluded that the media were weak, able to deliver only a few percent of the voters in an election, and able to gain only a few points' worth of market share for advertisers. Even these **limited effects** registered only at the margins, he said, primarily among the uninterested and the uninformed (Klapper, 1960).

Social media may facilitate passive selective exposure. For example, Google now personalizes searches based on individual search histories so that

> The **theory of limited effects** holds that the effects of the mass media on individuals are slight.

the search results conservatives see for the topic "planned parenthood" may differ from those seen by liberals. Social media recommender systems automatically feed us stories that like-minded friends also like. The proliferation of online news sources and social media also make active selective exposure easier, helping us to find sites with the ideological slant we prefer or to click on stories that our social media friends "like" (Mutz & Young, 2011).

SOCIAL LEARNING THEORY

Within a few years, Klapper's conclusions seemed unsatisfactory. In the 1960s, social critics cast about for explanations for mounting violence, political unrest, and a decline in public morality, especially among young adults. Television seemed a likely cause, because the young people belonged to the first "TV generation" that had grown up with the medium, and TV was loaded with images of violence and sex.

About the same time, a new theory of mass-media effects, social learning theory, lent credence to these claims. Previously, we applied this theory to media consumption behavior, but it originally entered the field of mass communication research to explain the effects of television. The theory explained that viewers imitate what they see on TV through a process known as *observational learning*. The "rewards" that television characters receive for their antisocial behavior, including not just the loot from their robberies but also their very appearance on a glamorous medium such as television, encourage imitation. On the other hand, when the bad guys on TV get caught and go to jail, this presumably inhibits viewers from imitating them. The more we identify with a character—the more it resembles us or someone we would like to be—the more likely we are to imitate his or her behavior. The Bobo doll experiments we examined previously and many others that followed validated this theory.

CULTIVATION THEORY

[**Cultivation theory** argues that mass-media exposure cultivates a view of the world that is consistent with mediated "reality."]

Another explanation of media effects is that heavy exposure imparts a worldview that is consistent with the "world" presented in the media (Gerbner et al., 1994). According to **cultivation theory**, heavy television viewers are likely to be influenced by what is consistently shown in media, such as overestimating their own chances of being victims of violent crime, since it seems so common on television. For example, children who were heavy viewers of stories about child kidnappings were more frightened for their safety than those who watched relatively little television news (Wilson, Martins, & Marske, 2005). Their real-world experiences combine with the television worldview over time in a process called *mainstreaming*. When real-life experience confirms the media view (e.g., the viewers live in violent neighborhoods), the effect intensifies through the process of *resonance*. From this analysis, we project media effects. The viewers who adopt this distorted TV worldview might tolerate violence in their communities and families and in their own behavior because they see it as "normal." This also helps explain why people ever believed in a hypodermic needle impact of propaganda in WW II; when Europeans heard Hitler's speeches on the radio, they had to take account of the real prospect that his army might invade their own country.

Cultivation assumes that media systems like conventional broadcast TV deliver a consistent message to a mass audience. So, how can it apply to new media with their diverse messages and fragmented audiences? Supporters of the theory argue that as Big Media corporations extend their influence to the Internet, the new media will present the same worldview as the old. For example, by using Hulu to push downloads of *24*, the new media present the same message of unrelenting violence as the old. Video games cultivate perceptions of danger in the real world, although those effects may be limited to the specific situations that are similar to those encountered in the gaming environment rather than generating a generalized fear (Williams, 2006).

PRIMING

Priming is another theory (Berkowitz, 1984) in which the activation of one thought triggers related thoughts. Seeing the Roadrunner cartoon character bash the hapless coyote with a hammer makes us more likely to bash our little brother after the show, or so the theory goes. Incidental cues may unleash the aggression. The next time we see a hammer and little brother is standing near—look out! Children may store "scripts" about how to respond with violence that they learn from the media in long-term memory and then act out those scripts when a real-world event triggers that memory (Van Erva, 1990). The General Aggression Model (GAM; Carnagey, Anderson, & Bushman, 2007) integrates priming theory with social learning theory to describe how previously learned violent behavior may be triggered by thoughts, emotions, or physiological states provoked by media exposure.

> **Priming** theory states that media images stimulate related thoughts in the minds of audience members.

AGENDA SETTING

Agenda setting is a process through which public figures and important events help to shape the content of the media. Agenda setting theory also describes the effects of that process on the media audience: the rank ordering that the audience assigns to important issues of the day tends to match the amount of coverage that the media give those issues (Wanta, 1997). For example, it has been found that political campaign press coverage affects the types of issues discussed in online discussion groups (Roberts, Wanta, & Dzwo, 2002) and that in some circumstances social media may set the agenda for conventional media (Sayre, et al., 2010).

CATHARSIS

The catharsis hypothesis argues that media sex and violence have positive effects by allowing people to live out their antisocial desires in a mediated fantasy world instead of the real world (Feshbach & Singer, 1971). This theory was popular in the 1930s and 1940s before it was widely believed that the media were responsible for society's ills. The catharsis hypothesis resurfaced in a review of the effects of violent video games in which it was found that those who played video games for relatively long periods of time exhibited less aggression than those who played for relatively short periods (Sherry, 2007). However, it could also be that the longer people play the more skilled and less frustrated and thus the less aggressive they become (Ferguson, 2009).

CRITICAL THEORIES

Critical theorists question the theories used in media effects studies as well as the methods used (see Chapter 2). Critical studies of media impacts focus less on behavioral effects on individuals and more on how individuals and communities interpret media, and to some degree, on large-scale cultural impacts of media. For example, a critical analysis of John Hinckley's attempted assassination of Ronald Reagan in 1980 examined the way in which Hinckley "read" (or interpreted) a violent movie (*Taxi Driver*) and mingled it with his fantasies about actress Jodie Foster and former actor Ronald Reagan (Real, 1989). By noting that Hinckley committed his act of violence on the eve of the Academy Awards ceremony, Real wove an explanation of how the would-be assassin was trying to communicate his unrequited love for Foster. Does *Avatar* glorify the military or is it a critique of capitalism? The critical theorist is able to examine broad questions such as these about the relationship between culture and society that may elude the social scientist.

Note that in interpretations such as these, the ebb and flow of cause and effect between media and society is not a one-way street. In a sense, the media themselves are the "effects" of class domination or racial prejudice. For example, media might be used by their owners to assert, or make hegemonic, an idea that fits with their interests. People who own factories might want to make unions look bad. And unions may ally with politicians to create media messages that seek to limit owners' power. So, in this view, the media are a part of broader systems of economic exploitation and cultural interaction.

There is a split in critical theory between those who focus on political economy and ideology, and those who focus on studies of culture. Among the former, researchers often assume fairly powerful effects, since they assume that powerful media owners can assert their ideological interests in their media's content. Among the latter, rather than the term *selective perception*, critical cultural theorists speak of audiences that are active "readers" of media "texts." Some focus on the role of the audience while others focus on a more qualitative, critical approach to media messages (Deacon, Pickering et al., 2007). Some critical theorists speak of "group mediation" (Martin-Barbero, 1993) or "interpretive communities" of groups who are similar in education, occupation, wealth, and family background (Lindlof & Taylor, 2010), whereas other social scientists use the term *multistep flow* to describe the way in which social interactions affect perceptions of the media. Likewise, critical theorists have relabeled the SMCR model (see Chapter 1) the "linear model" or "transmission paradigm," in which messages are perceived as flowing in a manner that seems more unidirectional and clear than what they observe from their own studies.

MEDIA AND ANTISOCIAL BEHAVIOR

Antisocial behavior is contrary to prevailing norms for social conduct. That includes unlawful actions such as murder, hate crimes, rape, and drug abuse, as well as behaviors that many members of society find objectionable even if they are not illegal, such as drunkenness, aggression, and sexual promiscuity.

VIOLENCE

The effects of televised violence have received far more attention by researchers than any other type of media impact. Effects on children are a special concern because youngsters have trouble distinguishing between the real world and the world of the small screen. To the child's mind, if Scooby-Doo recovers instantly from a bash on the head, then the same should be true for little brother. Television is packed with violence—three-fifths of all prime-time shows include it, at the rate of 4.5 violent acts per program (Signorielli, 2003). Children's television shows have even more violence than other programs, glamorize it just as much, and trivialize it even more (Wilson et al., 2002).

Hundreds of experimental studies, many patterned after Bandura's Bobo doll study described earlier, demonstrate that children can imitate violence they see. Televised violence prompts children not only to carry out parallel acts of aggression but also to perform other, novel forms of violent behavior; it predisposes them to select violent resolutions to conflicts in their daily lives and even primes them to engage in violent acts (Anderson et al., 2003). The strength of these effects is comparable to those associated with such well-documented public health hazards as lead poisoning and cigarette smoking (Baron et al., 2001).

Some discount experimental studies on the grounds that they are conducted under unrealistic conditions (Milavsky et al., 1982). However, survey studies conducted in real-world settings also tend to show a relationship between violent behavior and viewership of violent television (Paik & Comstock, 1994). Adult viewers who watch violent programs are likely to hold worldviews that match the TV portrayals they see (Gerbner et al., 1994), a result consistent with cultivation theory. However, these relationships are relatively weak ones (Morgan & Shanahan, 1997). More convincing are longitudinal panel studies in which television viewing at one time is related to violence exhibited at a second time that is days, months, or even years later. Earlier (page 410) we mentioned panel studies by Huesmann (2003) and his associates indicating that television viewing at an early age is related to violent behavior later in life. The effects continue to mount even in later years (Johnson et al., 2002).

Violence on television is not the most important factor contributing to violence in society, however. Family and peer influence, socioeconomic status, and substance abuse are more important (U.S. D.H.H.S., 2001). Still, it is probably safest to conclude that exposure to antisocial television portrayals can have at least short-term effects in promoting aggression. Many researchers would add that there are probably long-term effects as well, especially on children. However, these conclusions remain highly controversial. Significant effects are found in only about half of the experimental studies of television violence, are weak overall, and might be at least partially explained away by genetic factors or exposure to violence in the home (Ferguson, 2009).

If violence on television is a problem, shouldn't violent video games be even more dangerous to children? After all, video games are packed with violent role models (Lachlan, Smith, & Tamborini, 2005) and games of the first person shooter genre are nothing but violence without any attempt to show the real-life consequences. In those games the child *is* the violent perpetrator and presumably can readily imagine gunning down other humans while playing.

CHILD'S PLAY? The effects of violent video games on aggressive behavior are highly controversial. Some reviews of the research find substantial effects, whereas others find none.

A number of studies suggest that there are indeed negative effects. For example, in one study playing violent video games made players insensitive to the pain of others (Bushman & Anderson, 2009). In another study of boys, playing a violent video game had a greater effect on aggressive behavior observed during playtime at school than watching others play (Polman et al., 2008). However, some reviews of the studies examining the effects of violent video games find evidence of major effects on aggression (Anderson et al., 2010), whereas others find little evidence that such effects exist (Kutner & Olsen, 2008). Researchers disagree over the validity of the methods used in the studies and the interpretation of the findings. For example, many experimental studies (Polman et al. is a rare exception) focus on aggressive attitudes or use measures of "violence," such as blasts of loud noise, that have little in common with the real world violent acts that are the real concern. Survey studies rely on often faulty memories about the amount of exposure to violent games. Also, the studies typically involve children and college students drawn from normal populations that do not frequently engage in violence despite their video game exposure.

Concerned parents who may wish to err on the side of caution by protecting their children from media violence could benefit from warnings when violence is about to appear. Unfortunately the content labels supplied by television networks under-represent the amount of violence in program content (Kunkel et al., 2002) and less than a third of parents fully utilize them, in part because they find that the ratings do not provide detailed enough guidance (Gentile et al., 2011). Moreover, the labels may not be effective unless accompanied by improved parental supervision or automatic content filtering. Simply labeling the programs as violent attracts more young viewers to the "forbidden fruit" (Bushman & Cantor, 2003). Parental intervention can make a difference. Providing brief negative evaluations of violent characters (Nathanson, 2004) or enlisting parents and schools in campaigns to reduce exposure to media (Robinson & Borzekowski, 2006) can reduce violent effects. However, parental interaction may be ineffective in relationship to online risk factors that are more influenced by peers than by parents (Livingstone & Helsper, 2008).

PREJUDICE

The media may also promote sexism, racism, and other forms of intolerance. Media portrayals encourage **stereotyping**, the formation of generalizations about a group of people on the basis of limited information. Stereotypes are

Stereotyping is the making of generalizations about groups of people on the basis of limited information.

Leila Cutler/Alamy Limited

harmful when they become rationalizations for treating others unfairly. Furthermore, members of the groups to which they are applied may internalize negative stereotypes thereby undermining their own self-respect. Media are very effective at creating stereotypes because they are sometimes the only source of information we have about other groups and because they often present a distorted view of those groups.

Gender stereotypes are an example. Since the 1970s, women have begun appearing in higher-status jobs on television and in somewhat fewer stereotypically female occupations but still are more likely to be unemployed and less likely to have professional occupation than men. (for example, secretary and nurse; Signorielli, 2009; Signiorielli & Bacue, 1999). Sex-role stereotypes are rampant in video games as well where women are seldom seen in general, and usually appear scantily clad in sexy clothing when present (Downs & Smith, 2010). The reinforcement of stereotypes begins with programs aimed at toddlers: *Barney and Friends* and *Teletubbies* portrayed the few female characters as caregivers and followers whereas male roles included a wider range of possibilities (Powell & Abels, 2002). And, the reinforcement continues through film and video game characterizations as toddlers grow into tweens and teens (Okorafor & Davenport, 2001; Williamson, 2007).

To the male viewer, this might make it seem acceptable to treat women as inferiors. For their part, women may feel diminished because of their underrepresentation on TV. They may internalize the common media stereotypes that beautiful women are more valued and that women should sacrifice their careers for their families (Signorielli, 1989). Sex-role stereotypes in the media may have an effect on a wide range of outcomes including attitudes towards women and perceptions of the appropriateness of personality traits, occupations, and activities stereotypically associated more with one sex than the other (Oppliger, 2007). Gender stereotypes can also make us dissatisfied with our own bodies. Exposure to TV ads that portray women as sex objects makes women want to be thinner and men want to be larger than they actually are (Lavine, Sweeney, & Wagner, 1999) and may encourage unrealistically thin body images and lead to eating disorders among females (Grabe, Ward, & Hyde, 2008). As with violence effects, the impact of sex-role stereotyping can be counteracted by parental interventions that provide contradictory information; for example pointing out that "lots of girls do things besides paint their nails and put on make-up" (Nathanson et al., 2002, p. 928).

The life aspirations of minority children are also affected by the limited media portrayals of minorities (Clark, 1972). The level of representation of minority characters on network television now matches and even exceeds their numbers in the general population (Glascock, 2001). But racially stereotyped portrayals persist; for example, African-Americans are still more often portrayed as lazy, and Latinos as flashy dressers compared to whites (Mastro, 2008). Racially stereotyped television portrayals of minorities may lead white viewers to see minorities in more negative ways, such as making them more willing to see African-Americans as criminals (Ford, 1997) or to vote against public policies aimed at ending racial inequality (Mastro, 2008).

Media stereotyping affects all groups in society. Adults over 60 are relatively invisible on television, and when they do appear they are portrayed as relatively powerless and sexless compared to younger characters (Lauzen,

UNDOING STEREOTYPES The success of female role models like 2010 Oscar winner Kathryn Bigelow may hold the key to reducing gender stereotypes in front of the camera as well as behind it.

Dozier, & Reyes, 2007). Blue-collar families are underrepresented and are often portrayed in a way that denigrates their lifestyles (consider *The Simpsons*). The same is true of homosexuals, persons with disabilities, the homeless, the mentally ill, and seemingly any group that deviates from a mainstream society dominated by professional, "straight," healthy, and wealthy white males. We can easily summon to mind stock images of serious college students ("nerds" in media lexicon), millionaires, lawyers, and police that have little in common with their real-world counterparts. To some extent, the media cannot function without stereotypes. They are the "pictures in our heads" (Lippmann, 1922) that stories are made of, a type of conceptual shorthand that allows viewers to recognize characters immediately and connect with their situations.

It is when the negative stereotypes spill over from the flickering screen into our daily lives that they become a concern. In the midst of a continuing war on terrorism there is the danger that we may be unduly influenced by media images of Muslims and Arabs as terrorists and warmongers. Arab stereotypes have long been present in popular media (Shaheen, 2003) and U.S. media contain many negative images of Muslims (Nacos & Torres-Reyna, 2007). This might lead us to be prejudiced against Muslims or to back policies that punish them unfairly. Indeed, this situation is one in which the media images could be especially powerful. They highlight serious intergroup conflict in the starkest terms and provide the only information that many viewers have about members of a relatively small minority group. These are conditions in which media stereotypes can have very corrosive effects.

SEXUAL BEHAVIOR

Sex in the media erupted as an issue in the 1920s, in the aftermath of a wave of Hollywood sex scandals. Hollywood imposed strict self-censorship standards that now seem ludicrous in retrospect: no cleavage, no navels, separate beds for married couples, no kisses longer than four seconds, cut to the clouds overhead if sex is imminent. When Elizabeth Taylor said the word *virgin* in a 1954 movie, it caused a sensation. Since then, producers and publishers have continually pushed the limits to reap financial benefits at the box office and the newsstand.

The last decades have seen a dramatic increase in highly explicit pornographic material through magazines, home video, movies, and cable television. Today, online sex is a growing concern. In a recent national study about a fourth of children age 10–15 intentionally exposed themselves to X-rated material on the Internet and exposure to violent pornography (although not exposure to non-violent porn) greatly increased the chances of engaging in sexually related aggression over time (Ybarra et al., 2012). Among adults the consumption of pornography is related to participation in extra-marital sex and sex for hire (Wright, 2012). The latest cause for concern is "sexting," in which teens make their own pornography by taking pictures of themselves in various states of undress and sharing them via social media or cell phones. Although only about 2 percent of youth between the ages of 10 and 17 have sent pictures of that nature (Mitchell et al., 2012), the numbers are still alarming because parents, schools, and law enforcement officials treat the incidents as child pornography cases.

Experimental studies show that when males are exposed to explicit pornography, they are more likely to express negative attitudes toward women, to think that relatively uncommon sexual practices (such as fellatio and anal intercourse) are widespread, and to be more lenient with rape offenders in hypothetical court cases. In experiments that examine the combined impacts of pornography and violence, male subjects are more likely to administer simulated electric shocks (sometimes even supposedly lethal ones!) to females after exposure to pornography (Harris & Barlett, 2008).

Is there a relationship between pornography and sex crimes in the real world? Early exposure to X-rated material by adolescent males has been found to be related to more stereotyped attitudes towards women, more permissive sexuality, and more participation in sexual harassment later in life (Brown & L'Engle, 2009). Sex offenders are likely to consume pornography before engaging in sex and are highly aroused by material that matches the nature of their criminal sexual activities. Among those who are at "high risk" for sexual aggression (for example, men who are impulsive or hostile by nature), pornography exposure greatly adds to that risk. However, a link between the availability of pornography in a community and the incidence of sex crimes has not been established conclusively. The example of Japan is often cited, a culture in which sexual images in the media including violent ones are much more common than in the United States but sex crimes are far less frequent. That could be because of strict social norms against rape that inhibit the effects of pornography but also make victims reluctant to report it (Harris & Barlett, 2008).

The relatively mild sexual portrayals on television, in which sexual intercourse is at most strongly implied by showing "after" pictures of actors between the sheets, also pose a threat to society. Exposure to sexual content on television was found to be related to pregnancy rates during a study that followed a national sample of teens over three years (Chandra et al., 2008).

AF archive / Alamy

SEX AND VIOLENCE. Cable series like *Spartacus* that combine sex and violence may promote aggression against women. Exposure to sex on television has been linked to teen pregnancy.

DRUG ABUSE

A lifetime ago there was concern that movies such as *Easy Rider* glorified the drug scene and contributed to illegal drug use among college students. The media generally bowed to these concerns, if only because drug films were not as profitable as those featuring violence and sex, and because distributors of illegal drugs cannot buy advertisements for them!

The abuse of legal drugs is quite another story. Cigarette ads have long been banished from television by law. The ads can no longer glorify smoking by showing happy, glamorous people (or cuddly cartoon characters) puffing away; the Surgeon General's warnings about the hazards of smoking must be displayed; and there can be no imagery that obviously is designed to appeal to children. Hard-liquor distillers long avoided television (although this is now changing), but beer and wine commercials are one of the leading sources of advertising revenue for television, and so are ads for over-the-counter drugs, and restrictions on prescription drug ads have been relaxed so that they, too, can appear on television.

Advertisers claim that these ads do not boost overall consumption levels and affect only the relative market share the various brands enjoy. However, a comprehensive review of research about the effects of cigarette advertising concluded that cigarette ads may prompt both the initiation and continuation of smoking (Capella et al., 2011) and advertising also plays a role in the initiation of alcohol consumption (Smith & Foxcroft, 2009). Critics have long contended that some of the ads are secretly targeted to young viewers through characters (such as the dashing Captain Morgan pirate character and Joe Camel) that are carefully crafted to appeal to impressionable young viewers at an age when they are vulnerable to initiating lifelong addictions. Revelations of secret cigarette industry marketing studies on children have shown that the critics were right. Now attention has turned to antismoking campaigns directed at teens and children. Campaigns from the national "truth" anti-smoking campaign that attack the motives of the tobacco industry have proven effective but antismoking ads produced by the industry itself actually increase intentions to smoke (Davis et al., 2009). And, ads that are highly critical of the industry are prohibited under the terms of a settlement with the tobacco industry that set aside billions of dollars for smoking prevention.

Tobacco and alcohol industry apologists like to argue that their products are legal and they have a right to advertise, even if some children get in the way. After all, fast food may be harmful. Why don't we ban hamburger commercials aimed at children? Maybe we should. Now some critics have begun to argue that like drugs, fatty foods are indeed addictive. There is a relationship between television viewing and obesity in children (Caroli et al., 2004) and video game use is also associated with childhood obesity (Vanderwater et al., 2004).

COMMUNICATIONS MEDIA AND PROSOCIAL BEHAVIOR

[**Prosocial behaviors** are those that a society values and encourages.]

Prosocial behavior is in a sense the opposite of antisocial behavior. It includes behaviors and positive qualities that we want to encourage in our children and our society: cooperation, altruism, sharing, love, tolerance, respect, balanced nutrition, contraceptive use, personal hygiene, safe driving, improved reading skills, and so on. We can also include in this list the discontinuing of antisocial behaviors, such as smoking, drinking, reckless driving, or unsafe sex. Prosocial media fall along a continuum based on the relative mixture of entertainment and informational content. They range from transmitting heavily sugar-coated, subtle messages to explicit, direct educational efforts.

Efforts to promote prosocial media are the flip side of "media bashing" that we outlined earlier. Instead of criticizing the media for sex and violence, only to have them retreat behind the First Amendment, why not encourage them to produce more wholesome and educational programs? The Children's Television Act of 1990 does just that. It mandates that programs designed specifically for children be aired as a condition for broadcast license renewals (see Chapter 15). After years of wrangling over just how much children's programming is enough, what "specifically designed for children" means, and even who children are, meaningful guidelines were finally passed in 1996 (Kunkel, 1998).

INFORMATION CAMPAIGNS

Information campaigns use the techniques of public relations and advertising to "sell" people on prosocial behaviors. They seek to achieve specific changes in their audience, such as heightening public awareness of a health or social problem and changing related attitudes and behaviors. They usually adopt an informal and entertaining style to attract an audience. Perhaps the most familiar manifestations of information campaigns are the public service announcements that populate late-night television.

> **Information campaigns** use the techniques of advertising in an attempt to convince people to adopt prosocial behaviors.

Information campaigns have a spotty record of success. Experimental studies show, however, that some campaigns do affect the awareness, attitudes, and behaviors of their audiences. Campaigns can succeed if they have clear objectives and sharply defined target audiences and if they find relevant ways to overcome indifference (Rice & Atkin, 2000). *Social marketing*, an integrated marketing communication approach to behavior change (see Chapter 11), combines media, interpersonal influence, and carefully managed efforts to introduce recommended products directly into the lives of the target audience. This approach has achieved considerable success in the health communication field (Wakefield et al., 2010). For example, in a safe-sex campaign, public service ads might be combined with posters in nightclubs and with volunteers who circulate on dance floors to distribute condoms. Success can also depend upon striking just the right chord with their intended audiences. For example, antismoking ads that emphasize the personal stories of the effects of smoking are more effective than others (Durkin, Biener, & Wakefield, 2009). However, habitual behaviors like smoking are generally harder to change through information campaigns than infrequent behaviors such as obtaining flu vaccinations.

Even when well designed, some information campaigns face too many obstacles to have much impact. Many rely on free advertising space (hence their appearance late at night) and consequently have difficulty reaching their audiences. The public interest groups that produce information campaigns too often expend all their resources in developing the media materials, leaving little for paid media placements directed to their target audience.

James Leynse/ Corbis News/ Corbi

WE DARE YOU TO USE DRUGS Well-intentioned but poorly designed information campaigns sometimes unintentionally encourage the behaviors they hope to prevent. The D.A.R.E. antidrug program increased drug use when students learned that drugs were more prevalent than they had thought. The program had to be revised as a result of these findings.

And, not all information campaigns are effective to begin with. Advertising professionals who contribute their time in exchange for a chance to showcase their skills may not be familiar with scientific evidence about what works and what is needed to create successful campaigns. For example, health campaigns that emphasize social consequences and feature female sources tend to be effective whereas those featuring emotional appeals or that rely on credibility of the sources tend not to be. And, it is important to tailor messages according to the involvement level of audiences as well as their age, gender, and race (Keller & Lehmann, 2008). Other campaigns are worse than ineffective. Unintended effects also plague information campaigns. For example, informing children about the risks of drugs can also have the unintended effect of making drug use seem more prevalent and therefore more socially acceptable. One widely touted drug education program, Project D.A.R.E., was found to be ineffective at best (Lynam et al., 1999) and at worst may have encouraged drug use; it had to be re-designed.

In other cases, campaigns may have foggy objectives or uncertain target audiences, or they may have too many objectives, trying to satisfy multiple agendas ("We want users to stop using, potential users to stop thinking about it, and their parents to drum both messages into their children's heads"). Campaign developers seldom have the resources to fund the detailed research that goes into successful product commercials. And, they try to achieve much more than product advertisements, which merely aim to increase awareness of a brand name or a new product. Information campaigns often target deeply ingrained habitual behaviors, a goal that is generally unattainable through advertising alone.

INFORMAL EDUCATION

Without a "captive audience" of classroom students, informal education efforts must artfully combine the elements of education and entertainment. The best-known example is *Sesame Street*. Since its inception in 1969, *Sesame Street* has proved to be a popular and effective means of readying children for school (Fisch & Truglio, 2001). However, *Sesame Street* is also an example of a phenomenon that plagues prosocial media—the unintended effect. Sesame Street was originally designed to close the gap in school readiness between minority and majority children. Unfortunately, it does just the opposite. Middle-class white children who watch the show learn more about "words that begin with b" than low-income minority children, and the knowledge gap (see page 437) between the two widens as a result (Cook et al., 1975).

What about the prosocial effects of entertainment media? Do couch potatoes soak up valuable information from TV quiz shows? Do children learn about cooperation by watching *Spongebob Squarepants*? We call these effects *incidental learning* because they are side effects of exposure to entertainment. Content analyses of television entertainment programming reveal frequent examples of prosocial behavior, although these instances may be overwhelmed by glorified depictions of aggression (Greenberg et al., 1980). The Bill and Melinda Gates Foundation has an initiative to embed educational messages in the plot lines of TV shows, such as placing messages about HIV prevention in *Private Practice*. Relatively little research has been done in the United States on the prosocial effects of entertainment media. According to some studies, prosocial media can be highly effective (Friedlander, 1993; Huston et al., 1992). For example, an episode of *Friends* in which a broken condom led to an unwanted pregnancy proved to be an effective form of sex education (Collins et al., 2003). Internationally, a number of studies in Brazil, Mexico, India, and South Africa have shown that deliberate placement of plot lines in some operas and other serial entertainment encouraging smaller family sizes has had considerable impact over time—this approach has developed an entire approach to prosocial media called *entertainment-education* (Singhal et al., 2004).

Interactive media provide new venues for incidental learning. Prosocial video games can be effective in promoting desirable behaviors, such as cooperation, among children (Greitemeyer & Osswald, 2010). Many young Internet users engage in self-directed online research to learn about topics that interest them, often stimulated by their participation in online social media like Facebook (Ito et al., 2009).

FORMAL EDUCATION

The delivery of courses through the media is formally known as *distance education*. The new trend in distance education is putting courses on the World Wide Web, the virtual university. Overall, Web courses are at least as effective as classroom instruction and possibly more effective (Means et al., 2009).

However, there is wide variability in the effectiveness of distance education relative to classroom instruction: some online courses are more effective than the classroom, others far less so. With so many courses going online, either all or in part, the question becomes which forms of online coursework are most effective. For example, it appears that asynchronous courses that can be consumed at the convenience of the learner are more effective than synchronous courses even though the latter permit live interactions with the instructor (Bernard et al., 2009).

Online instruction could have a transformative effect on higher education that might someday eliminate many of our beloved alma maters as elite universities post online courses that are arguably "the best" and are also free. For example, MIT makes online materials (although not classroom access to its professors) for its courses available for all at no charge. Stanford University offered a free online course about artificial intelligence that drew over 100,000 students. In 2012, Stanford and MIT joined consortia of universities that plan to make a wide selection of courses freely available on the Internet.

There is growing interest in so-called "serious games" (see Chapter 13) that embed educational objectives in video games. Given the popularity of video games with learners of all ages and the ability of games to simulate real-world environments outside the classroom, this approach holds promise. It remains to be seen how effective and costly serious games are compared to other forms of instruction (VanderCruysse et al., 2012).

THE IMPACTS OF ADVERTISING

If the media have such mixed success in influencing behavior, why is there so much advertising? (For more on advertising, see Chapter 11.) The answer is that advertisers are happy to achieve rather limited impacts, at least when using conventional mass media. Most advertisers take our consumption behavior as a given. They merely seek to strengthen our brand awareness so that we think of their product when we are in the store and maintain brand loyalty so that we will keep coming back for more. At best, they hope to provide information that will sway the attitudes and purchase behavior among a small percentage of consumers and that those impacts will build slowly with repeated exposures to an ad campaign. However, conventional market research tools provide limited insight into the success of mass-media advertising campaigns based on the demographic characteristics of audiences and the media and products they consume (Stewart & Pavlou, 2008).

Does advertising work? Even with these relatively modest goals, many mass-media advertising campaigns are a flop. Sometimes they are outgunned by more powerful campaigns from competitors. Many other factors influence consumer purchases, including special promotional offers, the price of the product, its availability, the way it is packaged, and—let us not forget— consumer needs and the actual merits of the product. Any of these can negate the effects of the most polished advertising campaign. Sometimes the campaign is simply ineffective. Part of the problem lies with the way ads are tested. If they are highly memorable, they are deemed successful. Only much later do the advertisers find out whether they sell more hamburgers or athletic shoes.

It is unclear exactly how advertising works even when it is successful. The *hierarchy of effect* is a common notion in advertising research that states that purchase decisions follow a set series of steps: first comes awareness, then interest, then decision, followed by the action of actually buying the product. But there are many competing hierarchies, including some in which action comes first, as in the case of an impulse buy. One review of the literature concluded that none of the proposed hierarchies is especially compelling (Vakratsas & Ambler, 1999).

The impact of television advertising on young children is of great concern because most children first come into contact with the consumer society through TV. Young children have a difficult time understanding commercials. They confuse the commercials with the programs and react uncritically to advertising

OLD JOE Cigarette advertising often influences impressionable minds and may encourage young children to acquire an unhealthy lifelong habit. The tobacco industry secretly marketed to children before the practice was uncovered and its effects on children were documented, resulting in new restrictions on cigarette advertising (which marked the end of Joe Camel's life).

messages (Liebert & Sprafkin, 1988). Advertisers can exploit young viewers by using the hosts of children's shows to hawk their products, selecting deceptive camera angles to make tiny toys appear child-size. Sometimes, a new television show is really a big advertisement—part of a marketing campaign—where the characters of children's programs are dolls already on the store shelves waiting to be purchased. These shows prompt children to parrot advertising slogans to

STOP&REVIEW

1. Name three theories that contend that mass media have strong effects.

2. What are some of the factors that weaken media effects?

3. Do video games cause violence, or don't they? Explain your answer.

4. Name some examples of prosocial effects of the media.

wear down their parents: in a study of Christmas lists, two-thirds of 7- and 8-year-olds asked for products that were advertised on TV (Buijzen & Valkenburg, 2000) and, when their purchase requests went unfulfilled, also to family conflict and life dissatisfaction (Buijzen & Valkenburg, 2003). As we saw previously, advertising also plays a role in introducing children to harmful habits such as smoking and alcohol consumption.

Is advertising good for consumers in an economic sense? Overall, about 7 percent of what we spend on consumer goods goes into advertising (Shonfeld & Associates, 2012). In some product categories, cigarettes, beer, and soft drinks, for example, the advertising expenditures are considerably higher. When manufacturers establish brand loyalty, they can charge more for their products. However, advertising also makes consumers aware of alternative products and special offers, and it generally promotes competition, which helps to keep consumer prices down. Overall, it appears that advertisements are a slight "bargain" for the consumer (Jeffres, 1986). However, they are less of a bargain for advertisers than they used to be. The increase in sales stemming from increases in advertising has fallen to about half of what it was in the 1980s (Sethuraman et al., 2011). In the critical view, many researchers are concerned about the larger social impact of advertising in locking people into a consumerist point of view and a lifestyle that has them spending money they don't have for things they don't really need (Jhally, 2000).

Online advertising and marketing forces a rethinking of basic questions about advertising effectiveness (Stewart & Pavlou, 2008). In favor of advertisers, online search word advertising popularized by Google makes it possible to target ads to consumers who are in the market for a specific product, eliminating waste in advertising budgets. It is also possible to precisely determine the effectiveness of an ad by tracking the number of purchases completed as a result of clicking through to the advertiser's Web page instead of hoping that an impression of a television ad will come to mind during the next trip to the store. On the other hand, advertisers are losing control of the message as consumers turn to blogs, social media, product review sites, and other sources of online word of mouth (or word of mouse at is sometimes called) that may deflate the claims made by advertisers.

THE IMPACTS OF POLITICAL COMMUNICATION

Like it or not, political campaigns have largely evolved into advertising campaigns, the candidate being the "product." The techniques of market research and mass persuasion have been applied with a vengeance to politics. The political caucus has given way to the focus group.

What is the net effect of the political ads that glut the airwaves just before an election? The ads are most likely to impact those who are relatively unaware of an election and its issues, but are also likely to discourage highly aware voters from seeking other types of information (Valentino, Hutchings, & Williams, 2004). However, since unaware voters are also unlikely to vote, the overall impact may be minimal.

Political communication researchers have largely given up trying to understand how to sway massive blocs of votes through persuasive argumentation, concentrating instead on more complex interactions between voters, the media, and political systems. For example, newspaper readership (although not television news viewership) and engagement in political discussion foster involvement with local political issues (Scheufele, Shanahan, & Kim, 2002). Political practitioners have turned to negative ads in the hope of cutting through voter apathy, but overall these are ineffective and may stimulate a lack of trust in government (Laua et al., 2007). Negative ads probably do not diminish voter turnout as once thought (Franz et al., 2008). The campaign coverage that appears in the media, including news stories, opinion polls, public appearances by the candidates, debates, and editorial endorsements, is inherently more effective than political advertisements. That is because authoritative media sources are generally more credible, or believable, than politicians, and credible sources are more persuasive. Also, recall an earlier discussion (in Chapter 2) of the gatekeeping, framing, and agenda-setting functions of the mass media: their ability to define not what the important issues are but also how to think about those issues. For example, in the 2008 Presidential election the media set the agenda for an Obama victory by emphasizing the economic failures of the preceding administration (Kenski et al., 2010). Debates have some impact on perceptions of the candidate's character, but tend to only strengthen confidence in preexisting voting choices rather than change votes (Benoit & Hansen, 2004). However, the "spin" that the media place on the outcome of debates may affect voter attitudes (Fridkin et al., 2008).

The less important the election, the more important political coverage becomes. This is because voters are unlikely to be aware of candidates or issues outside of the presidential race and one or two other high-profile contests. Most Americans cannot name their own member of the House of Representatives, let alone the name of the challenger or the positions either candidate takes on the issues. Because people are naturally unwilling to vote for an unknown quantity, this often gives incumbents and candidates with names such as "Kennedy" and "Trueheart" a natural advantage. Issues have turned into TV "sound bites." In this vacuum, advertising can be effective in establishing name recognition. However, the effects of political ads in major campaigns may be obscured by the impact of other campaign activities. A study examining voters

POLITICALLY EFFECTIVE? The research shows that debates between the candidates change surprisingly few votes. Most viewers twist the debate in their minds to confirm their preexisting opinions about the candidates. However, the spin the media place on the result can sway attitudes.

in media markets in "battleground" states in the 2004 presidential elections but who lived in (non-battleground) neighboring states, who were thus not subjected to other campaign activities, revealed that campaign commercials are persuasive when considered in isolatoin from other campaign activities (Huber & Arcenaux, 2007).

The commonly held beliefs, attitudes, and misconceptions about the issues of the day are what we call *public opinion*. Like candidate preferences, public opinion is also shaped through interpersonal influence. The publicity attached to polls may help mold public opinion through a process called the *spiral of silence* (Noelle-Neumann, 1984). That is, when we believe that our opinions match the rising tide of public opinion—for example, when we see poll results that support our own opinions—our beliefs are strengthened. Conversely, when we sense that we hold an unpopular belief, a "red" voter in a "blue" state for example, we remain silent. Because one of the ways we gauge how popular our own opinions are is by hearing the same opinions voiced by others, a self-perpetuating cycle begins that eventually suppresses the less popular view.

Changes in the media landscape perhaps call for a re-assessment of the effects of political communication. The popularity of partisan media like Fox News (on the right) and MSNBC (on the left) may make it easier to maintain divergent views (Bennett & Iyengar, 2008), and social media make it possible to seek out social groups who will support and even amplify unpopular opinions (Mutz & Young, 2011). Online political participation extends beyond the older, wealthier participants who take part in offline political activities (Jensen, Danziger, & Venkatesh, 2007), and social media use is related to civic and political participation offline as well as online (DeZuniga et al., 2012). As the "Arab spring" uprisings in the Middle East (see Chapter 17), and the Occupy Wall Street movement in the U.S. illustrate, social media can also play an important role in sparking social movements outside the purview of the political establishment and mainstream media. However, the Internet is still not accessible to all; the digital divide (see Chapter 9) still persists among low income and minority citizens. That limits its value as a medium of political communication or as an electronic voting booth in an egalitarian society.

UNDERSTANDING SOCIETAL IMPACTS

Societal effects could be viewed as the aggregate of individual effects across large groups of people, the whole being equal to the sum of its parts. However, individual effects do not translate directly into broad social impacts. For example, although many studies have found that video games and television are related to aggression at the individual level, there is no consistent evidence that the availability of these media affect community-level rates of violent crime (Ferguson, 2009), and indeed different theories have been proposed to explain the broader implications of the media (see Chapter 2). The important issues related to media and society reflect issues that confront society at large. They are at the root of many of the controversies that swirl around the media and underlie many of the political debates in a free society. Indeed, we abandon the use of the term *media effects* at this point, since that is closely associated with social science research on the media and the individual, and instead consider broad "social impacts."

COMMUNICATIONS MEDIA AND SOCIAL INEQUALITY

One of the thorniest issues confronting society is inequality between social groups as defined by wealth, race, and gender. What are the roots of social inequality in society? As societies become more complex, they become more stratified—more divided into unequal social groups or classes (Braudel, 1994).

People may be categorized both in terms of their monetary wealth, or economic capital, and in terms of differences in their education and family backgrounds—their cultural capital (Bourdieu, 1984). Differences in both economic and cultural capital help perpetuate social inequality. As we saw in Chapter 9, gaps in Internet access still remain between income, racial, and education groups over time, a phenomenon known as the *digital divide*. We have seen that efforts to close the divide focus primarily on making up differences in economic capital by subsidizing computers and Internet connections in poor neighborhoods. Now there is growing concern about a second-level digital divide based on differential skill levels between better and less educated users (Hargittai & Hinnant, 2008). Low-income communities are also disadvantaged by lack of access to broadband connections that are necessary to take online courses and apply for jobs and social programs online (Dailey et al., 2010).

Equal access does not necessarily translate into social equality according to the *knowledge gap hypothesis*. The gap is between the information "haves" and the "have-nots." The information-rich "haves" are those with superior levels of education and access to libraries and home computers. The "have-nots" are the information-poor who have inferior levels of education and resource access and tend to be the economically poor as well (see Figure 14.2). The knowledge gap hypothesis states that the dissemination of information benefits both groups but that it will benefit the information-rich more, thereby widening the

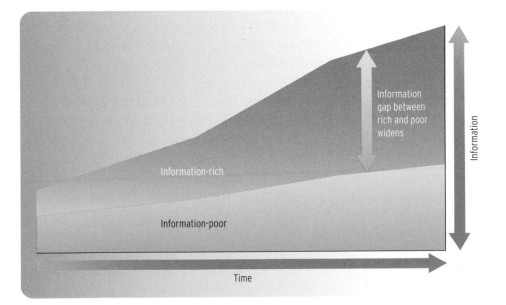

FIGURE 14.2 THE INFORMATION GAP According to the knowledge gap hypothesis, the introduction of new information technologies will help both the information-rich and the information-poor get richer, in terms of the information they posses, but the rich get richer faster, causing the knowledge gap to widen.

disparity between the two. Many studies have documented that information gaps are widened by the media (Hwang & Jeong, 2009), even by such well-intentioned efforts as *Sesame Street* that are specifically designed to close the gap. But, involvement may help to close the gap: those who are motivated to seek out information on a particular issue engage in more active information processing and learn more (Eveland, Shah, & Kwak, 2003).

The knowledge gap hypothesis suggests that efforts to close the digital divide (by placing computers in the schools, for example, or making e-mail available to all) will be at least partially self-defeating. That said, it will be difficult to close the knowledge gap short of changing the fundamental inequalities in society. One approach is community networking, which offers Internet access and content to disadvantaged groups through government agencies, schools, libraries churches, or residential communities (Straubhaar, Spence et al., 2012) the premise is that community-based resources tailored to local needs by community members themselves will close the gap. However, the substitution of Internet services for "real" public services may help justify cuts in public services while making the poor more reliant on a technology that they have difficulty accessing (Virnoche, 1998).

MEDIA AND COMMUNITY

What impact do media have on meaningful relationships? Television usage may lower community involvement (Brody, 1990), and virtual communities on the Internet may displace face-to-face relationships (Stepanikova, He & Nie, 2010). People tend to humanize media—talking back to their television sets and giving their computers affectionate nicknames (Reeves & Nass, 1996). Online relationships are perhaps a poor substitute for interpersonal relationships, lacking intimacy and the risks of real interactions (Turkle, 2011).

Early research suggested that the Internet caused depression among excessive users (Kraut et al., 1998). The researchers carried out a field experiment in which they introduced Internet access into homes and found that teenagers who were heavy Internet users exhibited more signs of depression than light users and also showed increased stress and loneliness. They called this finding the *Internet paradox*, meaning that a social technology such as the Internet—that is used mainly to communicate with others—could reduce social involvement and lead to loneliness and depression. However, later research on the same group found that the negative effects disappeared as users became better acquainted with the Internet, although community involvement still declined (Kraut et al., 2002). Among college students, Facebook use was positively related to measures of psychological well-being (Ellison, Steinfeld, & Lampe, 2007) and children use the Internet to perfect their social skills (Ito et al., 2009). However, not all the effects are positive, since uncontrolled use can also disrupt important real life activities (LaRose et al., 2010). Also, online forms of harassment including cyberstalking and cyberbullying that are perpetrated through social media (Kiriakidis & Kavoura, 2010) inflict psychological pain on millions of children, sometimes with tragic consequences.

How can these conflicting findings be resolved? Researchers must formulate new variables and new explanations that might resolve the apparent contradictions. One possibility is that online communication strengthens and complements real-world communication rather than replaces it. People with adequate preexisting levels of social support are likely to benefit from online interaction, whereas those lacking adequate social support may become more socially isolated as a result of indulging heavily in online social interaction (Bessiere et al., 2008). That means that excessive online interaction could be harmful for some and is not a cure for social isolation.

HEALTH AND ENVIRONMENT

Communications media affect physical health as well as mental health. We previously noted that television viewing is associated with obesity in children, for example. There is also preliminary evidence that television viewing by young children may cause attention disorders (Christakis et al., 2004). And the harmful effects are not limited to children. Adults who limit their television viewing to a couple of hours a day suffer less from depression and other psychological maladies compared to those with normal levels of viewing (Hammermeister et al., 2005).

Very low-frequency (VLF) radiation, the kind that electrical power lines emit, also poses a threat. At one point, EPA scientists concluded that VLF was as dangerous as chemical cancer-inducing agents, although this finding was overruled by EPA administrators. Computer video display terminals (VDTs) emit the same type of radiation, and some scientists suspect that this radiation causes cancer and miscarriages in heavy users. Overall the research is inconclusive on this point (Lim, Sauter, & Schnorr, 1998). Television sets emit the same magnetic fields, by the way, but not many people watch with the television in their laps. Cell phones have been implicated in brain cancer as well, and health authorities in many countries advise against their use by young children. But, again, the evidence is inconclusive although the question of damage from long-term exposure is still open (Ahlbom et al., 2009). When selecting your next cell phone you might wish to compare its radiation to others and in the meantime learn about ways to reduce your exposure (http://www.ewg.org/cellphoneradiation/Get-a-Safer-Phone). There is somewhat clearer evidence of another public health hazard stemming from mobile phone and mobile texting. Drivers who use mobile phones in their cars have the same degree of impairment as someone who is legally drunk. It has been estimated that texting while driving causes thousands of highway fatalities each year (Wilson & Stimpson, 2009). As a result, a growing number of areas are outlawing texting while driving.

Up to a quarter of all computer users suffer repetitive stress injuries, mostly a result of poor posture, bad workstation design, and repetitive tasks, but also a function of work demands and psychological stress (Lim, Sauter, & Schnorr, 1998). Others get stress injuries from surfing the Web, playing video games, or flipping the TV remote control. Extreme cases force sufferers to resort to medication, surgery, and career changes. Computer labs run by high schools and universities combine many of the factors known to increase the risk of injury: nonadjustable work surfaces, chairs with no armrests or footrests, displays perched too high, and instructors applying stressful grade pressure.

MEDIA AND THE ECONOMY

New media technologies in the workplace are impacting the economy. They are affecting both the quantity and quality of work.

The Quantity of Work. Information technology improves *productivity* by eliminating employees. For example, nonlinear editing systems are a common productivity-enhancing feature wherever video is edited. Clips are stored and edited from computer disks, eliminating the time-consuming drudgery of moving forward and backward to particular sequences on a long spool of tape. So, more shows are edited per day with fewer editors—that's productivity.

That also means that we do not need as many video editors as we once did. This phenomenon is euphemistically called *job displacement* by labor economists. The United States has seen almost complete elimination of a blue-collar middle class in a single generation, and nearly a third of U.S. workers are now "contingent employees" without long-term employment agreements. Beware of *offshoring*—the use of advanced communication networks to link Americans to customer service agents and loan officers located in developing countries. These people generally work for a fraction of the salaries paid for comparable jobs in the United States. Many media-related jobs including animation and documentary film production are starting to move offshore. A new trend is *in-sourcing* that brings jobs back from overseas, but that also has a downside. To offset the higher labor costs in North America the in-sourcers first redesign the production process so that it requires far fewer workers than when it was last based on our shores.

In the process, the old *corporate pyramid*, in which a few top executives command platoons of middle managers who in turn direct legions of rank-and-file workers, has toppled (see Figure 14.3). Information technologies have made it possible for top management to coordinate activities with far fewer middle managers, the *flattened pyramid*. Another model is the *core and ring*, in which middle management is eliminated and rank-and-file workers are all contingent employees who are added or subtracted as conditions warrant. Then there is the *virtual corporation* in which even top management is in constant flux, with networks of workers organized for particular tasks and disbanded when no longer needed. Hollywood production companies have long followed this model, but it is spreading to many sectors of the professional service economy populated by artists, writers, Web designers, and computer consultants.

However, if information technology reduces costs and increases product quality, then there should be demand for more products and thus higher employment (Kilborn, 1993). For example, if 3-D televisions following the *Avatar* model catch on, their costs will drop. Then Hollywood could fill hundreds of new channels with enticing 3-D entertainment, and we would watch TV more and see more ads, creating demand for yet more channels and generating new employment in the television industry. Historically, fears about higher unemployment resulting from automation have proved unfounded, whether the "new technology" was the textile machinery of the 1790s or computers of the 1990s.

But it isn't clear that all the investment in information technology actually improves productivity (Maes et al., 2011). Many high-tech investments

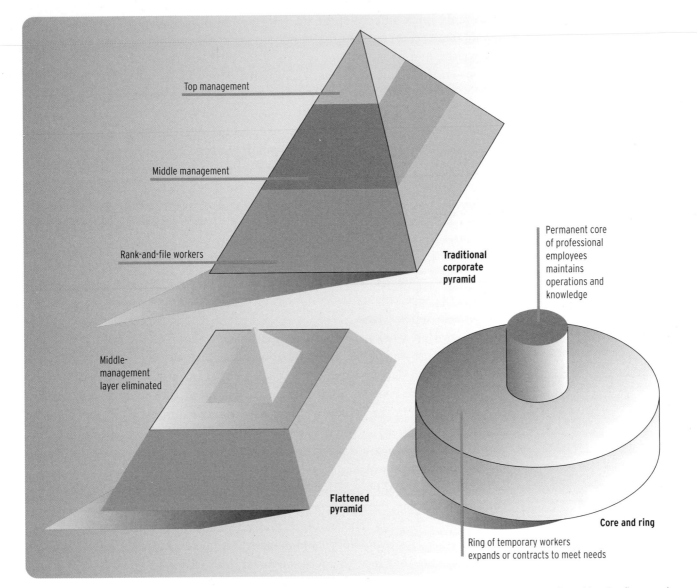

FIGURE 14.3 EVOLVING COPRORATE STRUCTURES The traditional corporate pyramid is being replaced by the flattened pyramid and the core-and-ring structure. In the process, layers of middle-management positions have been stripped away. New structures are more flexible but also dim prospects for job security.

never work quite right or incur hidden costs that sap their profitability. Economists call this the *productivity paradox*. Across the economy it looks as if the benefits of information technologies used in businesses have been found mainly in the high-tech industries themselves.

Work Gets Worse. What will work be like for those who still have it? Today's college students will have several different careers in their lives, not just several different jobs in the same career path with different employers, which was once the normal pattern. And lifelong employment with one employer is a relic of the past. All of this insecurity could place downward pressure on benefits and wages, except perhaps for the highly skilled elite.

Information technology could reduce skill requirements, a process known as *de-skilling*. For example, if we wanted to increase the productivity of sports reporters, we might specify a set of standard lead sentences: "Things looked extremely [pick adjective] for the [city name] nine that day. The score stood [home team score] to [visiting team score] with but an inning left to play." Fire the writer, and hire a college intern to fill in the blanks using reports transmitted on the Associated Press newswire. Then we would hold a stopwatch on the intern to see how many game summaries she could write in an hour and replace her if she fell below the standard for the job. And this example is by no means far-fetched. Statsheet uses an artificial intelligence program to write sports stories for the Web and smartphones. This process is also known as *Taylorism*, after Frederick Winslow Taylor, the early twentieth- century efficiency expert.

Fordism, named after Henry Ford, introduced the assembly-line system, in which each employee performs a single, narrowly defined task over and over again. Taylorized and Fordized workers do not know how to "make" anything (such as a good sports story). Their knowledge is limited to one small task, so that upward mobility is impossible. Only the owners and their white-collar managers (here, the sports editor) know how to organize those tasks to produce goods and services.

De-skilled workers can be paid less and replaced at will, a practice known as *post-Fordism*. Henry Ford was the first to pay rank-and-file factory workers a decent wage so that they could purchase the products that they assembled. Post-Fordism cuts pay to the point that workers can no longer participate in the consumer economy. In our example, the college intern might be paid so little (or perhaps be paid nothing—it's a media internship, after all!) that she could not afford an Internet connection to read her own sports stories on the Web.

Another dismal possibility is that skill requirements will be upgraded to the point that the current workforce does not possess them. This process is known as *up-skilling*. For example, many TV and film production specialists trained on analog technology cannot easily become a part of digital production teams because they lack the necessary computer skills.

Work Gets Better. But there are rays of hope, too, such as work decentralization. Computer networks make it possible to integrate the work of distant suppliers and far-flung backroom (or back lot) operations, moving them farther into the suburbs and rural areas. More employees can work where they want to live and avoid the stress of commuting and relocating at intervals. For example, the global nature of today's TV and film production industry, combined with traffic congestion, air pollution, and sky-high real estate costs in the Los Angeles basin, has prompted substitution of computer networks for travel in the industry. Overall, telecommuting is beneficial for workers and their families (Gajendran & Harrison, 2007). However, *telecommuting* has been slow to catch on amid concerns about effective supervision (Wells, 2001). But perhaps climbing gasoline costs and environmental concerns about the "carbon footprints" of commuters will finally stimulate telecommuting.

STOP&REVIEW

1. What is the difference between individual effects and social effects?
2. What does the knowledge gap hypothesis predict about the effects of new information technologies?
3. What impact do social media have on personal relationships?
4. What are the health effects of communications media?
5. How do Taylorism, Fordism, and post-Fordism differ?
6. Give examples of jobs that have been de-skilled, jobs that have been up-skilled, and jobs that have been re-skilled.

Another potential boon is *re-skilling*: reassigning to current employees tasks that were formerly parceled out to specialized workers. The employee reclaims the role of the preindustrial craftsperson (Zuboff, 1984) as knowledge becomes the cornerstone for business and social relations (Bell, 1973). For example, desktop publishing puts print publication back within the scope of a single person sitting at a personal computer. It hasn't been that way since the days of the medieval manuscript copyists. These changes rock the very foundations of industrial mass media by restoring control to the workers themselves. It is ironic that information technologies, the crowning achievement of industrial capitalism, may yet fulfill Karl Marx's prophecy. It was he, after all, who pointed out that capitalism creates the contradictions that inevitably lead to its own destruction!

SUMMARY&REVIEW

WHY DOESN'T SOMEONE "CLEAN UP" THE MEDIA?

Government control conflicts with the rights of the media to free speech. Media spokespersons question the validity of research that suggests the media's negative effects, and they argue that society's ills have deeper causes than mass-media exposure. The media sometimes adopt their own guidelines. However, these are voluntary standards that are usually eroded by commercial pressures.

WHAT ARE THE MAIN APPROACHES TO MEDIA EFFECTS?

Media effects are changes in knowledge, attitude, or behavior that result from exposure to the mass media. In the deductive approach, predictions about media effects are derived from theory, and exposure to media content is treated as the causal, or independent, variable that leads to the effects, or the dependent variable. The inductive approach infers the impacts of the media, and theories that explain them are inferred from detailed observations in real-world environments.

WHAT ARE BASIC METHODS OF MEDIA EFFECTS RESEARCH?

Content analysis is used to characterize the content of media systems by enumerating the types of behaviors, themes, and actors that appear in the media, though such analysis cannot be used to make inferences about the actual effects of the media. Experimental research examines the relationship between exposure to media content and audience effects under tightly controlled laboratory conditions that make it possible to rule out competing explanations for the effects that are observed. Survey studies administer questionnaires to large representative samples of subjects to examine relationships between media exposure and media effects; they take into account a wider range of factors than experimental studies. In ethnographic studies, researchers maintain extended contact with subjects so that they can gain insight into social processes involving media systems. Their results, however, may not be generalizable beyond the specific communities they study. Big Data research analyzes large databases to identify patterns of human behavior related to media use.

WHY DO PEOPLE USE THE MEDIA?

People attend to media that best meet their needs and expectations. Through their interactions with the media and their observations of others, people learn expectations about the consequences of media use that shape their media behavior. Positive outcomes include learning new things, diversion, and social interaction. People may also wish to avoid media that they find boring or offensive or that they cannot enjoy because they lack the required skills. Media habits form when media are consumed without conscious intent.

In organizational settings, the social presence of a medium is an important factor in deciding which tasks it is best suited for.

HOW HAVE THEORIES OF MEDIA EFFECTS CHANGED?

Theories of mass-media effects have evolved over the years. Early scholars believed the mass media could have immediate and profound effects on their audiences, after the fashion of a speeding bullet or a hypodermic injection. Later, researchers learned that the influence of the mass media is weakened by the intervention of social groups, via a multistep flow process, and by the audience's ability to selectively avoid, misinterpret, or forget content with which they disagree. Social learning theory describes how people can learn behavior from visual media, and cultivation theory shows how people's understanding of the world around them is shaped by media images. Priming theory focuses on the power of media images to activate related thoughts in our own minds. Critical theorists ask broader questions about the mutual relationship between media and society.

WHAT IS THE IMPACT OF MEDIA ON ANTISOCIAL BEHAVIOR?

Experimental studies have shown that even relatively short exposure to TV programs and video games featuring violence can provoke violent behavior in viewers, particularly young children. However, the long-term effects are still a matter of debate. Men exposed to violent pornography harbor more negative feelings toward women. Media also can reinforce sex-role and racial stereotypes that lead to sexism and racism.

WHAT IS THE IMPACT OF MEDIA ON PROSOCIAL BEHAVIOR?

Prosocial behaviors are socially desirable acts, such as cooperation, sharing, and racial tolerance. Information campaigns seek to convince mass audiences to adopt socially desirable behaviors. Although such campaigns are sometimes effective, they often suffer from poor planning and execution and from limited audience exposure. Furthermore, they must contend with resistance arising from social influence and selective perception among their audiences. Other varieties of prosocial media combine varying degrees of entertainment and educational content, ranging from distance-learning classes to incidental learning from entertainment programs.

WHAT ARE THE IMPACTS OF ADVERTISING AND POLITICAL CAMPAIGNS?

Despite the huge sums of money spent on commercial and political advertisements, their effects are relatively modest; they directly affect perhaps only a few percent of the audience. Those who are affected by advertisements are likely to be those who are relatively uninformed about or uninterested in the product or candidate to begin with. Interpersonal influence and selective perception act to reduce the impact of advertisements on most audiences. Still, that small percent that is influenced can translate into millions of dollars in a successful advertising campaign or into crucial deciding votes in a political race. Social media afford new avenues for impacting attitudes toward consumer products and political candidates.

HOW DO MEDIA AFFECT SOCIAL EQUALITY?

Information technologies do not benefit all groups in society equally. Minorities may be left behind in the transition to the information economy as the digital divide widens. The knowledge gap hypothesis predicts that efforts to improve the plight of the disadvantaged through improved access to communications media will instead result in widening the gap between rich and poor.

HOW DO MEDIA AFFECT SOCIAL RELATIONS?

The advent of the Internet has the potential for bringing about a situation in which everyone is our neighbor in a small, electronically mediated global village. The virtual communities that have formed on the Internet are an initial indication that new types of human relationships may be created and many can and do benefit from participating in social media. However, not all benefit equally. Some users may become more socially isolated by participating in online communities and withdrawing from real-world interactions while social media primarily benefit those with strong offline social relationships.

DO INFORMATION TECHNOLOGIES CAUSE UNEMPLOYMENT?

Improvements in productivity brought about by applications of information technology have the potential to displace large numbers of jobs. Historically, new waves of industrial technology have increased employment in the long term, and the same is likely to hold true today. In the short term, however, entire categories of workers will be eliminated or see their jobs moved offshore, and workers with useless skills may be forced to seek unstable contingent employment.

DO COMMUNICATIONS MEDIA MAKE WORK LESS SATISFYING?

In some applications, information technologies increase the twin tendencies of Taylorism and Fordism, de-skilling work to meaningless, repetitive, assembly-line tasks. In the extreme, jobs become so degraded that workers no longer command a decent living wage, a condition called *post-Fordism*. In other instances, information technology up-skills jobs, displacing workers whose skills no longer match job requirements. However, information technologies can also be applied in ways that re-skill jobs, restoring work to a meaningful and dignified pursuit.

THINKING CRITICALLY
ABOUT THE MEDIA

1. What were the uses and gratifications of each of the media you consumed yesterday?

2. What would you say is the most important effect the media have had on your life?

3. Using the media effects theory of your choice, explain the likely effects of your favorite video game or TV program.

4. Does political advertising have a positive or negative effect on elections? Why is that?

5. What career path do you expect to have in the information society?

KEY TERMS

bullet model (p. 418)

content analysis (p. 406)

correlated (p. 410)

cultivation theory (p. 420)

cultural studies (p. 414)

dependent variable (p. 405)

ethnography (p. 412)

experimental research (p. 407)

generalizability (p. 409)

independent variable (p. 405)

information campaigns (p. 429)

learning theory (p. 415)

limited effects (p. 419)

media effects (p. 404)

multistep flow (p. 419)

persuasion (p. 418)

priming theory (p. 421)

prosocial behaviors (p. 428)

reliability (p. 409)

social learning theory (p. 415)

stereotyping (p. 424)

survey studies (p. 411)

uses and gratifications (p. 414)

validity (p. 409)

IN GOD WE TRUST

CONGRESS PASSES LAWS THAT SHAPE THE MEDIA in many ways. What do media issues mean for us as individual citizens and as a society?

MEDIA POLICY AND LAW

15

GUIDING THE MEDIA

The media play such a critical role in U.S. society that their right to contribute to public debate is guaranteed by the First Amendment of the U.S. Constitution. However, in a country where the media are in private hands, there is also potential for abuse of power by media owners. So, perhaps more than any other industry, the media are guided within a fabric of policies, laws, technical standards, and self-regulation. Communications **policy** reflects government and public consideration of how to structure and regulate the media so that they contribute to the public good. Industry trade groups and public interest groups monitor media performance and lobby the government to change communications policy. In the U.S. system of government, **laws** are binding rules passed by legislatures (e.g., the U.S. Congress), administered and enforced by executive power (e.g., Federal Communications Commission), and adjudicated by courts (e.g., the U.S. Supreme Court). Policies are often turned into laws in order to make them legally binding. The Communications Act of 1934 and Telecommunications Act of 1996 are the basic laws of the land for all

1789	First Amendment to Constitution enshrines freedom of press; Fourth Amendment protects privacy against unwarranted searches and seizures by government	**1996**	Telecommunications Act deregulates industries to let them compete; Communications Decency Act declared unconstitutional by Supreme Court
1791	Copyright Act	**1998**	Copyright Term Extension Act; Digital Millennium Copyright Act, Children's Online Privacy Protection Act
1890	Sherman Antitrust Act limits monopolies' restraint of trade		
1934	Communications Act covers broadcasting and telecommunications	**2011**	The FCC extends universal service to Internet connections

Policy is a public framework for structuring and regulating media so they contribute to the public good.

Laws are binding rules passed by legislatures, enforced by the executive power, and applied or adjudicated by courts.

Standards are agreements about technical characteristics of communication systems.

Self-regulation pertains to communication industry codes and practices of monitoring and controlling the media's performance.

The **First Amendment** to the U.S. Constitution guarantees freedom of speech and of the press.

Freedom of speech is the idea that speech and media content should be free from government restriction.

communications media. **Standards** are technical characteristics, such as the number of lines on the television screen that must be agreed on for a technology to be widely manufactured and used. **Self-regulation** refers to the industry's own codes of conduct by which they monitor their own performance.

Some issues cut across all these media control mechanisms, for example, sex in the media. The Federal Communication Commission (FCC) has rules—a policy—against using indecent language on radio and television. Congress established fines for violating those standards by passing a law. In addition, the 1996 Telecommunications Act required a V-chip system to help people screen out objectionable content, a technical standard. And then there's the television rating system, which is a system of self-regulation.

COMMUNICATIONS POLICIES

Policies governing free speech, privacy, intellectual property, competition, diversity, access, technical standards, and spectrum allocation form the basic framework guiding communications media in the United States.

FREEDOM OF SPEECH

The most fundamental U.S. policy regarding the content and conduct of media is the **First Amendment** to the U.S. Constitution. It establishes **freedom of speech**, both in person and over media, as a basic requirement for a free society. In Chapter 4 we recounted how this principle developed during the American colonial period and the Revolutionary War that followed. The First Amendment seeks to preserve a **marketplace of ideas** in which different voices could compete for attention.

The First Amendment says:

> Congress shall make no law respecting an establishment of religion, or prohibiting the free exercise thereof; or abridging the freedom of speech, or of the press; or the right of the people peaceably to assemble, and to petition the Government for a redress of grievances.

Some kinds of speech are not protected by the First Amendment: defamation, obscenity, plagiarism, invasion of privacy, and inciting insurrection.

Defamation. Defamatory statements (**libel**, if it is written, or slander, if it is spoken, see Chapter 4) are untrue declarations about private citizens that might damage their reputations. Libel is information that is false or is intended to damage the reputation of the person being libeled. U.S. legal policy balances libel concerns against the watchdog role of the press, which is to expose corruption or incompetence by officials or public figures. Journalists often have to decide whether a certain kind of story about in-

STICKS AND STONES Many governments fear criticism from the press, so they control or censor it. A cartoon such as this, criticizing government policies, would not be allowed to run in many countries. The First Amendment protects all forms of political speech short of inciting political rallies to riot.

dividuals or certain treatment of individuals is ethical (see Chapter 16). Celebrities, politicians, and other public figures do not have the same protections as private citizens. To constitute libel against a public figure, false statements of fact have to be made knowingly and with malice.

Even if you do not work for a media organization, you have to be concerned about defamation, especially when you are online. If you post a scathing review of a product or criticize a company for its plundering of the environment you might find that you are the target of a libel suit. Corporations are resorting to libel laws to curb "bad buzz" about their products and company reputations online. Truth is the ultimate defense in defamation suits.

Political Speech. Some nations give people who have been criticized a right of reply. That principle has seldom been applied to U.S. print media, because they are numerous and tend to balance each other's excesses. However, the Radio Act of 1927 assumed that the First Amendment goal of promoting a diversity of viewpoints needed regulatory assistance in the case of radio, where only a few could have direct access to the airwaves. This principle is still applied to political debates, where all major candidates must be allowed to participate.

A far thornier issue has been paid political advertising, where richer candidates' financial resources give them greater access to the airwaves. There, two principles have evolved. First, stations cannot refuse a candidate's advertising, although stations can refuse to run ads by advocacy groups. Second, stations have to sell advertising time at their lowest rate to candidates. Congress has attempted several times to limit campaign financing abuses. Congress most recently tried to clamp down on "bundling" of small donations by Washington lobbyists, but loopholes have always emerged. In 2010 the Supreme Court lifted restrictions on political advertising, resulting in a spending binge on political TV ads during the 2012 presidential campaigns by corporations and labor unions.

Marketplace of ideas is the concept that the truth and the best ideas will win out in competition.

Libel is harmful and untruthful written criticism by the media that intends to damage someone.

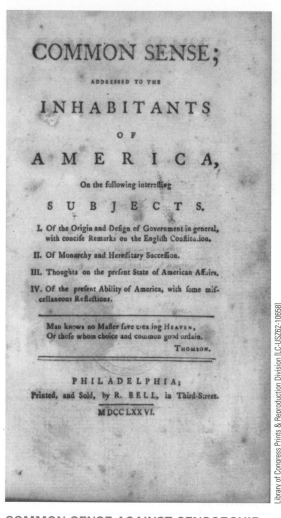

Library of Congress Prints & Reproduction Division [LC-US262-10658]

COMMON SENSE AGAINST CENSORSHIP
Publications such as Thomas Paine's *Common Sense* challenged British censorship and promoted the American Revolution. U.S. citizens have the right to question their form of government just as Paine questioned the legitimacy of the British monarchy to rule its American colonies.

Censorship is the formal restriction of media or speech content by government, political, or religious authorities.

Obscenity refers to material where the dominant theme taken as a whole appeals to prurient, or sexually arousing, interest.

The FCC also developed the Fairness Doctrine on the premise that the public's right to be informed overrides the right of broadcasters to carry their "own particular views on any matter" (Supreme Court decision in *Red Lion Broadcasting Co. v. FCC,* 395 U.S. 367, 1969). In theory, this concept required stations to schedule time for controversial programming on issues and then to ensure the expression of opposing views. In practice, the FCC did not require stations to carry issue-oriented programming, so the rule focused on the right of reply to controversial points of view. Broadcasters argued that the right of reply had a "chilling effect" on free speech that led stations to avoid controversial programming and that view finally prevailed as the Supreme Court struck down the right of reply.

Even with the "chilling effect" of the Fairness Doctrine removed, the mainstream media avoided giving platforms to political extremists for fear of offending their audiences. However, more politically charged speech emerged first on talk radio and then on some cable news channels like Fox News and MSNBC.

Political speech is highly protected even at the extremes, although it has limits that anyone who posts their opinions online should be aware of. It is permissible to criticize prominent politicians and their policies ("the president's policies are stupid") and attack their character and intelligence as long as the insult is a matter of opinion rather than of fact ("the candidate is a coward"). However, the same is not true of the clerk at the local Department of Motor Vehicles or your professors who, though they may be government employees, enjoy the same protections you do as a private citizen. You can criticize government policies ("Stop the war!") and also the system of government ("Smash capitalism!"), and call for its overthrow, even by violent means ("Up the Islamic revolution!"). But you may not directly incite people to violence with your words ("Go throw rocks at those police cars over there.").

Obscenity and Indecency. The First Amendment was originally framed to protect political speech and religious choice but has gradually been extended to speech that is regarded by some as morally wrong. For example, D. H. Lawrence's *Lady Chatterley's Lover* (1928) was **censored** in the United States for nearly 30 years, but is far less "steamy" than the romance novels that can be found on the shelves of local supermarkets today. In 1957, in *Roth v. United States*, the U.S. Supreme Court defined **obscenity** in community-based terms: ". . . whether, to the average person, applying contemporary community standards, the dominant theme of the material taken as a whole appeals to prurient interest [i.e., makes the average person sexually aroused]." In *Miller v. California* (1973), the Court added that states might prohibit works "which portray sexual conduct in a patently offensive way, and which, taken as a whole, do not have serious literary, artistic, political, or scientific value." That allows some communities to define books, magazines, and videos as pornographic and restrict their sales to adult bookstores or require their covers to be concealed when on public display.

MEDIA&CULTURE

GEORGE CARLIN AND THE "SEVEN DIRTY WORDS"

The *FCC v. Pacifica Foundation* case defined a number of key issues relevant to obscenity and indecency. The case centered on whether the Pacifica radio station could play a provocative 12-minute monologue about the "seven dirty words you can't say on radio," by the late comedian George Carlin that included multiple instances of each of the seven words.

The FCC argued that, judged by contemporary community standards, these words are offensive; that broadcasting is an intrusive medium; and that obscenity is separate from indecency. The FCC said that the rules are intended to protect children from "exposure to language that describes, in terms patently offensive as measured by contemporary community standards for the broadcast medium, sexual or excretory activities and organs, at times of the day when there is a reasonable risk that children may be in the audience ... language which most parents regard as inappropriate for them to hear." The FCC made a later clarification that media can use such words when children are in the audience when the words have legitimate artistic, political, or social value (for example, a Shakespearean play).

The Supreme Court decided (in *FCC v. Pacifica Foundation*, 98 Supreme Court 326, 1978) that the FCC may sanction licensees who use indecent words because broadcasting is the least protected by the First Amendment and it enters the privacy of people's homes where children have easy access. The FCC can review programming after broadcast and can use that review when considering licensing. It noted that Section 1464 of the U.S. Code lists "obscene, indecent, or profane" but that indecency is different from obscenity. It argued that a nuisance "may be merely a right thing in the wrong place. . . ." Although the FCC has not always taken advantage of this power, things changed in 2004 after singer Janet Jackson's breast was bared during the Super Bowl halftime show. The FCC began to receive more complaints about indecency and reacted to public complaints with more frequent and larger fines, to which the industry responded with more frequent and protracted legal appeals.

If you are not offended by "dirty words" (or are curious about what those are) or by fleeting nudity you can find both Carlin's and Jackson's greatest hits on YouTube. Interestingly, adult verification is needed for the former but not the latter.

Child pornography has no protection because of the harm done to the children who are its victims. In the United States (18 U.S.C. §2256) child pornography is defined as the visual depiction of persons under 18 engaging in actual or simulated explicit sexual acts or who display genitals or breasts. Producers of the *Skins* television series appearing on MTV in 2011 arguably violated this law by casting actual teens, as do advertisers who feature underage models in their fashion layouts. Teens who engage in "sexting" by sending naked pictures of themselves to their friends are also technically child pornographers although many states are crafting new laws to avoid treating them as sex offenders.

The 1934 Communications Act extended freedom of speech to broadcast media, but their use of the public airwaves makes them accessible to children and subjects them to limits on indecent speech as well as obscenity. The current standard for **indecent speech** was set when the FCC disciplined a radio station for broadcasting a comedy monologue that poked fun at the rules against saying "swear words" on the air (see Media&Culture: George Carlin and the "Seven Dirty Words"). The FCC defined indecency as "language that

> **Indecent speech** is graphic language that pertains to sexual or excretory functions.

describes, in terms patently offensive as measured by contemporary community standards. . .sexual or excretory activities or organs," and its action was upheld by the Supreme Court (Heins, 1993, p. 26). However, the prohibition only applies to radio and television broadcasts during hours when children are likely to be listening or watching. There is a "safe haven" for unfettered free speech from midnight to 6 A.M. Cable television and satellite radio are not covered because they require an extra fee and thus do not enter the home "unbidden" where they might be seen or heard by children.

Indecency rules continue to evolve. After Janet Jackson's "accidental" breast baring during the 2004 Super Bowl, Congress increased the fines tenfold (to $325,000) for each station that the offending party owned (CBS Television's 10 owned and operated stations). However, an incident the year before in which Bono used the "f-word" to describe his feelings about winning a music award undermined the crackdown. A federal judge ruled that Bono's offense was a fleeting one and that since the FCC had previously not punished brief instances of indecency they had no right to do so in the Bono case without providing notice of a change in their policy. The FCC changed the rule to cover fleeting obscenity but the Supreme Court ruled they could not do that after the fact and had to start over again. Meanwhile, the limits for broadcasters are unclear and a million indecency complaints are backlogged at the FCC.

Industry self-regulation also plays a role. The parental advisories that precede broadcast network television programs (see next section) are an example, as are the film ratings supplied by the Motion Picture Association of America (MPAA), and the video game ratings provided by the Entertainment Software Rating Board (ESRB), an industry trade group. In the United States, all such limits are a matter of self-regulation in a sense. The First Amendment prohibits government censorship before the fact. The FCC and federal prosecutors can respond to consumer complaints only after the fact.

The Internet poses unique challenges. Congress tried to hold the Internet to the same indecency standards as broadcasting, but the Supreme Court ruled that this infringed unfairly on the rights of adults. The 1998 Child Online Protection Act narrowed the prohibitions to cover commercial sites only, target only content harmful to children, and require age verification on adult sites in hopes of passing muster with the First Amendment, but the Supreme Court declined to uphold the law in a 2009 decision.

Christopher Polk/Getty Images

INDECENT? Did M.I.A. commit an indecent act when she flashed her middle finger during the 2012 Superbowl half time show? Now that the Supreme Court is making the FCC reconsider its indecency rules, should this gesture qualify?

For now, the only form of protection in effect is the Children's Internet Protection Act, which requires schools and libraries that receive government subsidies for their Internet connections to use filtering software.

Some social media have imposed their own self-regulation in an effort to make their networks friendly to all. YouTube screens submissions and removes pornography, although that happens after the material has been uploaded; thus obscene videos may live a fleeting life before they are removed. Facebook bans nudity, including pictures of breastfeeding, a prohibition that some mothers find excessive.

Obscenity laws also apply to us as individuals. Though seldom enforced, it is unlawful to use the "f-word" in phone conversations and some states have passed laws against using obscenity in texting. Possession of pornography is not a crime. Possession of child pornography is a crime, and its distribution is not protected by the First Amendment. Talking about sex ("sexting") on the Internet is also protected, but not if one of the parties is a minor. A growing number of states have laws against that and federal laws are pending.

Violence. Concerns about the effects of media on children (see Chapter 14) also underlie efforts to curb violence in the media. A provision in the 1996 Telecommunications Act required the V-chip that permits parents to block out television programs rated as containing sex or violence. Industry leaders reluctantly created a rating system in 1997, modeled on the age-based rating of films (see Chapter 7). Critics had hoped for a system that would have a separate rating for levels of sex, violence, and indecent language in each program but the industry chose not to comply with that request. And, surveys of viewers with V-chip sets have shown that very few were using this option. Now the attention of lawmakers has turned to the marketing of violent content to children. At issue are releases of "director's cut" versions of films to home video that contain depictions of sex and violence that were cut to earn child-friendly ratings in theaters. There was also a case involving a California law banning the sale of excessively violent video games to children that the Supreme Court struck down in a 2011 ruling.

Commercial Speech. Commercial speech advertises a product or service for profit or for a business purpose. It is entitled to much less protection than noncommercial speech, since it is not seen as part of the political marketplace of ideas. Misleading commercial speech or commercial speech that proposes unlawful actions has no protection. Businesses have free speech rights as long as their products are legal (see Chapter 11). That is why we still see cigarette and liquor ads even though those products harm their consumers when used in excess. The FTC intervenes if (1) the message is likely to mislead the consumer; (2) the consumer is found to be acting reasonably under the circumstances; and (3) the omission, falsehood, or representation is "material" or likely to affect actual purchase decisions. The FTC can issue a cease and desist order, prohibiting further communication of the deception, and mandate corrective advertising, requiring public clarification and admission of the falsehood.

PROTECTING PRIVACY

Although most Americans assume that they have a right to **privacy**, this right is not clearly established. Some argue that the first 10 amendments to the U.S. Constitution focus on protecting people from invasions of their privacy by

Privacy is the right to avoid unwanted intrusions or disclosure.

government. This broad view of privacy remains controversial. Private companies now pose privacy threats as well as the government.

Preventing Government Snooping. The clearest privacy protection against government snooping is found in the Fourth Amendment to the Constitution, which guarantees ". . . the right of the people to be secure in their persons, houses, papers, and effects, against unreasonable searches and seizures." It also states that "no (search) warrants shall issue but upon probable cause. . . particularly describing the place to be searched, and the persons or things to be seized."

Government intrusions on privacy had been carefully limited, but new federal initiatives against terrorism since the attacks of September 11, 2001, have raised many new issues. The contents of mail and telephone conversations are legally protected. Government criminal investigators can intercept conversations via wiretap, but only with a court warrant, as specified in the Fourth Amendment. The Electronic Communications Privacy Act of 1986 extended wiretap protections to electronic mail, teleconferences, and other new media. Although e-mail from home computers and personal accounts is protected, e-mail from office or school computers or accounts may be monitored by employers or school officials. Reformers would like to see the privacy act revised to draw clearer distinctions about the privacy rights of e-mail users and about the use of location-based information from cell phones.

The USA PATRIOT Act of 2001 loosened the rules in cases where the FBI or other officials convince special courts that U.S. national security is threatened. The standard of **probable cause** was reduced, so that approval of intercepts was almost automatic in national security cases. However, several court decisions have restored somewhat stricter requirements for probable cause. In 2002, Congress passed the Homeland Security Bill that permits federal officials to track and locate Internet users who pose an imminent threat to national security interests or who may perpetrate attacks on protected computers belonging to government or key private interstate commerce or communications companies. It also encourages cooperation from Internet and computer companies by protecting them from being sued for releasing personal information to the government. Congress fully legalized the monitoring in 2008. More recently, security agencies have begun monitoring social media on a massive scale to detect potential terror threats.

Preventing Commercial Snooping. The right to privacy encompasses a generalized "right to be let alone" that includes "the individual interest in avoiding disclosure of personal matters," the basis for a right to informational privacy (Chlapowski, 1991). The current threats to privacy come from government, as anticipated in the U.S. Bill of Rights, and from private companies that gather and sell information about individuals. The private sector intrusion grew with credit bureaus that gather credit information about individuals to sell to banks, loan agencies, and mortgage companies. Companies track sales data about individuals to determine their buying habits and preferences, and match that with information compiled from public records, such as drivers' licenses and property deeds. Firms that specialize in direct-mail sales also profit from selling mailing lists of potential customers (see Chapter 11).

The accuracy and control of computer databases is becoming a critical issue. When you apply for a credit card or loan, you may be refused

Probable cause is a judge's decision that provisional evidence of criminal violation or national security danger justifies a wiretap.

MEDIA&CULTURE

CONSUMER PRIVACY TIPS AND RIGHTS

- Periodically review your consumer credit files.

- If you dispute the information in your file, append your own explanation.

- If you want to have your name removed from telemarketing lists, contact the Do Not Call Registry of the FTC.

- Avoid giving out your Social Security number except to your employer or government agencies.

- Do not write your telephone number on credit applications, on subscription forms, or even on the checks you cash.

- Assume that everything you say on a cordless or cellular phone can be overheard.

- Assume that all of your computers or e-mail accounts from school or work are monitored by those institutions.

- Ask your phone company about caller ID service.

CONSUMER PRIVACY RIGHTS

A right to privacy has been articulated in a series of decisions by the federal courts and has been extended to information privacy by several pieces of legislation over the last decades. All consumers should be aware of their rights under these laws:

- **The right to inspect.** Under the Fair Credit Reporting Act of 1970, consumers have the right to inspect the information contained in a credit agency's file. The Fair and Accurate Credit Transactions (FACT) act of 2003 established a right to obtain free credit reports once a year and required financial institutions to institute protections against identity theft.

- **The right to challenge.** Consumers have the right to challenge the accuracy of the information and to append their own explanations.

- **The right to updates.** Credit agencies must purge items that are more than seven years old, including records of old arrests and lawsuits.

- **The right of control.** Inquiries for purposes other than hiring, insurance investigations, or credit checks can be made only with the permission of the subject or under a court order. The Privacy Act of

1974 constrains federal agencies—though not state and local governments or private companies—from transferring information without consent and from using information for purposes other than that for which it was originally collected. The Family Education Rights and Privacy Act (FERPA) gives students and their parents control over the release of academic information.

- **The right to refuse.** The Privacy Act of 1974 stipulates that citizens can refuse to disclose their Social Security number except where required by law. This limits the use of Social Security numbers to match data between sources.

- **The right to notification.** The Right to Financial Privacy Act of 1979 requires that federal law enforcement agencies notify individuals when their financial records are subpoenaed. The Privacy Act of 1974 prohibits secret files and requires government agencies to publish descriptions of the files they keep and the types of information they contain each year.

- **Freedom from Intrusion. The Federal Do Not Call Registry,** instituted by the Federal Trade Commission in 2003, gives you the right to register your telephone number to avoid marketing calls at home from commercial sales groups or marketers with whom you are not already doing business. The Controlling the Assault of Non-Solicited Pornography and Marketing (CAN-SPAM) Act requires commercial spammers (while exempting religious and political institutions and companies with whom we have a prior relationship) to identify themselves accurately and to offer the ability to opt out of future mailings. Also, sexually explicit content must be clearly labeled as such.

- **The right to electronic privacy.** A 1967 Supreme Court decision held telephone wiretaps to be unconstitutional, although Congress later legalized wiretaps conducted under court order. The Electronic Communication Privacy Act of 1986 extended this protection to electronic mail messages. The Health Insurance Portability Accountability Act (HIPAA) governs the release of medical records and gives patients the right to inspect and correct them. The Children's Online Privacy Protection Act (COPPA) prohibits websites from collecting personal information from children under 13 without parental permission.

because someone with a similar name or Social Security number has not made payments. Control over the use, release, and sale of information (see Media&Culture: Consumer Privacy Tips and Rights) was addressed by the Data Quality Act, which permits more scrutiny of government data for accuracy. The Health Insurance Portability and Accountability Act (HIPAA) set a national standard for electronic transfers of health data, but privacy advocates contend that it prioritizes medical needs over privacy concerns. However, political campaigns benefit enormously from the ability to target interest groups that such databases give them, so politicians are reluctant to regulate them. Still, public pressure for relief from intrusive telemarketing led to the Federal Trade Commission's Do Not Call Registry, which permits people to register telephone numbers that telemarketers cannot call.

Consumer privacy protections continue to evolve. In 2009, the FTC passed new guidelines for companies who use information about online behavior to target ads, a practice called behavioral targeting. Companies who collect information about consumers' Web surfing behavior are now encouraged to disclose the information they collect and to offer website visitors a chance to opt out. However, these are only guidelines intended to guide industry self-regulation and do not have the force of law.

In 2010 the FTC went even further in proposing a new "do not track" policy that would allow consumers to know when their online behavior was being tracked, to access and correct the information websites kept on them, and to be presented with a request to opt in at the point the data was collected. The FTC concluded that website privacy policy statements did not offer adequate protection because too few consumers read or understood them. The Internet industry contends that this will cripple their ability to offer targeted advertising and ruin a multi-billion dollar industry. Finally, in 2012 browser software developers promised to offer "do not track" buttons on a voluntary basis for the convenience of consumers.

Some privacy advocates now see Facebook as the worst privacy offender. Many social media fans seem blithely content to make this statement: "We have no privacy, get over it." However, a key principle of privacy law is one's expectation of privacy. So, in not expecting to have any privacy, social media fans are helping to assure that they will have no privacy rights, nor will anyone else. The issue is particularly acute for children. The Children's Online Privacy Protection Act (COPPA) prohibits websites from collecting private information from children under 13. On one hand, Facebook would like to see an end to the policy, arguing that millions of young children are already using the site. On the other hand, privacy advocates would like to see the protections applied to children through age 17 and bans on online tracking of children and the use of facial recognition and location information that might aid marketers, but also child molesters.

Disclosure of personal identities associated with online personae is another controversial privacy issue. Internet users who use the Web to gripe about products or people may become the targets of lawsuits when their information service providers expose their identities. Widely available Internet search tools can be used to track down everything you write in blogs or post on social networking sites, and it can archive your rash statements for years. Many a recent college graduate has learned to their dismay that employers now routinely look up the Facebook profiles of job applicants and demand that applicants show them content that is restricted to online friends. ISPs (including colleges and universities) are also required to provide information about Internet pirates under The Digital Millennium Copyright Act (DMCA) of 1998.

PROTECTING INTELLECTUAL PROPERTY

Intellectual property laws protect the original ideas of individuals and institutions through patents, copyrights, and trademarks. The goal of the laws is twofold: to encourage new ideas by allowing inventors and artists to profit from their innovations, while not unduly depriving society of the benefits of those ideas and making it possible to synthesize fresh ideas from old ones. The key to achieving that balance is to give creators exclusive rights to their works for a period of time, after which they enter the public domain where they may be used freely by all.

Encouraging Creativity. **Patents** give inventors the exclusive rights to their inventions for 20 years, during which time they can demand royalties from others who use them. For example, in 2012, Motorola (an acquisition target of Google) won a patent case against Apple that could force the latter to make royalty payments on iPhones and iPads.

The question of whether patents are restricted to tangible things, like Bell's telephone patent (see Chapter 12), is a controversial issue. Computer software was once considered unpatentable on the grounds that computers merely executed mathematical formulas that were the product of mental processes, rather than patentable devices. But that changed dramatically in the 1990s when patents were extended to business processes. For example, Amazon was awarded a patent on the "one-click" shopping method that lets return visitors to the site place orders without re-entering their credit card information. In 2010 the Supreme Court ruled that business processes that were merely abstract ideas (e.g. an idea for a new form of online dating) were not patentable but left the door open for business method patents in the future.

STOP&REVIEW

1. What is the distinction between policy and law?
2. What is the First Amendment and what does it specify?
3. What is libel?
4. What is indecent? Why is the standard different for the Internet?
5. What is the right to privacy?
6. What kinds of organizations present threats to our privacy?

> **Intellectual property** is a creative work of art, writing, film, or software that belongs to a legally protected owner.

> A **patent** gives an inventor the exclusive right to make, use, or sell an invention for 20 years.

COPY PROTECTION Copyright laws protect artists like Ludacris, who is shown here viewing his songs on the legal version of Napster. The record industry continues to clamp down on file sharing by suing file-sharing services. However, it no longer prosecutes individual downloaders.

AP Photo/Richard Drew

Article 1, Section 8 of the U.S. Constitution authorized a national **copyright** system to "promote the Progress of Science and useful Arts, by securing for limited Times to Authors. . .the exclusive Right to their. . .Writings." The United States (in 1791) and most developed countries established laws to protect authors' works. With the movement of books across borders, a need for international agreement on copyright became apparent, resulting in the Berne Convention in 1886. The United States expanded the range of works covered by copyright in 1976 to include computer programs, adding to more traditional protection of literature, music, drama, pantomimes, choreography, pictures, graphics, sculptures, motion pictures, audiovisual works, and sound recordings.

Patents are superior to a mere copyright in that they protect against reverse engineering—for example, making an imitation of an invention that performs the same basic functions as the inventor's but uses different underlying computer instructions. Copyright offers protection only against duplication of the underlying computer instructions and of the screen display and command sequences—the general "look and feel" of software, such as a spreadsheet program.

Efforts to prove that someone else has copied your idea may meet with varying degrees of success. Apple was unable to convince courts that Microsoft Windows copied the "look and feel" of the Macintosh graphical user interface, which Apple in turn had copied from Xerox. And aspiring Hollywood writers who write scripts "on spec" have had a notoriously difficult time proving that the resulting films based on their ideas were plagiarized. At the other end of the spectrum, the late Beatle George Harrison was found guilty of infringing the copyright of an earlier song ("He's So Fine") because he unknowingly copied its first three notes in his "My Sweet Lord."

Many believe that the balance is tipping too much in favor of the copyright owners. In 1998 the U.S. Congress passed the Copyright Term Extension Act (CTEA). It extended the period of protection to the life of the author plus 70 years. A major impetus for the law was to extend the "life" of cartoon characters such as Donald Duck and Bugs Bunny whose copyright protections were due to run out in the early 2000s. As mass-media conglomerates such as Disney (Donald Duck) and Warner (Bugs Bunny) have made a splash on the Internet, they have become very aggressive in closing down sites that use images from copyrighted works they control.

Another trap in intellectual property law is "work for hire," the principle that awards the property rights to the entity that pays the creator for his or her work. The heirs of Jack Kirby, originator of the X-Men comic book characters, were denied their inheritance when a court ruled that he had created them as work for hire. A word of caution to our readers: Students who write computer code or design Web pages for pay also lose their intellectual property rights.

Copyright laws are impeding an online initiative that some of our readers might find useful. Google has a plan to put the contents of major university libraries from around the world online, including many works whose authors cannot be tracked down for the purposes of gaining permissions to use their works. Having the works online could save us all trips to the library but the objections of the potentially disenfranchised copyright holders have stalled the plan thus far.

New digital technologies make it easy to duplicate copyrighted material without paying anything to the creators or to those who have bought the distribution rights. One solution has been to make unauthorized copying a crime. Another has been to legally regulate copying technologies to make illegal copying harder. A companion law to the Copyright Term Extension Act, the Digital Millennium Copyright Act (DMCA), made Internet service providers liable if they knowingly carry sites that violate copyright rules and forces them to identify the names of users who make illegal copies. The recording industry has stopped suing its customers but continues to pursue file-sharing services in court, and has successfully sued file-sharing services like Napster and Kazaa into submission. The DMCA also outlawed circumvention of copy protection technologies. Using this provision, the industry successfully sued the creators of software (known as DeCSS) that broke the anticopying technology incorporated in DVDs.

Internet piracy continues to plague media industries who claim each and every illegally copied file as a financial loss, and a criminal act. In 2012 the media industries urged the U.S. Congress to pass new restrictions that would make Internet service providers responsible for taking down illegal material, empower copyright owners to remove material themselves, and force search engines to block access to foreign websites that carried it. A mass protest by the Internet community focusing on the First Amendment implications of the proposed law resulted in the withdrawal of the proposal.

Piracy is also an international trade issue because software and entertainment products are among America's main exports. It is particularly difficult to ensure that no one copies these products in international markets without paying for their use. Illegal copying and nonpayment of royalties have been a thorny issue between the United States and China. New international agreements extend copyright protection to digital formats and treat intellectual property as an export commodity like any other so that powerful trade sanctions can be imposed on countries who act unfairly.

Protecting Consumer Rights. The protection of copyright holders is only half the story. The other side is that users of creative works are entitled to reasonable access to them. This concept of **fair use** permits academic and other noncommercial users to make copies of parts of copyrighted works for personal use and also for purposes of analyzing them in classrooms, in academic publications, or in artistic works, so long as they do not diminish the market for the complete work. Guidelines are given for how much of a copyrighted work can be reprinted or redisplayed without incurring the need to pay a license fee; for example, no more than 10 percent of a textbook. Consumers also have some rights under the Audio Home Recording Act of 1991. That law establishes the right of consumers to make copies of their own records and tapes for noncommercial use. But the Home Recording Act only protects hardware devices (like tape recorders) that make copies, not software that makes copies, which makes software-based programs, like Internet file-sharing programs, open to challenge.

To shield yourself from media industry lawyers, it is a good idea to avoid "sharing" copyrighted material online. It's also best to avoid well-known images from popular culture when making your own Web pages, recordings, or online videos. If you are dedicated to the idea that culture should be free,

[**Fair use** permits users limited copying of copyrighted works for academic, artistic, or personal use.]

THE BOSSES OF THE SENATE.

MONOPOLY IS NO GAME This nineteenth-century cartoon about industry monopolists shows the kind of problem that antitrust laws were enacted to prevent. Here, the fat monopoly (i.e., trust) owners are shown dominating the U.S Senate. The Sherman Antitrust Act prohibits monopoly practices.

your options are to join the Free Culture movement (see Chapter 6) or to practice what you preach by yielding some of your own intellectual property rights through the Creative Commons approach (see Chapter 9).

OWNERSHIP ISSUES

Media Concentration. In Chapter 2, we described the dangers of having a **monopoly**, where a single company controls an industry, or **oligopolies**, where a few companies dominate and have a much greater influence than would a broader, more competitive group of owners (Bagdikian, 2004). Dominant media firms may charge excessive amounts for their products, withhold innovations, or discourage new competitors. This kind of activity is an unlawful abuse of market power, according to the **Sherman Antitrust Act of 1890**.

U.S. courts, the U.S. Department of Commerce, and the FCC are charged with prohibiting any **restraint of trade** arising from excessive concentration of media ownership. The concentration of ownership may come about through **vertical integration**, when a company owns key assets in multiple aspects of a single industry. In approving Comcast's acquisition of NBC Universal in 2011, the FCC required that the company give fair access to its newly acquired television and Internet content properties to other cable, satellite, and Internet network providers. Another form of concentration is **horizontal integration**, in which a company owns many outlets of the same kind of medium or dominates a market on its own. For example, does Apple's iTunes wield excessive power in the online music market? Anti-competitive collusion is also forbidden. Did Apple and major book publishers collude over prices for e-books, as the U.S. Justice Department alleged in 2012?

The 1996 Telecommunications Act eliminated national ownership limits on the number of TV stations a company may own, raised the proportion of the nation that could be covered by a television network's own stations from 25 percent of homes to 35 percent (and raised it again to 39 percent), and set a cap (later struck down in court) of 30 percent on what proportion of U.S. households could be covered by a cable system owner. Even these expanded national limits are being challenged in Congress as interfering with free speech of media owners. In 2001, the FCC lifted its ban on one company owning more than one broadcast TV network. For radio, there are no national limits, and local ownership caps increase with market size (see Chapter 6).

Monopoly is the domination of a market by a single company.

Oligopoly is the domination of a market by a few firms.

The **Sherman Antitrust Act (1890)** prohibits monopolies and the restraint of free trade.

Restraints of trade limit competition.

Vertical integration occurs when a company with the same owner handles different aspects of a business within the same industry, such as film production and distribution.

Horizontal integration is the concentration of ownership by acquiring companies that are all in the same business.

Another ownership question has to do with **cross-ownership**: should a company be allowed to own various kinds of media? Traditionally, U.S. regulators did not allow a single company to own radio, television, and newspapers in the same area, in order to prevent one company from controlling too much content in one locality, thus limiting diversity of ideas. The 1996 Telecommunications Act largely deregulates vertical and horizontal integration and voids cross-ownership rules. In 2008, the FCC issued new rules that allowed limited TV–newspaper cross-ownership, but only when the TV station in question was not dominant in its market. That rule was struck down in court on the grounds that proper notice had not been given to the industry, but as of this writing the FCC is attempting once more to relax the cross-ownership restriction in the 20 largest markets.

Companies integrated very quickly after 1996, leading a few major firms, such as Disney and Fox, to dominate film and television production, film distribution, network and cable TV distribution, and syndication (see Chapters 7 and 8). Critics called for a reassessment of unbridled vertical integration (McChesney, 2000). Horizontal integration has also run rampant, particularly in the telecommunications industry, where Southwestern Bell has reconsolidated most of the old AT&T empire (see Chapter 12). However, amidst a long recession there is now a tendency to sell off media properties rather than accumulate them—if buyers can be found.

In the past, there was no apparent need to regulate newspaper ownership because there was lively competition. Even before the recent economic downturn that threatened major newspapers across the country, the government tried to sustain the industry by allowing competing newspapers within a city, such as Detroit's *Free Press* and *News*, to merge their business operations under what is called a *joint operating agreement*. The goal was to allow limited horizontal integration in exchange for preserving diversity of content in the form of separate newsrooms and editorial policies.

Network neutrality (see Chapter 9) presents a new type of ownership issue. That is the policy of requiring Internet providers to treat all of the data that passes through their networks on an equal basis to prevent them from favoring their own content. In 2011 the FCC imposed new rules on wireline Internet carriers that preserve net neutrality but allowed wireless carriers more freedom to control websites that strain network capacity. That could make Internet applications more expensive to use on smartphones and tablets than on personal computers.

Ownership and Diversity. Concentration of ownership is an issue in all industries, but diversity of content is an issue unique to the media. One of the major goals of the Federal Communications Commission since it was established by the Communications Act of 1934 has been to promote diversity of content among broadcasters. Limited frequencies and high initial costs pose *barriers to entry* so that relatively few people can actually participate in the "marketplace of ideas." The FCC decided that it needed to actively promote diversity of content under these conditions.

In an effort to preserve diversity, U.S. policy once gave preference to minorities, local owners, and female applicants for broadcast station licenses in the hope that they would increase diversity and better serve their communities. These preferences were gradually eliminated in the 1980s and 1990s, and

> **Cross-ownership** is the ownership by one firm of different media outlets in the same area.

UNIVERSAL SERVICE? Pictures like these of racially diverse, smiling tots using computers belie the fact that Internet access lags for children in minority homes.

minority and female ownership of broadcast stations remains very low (see Chapter 8). Furthermore, recent industry consolidation into a few large ownership groups has resulted in many minority owners selling their stations to larger groups (Irving, 1998). The FCC has renewed policy initiatives on minority ownership, but not much has actually changed.

Does diversity of ownership guarantee diversity of content? Even with fewer, less diverse owners, the number of channels of music and television has actually increased on FM radio and cable television. However, if one looks at diversity of ideas and artists within those channels, some critics still maintain that ownership concentration limits the number of people making decisions. The evidence is clear on one point: concentration of ownership has made for less local ownership, so decisions about what content to provide to local audiences are increasingly made by people farther away from listeners to radio and viewers of local TV news.

UNIVERSAL SERVICE

Universal service is the principle that everyone should have basic access to telecommunication services.

For most of the twentieth century, **universal service** meant trying to get a telephone into as many homes as possible. With national phone penetration hovering near 95 percent and more people using the Internet for their essential communication needs, attention has turned to making Internet service universal. As we saw in Chapter 9, the digital divide still exists, in that rural, low-income, and minority homes are less likely to have access to the Internet than urban, high-income, majority citizens and their access to broadband Internet also lags. But also, the U.S. lags behind many industrialized nations in broadband. How to close these gaps?

Following a mandate from the Telecommunications Act of 1996, the FCC created the e-Rate program to help fund Internet connections in schools and libraries using subsidies from telecommunication carriers. As part of the 2009 Recovery Act initiative, the Federal government invested $7.2 billion in improving broadband Internet service in underserved areas where adoption lags. The FCC has set a goal of having broadband in 90 percent of all U.S. homes in 2020, so sustained support is needed. In 2011 the FCC proposed a re-design of the Universal Service Fund that is paid for by monthly fees of $1 to $2 that appear on consumer phone bills. The new plan will target Internet connections rather than conventional landline phone service and will set aside funds to extend broadband connections in underserved areas. Yet, public infrastructure investments may not be enough by themselves. The FCC required Comcast to offer low-cost broadband service to millions of low-income households as a condition for approving its acquisition of NBC Universal in 2011. The FCC subsequently persuaded major cable companies to offer low cost (i.e., $9.99 a month) broadband Internet service to low income families whose children participate in subsidized lunch programs at school, for a trial period of two years. Making inexpensive refurbished computers available with software provide by Microsoft and free computer literacy training is also part of the plan. If further adoption is to take place the public needs to learn about effective uses of broadband Internet for personal and community development (LaRose et al., 2011).

WHO OWNS THE SPECTRUM?

One of the main reasons for regulation of broadcasting has been the need to allocate the scarce supply of radio and television channels. The Communications Act of 1934 established the Federal Communications Commission. It determined how close stations could be to each other geographically and still use the same channels. That put government regulators in the position of deciding who got to broadcast, so they made rules for awarding and renewing **licenses**. Historically, the main criterion was the public interest, but that term was left for the FCC to define, and it has never been given a precise definition. In practice, the FCC tried to promote **localism** by giving licenses to stations in cities of a variety of sizes. The FCC also reserved some licenses in FM and television specifically for noncommercial stations that emphasized education and culture.

> **License** is a legal permission to operate a transmitter.
>
> **Localism** is ownership and program decision making at the community level.

After 1980, the FCC decided that there was no longer a scarcity of radio stations, given the proliferation of FM stations. They also saw television as inherently competitive because an increasing number of U.S. homes had multichannel cable TV (Fowler & Brenner, 1982). Therefore, the **scarcity argument** for regulation was diminished. Furthermore, the pro-business commissioners proposed a lottery to pick applicants at random—or an auction, to "sell" frequencies to the highest bidder. Auctions are increasingly used to award frequencies for new telecommunication services.

> The **scarcity argument** states that because there are a small number of stations and the cost of entry to broadcasting is high, extra regulation is required.

The FCC held the "sale of the century" as it auctioned off television channels 52 to 69 as part of the transition to digital television in 2008. The scarcity of channel space for mobile communications has long been an issue in the United States, and the UHF television frequencies are "prime real estate" in the communications spectrum because those signals travel long distances and pass through walls with ease. With advances in wireless technology (see Chapter 12) this channel space could become the home for new entertainment services as well as mobile telephone and data services. The FCC has ruled that part of the spectrum will be "unlocked," that is, auction winners won't be able to lock their customers' cell phones into long-term contracts that prevent switching providers. In the Internet age the appetite for wireless spectrum space is bottomless. The FCC is also reallocating spectrum space reserved for government users and opening up the "white space" where television channel slots are unoccupied in local markets. A budget deal reached by Congress in 2012 calls for the clustering of TV stations in adjacent channels so that more spectrum can be auctioned off to wireless providers. Part of the proceeds will be set aside to compensate broadcasters for their trouble in moving channels.

The basic uses of radio spectrum frequencies are defined by the International Telecommunications Union (ITU). This body also allocates radio spectrum frequencies to countries, which their governments then allocate internally. Allocation issues are decided at the World Administrative Radio Congress (WARC), held every four years, and at regional conferences held in each of the ITU regions every two years. It is the WARC that decides, for example, which frequencies will be available for cellular radio service in various countries, which frequencies will be reserved for satellite communication, and how far apart the satellites must be. The regional conferences then deal with communications issues that crop up between neighboring countries.

TECHNICAL STANDARDS

Another regulatory function of governments is technical oversight for electronic media. The FCC works with private companies and with engineering-oriented standards organizations. Private companies often develop standards

HDTV DEBACLE Standards can determine the success of technology. The analog Japanese version of high-definition TV, shown here, was rendered obsolete by a U.S. decision to adopt a digital standard. The FCC adopted its own digital transmission standard that most of the rest of the world, including Japan, has rejected.

for their own equipment, then compete to set the industry-wide standard, such as the race between the HD-DVD and Blu-ray formats for high-definition home video that ended when key industry players gave their support to Blu-ray.

Agreement on basic technological standards signals manufacturers when to mass-produce a new technology. But when a technology continues to improve and evolve, when do we say the moment is right to set standards? Cell phones offer a clear example. Lack of agreement on which system to use and the proliferation of different digital technologies in the United States resulted in a less advanced system with more incompatibilities and less complete coverage than in Europe, which agreed early on to a common digital cellular standard, GSM. There are new efforts to adopt a world standard for fourth-generation (4G) cell phones (see Chapter 12).

Standards Bodies. In the United States, some standards are created by professional associations, such as the Institute for Electrical and Electronics Engineers (IEEE), and are subsequently ratified by the government. Some standards, like the Windows computer operating system of Microsoft, evolve from a single company. Sometimes the FCC forces industry to create a working group to resolve a conflict over standards. The Advanced Television Systems Committee that set the digital high-definition television (HDTV) standard is an example. In recent years, the government has tended not to set standards for new technologies, but rather has let industry work them out, sometimes leading to incompatible systems and consumer confusion, as in the case of cell phones.

International Standards. International bodies exist because of the need for connections among countries with telephony, fax, and data. The International Telecommunications Union (ITU), first formed in 1865 to standardize and enable telegraph traffic between countries, is the oldest international body in the world. The ITU standards process involves negotiation and ratification of technical approaches to providing telecommunications services. Representatives from equipment manufacturers, telecommunications carriers, and national regulatory bodies confer within committees to define the standards. The spectrum allocation process described in the previous section is part of the ITU's work.

STOP&REVIEW

1. What is the difference between a copyright and a patent?
2. What kinds of links might exist between forms of ownership and issues of media content?
3. What is the Sherman Antitrust Act?
4. How have ownership rules changed since 1996?
5. What is universal service? Why is it important?
6. Why did the relative scarcity of radio spectrum frequencies require government regulation?
7. How are international standards set?

THE POLICY-MAKING PROCESS

The United States has three branches of government: legislative, judicial, and executive. Government policy is made by representatives elected to Congress or state legislatures, judges appointed to various courts, and those appointed to regulatory agencies in the executive branch of government. Also, corporations make policy through their decisions, such as the types of services to offer and how much to charge, and work through professional lobbyists and industry trade associations to influence legislation. Researchers and journalists may help set the agenda for regulation by bringing issues to the attention of government or corporate policy makers: witness the decades of research done on the effects of television and video game violence on children.

FEDERAL REGULATION AND POLICY MAKING

All three branches of the federal government play an active role in communications regulation (see Figure 15.1, page 466). Laws are proposed by the executive branch or by Congress. Executive-branch regulatory agencies, such as the National Telecommunications and Information Administration (NTIA), propose legislation in consultation with Congress. Members of Congress frequently initiate legislation as well. Congress then considers, alters, and passes the legislation—first in specialized committees, such as the House Subcommittee on Telecommunication and the Internet, and eventually by the full House of Representatives and Senate. Legislation can be modified at all stages. Lobbyists for industries and various public interests also try to affect legislation in favor of their clients at each step of the process. Finally, bills of

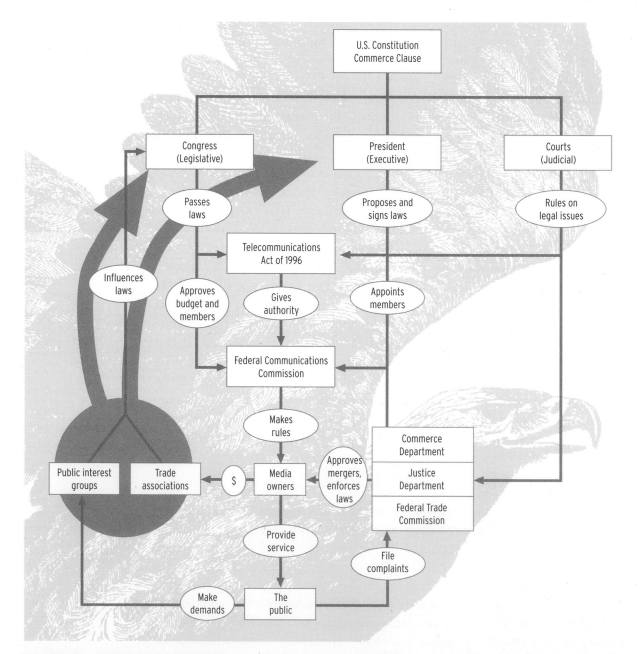

FIGURE 15.1 THE POLICY PROCESS The executive branch and the legislative branch write and pass media laws, such as the Telecommunications Act of 1996. If the laws are challenged, the courts then rule on their constitutionality.

MAKING POLICY The U.S. Congress passes legislation that regulates the media. The Telecommunications Act of 1996 remains the primary law governing the media in the United States.

proposed legislation are either defeated or passed by Congress and then sent to the president, who may either sign or veto them.

The executive branch implements the laws. Cabinet departments monitor industry compliance. For example, the Antitrust Division of the Justice Department examines whether companies are violating the Sherman Antitrust Act. If so, the department then brings a suit against the offender. It can also reject deals that it finds will undermine competition, as it did in turning down AT&T's acquisition of T-Mobile in 2011. Other laws are implemented by executive-branch regulatory agencies, such as the Federal Communications Commission (FCC) and the Federal Trade Commission (FTC). Because actions of the FCC or FTC are taken to federal district courts under the Telecommunications Act of 1996, these courts are often the key media-related element in the judicial branch. Ultimately, though, the Supreme Court hears cases that are appealed from lower courts, especially if there is a question as to whether the law that is being applied violates any principles of the U.S. Constitution, such as freedom of speech.

The Federal Communications Commission. The Federal Communications Commission (FCC) regulates broadcasting, satellite/cable TV, and telecommunications. The FCC Media Bureau oversees licensing and operation of broadcast stations and interprets legislation by Congress by making and enforcing regulations, such as those on cable system ownership. The FCC takes the wording of legislation and goes through a rule-making process. It solicits suggestions from industry, academics, and others; then FCC staff draft rules, which are put up for comment, then implemented.

The FCC's Wireline Competition Bureau has primary responsibility for the conventional telephone industry while its Wireless Telecommunications Bureaus oversee cell phone service. The Consumer and Governmental Affairs Bureau is in charge of educating members of the public about telecommunications and seeking their input about policy. With the 1996 Telecommunications Act, the FCC shifted away from direct regulation of telecommunications service rates and toward oversight of competition among telecommunications companies and market entry rules.

Increasingly, the FCC shares jurisdiction over key issues, such as antitrust and monopoly, with the Justice Department and Federal Trade Commission. Concerning local or regional telecommunications carriers, such as Verizon, the FCC shares jurisdiction with their respective state public utility commissions (PUCs). Cable television regulation is also shared between the FCC and local- or state-level cable commissions.

One problem with the FCC and other regulatory agencies is that they may end up attuned more closely to the interests of the industry than to the interests of the public. Critics say that regulators are often effectively captured by the industry they regulate—a concept referred to as **capture theory**.

Department of Commerce. The National Telecommunications and Information Administration (NTIA) was established within the Department of Commerce to advise on telecommunications policy. The Obama administration gave it the task of administering economic stimulus grants that will extend broadband Internet connections to underserved areas throughout the United States. The NTIA represents the United States in international bodies, such as the International Telecommunications Union, that set international telecommunications trade policies and make satellite orbit and communication frequency allocations.

Along with the Office of the United States Trade Representative, NTIA has been active in **multilateral trade negotiations**. These include the North American Free Trade Agreement (NAFTA) and the World Trade Organization (WTO). NTIA also negotiates issues such as the settlements of revenues from international phone calls. In addition, it is working on current topics such as limiting

The Yomiuri Shimbun via AP Images

OPENING MARKETS The NTIA is involved in negotiating access to Chinese markets for American media companies and in encouraging the Chinese government to clamp down on copyright piracy. Media products are a major source of foreign trade revenues for the U.S. economy.

overseas gambling sites, which has become an issue before the World Trade Organization.

The U.S. Patent and Trademark Office, and the United States Copyright Office of the U.S. Library of Congress address international copyright issues in communications media with the World Intellectual Property Organization.

The Federal Trade Commission (FTC). The FTC is the regulatory agency charged with domestic trade policy. It monitors trade practices such as **deceptive advertising**. It also investigates companies' actions in restraint of trade. It began an investigation of possible anticompetitive practices in computer operating systems that eventually led to an antitrust suit filed against Microsoft by the Justice Department. The FTC has scrutinized privacy policies and practices by companies online, as well as the advertising of violent media products to children.

The Justice Department. The Justice Department plays an important role in the enforcement of general laws that apply to communications as well. To enforce the Sherman Antitrust Act, the Justice Department initiated the suit that eventually broke up AT&T. In accordance with the 1996 Telecommunications Act, the Justice Department shares jurisdiction on monopoly issues with the FCC. It monitors competitiveness in important sectors of the information economy, such as monopoly practices in the computer industry, and competition in local TV and radio markets.

The Courts. The judiciary interprets challenges to laws written by Congress and rules made by the FCC and other federal agencies to see whether they are consistent with the U.S. Constitution. The Supreme Court is the ultimate court of appeals for decisions by lower courts, so it usually ends up reviewing decisions made in major cases such as penalties for indecency in broadcasting and local telephone competition. Courts can also interpret and enforce legal decisions. For example, the Third District Court of the District of Columbia supervised the breakup of the old Bell system in 1984, one of the most powerful government interventions in a communications industry.

The Congress. It is the U.S. Congress that ultimately writes and rewrites the communications laws of the land. After years of debate, Congress updated the 1934 Communications Act in 1996 because so many crucial issues required substantial definition or redefinition in law, not just regulatory decree or judicial interpretation. In 1996, those issues included competition within and across media and telecommunications industries, ownership restrictions, and regulation of violent and sexual content on TV. Many congressional committees are involved in communications issues. For the 1996 Telecommunications Act, for example, much of the crucial debate and lobbying took place in the House Telecommunications Subcommittee, since renamed the Subcommittee on Telecommunications and the Internet, which shaped the basic provisions that went before the full House of Representatives.

STATE AND LOCAL REGULATION

States and municipalities are increasingly involved in the regulation of telecommunications. They have been less involved in mass media, except in cable TV. For many years, state-level **public utility** commissions regulated local and regional telephone companies' rates. However, most states have

[**Public utilities** are regulated monopolies.]

drastically reduced their levels of regulatory oversight. They have **deregulated telecommunications** almost entirely by removing most of the restrictions on the nature and scope of activities that such companies engage in and the prices they charge. One area that states and localities are not involved in is regulation of the Internet. Congress has placed a moratorium on local regulation—and taxation—of the Internet in hopes of fostering the growth of the new medium. Yet, some states are beginning to impose their own regulations on privacy and consumer issues, as well as on financial issues like applying state sales taxes to Internet purchases.

LOBBIES

Industry and public interest groups lobby to influence proposed legislation in the executive branch and in Congress. Lobbies also try to affect how laws and rules are interpreted and enforced once they are made. For example, since passage of the 1996 Act, broadcasters and cable companies have lobbied Congress and the president to get the FCC to permit more concentration of ownership and more cross-ownership among local media.

Increasingly, telecommunications policy issues cut across industry boundaries, so the powerful lobbies of the publishing and motion picture industries end up getting involved. Technology companies such as Apple, Google, and Facebook are also organizing lobbying efforts of their own. These groups not only lobby directly about the substance of legislation and enforcement of laws; they also reinforce their arguments with campaign contributions and form political action committees (PACs) to lobby and to run advertisements for candidates. Sometimes they give favorable publicity, travel junkets, or financial deals to politicians in exchange for preferential treatment. Other lobby groups serve the public interest. The American Association of Retired Persons (AARP) and the Benton Foundation lobbied for years to preserve universal, low-cost "lifeline" local telephone service for older and poverty-stricken Americans.

Industry lobbyists and public interest groups are frequently at odds, and the competing special interests and public interests make it difficult to pass legislation. For example, public interest groups succeeded in pressing for restrictions on television indecency, even though they were resisted strenuously by the National Association of Broadcasters (NAB) and the television networks. Content restrictions are ordinarily considered unconstitutional, but the public interest groups have persuaded the FCC to threaten more and larger fines. Although industry lobbyists and public interest groups can legally exert influence on the executive and legislative branches, the judicial branch is beyond their reach.

THE FOURTH ESTATE

The mass media play an important role in the policy-making process by reporting stories about ongoing issues of interest to the general public, such as indecency and privacy. The media alert society and policy makers to social trends that raise new issues that could require government action, such as the digital divide. However, some of the policy issues we

STOP&REVIEW

1. How are media laws made and implemented?
2. What are the main institutions in the executive branch that participate in the media policy-making process?
3. What is the relationship of the FCC to other government agencies?
4. What is the role of the courts in media regulation?
5. What is a lobby group? What lobby groups are active in communications media issues?

WATCHING THE WATCHDOG PRESS The group Fairness and Accuracy in Reporting tracks what it considers conservative bias in media coverage. Accuracy in Media keeps a similarly watchful eye out for liberal bias.

have examined in this chapter, such as intellectual property, media ownership rules, and spectrum allocation, are not of much interest to the general public. Journalists working for trade publications, such as *Broadcasting and Cable* and *Telephony*, cover that territory, although often with a pro-industry slant. Increasingly, the "citizen journalists" who post their views on blogs (and social networking sites) play a role in public discussion, sometimes uncovering issues that the mainstream press may have overlooked and offering points of view not found in trade publications.

The mass media might act as lobbyists for their own interests, either directly in their own channels or through associations, such as the NAB and the MPAA. For example, few media reported on major telecommunications legislation in 1996 until it was drafted (Gustafsen, 2006), perhaps so that the media industry could present a unified message to the public. Media can have a much broader role as the forum in which much of the policy debate takes place.

The news media pursue the goal of reporting objectively, but they sometimes have a position or agenda of their own. For example, do news media tend to have a generally liberal or generally conservative bias, and are they intentionally biased for or against specific groups, such as business or the military? Observers disagree. For example, the group Fairness and Accuracy in Reporting (http://www.fair.org/) tracks what it considers conservative bias in media coverage, whereas Accuracy in Media (http://www.aim.org/) tracks perceived liberal bias.

SUMMARY&REVIEW

WHAT IS THE DISTINCTION BETWEEN POLICY AND LAW?

Policy is government and public consideration of how to structure and regulate media so that they contribute to the public good. Public policy involves a collective action of the whole society or its representatives. Laws are binding rules created by the legislature and enforced by the executive authority, like the FCC.

WHAT IS THE MARKETPLACE OF IDEAS?

The marketplace of ideas reflects the concept that, with free speech, the best ideas will win out in any competition with others. The concept of a free press is the extension of freedom of speech to media.

WHAT IS THE FIRST AMENDMENT?

The First Amendment to the U.S. Constitution says, "Congress shall make no law respecting an establishment of religion, or prohibiting the free exercise thereof, or abridging the freedom of speech, or of the press. . . ." Among the kinds of speech not protected by the First Amendment are libel, defamation, indecency, and inciting violence.

WHAT IS LIBEL?

Libel is harmful and untruthful written remarks that damage someone's reputation or good name. To be legally liable, the person or organization accused of libel must be shown to have known that the information was false, and its use must have been intended to damage the reputation of the person being libeled.

WHAT ARE THE RULES GOVERNING INDECENCY?

References to excretory or sexual organs or functions are indecent, and seven "dirty words" cannot be uttered on broadcast radio or television between the hours of 6 A.M. and midnight. The FCC responds to public complaints about indecent content and may impose fines of $325,000 per occurrence.

HOW ARE MEDIA AND TELECOMMUNICATIONS STANDARDS SET?

Companies often develop standards for their own equipment and compete to set the industry-wide standard. Industry committees sometimes set collective standards, often when spurred or required by government bodies such as the FCC. Internationally, most standards are set or endorsed by the International Telecommunications Union (ITU).

WHAT IS THE PRIMARY LAW REGULATING ELECTRONIC MEDIA?

The Communications Act of 1934 established the FCC, regulated broadcasting by regulating scarce frequencies, and regulated the monopolies of AT&T and, later, the regional Baby Bells. The 1996 Telecommunications Act encouraged competition between industries such as cable TV and telephony. It relaxed rules on how many stations a group could own and on cross-ownership of broadcasting, cable TV, telephone companies, and movie studios. It deregulated telephony ownership structures, areas of activity, and prices, but tried to maintain universal service. The Act also proposed restrictions on Internet pornography, which were struck down by the Supreme Court.

HOW IS PRIVACY PROTECTED?

Many people are concerned about privacy or control of personal individual information held in consumer credit databases and gathered on the Internet. No overall laws have yet been written on privacy rights, although use of data by government and the interception of messages are controlled by law. A right to privacy has been judicially interpreted from the Fourth Amendment. Congress has written laws both extending and limiting information privacy rights, which have been interpreted and reviewed by the courts.

WHAT ARE THE RESTRICTIONS ON MEDIA OWNERSHIP?

The Telecommunications Act of 1996 reduced or eliminated many restrictions on media ownership. No one company may own TV stations that collectively reach more than 39 percent of TV households or any more than two TV stations in a given market. The number of radio stations owned is restricted on a market-by-market basis, depending on the total number of stations in each market. One company may own a newspaper and a television station in the same market but only if the television station is not a dominant one.

HOW ARE MEDIA OWNERSHIP AND MEDIA CONTENT LINKED?

Some owners may try to influence content to promote their own ideas and interests. If owners are too much alike, they may not produce diverse content, whereas a greater diversity of ownership may produce more diverse content.

HOW DOES THE "SCARCITY ARGUMENT" JUSTIFY GOVERNMENT REGULATION?

There are far fewer frequencies than people who want to use them, both for broadcasting and for two-way services such as cellular telephony. Someone must allocate frequencies in such a way that radio spectrum users do not interfere with each other. Because the scarcity of frequencies requires that some people be given frequencies and others not, rules imposed by governments for allocating and renewing licenses were necessary.

WHAT ARE THE MAIN INSTITUTIONS IN THE MEDIA POLICY-MAKING PROCESS?

The main institutions in the executive branch are the Federal Communications Commission (FCC), which regulates most aspects of communication; the National Telecommunications and Information Administration (NTIA), which covers some aspects of policy research and international policy; and the Federal Trade Commission (FTC), which monitors trade and business practices. Congress passes laws about communication. The Justice Department and the court system, particularly the federal district courts, enforce and interpret the existing laws.

WHAT IS A LOBBY GROUP?

Lobbies are interest or business groups that try to influence lawmaking or enforcement. Some of the main business lobbies are the Baby Bells, the National Association of Broadcasters, and the Motion Picture Association of America.

THINKING CRITICALLY
ABOUT THE MEDIA

1. What is the best way to protect children from harmful media content?

2. Why do record companies have a right to prosecute file-sharing services?

3. What would be the best use of the communications spectrum that a new law will take away from television broadcasters?

4. What should the limits on media ownership be?

5. What does the FCC do, exactly?

KEY TERMS

capture theory (p. 468)

censorship (p. 450)

copyright (p. 458)

cross-ownership (p. 461)

deceptive advertising (p. 468)

deregulation (p. 470)

fair use (p. 459)

First Amendment (p. 448)

freedom of speech (p. 448)

horizontal integration (p. 460)

indecent (p. 451)

intellectual property (p. 457)

laws (p. 448)

libel (p. 449)

license (p. 463)

localism (p. 463)

marketplace of ideas (p. 449)

monopoly (p. 460)

multilateral trade negotiations (p. 468)

obscenity (p. 450)

oligopoly (p. 460)

patents (p. 457)

policy (p. 448)

privacy (p. 453)

probable cause (p. 454)

public utilities (p. 469)

restraints of trade (p. 460)

scarcity argument (p. 463)

self-regulation (p. 448)

Sherman Antitrust Act of 1890 (p. 460)

standards (p. 448)

universal service (p. 462)

vertical integration (p. 460)

The ways that professionals use media to send messages to the public can affect a company's survival. Several deaths and about 250 injuries occurred while Chinese workers assembled iPads and other devices. Apple turned to social media to respond to charges that it knew about the unsafe working conditions at Foxconn.

16

MEDIA ETHICS

ETHICAL THINKING

The First Amendment gives media professionals a great deal of freedom, but media professionals and others are always guided in their choices by community standards, professional ethics, and personal values and morals. Still, many wonder at the quantity of inaccurate stories, character assassinations, violence, sex, racial stereotypes, and other questionable content that results from many of these professionals' choices. In this chapter we ask, how do media professionals make these choices and how can we in the audience judge them?

Morality is defined as the ability to understand the difference between right and wrong. **Ethics** are standards of good conduct and moral rules for media professionals in all situations whether or not they are governed by formal laws or policies. Some of these guidelines are codified by professional organizations, whereas others represent broad systems of ethics. Churches, private companies, industry trade groups, minority groups, and public-interest groups also monitor media performance. But individual media professionals themselves must always act as their own ethical watchdogs, guided by organizational codes and community standards. Indeed, we can hope for the day that the ethical conduct of all individuals would make laws unnecessary.

> **Morality** is being able to distinguish right from wrong.
>
> **Ethics** are moral rules of good conduct that guide one's actions.

MEDIA THEN MEDIANOW

384–322 BCE	Aristotle discusses the golden mean in *Nicomachean Ethics*
1787	First Amendment to the U.S. Constitution
1790	Kant introduces the categorical imperative in *Critique of Practical Reason*
1863	John Stuart Mill publishes *Utilitarianism*
1947	Hutchins Commission promotes social responsibility of the press
1974	Deep Throat becomes source for Watergate reporters

2007	*Kid Nation* accused of child abuse
2009	Federal bailouts for AIG and Detroit automakers
2010	Toyota gets slammed for knowing about its auto problems
2012	United Kingdom Parliamentary report condemns Rupert Murdoch's fitness to run News Corp. because of bribery and phone hacking

Take a look at the news headlines today. Much of the negative news seems to be about people who don't have a moral compass (they can't tell the difference between right and wrong). Most people think they are ethical; yet, individuals have varying standards of what is right and wrong. In bygone days, all college students were required to take ethics classes. Now, students rarely have training in ethics; they receive their knowledge from religious beliefs, family, and society. Thus, codes try to set a standard or act as a guide for ethical decision making. The ethics of journalists receive a lot of coverage and debate because their work is in front of millions of people, but professionals involved in all aspects of the media face moral dilemmas every day. Increasingly, media audiences face ethical dilemmas of their own as they get involved in providing content for the Internet. Imagine what you would do in the following situations, and why:

- You work for the student online news site and an Apple representative sends you a new iPad3. Do you keep it? What if an Apple public relations person calls you and asks if you like the new iPad3, and then asks you to tweet or blog about it? Do you do it? If so, do you also say that Apple sent you an iPad3, and that Apple asked you to endorse it?
- How do you think people would regard your story criticizing the Nook if they knew you had been given an iPad3? (Does it appear as if you were compensated for your story?)
- Does the iPad3 gift affect your objective story about Apple and the deplorable conditions of China's Foxconn workers who assemble Apple products?
- You work for the independent campus TV news show. You shot video of the latest campus riot. The police want it to identify the ringleaders. Do you turn it over to them?
- There is not much time left during the noon hour radio news for the update on the Trayvon Martin story of George Zimmerman's 911 call. Is it okay to cut and paste the call, pulling some of the quotes out of context? (Those who did, got fired.)

- The tweet that you just received is perfect for your research paper on the effects of the economy on the media industry! Since it is just someone's opinion, do you need to reference it in your research paper? Would it make a difference if you found it in a blog? Does it matter if you don't know the person's real name?

What are our guidelines, and where do they come from? We will look first at some general systems of ethics that are prevalent now. Then we will look specifically at some of the current ethical issues and how individual media professionals have resolved them.

ETHICAL PRINCIPLES

Many ethical decisions are based on people's underlying religious, philosophical, and cultural ideals. Thousands of journalists and others who work in media make good, ethical decisions every day. Because of the nature of the industry, however, bad judgment is publicized in the hopes of being corrected or honest with the public. Let us consider several ideals that have been useful in media ethics.

- Socrates, Thomas Hobbes, and John Locke believed in a social contract theory—that people in society have an unwritten agreement with one another. For example, as long as news organizations uphold their social responsibility of reporting news with integrity, society might not call for government regulation of news content.
- Aristotle's golden mean holds that "moral virtue is an appropriate location between two extremes." Moderation and balance are the key points (Merrill, 1997). This means giving balanced points of view or including various points of view to provide balance. For example, Norwegian Anders Behring Breivik killed 80 people on an island youth camp. We continue to see his photo and read stories that questioned his sanity (imagine that!). Should news programs spend time reporting his actions that led up to this catastrophe or should the time be spent remembering the victims?
- The golden rule, "Do unto others as you would have them do unto you," comes from the Bible but can be found in many other cultural traditions as well. Translated into media terms it means doing no harm to the subjects of your stories and treating them respectfully. How would the developers of social media like it if all of their keystrokes and personal information were recorded and sold? Yet, some companies profit from doing this same thing to private individuals. The social media industry appears to be a massive ethics breach. Facebook collected information from innocent teens and sold it to marketers, while simultaneously citing that its "privacy policies" protect users. For three years, Google's Street View cars photographed street views, but as the specially equipped cars roamed the streets, they also intentionally collected personal information from millions of unsuspecting people on their computers. And, Apple tracked and recording detailed information from iPhones and iPads on customer's locations with a time stamp in

an unprotected file. Any hacker could find out where you live and the places that you regularly go. Developers should treat and respect others as they would like to be treated.

- Using the "veil of ignorance" (Rawls, 1999) means treating all members of society equally, as if you didn't know who had a stake in an issue. Rawls would have admonished Rush Limbaugh for calling a Georgetown University law student a "slut" after she spoke out in favor of insurance coverage for contraception. (Limbaugh might not have said anything, if he had known that many of his sponsors would pull their support of his program.)

- Immanuel Kant's categorical imperative holds that you should "act on that maxim which you will [wish] to become a universal law." A 14-year-old girl and more than 90,000 other petitioners wish that magazines such as *Seventeen* would stop airbrushing models, making them fake. In other words, what's wrong with being natural and real? Isn't that pretty enough? Her petition on change.org says, "Girls want to be accepted, appreciated, and liked. And when they don't fit the criteria, some girls try to "fix" themselves. This can lead to eating disorders, dieting, depression, and low self-esteem." A male petitioner wrote: "But, it goes beyond this. Unreal images of ideal female beauty damage boys' (men's) expectations as well. Raised by the media to desire this conception of ideal beauty, we men, much like women, must struggle with the disjunction between, on the one hand, what we have been taught to expect, to desire, to demand, and on the other hand, reality." Fashion magazines should take this example to heart as a reminder that fake photos set an unattainable standard and have very negative repercussions for girls' and boys' images of beauty.

- John Stuart Mill's principle of utility holds that we should "seek the greatest happiness for the greatest number." Mill was concerned about what would bring the greatest good for society, which he defined as benefiting the largest number of people (Christians, Rotzoll, & Fackler, 1991). Here, we consider potential benefits and harm, determine which action would benefit the most people (or harm the fewest), and choose that. For example, journalists who revealed the U.S. government's surveillance of global money transfers had to weigh the benefits of informing the public against the government's need to keep anti-terror tactics secret.

- Pragmatic ethics were postulated by John Dewey, an early twentieth-century American social philosopher and educator. He argued that actions had to be judged by their results, not by whether they adhered to a particular philosophy or guideline. This directs us to think ahead about the consequences of our actions. For example, will publishing photos of unidentified FBI suspects who "look like" they are of Middle Eastern descent cause prejudice against Arab-Americans?

- Situation ethics considers moral principles to be relative to the situation at hand, not absolute. Individuals may trust their intuitive sense of what is right, and guidelines might have exceptions if the overall purpose is good (Day, 1991). Situation ethics is not an ethical code like the others here, but rather urges consideration of alternate frameworks depending on the situation. For instance, using hidden recording devices to document lawbreaking is against the categorical imperative of respecting the privacy of subjects but might be acceptable as an application of the principle of utility if revealing the story will serve the public interest.

THINKING THROUGH ETHICAL PROBLEMS: POTTER'S BOX

Potter's Box is a process approach to deciding on ethical actions, developed by Harvard divinity professor Ralph Potter (see Figure 16.1). It is a four-stage model in which each stage helps clarify one aspect of the ethical problem at hand. Potter represented the stages as four quadrants of a box, hence the name.

In quadrant 1 of the box, we identify the facts of the situation. For example, in designing a public campaign against drunk driving, the media planners want to address a serious public safety problem by making the consequences of drunk driving visible. They consider featuring a young woman who was disfigured in an accident caused by a drunk driver. She is willing to have her image used and signs a release form.

In quadrant 2, we identify our choices and the ethical options. Will the shock value of the images deter potential drunk drivers? Will the images be sensationalistic violating community sensibilities, going beyond moderation? Despite being warned of possible outcomes, could the publicity harm the woman and affect her willingness to participate?

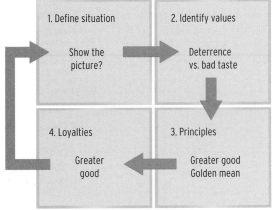

FIGURE 16.1 POTTER'S BOX Potter's Box gives a four-step model for thinking through ethical situations.

Next, in quadrant 3, we look for general principles that underlie our options. Based on Mill's utility principle or situation ethics, one could argue that the greater good of public safety outweighs the lesser evil of bad taste. Aristotle's golden mean might argue against using an extreme image, going beyond past practices. The golden rule might make us hesitate to put the young woman through an ordeal that we would not wish to suffer ourselves. This helps link concrete options to overarching principles, getting us to think about our own basic values.

In quadrant 4, we clarify our loyalties. Are we more concerned about being true to our own values or about the effectiveness of the campaign? Are we more excited about being connected to something edgy or new, or is it too close to sensationalism? Is the greater good more important than the golden mean?

Potter's Box is not a solution—but, it is a process that helps us think about our options more clearly. It focuses on ethical or moral issues, not legal ones. Everyone will run into ethical dilemmas where laws, professional training, or organizational rules are not always clear. Potter's Box can help us think through what to do.

CODES OF ETHICS

To assist their members in ethical decision-making, various professional groups and media organizations have adopted more concrete ethics guidelines or codes. The recommendations of the 1947 Hutchins Commission on social responsibility in journalism have been quite influential among both newspaper journalists and broadcasters and serve as a model for other media professions, so we will use them as an illustration.

The guidelines were based on two fundamental ideas: one, whoever enjoys a special measure of freedom, like a professional journalist, has an obligation to society to use their freedoms and powers responsibly. Second, society's welfare is paramount, more important than individual careers or even individual rights. The Commission went further to list five guidelines for the press: (1) present meaningful news, accurate and separated from opinion; (2) serve as a forum for the exchange of comment and criticism and to expand access to diverse points of view; (3) project "a representative picture of the constituent groups in society," by avoiding stereotypes and by including diverse voices; (4) clarify the goals and values of the society; implicit was an appeal to avoid pandering to the lowest common denominator, with sensationalism, for example; (5) give broad coverage of what was known about society. This has been interpreted as prying open government secrets and presenting scientific discoveries.

These principles inspired the Society of Professional Journalists' Code of Ethics. It tries to anticipate situations and offer guidance on how to deal with them (see Media&Culture: Society of Professional Journalists' Code of Ethics, page 480). If journalists follow the Society's guidelines, many ethical missteps could be avoided.

MEDIA&CULTURE

SOCIETY OF PROFESSIONAL JOURNALISTS' CODE OF ETHICS
SEEK TRUTH AND REPORT IT

Journalists should be honest, fair, and courageous in gathering, reporting, and interpreting information. Journalists should:

- Test the accuracy of information from all sources and exercise care to avoid inadvertent error. Deliberate distortion is never permissible.

- Diligently seek out subjects of news stories to give them the opportunity to respond to allegations of wrongdoing.

- Identify sources whenever feasible. The public is entitled to as much information as possible on sources' reliability.

- Always question sources' motives before promising anonymity. Clarify conditions attached to any promise made in exchange for information. Keep promises.

- Make certain that headlines, news teases, and promotional material, photos, video, audio, graphics, sound bites, and quotations do not misrepresent. They should not oversimplify or highlight incidents out of context.

- Never distort the content of news photos or video. Image enhancement for technical clarity is always permissible. Label montages and photo illustrations.

- Avoid misleading reenactments or staged news events. If reenactment is necessary to tell a story, label it.

- Avoid undercover or other surreptitious methods of gathering information except when traditional open methods will not yield information vital to the public. Use of such methods should be explained as part of the story.

- Never plagiarize.

- Tell the story of the diversity and magnitude of the human experience boldly, even when it is unpopular to do so.

- Examine their own cultural values and avoid imposing those values on others.

- Avoid stereotyping by race, gender, age, religion, ethnicity, geography, sexual orientation, disability, physical appearance, or social status.

- Support the open exchange of views, even views they find repugnant.
- Give voice to the voiceless; official and unofficial sources of information can be equally valid.
- Distinguish between advocacy and news reporting. Analysis and commentary should be labeled and not misrepresent fact or context.
- Distinguish news from advertising, and shun hybrids that blur the lines between the two.
- Recognize a special obligation to ensure that the public's business is conducted in the open and that government records are open to inspection.

MINIMIZE HARM

Ethical journalists treat sources, subjects, and colleagues as human beings deserving of respect. Journalists should:

- Show compassion for those who may be affected adversely by news coverage. Use special sensitivity when dealing with children and inexperienced sources or subjects.
- Be sensitive when seeking or using interviews or photographs of those affected by tragedy or grief.
- Recognize that gathering and reporting information may cause harm or discomfort. Pursuit of the news is not a license for arrogance.
- Recognize that private people have a greater right to control information about themselves than do public officials and others who seek power, influence, or attention. Only an overriding public need can justify intrusion into anyone's privacy.
- Show good taste. Avoid pandering to lurid curiosity.
- Be cautious about identifying juvenile suspects or victims of sex crimes.
- Be judicious about naming criminal suspects before the formal filing of charges.
- Balance a criminal suspect's fair trial rights with the public's right to be informed.

ACT INDEPENDENTLY

Journalists should be free of obligation to any interest other than the public's right to know. Journalists should:

- Avoid conflicts of interest, real or perceived.
- Remain free of associations and activities that may compromise integrity or damage credibility.
- Refuse gifts, favors, fees, free travel, and special treatment, and shun secondary employment, political involvement, public office, and service in community organizations if they compromise journalistic integrity.
- Disclose unavoidable conflicts.
- Be vigilant and courageous about holding those with power accountable.
- Deny favored treatment to advertisers and special interests and resist their pressure to influence news coverage.
- Be wary of sources offering information for favors or money; avoid bidding for news.

BE ACCOUNTABLE

Journalists are accountable to their readers, listeners, viewers, and each other. Journalists should:

- Clarify and explain news coverage and invite dialogue with the public over journalistic conduct.
- Encourage the public to voice grievances against the news media.
- Admit mistakes and correct them promptly.
- Expose unethical practices of journalists and the news media.
- Abide by the same high standards to which they hold others.

Source: http://www.spj.org/ethicscode.asp, revised and adopted 1996. Used by permission.

CORPORATE ETHICS

Wow! Wouldn't it be great to be an executive at American International Group (AIG)? You ask the government for taxpayers' hard-earned money to bail out your company as a reward for your bad business decisions, and then give yourself an $800,000 bonus! Or, how about being one of the Big Three automakers who spent about $20,000 to fly in a private jet to Washington to ask the federal government for a handout from taxpayers because the CEOs don't have good business sense on how to balance their budgets? Imagine being their PR practitioner having to respond to the media and to the public. So far, our discussion in this chapter has emphasized individual ethical choices. However, most media professionals work within large corporations that present a fundamental

FLYING HIGH Big Three automaker executives flew in private jets to Washington, D.C., holding out their tin cups for taxpayers' money. Where's the business sense?

moral conflict on a daily basis: my ethics or my job? Professional ethics codes provide guidance when corporate ethics have lapsed such that media workers know when it is time to "blow the whistle" on unethical corporate practices.

Large media firms share some basic ethical dilemmas with other large corporations. Many critics believe that an ethical crisis exists, and it is the result of a fundamental shift in the values of large corporations and their top managers. The temptation to improve their numbers by hiding losses, recording phony profits, or shortchanging public service obligations has proven irresistible to some ethically challenged executives. In addition, many of these executives are obsessed with their own comforts and exorbitant incomes.

Perhaps it is time to return to the corporate responsibility model that preceded the obsession with the bottom line. This imperative parallels the social responsibility model that guides individual journalists. Ethical corporations are expected to "give back" to the communities in which they do business by making charitable contributions and performing public service. Their executives have an obligation to serve with community organizations and, individually and collectively, make their communities a better place to live.

Furthermore, corporations do have a responsibility to foster ethical behavior among their own employees. By emphasizing fair play and a respect for law and other individuals, they aim to develop a corporate culture that rewards ethical behavior, not just the pursuit of the bottom line. Many corporations behave responsibly toward their communities, although their good works sometimes do not attract as much attention. The Corporate Social Responsibility Newswire (http://www.csrwire.com/) is a resource that catalogs the good that corporations do.

MAKING ETHICS WORK

In some professions, notably medicine and law, ethical codes are tied to licensing requirements. The penalty for ethical violations can be revocation of one's license to practice. There is no licensing in media professions, although serious ethical lapses can be career-threatening. This brings us to the question of how codes of ethics have any impact if they do not have the force of law or carry threats to one's livelihood.

Perhaps the most important impact of professional codes is the idea that media professionals have a responsibility to society. Because relatively few people create professional media content, those who do need to consider the impact of their actions on society. In the United States, this sense of social responsibility is the prevailing ethic for media.

Although compliance with professional media codes is voluntary, there are nonetheless severe consequences for violating them. This is because media managers hold them up as norms for employee conduct. In several well-publicized cases, reporters who fabricated stories or plagiarized material for their columns were not only fired from their jobs, but were unable to find work at any other newspaper in the country. Even editors may lose their jobs if their oversight is too lax. But who oversees the boss's boss in a large media organization, especially if the "higher ups" have no background as journalists themselves?

One approach is that employees in news organization are required to read and sign the ethics code. Another approach is for instructors to make ethics an important component of journalism education, which is a required part of the curriculum in accredited journalism programs everywhere. So, if you plan a career in journalism it is not too soon to start thinking about the choices you will face and the personal values you will bring to those decisions.

ETHICAL ISSUES

Now that we understand some of the principles, challenges, and procedures involved in media ethics, we turn to consider some recurring ethical issues. These are organized around the various media professions.

JOURNALISM ETHICS

Whether they write stories for traditional media or tweet an update, journalists face ethical dilemmas at every turn.

Ethical Limits on Free Speech. The First Amendment was originally framed to ensure freedom of the press, but that is not an absolute freedom, and is still not enjoyed in many parts of the world today. In Chapter 15 we discussed legal limits on freedom of the press having to do with libel, public safety, indecency, and obscenity. But even perfectly legal stories are still subject to ethical restraints.

Indecency is a particularly sensitive issue since the courts have ruled that moral standards vary among communities, which are permitted to develop local standards for treatment of sexuality. Media professionals need to think about the ethics of indecency in individual terms ("Do I really think this is a good idea?"), in institutional terms ("What do we as a company want to say to the public?"), and in terms of community standards and values ("Is this an appropriate thing to say to this community?"). Pulitzer Prize winners M. L. Elrick and Jim Schaefer used the Freedom of Information Act to obtain former Detroit Mayor Kwame Kilpatrick's text messages that showed he lied under oath. Much of the "sexting" between Kilpatrick and his aide, Christine Beatty, was scandalous and indecent, and most news organizations chose not to publish the most graphic examples. Of course, many people remember the Super Bowl half-time incident in which Janet Jackson's breast was exposed (see Chapter 15); the media might have shown the offending naked breast, a digitally blurred image—which was still indecent to some—or no picture at all. In the wake of the incident, the electronic media adopted further ethical guidelines covering indecency in all programming (and barred MTV from ever doing a half-time show again). But what about the performers? Should M.I.A. have

DOING A GOOD DEED FOR SOCIETY Detroit News Investigative Journalists Jim Schaefer (left) and M.L. Elrick (right) used the FOIA to expose former Detroit mayor Kwame Kilpatrick's unethical behavior.

thought about the children in the audience before she flashed an obscene gesture to audiences (you) during the 2012 Super Bowl halftime show? And, why do it anyway? Can you respect someone who doesn't respect you?

Print media are not subject to the same legal standards of indecent speech as broadcasters, but they have similar ethical considerations. The issue of decency in journalism extends far beyond the FCC's definition that prohibits the use of words or images relating to excretory or sexual organs or functions. For example, showing pictures of American soldiers posing with the body parts of Afghans killed in action shocks the average person's sensibilities and violates the golden rule with respect to the families of the victims and to the Islamic religion. Could the reporting of the soldiers' actions or their mental instability be conveyed differently?

Accuracy. In conventional news media, prevailing journalistic ethical principles about the accuracy of information are quite strict. Journalists do not fabricate evidence, make up quotes, create stories or events, or manipulate misleading photographs, any of which might deceive the public. In a classic case, *New York Times* columnist Jayson Blair copied many of his stories from other newspapers, fabricated interviews and sources, and wrote as if he were reporting from the scene. Blair was fired, and so were his editors (Boyd, 2010). More recently, Facebook retained its public relations firm, Burson-Marsteller, to plant negative news stories about its rival Google's social media service.

When students read news and information online, they should know that ethics standards are far less strict on Internet sites that are not traditional news organizations with ethics codes in place. Internet columnist Matt Drudge, for example, routinely violates the norms of professional journalism by publishing unconfirmed reports that may turn out to be only rumors. Matt Drudge, however, doesn't have a degree in journalism and might not have taken a media ethics class.

Fairness. Journalists and editors constantly make choices about what to cover. They can advance certain companies, people, and causes over others by the decisions they make on whom and what to cover, and whom to quote first and how much to quote. So it is important to be fair.

On the one hand, how far should reporters go in their criticism of the subject of a story? And, to what degree are they responsible for consequences to that person? Journalists weigh the public's right to know with an individual's privacy. When their privacy has been invaded, some subjects move away from the local area, change their names, or even commit suicide. Often, journalists can report the "who," "what," "where," and "when" for a story immediately, but instead of interpreting or assuming, they have to wait on the "how" and "why" until facts can be verified.

On the other hand, should reporters publicize someone they know, a cause they agree with, or a company they are employed by at the expense of others? For example, should ABC News run stories about Disneyland theme parks owned by its parent company, but not other theme parks?

UNETHICAL SMEAR CAMPAIGN Mark Zuckerberg had some explaining to do when Facebook hired Burson-Marsteller PR agency to do an anti-Google smear campaign. Burson-Marsteller said they should not have gone along with their client's idea and its request to stay anonymous.

Confidentiality. News reporters protect the confidentiality of their sources so that they have the trust of citizens who may have inside information about important stories. For example, if a reporter is doing a story on the drug trade, she will end up talking to drug dealers. Because the knowledge the reporter gains from her sources could help convict them, law enforcement officials sometimes try to get reporters to reveal the identity of the sources. However, this is one ethical issue on which there is fairly widespread agreement: the reporter has promised either implicitly or explicitly to keep secret the source's identity and any of the details that could incriminate the source. After all, a journalist who breaks her promise of confidentiality to a source will get no more interviews or tips from others. Furthermore, news organizations do not relish the idea of being considered an arm of the police or authorities.

Indeed, reporters go to great lengths to avoid revealing a source. Even when threatened with jail time or fines for contempt of court for not cooperating with a deposition, *Detroit Free Press* reporter David Ashenfelder repeatedly refused to name his source in a story concerning a former federal prosecutor. Finally, several years later, a U.S. District Judge agreed that the Pulitzer Prize winner had sufficient evidence to support his Fifth Amendment defense.

A related question is source attribution—how to cite sources. Rarely should journalists attribute something that is said without revealing the identity of their source; this is an anonymous source. A reporter reveals as much as possible about the competence and position of his source in order to support the credibility of the story. After all, the public wonders why unnamed "official sources" do not have to be held accountable for their statements.

However, many sources will talk only if they cannot be identified from what is said about them in the story. This issue becomes more complex when the source is a well-known public figure who wants to "leak" a story on which he or she is not yet ready to be quoted. For example, Iraq's alleged noncompliance with U.N. resolutions on weapons of mass destruction was leaked to the

CONFIDENTIALITY Robert Woodward (right) and Carl Bernstein (left) became famous when they broke the story on Watergate. A primary ingredient for the success of the story was an inside source referred to as "Deep Throat," unnamed for more than 30 years.

AP Photo

press because intelligence sources worried that if they "went on the record," that is, to be named and quoted directly, it would compromise their own sources in Iraq. That's why we see stories attributed to a "highly placed official," or perhaps a "cabinet-level source." The most famous example was the Watergate scandal of the 1970s, wherein key inside information was supplied by a confidential source known only as "Deep Throat"—it wasn't until 2005 that Deep Throat was revealed as W. Mark Felt, former assistant director of the FBI during the Nixon administration.

Political leaders are known for wanting to leak ideas about what they might try to do concerning certain issues. The official might follow through on the idea or abandon it, depending on the public's response. Journalists dislike being used surreptitiously by the officials because it is not their job to help politicians.

Sensationalism. Hearst and Pulitzer relied on sensational stories, titillating details, and graphics to compete for readers (see Chapter 4). Some consider sensationalism simply a matter of pandering to bad taste.

International press exercises different standards concerning sensationalism. When a hotel maid accused the French former International Monetary Fund advisor of rape, the French named the alleged victim and her daughter, described her personality and looks (which has nothing to do with rape), but discouraged photos of the politician in handcuffs.

Meanwhile, the Americans refrained from naming the housekeeper with whom former California governor Arnold Schwarzenegger had an affair, even though it was

Richard Levine/Alamy

PRACTICE RESTRAINT Ethical news professionals kept the name and photo of Schwarzenegger's and his housekeeper's son out of the media, to protect him as a minor and a private citizen.

consensual, until after her name came out in blogs. They also held back the name of Schwarzenegger's and the housekeeper's boy, now 14, and blurred his face in baby photos.

Sometimes media get carried away: do you really want to know that Jessica Simpson uses only Listerine and her sweater to brush her teeth?

Sometimes to get sensational headlines, reporters lose their moral compass. In Britain, Rupert Murdoch's News Corporation scandal developed in 2011 when it was found that reporters had hacked into the royals' phones—and apparently had been doing so for years. Subsequent investigations showed more wrong-doings that included more phone hacking and bribery (of police). A government inquiry concluded that Murdoch was not a "fit and proper" owner of a news organization for what appeared to be a pattern of willful ignorance of wrong doing by his employees. Legislators in the United States now want to know if Murdoch's unethical web stretched across the Atlantic Ocean, including trying to get private phone records of 9/11 victims.

Conflicts of Interest. Some freelancers and journalists are tempted to let someone else pay for their travel to exotic locations, such as the Bahamas, or to high-profile events, like the North American Auto Show. Sponsors hope that **junkets**— paid trips for journalists will attract the attention of reporters or influence how a subject is portrayed. For example, a resort operator might pay for travel writers to visit in hopes of getting a favorable story into a newspaper or magazine—free advertising—that might entice visitors. Or, a company might fund a trip that is only vaguely related to a particular topic but might make the writer feel more positive toward the sponsoring organization when a story in the future pops up. If you liked their luxury resort (and want to be invited back), you should also like their parent company's stock, right? Another form of conflict of interest is **freebies**—gifts from sources and news subjects. It is sometimes tempting for journalists to accept free gifts, such as dinners, T-shirts, books, and passes to sports events or to the theater. Even the smallest of gifts can leave a big impression, and you should say no.

The problem with junkets and freebies is that the journalists are not experiencing the event as regular customers who have to pay fees and haggle with managers. Another problem is that journalists who are feeling good from having been lavishly wined and dined are reflecting positively instead of objectively on the free experience.

Most publications have very strict rules against all freebies and junkets. When journalists are given gifts—before or after stories—the gifts are returned or given to charity, citing company policy. These journalists avoid even the appearance of a conflict of interest. Also, an accepted practice is to disclose the

Jon Kopaloff/FilmMagic/Getty Images

SMILING ALL THE WAY TO THE BANK Is it really newsworthy to report that Jessica Simpson sometimes doesn't brush her teeth? Is this pandering to audiences and could more important news be published?

A **junket** is an expense-paid trip intended to influence media coverage.

Freebies are gifts of any value from sources and potential news subjects.

STOP&REVIEW

1. What are the main areas of concern in media ethics?
2. What are some of the classic ethical principles that people apply to issues that arise in media ethics?
3. What is Potter's Box?
4. What are the main ethical responsibilities of journalists?

relationship that raises a conflict of interest so that the audience can be alerted to the potential bias. If there is too much of a conflict, then another journalist is assigned to the story.

Commercialism. Ethics can be compromised in several ways because of commercialism. A conflict can occur between news value and shareholder values. Many stations run sensationalized stories ("How clean are the kitchens in your favorite restaurants?") during ratings sweep periods, even though there is not really anything new to report. Broadcast news focuses on stories that have a dramatic visual element that makes for good ratings. There is an inclination to lead newscasts with footage of car wrecks, wars, or airplane crashes because of the visual nature of the medium. There is also a temptation to ignore or downplay an important story because it doesn't have eye-catching footage to go with it. This ideology is changing with multimedia stories on the Internet. Now, news editors ask what is the important story and what is the best way to tell the story.

Yet, as conglomerates become owners of television stations, it might become difficult for television newscasts to not run "news stories" that are thinly disguised promotions for entertainment shows on the same station. Vertical integration creates the potential for interference with negative news coverage affecting media owners. When journalists in a company's media holdings cover other parts of the company's operations, there is a natural tendency to mute any criticism. For example, to please its corporate parent, Disney Corporation, ABC News canceled a story about child molesters employed by Disneyland. Although the news editor protested, the story did not air. This creates a climate of self-censorship in which reporters come to know that it isn't a good idea to prepare critical stories about their corporate cousins. On the flip side, positive news about competitors could also be squelched—which contributes to a decline in trustworthy, objective reporting.

Privacy. Many reporters are concerned about the privacy of those they are covering, which competes with their natural desire to expose and describe the topic of the story. It adds legitimacy and human interest to a story to provide personal details about the people involved. Some kinds of details may cause harm to those covered or their families. In the Iraq war, for example, most media refrained from revealing the names of military casualties until their families could be contacted. Revealing the identities of witnesses who testify at criminal trials or in grand jury proceedings or the names of jurors also raises ethical challenges because their personal safety as well as their privacy is at stake—to say nothing of the integrity of the courts.

ETHICAL ENTERTAINMENT

Why should we care how much violence children or adults are exposed to in computer games? What about television's thousands of murders that elementary school children see and the hundreds of thousand acts of media violence that teenagers are exposed to by the time they graduate from high school? (See Chapter 14.) Will they think that hurting others is no big deal as they confuse fantasy with real life? Do filmmakers need to think about the social impacts of their films?

Who's Responsible for Media Effects? Should producers take responsibility for the social effects of their creations? Or is their role to create "art" and let the chips fall where they may? Most filmmakers, musicians, and television entertainment producers, for example, say that they are not responsible for the social impacts of their creations. If someone gets hurt imitating a stunt on *The Final Destination*, then that is their problem, not the producers'. The same issue applies to depictions of rude behavior or vulgarity in popular movies, TV shows, computer games, and music. Young viewers might be influenced to think that the behavior they see so often on the screen or hear in songs is attractive or even socially acceptable. What happens when we have a whole society thinking that such dispositions on how to treat one another are commonplace?

As Chapter 14 discusses, researchers do not always agree on how deep or pervasive the effects of violence or sex in the media are, but they do agree that the amount of graphic violence in media has increased. Headlines constantly remind us that some people seem to imitate specific acts of violence or reckless behavior that they have seen on the screen or heard about in music. What if larger numbers of people don't directly imitate the act but come to see it as more normal or acceptable?

Industry representatives usually make two counterarguments: first, that individuals are not as vulnerable as is commonly supposed; and second, that individuals and families have a responsibility to make their own decisions about what to watch and what to make of it. For the mainstream of society, making responsible choices is probably the right answer. But how can people make informed choices? One current response within public schools is to teach media literacy so that children and adolescents understand the industry and what they are watching. A number of churches and other groups are also doing this to supplement what children do or don't learn at home about making such choices.

Until recently, the prevailing trend in America was toward unrestricted artistic freedom divorced from social considerations. But religious critics and social philosophers, present and past, have argued that the artist is not absolved from responsibility to contribute positively to society. These critics argue that artists should either raise people's consciousness about issues or, at the very least, refrain from contributing to social harm. And, some argue that TV simply isn't art.

Reality programs deepen the ethical quagmire when they cross the line from merely recording human suffering to causing it, and each year producers push the envelope. Many children are hurt or killed trying to replicate acts on reality shows. A 13-year-old boy hanged himself on the monkey bars of his school playground reportedly while trying to imitate a stunt on *Fear Factor*. The reality show *Roadies* also has incited children, with one recent case seemingly resulting in the death of a 9-year-old boy who also hanged himself. Should there be censorship? Should government step in with laws if media cannot regulate themselves? How would Locke apply the social contract theory?

Social Media Ethics. Social media are profoundly ethically challenged. Facebook chooses to remain willfully ignorant of the many children under age 13 who use its website, making the youngsters vulnerable to stalkers, bullies, and unscrupulous marketers. Social media follow the lead of the mass media when it comes to explaining away media effects, even including cases of suicide induced by cyber bullies: It's the parents' (or the schools' or law enforcement's) fault but never theirs. When it comes to privacy, the entire social media phenomenon is predicated on a massive ethical breach: selling private information to commercial interests under the false pretense of running a place where friends and family can meet, then hiding behind baffling privacy protection policies.

PUBLIC RELATIONS ETHICS

In any job, choices of doing good or evil exist. Public relations can be used for the public good while advancing private advantage. Or, it can be used to manipulate the public interest or hide selfish commercial objectives. Most practitioners are very ethical.

When a practitioner knowingly makes a wrong decision, it often stays on the conscience until corrected. For example, Facebook hired the public relations firm of Burson-Marsteller to smear Google's reputation. The PR company used e-mail to journalists and blogs to spread the fable that Google used a special software to collect information from social media websites about users without their knowledge. When confronted, Facebook denied the allegations, but Burson quickly admitted its dastardly deeds, carried out on behalf of Facebook. Burson also expressed regret that it hid the fact it was working for Facebook and that it never should have agreed to do this type of work.

The problem was that Facebook wanted to steal away advertising revenues from Google. Decisions have consequences. Burson now has its unethical decision and then ethical retraction tied to its name.

The Center for Media & Democracy is a modern-day critic that identifies and investigates spin by corporations and government agencies that affect the democratic process. Its website (http://www.prwatch.org) and e-mail newsletter ("The Weekly Spin") criticize assaults against the public interest.

The key to ethical behavior for both individual practitioners and the institutions they serve is organizational performance. If a company, for example, acts in a manner that harms rather than helps the people it depends on for success, no amount of public relations can save the day, no matter how well the effort is designed or executed. The only real solution for the guilty party is for management to correct the problem. For example, many critics assume top executives knew, but did nothing, about Toyota's accelerator problems—and people were killed and injured as a result. If so, this is a very different scenario from

VIOLATING YOUR PERSONAL RIGHTS? Google's Street View cars collected personal information (emails, passwords, etc.) from open WiFi networks for years as they also took pictures of streets.

guy harrop / Alamy

MEDIA&CULTURE

PR ETHICS

We believe our professional values are vital to the integrity of the profession as a whole.

Advocacy We serve the public interest by acting as responsible advocates for those we represent. We provide a voice in the marketplace of ideas, facts, and viewpoints to aid informed public debate.

Honesty We adhere to the highest standards of accuracy and truth in advancing the interests of those we represent and in communicating with the public.

Expertise We acquire and responsibly use specialized knowledge and experience. We advance the profession through continued professional development, research,

and education. We build mutual understanding, credibility, and relationships among a wide array of institutions and audiences.

Independence We provide objective counsel to those we represent. We are accountable for our actions.

Loyalty We are faithful to those we represent, while honoring our obligation to serve the public interest.

Fairness We deal fairly with clients, employers, competitors, peers, vendors, the media, and the general public. We respect all opinions and support the right of free expression.

Source: PRSA Member Code of Ethics (revised 2000).

---

the classic Tylenol case where top brass immediately cleared all store shelves of the product in an effort to minimize harm.

Down through the years, ethical and legal breaches of conduct led to the formation of the Public Relations Society of America (PRSA) in 1948 and to the promulgation by that organization in 1950 of a Code of Professional Standards (see Media&Culture: PR Ethics). PRSA completely revised its code so that its power to expel a member applies if he or she has been "sanctioned by a government agency or convicted in a court of law." The code is framed as a self-directed teaching tool that expresses the "universal values that inspire ethical behavior and performance." Other public relations membership organizations, such as the International Public Relations Association (IPRA) and the International Association of Business Communicators (IABC), have codes of conduct with specific examples of what they consider unprofessional and/or unethical behaviors.

ADVERTISING ETHICS

In advertising, ethical decisions revolve around selecting one moral value over another when writing, designing, or placing advertisements.

Harmful Products. The promotion of harmful products creates obvious ethical dilemmas for advertising professionals. Emerson Foote resigned as chairman of McCann-Erickson, one of the world's largest and most prestigious ad agencies, in protest over its willingness to create cigarette advertising. He was making a choice between the value of free expression on the one hand (tobacco companies produce legal products and have a right to advertise) and the value of health concerns (mounting evidence of the link between smoking and cancer) on the other.

Other advertising professionals have not been so scrupulous. The Joe Camel cigarette advertising campaign was secretly targeted at children in an effort to get youngsters to develop a life-shortening tobacco habit. Perhaps their sense of professional responsibility to the advertising client, or perhaps the desire to continue their own employment, outweighed the advertising professionals' ethical responsibility to the children of America. Recently, though, after a series of legal battles, tobacco advertisers have become more sensitive to their responsibilities toward children. For example, they pulled cigarette advertising from magazines with substantial numbers of young readers. However, they are also resisting efforts to place graphic warnings about the effects cigarette smoking, such as pictures of cancerous lungs, on cigarette packages. They are claiming their First Amendment rights, but is it ethical to do so?

Stereotyping. There are also questions about the ethics of using ethnic and sex-role stereotypes in advertising. Did you ever notice how almost all the women who appear in ads are unnaturally thin and beautiful, while the African-American males tend to be professional athletes? Are such portrayals harmless appeals to advertising target markets, or do they perpetuate harmful racial stereotypes that foster racism and sexism?

What about the stereotype that all women must be thin to be beautiful? Many young girls strive to achieve the impossible and boys think the unnatural is the standard. It's bad enough that many models look anorexic, and that if a real woman looked like Barbie she'd topple over. (Slumber Party Barbie came with a book on "How to Lose Weight" that included the tip: "Don't Eat.") (McDonough, 2010) Photographers add to girls' and women's insecurities by airbrushing and cutting those thin models in half: just liquefy, freeze, and wrap in Photoshop. The images also socialize boys and men to have unnatural expectations. In 2012, teenager Julia Bluhm started an online petition drive on demanding that *Seventeen* magazine start publishing un-retouched photo spreads. She gained more than 90,000 male and female supporters within weeks (see more discussion in Immanuel Kant's categorical imperative earlier in the chapter).

Images of groups portrayed in advertising may have negative effects even when they do not include blatant stereotypes. Numerous studies show that the models appearing in ads do not reflect the racial and gender balance of the American population. Indeed, some groups, Native-Americans, female business executives, and people with glasses are nearly invisible in ads. Perhaps that sends the message that minorities, females and those with physical impairments are invisible in society. There are also valid concerns about targeting vulnerable groups with potentially harmful products, like selling high-alcohol malt liquor or cheap wine in low-income areas or potentially unhealthful diet aids to females.

Consumer Privacy. So, what's the first thing the clerk asks when you step up to the counter to purchase your party shoes at DSW or your tennis shoes at Dick's Sporting Goods? "Let me sign you up for our rewards program!" The coded language

REAL IMAGES Julia Bluhm (center) and thousands of others successfully petitioned *Seventeen* magazine to include only real photos of young women. *Seventeen* vowed to not retouch face or body shapes and use only healthy body images.

MEDIA&CULTURE

GUIDELINES FOR INTERNET ADVERTISING AND MARKETING

The International Chamber of Commerce developed guidelines to promote high standards of ethics on all forms (text, audio, visual) of advertising and marketing communications. The following is a subset of the original guidelines. The complete guidelines can be found at: http://www.codescentre.com/index.php/icc-code.

1 – Basic principles All marketing communications should be legal, decent, honest and truthful.

All marketing communications should be prepared with a due sense of social and professional responsibility and should conform to the principles of fair competition, as generally accepted in business.

No communication should be such as to impair public confidence in marketing.

2 – Decency Marketing communications should not contain statements or audio or visual treatments which offend standards of decency currently prevailing in the country and culture concerned.

3 – Honesty Marketing communications should be so framed as not to abuse the trust of consumers or exploit their lack of experience or knowledge.

Relevant factors likely to affect consumers' decisions should be communicated in such a way and at such a time that consumers can take them into account.

4 – Social responsibility Marketing communications should respect human dignity and should not incite or condone any form of discrimination, including that based upon race, national origin, religion, gender, age, disability or sexual orientation. Marketing communications should not without justifiable reason play on fear or exploit misfortune or suffering. Marketing communications should not appear to condone or incite violent, unlawful or anti-social behavior. Marketing communications should not play on superstition.

5 – Truthfulness Marketing communications should be truthful and not misleading.

Marketing communications should not contain any statement, claim or audio or visual treatment which, directly or by implication, omission, ambiguity or exaggeration, is likely to mislead the consumer.

6 – Use of technical/scientific data and terminology Marketing communications should not: misuse technical data, e.g. research results or quotations from technical and scientific publications; present statistics in such a way as to exaggerate the validity of a product claim; use scientific terminology or vocabulary in such a way as falsely to suggest that a product claim has scientific validity.

7 – Use of "free" and "guarantee" substantiated.

8 – Substantiation Descriptions, claims or illustrations relating to verifiable facts in marketing communications should be capable of substantiation. Such substantiation should be available so that evidence can be produced without delay and upon request to the self-regulatory organizations responsible for the implementation of the Code.

9 – Identification Marketing communications should be clearly distinguishable as such, whatever their form and whatever the medium used. When an advertisement appears in a medium containing news or editorial matter, it should be so presented that it is readily recognizable as an advertisement and the identity of the advertiser should be apparent.

Marketing communications should not misrepresent their true commercial purpose. Hence a communication promoting the sale of a product should not be disguised as for example market research, consumer surveys, user-generated content, private blogs or independent reviews.

10 – Identity The identity of the marketer should be apparent. Marketing communications should, where appropriate, include contact information to enable the consumer to get in touch with the marketer without difficulty.

11 – Comparisons Marketing communications containing comparisons should be so designed that the comparison is not likely to mislead, and should comply with the principles of fair competition. Points of comparison should be based on facts that can be substantiated and should not be unfairly selected.

12 – Denigration Marketing communications should not denigrate any person or group of persons, firm, organization, industrial or commercial activity, profession or product, or seek to bring it or them into public contempt or ridicule.

13 – Testimonials

14 – Portrayal or imitation of persons and references to personal property

15 – Exploitation of goodwill

16 – Imitation Marketing communications should not imitate those of another marketer in any way likely to mislead or confuse the consumer, for example through the general layout, text, slogan, visual treatment, music or sound effects.

17 – Safety and health Marketing communications should not, without justification on educational or social grounds, contain any visual portrayal or any description of potentially dangerous practices, or situations which show a disregard for safety or health, as defined by local national standards. Instructions for use should include appropriate safety warnings and, where necessary, disclaimers.

Children should be shown to be under adult supervision whenever a product or an activity involves a safety risk.

18 – Children and young people Special care should be taken in marketing communications directed to or featuring children or young people. The following provisions apply to marketing communications addressed to children and young people as defined in national laws and regulations relevant to such communications.

- Such communications should not undermine positive social behavior, lifestyles and attitudes;

- Products unsuitable for children or young people should not be advertised in media targeted to them, and advertisements directed to children or young people should not be inserted in media where the editorial matter is unsuitable for them

19 – Data protection and privacy When collecting personal data from individuals, care should be taken to respect and protect their privacy by complying with relevant rules and regulations.

Collection of data and notice When personal information is collected from consumers, it is essential to ensure that the individuals concerned are aware of the purpose of the collection and of any intention to transfer the data to a third party for that third party's marketing purposes.

Security of processing Adequate security measures should be in place, having regard to the sensitivity of the information, in order to prevent unauthorized access to, or disclosure of, the personal data.

CHILDREN'S PERSONAL INFORMATION

Privacy policy

Rights of the consumer Appropriate measures should be taken to ensure that consumers understand and exercise their rights to opt out of marketing lists (including the right to sign on to general preference (services); to require that their data are not made available to third parties for their marketing purposes; and to rectify incorrect data which are held about them.

20 – Transparency on cost of communication

21 – Unsolicited products and undisclosed costs

22 – Environmental behavior

23 – Responsibility

24 – Effect of subsequent redress for contravention

25 – Implementation

26 – Respect for self-regulatory decisions

Source: International Chamber of Commerce, The World Business Organization, found at **http://www.codescentre.com/index.php/icc-code.**

---

from some companies is "Our company wants all of your contact information, and we want to record your purchases." Yikes! The ability to compile massive individual files of consumer and media behavior data takes market segmentation to the extreme, making it possible to address consumers as individuals, which is the practice of relationship marketing. However, this type of research is also important in data mining, which allows advertisers to sift through huge databases to come up with unique market segments, such as hair-care product users who use hair treatments and like to talk about them with their friends.

These capabilities raise concerns about the misuse of personal information collected and stored through databases and websites. Many websites require the disclosure of your personal information including name, address, telephone number, and credit card numbers. They can also track your keystrokes while at their websites, collate that information with information obtained from your visits to other websites and from your own computer, merge it with consumer credit information from the offline world, and sell the information on you to third parties (see Chapter 11).

Industry self-regulation has thus far been the preferred method of dealing with privacy issues. The Federal Trade Commission issued "Rules of the Road" guidelines that require websites to disclose their privacy policies, and privacy certification authorities have been established to monitor compliance: www.ftc.gov/bcp/edu/pubs/business/ecommerce/bus28.shtm. However, websites presenting these disclosures may seem to give the appearance of trustworthiness, whereas in fact they only inform the website visitor *how* their privacy will be invaded (LaRose & Rifon, 2006). Thus, consumer privacy protection is still largely a matter of the ethical choices made by website proprietors.

Intrusiveness. It's even at the gas pumps! The ubiquitous nature of advertising has raised another type of privacy question: are there places that should be protected from advertising? In recent years, advertising has appeared on speaker boxes at gas stations, on eggs, on parking meters, and in public bathroom stalls. Proposals have been made to put commercial messages on postage stamps. Now marketers send attractive, young undercover marketing representatives to cyber cafés and bars to plant plugs for computers and liquor products in casual conversations. Consumers are often annoyed when they are powerless to separate themselves from commercialism. Telemarketers interrupt family meals. Advertisers tie up fax machines and spam e-mails, and they use satellite channels, such as Channel One, for commercials shown in public schools, a domain that was previously commercial-free.

With the exception of the Do Not Call lists for telemarketers, recent anti-spam legislation, and restrictions on cigarette advertising, there is little legal protection from the advertising barrage. Advertising on broadcast network television is limited by a voluntary agreement among broadcasters, and most media organizations have standards that prohibit ads for certain products, such as condoms. Other than that, advertisers enjoy broad free-speech protections, so incessant advertising bombardment comes down to a choice between ethics and commerce for the advertiser.

Subliminal Messages in Media. You can receive messages without even knowing it. Subliminal ads are words and messages that are

IT'S EVERYWHERE! IT'S EVERYWHERE! Should we be confronted with advertising every moment of our lives?

presented below the audience's level of awareness, and were banned by the Federal Communications Commission. One type of subliminal messaging is product insertions in movies that promote power of suggestion: you see actors drinking cokes in a movie and soon you want a coke to drink. Some subliminal messages are in the form of faint writing on images that only your subconscious sees. And, another type is the insertion of frames into a movie that flip by so quickly that you don't realize you are seeing something other than what is in the surrounding frames. Disney animated movies insert all types of sexual messaging, from the word "SEX" in *The Lion King* to nude women in *The Rescuers*, according to The Official Subliminal Messaging Blog (www.subliminal-messaging.com).

Deceptive Advertising. In order to preserve their good name, most advertisers go to great lengths to avoid deceptive advertising. However, blunders and differences of opinions can happen. For example, Weight Watchers sued Jenny Craig over "misleading and deceptive ads" in which Jenny Craig compares the two programs in a study that Weight Watchers said never happened and is not backed by scientific fact. The government does not usually regulate what is called puffery, or exaggerated assertions in advertising that can't be proved. Puffery ranges from small-business claims, such as "best pizza in the world," to national slogans, such as Gillette's "the best a man can get." These statements, though seemingly harmless on the surface, raise a number of questions about truth in advertising. At which point should advertisers be required to substantiate their claims? Are particular audiences, such as children, more vulnerable to puffery? Is it up to the government to monitor the total range of deception in the advertising industry? Is puffery "deceptive" in the same way as falsehood?

RESEARCH ETHICS

Communications research is a vital component of many media professions. It is everywhere,: from surveys appearing in your e-mail to phone calls at home to the questionnaires your professor asks you to fill out in class. Sometimes you try to make it stop, but that only triggers more mailings and phone calls (because you responded at all), and urgings to "please take the survey if you want extra credit," as the researchers make further attempts to get you to complete their study.

What gives the researchers the right to intrude? It is important to remember that both society and you can benefit from your cooperation in research studies. Ratings, reader surveys, and cable subscriber surveys provide the feedback that the media industry needs to serve you better. The studies that social scientists conduct help increase our knowledge of the role that communications media play in society (see Chapter 14), or they help to inform public policy debates. Your opinions truly do count in communications research studies, so you should provide them willingly and honestly when you can.

However, not all surveys are legitimate, and not all researchers adhere to accepted ethical guidelines. This is a special problem with phone surveys. Too many times, what starts out as a survey winds up being a sales pitch. If you don't go along, the so-called interviewer may resort to abuse, begging, or intimidation to keep you on the line. The information you give, along with your name, address, and phone number, may be turned over to direct marketers who put you at the top of their "sucker lists." In the most blatant cases, the interviewer will suddenly turn salesperson on you while you are still on the phone.

The Do Not Call list offers a little protection, except in the last case, since researchers are exempt. Such "researchers" are acting unethically by misrepresenting themselves and the purpose of their calls (see Media & Culture, Article 9, Identification, on p. 493). According to the ethical guidelines of the American Association for Public Opinion Research, professional researchers may not lie to you or coerce you in any way. All information that can be used to identify you through your responses must be kept confidential and your name may not be disclosed for nonresearch purposes (marketing, for instance).

Academic researchers must adhere to even stricter standards. The American Psychological Association (APA), for example, expects ethical researchers to stress that your participation is voluntary and that you may withdraw at any time. They should seek your informed consent to participate, after telling you of the nature of the study and the amount of time—or other commitment—that is expected of you. And, if you are participating in the study for extra credit in a class, an alternative activity should be available by which you could earn the same credit.

Experimental and ethnographic studies raise their own issues. Experimental manipulations (such as those that administer simulated electrical shocks) can have harmful psychological effects on participants. Ethnographic studies that observe people in Internet discussion groups may violate the privacy of participants if they have an expectation that they are "speaking" to a closed group of associates. Only content analysis studies are completely free of human subjects' ethics concerns.

Most colleges and universities have a human subjects committee and a set of guidelines mandated by the federal government to safeguard your rights as a research subject. Such committees review and approve research studies prior to their implementation, especially if an experimental design involving deception is used or if sensitive information (such as questions about sexually transmitted disease) is collected. Some human subjects committees also uphold the APA guidelines and have special provisions of their own. Other human subjects committees may require that all projects, including interviews and surveys, be approved by them.

CONSUMER ETHICS

In the evolving world of innovative digital media, an important change is that the receiver, or audience, for the media is also the source of media content (see Chapter 1). That raises ethical issues for you, the audience.

Web Surfing. Sometimes it may seem that the Internet has no rules, but that is not true. Most Internet providers have a code of ethics on their home page under "Acceptable Uses" or "User Policy." These are guidelines, not laws, but the penalty for disobeying them can be the heavy Internet users' equivalent of "death": termination of your account. Some general rules to follow:

Harassment. Here the golden rule might apply. If you don't like receiving abusive e-mail, spam, or "mail bombs" of repetitive, unwanted messages, then it might be a good idea not to send them either. "Trolling"—making provocative statements in newsgroups to get people to visit your website or buy your client's project, for example—might also be avoided. If your account is at a university, school authorities will take an especially dim view of sexual or racial harassment,

EXPLAINING BAD DECISIONS Thousands of readers denounced Rupert Murdoch's decision to publish pictures of a naked Prince Harry on vacation in Las Vegas. Less than a year earlier, the U.K. Parliament declared Murdoch unfit to lead a media company because News Corp. used bribery and phone hacking to get private information.

and it may have legal or disciplinary consequences far beyond cancellation of your e-mail privileges.

Misrepresentation. Americans are swindled out of millions of dollars each year because of fraud— sometimes as people posing as FBI agents or banks wanting your account numbers or "friends" needing you to send money. However, if "no misrepresentation" is your "categorical imperative" it also precludes using someone else's name to sign up for services or listservs. Of course, if you are in a multiuser game or another Internet environment where everyone has a false identity and everyone knows and agrees on the rules, this "misrepresentation" is acceptable. That's an example of adapting your ethics to the situation. However, "stealing" someone's identity online is a serious issue that could create real damage to the person you are pretending to be.

Hacking. Some forms of hacking are unlawful, such as gaining unauthorized access to people's telephones (a la Rupert Murdoch style), bank accounts, or computers and stealing credit card numbers. But sabotaging other people's websites and writing malicious programs to distribute on the Internet are unethical as well. You may think that "the greater good" is served by defacing a particular website, but the owners of the site and their visitors certainly won't agree.

Your own provider may have additional guidelines. Universities, for example, generally have a policy that prohibits the commercial use of the Internet. Using your Web page to promote your rock band or your favorite politician might get you into trouble, and using it to sell pirated recordings of Grateful Dead or Rihanna concerts almost certainly will.

Providers also vary in how they check for violations. Some respond only to complaints, whereas others take it upon themselves to seek out abusers by monitoring chat rooms and discussion areas. Also, be advised that if your e-mail or website is an organizational account (and that does include student accounts) you have no right to privacy. Employers (and university administrators) have the legal right to inspect your e-mail for violations of their acceptable uses policies. The FBI is working with a trade group, the Information Technology Association of America, to promulgate ethical guidelines to young Internet users, their schools, and their parents. These are phrased as biblical commandments, examples of what Kant called "categorical imperatives":

Thou shalt not vandalize Web pages.

Thou shalt not shut down websites.

Sharing or Stealing? Intellectual property rights are now on a collision course with the freewheeling culture of the Internet. Let there be no doubt, it is unlawful to share copyrighted music and video files over the Internet without permission from (and also payment to) the copyright owner (see Chapter 15). You may call it "sharing" or "downloading," but in fact it is stealing. The Recording Industry Association of America and the Motion Picture Association of America have abandoned the strategy of prosecuting individual downloaders, at least for now, so the ethics issue remains important. Like speeding and underage drinking, file sharing is illegal but the odds of getting caught seem small. So what weak ethical justification can you produce? I won't get caught? Everyone else is doing it? The Big Media are ripping us all off? I can't afford the CD anyway?

Social Media User Ethics. As we saw earlier, proprietors of social media websites are ethically challenged, so you the user need to supply ethical standards. You might consider refusing requests from underage friends (i.e., under age 13) to discourage them from using social media that have a real potential of harming them. You should mind your own online behavior, refraining from making posts that are certain to provoke hostility or encourage lewdness and drunkeness. Don't disclose the private information of others: if they are careful not to reveal their home address, phone number, or current whereabouts you should not disclose those, either. When you see inappropriate content take your "friends" to task and report it to the system administrator. Be sure to observe the journalistic ethics discussed previously. Even if you do not aspire to be an online journalist, you must respect the rights of private citizens in your tweets and blog posts. You are not free to "dish the dirt" on everyone you know as they do in the tabloids. And, private citizens and businesses can sue you if they feel you have besmirched their reputations.

Plagiarism. Another ethical dilemma for students is downloading material from the Internet into term papers, or downloading (or even buying) entire papers. Some sites offer term papers for sale (we won't tell you where), but many students use Google to find relevant snippets of documents and cut and paste them into their own papers. It's so easy! However, both are plagiarism.

Perhaps you would like some nice graphics to spice up your paper (and fill out the minimum page requirement)? Don't be tempted! Copying just about anything from a website or from a print publication is probably a copyright violation unless you obtain permission from the author. Sometimes the site explicitly says that you are free to use the images there as long as you credit the source, but you have to be sure that the site from which you copied owns the rights to the work in the first place. There are many online sources of "free" graphics, called *clip art* (for example, http://www.clipart.com), but be careful to read the fine print at the bottom of the page. Some demand citation or permission, and others limit use to offline applications. However, even if citation is not required, copying someone else's diagram, photo, or artwork into your paper is as much an act of plagiarism as copying their words.

Most colleges and universities have honor codes that specifically prohibit plagiarism, with penalties ranging from flunking the assignment to failing the course to expulsion from the program or university. Just so we are clear, plagiarism is not only a copyright violation but also a breach of your school's honor code, even when you take the trouble to look up synonyms for a few words and rewrite the lead sentences. Don't use Wikipedia as a guide to organize your paper. Even copying the order in which the arguments are made in someone else's work is plagiarism. You need to quote and cite exactly what you copy and paraphrase and

STOP&REVIEW

1. Why should we care about entertainment ethics? What are some of the concerns?

2. What does the International Chamber of Commerce guidelines say about data protection and privacy information?

3. What are your rights as a research subject?

4. What is the problem with stereotyping in advertising and other media?

5. What are some forms of plagiarism in class assignments, and what can happen if caught?

cite ideas that you borrow. And, having a reference to the work containing the paragraph you are stealing somewhere else in your paper does not cover you; every quote you copy or paraphrase must be properly cited at the point it is found in the text.

Beware—professors can Google, too, and can turn up the works you steal from. And they have tools like http://www.turnitin.com that can pick out passages that were edited to replace keywords. So how many words is it ethically acceptable to copy? None! You need to reinterpret everything, process it in your own words and thoughts, and cite the sources you have used for inspiration. Don't copy and paste information for your notes; reinterpret the information in your own words as you attribute.

SUMMARY&REVIEW

WHAT ARE MEDIA ETHICS?

Ethics guide communicators in how to behave in situations in which their activities may have a negative impact on others.

WHAT ARE THE MAIN AREAS OF CONCERN IN JOURNALISM ETHICS?

The main ethical issues that arise in communications media are accuracy or truthfulness, fairness and responsibility of treatment, privacy for media subjects and people in information services, and respect for the intellectual property or ideas of others.

WHAT ARE SOME OF THE BASIC ETHICAL PRINCIPLES?

Some are absolute standards. Kant's categorical imperative directs us to act according to rules that we would like to see universally applied. The "veil of ignorance" involves treating all members of society equally. Other principles make judgments more relative to situations. With situation ethics, for example, moral ideas and judgments must be made in the context of the situation at hand. According to Aristotle's golden mean, "moral virtue is appropriate location between two extremes." Mill's principle of utility states that we should "seek the greatest happiness for the greatest number." Dewey's Pragmatic Ethics ask us to judge actions by their results.

WHAT ARE THE MAJOR CODES OF ETHICS FOR COMMUNICATORS?

The Society of Professional Journalists' Code of Ethics and the Public Relations Society of America's Code of Professional Standards.

WHAT IS POTTER'S BOX?

Developed by Harvard divinity professor Ralph Potter, Potter's Box is a process approach to deciding on ethical actions. In four stages, one defines the facts of the issue, identifies the different values for choices that can be made, looks for general principles that underlie the options identified, and clarifies the ethical priorities.

WHAT ARE THE BASIC ETHICAL PRINCIPLES FOR JOURNALISM?

Journalists are not to fabricate evidence, make up quotes, create hypothetical individuals to focus stories around, or create or manipulate misleading photographs, any of which might deceive the public. They avoid favoritism or partisanship in coverage; protect sources; and avoid corruption, bribery, or accepting favors. Sensationalism in news coverage can affect the process of legal trials. It can affect perceptions of violence, fear, and racial tensions. Pressure to improve ratings or sales can lead to overdramatizing sensational elements and compromising news values. Corporate strategies and vertical integration can lead to unfairly favoring in-house interests.

Reporters are usually concerned about protecting their sources, but they also need to refer to them as explicitly as possible to increase the credibility of what they write. Confidentiality of sources is crucial to reporters, both to protect those sources and to gain and maintain access to them. Reporters must make decisions about when to disturb the privacy of individuals.

WHAT ARE THE ETHICAL ISSUES IN PUBLIC RELATIONS?

PR practitioners should deal fairly and responsibly with both clients and the public, not harming the public interest. If a practice is in the best interest of the community, then it probably is in the best interests of the organization. Most practitioners would prefer to be pro-active in their public responsibilities, rather than deal with crisis communications—having to react to and clean up a disaster. Some practitioners have to decide between their own moral compass of what is right and the requests of corporate executives who want to make more money at all costs (and who might not have had an ethics class).

WHAT ARE THE ETHICAL RESPONSIBILITIES OF ENTERTAINMENT PRODUCERS?

Should producers avoid content that can harm their audience? Those who hold the idea of social responsibility for media professionals would say yes, but most entertainment creators say no. Research shows that entertainment may have considerable impact, but industry groups minimize social effects and say that people should make more responsible choices about what they consume.

WHAT ARE THE ETHICS ISSUES FOR ADVERTISING?

In advertising, ethics is about the process of selecting and balancing moral values against profits when writing, designing, or placing advertisements; protecting privacy in direct marketing; and avoiding promotion of harmful products and deceptive advertising.

WHAT ETHICAL BEHAVIOR SHOULD INTERNET USERS CONSIDER?

Internet users should avoid harassment of other users, not misrepresent themselves or others, not violate others' privacy, not use Web sources for plagiarism, and they should obtain permission for material they copy onto their websites.

WHAT ARE THE MAIN ETHICAL ISSUES FOR MEDIA CONSUMERS?

Consumers owe reasonable compensation to people who produce intellectual property—the things you read, watch, and listen to—so don't illegally download copyrighted music or videos.

THINKING CRITICALLY
ABOUT THE MEDIA

1. Use Potter's Box to analyze the examples of page 476.

2. Using the ethical principle of your choice, decide if a journalist could justify revealing a source, rather than spending months in jail for contempt.

3. If it is true that exposure to violent TV harms young children? Please explain.

4. How do you ethically justify "sharing" music on the Internet? How would you explain that position to Carly Rae Jepsen?

5. What is plagiarism and how can you avoid it?

 **KEY TERMS**

ethics (p. 475)	junket (p. 487)
freebies (p. 487)	morality (p. 475)

WHAT'S ON IN JAPAN IS SOMETIMES THE SAME as what's on where you live. A growing number of countries are not only taking in U.S. imports, but also creating their own media and exporting to other countries.

17

GLOBAL COMMUNICATIONS MEDIA

ACTING GLOBALLY, REGIONALLY, AND NATIONALLY

The global aspect of media is very striking. *The Simpsons* was on television in over 60 countries in 2011, while the last *Harry Potter* covered many movie and video screens worldwide, making far more money outside than inside the United States. Young women in South Korea outraged their elders by modeling their lives on *Sex and the City*. Australian media magnate Rupert Murdoch's various companies reach about three-fourths of the globe with satellite TV signals and even more countries with movies and TV programs.

Global media are not just a Hollywood monopoly anymore. In fact, some major U.S. media companies are or have recently been owned by Japanese (Sony) or Canadian (Warner Records) companies. Mexican and Brazilian soap operas (telenovelas) reach as many countries as *Friends* and are extremely popular in some places, such as Eastern Europe and Central Asia (see Figure 17.1). Facebook operates in dozens of countries worldwide, but faces significant local competition in parts of the world, from companies such as Renren in China. When AT&T invested in foreign telecommunications companies, it had to compete closely with British Telecom (Great Britain) and Telefónica (Spain) abroad and with T-Mobile (Germany) in the United States.

1865	ITU (International Telecommunication Union) started as the International Telegraph Union	1983	United States pulls out of UNESCO to protest its critique of unfair media flows across borders
1914– 1945	World War I and II permit Hollywood to outpace competitors	1990	Satellite TV begins to compete with national control of television
1939	Hollywood pulls ahead of other film producers	2003	ITU hosts World Summit on the Information Society to promote use of Internet in poorer countries
1945	Hollywood gains advantage over other distributors	2010	Google violates European Union privacy protections by collecting street-level data.
1948	UN founded, incorporating ITU, starting UNESCO	2012	Facebook has 800 million members worldwide
1976– 1983	UNESCO hosts critical discussion for proposals for a New World Information Order		

Although American-made films, TV programs, and music remain attractive to world audiences, global, regional, national, and local media industries, audiences, and regulatory bodies are emerging, with a wide variety of ideas, genres, and agendas. More countries are competing to sell or transmit media to others. Some, such as Mexico, Brazil, India, and Hong Kong, compete worldwide. Egypt and Lebanon dominate a regional market in the Middle East characterized by shared geography, language, and culture, similar to the regional market for Mexico that includes U.S. Hispanics.

Globalization of media is probably most pervasive at the level of technology and media industry models—ways of organizing and creating

> [**Globalization** is reducing differences that existed between nations in time, space, and culture.]

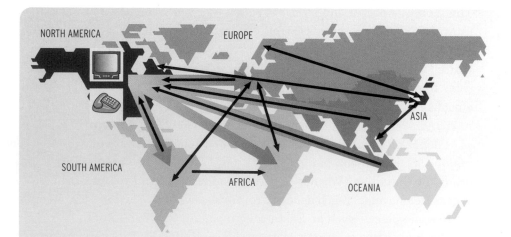

FIGURE 17.1 INTERNATIONAL MEDIA FLOWS Although the United States has initially dominated international flows in most media, other countries are beginning to sell more media and information to each other. (In the figure, wider arrows indicate heavier flows.)

media. The world is becoming a more integrated market based in capitalist, or marketplace, economics. This exerts pressures on nations to make media more commercial, supported by advertising, aimed at consumers, and to privatize telecommunications companies that were once government owned.

Most countries produce increasing amounts of their own television, music, and magazines. But if they produce them by drawing on U.S., British, or Japanese models and genre ideas or formats licensed from media companies headquartered in those countries, those "national" media products are still at least somewhat globalized. And even if a national soap opera reflects largely local culture in its plot and characters, it still helps Colgate-Palmolive and other multinational firms sell soap in yet another part of the global market. Roland Robertson (1995) called such combinations **glocal**—local productions done with global forms and ideas.

[**Glocal** is local people borrowing or adapting global ideas.]

But at the same time, truly globalized markets are emerging as many youth the world over are exposed to the Internet and shop online for the latest fashions and consumer products. Procter and Gamble finds that teenage girls everywhere seem to have the same questions about puberty, for example, so they can simply translate the material on their website into 40 different languages instead of developing a separate website in each country. Controversy rages about global campaigns, however, and other firms find it better to go local in their strategies.

Global institutions and companies also have a major impact. Global standards bodies such as the International Telecommunications Union (ITU) allocate satellite orbits, determine broadcast frequencies, and define the standards for telephones, mobile phones, faxes, and Internet connections. The ITU would like to allocate Internet domains and other resources, too, but the U.S. opposes that idea. Global telecom companies, like Cable & Wireless, run much of the world's communications infrastructure of optical fiber cables, satellites, and high-speed lines. Global media companies, like Rupert Murdoch's News Corporation, not only reach people directly with media but also force domestic competitors to react to them. When Murdoch's Star TV started broadcasting in India, the state television broadcaster had to respond with more competitive entertainment or lose its audience. However, when Murdoch went into China, he had to bend to their rules to do business, which shows that global companies are not equally powerful everywhere.

The other major aspect of globalization is the increasingly worldwide penetration of media technology. All nations now have some people using the Internet and satellite television. Those new media can greatly increase global reach and access for some. Global new media reach co-exists with a global digital divide that makes the media experience of the rich much more different from that of the poor than it was 20 years ago, when both primarily relied on some form of television.

REGIONALIZATION

Regionalization of media is growing as well. In several regions of the world (such as Europe, North and South America, and the Middle East), magazines, newspapers, and books have been transported easily across borders for centuries. Radio, television, and satellite television signals also spilled directly

[**Regionalization** links nations together based on geographic, cultural, linguistic, and historical commonalities.]

from one country to its neighbor. Well over half of the Canadian population can directly receive U.S. radio and television signals, for example.

In the European Union (EU) and the North American Free Trade Agreement regions (NAFTA—Canada, the United States, Mexico), governments have negotiated agreements on how to handle such media border crossings. The EU went further in 1989 to try to have "television without frontiers" within the EU. However, the attempt to produce programming for a Europewide television market proved difficult, despite being promoted heavily by the European Union. Europeans are still divided by language and culture. Historically, many haven't wanted to watch, read, or listen in another language (Schlesinger, 1991). The French still prefer French television to German or British television. However, Europeans are more willing to listen to other nations' music, with Gotye and Kimbra (from Australia and New Zealand, respectively) topping the charts in several European countries as well as the United States in 2012. So the music industry has regionalized somewhat farther in Europe than television, even as some countries, particularly France, still tend to protect their national film industries.

CULTURAL PROXIMITY

Although geographical closeness or proximity helps media cross borders, language and culture seem more important than geography, as the example of Europe shows. It seems that people there and elsewhere tend to look for television programming, Internet sites, and music that are more culturally proximate.

Cultural proximity is the desire for cultural products as similar as possible to one's own language, culture, history, and values. Thus, even though people often like the cosmopolitan appeal of some European or American television, movies, and music, they tend to choose most of their media from their own or a similar culture.

Language is a crucial divider of media markets. Historically, trade in television between countries has been shaped by language (Wildman & Siwek, 1988), and language seems to be shaping music and Internet patterns as well. Language provides a strong natural barrier to media imports. The United States is a prime example. Most of what little imported television and film Americans watch comes from Great Britain, New Zealand, or Australia, culturally similar English-speaking countries. Likewise, British pop music is widely accepted, whereas other musicians such as the Swedish group The Hives have to sing in English to break into the U.S. market. This also indicates a counter-trend, that many global youth are getting more used to listening to music in English.

Besides language, other aspects of culture are important in defining audiences: jokes, slang, historical references, political references, gossip about stars, and remarks about current people and events are often culture- or nation-specific. Such cues, where they are shared across borders, can help build cross-national markets. For instance, Latin American countries used to import American situation comedies in the 1950s–60s. Now they tend to import comedy shows from each other, because the cultural proximity of Spanish-speaking Latin American nations makes slang, jokes, and references to

> **Cultural proximity** is the preference of audiences for media in their own language and culture.

current events easier to understand. This is also true for U.S. Spanish-speaking audiences, who often prefer Mexican shows to Hollywood, since Mexican (or Colombian or Venezuelan) shows feel more familiar.

However, many producers have discovered that when they make too many references to current politics, use too much slang, or otherwise focus too narrowly on current local issues, their programs are less well-received around the world. Hollywood has long experienced this dilemma. Sometimes a very popular sitcom, such as *Seinfeld,* is too specific to the United States for broad export in the global market, whereas a show such as *Sex and the City* does better abroad. Although cultural proximity is a strong factor, audiences in many countries still respond very well to some kinds of imported programs, particularly those whose emphasis is on action, sex, and violence. (Conversely, a rising trend calls for local versions of popular shows, such as the Brazilian version of *Big Brother,* in its twelfth season in 2012.) Those who prefer an imported program are also more likely to be well off, better educated, and urban. Among the few foreign, non-English-speaking genres to be hits in the United States are stylish, violent action films from Hong Kong and China, and sexy, violent cartoons from Japan. Sports are another genre with nearly universal appeal. And some elements of pop music are globalized, whereas others are localized, another example that complicates the logic of cultural proximity.

Smaller than global but larger than national, cultural-linguistic markets build on transnational cultural proximity. These markets build on common languages and common cultures that span borders. Just as the United States grew beyond its own market to export globally, a number of companies have grown beyond their original national markets to serve these cultural-linguistic markets, such as Mexico for Latin America and much of the Hispanic U.S.

NATIONAL PRODUCTION

However, even as global and cultural linguistic markets for media are all increasingly important, the main point at which media are created, regulated, and consumed remains the nation. The vast majority of media companies have been structured, at least at first, to serve national markets. National governments have far more effective control over media through station licensing, economic controls, technology controls, and subsidies than regional or global institutions or treaties. And ratings and audience research over the years tend to show that,

SEX SELLS GLOBALLY Although most countries produce an increasing number of their own TV shows, highly produced U.S. shows that emphasize sex or action adventure can still sell to many countries as has *Sex and the City*. It was so popular among Korean young women that the press and political figures were scandalized.

given a choice, people tend to prefer to see national content in media (de Sola Pool, 1983; Straubhaar, 2007; Tracey, 1988).

Nations vary considerably, however, in what they can or will do to create media. Larger, more prosperous nations can create more media content than small, poorer nations. The United States, the United Kingdom, Japan, and other industrialized countries can afford lavish production values that may overwhelm the modest productions of local media. This has been especially notable in film, where U.S. exports dominate more than in television or websites. There can be a contradictory tug-of-war between cultural proximity and imported production values.

National governments can help or hinder media growth. National goals for media, reflected in government policies, are often very different, and they significantly affect how media are structured and what they create. Some nations, like China, expect media to cooperate with government political and economic goals. Some, like Saudi Arabia, expect media to project a certain set of religious values.

THE GLOBAL MEDIA

Twenty years ago people talked about Americanization of media in the world. Today people talk more about globalization. Although American media still play a prominent role in the global scene, media industries from a number of other countries are also heavily involved across the world. There are also media whose goal is to cover a region, like Al Jazeera in the Middle East, or the globe, like the BBC World Service.

A handful of publicly traded firms dominate the most globalized part of the media system. Some of the largest are Time Warner (U.S.), Disney (U.S.), Comcast (U.S.), Rupert Murdoch's News Corporation (Australian/U.S.), DirecTV (U.S), Bertelsmann (German), Viacom (U.S.), and Sony/Columbia/TriStar (Japanese). The other main global firms are Apple (U.S.), Microsoft (U.S.), and Vivendi (French). Of the top 10–12 global media firms, seven are American. These types of companies are growing and globalizing quickly. Time Warner and Disney generated around 15 percent of their income outside of the United States in 1990, a figure that rose to over 35 percent by 2009.

Behind the top global firms is a second tier of 30 to 40 media firms that do between $1 billion and $8 billion yearly in media-related business.

Frank Micelotta/Getty Images

BONO, FROM GLOBAL SUPERSTAR TO GLOBAL DEVELOPMENT AID ACTIVIST A number of entertainment superstars such as Bono, Shakira, or Angelina Jolie, are trying to convert the fame and symbolic capital they have acquired into a different kind of star power to try to draw people to the cause of increasing development aid for the world's poor, which all are promoting in different ways. This kind of activism goes back at least to George Harrison's Concert for Bangladesh in the early 1970s.

These firms have national or cultural-linguistic strongholds or specialize in specific global niches, as the BBC specializes in news and documentaries. Some are American (including Gannett and Cox). Most of the rest come from Europe (Hachette, Havas, EMI) or Canada (Rogers, Shaw). Some are based in East Asia (NHK, Chinese Central TV) and Latin America (TV Globo, Televisa). It is no stretch to add computer media and telecommunications, so we should add Google, Apple, and Microsoft; game companies Nintendo and Electronic Arts; and AT&T, Deutsche Telecom, and Telefónica to the list. Social media giant Facebook is also a rising force in global media.

Some media industries, such as the Hollywood film and TV studios represented by the Motion Picture Association of America, have been global since the 1920s. They control many of the companies in other countries that distributed and exhibited (in theaters) the films produced in the United States. However, the ownership of Hollywood itself became globalized. Critics scrutinized the results to see whether films produced by Sony reflected Japanese rather than American sensibilities. No real changes were found.

Record companies are similarly structured except that they have a more diverse set of origins and an even more international ownership. Parts of the music Big Three are based outside the United States, including Warner-EMI (Canada), Sony-BMG Music Group (Japan-Germany), and Vivendi-Universal (France). These companies also have large foreign branches that produce and distribute records within other markets as well as distribute American and European music.

However, as music production becomes much cheaper all over the world, more groups are recording at all levels: local, national, and regional. Those sell now in many forms—cassettes, CDs, MP3s, and streaming online. Piracy is also so prevalent in many places that groups earn a living mostly from live performances.

Still, there are some important distinctions in the ways that various media are organized around the world. In the following sections we will consider those differences and analyze the flow of media between them.

NEWS AGENCIES

News has flowed across borders for a long time. Many early newspapers and newsletters installed correspondents in other countries so that they could publish foreign news for their readers.

International news flow took a significant step forward in speed and volume with the development, in the 1840s, of newswire services based on the then-new technology of the telegraph. The U.S. Associated Press (AP), British Reuters, and Agence France Presse (AFP) were the first electronic news services, anticipating in many ways the increase in speed and volume of information that the Internet would amplify. By the 1970s, many critics asserted that the major newswire services had too much control over international news flow. They followed standard American and European definitions of what was news: disasters, sensational or unusual events, political upheaval, wars or conflicts, famous personalities, and current (versus long-term) events. Although this approach fits the Western ideal of the press as a critic and watchdog, it often produces negative coverage and images of other countries.

STOP&REVIEW

1. What is globalization?

2. What is cultural proximity?

3. What are some of the bases that define cultural-linguistic markets for media?

4. What are the main reasons why companies buy or start up media in other countries?

5. Which companies are the main global owners of media?

6. How does news flow between countries?

As radio and television became the dominant news media in many countries, the wire services developed material for them, and later, so did satellite news channels like CNN. News agencies, particularly Reuters, began to bypass the newspapers and TV networks, and reach readers directly via the Internet, although they have to compete with the many news sources now available to everyone online. Now information and reporting by a variety of people on Facebook and, particularly, Twitter have become both direct news sources for many and sources that professional news reports use in their own stories. This became particularly clear with micro-blogging in China and the Twitter role in the Arab Spring political and social revolutions of 2011.

RADIO BROADCASTING

Because the print media's reach is limited in many countries by low literacy and income levels (see Figure 17.2 on page 513), broadcast media took on increased importance. In the poorest countries, radio is still the main mass medium for many people. However, in parts of Africa and South Asia, some people do not even have access to radio because the signal doesn't reach them, they can't afford a receiver, or they don't have electricity.

International Radio. In some of the poorest countries, where domestic radio stations don't cover the whole country, people in remote areas often listen to international broadcasters. Such international radio is usually on shortwave frequencies that can carry across thousands of miles, compared to the limited range of FM and AM radio. In Africa, people in remote areas listen on shortwave to continent-spanning commercial radio stations such as Africa One, as well as to foreign-government stations such as the Voice of America (VOA), Radio France, and the BBC (Straubhaar & Boyd, 2007).

VOA and other international stations are now streamed over the Internet too. There, however, they have to compete with thousands of stations streamed in dozens of languages from many countries. Many shortwave services, including the BBC English-language radio service, have been discontinued as a result. New services have begun, however, in hotspot areas, like Radio Sawa by the United States in Arabic in the Middle East. Such international radio programs now try to use medium wave radio, which can be received by more people than short wave.

National Radio. In most countries, national and local radio become much more important than international radio. Many countries have important national radio networks, which are widely listened to, but in many places radio is becoming more local. Radio can cater to the apparently widespread audience desire for local news, local weather and information, local talk shows, and local music. In radio, the urge for cultural proximity by audiences and market segmentation by advertisers often favors the very local, although people still want to hear national and global music and news. Local music can reflect local preferences in local languages, and local news and talk tend to cover the things that most concern people in daily life. In Wales, some radio stations try to attract people to listening in Welsh in order to help keep the language alive and sell ads to the locals. Similar stations promote local languages in many places.

MUSIC

Music around the world seems to be both the most globalized and the most localized of media. Travelers to almost any country will hear a great deal of American and European music, but they will also hear an astonishing variety of local music—nearly all cultures have a musical tradition (and a market niche for it). Such traditional music usually adapts well to being recorded, played on the radio, and sold on CDs.

The strength of national and local radio has a great deal to do with a revival in national and local music around the globe. Gotye and Kimba can be heard around the world on many stations that appeal to affluent and globalized young people, but other stations are playing music by local artists as well, which tend to appeal to more middle-class, working-class, and poor people (Straubhaar, 2005).

There is a truly global music industry, based primarily in the United States and Europe, which speaks to a globalized youth culture. But there are also thriving national and regional music industries, with a wide variety of genres and audiences, which also remain popular in most countries. Distinct music genres and variations on genres have emerged, such as reggae in Jamaica and ska in Great Britain. Historically, audience tastes tend to be multilayered, with many people listening to global music, regional or national music, and local music to suit different needs and interests, including local advertisers (Colista & Leshner, 1998). Technology changes, like global flow of music files over the Internet, can increase access to U.S. music, but new technologies like Internet radio or videos on YouTube are also increasingly used for regional and national music.

Governments sometimes require that a certain proportion of nationally produced music be played on radio stations. For example, Canada requires satellite radio Sirius to include Canadian content. Some also subsidize national music industries to make sure that local music is produced. Most often, music development has been left to musicians' initiative, market forces, and audience demand. Audience members are often willing to pay for local and national music, although they also listen to and purchase global music. Music, too, is much cheaper to produce than film or television—so much so that it serves a wide variety of subcultures and market niches within and across nations, such as Turkish music among Turkish residents in Germany.

AP Photo/Andrew Medichini

POP GOES THE WORLD The success of Colombian rock/pop singer Shakira in English in the United States shows an ongoing crossover and blurring of musical categories like world, pop, and Latin music. Like Bono and others, she is using her fame to promote social causes. She focuses on children and poverty in Latin America, where she is still most intensely well-known.

One threat to both global and local music industries is piracy. In many countries, like Russia, local and national musicians simply cannot make any money at all by selling recordings, since nearly all copies sold are pirated illegally. The only way such artists support themselves is by touring and giving concerts, which deters many from being professional musicians.

A few major companies dominate international music: Vivendi-Universal, Warner, and Sony. They import and sell the dominant American and European pop music around the world. In many countries and regions, they also record and sell works by national or cultural-linguistic market artists. That gives them something of a stake in promoting those artists, both at home and abroad, when they perceive that there might be an export market. Multinational firms record Jamaican reggae and dance hall as well as Caribbean salsa and merengue, sell them at home, and also export them to the United States. Those international companies are willing to risk distributing national music recordings, because musical tastes are more diverse and the costs (and financial risks) of recording, distributing, and promoting music recordings are much lower than film or TV. So global firms end up selling both global and local music.

FILM

Of all the international media examined here, film is perhaps the most globalized and the most difficult to produce on a sustained national basis. First, film is a relatively expensive medium to produce. Even cheap feature films, paying almost nothing to actors and technicians, cost tens of thousands of dollars, and an average Hollywood film costs over $80 million. (Cheaper digital production equipment has started to change this, as seen with the proliferation of hundreds of quickly shot, low-budget Nigerian films on video, but global promotion costs continue to rise sharply.) Second, the economic success of a film is never guaranteed, so it represents an expensive, risky investment to the producer, investors, and other funding sources, which many countries are unable to sustain. Third, the distribution channels to enable a film to make money have been globalized to a degree unlike that of any other medium. Films from independent producers or from outside the English-speaking world have a hard time breaking into the international distribution system, which is largely controlled by companies associated with the Motion Picture Association of America.

However, an increasing number of firms, like Fox and Sony, do actively look for international films to distribute in the United States and abroad, as well as for opportunities to co-produce films with foreign companies. Even Disney has begun to look for international cartoons to distribute, like those of Japanese Hayao Miyazaki, such as *Ponyo* (2009). Some foreign films, like *Let the Right One In* (Sweden—2008) or *Pan's Labyrinth* (Mexico/Spain—2007), are internationally distributed and do well, but most films produced in other countries never get distributed outside their home countries. Even some of the more successful ones, such as the well-regarded original Swedish version of *Girl with the Dragon Tattoo* (2009) do less well with American audiences than U.S. remakes like the 2011 U.S. version of *Girl with the Dragon Tattoo*.

Films of significant quality and interest have been produced in many countries, but few countries are currently producing many feature films. A number of poor nations, such as the Dominican Republic, have produced only a few feature-length films in their histories—and some have made none at all. Furthermore, film production has slowed down in many countries, such as most of Latin America and Africa, as many companies have fallen into debt or suffered other economic crises. In a number of countries where film production had been heavily subsidized, governments have found themselves unable to continue support. Some countries, including France and Spain, still continue to subsidize their film industries, but this led to conflicts in trade talks (such as the World Trade Agreement)

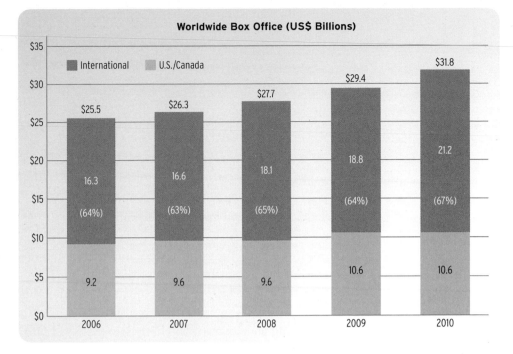

Worldwide Box Office (US$ Billions)

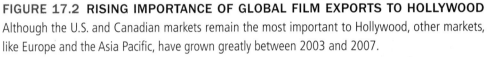

FIGURE 17.2 RISING IMPORTANCE OF GLOBAL FILM EXPORTS TO HOLLYWOOD
Although the U.S. and Canadian markets remain the most important to Hollywood, other markets, like Europe and the Asia Pacific, have grown greatly between 2003 and 2007.

with the United States, which considers these subsidies an unfair form of protectionism(U.S. Department of Commerce, 2004). The big problem is that international films, even when produced at national expense, do not break through the largely Hollywood-based control of international distribution, and most national markets, with the exception of Brazil, India, Nigeria, and China, are not big enough to make money with films that have little chance of international distribution.

The United States has dominated international film production and distribution since World War I (1914–1918). Both world wars disrupted a number of the other major international film producers (Italy, Germany, Japan, France, and Great Britain) and cut off their industries from world trade in films. This put the U.S. film industry on the road to its current dominance.

American films have succeeded in a variety of markets around the world for several reasons. One is the enormous size of the U.S. market for movies, which for many years permitted Hollywood to recover most of the costs of films in their domestic release, although now Hollywood depends increasingly on overseas sales for much of their profits. Even now, however, no other country has such a large and affluent national film audience. Second is the heterogeneous nature of the U.S. audience, which includes diverse groups that demand simple, more entertainment-oriented, and more universal films. Because of these elements, Hollywood has been the world's film production center, drawing money and talent from around the world and away from competing film industries abroad. Since the 1920s, Hollywood has drawn actors, directors, writers, and musicians from Europe, Latin America, and Asia (Guback & Varis, 1982).

Furthermore, Hollywood studios, organized under the Motion Picture Association of America, have worked together to promote exports and control overseas distribution networks. They have done so with a degree of cooperation or collusion that might be considered an anticompetitive violation of antitrust laws if it were done domestically but that has been specifically permitted overseas by the U.S. Congress under the Webb-Pomerene Act of 1918 (Guback & Varis, 1986). Specifically, American producers used that cartel monopoly power to fix prices, allocate and dominate markets, undercut and destroy other nations' film industries, and control global distribution in favor of Hollywood films, over all others.

Today the United States clearly dominates world film. American films filled over 80 percent of the theater seats in Europe in 2009. Overseas sales can more than triple those in the United States for films like *Avatar* and *How to Train Your Dragon,* so Hollywood studios come to depend on overseas markets (*MPAA, 2012*). Government protection of film industries in other countries is not surprising: they simply want to ensure that national film industries survive. Quite a few films are produced in Asia, primarily in Hong Kong and India (which has produced more films than the United States in some years). Egypt is the film center of the Arab world and Nigeria of West Africa. Brazil and Mexico produce far more than other Latin American countries. These countries show that film industries can be maintained, even in some developing countries, if the domestic market is large or if the film companies produce for a multi-country audience and market. Some countries are also getting creative with financial incentives to promote national film production. Since Brazil, for example, began letting national and international companies deduct any losses on Brazilian film investment from their taxes, film investment and production has shot up to over 30 films a year, a small number compared to the United States, Nigeria or India, but significant by international standards.

Many international producers have also started working with Hollywood in financing, distribution, or even broader co-production. Other countries, like Canada, offer sizable production incentives, which have moved Hollywood companies to shoot there. It is becoming common to shoot exteriors in one country and sound stage scenes in another, edit sound in another, and add special effects in yet another. The *Narnia* and *Lord of the Rings* films all feature British stories, actors from the United Kingdom, the United States, Australia, and New Zealand; New Zealand locations, and special effects; and U.S. financing and distribution.

VIDEO

In many countries, films are now most commonly seen on video or on television, rather than in cinema houses. In the more affluent parts of most countries, increasing numbers of the middle class and economic elite have DVDs, satellite or cable TV, and Internet downloads or streaming to watch films or TV. U.S. productions largely dominate video rental stocks as well, since the same Hollywood firms that dominate theatrical distribution supply them. Video rentals are actually somewhat more diverse, since there are parallel circuits for distributing films and television programs from local producers in China, Korea, Turkey, Nigeria and India to immigrant populations around the world who miss media from home. For example, almost any medium-size city in the United States has ethnic stores that also rent videos, movies, and television programs from "home." Plus an increasing number of countries are creating cable channels that show nationally produced movies almost exclusively, which provides a notable distribution vehicle for national films that many viewers would not otherwise see.

Film finance is also drifting off shore. Mainland China is beginning to emerge as a financial power in film production. Both private investors and a government-backed media fund are backing co-productions with Hollywood studios. The next installment of the *Iron Man* franchise, for example, is slated to be a Chinese-American co-production.

TELEVISION

Television broadcasting in many countries is divided among public, governmental, and private ownership. Because most broadcasters use the scarce VHF frequencies of the radio spectrum, relatively few channels are available and few people or groups can be involved. Television is also very expensive, too expensive for private media to make it profitable in some very poor countries. Almost all governments get involved in planning who gets to own or operate radio or television stations, which also leads many of them to get involved in controlling content.

In Africa, Asia, and Eastern Europe, governments often have owned-and-operated broadcasting systems in order to control radio and TV content. Their stated intention has usually been to use radio and television as powerful tools to develop their societies, but controlling politics is often the hidden agenda. India's state television, Doordarshan, initially tried to use television to teach better health and agricultural practices to villagers, but then-Prime Minister of India, Indira Gandhi, in the 1970s and 1980s also discovered it to be a very powerful political tool (Kumar 2006). In addition, urban and middle-class viewers of the single national channel rebelled, demanding more entertainment. Since then, Doordarshan must be content to insinuate subtle pro-development themes, such as child health care and family planning into soap operas that people like to watch (Singhal & Rogers, 2001). Satellite television after 1990 also brought in new forms of competition in much of the world, which forced broadcast television to change. This has been true in Europe, India, Turkey, several Arab nations, and several parts of Asia.

Access to television is still somewhat unequal around the globe. In some parts of the world, including much of Africa, most of the population doesn't see television, particularly outside the main cities. In Mozambique, one of the poorest countries, only around 30 to 35 percent of the population has a television, the same 30 to 35 percent who speak Portuguese, the language used on television. In contrast, most people, even among the poor, in Latin America, and East and South Asia have television. Most people in the world work very hard now to gain access to television, perhaps more than any other medium. One of the authors of this book has visited Brazilian, Peruvian, and South African homes where auto batteries power the TV sets in homes with no other electricity.

In many countries, including most of Western Europe, either governments or not-for-profit public corporations tend to operate television broadcasting, but with increasing competition. Since the 1990s, a number of these countries have also introduced commercial television, which is becoming economically and culturally powerful. The goal of public broadcasters has been to use broadcasting to promote education and culture. An example is the BBC in Great Britain. To a large extent, the public broadcasters in Europe and Japan have outpaced the U.S. Public Broadcasting System (PBS) and National Public Radio in creating more educational, informational, and cultural programming. However, in some countries, such as Italy, public broadcasters sometimes have let political parties control their news and information programs.

State broadcasters are usually supported from government funds. Public radio and television networks are often supported by audience license fees. This is in order to maintain independence from both government budget control and commercial pressures by advertisers. In Britain and Japan, everyone who owns a radio or a television set pays an annual license fee. That fee goes directly to the public broadcasters (BBC in Britain and NHK in Japan), who use it to finance program production and development. Some audiences in Great Britain have complained that programming tends to be elitist and stiff. In 2007, the hallowed and venerable "beeb," as it is known, was told point blank by the British government to be more entertaining if it wanted its license renewed in the future. Faced with a growing unwillingness on the part of the government to support higher license fees the "beeb" was forced to make deep cuts in its staff and cut back on original programming in 2012.

Broadcasting has mostly been privately owned in Canada, Central America, and South America, in part because of the strong influence of U.S. media corporations and advertisers, who promoted commercial approaches in the 1930s and 1940s (Schwoch, 1990). However, government controls over private broadcasters have varied among these countries. In contrast to the minimal controls in the United States, there are strict controls in Canada, where the government has tried to restrict the importation of programs from the United States. Many Latin American and Eastern European governments have exerted strong control over private broadcasters to obtain political support, mostly through economic pressures such as selectively awarding government advertising to supportive broadcasters. In most of the private broadcasting systems, entertainment programming has dominated to meet the demands of advertisers for large audiences.

There is a general recent tendency in European, Asian, and other countries to increase private commercial broadcasting and reduce government and public ownership. Publics often push for more broadcast choices, and advertisers, both foreign and local, push to have commercial stations to put advertising on. Most countries have liberalized competition in broadcasting by permitting new private companies and individuals to enter the market. They often come from print publishing, such as Silvio Berlusconi, ex-prime minister of Italy, who still controls the three major private Italian television networks. Many countries also **privatized** some public or government broadcast stations and networks.

DRAWING POWER In many places, people see TV as so important that it comes before almost all other purchases. Even temporary shelters like this one may have a dish to receive satellite TV.

AP Photo/Enric Marti

[**Privatizing** government assets refers to selling them to private owners.]

Sometimes this was to reduce government political control over state stations, such as when France privatized some of the state television networks. Sometimes, too, privatizing was done to take broadcasting out of the public budget and make it privately supported through advertising. Some public broadcasters are feeling budget pressures, which also tends to turn them to advertising as an alternative source of funding.

Television Flows. Television has a much more complicated flow between countries than film. American television programs are very common and visible globally, but many other producers now sell programs to national and transnational cultural linguistic markets as well. At first, U.S. film studios and independent producers sold television programs worldwide with the same economic and cultural advantages that American film producers had enjoyed. In the 1960s–1970s, American films, sitcoms, action-adventures, and cartoons flooded into many other countries. Since then, many countries have begun to create much of their own television and, to lesser degree, to buy more from other countries besides the United States.

A number of countries, from Great Britain to Taiwan, established quotas limiting the amount of imported television programming that can be shown. In 1989, the European Economic Community required member nations to carry at least 50 percent of television programming produced within Europe. Hollywood and U.S. government officials protested these rules at trade talks in the World Trade Organization and in regional treaties like the North American Free Trade Agreement (NAFTA). However, quotas or barriers to the import of film and television lose some of their force when young, tech-savvy viewers can download *Sex and the City* in Beijing even though those shows are not broadcast or carried on local cable.

American television exports represent a steadily increasing share of television producers' profits. Because many shows made more money overseas than in the United States, a number of American producers began to shape their programs to anticipate and maximize overseas sales in the 1980s and 1990s (Waxman, 1998). However, now the high cost of U.S. TV programs also limits their distribution. The fees charged to foreign stations are set in relation to ratings, which sometimes makes U.S. shows more expensive than domestic ones. In other cases, lower local ratings often relegate foreign shows to late-night hours when few are watching.

American television programs are also facing increased competition in a number of areas. More nations at

IMPORTED AND EXPORTED TELEVISION Just as adaptations of formats foreign television shows like *American Idol* (originally a British show called *Pop Idol*) have become smash hits in the US, American created formats are very successful in foreign markets. Adaptation is a game that everyone seems to be playing.

WORLD VIEW

SOAP OPERAS AROUND THE WORLD

Although American soap operas are still popular in many other countries, now they have to compete with soaps from Mexico and Hong Kong. In Latin America, telenovelas run in prime time and usually depict romance, family drama, and upward mobility. The archetypal telenovela for many was *Simplemente Maria*, about a Peruvian peasant girl who moves to the city, works as a maid, saves money, buys a sewing machine, and becomes a successful seamstress. All sewing machines in Lima sold out after that plot development. Mexico, India, and South Africa have all used soap operas to convey themes that development planners want to communicate, such as family planning in Mexico and India, and working against domestic violence in South Africa. On the commercial side, Brazilian telenovelas' product placement often represents close to 50 percent of the advertising money spent on the program. Telenovelas are also hot exports, still playing to large audiences in Romania, Russia, and even China.

Martial arts dramas from Hong Kong and China follow some soap opera themes—romance, love, family intrigues, and rivalries—but add martial arts action, dramatic battles, historical plots, and period costumes. These are popular throughout Asia. Japan makes its own versions, focused on the Samurai era and featuring a similar mix of rugged heroes, beautiful heroines, and battles. These programs are also becoming popular worldwide. Korea has exported contemporary family and romance melodrama throughout East Asia.

Indian soap operas can be epic, mythological, and even religious. One of the first popular soap operas retold the national Hindu religious epic *The Ramayana*, the story of the Hindu gods. It had a powerful effect according to critics, who saw it as reinforcing nationalist Hindu political parties and standardizing throughout India a previously diverse set of versions of *The Ramayana*.

Many of these series are also popular in other markets, especially those that share languages and cultures. Telenovelas now sell to all of Latin America; Hong Kong soaps sell in southern China and feature on satellite Star TV; and Indian soaps are popular even in neighboring (and rival) Pakistan. Some of these exporters are also breaking into the global market. Mexican soap operas are popular now in Eastern Europe, and Hong Kong martial arts serials can be seen in Los Angeles dubbed into Spanish. If the theme is interesting enough—like in a recent Colombian telenovela, *Yo soy Betty la fea* (I Am Betty the Ugly Girl), about a spunky girl dismissed by the fashionistas she works with—then people who don't even speak the language watch the program for its emotional impact. This was true of many English-language viewers when *Betty* played on Spanish-language television in the United States in 2001. (*Betty* touched such a nerve in the United States that in 2006–2010 ABC aired its own version, called *Ugly Betty*, and the series was quickly nominated for a Golden Globe award.)

What do people find most interesting about international soap operas, like telenovelas? Colombian professor Jesus Martín-Barbero thinks that melodrama speaks very deeply to key issues for almost everyone: the need to get ahead; the need to keep your family together while you do that; the ups and downs of romance; and the complex emotions that family life stirs up (Martín-Barbero, 1993).

virtually all levels of wealth are creating their own programming. Production technology costs are going down, groups of experienced technicians and artists have been trained in most countries, and a number of low-cost program forms or genres have been developed, including talk, variety, live music, reality shows, and game shows. Even more expensive shows, like soap operas, are increasingly produced nationally (see Worldview: Soap Operas Around the World). As ratings and program schedules in many countries reflect, audiences usually tend to prefer local programming when they can get it (Straubhaar, 2007). And now, foreign format shows are invading television in the United States and elsewhere in a big way. *American Idol* is a ratings hit based on a format developed in Great Britain, for example, with productions in over 20 countries and unlicensed copies in another half dozen. Licensing formats like *Wheel of Fortune* or

Survivor are now a rapidly increasing global business. A great deal of "local" or "glocal" programming is now based on such international formats and models. Imported TV formats are often replacing imported TV programs, since they have some advantages of cultural proximity (local stars, jokes, etc.) while retaining the value of using formulas that are proven ratings successes elsewhere.

A significant exception to the localization of television in many places is TV news. Since the 1970s, television news flow began to increase steadily from wire services, such as the Associated Press and news film sources from Great Britain. They offered filmed (and later video) footage for various national television news operations to use in their newscasts.

NEWS WITH AN ARAB SPIN? Since 1996, Al Jazeera, based in Qatar, has become "the CNN of the Arab World." By taking a very independent line on covering the Israeli–Palestinian conflict and on the wars in Afghanistan and Iraq, it has also become very controversial outside the Arabic-speaking world. It now has an international service in English, which many Americans use to get a local take on Afghanistan and Iraq.

Television news flow increased dramatically as CNN, the BBC, Al Jazeera, and other satellite-based news operations began to offer entire newscasts and even all-day news coverage across borders, primarily to satellite television receivers and cable television operations. Now television news also flows on the Internet, so U.S. viewers can see Al Jazeera International, even if U.S. operators refuse to carry it.

CABLE AND SATELLITE TV

Cable TV, familiar to most Americans, Canadians, and some Europeans for years, has been expanding in most other countries of the world. **Direct broadcast satellite(DBS)** or direct-to-home (DTH) started in Japan and Britain and has rapidly spread to many other countries, often spanning the borders of neighboring countries.

By the 1990s, cable systems and private satellite TV channels to feed them were blossoming in Europe, Latin America, and Asia. These cable systems delivered what is for the most part a one-way expansion of new video channels, especially U.S. cable channels, into these new markets. A number of channels quickly became global in reach: CNN, MTV, HBO, ESPN, TNT, Nickelodeon, the Cartoon Network, Discovery, Disney, and others began to sell their existing channels in these countries or even to translate and adapt their U.S. channels to the languages and cultures of the new audiences. MTV is a prolific example, with over 50 different versions worldwide.

> **Direct broadcast satellite (DBS)** is a television or radio satellite service that transmits television signals from satellites to compact home receivers.

STOP&REVIEW

1. What role has radio played in communication between countries?

2. Why is music more likely to be produced in a wider variety of countries than film or TV?

3. Why did American films come to dominate world film markets?

4. What competes with American media products, such as The Simpsons, around the world?

5. Why is television more often locally produced around the world than film?

6. How do changes like privatization affect TV production and flow?

A number of cable channels and DBS services started with a specific language or regional target. Some European channels focused on news, music, sports, films, children's shows, and other targeted programming. One satellite television service in Asia, Star TV, owned by Rupert Murdoch, originally targeted the whole of Asia with American (MTV, film), European (BBC, sports), and Chinese-language channels. It has since begun to target more specific markets, such as India, Taiwan, China, South Asia, Indonesia, and Japan, with more **localized** programming, such as its own adaptations of the music video format and more language and culture-specific programs.

Satellite TV and cable television have also expanded in Latin America and the Middle East. Channels exported from industrialized nations (CNN, BBC, MTV, etc.) are popular, but several nations (China, Hong Kong, Mexico, Egypt, Saudi Arabia) have developed their own satellite television channels aimed both at national audiences and neighbors within the same cultural-linguistic markets. For example, the Qatar channel Al Jazeera has provided regional news to the Middle Eastern regional market of Arabic speakers for over a decade, effectively creating a region-wide television news audience. By covering the U.S. war against Iraq in a way that gave considerable coverage to Iraqi civilian casualties as well as providing pro-Palestinian coverage of the Israeli–Palestinian conflict, Al Jazeera has won many viewers in the region, and has come into major conflict with Western governments who found they had little leverage over it. Other countries use Al Jazeera footage as a news source.

Some countries moved into fully digital television and cable TV long before the United States. Japan and some European countries were operating broadcast digital TV early in 1998.

TELECOMMUNICATIONS SYSTEMS

The infrastructure for international media and information services has also become increasingly globalized. For transoceanic transmission there are several worldwide satellite networks, such as INMARSAT, which handle much of the world's maritime and other mobile communications (see Chapter 12). There are also a number of regional satellite systems, including the Arab League's ArabSat and the European Union's Eutelsat. Quite a few national satellite systems also offer telephone and television transmission services to neighboring countries.

Satellites compete with an extensive set of world and regional fiber-optic networks owned by AT&T, Cable & Wireless of Great Britain, and others. Fiber-optic cables carry the same kinds of signals carried by satellites across transoceanic distances, with greater speed and less distortion.

In another globalizing development, a number of national telecommunications companies are going international. The Baby Bells, France Telecom,

Telefónica of Spain, and others bought telephone, cellular telephone, and data communications companies in Latin America, Africa, and Asia in the 1990s. These firms invested in a number of the telephone companies that were privatized in various nations. They sought to supply cellular mobile telephony, in countries where foreign investments have been allowed under newly liberalized rules (Mody, Bauer, & Straubhaar, 1995). However, after the early 2000s global telecommunications capacity glut and bust, as well as the decline in profitability of many telecommunications operating companies, some of these firms, like AT&T, sold off some of their international interests. One pattern that emerged was of companies refocusing on markets where they traditionally had influence, like Telefónica in Latin America and Cable & Wireless in the Caribbean. Major companies also suffered setbacks speculating in licenses for emerging wireless technologies like third-generation (3G) wireless, although those networks are now finally being built and becoming profitable in both developed and developing countries, especially as mobile smartphones become a primary means of access to the Internet, especially in developing areas where fixed lines and cable never existed.

At the national level, telephone, telegraph, and other telecommunications systems have also developed at different rates in various countries. The United States, Japan, and a few other countries have more than 60 wired telephones and 90 to 110 mobile phones per 100 people and have an Internet built on the telephone and cable television infrastructures. But some African and South Asian nations have less than one wired telephone line per 100 people (see Figure 17.3).

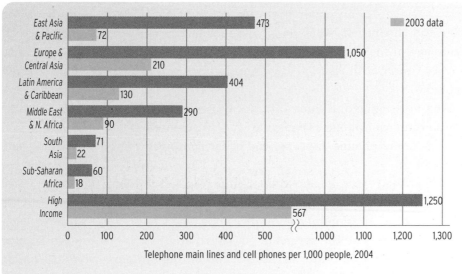

Source: International Telecommunication Union, World Telecommunications Indicators Database.

FIGURE 17.3 TELEPHONES AND CELL PHONES AROUND THE WORLD Telephone lines are unequally available around the world, which keeps much of the world's population cut off from all the different services that phone lines provide (landline phones, fax machines, e-mail, etc.). This graph shows regular telephone lines and cell phone subscribers combined, since many countries now have more cell phones than regular phone lines.

CAN YOU HEAR ME NOW? In many countries, where telephone lines are limited, the first phone for most people is now a cell phone.

AP Photo/Greg Baker

Until the 1990s, most telephone systems were operated by postal, telephone, and telegraph administrations (PTTs)—state-owned telecommunications monopolies. Governments tended to see telephones as essential to their social and economic development. They were willing to invest in telephones even when the services were not profitable, such as those to rural areas. Since the 1990s, many governments privatized their phone companies, selling them to private operators. The reasons were usually financial—to reduce debt or gain new resources to expand the phone or information systems. Others just opened up new services, such as cellular telephony and Internet access, to competition. Investment has gone up but most is targeted at Internet services or mobile phones.

In most countries the regular wired telephone system never reached most of the population, so cellular or mobile telephony is the standard telephone service. It can cover large numbers of new telephone subscribers faster and cheaper. It avoids long waits for delivery of service and offers the advantage of mobility. In most countries in Africa, Eastern Europe, Latin America, and South Asia, people mainly have cell service as their primary telephone.

Text messaging and some Internet access is widespread over cell phones, more so than over phone or cable wires. Also spreading fast is wireless (Wi-Fi) access to smartphones, laptops, and other computers in both rich and poor countries.

Part of the reason is near-universal (excepting the United States) acceptance of a worldwide standard for digital cellular telephone systems, GSM (Global System for Mobile) communications (see Chapter 12). Other reasons are new services, like the spread of new third-and fourth- generation wireless services for high-speed Internet access, and billing systems where the calling party pays the costs.

Under pressure from the World Trade Organization and the threat of competition from low-cost (and unregulated) Internet telephone services (see Chapter 12), international telephone costs are decreasing. Increasing numbers of global calls are made via computers on Internet networks like Skype for very low cost or even free.

COMPUTER ACCESS

The production of computers has been limited to a few countries in North America, Europe, Latin America, and East Asia. Although China, Korea, and Taiwan have developed successful computer hardware industries, the efforts of most other less industrialized countries, such as Brazil, to develop computer hardware industries have often been frustrating and expensive, although India and others have developed successful software industries. The use of computers is still concentrated in the industrialized countries because of the relatively high cost of hardware and software and the unequal distribution of income that allows fewer in the developing world to afford computers. Even though personal computers can cost less than $400 in the United States, they tend to be considerably more expensive in many other countries. Citizens of many countries have average monthly incomes well under $200, which makes acquiring even a $400 computer difficult for most of the world's population. Figure 17.4 shows how computers are still concentrated in the industrialized countries, although their use is beginning to spread. There are initiatives, like the MIT Media Lab program for One Laptop per Child or the competing Intel low-cost laptop, which created very low-cost laptops and spread them around the world, but with less dramatic impact than anticipated.

Thus the purchase and use of computers have been spreading worldwide, but unequally. In some countries, only government bureaucrats and the wealthiest professionals and business owners can afford access to computers. In others, such as North Korea or Cuba, dictatorial regimes prevent their citizens from owning computers for fear their citizens will learn inconvenient truths about their living conditions. In fact, many experts fear that relatively limited access to computers will keep businesses and

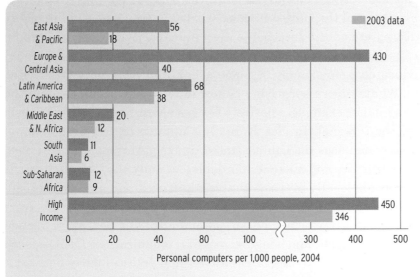

Source: International Telecommunication Union, World Telecommunications Indicators Database.

FIGURE 17.4 COMPUTER ACCESS Most people in the world lack access to computers, which also cuts them off from the Internet.

professionals in the poorest developing countries from competing in a globalized market where others have a sophisticated computer infrastructure to work with, particularly those in Europe, North America, and East Asia (Castells, 2004).

THE INTERNET

However, computers have entered into business globally at a considerable rate, along with Internet use. The first significant global impact of information services and data communications worldwide was the interconnection of far flung operations of multinational corporations via data networks. Today it is most likely that the customer service representative we are talking to on the phone is based in India, where a large industry of training people to talk to Americans or Australians has grown up.

In India, telecommunications networks and the Internet permit outsourcing of work from the United States ranging from computer programming to telephone call centers. The arrival of the Internet standardized many of these technologies into a single network that was much cheaper to use, so small business and individual users outside of big business and government can now afford access to rapid, high-capacity international data, text, and graphics communications. However, lack of access to information communication technology still hampers many poorer countries (World Bank, 2009).

The Internet has exploded out of the United States into the rest of the world. It has proved attractive almost everywhere. However, the computers and telephone lines that form the backbone of the Internet are in much shorter supply in most developing countries. The spread of the Internet was initially slower outside Japan, Australia, North America, and northern Europe, although it is now growing rapidly almost everywhere.

The proportion of small businesses with Web pages is perhaps even larger in Scandinavia than in the United States. Nearly all the citizens of Singapore and South Korea are on the Internet, with high-capacity multimedia broadband networks. However, it is not surprising that in fairly prosperous countries, well-educated people, many of whom speak English, would start using the Internet. What is more surprising is how many other people around the world are using it. For example, relatively few people in Korea speak English, but most use the Internet. In fact, Korea has a much higher proportion of broadband users than does the United States, due to government programs to push this infrastructure and make it affordable. Actually, the United States is barely in the top 20 globally in terms of access to, speed and quality of broadband Internet (OECD, 2010).

The Internet has attracted a wide variety of unexpected new users in a variety of countries. Nonprofit and nongovernmental organizations (NGOs), such as human rights groups, churches, labor unions, and political party networks, have found the Internet a useful communications tool. For example, mass protests against elections held in Iran in 2009, which many citizens perceived as rigged, were organized through the Internet (especially e-mail and Twitter) and cell phones. Now social networking is used by political activists around the world, as was visible across the Middle East in 2011.

The Internet raises a number of new prospects for communication across borders. The structure of the Internet permits anyone with access to a computer or smartphone to send or receive e-mail to or from anyone else on the planet who has an Internet connection. Use of the World Wide Web, social networks, or music and video downloading are much more problematic for many global users, because Internet connections in developing countries may rely on unreliable telephone lines that permit only the slowest connections, making the transmission of graphics, let alone music and video, impractical.

A student in Lebanon can read news about his country not only from official sources, but from foreign newspapers, international newswire services, political dissidents and Islamic movements such as Al Manar, and other sources not approved by his government. This makes the Internet a revolutionary force in global information flow, as we shall see in the next section. It also makes the Internet the main current challenge for many governments, such as China, India, and Singapore, that are concerned about controlling information flows into their country (see Technology Demystified: A Closed or an Open Internet—The Great Firewall of China). China and other nations that wish to control political content on the Internet are working hard on ways to give access to the information people need to participate in a global Information Age economy—while controlling access to politically threatening information and news from the rest of the world. Access to the Internet has grown rapidly, but the government continues to use various controls to limit access to critical political commentary, particularly from outside China. This effort continues to cast considerable doubt on the idea that the Internet would tend to eliminate political control over information.

INTERNATIONAL REGULATION

International media and telecommunications systems are regulated differently from national media systems. As with most aspects of **international law**, there is usually no direct enforcement power, and regulation requires a consensus among nations that the proposed regulations or changes serve their various interests. Failing that, nations tend to assert their self-interest, and the larger, more powerful nations tend to get their way (McPhail, 1989).

One of the few international organizations to have achieved any real power and real changes is the International Telecommunications Union (ITU). Technical standards are required so that users of telegraph, telephone, fax, and e-mail equipment in various countries can communicate with each other across borders. For instance, the ITU encouraged ICANN (see Chapter 9) to create URLs in all languages to enable truly global use of the Internet. One of the main ITU divisions, ITU-T (telecommunications), is primarily involved with technical standards for telecommunications.

The ITU controls some of the same crucial regulatory problems that individual nations solve within their borders. For example, radio spectrum frequencies have to be allocated to different uses in various nations to avoid interference among users. Even more important, the ITU allocates the space orbits for satellites, since those orbits lie above and across national boundaries.

International law includes treaties between countries, multi-country agreements, and rules established by international organizations.

A CLOSED OR AN OPEN INTERNET—THE GREAT FIREWALL OF CHINA

For a number of years, the PRC (People's Republic of China) has blocked thousands of foreign websites that carry objectionable material by preventing IP addresses from being routed through its servers. It does this using standard firewalls and proxy servers at Internet gateways. Public security uses keyword filtering technology to identify sites and sends the current list of objectionable sites to the entry points periodically while human spies paid by the government are planted in Internet cafes. Chinese news outlets are also required to hire inhouse censors who block politically sensitive stories from being posted online or take them down when they appear. Social networking sites are also monitored.

China monitors new perceived technological threats to its information control. "As more and more illegal and unhealthy information spreads through the blog and search engine, we will take effective measures to put the BBS, blog and search engine under control," according to Cai Wu, director of the Information Office of China's Cabinet (French, 2006).

A 2004 crackdown, a "People's war" on pornography, showed earlier Chinese attempts at control. Government regulations require Internet service providers to implement registration systems forbidding the collection of service charges from pornographic websites. Those caught violating the rules will be blacklisted by supervisory officials. They have requested that Internet cafés install software to monitor their customers. Internet cafés are not allowed to permit people under 18 to use their services. More recently, they have cracked down on domestic micro-blog services that people used to criticize government policies and organize protests.

Some reviews have indicated that the Chinese firewall is largely ineffective and can be avoided by using proxy servers outside of China. However, the government also relies on the fact that most people will not actively seek out objectionable material against government wishes. That has been reinforced by prosecution and severe punishment of those who use the Internet in forbidden ways. The government has also required search engines like Google or Yahoo! to censure search possibilities in their Chinese versions, in order to gain permission to operate legally and accept advertising in China. In 2009 a group of hackers with links to the Chinese government broke into files containing information about Google e-mail accounts held by Chinese citizens. This led Google to decide to stop cooperating with government censorship requests and withdraw direct search services from China. As of June 2010, it referred queries to its Hong Kong Chinese language site, in the hopes that more lenient rules would obtain there, but the sites Chinese users on the mainland try to link to can still be blocked by government filters.

E-mail is generally unaffected by blocking. Dissident organizations outside China collect thousands of e-mail addresses and send them to Chinese netters, although several people have been prosecuted over the years for providing such e-mail lists to outsiders. One academic said that the Chinese are not held responsible for undesirable material that shows up in their e-mail mailbox but might incur a penalty for sending it along to other people. Since blocking access to sites has been technologically difficult, the Chinese government is more recently working on controlling access, particularly at public cybercafés, by making people register and making cybercafé owners responsible for what is accessed.

Source: This builds on several sources, including newspaper coverage, and "Internet Censorship–China" in M/Cyclopedia of New Media.

[A **satellite footprint** is the surface area covered by the satellite's signal.]

Satellite footprint areas almost automatically cover multiple countries, requiring international agreements on coverage and standards. Frequency and orbit allocations are routinely recorded by the ITU's B (broadcasting) division and are overseen by periodic World Administrative Radio Conferences that decide ultimately which country gets which orbits and frequencies. Poorer countries have complained since the 1970s that this process favors the larger, more industrialized countries. The ITU responded by creating a third major division, Development, to work with developing countries to accelerate their adoption of new telecommunications and broadcast-related technologies. That group organized the World Summit on the Information Society (WSIS) in 2003–2005, which focused a great deal of attention on the need to promote greater Internet access in developing countries, as well as challenging U.S. control over Internet standards via ICANN (Internet Corporation for Assigned Names and Numbers), a private corporation in the United States created in 1998.

The Internet has posed interesting challenges to international regulation. It has required some new regulatory mechanisms for basic tasks like setting standards and assigning domain names, such as ICANN, ISOC, and IETF (see Chapter 9 for details). Much of the discussion in the WSIS ended up focusing on the need to globalize the functions of ICANN in assigning domain names that use world languages, for example.

The other major player in global regulation is now the European Union, which has begun to set de facto global standards on antitrust and privacy issues. Since global corporations have to meet EU rules to operate in that large part of the global economy, those rules may become their working global standards.

Privacy laws have already required intense negotiation between EU standards, which are very protective of privacy, and American standards, which have been much looser and less defined. In order for American firms to do Internet business in Europe, they have to negotiate an adjustment to those European rules. In fact this is an area in which European standards may well push the United States toward stricter rules on privacy than would otherwise have been the case. In 2010 Google was forced to turn over private data it had collected while making street-level images of cities in Europe that violated EU privacy standards. The EU has also pushed against

THE MAIN SOURCE Most people in the world now have access to TV, which brings images from around the world.

AP Photo/Hasan Sarbakhshian

monopoly dominance by U.S. companies, threatening to take Apple to court for closing iTunes to competitors and fining Microsoft for restricting competition with its proprietary technologies like Internet Explorer or Windows Media Player.

There are other tough regulatory issues on the near horizon for the global Internet, like setting and collecting taxes on Internet commerce. Even more than with American states, many European and other countries get much of their revenue from sales taxes that are evaded by Internet commerce. Countries around the world also have very different positions on things like pornography or hate speech. For example, Germany attempts to regulate cross-border anti-Semitic hate speech, which violates strict laws put in place after the nightmare of Hitler's Holocaust against the Jews in World War II.

The Internet is challenging not only global rules but also regional ones like the privacy rules of the European Union. It is perhaps even more challenging to the internal rules of a number of countries. Nations as varied as Saudi Arabia, China, and Malaysia have tried to create restrictions on access to and use of the Internet in order to protect political control, national cultures, and religions. China has been a much-observed and commented-on example of a country that has embraced the Internet for electronic commerce, while restricting its use for the flow of political information into and within China. In contrast, Saudi Arabia has been more concerned with the affront to Islamic values created by easy access to pornography over the Internet—an issue that also vexes many in the U.S. Congress.

MEDIA LITERACY

WHOSE WORLD IS IT?

> **Cultural imperialism** occurs when some countries dominate others through the media.

Among the main issues in globalization of communications media are **cultural imperialism**, media and information flows, free flow of information, media trade, and the effects of media on national development.

POLITICAL ECONOMY OF THE INTERNET

Critics such as Herbert Schiller, in his book *Information in the Age of the Fortune 500* (1981), anticipated that the ancestor of the Internet, private transborder data flows, would be a tool for increasing U.S. corporate power throughout the world, to the detriment of developing economies, political systems, and cultures. However, although computers can promote U.S. corporate centralization of global operations, computer networks and data transfers also permit high-level jobs such as computer programming to be transferred to low-wage nations such as India, which has become an offshore outsourcing center for many corporations.

This situation represents an economic opportunity for millions of Indians but a loss of jobs for many Americans who had previously done the work.

And high-level programming and systems analyst jobs are also being increasingly exported to countries such as India, reversing the pattern of dominance that Schiller alerted us to. In fact, an increasingly dense and complex integration of companies' operations between the United States, India, and lots of other places via the Internet is now one of the most crucial defining characteristics of globalization for many people. This enables outsourcing of jobs in areas like telephone call centers, database entry, software development, and television and film production, from the United States to India and other countries where labor costs are low (see Chapter 1). Workers there can easily and relatively cheaply be connected to companies in the United States, given the relatively low cost of telecommunications between the two countries.

POLITICAL ECONOMY OF CULTURAL IMPERIALISM

Perhaps the biggest international issue in communications media has been what many nations call *cultural imperialism*, particularly the unequal flows of film, television, music, news, and information from the U.S. and Europe to other nations. This unbalanced flow bothers many nations on several levels. First, it is seen as a cause of cultural erosion and change. So many media products and cultural influences flow into some countries from the United States that traditionalists fear American ideas, images, and values will replace their own. Some of the fears seem trivial to U.S. observers, as when French authorities fought to keep American words such as "drugstore" and "weekend" from creeping into common use by French. However, some consequences of media flows can be deadly serious. Some poor countries in Africa saw epidemics of infant diarrhea and death when mothers gave up breast-feeding for bottle-feeding, which they had seen in European and American television programs and advertising. (Mixing infant formula with unsanitary water caused the problem.)

Other critics of cultural imperialism have been more concerned about the increasingly global economics underlying the structures of media. Underlying the fear of commercial media, in particular, is the idea that they tend to tie countries into a global economy based on advertising and consumption, which pushes poor people to want goods they cannot afford.

The cultural imperialism argument lost much of its force as many countries increased the amount and kinds of media contents they produce. Some governments, such as Japan and Taiwan, pressured national television broadcasters to produce more programming. Others, such as France, subsidize their national film industries to keep them strong. Another solution is to limit media imports, such as the amount of foreign television and film. For example, until recently China only allowed in 20 feature films per year. However, such limits have been strongly opposed by the United States in the World Trade Organization. The MPAA has been negotiating increased film imports into China. Many countries have discovered that national and regional television and music production tend to increase more or less naturally, because they are increasingly feasible economically and because audiences want them. However, for many critics, the global transformation of the economics of media into steadily more capitalist, commercial forms of operation in most countries reflects the continuation of many of the economic issues of cultural imperialism into the new framework of globalization.

CULTURAL IMPACT OF MEDIA AND INFORMATION FLOWS

Even though nations differ culturally and politically, they are seldom isolated. As we look at the globalization of media, we see that one of its most obvious aspects is an extensive flow of a variety of media contents between countries. Elements of media, such as books, songs, stories, and news, have always flowed across borders; cultures have never been truly isolated. Even before Gutenberg's printing press, the Christian Bible and the Islamic Koran had both moved powerfully across a number of countries and cultures, as handwritten copies motivated leaders who led millions into massive religious and cultural change.

However, many people worry that modern media move new ideas and values across borders in such quantities, and at such speed, that we have entered a new age of much more pervasive and rapid change in the world's cultures. Marshall McLuhan (1964) looked at the electronic media and anticipated a "global village." What kind of global village might the media construct? Much of what flows across borders originates in Hollywood, so some fear that the "village" will be as Americanized as a San Fernando Valley mall multiplex theater. However, as detailed earlier in this chapter, observers like Castells (1997) and Straubhaar (1991) pointed outed that media flows from television to the Internet began to be more balanced, although film remains an exception.

A major issue is the impact of Hollywood-style material on other cultures. Because Hollywood films, television, and Anglo-American pop music often include sex, violence, drugs, and gender roles and racial images that clash strongly with local values around the world, many people fear its influence, particularly on the young. After September 11, 2001, some in the Arab nations cited such clashing images as part of what made a number of religious Muslims fear U.S. cultural influence on their national values. Many worry that media like satellite television and the Internet simply amplify the availability of these messages. However, after 9/11, satellite television in the Arab nations also became notable for carrying Al Jazeera's Arab version of the news, which competed very strongly with both commercial American news media like CNN and official U.S. media in the region like Al Sawa and Al Hura.

An alternative vision of the global future is that media and information technologies will decentralize the global village, so that information and culture will flow in many directions, from a variety of sources, with many different messages. This scenario sees a variety of different kinds of companies and groups, such as environment or human rights groups, reaching broader audiences across borders. An example might be the Doctors without Borders, which provides medical and other support to refugees in places like Darfur. Another example is U.S. human rights groups like MTVU (http://www.mtvu.com/on_mtvu/activism/sudan.jhtml), which work with issues in developing countries.

FREE FLOW OF INFORMATION

One of the fears in many countries is that unbalanced media flows will diminish **national sovereignty**, reducing countries' cultural autonomy and governments' abilities to support and protect their cultures. In contrast, the idea of a **free flow of information** reflects the basic concept of freedom of speech, whereby all people ought to be as free as possible to both send and receive information across borders. So U.S. news media oppose any attempt to balance or regulate news flows. But according to the idea of national sovereignty, governments or other domestic forces are entitled to assert national control over natural resources, culture, politics, and so on. Both approaches are established as basic principles in the UNESCO (United Nations Educational, Scientific, and Cultural Organization) charter and the 1948 U.N. Declaration on Human Rights. A 2005 convention on protection of endangered cultures in UNESCO raised these issues again.

Those who consider the current international flows of information and culture unequal tend to emphasize national sovereignty as a justification for a country's asserting control over media flows. The United States has opposed many such proposals. It does so in part because American commercial media interests are threatened by proposed restrictions on media sales and flows. But the United States has also opposed certain proposed restrictions on principle. The United States and a number of other nations believe it is important to keep as free a flow of information as possible to promote freedom of speech globally, independent of government censorship.

Debate raged in UNESCO over these issues in 1976–1983 until the United States decided to withdraw in protest of proposed policies that it thought violated the values of the free flow of information and journalistic freedom. UNESCO proposed that countries create national policies to balance the flow of information. The United States feared that these policies would give too much power to governments, which would be likely to restrict free speech and the free flow of information. The compromise proposal by UNESCO (subsequently rejected by the United States after 1980) promoted a free and balanced flow by helping developing countries build up their own abilities to produce and export media and cultural products.

Although this idea received little financial support, a number of developing nations succeeded in producing more media anyway. Most countries now do much more of their own television, music, news, and websites. The most notable regional news agency launched in the Middle East, the Caribbean, and Africa has been Al Jazeera. More recently, the Internet has permitted a much more diverse flow of news, although most major news media continue to use the same old commercial news agencies. As described earlier in this chapter, a number of national media ventures have begun to balance the flow of television, film, and music among nations.

TRADE IN MEDIA

Media flow and trade issues have been raised in regional treaty organizations, such as the European Union (EU) and the North American Free Trade Agreement (NAFTA), as well as in the World Trade Organization (WTO). The United States tends to see cultural industries as a trade policy issue, because such exports are a significant part of the American balance of trade, compensating

> **National sovereignty** is the policy of keeping domestic forces in control of a nation's economy, politics, and culture.
>
> **Free flow of information** occurs when information flows as freely as possible between countries.

for American purchases of Japanese, Korean and Chinese DVD players, radios, and other consumer electronics, for example. European and Canadian governments, desiring to boost their own producers, see these matters partially as a trade issue, but they also see a cultural policy issue and believe the distinctness of national cultures ought to be preserved on television, music, and film.

The issue came up repeatedly in the General Agreement on Tariffs and Trade (GATT), which was dedicated to lower **tariffs** on trade, and its successor, the World Trade Organization (WTO). In the last round of GATT negotiations, in the early 1990s, the United States pushed hard to impose new international trade rules on audiovisual materials (television and film) that would keep countries from protecting their own national film and television industries or setting quotas to keep out imported films and programs. The European Union rallied around the French, who opposed such a change (existing GATT rules permitted protection and subsidy of film industries), but audiovisual materials are subject to more liberal trade rules under the WTO. At the same time, the European Union has been opening up Europe for greater competition, trade, and non-European investment in telecommunications, since telecommunications is not seen as having the same cultural impact as film and television.

In the late 1990s, the WTO moved into another crucial area for new digital media: copyright and intellectual property protection. It created significantly stronger copyright protection in digital media, such as the Internet and digital recordings (CDs, CD-ROMs, digital audiotape), in 1998. However, enforcement in places like China has been difficult. A specific organization, the World Intellectual Property Organization (WIPO), was created in 1974 to safeguard copyright and related interests. It has become an increasingly central part of world trade in information, media, and cultural products, as those products now assume a larger role in world trade. U.S. industry organizations like the MPAA also push hard for international enforcement of copyright protection.

> **Tariffs** are taxes imposed by governments on goods imported from other countries.

MEDIA AND NATIONAL/LOCAL DEVELOPMENT

Another main issue is whether media, information technologies, and telecommunications can be made to better serve national or local development. As we noted earlier, part of the fear expressed in international debates is that media are primarily serving global commercial interests, not the needs of the populations of the various countries, whether rich or poor. Many government planners and social critics feel that most people in developing nations need media that offer more than slick American entertainment and advertising.

Many governments and international organizations, such as UNESCO, worked hard to create models using media to promote education, health, agriculture, local religious and cultural values, and so on. Some of these programs succeeded, particularly radio programs based in rural areas (McAnany, 1980). The latest development focus has been to try to address health issues in areas like Africa and to get laptops or other computers to students and others in developing countries (ITU, 2010).

STOP&REVIEW

1. Why would countries privatize telephone companies?
2. What are the barriers to increasing Internet access in many countries?
3. What kinds of new challenges does the Internet bring to international regulators? To nations?
4. What is cultural imperialism?
5. What are the counterarguments to cultural imperialism?
6. What are considered unequal flows of media?
7. What is the conflict or trade-off between national sovereignty and the free flow of information?

The International Telecommunications Union and the World Bank are encouraging national governments and foreign investors to invest more funds in the expansion of developing world telephone and telecommunications systems, such as rebuilding Afghanistan's telecommunications system. World Bank and other research shows that such investment contributes to economic growth. This issue is currently discussed primarily in terms of poor countries' access to the Internet. Debate at the 2003 World Summit on the Information Society showed countries feared falling behind in their abilities to compete in economic areas where widespread and fast Internet connection was crucial. Since many people in most countries do not have access to the Internet, one of the main immediate impacts is increased economic and social stratification between those who can e-mail and surf the Net and those who do not.

SUMMARY&REVIEW

WHY DO GOVERNMENTS OWN MORE BROADCASTING THAN PRINT MEDIA IN MANY COUNTRIES?

Broadcast media always require frequency regulations or standards by governments, which led many governments to take control of radio and television they regulated. In some poor countries, governments are the only institution with enough money to support television. Electronic media also have the potential to affect more people. Some governments see electronic media as valuable tools for either development or political control. In some of the poorest countries, governments may be among only a few bodies that have enough money to run broadcasting or telecommunications.

WHY DOES HOLLYWOOD DOMINATE WORLD FILM MARKETS MORE THAN IN TELEVISION?

American films were made to appeal to a large immigrant audience through a universal and entertainment-oriented style, which made it easy for diverse international audiences to accept its films. The United States also benefited from the destruction or blockage of foreign film industries during World War I and World War II. U.S. producers developed an efficient export cartel, the Motion Picture Association of America (MPAA), which owned much of the world distribution and exhibition structure.

U.S. television programs were also produced primarily by the MPAA film studio companies, which gave them the benefit of an existing international distribution structure. American television also used many of the popular techniques and formulas of Hollywood film producers, which gave its productions much of the same universal entertainment appeal. Many other countries found that showing American television programs was cheaper than the cost of local production and provided an easy solution to filling schedules, although U.S. programs are increasingly expensive, so they are sometimes not cheaper than local productions in some countries. However, because U.S. programs are frequently much less popular than local ones, most countries have increasingly produced more and more national television.

As technology costs for television production decline and experience in producing shows increases, people in many countries are finding it easier to make their own shows. Furthermore, once countries develop television genres that are popular at home and in nearby cultural linguistic markets, audiences tend to prefer the local programs, and companies now export formats to the United States, reversing the conventional flow of entertainment programs.

Soap operas, variety shows, and music and talk shows tend to be more prominent in programming abroad than in the United States. Some countries are too small to produce certain kinds of programming. Smaller countries tend to focus on these lower-cost genres.

WHY DO MORE COUNTRIES PRODUCE MUSIC THAN TELEVISION?

Recorded music is cheaper to produce than television shows. Musical preferences are often more localized to regions within countries and to subcultures defined by age, ethnicity, and religion. Thus there is demand for a large, diverse set of artists and recording companies.

WHAT ARE THE MAIN GLOBAL IMPACTS OF THE INTERNET?

Since many people in most countries do not have access to the Internet, one of the main immediate impacts is increased economic and social stratification between those who can e-mail and surf the Net and those who do not. For those with access, the Internet helps globalize economic activity, making it easier to sell things and outsource jobs across borders. It also challenged attempts at news control and censorship. The Internet enables nontraditional groups, from EcoNetto Al Qaeda to network and coordinate across the world.

WHICH COMPANIES ARE THE MAIN GLOBAL OWNERS OF MASS MEDIA?

The main companies are Time Warner (U.S.), Disney/ABC (U.S.), Rupert Murdoch's News Corporation (Australia), DirecTV (U.S.), and Comcast (U.S.). Others include Seagram-Universal (Canada), Bertelsmann (Germany), Vivendi (France) and General Electric/NBC (U.S.). Companies beyond traditional mass media, such as Apple, Google, Microsoft and Telefónica (Spain), should be considered too.

WHAT ORGANIZATIONS MOST AFFECT INTERNATIONAL MEDIA?

The main international regulatory organization is the ITU (International Telecommunications Union), which has telecommunication, broadcasting, and development divisions. It allocates frequencies and satellite orbits to countries and, together with the International Standards Organization, sets international standards for telecommunications. UNESCO (United Nations Educational, Scientific, and Cultural Organization) debates the unbalanced flows of media and news between countries and whether countries have a right to protect their cultures from outside influence. The EC (European Commission) sets standards, establishes rules about media flow, and creates regional markets. The World Trade Organization (WTO) has also become important in regulation of trade in media products and information services.

WHAT IS CULTURAL IMPERIALISM?

Cultural imperialism is an unbalanced relationship in culture and media between countries. The main specific issue is unequal flows of film, news, television programs, cable channels, and music from the United States to other countries. Other aspects include the globalization of media ownership, foreign investment in national media, and the use of foreign media models. International media flows seem to become more balanced as other countries produce and export more. This tendency toward balance is more notable in music and television than in film or news.

WHAT IS THE TRADE-OFF BETWEEN NATIONAL SOVEREIGNTY AND THE FREE FLOW OF INFORMATION?

The United States promotes the free flow of information as an international extension of its national values about freedom of expression. Other countries complain that the free flow of ideas permits the United States to dominate international flows of media. These countries wish to exercise their national sovereignty. However, giving such power to government raises the prospects of censorship and control of information.

THINKING CRITICALLY
ABOUT THE MEDIA

1. What type of conditions in the media relations between countries led people to call it media imperialism?

2. Why do people characterize the media relations between countries and cultures in the last 20 years as increasing globalization?

3. Why does Hollywood dominate global film production and distribution much more than it does television, music, and the Internet?

4. What is the difference between a free flow of media and a free and balanced flow?

5. What are the different impacts of media on developing countries?

cultural imperialism (p. 528)

cultural proximity (p. 506)

direct broadcast satellite (p. 519)

free flow of information (p. 531)

globalization (p. 504)

glocal (p. 505)

international law (p. 525)

national sovereignty (p. 531)

privatizing (p. 516)

regionalization (p. 505)

satellite footprint (p. 526)

tariff (p. 532)

Glossary

AAC is Advanced Audio Coding.

Account executives are the liaisons between the agency and the client.

Acoustic is a sound that is not electronically amplified.

Advertising is communication that is paid for and is usually persuasive in nature.

Advertising media are the communication channels that carry messages to consumers.

The **advertising plan** is a written document outlining the objectives and strategies for a product's advertising.

An **affiliate** is a station that contracts with networks to distribute their programming.

Affiliate fees are monthly per-subscriber fees that cable programming services charge local cable operators.

Affordances are the technical features of communication channels that allow their users to perform useful functions.

Almanacs are book-length collections of useful facts, calendars, and advice.

AM, or **amplitude modulation**, carries information in the height, or amplitude, of the radio wave.

Analog communication uses continuously varying signals corresponding to the light or sounds originated by the source.

Anonymous sources are people who gives reporters information but do not allow the publication of their names

Apps (short for applications) are software applications for use on smartphones.

Artificial intelligence (AI) is the property of an interactive medium that convinces users that they are interacting with a real person.

Asynchronous media are not consumed simultaneously by all members of the audience.

Audience is the number of readers of a magazine.

Audio books are printed books narrated onto CDs. Some can be downloaded.

Augmented reality superimposes game objects on a real-world environment.

B movies are cheaply and quickly made genre films.

Backlist books are older books that are not actively promoted but are still in print.

Backpack journalism is the term for reporters who carry a digital video camera (a mini DV; see Chapter 7), tape recorder, and notebook, often in a backpack.

Barriers to entry are obstacles companies must overcome to enter a market.

Basic cable is the lowest level of cable service that includes local broadcast stations.

A **blog**, short for Web log, is a personal home page with commentary addressed to the Web audience.

A **blog**, short for Web log, is commentary addressed to the Web audience. A blog is similar to an online opinion journal.

Bluegrass came from white music in the South and Appalachia, building on Irish and Scottish instruments and traditions.

Blues came from music by black slaves in the South, which was characterized by specific chord progressions and moods.

Book publishers offer an array of services, from editing to promoting to selling a book.

A **brand** consists of all the dimensions that identify and give unique value to a product or company.

Brand loyalty is the consumer's propensity to make repeat purchases of a specific brand of product.

Broadband refers to high speed Internet connections.

Browsers are computer programs that display information found on the Web.

The **bullet** model, or hypodermic model, posits powerful, direct effects of the mass media.

The **buying motive** explains the consumer's desire to purchase particular products.

Cable modems connect personal computers to cable TV systems.

Cable television transmits television programs via coaxial cable or fiber.

CANSPAM Law regulates commercial e-mail.

Capture theory explains that regulators are unduly influenced by the industry they regulate.

Casual games are informal games that can be completed in short periods of time.

Censorship is the formal restriction of media or speech content by government, political, or religious authorities.

Chain broadcasting is synonymous with a broadcasting network.

A **channel** is an electronic or mechanical system that links the source to the receiver.

Circulation is the number of copies distributed to the public, for a price or free.

Click-through rate is the percentage of readers who click on the ad to visit the advertiser's page.

Coaxial cable is the high-capacity wire used for cable television transmission.

Common carriers provide service to all on an equal basis.

Communication is an exchange of meaning.

The **communications spectrum** includes the range of electromagnetic radiation frequencies that are used in wireless communication systems.

Community access means created by community residents without the involvement of the cable operator.

Compositing is merging several layers of images that were shot separately.

Computer-to-plate technology transfers page images composed inside a computer directly to printing plates.

Concentration of ownership occurs when several kinds of media or many outlets of the same kind of media are owned by a single owner.

Conglomerates are big businesses or corporations that own seemingly unrelated holdings. They are made up of diverse parts from across several media industries and are involved in multiple areas of business activity.

Consumer magazines are magazines that contain general-interest topics.

Content analysis is a quantitative description of the content of the media.

Convergence is the integration of mass media, computers, and telecommunications.

Cookies are small files that websites leave on their visitors' computers.

Copy testing evaluates the effectiveness of advertisements.

Copyright is the legal right to control intellectual property.

A **copyright royalty fee** is a payment for use of a creative work.

Corantos were news sheets that appeared around 1600.

Correlated means that there is a statistical measure of association between two variables.

Cost per thousand is how much a commercial costs in relation to the number of viewers that see it, in thousands.

Covers are artists' performances of others' songs.

Critical studies examines the overall impact of media.

Cross-ownership is the ownership by one firm of different media outlets in the same area.

Cultivation theory argues that mass-media exposure cultivates a view of the world that is consistent with mediated "reality."

Cultural imperialism occurs when some countries dominate others through the media.

Cultural proximity is the preference of audiences for media in their own language and culture.

Cultural studies is a branch of scholarship that argues that media and audiences work together to define culture.

Culture is a group's pattern of thought and activity.

Database marketing is used when advertisers store information about consumers so that they can personalize messages.

Datelines appear at the beginning of a story and note the location of a story if it happens.

Deceptive advertising makes misleading or untruthful claims.

Demographic segmentation is based on social or personal characteristics, such as age, sex, education, or income.

Dependent variables are the consequences, or effects, of media exposure.

Deregulation removes restrictions on the nature and scope of activities that companies engage in and the prices they charge.

Desktop publishing is the process of editing, laying out, and inserting photos using a desktop computer.

Diffusion is the spread of innovations.

The **digital divide** is the gap in Internet usage between rich and poor, Anglos and minorities.

Digital game is a game in which a digital computer facilitates the game play.

Digital means computer-readable information formatted in 1s and 0s.

Digital subscriber line (DSL) sends high-speed data over existing phone lines.

Digital video is recorded, edited, and often transmitted in digital form as used by computers.

Dime novels were inexpensive paperback novels of the nineteenth century.

Direct broadcast satellite (DBS) is a television or radio satellite service that transmits television signals from satellites to compact home receivers.

Direct marketing is a form of advertising that requests an immediate consumer response.

A **disc jockey (DJ)** is a radio station announcer who plays records and often emphasizes delivery and personality.

A **duopoly** exists when two companies dominate a market.

E-books are book content that appears in digital text format. It can be read on mobile devices, computer tablets, and e-readers.

E-commerce (electronic commerce) completes online purchases and financial transactions on the Web.

E-readers are devices that are used to read digital content found in books, magazines, and newspapers.

Economics studies the forces that allocate resources to satisfy competing needs.

Economies of scale result when unit costs go down as production quantities increase.

Electromagnetic recording is a method of storing information as magnetized areas on a tape or disk.

Encryption is used when a message is written in a secret code.

In the **era of creativity** advertisers emphasized entertainment as well as information.

Ethics are moral rules of good conduct that guide one's actions.

Ethnography is a naturalistic research method in which the observer obtains detailed information from personal observation or interviews over extended periods of time.

Experimental research studies the effects of media in carefully controlled situations that manipulate media exposure and content.

Fabrication is information that is made up instead of emerging from facts.

Fair use permits users limited copying of copyrighted works for academic, artistic, or personal use.

Feature films are story films, usually over one and a half hours.

The **Federal Communications Commission (FCC)** regulates communication in the United States.

Fiber-optic systems use light instead of electricity to transmit information

Film noir comprised the "dark," moody American films of the 1940s, often focused on detectives or similar themes.

The **First Amendment** to the U.S. Constitution guarantees freedom of speech and of the press.

First-run distribution for film productions is made specifically for movie theaters.

First-run syndication is the rental or licensing for original productions made specifically for the syndication market.

FM, or **frequency modulation**, carries information in variations in the frequency of the radio wave.

Format clock is an hourly radio programming schedule.

Formats are radio label content aimed at a specific audience.

Free flow of information occurs when information flows as freely as possible between countries.

Freebies are gifts of any value from sources and potential news subjects.

Freedom of speech is the idea that speech and media content should be free from government restriction.

Frequency is the number of cycles that radio waves complete in a second.

Front projection lets actors be photographed in front of an image so that they appear as part of it.

Game engine refers to the software components that govern the physical properties of the game world, interact with the user, and render images for the player.

Gatekeepers decide what will appear in the media.

Gatekeeping is deciding what will appear in the media.

Generalizability is the degree to which research procedures and samples may be generalized to the real world.

Genres are distinctive styles of creative works. The term is also used to represent different types or formats of media content.

Globalization is reducing differences that existed between nations in time, space, and culture.

Glocal is local people borrowing or adapting global ideas.

Gospel music derives from white and black southern church hymns.

Gross is the total box office revenue before expenses are deducted.

Group owners own a number of broadcast stations.

Hard news is the coverage of recent events, such as accidents and crime.

Hegemony is the use of media to create a consensus around certain ideas, so that they come to be accepted as common sense.

Hertz (Hz) is a measure of the frequency of a radio wave in cycles per second.

High fidelity is accurate reproduction of natural sound.

High-definition television (HDTV) is digital television that provides a wider and clearer picture than standard television.

Horizontal integration is the concentration of ownership by acquiring companies that are all in the same business.

Hybrid genres or music blends different traditions into a new form.

Hypertext markup language (HTML) is used to format pages on the Web.

Hypertext transfer protocol (http) is the Internet protocol used to transfer files over the Web.

Indecent speech is graphic language that pertains to sexual or excretory functions.

Independent (indie) film refers to films not made by the major studios.

Independent variables are the causes of media effects.

Infomercials are paid television programs that promote a product.

Information campaigns use the techniques of advertising in an attempt to convince people to adopt prosocial behaviors.

In an **information society**, the exchange of information is the predominant economic activity.

Information workers create, process, transform, or store information.

The **infrastructure** is the underlying physical structure of communication networks.

Integrated marketing communications (IMC) assures that the use of all commercial media and messages is clear, consistent, and influential.

Intellectual property is a creative work of art, writing, film, or software that belongs to a legally protected owner.

Interactive communication uses feedback to modify a message as it is presented.

International law includes treaties between countries, multi-country agreements, and rules established by international organizations.

Internet service providers (ISPs) provide connections to the Internet

Internet Television is a television program viewed over the Internet.

Internet2 is a new, faster version of the Internet.

Joint operation agreements (JOAs) allow competing newspapers to share resources while maintaining editorial independence.

A **junket** is an expense-paid trip intended to influence media coverage.

The **law of supply and demand** describes the relationship among the supply of products, prices, and consumer demand.

Laws are binding rules passed by legislatures, enforced by the executive power, and applied or adjudicated by courts.

Libel is harmful and untruthful written criticism by the media that intends to damage someone.

License is a legal permission to operate a transmitter. Licenses grant legal permission to operate a radio transmitter.

Literacy is the ability to read and understand a variety of information.

Local area networks (LANs) link computers within a department, building, or campus.

Local market monopoly occurs when one company owns (controls) the media in that community.

Local origination means created within the community by the cable operator.

Localism is ownership and program decision making at the community level.

Location-based services use information about the location of mobile phone users to tailor content to specific locations.

Low-power stations have more limited transmission power and cover smaller areas than regular FM stations.

Major film studios like Fox or Disney integrate all aspects of production and distribution.

Marginal costs are the incremental costs of each additional copy or unit of a product.

Marketplace of ideas is the concept that the truth and the best ideas will win out in competition.

A **mashup** combines several audio and/or video segments or tracks into a new creation.

Mass communication is one-to-many, with limited audience feedback.

Massively Multiplayer Online Role-Playing Games (MMORPGs) are online games that thousands play at the same time in a virtual world.

Mattes are background paintings or photographs that are combined with performers in the foreground.

m-commerce means electronic shopping transactions completed with a cell phone.

Media departments negotiate on behalf of the advertiser to buy space from media companies.

Media effects are changes in knowledge, attitudes, or behaviors resulting from media exposure.

Media literacy means learning to think critically about the role of media in society.

Media relations focus on establishing and maintaining good relations with the media.

Mediated refers to communication transmitted through an electronic or mechanical channel.

Microwave systems transmit information between relay towers on highly focused beams of radio waves.

Miscellanies were magazines with a wide variety of content.

Mobile devices are hand-held computers or cell phones with display screens. They access and send information using cell phone or WiFi connections to the Internet.

Mobile Virtual Network Operators (MVNOs) offer mobile services by leasing capacity from network owners.

Modems (modulator-demodulators) convert digital data to analog signals and vice versa.

Mods are modifications to game play or game environments made by users and amateur game developers.

Monopoly is the domination of a market by a single company.

Morality is being able to distinguish right from wrong.

Motion Picture Code of 1930 (Hays Code) was a self-regulation of sex on screen by the motion picture industry.

MP3 is a sound digitization and compression standard, short for MPEG-2 Layer 3.

MPAA (Motion Picture Association of America) is a trade organization that represents the major film studios.

MPAA ratings are part of a movie rating system instituted in 1968.

Muckraking is investigative journalism that "rakes up the muck"—dirt and filth—to expose corruption and scandal.

Multilateral trade negotiations occur among a number of countries at the same time.

Multiple system operators (MSOs) are cable companies that operate systems in two or more communities.

The **multistep flow** model assumes that media effects are indirect and are mediated by opinion leaders.

Must carry is the policy that requires cable companies to carry local broadcast signals.

Narrowcasting targets media to specific segments of the audience.

National sovereignty is the policy of keeping domestic forces in control of a nation's economy, politics, and culture.

Net neutrality means users are not discriminated against based on the amount or nature of the data they transfer on the Internet.

New journalism was the investigative reporting of the nineteenth century.

Newsmagazine is a weekly periodical with in-depth coverage (text and visual) on current news events.

Nickelodeon is a phonograph or player piano operated by inserting a coin, originally a nickel.

Nonlinear editing uses digital equipment to re-arrange scenes to make the master copy.

Novels are extended fictional works, usually of book length.

O&O is a TV or radio station that is owned and operated by a network.

Objectivity fosters news stories free of biases and opinions.

Obscene or **indecent speech** depicts sexual conduct in a way that appeals to sexual interests in a manner that is "patently offensive" to community standards, and lacks serious artistic, political, or scientific value.

Obscenity refers to material where the dominant theme taken as a whole appeals to prurient, or sexually arousing, interest.

Oligopoly is the domination of a market by a few firms.

Orphaned books are older books, perhaps still under copyright—whose authors are unknown.

Packet switching breaks up digital information into individually addressed chunks, or packets.

Pass-along rate is the number of people who see a single copy of the magazine.

A **patent** gives an inventor the exclusive right to make, use, or sell an invention for 20 years.

Pay TV charges cable customers an extra monthly fee to receive a specific channel.

Payola occurs when record companies give bribes to DJs to get their records played.

Penny Press included daily newspapers that sold for one cent.

Persuasion is the use of convincing arguments to change people's beliefs, attitudes, or behaviors.

Phishing is an online scam in which criminals pretend to be someone you trust in an effort to obtain money or sensitive information.

Plagiarism is using the ideas of another without citation.

Platform is a basic type or brand of game system.

Playlists are the songs picked for air play.

Podcasts are recorded messages or audio programs distributed through download to computers, iPods, or other portable digital music players.

Policy is a public framework for structuring and regulating media so they contribute to the public good.

Political economy analyzes patterns of class domination and economic power.

Popular culture is made up of elements mass-produced in society for the mass population.

Portals are Web pages that users launch when they first log on to the Web.

Postproduction includes editing, sound effects, and visual effects that are added after shooting the original footage.

Priming theory states that media images stimulate related thoughts in the minds of audience members.

Print-on-demand technology prints books only when they are ordered by customers.

Privacy is the right to avoid unwanted intrusions or disclosure.

Privatizing government assets refers to selling them to private owners.

Probable cause is a judge's decision that provisional evidence of criminal violation or national security danger justifies a wiretap.

Profits are what is left after operating costs, taxes, and paybacks to investors.

Propaganda is the intentional influence of attitudes and opinions.

Prosocial behaviors are those that a society values and encourages.

Protocols are technical rules governing data communication.

Public broadcasters aim to serve public interests with information, culture, and news.

Public opinion is the aggregate view of the general population.

Public relations are organized activities intended to favorably influence the public.

Public utilities are regulated monopolies.

Publics are the different audiences that PR practitioners communicate with as part of their daily work.

Radio Act of 1912 first licensed radio transmitters.

Radio waves are composed of electromagnetic energy and rise and fall in regular cycles.

Ratings measure the proportion of television households that watch a specific show, or how many people are listening to a radio station.

Rear-projection effects have images projected behind performers who are in the foreground.

Regional Bell operating companies (RBOCs) are the local telephone operating companies that AT&T divested in 1984.

Regionalization links nations together based on geographic, cultural, linguistic, and historical commonalities.

Regulation is government restriction or supervision of privately owned activity.

With **relationship marketing** consumers develop a strong preference for brand through one-to-one communication.

Reliability is the extent to which a result is stable and consistent.

Research organizations compile statistics about consumers and their media habits and evaluate advertising messages.

Restraints of trade limit competition.

Retransmission fees are monthly per-subscriber fees that local broadcasters charge cable companies for the right to carry their programs.

Sales promotions are specific features like coupons that directly spur sales.

Satellite systems send information back and forth to relays in orbit around the earth.

A **satellite footprint** is the surface area covered by the satellite's signal.

The **scarcity argument** states that because there are a small number of stations and the cost of entry to broadcasting is high, extra regulation is required.

Seditious speech is aimed at overthrowing the government.

Self-regulation pertains to communication industry codes and practices of monitoring and controlling the media's performance.

The **Sherman Antitrust Act (1890)** prohibits monopolies and the restraint of free trade.

Shoppers are free to readers and are supported by advertisers. Content sometimes includes news stories, but advertising is the main objective.

Smartphones are cell phones that can also access the Internet.

Social learning theory explains media consumption in terms of its expected outcomes.

Social media are media whose content is created and distributed through social interaction.

Social responsibility model calls on journalists to monitor the ethics of their own writing.

Softcover books are usually printed and distributed in a manner similar to that of hard cover books. They are larger, exhibit more intricate artwork on the cover and are more expensive than mass market paperbacks.

The **Source-Message-Channel-Receiver (SMCR)** model of mass communication describes the exchange of information as the message passes from the source to the channel to the receiver, with feedback to the source.

Spamming is unsolicited commercial e-mailing.

Spyware is malicious software that secretly sends information about your online activities.

Standards are agreements about technical characteristics of communication systems.

The **star system** was the film studios' use of stars' popularity to promote their movies.

Stereo is splitting recorded sound into two separate channels.

Stereotyping is the making of generalizations about groups of people on the basis of limited information.

Stop Online Piracy Act (SOPA) was an anti-piracy initiative by the film and music industries, defeated in 2011 because it seemed to limit Internet rights.

The **studio system** in Hollywood emphasized key stars as a way to promote studio films.

Subscription libraries lent books to the public for a fee.

Survey studies make generalizations about a population of people by addressing questions to a sample of that population.

Syndication is rental or licensing of media products.

Tabloids are newspapers focused on popular, sensational events.

Talkies are motion pictures with synchronized sound for dialogue.

Tariffs are taxes imposed by governments on goods imported from other countries.

Technological determinism explains that the media cause changes in society and culture.

The **Telecommunications Act of 1996** is federal legislation that deregulated radio ownership rules and the communications media. It opened the U.S. telecommunications industry to competition.

Teletext was an early way to transmit digital news by cable or broadcast signals for display on a TVs.

The theory of limited effects holds that the effects of the mass media on individuals are slight.

Theatrical films are those released for distribution in movie theaters.

Theories are general principles that explain and predict behavior.

Third-generation (3G) cell phones have high-speed data transmission capacity for video and Internet.

Top 40 is a radio format that replays the top 40 songs heavily.

Trade magazines are magazines that are targeted toward a particular profession.

Transmission-control protocol/Internet protocol (TCP/IP) is the basic protocol used by the Internet.

UHF stands for ultra-high frequency, channels 14 to 69.

Underwriting is corporate financial support of public television programs in return for a mention of the donor on the air.

Uniform resource locators (URLs) are the addresses of Web pages.

Unique visitors per month is the measure of how many different people visit the site within a month. A visitor can make many visits to the site, but is counted once. (It is the computer origination that is counted and not the person.)

Universal service is the principle that everyone should have basic access to telecommunication services.

Uses and gratifications is the theory that media are actively selected to satisfy our needs.

Validity is the degree to which we are actually measuring what we intend to measure.

Vertical integration is when a company with the same owner handles different aspects of a business (within the same industry), such as film production and distribution.

VHF is the very high frequency television band, channels 2 to 13.

Victrola was the trade name for an early phonograph.

Video game uses a television or similar screen to display the game play.

Videotex was an early way to transmit digital news by phone lines for display on TVs or early desktop computers. A modem and special software was needed to transmit the analog signals to digital ones and vice-versa.

Virtual reality is a computer-generated environment that immerses the user in make-believe world.

Web 2.0 is a new way of using the Internet for collaboration and sharing of data among individual users.

A **webcast** is a real-time event transmitted over the Internet.

Wide area networks (WANs) connect computers that are miles apart.

Wi-Fi is short for wireless fidelity, a standard for wireless data.

Windows are separate film release times for different channels or media.

Wire services supply news to multiple publications; they were named originally for their use of telegraph wires.

With **viral marketing** ideas are spread about products through chat rooms, blogs, social networking sites, or other Internet-based avenues.

Woodcuts were used to make illustrations by carving a picture in a block of wood, inking it, and pressing it onto paper.

Yellow journalism was the sensationalistic reporting of the nineteenth century.

References

Adorno, T., & Horkheimer, M. (1972). The culture industry: Enlightenment as mass deception. In *The dialectics of enlightenment*. New York: Herder and Herder.

Ahlbom, A., & Feychting, M. (2001, April 14). Current thinking about risks from currents. *The Lancet, 357*(9263), 1143–1144.

Ahlbom, A., Feychting, M., Green, A., Kheifets, L., Savitz, D. A., & Swerdlow, A. J. (2009). Epidemiologic evidence on mobile phones and tumor risk: A review. *Epidemiology, 20*(5), 639–652.

Allen, M., D'Alessio, D., & Brezgel, K. (1995). A meta-analysis summarizing the effects of pornography. Aggression after exposure. *Human Communication Research, 22*(2), 258–283.

Allen, M., D'Allessio, D., & Emmers-Sommer, T. (1999). Reaction of criminal sexual offenders to pornography: A meta-analytic summary. In M. E. Roloff (Ed.), *Communication Yearbook 22* (pp. 139–170). Thousand Oaks, CA: Sage.

Allen, R. (1992). *Channels of discourse, reassembled.* Chapel Hill: University of North Carolina Press.

Alsop, R. (Ed.). (1997). *The Wall Street Journal almanac, 1998.* New York: Ballantine Books.

Altheide, D. (1974). *Creating reality.* Beverly Hills, CA: Sage.

Altschull, H. (1995). *Agents of power* (2nd ed). New York: Longman.

American Library Association. ALA Press Release. (April 11, 2011). Jobs-seekers, entrepreneurs continue to turn to their local library for help: State of America's Libraries Report 2011. Retrieved from http://www.ala.org/news/pr?id=6865

American Library Association. (2008). Frequently challenged books of the 21st century. Retrieved from http://www.ala.org/ala/issuesadvocacy/banned/freque ntlychallenged/21stcenturychallenged/index.cfm

Anderson, B. (1991). *Imagined communities: Reflections on the origin and spread of nationalism.* New York: Verso.

Anderson, C. (2004). An update on the effects of playing violent video games. *Journal of Adolescence, 27*(1), 113–122.

Anderson, C. A., Berkowitz, L., Donnerstein, E., Rowell Huesmann, L., Johnson, J. D., Linz, D., Malamuth, N. M., & Wartella, E. (2003). The influence of media violence on youth. *Psychological Science, 4*(3), 81–110.

Anderson, C. A., & Dill, K. E. (2000). *Journal of Personality and Social Psychology, 78*(4), 772–790.

Anderson, C. A., Shibuya, A., Ihori, N., Swing, E. L., Bushman, B. J., Sakamoto, A., Rothstein, H. R., & Saleem, M. (2010). Violent video game effects on aggression, empathy, and prosocial behavior in Eastern and Western countries: A meta-analytic review. *Psychological Bulletin, 136*(2), 151–173. doi: 10.1037/a0018251

Anderson, C. A., Gentile, D. A., & Buckley, K. E. (2007). Violent video game effects on children and adolescents: Theory, research, and public policy. New York: Oxford University Press.

Anderson, J., & Meyer, T. (1988). *Mediated communication.* Newbury Park, CA: Sage. Anderson et al. 2006-2.

Anderson, C., & Wolff, M. (2010, September). The web is dead. Long live the Internet. *Wired Magazine.* Retrieved April 22, 2012, from http://www.wired.com/magazine/2010/08/ff_webrip/all/1

Aoyama, Y., & Castells, M. (2002). An empirical assessment of the informational society: Employment and occupational structures of G-7 countries, 1920–2000. *International Labour Review, 141*(1/2), 123–160.

Apperley, T. H. (2006). Genre and game studies: Toward a critical approach to video game genres. *Simulation Gaming, 37*(1), 6–23.

Arbitron (2011). The Infinite Dial 2011. Retrieved from http://www.edisonresearch.com/Infinite_Dial_2011_ ExecSummary.pdf

Arbitron. (2011). Radio ratings. Retrieved from http://www.arbitron.com/home/content.stm. Accessed 7/14/2012

Arsenault, D. (2009). Video game genre, evolution and innovation. *Eludamos Journal for Computer Game Culture, 3*(2), 149–176.

Ashbee, E. (2003). The Lott resignation, "blogging" and American conservatism. *The Political Quarterly, 74*(3), 361–370.

Association of American Publishers. (2006). *AAP annual report: Fiscal year 2005/2006.* Retrieved from http://www.publishers.org/main/AboutAAP/documents/AnnualReportDraft70.pdf

Attorney General of the United States. (1986). *Final report of the Attorney General's Commission on Pornography.* Washington, DC: U.S. Government Printing Office.

Aufderheide, P. (1999). *Communications policy and the public interest: The Telecommunications Act of 1996.* New York: Guilford Press.

Baar, A. (2007, October 15). *Hallmark sees red for social-marketing effort.* Retrieved from http://www.adweek.com/aw/magazine/article_display.jsp?vnu_content_id=1003658209

Bachmair, B. (2006). Medien padagogik. *Medienpaed.* Retrieved from www.medienpaed.com/06-1/bachmair2.pdf

Bagdikian. (2004). *The new media monopoly.* Beacon Press: New York.

Bandura, A. (1965). Influence of models' reinforcement contingencies on the acquisition of imitative responses.

Journal of Personality and Social Psychology, 1, 589–595.

———. (1986). *Social foundations of thought and action.* Englewood Cliffs, NJ: Prentice Hall.

Bank, D. (1997, September 15). Microsoft's webTV unit to introduce process that uses web to enhance TV. *Wall Street Journal,* Ae.

Barak, A., & Fisher, W. (1997). Effects of interactive computer erotica on men's attitudes and behavior toward women: An experimental study. *Computers in Human Behavior,* 13(3), 353–369.

Barlett, C.P. (2009). Video game effects—Confirmed, suspected, and speculative: A review of the evidence. *Simulation Gaming,* 40, 377–403.

Barner, M. R. (1999). Sex-role stereotyping in FCC-mandated children's educational television. *Journal of Broadcasting & Electronic Media,* 43, 551–564.

Barnhurst, K., & Nerone, J. (2001). *The form of news: A history.* New York: Guilford Press.

Barnouw, E. (1966). *A history of broadcasting in the United States.* New York: Oxford University Press.

Baron, M., Broughton, D., Buttross, S., Corrigan, S., et al. (2001). Media violence. *Pediatrics,* 108(5), 1222–1226.

Baudrillard. (1983). *Simulations.* New York: Semiotext(e), Inc.

Bartsh, A., & Oliver, M. B. (2010). Making sense of entertainment on the interplay of emotion and cognition in entertainment. *Experience Journal of Media Psychology* 2011. 23(1), 12–17. doi:10.1027/1864-1105/a000026

Bell, D. (1973). *The coming of post-industrial society.* New York: Basic Books.

Bellis. (2000). *The walkie-talkie: Al Gross.* Retrieved July 26, 2006, from http://web.mit.edu/invent/iow/gross.html

Bennett, W. L., & Iyengar, S. (2008). A new era of minimal effects? The changing foundations of political communication. *Journal of Communication,* 58, 707–731.

Benoit, W., & Hansen, G. (2004). Presidential debate watching, issue knowledge, character evaluation, and vote choice. *Human Communication Research,* 30(1), 121–144.

Benson, K., & Whitaker, J. (1990). *Television and audio handbook.* New York: McGraw-Hill.

Berger, A. (1992). *Popular culture genres.* Newbury Park, CA: Sage.

Berkowitz, L. (1984). Some effects of thought on anti- and pro-social influences of media effects. *Psychological Bulletin,* 95, 410–427.

Berlo, David K. (1960). *The process of communication: An introduction to theory and practice.* New York: Holt, Rinehart and Winston.

Bernard, R. M., Abrami, P. C., Borokhovski, E., Wade, C. A., & Ta, R. M. (2009). A meta-analysis of three types of interaction treatments in distance education. *Review of Educational Research,* 79(3), 1243.

Bernays, E. (1961). *Crystallizing public opinion.* Norman: University of Oklahoma Press.

Bernstein, C., & Woodward, B. (1974). *All the president's men.* New York: Simon & Schuster.

Bessiere, K., Kiesler, S., Kraut, R., & Boneva, B. (2008). Effects of Internet use and social resources on changes in depression. *Information, Communication and Society,* 11, 47–70.

Beuf, A. (1974). Doctor, lawyer, household drudge. *Journal of Communication,* 24(2), 142–145.

Block, J., & Crain, B. (2007). Omissions and errors in "Media violence and the American public." *American Psychologist,* 62, 252–253.

BLS, Bureau of Labor Statistics. (2003). *Tomorrow's jobs.* Retrieved from http://www.bls.gov/oco/oco2003.htm

——— or U.S. Occupational Outlook Handbook. (2010). U.S. Occupational Outlook Handbook. Washington, DC: U.S. Department of Labor. Retrieved from http://www.bls.gov/ooh/

Bogost, I. (2007). *Persuasive games: The expressive power of videogames.* Cambridge, MA: MIT Press.

Bohn, R. E., & Short, J. E. (2009). *How much information? 2009 report on American consumers.* San Diego, CA: Global Information Industry Center, University of California, San Diego. Retrieved January 29, 2010, from http://hmi.ucsd.edu/howmuchinfo_research_report_consum.php

Borgida, E., Sullivan, J., Oxendine, A., Jackson, M., et al. (2002). Civic culture meets the digital divide: The role of community electronic networks. *The Journal of Social Issues,* 58(10), 125–141.

Bourdieu, P. (1984). *Distinction: A social critique of the judgment of taste.* Cambridge, MA: Harvard University Press.

———. (1998). *On television.* New York: New Press.

Bowen, B. (1999). Four puzzles in adult literacy: Reflections on the National Adult Literacy Survey. *Journal of Adolescent & Adult Literacy,* 42(4), 314–324.

Bouman, H., & Christofferson, M. (Eds.). (1992). *Relaunching videotext.* Boston: Kluwer Academic Publishers.

Boyd, D. (1999). *Broadcasting in the Arab world: A survey of the electronic media in the Middle East* (3rd ed). Ames: Iowa State University Press.

Braestrup, P. (1977). *Big story: How the American press and television reported and interpreted the crisis of Tet 1968 in Vietnam and Washington.* Boulder, CO: Westview Press.

Braudel, F. (1994). *A history of civilizations.* New York: Penguin.

Braunstein, Y. (2000). The FCC's financial qualification requirements: Economic evaluation of a barrier to entry for minority broadcasters. *Federal Communications Law Journal,* 53(1), 69–90.

Brenner, V. (1997). Psychology of computer use. XLVII. Parameters of Internet use, abuse and addiction: The first 90 days of the Internet usage survey. *Psychological Reports,* 80, 879–882.

Brinkley, J. (1997, July 21). Companies' quest: Lend them your ears. *New York Times,* Cg.

Brockway, A., Chadwick, T., & Hall, D. (1997). *Persistence of vision: Moving images through the ages.* Retrieved from http://www.iup.edu/~gcfg/vision/frames.html

Brody, G. (1990). Effects of television viewing on family interactions: An observational study. *Family Relations,* 29, 216–220.

Brooks, J. (1976). *Telephone: The first hundred years.* New York: Harper & Row.

Broom, G. (2009). *Cutlip and Center's effective public relations* (10th ed). Englewood Cliffs, NJ: Prentice Hall.

Brown, J., Broderick, A., & Lee, A. (2007). Word of mouth communication within online communities: Conceptualizing the online social network. *Journal of Interactive Marketing*, 21, 2–20.

Brown, J. D., & L'Engle, K. L. (2009). Sexual attitudes and behaviors associated with U.S. early adolescents' exposure to sexually explicit media. *Communication Research*, 36(1), 129–151.

Bryce, J., Rutter, J., & Sullivan, C. (2006). Digital games and gender. In J. Rutter & J. Bryce (Eds.), *Understanding digital games*. Thousand Oaks, CA: Sage, pp. 185–204.

Bucy, E. P., & D'Angelo, P. (1999). The crisis of political communication: Normative critiques of news and democratic processes. In M. E. Roloff (Ed.), *Communication yearbook 22* (pp. 301–340). Thousand Oaks, CA: Sage.

Buijzen, M., & Valkenburg, P. (2000). The impact of television advertising on children's Christmas wishes. *Journal of Broadcasting & Electronic Media*, 44(3), 456–470.

Buijzen, M., & Valkenburg, P. (2003). The unintended effects of television advertising: A parent-child survey. *Communication Research,* 30(5), 483–503.

Bulkeley, W. (1997, November 11). Hard lessons. *Wall Street Journal*, R1.

Burke, M., Marlow, C. & Lento, T. (2010). Social network activity and social wellbeing. Paper presented at the Computer Human Interaction Conference, Atlanta, Georgia, April 27.

Burns, E. (2006, April 4). *Newspaper sites gain audience. Click Z stats—Traffic patterns.* Retrieved April 4, 2006, from www.clickz.com/3596391

Bushman, B. J., & Anderson, C. A. (2009). Comfortably numb: desensitizing effects of violent media on helping others. *Psychological Science*, 20(3), 273–277.

Bushman, B., & Cantor, J. (2003). Media ratings for violence and sex: Implications for policymakers and parents. *The American Psychologist*, 58(2), 130–141.

Cable Television Advertising Bureau. (1998). *1997 cable TV facts on access CAB.* Retrieved from http://www.cabletvadbureau.com/infofact.html

Campbell, J., & Carlson, M. (2002). Panopticon.com: Online surveillance and the commodification of privacy. *Journal of Broadcasting & Electronic Media,* 46(4), 586–606.

Canclini, N. Garcia. (1995). *Hybrid cultures: Strategies for entering and leaving modernity.* Minneapolis: University of Minnesota Press.

Carey, J. (1972). *Politics of the electronic revolution or 1989 commas culture?* Urbana: University of Illinois.

Carey, J. W. (1989). *Communication as culture: Essays on media and society.* Boston: Unwin Hyman.

Carnagey, N., Anderson, C., & Bushman, B. (2007). The effect of video game violence on physiological desensitization to real-life violence. *Journal of Experimental and Social Psychology*, 43(3), 489.

Caroli, M., Argentieri, L., Cardone, M., & Masi, A., (2004). Role of television in childhood obesity prevention. *International Journal of Obesity*, 28, S104–S108.

Capella, Michael L., Cynthia Webster, & Brian R. Kinard. A review of the effect of cigarette advertising. *International Journal of Research in Marketing*, 28(3), 269–279.

Cassell, J., & Jenkins, H. (1998). *From Barbie to Mortal Kombat: Gender and computer games.* Cambridge, MA: MIT Press.

Cassidy, J. (1997, October 20). Media indelible ink. *The New Yorker*. Retrieved from http://www.newyorker.com/archive/1997/10/20/1997_10_20_086_TNY_CARDS_000380128

Castells, M. (2000). *Rise of the network society: The information age: Economy, society and culture* (2nd ed). Cambridge, MA: Blackwell Publishers, Inc.

Castells, M. (2004). *The power of identity* (2nd ed). Cambridge, MA: Blackwell Publishers, Inc.

Chandra, A., Martino, S. C., Collins, R. L., Elliott, M. N. Berry, S. H., Kanouse, D. E., & Miu, A. (2008). Does watching sex on television predict teen pregnancy? Findings from a national longitudinal survey of youth. *Pediatrics*, 122(5), 1047–1054.

Children Now. (2002). *Fall colors 2001–2002. Prime time diversity report.* Retrieved June 1, 2002, from http://www.childrennow.org/media/fc2002/fc-2002-report.pdf

Chlapowski, F. (1991). The constitutional protection of informational privacy. *Boston University Law Review,* 71, 133.

Chomsky, N., & Herman, E. (1988). *Manufacturing consent: The political economy of the mass media.* New York: Pantheon Books.

Christakis, D. A., Zimmerman, F. J., DiGiuseppe, D. L., & McCarty, C. A. (2004). Early television exposure and subsequent attentional problems in children. *Pediatrics,* 113(4), 708–713.

Christians, C., Rotzoll, K., & Fackler, M. (1991). *Media ethics: Cases and moral reasoning* (3rd ed). New York: Longman.

Clark, C. (1972). Race, identification and television violence. In G. Comstock, E. Rubenstein, & J. Murray (Eds.), *Television and social behavior* (Vol. 5). Washington, DC: U.S. Government Printing Office.

Cleaver, H. (1998). The Zapatistas and the electronic fabric of struggle. In J. Holloway & E. Peláez (Eds.), *Zapatista! reinventing revolution in Mexico.* London: Pluto Press.

Colista, C., & Leshner, G. (1998). Traveling music: Following the path of music through the global market. *Critical Studies in Mass Communication,* 15, 181–194.

Collins, et al. (2003). Entertainment television as a healthy sex educator: The impact of condom-efficacy information in an episode of *Friends. Pediatrics,* 112(5), 1115–1121.

Collins, R., Ellickson, P., McCaffrey, D., & Hambarsoomians, K. (2007, June). Early adolescent exposure to alcohol advertising and its relationship to underage drinking. *Journal of Adolescent Health,* 40(6), 527–534.

Collins, R. L., Elliott, M. N., Berry, S. H., Kanouse, D. E., Kunkel, D., Hunter, & S. B., Miu, A. (2004). Watching sex on television predicts adolescent initiation of sexual behavior. *Pediatrics,* 114(3), 843.

Columbia Journalism Review. (2007). *CJR resources: Who owns what*. Retrieved from http://www.cjr.org/resources/

Common Sense Media. (2006). *New national poll: The Internet now seen as #1 media concern for parents*. Retrieved from http://www.commonsensemedia.org/news/press-releases.php?id=23

Computing Research Association. (2011). Taulbee survey report 2009-2010. Retrieved from http://www.cra.org/resources/taulbee/

ComScore (2011). *comScore Releases November 2011 U.S. Online Video Rankings*. Retrieved from http://www.comscore.com/Press_Events/Press_Releases/2011/12/comScore_Releases_November_2011_U.S._Online_Video_Rankings

Cook, T., Appleton, H., Conner, R., Shaffer, A., Tamkin, G., & Weber, S. (1975). *Sesame Street revisited: A case study in evaluation research*. New York: Russell Sage Foundation.

Coombs, W., & Holladay, S. J. (2007). *It's not just PR: Public relations in society*. Malden, MA: Blackwell.

Cosmopolitan magazine Media Kit. (2007). *Rates*. Retrieved from http://www.cosmomediakit.com/r5/showkiosk.asp?listing_id=474162&category_code=rate&category_id=27809

Cox, K. (2011). *The Gamer's Gaze*. Downloaded March 3, 2012, from http://www.your-critic.com/2011/06/gamers-gaze-part-1.html

Crawford, G., & Rutter, J. (2006). Digital games and cultural studies. In J. Rutter & J. Bryce (Eds.). *Understanding digital games* (pp.148–165). Thousand Oaks, CA: sage

Cringely, R. (1998). *Nerds 2.0.1*. Retrieved September 17, 2002, from http://www.pbs.org/opb/nerds2.0.1/

Curtis, A. (2011). The brief history of social media. Downoaded April 22, 2012, from http://www.uncp.edu/home/acurtis/NewMedia/SocialMedia/SocialMediaHistory.html

Cutlip, S. (1995). *Public relations history: From the seventeenth to the twentieth century*. Hillsdale, NJ: Erlbaum.

———. (2007). *Effective public relations* (9th ed). Englewood Cliffs, NJ: Prentice Hall.

Czitrom, D. (1982). *Media and the American mind*. Chapel Hill: University of North Carolina Press.

Dailey, D., Bryne, A., Powell, A., Karaganis, J., & Chung, J. (2010). *Broadband adoption in low-income communities*. A Social Science Research Council report. Retrieved from http://www.ssrc.org/publications/view/1EB76F62-C720-DF11-9D32-001CC477EC70/

Dates, J., & Barlow, W. (1997). Does mass media realistically portray African American culture? No. In A. Alexander & J. Hanson (Eds.), *Taking sides: Clashing views on controversial issues in mass media and society*. Guilford, CT: Dushkin/Brown & Benchmark.

Davenport, L. (1987). *A co-orientation analysis of newspaper editors and readers' attitudes toward videotex, online news and databases: A study of perceptions and opinions*. Doctoral dissertation, Ohio University.

Davenport, L. (1988, July). *An update: 1976 and 1987 editors' predictions of audience reactions to videotex; and a comparison: 1987 audience reactions and 1976 and 1987 editors' predictions*. Paper presented to the Newspaper Division, Association for Education in Journalism and Mass Communication National Convention, Portland, Oregon.

Davenport, L., Fico, F., & DeFleur, M. (2002, Spring). Computer-assisted reporting in classrooms: A decade of diffusion. *Journalism Educator*, 57(1), 6–22.

Davenport, L., Randle, Q., & Bossen, H. (2007). Now you see it, now you don't: The problems with newspaper photo archives. *Visual Communication Quarterly*, 14(4), 218–230.

Davies, P. G., Spencer, S. J., Qiunn, D. M., & Gerhardstein, R. (2002). Consuming images: How television commercials that elicit stereotype threat can restrain women academically and professionally. *Personality and Social Psychology Bulletin*, 28(12), 1615–1628.

Davis, K. (1985). *Two-bit culture*. Boston: Houghton-Mifflin.

Davis K.C., Farrelly M.C., Messeri P., & Duke J. (2009). The impact of national smoking prevention campaigns on tobacco-related beliefs, intentions to smoke and smoking initiation: Results from a Longitudinal Survey of Youth in the United States. *International Journal of Environmental Research and Public Health*, 6(2), 722–740.

Davis, S., Elin, L., & Reeher, G. (2002). *Click on democracy: The Internet's power to change political apathy into civic action*. Boulder, CO: Westview Press.

Day, B. (2007, October 30). *The next video ad innovation: Automation of ad assembly*. Retrieved from http://blogs.mediapost.com/video_insider/?p=124

Day, L. (1991). *Ethics in media communications: Cases and controversies*. Belmont, CA: Wadsworth.

Deacon, D., Pickering, M., et al. (2007). *Researching communications: A practical guide to methods in media and cultural analysis*. New York: Bloomsbury USA.

de Sola Pool, I. (1983). *Forecasting the telephone: A retrospective technology assessment of the telephone*. Norwood, NJ: Ablex.

Dessauer, J. (1981). *Book publishing—What it is, what it does* (2nd ed). New York: R. R. Bowker.

De Zuniga, H. G., Nakwon Jung, Sebastián Valenzuela. (2012). Social media use for news and individuals' social capital, civic engagement and political participation. *Journal of Computer-Mediated Communication*. 17(3), 319–336

Diana C. Mutz and Lori Young. (2011). Communication and Public Opinion: Plus Ça Change? *Public Opinion Quarterly*, 75(5), 1018–1044. doi:10.1093/poq/nfr052

Dibbel, J. (1993, December 21). A rape in cyberspace. *The Village Voice*, pp. 36–42.

Dietrich, D. (1997). (Re)-Fashioning the techno-erotic woman: Gender and textuality in the cybercultural matrix. In S. Jones (Ed.), *Virtual culture*. Thousand Oaks, CA: Sage.

Difranza, Jr., Richards, J., Paulman, P., Wolfgillespie, N., Fletcher, C., Jaffe, R., & Murray, D. (1991). RJR Nabisco's cartoon camel promotes Camel cigarettes to children. *Journal of the American Medical Association*, 266(22), 3149–3153.

DirectTV vs Time Warner: DirectTV wins round one. (2007, August 21). Retrieved from http://lawvibe.com/directtv-vs-time-warner-directtv-wins-round-one/

Distimo. (2011). *Full year 2011*. Downloaded February 26, 2012, from http://www.distimo.com/publications/

Dizard, W. (1997). *Old media, new media.* New York: Longman.

Douglas, S. (2004). *Listening in: Radio and the American imagination.* Minneapolis: University of Minnesota Press.

Downing, J., Mohammadi, A., & Sreberny-Mohammadi, A. (1990). *Questioning the media: A critical introduction.* Newbury Park, CA: Sage. Downloaded February 25, 2012, from http://hraunfoss.fcc.gov/edocs_public/attachmatch/DOC-305297A1.pdf

Downs, E., & Smith, S. L. (2010). Keeping abreast of hypersexuality: A video game character content analysis. *Sex Roles, 62,* 721–733. doi:10.1007/s11199-009-9637-1

Durkin, S. J., Biener, L., & Wakefield, M. A. (2009). Effects of different types of antismoking ads on reducing disparities in smoking cessation among socioeconomic subgroups. *American Journal of Public Health,* 99(12), 2217–2223.

E-Marketer. (2006). *Media audiences and new media.* Retrieved from http://www.emarketer.com

Eastin, M., & LaRose, R. (2000). Internet self-efficacy and the psychology of the digital divide. *Journal of Computer Mediated Communication,* 6(1). Retrieved from http://www.ascusc.org/jcmc/vol6/issue1/eastin.html

Eastman, L. (1993). *Broadcast/cable programming.* Belmont, CA: Wadsworth.

eBay company overview, management. Retrieved from http://pages.eBay.com/community/abouteBay/overview/management.html

Editor & Publisher. (2007). *International year book: The encyclopedia of the newspaper industry* (87th ed.). New York: Editor & Publisher

Edwards, B. (2009). *30 years of handheld game systems.* Retrieved from http://www.pcworld.com/article/183679/30_years_of_handheld_game_systems.html

Edwards, B. (2004). *Edward R. Murrow and the birth of broadcast journalism.* New York: Wiley.

Egenfeldt-Nielsen, S., Smith, J. H., & Tosca, S. P. (2008). *Understanding the video games.* New York: Routledge.

Elliott, S. (2001, February 26). Advertising: Agencies seek strength through media diversity. *The New York Times.* Retrieved from www.nytimes.com/2001/02/26/business/26ADCO.html

———. (2007a, November). *Making social connections and selling cookies.* Retrieved from http://www.nytimes.com/2007/11/21/business/media/21adco.html?_r=1&ref=technology&oref=slogin

———. (2007b, October). *Student's ad gets a remake, and makes the big time.* Retrieved from http://www.nytimes.com/2007/10/26/business/media/26appleweb.html?_r=1&oref=slogin

Ellison, N., Steinfeld, C., & Lampe, C. (2007). The benefits of Facebook "friends": Social capital and college students' use of online social network sites. *Journal of Computer-Mediated Communication,* 12(4), article 1. Retrieved from http://jcmc.indiana.edu/vol12/issue4/ellison.html

Ellul, J. (1990). *The technological bluff.* Grand Rapids, MI: Eerdmans.

ESA. (2011). *Essential facts about the computer and video game industry.* Dowloaded March 3, 2012, from http://www.theesa.com/facts/pdfs/ESA_EF_2011.pdf

Eveland, W., Shah, D., & Kwak, N. (2003). Assessing causality in the cognitive mediation model: A panel study of motivations, information processing, and learning during campaign 2000. *Communication Research,* 30(4), 359–386.

Everett, G. (1993). The age of new journalism, 1883–1900. In W. Sloan, J. Stovall, & J. Startt (Eds.), *Media in America: A history* (2nd ed). Scottsdale, AZ: Publishing Horizons.

Ewen, S. (1976). *Captains of consciousness.* New York: McGraw-Hill.

———. (1996). PR! *A social history of spin.* New York: Basic Books.

FCC. (2010). Local Telephone Competition: Status as of June 30, 2010.

FCC. (2011). *Annual report and analysis of competitive market conditions with respect to mobile wireless, including commercial mobile services.* Downloaded February 26, 2012, from http://www.fcc.gov/reports/mobile-wireless-competition-report-15th-annual

Feather, F. (2000). *Future Consumer.com: The webolution of shopping to 2010.* Toronto, ON: Warwick.

Featherstone, M. (1990). Perspectives on consumer culture. *Sociology,* 24.

———. (1991). *Consumer culture and post-modernism.* Newbury Park, CA: Sage.

Federman, J. (1998). *National television violence study, vol. 3, Executive summary.* Santa Barbara: University of California Santa Barbara, Center for Communication and Social Policy.

Ferguson, C. J. (2009). Media violence effects and violent crime: Good science or moral panic? In C. J. Ferguson (Ed.),*Violent crime: Clinical and social implications.* (pp. 37–57). Thousand Oaks, CA: Sage Publications.

Feshbach, S., & Singer, R. (1971). *Television and aggression.* San Francisco: Jossey-Bass.

Fisch, S., & Truglio, R. (Eds). (2001). *"G" is for growing: Thirty years of research on children and Sesame Street.* Mahwah, NJ: Erlbaum.

Fischer, C. (1992). *America calling.* Berkeley: University of California Press.

Folkerts, J., & Teeter, D. (1994). *Voices of a nation: A history of mass media in the United States.* New York: Macmillan.

Ford, T. (1997). Effects of stereotypical television portrayals of African-Americans on person perception. *Social Psychology Quarterly,* 60(3), 266–275.

Fowler, M., & Brenner, D. (1982). A marketplace approach to broadcast regulation. *Texas Law Review,* 60, 207–257.

Fowles, J. (1999). *The case for television violence.* Thousand Oaks, CA: Sage Publications.

Fox, S. (1984). *The mirror makers: A history of American advertising.* London: Heinemann.

Franz, M. M., Freedman, P., Goldstein, K., & Ridout, T. N. (2008). Understanding the effect of political advertising on voter turnout: A response to Krasno and Green. *The Journal of Politics,* 70, 262–268.

Freemuse: Freedom of Musical Expression. Retrieved October 12, 2007, from http://www.freemuse.org/

FreePress. (2006). *How conglomerates have grown.* Retrieved from http://freepress.org/

FreePress. (2011). *Who owns the media?* Retrieved July 14, 2012, from http://www.savetheinternet.com/ownership/chart.

French, H. W. (June 30, 2006). China vows broad new censorship measures. *The New York Times.* Retrieved from http://www.nytimes.com/2006/06/30/world/asia/30iht-china.2093703.html?_r=1

Freud, S. (1949). *An outline of psychoanalysis.* Authorized translation by James Strachey (1st ed.). New York: W. W. Norton.

Freuh, T., & McGhee, P. (1975). Traditional sex role development and the amount of time spent watching television. *Developmental Psychology, 11*(1), 109.

Fridkin, K. L., Kenney, P. J., Gershon, S. A., & Woodall, G. S. (2008). Spinning debates: The impact of the news media's coverage of the final 2004 presidential debate. *The International Journal of Press / Politics, 13*(1), 29–51.

Friedlander, B. (1993). Community violence, children's development and mass media. *Psychiatry, 56*(1), 66–81.

Frost, R. (1996, November 21). The electronic Gutenberg fails to win mass appeal. *Wall Street Journal,* B6.

Funk, J. B., Baldacci, H. B., Pasold, T., Baumgardner, J. (2004). Violence exposure in real-life, video games, television, movies, and the Internet: Is there desensitization? *Journal of Adolescence, 27*(1), 23–39.

Fyfe, K. (2006). *Wolves in sheep's clothing.* Retrieved from http://www.parentstv.org/PTC/publications/reports/childrensstudy/main.asp

Gajendran, R. S., & Harrison, D. A. (2007). The good, the bad, and the unknown about telecommuting: Meta-analysis of psychological mediators and individual consequences. *Journal of Applied Psychology, 92,* 1524–1541.

Galtung, J., & Ruge, M. H. (1965). The structure of foreign news. *Journal of Peace Research, 2*(1), 64–91.

Gamespot. (2010). *The history of video games.* Retrieved from http://www.gamespot.com/gamespot/features/video/hov/

Gandy, O. (1982). *Beyond agenda setting: Information subsidies and public policy.* Norwood, NJ: Ablex.

———. (1993). *The panoptic sort.* Boulder, CO: Westview.

Gannett, Inc. (2007). *Gannett: The Information Company 2006 Annual Report.* McLean, VA. Bennett, Inc.

Garth, J. (2003). *Tolkien and the Great War: The threshold of Middle-Earth.* New York: Houghton-Mifflin.

Gee, J. P. (2003). *What video games have to teach us about learning and literacy.* New York: Macmillan.

Genuis, S. J. (2008). Fielding a current idea: exploring the public health impact of electromagnetic radiation. *Public Health, 122*(2), 113–124.

Gentile, Douglas A., Julia A. Maier, Mary Rice Hasson, & Beatriz Lopez de Bonetti. (2011). Parents' Evaluation of Media Ratings a Decade After the Television Ratings Were Introduced. *Pediatrics, 128,* 36–44. doi 10.1542/peds.2010-3026

Gentile, D. A., Lynch, P., Linder, J., & Walsh, D. (2004). The effects of violent video game habits on adolescent hostility, aggressive behaviors, and school performance. *Journal of Adolescence, 27,* 5–22.

Gentry, C. (1991). Pornography and rape: An empirical analysis. *Deviant Behavior, 12,* 277–288.

Gerbner, G., Gross, L., Morgan, M., & Signorelli, N. (1994). Growing up with television: The cultivation perspective. In J. Bryant & D. Zillmann (Eds.), *Media effects: Advances in theory and research.* Hillsdale, NJ: Lawrence Erlbaum.

Gilder, G. (2000). *Telecosm: How infinite bandwidth will revolutionize our world.* New York: Free Press.

Gitlin, T. (1983). *Inside prime time.* New York: Pantheon Books.

Glascock, J. (2001). Gender roles on prime-time network television: Demographics and behaviors. *Journal of Broadcasting & Electronic Media, 45*(4), 656–669.

———. (2003). Gender, race, and aggression in newer TV networks' primetime programming. *Communication Quarterly, 51*(1), 90–100.

Glascock, J. (2003). Gender, race, and aggression in newer tv networks' primetime programming. *Comunication Quarterly, 51,* 90–100.

Gomery, D. (1991). *Movie history: A survey.* Belmont, CA: Wadsworth.

Gortmaker, S., Must, A., Sobol, A., Peterson, K., Colditz, G., & Dietz, W. (1996). Television viewing as a cause of increasing obesity among children in the United States, 1986–1990. *Archive of Pediatric and Adolescent Medicine, 150,* 356–362.

Gough, P. J. (2007, October 15). *Nielsen spots and watchers.* Retrieved from http://www.hollywood-reporter.com/hr/content_display/business/news/e3ie1bcfaee594e25d91207aa4eeb2de217

Grabe, S., Ward, L. M., & Hyde, J. S. (2008). The role of the media in body image concerns among women: A meta-analysis of experimental and correlational studies. *Psychology Bulletin, 134,* 460–76.

Gramsci, A. (1994). *Letters from prison.* New York: Columbia University Press.

Gramsci, A. (1971). *Selections from the prison notebooks.* New York: International Publishers.

Gray, H. (1995). *Watching race: television and the struggle for "Blackness."* Minneapolis: University of Minnesota Press.

Greenberg, B., Edison, N. Korzenny, F., Fenandez-Coooado, C., & Atkin, C. (1980). Antisocial and prosocial behaviors on television. In B. Greenberg (Ed.), *Life on television: Content analysis of U.S. TV drama.* Norwood, NJ: Ablex.

Greitemeyer, T., & Osswald, S. (2010). Effects of prosocial video games on prosocial behavior. *Journal of Personality and Social Psychology, 98*(2), 211.

Griffin, N., & Masters, K. (1997). *Hit and run: How Jon Peters and Peter Guber took Sony for a ride in Hollywood.* New York: Touchstone Books.

Griffiths, M. (1998). Violent video games and aggression: A review of the literature. *Aggression and Violent Behavior, 4*(2), 203–212.

Grohol, J. (1996). *Psychology of the Internet research and theory: Internet additions.* Retrieved from http://www.cmhc.com/mlists/research

Grossman, L. (2007, August 23). *Why Facebook is the future.* Retrieved from http://www.time.com/time/magazine/article/0,9171,1655722,00.html

Guback, T., & Varis, T. (1986). *Transnational communication and cultural industries*, UNESCO.

Guback, T., & Varis, T. (1982). Transnational communication and cultural industries. *Reports and Papers on Mass Communication.* UNESCO, Paris, No. 92.

Guernsey, L. (2001, September 20). An unimaginable emergency put communications to the test. *New York Times.* Retrieved from http://www.nytimes com/2001/09/20/technology/circuits/201NFR.html

Gustafsen, K. (2006). *Deregulation and the market in public discourse: The AT&T divestiture, the 1996 Telecommunications Act, and the development of a commercial Internet.* PhD dissertation, University of Texas Libraries, Austin, TX

Hall, S. (1980). Encoding/Decoding. In S. Hall, D. Hobson, A. Lowe, & P. Willis (Eds.), *Culture, media language.* London: Hutchinson.

Hammermeister, J., Brock, B., Winterstein, D., & Page, R. (2005). Life without TV? Cultivation theory and psychosocial health characteristics of television-free individuals and their television-viewing counterparts. *Health Communication, 17*(3), 253–264.

Handbook of Research on Serious Games as Educational, Business and Research Tools Maria Manuela Cruz-Cunha (Polytechnic Institute of Cavado and Ave, Portugal) 628–647

Hargittai, E., & Hinnant, A. (2008). Differences in young adults' use of the Internet. *Communication Research, 35*(5), 602–621.

Harris, R. J., & Barlett, C. P. (2008). Effects of sex in the media. In J. Bryant and M. B. Oliver, *Media effects advances in theory and research,* (3rd ed., p. 324). New York: Erlbaum.

Hart, M. (1990). *Drumming at the edge of magic.* New York: Harper-Collins.

Hayes, T. (1991, December 15). Making a difference: A new start at a TRW hot spot. *The New York Times.* Business section.

Heins, M. (1993). *Sex, sin and blasphemy.* New York: New Press.

Hesmondhalgh, D. J. (2008). Cultural and creative industries. In T. Bennett & J. Frow (Eds.), *The SAGE handbook of cultural analysis* (pp. 553–569). London: Sage Publications.

HHS. (2010). *Childhood obesity.* Retrieved from http://aspe.hhs.gov/health/reports/child_obesity/

High, K. (2007, November 19). *Jonathan Epstein, game on.* Retrieved from http://www.adweek.com/aw/magazine/article_display.jsp?vnu_content_id=1003674403

Hilmes, M. (1997). *Radio voices: American broadcasting, 1922–1952.* Minneapolis: University of Minnesota Press.

Hirsch, P. (1980). The "scary world" of the nonviewer and other anomalies: A reanalysis of Gerbner et al.'s findings on cultivation analysis. *Communication research, 7,* 403–456.

Ho, A. (2002). Reinventing local governments and the e-government initiative. *Public Administratrion Review, 62*(4), 434–444.

Holbrook, T. (2002). Presidential campaigns and the knowledge gap. *Political Communication, 19*(4), 437–454.

Holzmann, G., & Pherson, B. (1994). *The early history of data networks.* Retrieved from http://www.it.kth.se/docs /early_net/toc.html

Horchow, R., & Horchow, S. (2006). *The art of friendship: 70 simple rules for making meaningful connections.* New York: St. Martin's Press.

Horkheimer, M., & Adorno, T. W. (1972). *Dialectic of enlightenment.* Translated by John Cumming. New York: Herder and Herder.

Hovland, C., Lumsdane, A., & Sheffield, F. (1949). *Experiments on mass communications.* Princeton, NJ: Princeton University Press.

Hoynes, D. C. a. W. (2002). *Social inequality and media representation. Media society: Industries, images, and audiences.* Thousand Pine Oaks, CA, Pine Forge Press.

Huber, G., & Arceneaux, K. (2007,). Identifying the persuasive effects of presidential advertising. *American Journal of Political Science, 51*(4), 957.

Huesmann, L., & Eron, L. (1986). The development of aggression in American children as a consequence of television violence viewing. In L. Huesmann, & L. Eron (Eds.), *Television and the aggressive child.* Hillsdale, NJ: Lawrence Erlbaum.

Huesmann, L., Moise-Titus, J., Podolski, C., & Eron, L. (2003). Longitudinal relations between children's exposure to TV violence and their aggressive and violent behavior in young adulthood: 1977–1992. *Developmental Psychology, 39*(2), 201–221.

Huntzicker, W. (1993). The frontier press 1800–1900. In W. Sloan, J. Stovall, & J. Startt (Eds.), *Media in America: A history* (2nd ed.). Scottsdale, AZ: Publishing Horizons.

Huston, A., Huston, A. C., Donnerstein, E., Fairchild, H., & Feshbach, N. (1992). *Big world, small screen: The role of television in American society.* Omaha: University of Nebraska Press.

IGN Entertainment. (2010). *IGN's top 100 games.* Retrieved from http://top100.ign.com/2005/001-010.html

International Telecommunication Union (ITU). (2006). *World Summit on the Information Society.* Retrieved March 6, 2006, from www.itu.int/wsis/basic.about/htm

Irving, L. (1998, September 18). *Minority commercial broadcast ownership report.* Washington, DC: National Telecommunications and Information Administration.

Ito, M., Horst, H., Bittanti, M., Boyd, D., Herr-Stephenson, B., Lange, P. G., Pascoe, C. J., & Robinson, L., with Baumer, S., Cody, R., Mahendran, D., Martínez, K., Perkel, D., Sims, C., & Tripp, L. (2009). *Living and learning with new media: Summary of findings from the digial youth project.* Retrieved March 7, 2012, from http://digitalyouth.ischool.berkeley.edu/report

It's in the links. Blogging is just another word for having conversations. (2006, April 20). *Economist.* Retrieved from http://www.economist.com/surveys/displaystory.cfm?story_id=6794172

ITU. (2010). *World telecommunication/ICT development report 2010.* Geneva: ITU.

Iyengar, S., & Reeves, R. (Eds.). (1997). *Does the media govern? Politicians, voters and reporters in America.* Thousand Oaks, CA: Sage.

Jeffres, L. (1986). *Mass media processes and effects.* Prospect Heights, IL: Waveland Press.

Jenkins, H. (1999, July) Professor Jenkins goes to Washington. *Harper's Magazine,* pp. 19–23. Jensen, M., Danziger, J., & Venkatesh, A. (2007, January/February). Civil society and cyber society: The role of the Internet in community associations and democratic politics. *Information Society, 23*(1), 39.

Jhally, S. (2000). Advertising at the edge of the apocalypse. Critical studies in media commercialism.

John, D. (1999). Through the eyes of a child: Children's knowledge and understanding of advertising. In M. C. Macklin and L. Carlson (Eds.), *Advertising to children: Concepts and controversies.* Thousand Oaks, CA: Sage.

Johnson, J. G., Cohen, P., Smailes, E. M., Kasen, S., & Brook, J. S. (2002, March 29). Television viewing and aggressive behavior during adolescence and adulthood. *Science,* 2468–2471.

Johnston, J. (1987). *Electronic learning.* Hillsdale, NJ: Lawrence Erlbaum.

Jones, C. (1996). *Winning with the news media.* Tampa, FL: Video Consultants, Inc.

Jones, S. (1992). *Rock formation: Music, technology and mass communication.* Newbury Park, CA: Sage.

Jung, C. G. (1970). *Analytical psychology: Its theory and practice; the Travistock lectures.* Foreword by E. A. Bennet. New York: Vintage Books.

Kafai, Y. B., Heeter, C., Denner, J., & Sun, J. Y. (2008). *Beyond Barbie and Mortal Kombat: New perspectives on gender and gaming.* Cambridge, MA: MIT Press.

Kahin, B., & Varian, H. (Eds.). (2000). *Internet publishing and beyond: The economics of digital information and intellectual property.* Cambridge, MA: MIT Press.

Katz, E., & Lazarsfeld, P. (1955). *Personal influence.* New York: Free Press.

Kaye, B., & Medoff, N. (2001). *Just a click away: Advertising on the Internet.* Boston: Allyn & Bacon.

Keller, P., & Lehmann, D. (2008). Designing effective health communications: A meta-analysis. *Journal Of Public Policy & Marketing, 27*(2), 117–130. doi:10.1509/jppm.27.2.117

Kenski, Kate, Bruce W. Hardy, & Kathleen Hall Jamieson. (2010). *The Obama victory: How media, money and message shaped the 2008 election.* New York: Oxford.

Kent, S. L. (2001). *The ultimate history of video games.* Rocklin, CA: Prima Publications.

Kernan, M., & Howard, G. (1990). Computer anxiety and computer attitudes: An investigation of construct and predictive validity issues. *Educational and Psychological Measurement, 50,* 681–690.

Kerr, A. The economics of digital games. In J. Rutter & J. Bryce (Eds.), *Understanding digital games* (pp. 58–74). London, Thousand Oaks: Sage Publications Ltd.

Kilborn, P. (1993, March 15). New jobs lack the old security in time of "disposable workers." *New York Times,* A1.

Kim, K., & McCombs, M. (2007, Summer). News story descriptions and the public's opinions of political candidates. *Columbia Journalism and Mass Communication Quarterly, 84*(2), 299–315.

Kiriakidis, S., & Kavoura, A. (2010). Cyberbullying: A review of the literature on harassment through the Internet and other electronic means. *Family & Community Health, 33,* 82–93.

Kirriemuir, J. (2006). A history of digital games. In J. Rutter & J. Bryce (Eds.), *Understanding digital games* (pp. 21–36). London, Thousand Oaks: Sage Publications Ltd.

Klapper, J. (1960). *The effects of mass communication.* New York: Free Press.

Knight, A. (1979). *The liveliest art.* New York: New American Library.

Koponen, J. M. (2010). *The future of personal digital information—Scarce resource, valuable commodity or an efficient utility?* University of Art & Design Helsinki. Retrieved January 4, 2010, from http://www.jarnokoponen.net/file_download/9/OPEN_TheFutureOfDigitalInformation_JMKoponen_021109_final.pdf

Koster, R. (2002). *Online world timeline.* Retrieved from http://www.raphkoster.com/gaming/mudtimeline.shtml

Kraut, R., Kiesler, S., Boneva, B., Cummings J., Helgeson, V., & Crawford, A. (2002). The Internet paradox revisited. *Journal of Social Issues, 58,* 49–74.

Kraut, R., Patterson, M., Lundmark, V., Kiesler, S., Mukophadhyay, T., & Scherlig, W. (1998). Internet paradox: A social technology that reduces social involvement and psychological well-being? *American Psychologist, 53*(9), 1017–1031.

Kuchinskas, S. (2000, November 14). The end of marketing. *Business 2.0,* 134–139.

Kunkel, D. (1998). Policy battles over defining children's educational television. (Children and Television). *The Annals of the American Academy of Political and Social Science, 57*(15), 37.

Kunkel, D., Maynard Farinola, W. J., Farrar, K., Donnerstein, E., Biely, E., & Zwarun, L. (2002). Deciphering the V-chip: An examination of the television industry's program rating judgments. *Journal of Communication, 52*(1), 112–138.

Kutner, L., & Olson, C. K. (2008). Grand theft childhood: The surprising truth about violent video games and what parents can do. New York: Simon & Schuster.

Lachlan, K., Smith, S., & Tamborini, R. (2005, December). Models for aggressive behavior: The attributes of violent characters in popular video games. *Communication Studies, 56*(4), 313–330.

LaRose, R. (1999). *Understanding personal telephone behavior.* In H. Sawhney & G. Barnett (Eds.), *Progress in communication science, vol. XV: Advances in telecommunication theory and research.* Norwood, NJ: Ablex.

LaRose, R. (2010). The problem of media habits. *Communication Theory, 20,* 194–222.

LaRose, R., & Atkin, D. (1992). Audiotext and the reinvention of the telephone as a mass medium. *Journalism Quarterly, 69*(2), 413–421.

LaRose, R., & Atkin, D. (1988). Satisfaction, demographic and media environment predictors of cable subscription. *Journal of Broadcasting and Electronic Media, 32*(4), 403–413.

LaRose, R., & Eastin, M. (2004). A social cognitive theory of Internet uses and gratifications: Toward a new model of media attendance. *Journal of Broadcasting and Electronic Media,* 48(3), 358–377.

LaRose, R., Gregg, J. L., Strover, S., Straubhaar, J., & Carpenter, S. (2007). Closing the rural broadband gap: Promoting adoption of the Internet in rural America. *Telecommunications Policy*, 31(6–7), 359–373.

LaRose, R., Kim, J. H., & Peng, W. (2010). Social networking: Addictive, compulsive, problematic, or just another media habit? In Z. Pappacharissi (Ed.), A Networked Self: Identity, Community, and Culture on Social Network Sites (pp. 59–81). New York: Routledge.

LaRose, R., Lai, Y.J., Lange, R., Love, B., & Wu, Y. (2005). Sharing or piracy? An exploration of downloading behavior. *Journal of Computer Mediated Communication,* 11(1).

LaRose, R., Lin, C. A., & Eastin, M. S. (2003). Unregulated internet usage: Addiction, habit, or deficient self-regulation? *Media Psychology*, 5, 225–253.

LaRose, R., & Rifon, N. (2006). Your privacy is assured—of being invaded. *New Media and Society,* 8(4), 1009–1030.

LaRose, R., Strover, S., Gregg, J., & Straubhaar, J. (2011). The impact of rural broadband development: Lessons from a natural field experiment. *Government Information Quarterly*, 28, 91–100.

Lau, R., Sigelman, L., Heldman, C., & Babbitt, P. (1999). The effects of negative political advertisements: A meta-analytic assessment. *The American Political Science Review,* 93(4), 851–875.

Laua, R. R., Sigelman, L., & Rovnera , I. B. (2007). *The Journal of Politics*, 69, 1176–1209.

Lauzen, M., Dozier, D., & Reyes, B. (2007). From adultescents to zoomers: An examination of age and gender in prime-time television. *Communication Quarterly*, 55(3), 343.

Lavine, H., Sweeney, D., & Wagner, S. (1999). Depicting women as sex object in television advertising: Effects on body dissatisfaction. *Personality and Social Psychology Bulletin,* 25(8), 1049–1058.

Lazarsfeld, P. (1941). Remarks on administrative and critical communication research. *Studies in Philosophy and Social Science,* 9, 2–16.

Lee, K. (2004). Presence, explicated. *Communication Theory,* 14(1), 27–50.

Leiner, B., Cerf, V., Clark, D., Kahn, R., Kleinrock, L., Lynch, D., Postel, J., Roberts, L., & Wolf, S. (2000). *A brief history of the Internet.* Retrieved September 16, 2002, from http://www.isoc.org/internet/history/brief.shtml

Levy, P. (2001). *Cyberculture.* Translated by Bononno, R. Minneapolis: University of Minnesota Press.

Lemmens, Jeroen, S., Patti M. Valkenburg, & Jochen Peter. (2009). Development and Validation of a Game Addiction Scale for Adolescents. *Media Psychology*, 12, 77–95.

Lieberman, D. A. (1997). Interactive video games for health promotion. In R. L. Street, Jr, W. R. Gold, & T. Manning (Eds.), *Health promotion and interactive technology* (pp. 103–120). Mahwah, NJ: Lawrence Erlbaum.

Liebert, R., & Sprafkin, J. (1988). *The early window.* New York: Pergamon Press.

Lim, S., Sauter, S., & Schnorr, T. (1998). Occupational health aspects of work with video display terminals. In W. Rom (Ed.), *Environmental and occupational medicine* (3rd ed.). Philadelphia: Lippincott-Raven.

Limmer, J. (Ed.). (1981). *The Rolling Stone illustrated history of rock and roll.* New York: Random House.

Lin, C. (2003). An interactive communication technology adoption model. *Communication Theory,* 13(4), 345–365.

Lin, J. (2007). *College students perceptions of credibility of blogs and traditional media as a function of the blog usage.* Master's thesis, Michigan State University.

Lindlof, T. (1995). *Qualitative communications research methods.* Thousand Oaks, CA: Sage.

Lindlof, T. R., & B. C. Taylor (2010). *Qualitative communication research methods*. Thousand Oaks, CA, Sage.

Ling, R. (2004). *The mobile connection: The cell phone's impact on society.* San Francisco: Morgan Kaufmann.

Lippmann, W. (1922). *Public opinion.* New York: Macmillan.

Littlefield, M. B. (2008). The media as a system of racialization: Exploring images of African American women and the new racism. *American Behavioral Scientist*, 51(5), 675–685.

Livingstone, S. (1998). *Making sense of television: The psychology of audience interpretation* (2nd ed.). New York: Routledge.

Livingstone, S., & Helsper, E. J. (2008). Parental mediation of children's Internet use. *Journal of Broadcasting & Electronic Media*, 52(4), pp. 581–599.

Lodish, L., Abraham, M., Livelsberger, J., Lubetkin, B., Richardson, B., & Stevens, M. (1995). A summary of 55 in-market experimental estimates of the long-term effect of TV advertising. *Marketing Science*, 14(3), G133–G140.

Lotz, A. D. (2001). Postfeminist television criticism: Rehabilitating critical terms and identifying postfeminist attributes. *Feminist Media Studies*, 105–121.

Lynam, D., Milich, R., Zimmerman, R., Novak, S., et al. (1999). Project DARE: No effects at 10-year follow-up. *Journal of Consulting and Clinical Psychology,* 67(4), 590–593.

Lyotard, J. (1984). *The postmodern condition.* Manchester, UK: Manchester University Press.

Mack, O. (2007, October 29). *Video ads for people without TVs.* Retrieved from http://blogs.mediapost.com/video_insider/?p=123

Maes, K., De Haes, S., & Van Grembergen, W. (2011). How IT enabled investments bring value to the business: A literature review. This paper appears in: System Sciences 44th International Conference on System Sciences, Kauai, Hawaii, January. Pages 1–10. Digital Object Identifier: 10.1109/HICSS.2011.227

Magazine Publishers of America. (2011/2012). Factbook. Retrieved online at http://www.magazine.org/

Magazine Publishers of America (MPA). (2011). Retrieved online at http://www.magazine.org/CONSUMER_MARKETING/CIRC_TRENDS/1318.aspx

Maibach, E., & Holtgrave, D. (1995). Advances in public health communication. *Annual Review of Public Health, 16,* 219–238.

Malamuth, N., Addison, T., & Koss, M. (2000). Pornography and sexual aggression: Are there reliable effects and can we understand them? *Annual Review of Sex Research, 11,* 26–91.

Martin, D., & Coons, D. (1998a, April 20). Court KO's EEO. *Broadcasting & Cable,* 6.

———. (1998b). *Media flight plan.* Provo, UT: Deer Creek Publishing.

Martín-Barbero, J. (1993). *Communication, culture, and hegemony: From the media to the mediations.* Thousand Oaks, CA: Sage.

Mast, G., & Kawin, B. (1996). *The movies: A short history.* Needham Heights, MA: Simon & Schuster.

Mastro, D. (2008). Effects of racial and ethnic stereotyping. In J. Bryant and M. B. Oliver (Eds.), *Media effects advances in theory and research* (3rd ed., pp. 325–341). Mahwah, NJ: Erlbaum.

Mastro, D., & Greenberg, B. (2000). The portrayal of minorities on prime time television. *Journal of Broadcasting and Electronic Media, 44,* 690–703.

Mastro, D., & Stern, S. (2003). Representations of race in television commercials: A content analysis of prime-time advertising. *Journal of Broadcasting & Electronic Media, 47*(4), 638–647.

McAnany, E. (1980). *Communication in the rural third world: The role of information in development.* New York: Praeger.

McAvoy, K. (2011). TV's top 30 group owners. *TV News Check.* Retrieved from http://www.tvnewscheck.com/article/2011/03/30/50206/tv-group-ranking-could-see-shakeup-in-11

McChesney, R. (1996). The Internet and U.S. communication policy making in historical and critical context. *Journal of Communication, 46*(1), 98–124.

———. (2000). *Rich media, poor democracy: Communication politics in dubious times.* Urbana: University of Illinois Press.

McChesney, R. (2007). *Communication revolution: Critical junctures and the future of media.* New York: New Press, distributed by W. W. Norton & Co.

McDaniel, D. (2002). *Electronic tigers of Southeast Asia.* Ames: Iowa State University.

McDonough, P. (2009). *TV viewing among kids at an eight-year high.* Retrieved February 14, 2011, from http://blog.nielsen.com/nielsenwire/media_entertainment/tv-viewing-among-kids-at-an-eight-year-high/

McKearns, J. (1993). The emergence of modern media, 1900–1945. In W. Sloan, J. Stovall, & J. Startt (Eds.), *Media in America: A history* (2nd ed.). Scottsdale, AZ: Publishing Horizons.

McLeod, J., Kosicki, G., & McLeod, D. (1994). The expanding boundaries of political communication effects. In J. Bryant & D. Zillman (Eds.), *Media effects.* Hillsdale, NJ: Lawrence Erlbaum.

McLuhan, M. (1962). *The Gutenberg galaxy: The making of a typographic man.* Toronto, ON: University of Toronto Press.

———. (1964). *Understanding media: The extensions of man.* New York: McGraw-Hill.

McPhail, T. (1989). *Electronic colonialism.* Newbury Park, CA: Sage.

Means, B., Toyama, Y., Murphy, R., Bakia, M., et al. (2009). *Evaluation of evidence-based practices in online learning: A meta-analysis and review of online learning studies.* Washington, DC: U.S. Department of Education.

Merrill, J. (1997). *Journalism ethics: Philosophical foundations for news media.* New York: St. Martin's Press.

Milavsky, J., Kessler, R., Stipp, H., & Rubens, W. (1982). Television and aggression: Results of a panel study. In D. Perarl, L. Bouthliet, & J. Lazar (Eds.), *Television and behavior: Ten years of scientific progress and implications for the eighties* (Vol. 2.) Washington, DC: National Institute for Mental Health.

Miller, T. N., Govil, J., Mcmurria, R., Maxwell, T., & Wang. (2005). *Global Hollywood 2.* Berkeley: University of California Press.

Millman, S. (1984). *A history of engineering & science in the Bell System: Communications sciences, 1925–1980.* Murray Hill, NJ: AT&T Bell Laboratories.

Mitchell, Finkelhor, & Wolak. (2003). The exposure of youth to unwanted sexual material on the Internet: A national survey of risk, impact, and prevention. *Youth and Society, 34*(3), 330–359.

Mitchell, Kimberly J., David Finkelhor, Lisa M. Jones, & Janis Wolak J. D. (2012). Prevalence and characteristics of youth sexting: A National Study. *Pediatrics, 129*(1), pp. 13–20. doi:10.1542/peds. 2011-1730

Mody, B., Bauer, J., & Straubhaar, J. (1995). *Telecommunications politics: Ownership and control of the information highway in developing countries.* Hillsdale, NJ: Lawrence Earlbaum.

Moore, G. (1996). *Nanometers and gigabucks—Moore on Moore's Law.* University Video Corporation Distinguished Lecture. Retrieved from http://www.uvc.com/

Morgan, D. (2007, October 25). *The trust issue.* Retrieved from http://publications.mediapost.com/index.cfm?fuseaction=Articles.showArticle&art_aid=69785

Morgan, M., & Shanahan, J. (1992). *Television, audiences and cultural studies.* New York: Routledge.

———. (1997). Two decades of cultivation research. In B. R. Burelson (Ed.), *Communication yearbook 20* (pp. 1–47). Thousand Oaks, CA: Sage.

Morley, D. (1992). *Television, audiences and cultural studies.* New York: Routledge.

Morley, N. (1986). *Family television: Cultural power and domestic leisure.* London: Routledge.

Morozov, E. (2011). The net delusion: The dark side of Internet freedom. New York: Public Affairs.

Morrissey, B. (2007, November 5). *Social network ads: Too close, too personal?* Retrieved from http://news.yahoo.com/s/adweek/20071106/ad_bpiaw/socialnetworkadstoocloetoopersonal

Motion Picture Association of America. (2011). *2010 U.S. theatrical market statistics report.* Retrieved from http://www.magazine.org

———. (2007b). *U.S. theatrical snapshot.* Retrieved from http://www.magazine.org

Mueller, M., & Schement, J. (1995). *Universal service from the bottom up: A profile of telecommunications access in Camden, New Jersey.* New Brunswick, NJ: Rutgers University School of Communication, Information and Library Studies.

Mulligan, J. (2000). *History of online games.* Retrieved from http://tharsis-gate.org/articles/imaginary/HISTOR~1.HTM

Nacos, B. L., & Torres-Reyna, O. (2007). Fueling our fears: Stereotyping, media coverage, and public opinion of Muslim Americans. Lanham, MD: Rowman & Littlefield.

Napoli, P. (2002). Audience valuation and minority media: An analysis of the determinants of the value of radio audiences. *Journal of Broadcasting & Electronic Media, 46*(2), 169–184.

Nathanson, A. (2004). Factual and evaluative approaches to modifying children's responses to violent television. *Journal of Communication, 54*(2), 321–336.

Nathanson, A. I., Wilson, B. J., McGee, J., Sebastian, M. (2002). Counteracting the effects of female stereotypes on television via active mediation, *Journal of Communication,* 52(4), 922–937.

National Telecommunications and Information Administration (NTIA). (2000). *Falling through the net: Toward digital inclusion.* Retrieved from http://www.ntia.doc.gov/ntiahome/digitaldivide/execsumfttn00.htm

National Center for Educational Statistics. (2005). National Assessment of Adult Literacy Results. Commissioner Mark Schneider Speech on 2003 data. Retrieved from http://nces.ed.gov/whatsnew/commissioner/remarks2005/12_15_2005.asp

———. (2002). *A nation online: How Americans are expanding their use of the Internet.* Retrieved from http://ntia.doc./gov/ntiahome/dn/index.html

———. (2004). *A nation online: Entering the broadband age.* Retrieved from http://www.ntia.doc.gov/reports/anol/index.html

Nielsen. (2012a). *State of the media: U.S. digital consumer report Q3–Q4 2011.* Retrieved February 25, 2011, from http://www.nielsen.com/content/dam/corporate/us/en/reports-downloads/2012%20Reports/Digital-Consumer-Report-Q4-2012.pdf

Nielsen. (2012b). *Are US consumers choosing smartphones as Apple closes the gap on Android.* Retrieved Februrary 25, 2012, from http://blog.nielsen.com/nielsenwire/consumer/more-us-consumers-choosing-smartphones-as-apple-closes-the-gap-on-android/

Nielsen Mobile. (July 2008). *Critical Mass: The Worldwide State of the Mobile Web.* Retrieved from www.nielsen-mobile.com/documents/CriticalMass.pdf

NTIA. (2011). *Exploring the digital nation—Computer and Internet use at home.* Retrieved April 20, 2012, from http://www.ntia.doc.gov/report/2011/exploring-digital-nation-computer-and-internet-use-home

Neff, J. (2007, September). *Soft soap.* Retrieved from http://adage.com/results?search_offset=0&search_order_by=score&search_phrase=dove+soap

NetRatings. (2002). *Hot off the net.* Retrieved from http://www.neilsen-netratings.com/hot_off_the_net_i.jsp

———. (2008). *United States: Average web use.* Retrieved from http://www.nielsen-netratings.com/reports.jsp?section=pub_reports&report=usage&period=monthly&panel_type=2

Newcomb, H. (1992). *Television: A critical view* (5th ed.) New York: Oxford University Press.

Newman, E. (2007, August 20). *New media: Facebook enjoys fresh-faced appeal among advertisers.* Retrieved from http://www.insidebrandedentertainment.com/bep/article_display.jsp?JSESSIONID=yY3ZHMVMGmLZszkQ4xC5QG2rhfJsnfHS924FJzT1XTv5vrkqx3TS!363335482&vnu_content_id=1003627727

Newman, R., & Johnson, F. (1999). Sites for power and knowledge? Towards a critique of the virtual university. *British Journal of Sociology of Education,* 20(1), 79–88. Newspaper Association of America. (2004). Retrieved from http://www.naa.org

New York Times. (1901). *Tweed ring—Its beginnings and its methods* [sic.]. Retrieved from http://query.nytimes.com/mem/archive-free/pdf?res=F3071EF73C5415738DDDA10994D1405B818CF1D3

Nie, N. H. (2001). Sociability, interpersonal relations, and the Internet: Reconciling conflicting findings. *The American Behavioral Scientist,* 45, 420–436.

Nie, N. H., & Ebring, L. (2002, Summer). *IT & Society,* 1(1), 275–283.

Nielsen (2011). *The social media report.* Retrieved from http://blog.nielsen.com/nielsenwire/social/

Nielsen Media Research. (2007). *Nielsen reports television tuning remains at record levels.* Retrieved from www.nielsenmedia.com/nc/portal/site/Public/menuitem.55dc65b4a7d5adff3f65936147a062a0/?vgnextoid=13280e5b2cea5110VgnVCM100000ac0a260aRCRD

Nielsen Media Research. (2010). *Television audience 2009.* New York: The Nielsen Company.

Noam, E. (1983). *Telecommunications regulation today and tomorrow.* New York: Law and Business.

Noelle-Neumann, E. (1984). *The spiral of silence: Public opinion—Our social skin.* Chicago: University of Chicago Press.

NPD Group. (2012). *U.S. video game industry new physical retail content sales reach $9.3 billion.* Retrieved March 3, 2012, from https://www.npd.com/wps/portal/npd/us/news/pressreleases/pr_120116

Nuzum, E. (2001). *Parental advisory: Music censorship in America.* New York: Harper Collins.

Odlyzko, A. (2001). *Content is not king.* Retrieved from http://firstmonday.org/issues/issue6_2/odlyzko/index.html

OECD. (2011). *OECD broadband portal.* Retrieved from http://www.oecd.org/document/54/0,3746, en_2649_34225_38690102_1_1_1_1,00.html

Okorafor, N., & Davenport, L. (2001, August). *Virtual women: Replacing the real.* Commission on the Status of Women, Association for Education in Journalism and Mass Communication National Convention, Washington, DC.

Olasky, M. (1987). *Corporate public relations & American private enterprise.* Hillsdale, NJ: Erlbaum.

O'Neill, M. (2010). How much money do the top grossing YouTube partners make? Retrieved from http://socialtimes.com/money-youtube-partners_b21335

Oppliger, P. A. (2007). Effects of gender stereotyping on socialization. In R. W. Preiss, B. M. Gayle, N. Burrell, M. Allen, & J. Bryant (Eds.), *Mass Media Effects Research: Advances through meta-analysis* (pp. 199–214). Florence, KY: Routledge.

Ouellette, J. A., & Wood, W. (1998). Habit and intention in everyday life: The multiple processes by which past behavior predicts future behavior. *Psychological Bulletin*, 124, 54–74.

Outing, S. (2011). *The 11 layers of citizen journalism*. Retrieved from http://www.poynter.org/uncategorized/69328/the-11-layers-of-citizen-journalism/

Owen, B., & Wildman, S. (1992). *Video economics*. Cambridge, MA: Harvard University Press.

Packard, V. (1957). *The hidden persuaders*. New York: Simon & Schuster.

Paik, H., & Comstock, G. (1994). The effects of television violence on social behavior: A meta-analysis. *Communication Research,* 21, 516–545.

Palmgreen, P., & Rayburn, J. (1985). An expectancy-value approach to media gratifications. In K. Rosengren, L. Wenner, & P. Palmgreen (Eds.), *Media gratifications research: Current perspectives*. Thousand Oaks, CA: Sage.

Papacharissi, Z., & Rubin, A. M. (2000). Predictors of Internet usage. *Journal of Broadcasting and Electronic Media,* 44, 175–196.

Pappas, C. (2000, July 10). Ad nauseam. *Advertising Age,* 16–18.

Pariser, E. (2011). *The filter bubble: What the Internet is hiding from you*. New York: Penguin Press.

Parlett, D. S. (1999). *The Oxford history of board games*. New York: Oxford University Press.

Parks, M., & Floyd, K. (1996). Making friends in cyberspace. *Journal of Communication,* 46(1), 80–97.

Parsons, P., & Frieden, R. (1998). *The cable and satellite television industries*. Needham Heights, MA: Allyn & Bacon.

Parton, J. (1874, July). Falsehood in the Daily Press. *Harper's New Monthly Magazine*, 49, 274. Retrieved from http://harpers.org/archive/1874/07/0044438.

Patchin, J. W., & Hinduza, S. (2006). Bullies move beyond the schoolyard. *Youth Violence and Juvenile Justice,* 4, 148–169.

Pavlik, J. (1987). *Public relations: What research tells us*. Newbury Park, CA: Sage.

———. (1998). *New media technology: Cultural and commercial perspectives* (2nd ed.). Boston: Allyn & Bacon.

Payne, D. (1993). The age of mass magazines, 1900–present. In W. Sloan, J. Stovall, & J. Startt (Eds.), *Media in America: A history* (2nd ed.). Scottsdale, AZ: Publishing Horizons.

Peal, D., & Savitz, K. (1997). *Official America Online Internet guide*. New York: McGraw-Hill.

People 2007 Media Kit. (2007). *Rates and discounts*. Retrieved from ftp://ftp.timeinc.net/pub/people/mediakit/pdfs/ratecard.pdf

Perez-Pena, R. (2007). More readers trading newspapers for web sites. *New York Times*. Retrieved from www.nytimes.com/2007/11/06/business/media/06adco.html

Petry, N. M. (2011). Commentary on Van Rooij et al. (2011): "Gaming addiction"—a psychiatric disorder or not? *Addiction*, 106, 213–214. doi:10.1111/j.1360-0443.2010.03132.x

Pew Research Center. (2002). *The economics and financing of media companies*. New York: Fordham University Press.

Pew Research Center. (2012). *The State of the News Media: Mobile devices and news consumption: some good signs for journalism*. Retrieved from http://stateofthemedia.org/2012/mobile-devices-and-news-consumption-some-good-signs-for-journalism/

Pew Research Center. (2010). *The State of the News Media: Americans spending more time following the news*. Retrieved from www.people-press.org/2010/09/12/americans-spending-more-time-following-the-news/

Pew Research Center's Project for Excellence in Journalism. (2012). Edmonds, R., Guskin, E., Rosenstiel, T., and Mitchell, A. Newspapers: building digital revenues proves painfully slow. Retrieved from http://stateofthemedia.org/2012/newspapers-building-digital-revenues-proves-painfully-slow/#fn-10488-31

Pew Research Center for Excellence in Journalism. (2011). *Overview by Tom Rosenstiel and Amy Mitchell on the annual report of american journalism 2011*. Retrieved from http://stateofthemedia.org/2011/overview-2/

———. (2005). *How women and men use the Internet*. Retrieved from http://www.pewinternet.org/pdfs/PIP_Women_and_Men_online.pdf

———. (2006a). *Internet penetration and impact*. Retrieved from http://www.pewinternet.org/PPF/r/182/report_display.asp

———. (2007a). *Election 2006 online*. Retrieved from http://www.pewinternet.org/pdfs/PIP_Politics_2006.pdf

———. (2007b). *Online video*. Retrieved from http://www.pewinternet.org/pdfs/PIP_Online_Video_2007.pdf

———. (2011). The state of the news media 2011. Retrieved from http://stateofthemedia.org/

Picard, R. G. (2002). *The economics and financing of media companies*. New York: Fordham University Press.

Pieterse, J. N. (2004). *Globalization and culture: Global melange*. Lanham, MD: Rowman & Littlefield.

Pogrebin, R. (1998, March 9). At work and at play, *Time's* editor seeks to keep magazine vigorous at 75. *New York Times*. Retrieved from http://query.nytimes.com/gst/fullpage.html?res=9E05E3D71430F93AA35750C0A96E958260&sec=&spon=&pagewanted=1

Polman, Hanneke, de Castro, Bram Orobio, van Aken, & Marcel, A. G. (2008). Experimental study of the differential effects of playing versus watching violent video games on children's aggressive behavior. *Aggressive Behavior*, 34, 256–264.

Postman, N. (1986). *Amusing ourselves to death: Public discourse in the age of show business*. New York: Penguin Books.

———. (1992). *Technopoly*. New York: Knopf.

Pulse of America Research. (2011). National newspaper reader survey results find newspapers are delivering customers. Retrieved from http://www.editorandpublisher.com/Article/National-Newspaper-Reader-Survey-Results-Find-Newspapers-Are-Delivering-Customers

Powell, K., & Abels, L. (2002). Sex-role stereotypes in television programs aimed at the preschool audience:

An analysis of teletubbies and Barney & Friends. *Women and Language*, 25(1), 14–22.

Purcell, Kristen, Lee Rainie, Amy Mitchell, Tom Rosenstiel & Kenny Olmstead. "Understanding the Participatory News Consumer." Pew Research Center's Internet & American Life Project 2010.

Putnam, R. (2000). *Bowling alone: The collapse and revival of American community*. New York: Simon & Schuster.

Putnam, R. (2002). *Bowling alone: The collapse and revival of American community*. New York: Simon & Schuster.

Racial & Ethnic Populations. (2005). *Office of Minority Health and Health Disparities (OMHD)*. Retrieved from www.cdc.gov/omhd/Populations/populations.htm

Radway. (1984). *Reading the romance: Women, patriarchy, and popular literature*. Durham: University of North Carolina Press.

Rafaeli, S. (1988). Interactivity: From new media to communication. In Hawkins, Pingree, & Weimann (Eds.), *Advancing communication sciences, vol. 16*. Beverly Hills, CA: Sage.

Rafaeli, S., & LaRose, R. (1993). Electronic bulletin boards and "public goods" explanations of collaborative mass media. *Communication Research*, 28(2), 277–297.

Rajeev, P., & Lonial, S. (1990). Advertising to children: Findings and implications. *Current Research and Issues in Advertising*, 12, 231–274.

Rakow, L. (1992). *Gender on the line*. Urbana: University of Illinois Press.

Rawls. (1999). *A theory of justice: A revised edition*. Boston: Belknap Press.

Real, M. (1989). *Super media: A cultural studies approach*. Thousand Oaks, CA: Sage.

Reed, B. (2010). A brief history of smartphones. *Network World*. Retrieved from http://www.networkworld.com/slideshows/2010/061510-smartphone-history.html

Reeves, B., & Nass, C. (1996). *The media equation*. New York: Cambridge University Press.

Reich, R. (1991). *The work of nations*. New York: Knopf.

Rice, R., & Atkin, C. (2000). *Public communication campaigns* (3rd ed.). Thousand Oaks, CA: Sage.

Ricks, D. (1999). *Blunders in international business* (3rd ed.). Malden, MA: Blackwell.

Riddler, I., & Denison, S. (February 1998). *When there is no end to a good game. British Archaeology* (United Kingdom: Council for British Archaeology) (31), ISSN 1357–4442.

Rideout, V. (2007). Parents, children & media. Kaiser Family Foundation. Retrieved from http://www.kff.org/entmedia/upload/7638.pdf

Riley, S. (1993). American magazines, 1740–1900. In W. Sloan, J. Stovall & J. Startt (Eds.), *Media in America: A history* (2nd ed.). Scottsdale, AZ: Publishing Horizons.

Robert, L., & David, A. (1992). Audiotext and the reinvention of the telephone as a mass medium. *Journalism Quarterly*, 69(2), 413–421.

Roberts, M., Wanta, W., & Dzwo, T. (2002). Agenda setting and issue salience online. *Communication Research*, 29(4), 452–465.

Robertson, R. (1995). Globalization: Time-space and homogeneity-heterogeneity. In M. Featherstone, S. Lash, & R. Robertson (Eds.), *Global modernities*. Thousand Oaks, CA: Sage.

Robins, K. (1996). Cyberspace and the world we live in. In J. Dovey (Ed.), *Fractal dreams*. London: Lawrence & Wishart.

Robinson, J., Dimaggio, P., & Hargittai, E. (2003, Summer). New social survey perspectives on the digital divide. *IT & Society*, 1(5), 1–22.

Robinson, T. N., & Borzekowski, D. L. G. (2006). Effects of the SMART classroom curriculum to reduce child and family screen time. *Journal of Communication*, 56(1), 1–26.

Rogers, E. (1986). *Communication technology—The new media in society*. New York: Free Press.

———. (1995). *Diffusion of innovations* (4th ed.). New York: Free Press.

Rojas, V., Straubhaar, J., Fuentes, M., & Pinon, J. (2005). Still divided: Ethnicity, generation, cultural capital and new technologies. In O. Janiero & J. Straubhaar (Eds.), *Politics de informaggao e comunicacao jornalismo e inclusoo digital: o local e global em Austine Salvador*. Salvador, Brazil: Edufba.

Romanowski, P., & George-Warren, H. (1995). *The new Rolling Stone encyclopedia of rock & roll*. New York: Fireside.

Rosser, Jr, J. C., Lynch, P. J., Cuddihy, L., Gentile, D. A., Klonsky, J., & Merrell, R. (2007). The impact of video games on training surgeons in the 21st century. Archives of Surgery, 142(2), 181.

Rubin, A. (1983). Television uses and gratifications. *Journal of Broadcasting*, 27, 37–51.

Sadowski, C. (2011, July). *Newspaper websites post consecutive quarterly traffic increase*. Retrieved at http://www.naa.org/News-and-Media/Press-Center/Archives/2011/Newspaper-Websites-Post-Consecutive-Quarterly-Traffic-Increase.aspx

Sandage, C. H., Fryburger, V. R., & Rotzoll, K. B. (1989). *Advertising theory and practice*. White Plains, NY: Longman.

Sass, K. (2009), *Media age of magazine readers rise. Media daily news in media post news*. Retrieved from http://www.mediapost.com/publications/?fa=Articles.showArticle&art_aid=106724

Sayre, B., Bode, L., Shah, D., Wilcox, D., & Shah, C. (2010). Agenda setting in a digital age: Tracking attention to California proposition 8 in social media, online news and conventional news. *Policy & Internet*, 2(2). doi:10.2202/1944-2866.1040

Schement, J., & Curtis, T. (1997). *Tendencies and tensions of the information age*. New Brunswick: Transaction books.

Scheufele, D., Shanahan, J., & Kim, S. (2002). Who cares about local politics? Media influences on local political involvement, issue awareness, and attitude strength. *Journalism and Mass Communication Quarterly*, 79(2), 427–444.

Schiller, D. (1996). *Theorizing communication: A history*. New York: Oxford University Press.

Schiller, H. (1981). *Information in the age of the Fortune 500*. Norwood, NJ: Ablex.

Schlesinger, P. (1991). *Media, state and nation.* Newbury Park, CA: Sage.

Schmitz, J. (1997). Structural relations, electronic media, and social change: The public electronic network and the homeless. In S. Jones (Ed.), *Virtual culture.* Thousand Oaks, CA: Sage.

Schramm, Wilbur (Ed.). (1954). *The process and effects of communication.* Urbana, IL: The University of Illinois Press.

Schramm, W. (1982). *Men, women, messages and media.* New York: Harper & Row.

Schramm, W., Lyle, J., & Parker, E. (1961). Television in the lives of our children. Palo Alto, CA: Stanford University Press.

Schudson, M. (1984). *Advertising, the uneasy persuasion.* New York: Basic Books.

Schwartz, J. (1999, May 22). Study: Cell phones may have cancer link. *Washington Post,* E1.

Schwoch, J. (1990). *The American radio industry and its Latin American activities, 1900–1939.* Champaign: University of Illinois Press.

Sears, D., & Freedman, J. (1972). Selective exposure to information: A critical review. In W. Schramm & D. Roberts (Eds.), *The process and effects of mass communication.* Chicago: University of Illinois Press.

Seelye, K. Q. (2006, August 23). *Microsoft to provide and sell ads on Facebook, the website.* Retrieved from http://www.nytimes.com/2006/08/23/technology/23soft.html

Seiter, E. (1992). Semiotics, structuralism, and television. In R. Allen (Ed.), *Channels of discourse, reassembled.* Chapel Hill: University of North Carolina Press.

Settle, R., & Alreck, P. (1986). *Why they buy.* New York: Wiley.

Sethuraman, Raj, Gerard J . Tellis, & Richard A. Briesch. (2011). How well does advertising work? Generalizations from meta-analysis of brand advertising elasticities. *Journal of Marketing Research*, 48(3), 457–471.

Shaheen, J. G. (2003). Reel bad Arabs: How Hollywood vilifies a people. *The Annals of the American Academy of Political and Social Science,* 588(1), 171–193.

Shannon, C. E., & Weaver, W. (1949): *The mathematical theory of communication.* Urbana IL: University of Illinois Press.

Shefrin, D. (1993). Rediscovering an olde technology: Facsimile newspaper lessons of invention and failure. In J. Pavlik & E. Dennis (Eds.), *Demystifying media technology.* Mountain View, CA: Mayfield Publishing.

Sher, J., & Carey, B. (2007, July 19). Federal study stirs debate on child pornography's link to molesting. *New York Times.* Retrieved from http://www.nytimes.com/2007/07/19/us/19sex.html?n=Top2fReference2fTimes20Topics2fSubjects2fP2fPornography20and20Obscenity

Sherry, J. (2004). Flow and media enjoyment. *Communication Theory,* 14, 328–347.

Sherry, J. (2007). Violent video games and aggression: Why can't we find links? In R. Preiss, B. Gayle, N. Burrell, M. Allen, & J. Bryant (Eds.), *Mass media effects research: Advances through meta-analysis* (pp. 231–248). Mahwah, NJ: Routledge.

Shoemaker, P. (1991). *Gatekeeping.* Newbury Park, CA: Sage.

Shoemaker, P. J., & Vohs, T. P. (2009). *Gatekeeping theory.* New York: Taylor & Francis.

Shonfeld & Associates. (2012). 2011 advertising to sales ratios by industry sector. Retrieved March 7, 2012, from http://www.saibooks.com/adv-ind-sector-ratios.html

Sichel, D. (1999, April). Computers and aggregate economic growth: An update. *Business Economics,* 34(2), 18–24.

Signorelli, Nancy. (2009). Race and sex in prime time: A look at occupations and occupational prestige. *Mass Communication and Society,* 12(3), 332–352. doi:10.1080/15205430802478693

Signorielli, N. (1989). Television and conceptions about sex roles: Maintaining conventionality and the status quo. *Sex Roles,* 21(5–6), 341–360.

Signorielli, N. (2003). Prime-time violence 1993–2001: Has the picture really changed? *Journal of Broadcasting & Electronic Media*, 47(1), 36–58.

Signorielli, N., & Bacue, A. (1999). Recognition and respect: A content analysis of prime-time television characters across three decades. *Sex Roles,* 40, 527–544.

Silva, C. E. Lins da. (1990). *O adiantado da hora: a influencia americana sobre o jornalismo brasileiro.* (The avant-guard: American influence on Brazilian journalism.) Sao Paulo: Summus.

Sim, Timothy, Douglas A. Gentile, Francesco Bricolo, Giovanni Serpelloni, & Farah Gulamoydeen. (2011). A conceptual review of research on the pathological use of computers, video games, and the internet. *International Journal of Mental Health and Addiction.* doi:10.1007/s11469-011-9369-7

Singhal, A., & Rogers, E. M. (2001). *India's communication revolution: From bullock carts to cyber marts.* New Delhi: Sage/India.

Sitzmann, T., Kraiger, K., Stewart, D., & Wisher, R. (2006, Autumn). The comparative effectiveness of Web-based and classroom instruction: A meta-analysis. *Personnel Psychology,* 59(3), 623–664.

Sloan, D. (Ed.). (2005). *The media in America: A history* (6th ed.). Northport, AL: Vision Press.

Sloan, W., Stovall, J., & Startt, J. (Eds.). (1993). *Media in America: A history* (2nd ed.). Scottsdale, AZ: Publishing Horizons.

Smillie, B. (1997, December 18). Japanese TV cartoon show stuns hundreds. *Lansing State Journal*, 15A.

Smith, Aaron. (2011). *The Internet and Campaign 2010.* Retrieved from http://www.pewinternet.org/Reports/2011/The-Internet-and-Campaign-2010.aspx

Smith, L. A., & Foxcroft, D. R. (2009). The effect of alcohol advertising, marketing and portrayal on drinking behaviour in young people: Systematic review of prospective cohort studies. *BMC Public Health*, 9, 51–62.

Sports Illustrated Media Kit. (2007). *Rate card.* Retrieved from http://sportsillustrated.cnn.com/adinfo/si/rate-card2008.pdf

Spretnak, C. (1997, July). Resurgence of the real. *UTNE Reader,* 106, 59–63.

Sproull, L., & Faraj, S. (1997). Atheism, sex, and databases: The net as a social technology. In S. Kiesler (Ed.), *Culture of the Internet*. Mahwah, NJ: Lawrence Erlbaum.

Standage, T. (1998). *The Victorian Internet*. New York: Berkley Books.

Steinberg (2006, July 10). The marketing maze. *Wall Street Journal*, 248(7), R1(2).

Stepanikova, Irena, Norman H. Nie, Xiaobin He. (2010, May). Time on the Internet at home, loneliness, and life satisfaction: Evidence from panel time-diary data. *Computers in Human Behavior*, 26(3), 329–338. ISSN 0747-5632, doi: 10.1016/j.chb.2009.11.002

Sterling, C., & Kittross, J. (2002). *Stay tuned—A concise history of American broadcasting* (2nd ed.). Belmont, CA: Wadsworth.

Stewart, D. W., & Pavlou, P. A. (2008). The effects of media on marketing communication. In J. Bryant and M. B. Oliver, *Media effects advances in theory and research* (3rd ed.). New York: Erlbaum.

Story, L. (2007, October 22). *How many site hits? Depends on who's counting*. Retrieved from http://www.nytimes.com/2007/10/26/business/media/26appleweb.html?_r=1&oref=slogin

Story, L., & Helft, M. (2007, April 14). *Google buys an online ad firm for $3.1 billion*. Retrieved from http://www.nytimes.com/2007/04/14/technology/14deal.html?_r=1&oref=slogin

Straubhaar, J. (1991). Beyond media imperialism: Asymmetrical interdependence and cultural proximity. *Critical Studies in Mass Communication*, (8), 39–59.

Straubhaar, J. (2005). (Re)Asserting National Television and National Identity Against the Global, Regional and Local Levels of World Television. Media and Cultural Studies: Keyworks, Revised Edition G. Durham and D. Kellner. NYC, Blackwell: 681–702.

Straubhaar, J. D. (2007). *World television: From global to local*. Sage Publications, Thousand Oaks, CA.

Straubhaar, J., & Boyd, D. (2007). International Broadcasting. *Global Communication* (2nd ed.). Yahya R. Kamalipour, Ed. Belmont, CA: Wadsworth.

Straubhaar, J., & Duarte, L. G. (2005). Adapting U.S. transnational television to a complex world: From cultural imperialism to localization to hybridization. In J. Chalaby (Ed.), *Transnational Television Worldwide: Towards a New Media Order* (pp. 216–253). London: I.B. Taurus.

Straubhaar, J. D., Spence, J. et al. (Eds.). (2012). Inequity in the Technopolis: Race, class, gender and the digital divide in Austin, TX. Austin: University of Texas Press.

Streeter, Thomas. (1996). *Selling the air: A critique of the policy of commercial broadcasting in the United States*. Chicago: University of Chicago Press.

Strover, S., & Straubhaar, J. (2004). *Critically evaluating market diffusion policy and the digital divide in Texas 2000–2004*. Communication and Technology Division. Paper presented at the 55th Annual Conference of the International Communication Association, New York.

Synovate. (2007, August 30). *New study shows Americans' blogging behaviour*. Retrieved from http://www.synovate.com/news/article/2007/08/new-study-shows-americans-blogging-behaviour.html

Taylor, T. A. (2007). *Career opportunities in the Internet, video games, and multimedia*. New York: Ferguson.

Tebbel, J. (1969). *The American magazine: A compact history*. New York: Hawthorne Books.

The impact of video games on training surgeons in the 21st century. *Archives of Surgery*, 142(2), 181–186.

The Week. (2011). Occupy Wall Street: A protest timeline. Retrieved from http://theweek.com/article/index/220100/occupy-wall-street-a-protest-timeline

Tiffin, J., & Rajasingham, L. (1995). *In search of the virtual class*. New York: Routledge.

Tolbert & McNeal. (2003). Unraveling the effects of the Internet on political participation? *Political Research Quarterly,* 56(2), 175–185.

Turing, A. M. (1950). Computing machinery and intelligence. *Mind,* 59(236), 433.

Turkle, S. (1995). *Life on the screen: Identity in the age of the Internet*. New York: Simon & Schuster.

Turkle, S. (2011). *Alone together: Why we expect more from technology and less from each other*. New York: Basic Books.

Turner, S., & Cooper, M. (2007). *Out of the picture: Minority and female TV ownership in the United States*. Retrieved from http://www.freepress.net/files/otp2007.pdf

TV-Free America. (n.d.). *Television statistics*. Retrieved from http://www.csun.edu/science/health/docs/tv&health.html

U.S. Department of Commerce. (2004). National Telecommunications and Information Administration, *A nation online: Entering the broadband age*.

U.S. Department of Health and Human Services (U.S.D.H.H.S.). (2001). *Youth violence: A report of the surgeon general*. Rockville, MD: U.S.D.H.H.S.

U.S. Occupational Outlook Handbook. (2010). U.S. occupational outlook handbook. Washington, DC: U.S. Department of Labor. http://www.bls.gov/ooh/

USA Today. (12/11/2004). *Wal-Mart sued over Evanescence lyrics*. Retrieved from http://www.usatoday.com/life/music/2004-12-11-walmart-music_x.htm. Accessed 7/14/2012

University of Texas. (2000). *The Internet economy indicators*. Austin, TX: Center for Research in Mass Commerce, University of Texas. Retrieved from http://www.internetindicators.com/the_indicators_june_00.htm

Vakratsas, D., & Ambler, T. (1999). How advertising works: What do we really know? *Journal of Marketing,* 63(1), 26–43.

Valentino, N., Hutchings, V., & Williams, D. (2004). The impact of political advertising on knowledge, Internet information seeking, and candidate preference. *Journal of Communication,* 54(2), 337–354.

van der Molen, J. (2004). Violence and suffering in television news: Toward a broader conception of harmful television content for children. *Pediatrics,* 113(6), 1771–1776.

Vandewater, E. A., Shim, M. S., & Caplovitz, A. G. (2004). Linking obesity and activity level with children's television and video game use. *Journal of Adolescence*, 27(1), 71–85.

Van Erva, J. (1990). *Television and child development.* Hillsdale, NJ: Lawrence Erlbaum.

Van Rooij, Antonius, J., Tim M Schoenmakers, Ad A Vermulst, Regina J J M Van Den Eijnden, Dike Van De Mheen. 106(1), 205–212. (2011). Online video game addiction: identification of addicted adolescent gamers. Addiction

Vara, V. (2007). *Facebook gets personal with ad targeting plan.* Retrieved from http://online.wsj.com/article/SB118783296519606151.html

Vandercruysse, S., Vandewaetere, M., & Clarebout, G. (2012). Game-based learning: A review on the effectiveness of educational games. In M. Cruz-Cunha (Ed.), Handbook of Research on Serious Games as Educational, Business and Research Tools (pp. 628–647). Hershey, PA: Information Science Reference.

Variety. (2006). *Variety's global 50.* Retrieved July 24, 2006, from http://www.variety.com

Venkatesh, V., & Johnson, P. (2002). Telecommuting technology implementations: A within-and-between-subjects longitudinal field study. *Personnel Psychology,* 55(3), 661.

Virnoche, M. (1998). The seamless web and communications equity: The shaping of a community network. *Science, Technology & Human Values,* 23(2), 199–218.

Vlad, T., Becker, L. B., Olin, D., Wilcox, D., & Hanisak, S. (2009). 2008 Annual Survey of Journalism and Mass Communication Enrollments. Athens, Georgia, Grady College of Journalism & Mass Communication, University of Georgia. Retrieved January 29, 2010, from www.grady.uga.edu/annualsurveys/

Vogel, H. (2007). *Entertainment industry economics: a guide for financial analysis* (7th ed.). New York: Cambridge University Press.

Wakefield, M., Terry-McElrath, Y., Emery, S., Saffer, H., et al. (2006, December). Effect of televised, tobacco company-funded smoking prevention advertising on youth smoking-related beliefs, intentions, and behavior. *American Journal of Public Health,* 96(12), 2154–2161.

Waldman, S. (2011). The information needs of communities. Washington, DC: Federal Communications Commission. Retrieved from http://www.fcc.gov/info-needs-communities

Wall Street Journal. (2006, May 24). Poll shows more U.S. adults go online at home. Retrieved from www.wsj.com
———. (2007). *Circulation quality continues growth.* Retrieved from http://finance.paidcontent.org/paidcontent?GUID=3690810&Page=MediaViewer&Ticker=DJ

Walther, J. (1996). Computer mediated communication: Impersonal, interpersonal and hypersonal. *Communication Research,* 23(1), 3–41.

Wanta, W. (1997). *The public and the national agenda.* Mahawh, NJ: Lawrence Erlbaum.

Waverman, L., & Dasgupta, K. (2009). *Connectivity scorecard 2009.* Retrieved from http://www.connectivityscorecard.org/images/uploads/media/TheConnectivityReport2009.pdf

Wakefield, Melanie A., Barbara Loken, & Robert C. Hornik. (2010, October 9–15). Use of mass media campaigns to change health behaviour. *The Lancet,* 376(9748), 1261–1271. ISSN 0140-6736, doi: 10.1016/S0140-6736(10)60809-4 (http://www.sciencedirect.com/science/article/pii/S0140673610608094)

Waxman, S. (1998, November 29). As Hollywood looks afar, minorities often lose out. *Washington Post News Service* in *Austin American-Statesman,* G-1.

Weber, R. 2008, Audience Segmentation, The International Encyclopedia of Communication, W. Donsbach, ed. NY: Blackwell.

Weber, T. (1996, December 9). Who uses the Internet? *Wall Street Journal,* R6.

Wells, S. (2001). Making telecommuting work. *HRMagazine,* 46(10), 34–45.

Wells, W., Burnett, J., & Moriarty, S. (1995). *Advertising principles and practice.* Engelwood Cliffs, NJ: Prentice Hall.

Whetmore, E. (1981). *The magic medium: An introduction to radio in America.* Belmont, CA: Wadsworth.

White, C., & Kinnick, K. (2000). One click forward and two clicks back: Portrayal of women using computers in television commercials. *Women's Studies in Communication,* 23, 392–412.

White, D. (1949). The gate-keeper: A case study in the selection of news. *Journalism Quarterly,* 27.

White Gets Black Curtain Success. (2007, September 20). Retrieved from http://www.countingdown.com/movies/3915214/news?item_id=3992726

Wildman, S., & Siwek, S. (1988). *International trade in films and television programs.* Cambridge, MA: Ballinger.

Williams, B., & Delli Carpini, M. (2004). Monica and Bill all the time and everywhere: The collapse of gatekeeping and agenda setting in the new media environment. *American Behavioral Scientist,* 47(9), 1208–1230.

Williams, D. (2006). Virtual cultivation: Online worlds, offline perceptions. *Journal of Communication,* 56, 69–87.

Williams, R. (1989). *On television: Selected writings.* Edited by Alan O'Connor. New York: Routledge.

Williamson, P. (2007). *Ratings and their reasons: An investigation of the efficiency, application and unintended consequences of the Motion Picture Association of America's film rating system.* Dissertation, Michigan State University.

Wilson, B., Martins, N., & Marske, A. (2005). Children's and parents' fright reactions to kidnapping stories in the news. *Communication Monographs,* 72(1), 46.

Wilson, B., Smith, S., Potter, W., Kunkel, D., et al. (2002). Violence in children's television programming: Assessing the risks. *Journal of Communications,* 52(1), 5–35.

Wilson, Fernando A., & Jim P. Stimpson. (2010, November). Trends in fatalities from distracted driving in the United States, 1999 to 2008. *American Journal of Public Health,* 100(11), 2213–2219. doi 10.2105/AJPH.2009.187179

Wimmer, R. D., & Dominick, J. R. (2011). *Mass media research* (9th ed.). Boston: Cengage.

Wimmer, R., & Dominick, J. (2006). *Mass media research: An introduction* (8th ed.). Belmont, CA: Wadsworth.

Winseck, D. (2011). *The political economies of media and the transformation of the Global Media Industries*. Edited by D. Winseck and D. Y. Jin. London: Bloomsbury Academic.

Wolf, M. J. (2001). Genre and the video game. In M. J. Wolf (ed.), *The medium of the video game* (pp. 113–134). Austin: University of Texas Press.

Wolff, E. N. (2006). The growth of information workers in the US economy, 1950–2000: The role of technological change, computerization, and structural change. *Economic Systems Research*, 18(3), 221–255.

Wood, J. (2005). *Gendered lives: Communication, gender, and culture*. Belmont, CA: Wadsworth/Thomson Learning.

Wood W., Wong F. Y., & Chachere, J. G. (1991). Effects of media violence on viewers' aggression in unconstrained social interaction. *Pychological Bulletin*, 109(3), 371–383.

World Bank. (2006). *World development report*. Washington, DC: World Bank.

World Bank. (2009). *World development report 2010: development and climate change*. Washington, DC: World Bank Group.

Wright, C. (1974). Functional analysis and mass communications revisited. In J. Blumler & E. Katz (Eds.), *The uses of mass communications*. Beverly Hills, CA: Sage.

Wright, Paul J. (2012). U.S. males and pornography, 1973–2010: Consumption, predictors, correlates. *Journal of Sex Research*. doi:10.1080/00224499.2011.628132

Ybarra, Michele L. Mitchell, Kimberly J. Hamburger, Merle Diener-West, & Marie Leaf, Philip J. (2012). X-rated material and perpetration of sexually aggressive behavior among children and adolescents: Is there a link? *Aggressive Behavior*, 37, 1098–2337. Retrieved from http://dx.doi.org/10.1002/ab.20367

Ybarra, Michele L., Marie Diener-West, Dana Markow, Philip J. Leaf, & Merle Hamburger, Paul. (2008). Linkages between Internet and other media violence with seriously violent behavior. *Youth Pediatrics*, 122(5), 929–937. doi:10.1542/peds.2007-3377

Yee, N., (2007). Motivations of play in online games. *Journal of CyberPyschology and Behaviour*, 9, 772–775.

Yioutas, J., & Segvic, I. (2003). Revisiting the Clinton/Lewinsky scandal: The convergence of agenda setting and framing. *Journalism and Mass Communication Quarterly,* 80(3), 567.

Yoori Hwang, & Se-Hoon Jeong. (2009). Revisiting the knowledge gap hypothesis: A meta-analysis of thirty-five years of research. *Journalism & Mass Communication Quarterly*, 86(3) pp. 513–532. doi: 10.1177/107769900908600304

Zickuhr, Kathryn. (2010). *Generations 2010*. Retrieved from http://www.pewinternet.org/Reports/2010/Generations-2010.aspx

Zillmann, D., & Bryant, J. (1985). Affect mood and emotion as determinants of selective exposure. In D. Zillmann & J. Bryant (Eds.), Selective exposure to communication (pp. 157–189). New York: Routledge.

Zuboff, S. (1984). *In the age of the smart machine*. New York: Basic Books.

Zuckerman, S. (2007, October 21). *Yes, some blogs are profitable—Very profitable*. Retrieved from http://www.sfgate.com/cgi-bin/article.cgi?f=/c/a/2007/10/21/BUVJSNSTC.DTL

Index

and PR, 297–298
women and, 44
bluegrass music, 133
blues music, 133, 134, 154
Bluetooth, 364, 388
Bluhn, Julia, 492
Blu-Ray technology, 16, 201–202, 228, 257, 387, 465
Bly, Nellie, 100
B movies, 190, 194
board games, 394
"Bobo doll" experiment, 407–409
Bodley, Thomas, 60
Bogart, Humphrey, 189
Bono, 321, 452, 508
Book of Kells, 58–59
book-of-the-month clubs, 68
books
    audio, 69, 80
    backlist, 72
    book-of-the-month clubs, 68
    categories of, 83–85
    censorship, 88–89
    as commodities, 86
    copyright on, 62. *see also* copyright
    digital publishing, 69
    e-books, 69
    economics of publishing, 77
    electronic (*see* e-books)
    E-reader, 79
    genres of, 83–85
    as ideas, 86
    Internet, 256
    Nook, 79–80
    orphaned, 72
    paperbacks, 68
    publishers, 69
    publishing and, 68–69, 77, 78–79
    purchasers of, 80
    social media and, 77
    softcover, 79
    teen purchasing habits, 80
    textbooks, 69
    top books of 19th and 20th Century, 83
    women and, 80
bookstores, 71, 79–80
Boost Mobile, 367
Borders, 79–80
Boston News-Letter (newspaper), 14, 95, 314
Boston Phoenix (newspaper), 114
Bourdieu, Pierre, 51
BP (British Petroleum), 291, 306–307
Brady, Matthew, 63, 99
brand/branding, 326
brand loyalty, 336
brand manager, 326
Breivik, Andres Behring, 477
Brewer, David, 120
Bridgestone/Firestone, 305
Brin, Sergey, 254
British Broadcasting Corporation (BBC), 160, 234
British Petroleum (BP), 291, 297–298, 306–307
broadband over power lines (BPL), 258
broadband technology, 358
Broadcasting and Cable (magazine), 82
Broadcast Music Incorporated (BMI), 148–149, 180
Broadside ballads, 60
B-roll, 296
browsers, 254
b to c (business to consumer), 274
Buena Vista Studios, 192, 202, 212
Buffy the Vampire Slayer (film), 194
Bulldog Reporter (newsletter), 301–302
Bulletin Board Systems (BBSs), 252–253

bullet model, 418
Bureau d'Esprit, 286
Bureau of Labor Statistics, 308
BurrellesLuce, 298
Burson-Marsteller, 490
Bush, George W., 124, 307
Bushnell, Nolan, 380
business to consumer, 274
Business Week (magazine), 82
Business Wire, 298
buttons, 320
buying motive, 336–338
Buy Nothing Day, 341
Bwana Devil (film), 197

C

Cable & Wireless, 505, 521
Cable Act of 1992, 222
cable modem, 359
cable television
    advertising (*see* product placements)
    vs. broadcast TV, 248
    Cable Act of 1992, 222
    defined, 220
    development of, 220–221
    digitization of, 16
    genres, 240–243
    globalization of, 519–520
    indecent content on, 221, 452
    infomercials, 335
    Internet and, 229
    narrowcasting, 241–242
    pay-per-view programming, 236
    production of, 235
    regulation of, 468
    revenue sources, 235–236
    target audience, 241
    technology of, 359
    violence on, 407
Cadillac Records (film), 134
Caesar, Julius, 94, 286
Cajun All-Stars, 131
caller ID, 355, 370
"Call of Duty" (video game), 384, 404
Cameron, James, 35–36, 197, 199, 205–206
Campbell, John, 95
CANSPAM law, 279, 322
Capital One, 329
Capital Records, 134
capture theory, 468
careers in media
    advertising, 328
    app developer, 368
    editors, 66–67
    film, 195
    introduction to, 9
    journalism/journalists, 125–126
    media scholar, 32
    mobile media, 368
    music, 148
    play tester, 392
    public relations, 308
    radio, 177
    recording industry, 148
    video game designers, 392
    video production, 233, 368
    web designer, 267
    writers, 66–67
Carlin, George, 180, 451
Carlisle, Brandi, 147
Carnegie-Frick Steel Company, 288
Carter family, 133
Cassavetes, John, 196
Castells, Manuel, 52
casual games, 385
The Catcher in the Rye (Salinger), 89

category killers, 274
catharsis hypothesis, 421
cathode ray tube (CRT), 227, 257
CB radios, 353–354
CBS Television. *See also* Big Three television companies; *specific shows*
    advertising on, 38
    distribution of, 235
    economics of, 30
    indecent content on, 245, 452
    O & Os, 160
    ownership of, 222
    Paley and, 216
    vertical integration of, 170
CDs. *See* compact discs (CDs)
cell phones
    3G, 363–364
    4G, 364
    AMPS, 362
    application programs, 367–368
    Bluetooth, 364
    capabilities of, 355
    carriers, 367
    college students on, 351
    companies, 367
    cramming, 371
    diffusion of, 47
    e-mail, 355–356
    encryption systems, 375
    first, 353
    globalization of, 521
    Google and, 367
    GSM, 363
    health effects of, 439
    history of, 376
    Internet and, 363–365
    location-based marketing and, 323, 369–370
    locator services, 375
    "locking" of, 371, 376
    multimedia, 363–364
    in other countries, 354
    privacy, 375
    satellite, 365
    social impact of, 351, 355–356
    technical standards for, 465
    technology of, 362–364
    text messaging, 363, 373–374, 375, 439, 522
    video, 364
    visual display on, 355
    Wi-Fi and, 364
    vs. wired phones, 522
    wireless technology and, 364
celluloid film, 200
censorship
    books and, 88–89
    defined, 450
    films and, 187, 193, 426
    of Internet, 255
    libraries and, 88–89
    in music, 152–153, 155
    newspaper, 94
    self-, 426
    on television, 245, 249
Center for Media & Democracy, 490
Center for Media Literacy, 85, 345
"Centipede" (video game), 396
central processing units (CPUs), 257
CenturyLink, 355
chain broadcasting, 161
Chandler, Harry, 102
channel, 8, 17
Channel One, 495
channels of communication, 8
channel surfing device fee, 229
chapbooks, 60

electronic news gathering (ENG) systems, 228
electronic numerical integrator and calculator (ENIAC), 251
electronic publishing, 268–269
Electronic Software Review Board, 383
The Ellen DeGeneres Show (TV show), 236–237
Ellul, Jacques, 52
Elrick, M.L., 104, 483
e-mail
    cell phones and, 355–356
    Chinese government and, 526
    ECPA and, 454
    harassment and, 497–498
    Homeland Security Act and, 279
    as Internet activity, 275
    ISPs and, 265–266
    privacy and, 454, 497–498
    as public relations tool, 296, 310
    social presence and, 417
    spamming, 280
    TCP/IP and, 259
    telephones and, 355–356
    web bugs in, 263
Eminem, 135
EMI Records, 146
Emmis, 170
employment, effects of media on, 440–443, 444
EMUSIC, 152
encoder, 17
encryption
    on cell phones, 375
    defined, 281
Energizer Batteries, 329
ENG systems, 228
Enron, 291
Entercom, 170
entertainment, 49
entertainment-education, 431
Entertainment Software Rating Board (ESRB), 398, 452
Epic Games of North Carolina, 391
e-publishing, 71–73. *See also* e-books
e-Rate program, 462–463
ESPN, 221, 234, 241
ESPN (magazine), 344
Ethernet, 252, 360
ethics
    in advertising, 491–496, 501
    blogging and, 297–298, 305
    codes of, 480–481, 491, 500
    commercialism and, 488
    compliance with, 482–483
    confidentiality, 485–486
    conflicts of interest and, 487–488
    consumers and, 497–500
    corporate, 481–482
    defined, 475
    in education, 499–500
    entertainment and, 488–490
    fair practices, 484–485
    First Amendment to the Constitution, 483
    hacking, 498
    harassment and, 497–498
    Internet and, 484, 497–500, 501
    in journalism, 100, 122–123, 483–488, 500
    media effects and, 489
    misrepresentation, 498
    newspapers, 122–123, 129, 484
    New York Times, 484
    piracy, 144, 209–212
    plagiarism, 499
    Potter's box, 479
    pragmatic, 478
    privacy and, 488, 492–495
    professional, 478–480

    in public relations, 291, 297, 305–306, 311, 490–491, 501
    in research, 496–497
    situation, 478–479, 500
    social media, 489–490, 499
    violations to, 482–483
    web surfing, 497
    yellow journalism, 100–101, 128
ethnicity
    advertising and, 44
    Internet access and, 42
    media studies of, 44
    telephone access and, 42
ethnographic research, 412–414, 443, 497
"E.T. The Extraterrestrial" (video game), 380–381
European Economic Community, 517
European Union (EU)
    Internet regulation and, 527–528
    regionalization and, 506
    and trade, 531–532
Eutelsat, 520
Evanescence (band), 153
EV-DO services, 261
"EverQuest" (video game), 382
EveryBlock.com, 117
Ewen, Stewart, 340–341
Expedia, 274
experimental research, 407–409, 413–414, 443, 497
ExxonMobil, 291, 306
Exxon Valdez crisis, 291, 306
EyeToy, 388

F

fabrication, 122–123
Facebook. *See also* social networking sites
    advertising on, 264, 317–318, 320
    content on, 273
    effects on community, 438
    ethics, 477, 490
    globalization of, 504
    global media and, 509
    privacy and, 342, 456–457
    as public relations tool, 296
    social media and, 256
    video games and, 391
facial recognition technology, 388
Fair and Accurate Credit Transactions (FACT) Act of 2003, 455
Fairbanks, Douglas, 188
Fair Credit Reporting Act of 1970, 455
Fairness and Accuracy in Reporting, 244, 471
Fairness Doctrine, 244, 450
FairPlay (software), 144
fair use rights, 88, 459–460
Fanning, Shawn, 139
"FarmVille" (video game), 270, 385, 391
Farnsworth, Philo, 225
Fat Boy Slim, 138
FCC (Federal Communications Commission)
    broadband strategy, 372–373
    on cable TV, 221
    on children's programming, 246
    on decency standards, 245
    defined, 473
    development of, 182, 352
    on diversity of content, 461–462
    Do Not Call List, 343, 375
    electronic media and, 464
    e-Rate program, 462–463
    Fairness Doctrine and, 450
    family viewing hour, 220
    FCC v. Pacifica Foundation, 451
    FinSyn rules, 218–220, 221

    functions of, 178, 467–468
    on indecent content, 180, 448, 452
    Justice Department and, 468
    Media Bureau, 467–468
    on monopolies, 121
    Prime Time Access Rule, 220
    Sixth Report and Order, 215–216, 220
    subliminal advertising and, 495–496
    and telephone industry, 352
    television "freeze," 215
    transition to digital television, 463–464
    and video on demand, 202
    Wireline Competition Bureau, 468
FCC v. Pacifica Foundation, 451
Fear Factor (TV show), 489
feature film, defined, 186
Federal Communications Commission (FCC). *See* FCC (Federal Communications Commission)
"Federalist Papers" (Hamilton), 62, 287
Federal Trade Commission (FTC)
    on advertising regulations, 344
    deceptive advertising, 343, 453
    defined, 473
    Do Not Call Registry, 456
    ethics and, 305–306
    Fair Credit Reporting Act, 455
    functions of, 469
    and Internet advertising, 495
    rating systems and, 398
feedback, 17
feedback mechanism, 17
Felt, W. Mark, 486
feminists. *See also* women
    media studies by, 43–44
    Torches of Freedom march, 289–290
fiber-optic carriers, 359
Fiber Optic Systems (FiOS), 359, 376
file sharing, 281, 459, 498–499. *See also specific file sharing site names*
file transfers, 259
film noir, 189
films
    3-D, 196–197
    advertising of, 36
    audience for, 191
    blockbusters, 193
    B movies, 190, 194
    careers in, 195
    celluloid, 200
    censorship of, 187, 193, 426
    cloud computing, 202
    comedies, 188
    conglomerates, 202
    content of, 192–193, 205–206
    copyright of, 196, 209–212
    creation of, 198–199
    cultural imperialism and, 211
    vs. digital cameras/projectors, 200
    digitization of, 195–198
    distribution of, 204–205, 512
    domination of international, 513
    early history of, 185–186
    editing of, 199
    feature film, 186
    financing, 203–204
    first-copy costs, 36
    first-run distribution, 194
    franchise, 196
    genres of, 187, 206–209, 212–213
    globalization of, 509, 512–514
    "green screen" techniques, 199
    IMAX format films, 196–197
    indecent content in, 208–209
    independent, 203, 212
    international, 189